T0296857

Software Architecture for Big Data and the Cloud

Software Architecture for Big Data and the Cloud

Edited by

Ivan Mistrik

Rami Bahsoon

Nour Ali

Maritta Heisel

Bruce Maxim

MORGAN KAUFMANN PUBLISHERS
AN IMPRINT OF ELSEVIER

Morgan Kaufmann is an imprint of Elsevier
50 Hampshire Street, 5th Floor, Cambridge, MA 02139, United States

Library of Congress Cataloging-in-Publication Data
A catalog record for this book is available from the Library of Congress

British Library Cataloguing-in-Publication Data
A catalogue record for this book is available from the British Library

ISBN: 978-0-12-805467-3

For information on all Morgan Kaufmann publications
visit our website at https://www.elsevier.com/books-and-journals

Working together
to grow libraries in
developing countries

www.elsevier.com • www.bookaid.org

Publisher: Todd Green, Jonathan Simpson
Acquisition Editor: Todd Green, Jonathan Simpson
Editorial Project Manager: Lindsay Lawrence
Senior Production Project Manager: Priya Kumaraguruparan
Designer: Vicky Pearson Esser

Typeset by VTeX

CONTENTS

Contributors   xv
About the Editors   xxi
Foreword by Mandy Chessell   xxv
Foreword by Ian Gorton   xxix
Preface   xxxi

CHAPTER 1   Introduction. Software Architecture for Cloud and Big Data: An Open Quest for the Architecturally Significant Requirements .   1
Rami Bahsoon, Nour Ali, Maritta Heisel, Bruce Maxim, Ivan Mistrik
1.1   A Perspective into Software Architecture for Cloud and Big Data   1
1.2   Cloud Architecturally Significant Requirements and Their Design Implications   2
         1.2.1   Dynamism and Elasticity as Cloud Architecturally Significant Requirements   3
         1.2.2   Multitenancy as Cloud Architecturally Significant Requirement   4
         1.2.3   Service Level Agreements (SLAs) Constraints as Cloud Architecturally Significant Requirement   4
         1.2.4   Cloud Marketplaces as Architecturally Significant Requirement   5
         1.2.5   Seeking Value as Cloud Architecturally Significant Requirement   6
1.3   Big Data Management as Cloud Architecturally Significant Requirement   7
         1.3.1   Big Data Analytics Enabled by the Cloud and Its Architecturally Significant Requirements   8
         1.3.2   Architecturally Significant Requirements in Realm of Competing Big Data Technologies   8
         References   9

PART 1 CONCEPTS AND MODELS   11

CHAPTER 2   Hyperscalability – The Changing Face of Software Architecture   13
Ian Gorton
2.1   Introduction   13
2.2   Hyperscalable Systems   14
         2.2.1   Scalability   14
         2.2.2   Scalability Limits   15
         2.2.3   Scalability Costs   17
         2.2.4   Hyperscalability   19
2.3   Principles of Hyperscalable Systems   20
         2.3.1   Automate and Optimize to Control Costs   21

	2.3.2 Simple Solutions Promote Scalability	23
	2.3.3 Utilize Stateless Services	25
	2.3.4 Observability is Fundamental to Success at Hyperscale	26
2.4	Related Work	29
2.5	Conclusions	30
	References	30

CHAPTER 3   Architecting to Deliver Value From a Big Data and Hybrid Cloud Architecture   33

Mandy Chessell, Dan Wolfson, Tim Vincent

3.1	Introduction	33
3.2	Supporting the Analytics Lifecycle	33
3.3	The Role of Data Lakes	35
3.4	Key Design Features That Make a Data Lake Successful	36
3.5	Architecture Example – Context Management in the IoT	37
3.6	Big Data Origins and Characteristics	38
3.7	The Systems That Capture and Process Big Data	39
3.8	Operating Across Organizational Silos	41
3.9	Architecture Example – Local Processing of Big Data	42
3.10	Architecture Example – Creating a Multichannel View	43
3.11	Application Independent Data	45
3.12	Metadata and Governance	45
3.13	Conclusions	46
3.14	Outlook and Future Directions	47
	References	48

CHAPTER 4   Domain-Driven Design of Big Data Systems Based on a Reference Architecture   49

Cigdem Avci Salma, Bedir Tekinerdogan, Ioannis N. Athanasiadis

4.1	Introduction	49
4.2	Domain-Driven Design Approach	50
4.3	Related Work	53
4.4	Feature Model of Big Data Systems	54
	4.4.1 Data	56
	4.4.2 Information Management	56
	4.4.3 Interface and Visualization	56
	4.4.4 Data Processing	56
	4.4.5 Data Storage	57
	4.4.6 Data Analysis	57
	4.4.7 Feature Constraints	57
4.5	Deriving the Application Architectures and Example	60
	4.5.1 Feature Modeling	60
	4.5.2 Design Rule Modeling	60

4.5.3 Associating Design Decisions With Features   61
4.5.4 Generation of the Application Architecture and the Deployment
       Diagram   62
4.5.5 Deriving Big Data Architectures of Existing Systems   63

4.6   Conclusion   66
       References   67

CHAPTER 5   **An Architectural Model-Based Approach to Quality-Aware**
DevOps in Cloud Applications   69
Robert Heinrich, Reiner Jung, Christian Zirkelbach,
Wilhelm Hasselbring, Ralf Reussner

5.1   Introduction   69
5.2   A Cloud-Based Software Application   70
5.3   Differences in Architectural Models Among Development and Operations . . .   71
5.4   The iObserve Approach   72
5.5   Addressing the Differences in Architectural Models   75
       5.5.1 The iObserve Megamodel   75
       5.5.2 Descriptive and Prescriptive Architectural Models in iObserve   77
       5.5.3 Static and Dynamic Content in Architectural Models   78
5.6   Applying iObserve to CoCoME   80
       5.6.1 Applying the iObserve Megamodel   81
       5.6.2 Applying Descriptive and Prescriptive Architectural Models   82
       5.6.3 Applying Live Visualization   82
5.7   Limitations   84
5.8   Related Work   85
5.9   Conclusion   87
       References   87

CHAPTER 6   **Bridging Ecology and Cloud: Transposing Ecological**
Perspective to Enable Better Cloud Autoscaling   91
Tao Chen, Rami Bahsoon

6.1   Introduction   91
6.2   Motivation   92
6.3   Natural Ecosystem   93
6.4   Transposing Ecological Principles, Theories and Models to Cloud Ecosystem   94
6.5   Ecology-Inspired Self-Aware Pattern   97
6.6   Opportunities and Challenges   99
6.7   Related Work   100
6.8   Conclusion   100
       References   101
       Acknowledgement   102

PART 2 ANALYZING AND EVALUATING   103

CHAPTER 7   Evaluating Web PKIs **105**
                Jiangshan Yu, Mark Ryan
         7.1 Introduction 105
         7.2 An Overview of PKI 106
         7.3 Desired Features and Security Concerns 108
         7.4 Existing Proposals 110
                 7.4.1 Classic 110
                 7.4.2 Difference Observation 110
                 7.4.3 Scope Restriction 114
                 7.4.4 Certificate Management Transparency 115
         7.5 Observations 120
                 7.5.1 Property Perspective 120
                 7.5.2 System Perspective 122
         7.6 Conclusion 123
                 References 123

CHAPTER 8   Performance Isolation in Cloud-Based Big Data Architectures   127
                Bedir Tekinerdogan, Alp Oral
         8.1 Introduction 127
         8.2 Background 128
                 8.2.1 Cloud Computing 128
                 8.2.2 Big Data Architecture 129
         8.3 Case Study and Problem Statement 130
                 8.3.1 Case Study 130
                 8.3.2 Problem Statement 132
         8.4 Performance Monitoring in Cloud-Based Systems 132
         8.5 Application Framework for Performance Isolation 134
         8.6 Evaluation of the Framework 137
                 8.6.1 Evaluation Results 140
         8.7 Discussion 143
         8.8 Related Work 143
         8.9 Conclusion 144
                 References 145

**CHAPTER 9   From Legacy to Cloud: Risks and Benefits in Software Cloud
                Migration** **147**
                Anastasija Efremovska, Patricia Lago
         9.1 Introduction 147
         9.2 Research Method 147
                 9.2.1 Pilot Study 148
                 9.2.2 Search Strategy 148
                 9.2.3 Data Extraction 151
                 9.2.4 Data Analysis Method 152

9.3 Results 154
    9.3.1 Overview of Primary Studies and Quality Evaluation 154
    9.3.2 Benefits and Risks 156
    9.3.3 General Measures 159
    9.3.4 Models and Frameworks for Cloud Migration 160
9.4 Discussion 162
    9.4.1 Findings and Lessons Learned 162
    9.4.2 Threats to Validity 163
9.5 Conclusion 164
    References 164

CHAPTER 10 Big Data: A Practitioners Perspective **167**
Darshan Lopes, Kevin Palmer, Fiona O'Sullivan
10.1 Big Data Is a New Paradigm – Differences With Traditional Data Warehouse,
    Pitfalls and Consideration 167
    10.1.1 Differences With Traditional Data Warehouse 167
    10.1.2 Pitfalls 168
    10.1.3 Considerations 169
10.2 Product Considerations for Big Data – Use of Open Source Products for Big
    Data, Pitfalls and Considerations 169
    10.2.1 The Use of Open Source Product for Big Data 169
    10.2.2 Pitfalls 170
    10.2.3 Considerations 171
10.3 Use of Cloud for hosting Big Data – Why to Use Cloud, Pitfalls and
    Consideration 171
    10.3.1 Why to Use Cloud? 171
    10.3.2 Pitfalls 172
    10.3.3 Consideration 172
10.4 Big Data Implementation – Architecture Definition, Processing Framework
    and Migration Pattern From Data Warehouse to Big Data 172
    10.4.1 Patterns for Transitioning From Data Warehouse to Big Data 175
10.5 Conclusion 178
    References 179

PART 3 TECHNOLOGIES   181

CHAPTER 11 A Taxonomy and Survey of Stream Processing Systems **183**
Xinwei Zhao, Saurabh Garg, Carlos Queiroz,
Rajkumar Buyya
11.1 Introduction 183
11.2 Stream Processing Platforms: A Brief Background 185
    11.2.1 Requirements of Stream Processing Platforms/Engines 186
    11.2.2 Generic Model of Modern Stream Processing Platforms/Engines 187
11.3 Taxonomy 188

11.3.1 Functional Aspects 189
11.3.2 Nonfunctional Aspects 195
11.4 A Survey of Stream Processing Platforms 197
11.4.1 Data Stream Management Systems 198
11.4.2 Complex Event Processing Systems 198
11.4.3 Stream Processing Platforms/Engines......................... 199
11.5 Comparison Study of the Stream Processing Platforms 200
11.5.1 Scalability 200
11.5.2 Messaging & Distribution 201
11.5.3 Data Processing/Stream Processors........................... 201
11.5.4 Fault Tolerance 202
11.6 Conclusions and Future Directions 202
References 204

CHAPTER 12   Architecting Cloud Services for the Digital Me in a Privacy-Aware Environment 207
Robert Eikermann, Markus Look, Alexander Roth, Berhard Rumpe, Andreas Wortmann

12.1 Introduction 207
12.2 Example 208
12.3 Challenges 210
12.3.1 Service Composition 211
12.3.2 Technology Abstraction 211
12.3.3 Service and Data Integration 211
12.3.4 Trusted Use of Personal Data................................ 212
12.4 Preliminaries 212
12.5 System-of-Systems Approach 213
12.5.1 Persistence Service 214
12.5.2 DataConversion Service 216
12.5.3 Privacy Service 217
12.5.4 LookUp Service.. 217
12.5.5 PersonalData Service 218
12.6 Generative Approach 219
12.7 Related Work 221
12.7.1 Service Composition 222
12.7.2 Technology Abstraction 222
12.7.3 Service and Data Integration 222
12.7.4 Trusted Use of Personal Data................................ 222
12.8 Discussion 223
12.9 Conclusion 223
References 224

CHAPTER 13   Reengineering Data-Centric Information Systems for the Cloud – A Method and Architectural Patterns Promoting Multitenancy 227
Andrei Furda, Colin Fidge, Alistair Barros,
Olaf Zimmermann

13.1 Introduction 227
13.2 Context and Problem: Multitenancy in Cloud Computing 228
13.3 Solution Overview: Reengineering Method and Process 230
13.4 Solution Detail 1: Architectural Patterns in the Method 232
　　　13.4.1 Architectural Reengineering Steps for the Cloud (Architectural
　　　　　　Refactoring) 233
　　　13.4.2 Multitenancy Requirements and Patterns for Cloud Environments 234
　　　13.4.3 The Multitenancy Capable Model 235
　　　13.4.4 The Multitenancy Capable Controller 235
　　　13.4.5 The Multitenancy Capable View 236
13.5 Solution Detail 2: Testing and Code Reviews 237
　　　13.5.1 Testing for Multitenancy Defects 237
　　　13.5.2 Code Review for Multitenancy Defects 239
　　　13.5.3 Summary 240
13.6 Case Study (Implementation) 240
　　　13.6.1 Multitenancy Transformation Without Patterns 241
　　　13.6.2 Multitenancy Transformation With Patterns 243
　　　13.6.3 Comparison 243
13.7 Discussion 246
13.8 Related Work 247
13.9 Summary and Conclusions 247
Appendix 13.A Architectural Refactoring (AR) Reference 248
　　　References 249

CHAPTER 14   Exploring the Evolution of Big Data Technologies   253
Stephen Bonner, Ibad Kureshi, John Brennan,
Georgios Theodoropoulos

14.1 Introduction 253
14.2 Big Data in Our Daily Lives 254
14.3 Data Intensive Computing 256
　　　14.3.1 Big Compute Versus Big Data 256
　　　14.3.2 Data Intensive Applications 258
　　　14.3.3 Data Intensive Frameworks 258
　　　14.3.4 MapReduce and GFS 259
14.4 Apache Hadoop 263
　　　14.4.1 Hadoop V1 263
　　　14.4.2 Hadoop 2.0 266
14.5 Apache Spark 267
　　　14.5.1 Resilient Distributed Datasets 268
　　　14.5.2 Data Flow and Programming With Spark 269

	14.5.3	Spark Processing Engines	270
	14.5.4	Hadoop Ecosystem Taxonomy	271
14.6	The Role of Cloud Computing		271
14.7	The Future of Big Data Platforms		274
	14.7.1	Big Data Applications	274
	14.7.2	Big Data Frameworks and Hardware	275
	14.7.3	Big Data on the Road to Exascale	279
14.8	Conclusion		280
	References		281

CHAPTER 15   A Taxonomy and Survey of Fault-Tolerant Workflow Management Systems in Cloud and Distributed Computing Environments ..   285

Deepak Poola, Mohsen Amini Salehi,
Kotagiri Ramamohanarao, Rajkumar Buyya

15.1	Introduction		285
15.2	Background		286
	15.2.1	Workflow Management Systems	286
	15.2.2	Workflow Scheduling	287
15.3	Introduction to Fault-Tolerance		288
	15.3.1	Necessity for Fault-Tolerance in Distributed Systems	290
15.4	Taxonomy of Faults		290
15.5	Taxonomy of Fault-Tolerant Scheduling Algorithms		291
	15.5.1	Replication	292
	15.5.2	Resubmission	295
	15.5.3	Checkpointing	297
	15.5.4	Provenance	300
	15.5.5	Rescue Workflow	301
	15.5.6	User-Defined Exception Handling	301
	15.5.7	Alternate Task	301
	15.5.8	Failure Masking	301
	15.5.9	Slack Time	302
	15.5.10	Trust-Based Scheduling Algorithms	302
15.6	Modeling of Failures in Workflow Management Systems		303
15.7	Metrics Used to Quantify Fault-Tolerance		304
15.8	Survey of Workflow Management Systems and Frameworks		305
	15.8.1	Askalon	305
	15.8.2	Pegasus	308
	15.8.3	Triana	309
	15.8.4	UNICORE 6	310
	15.8.5	Kepler	310
	15.8.6	Cloudbus Workflow Management System	310
	15.8.7	Traverna	311
	15.8.8	The e-Science Central (e-SC)	311
	15.8.9	SwinDeW-C	311

15.8.10 Big Data Workflow Frameworks: MapReduce, Hadoop, and Spark . . 312
15.8.11 Other Workflow Management Systems 313
15.9 Tools and Support Systems 313
15.9.1 Data Management Tools 313
15.9.2 Security and Fault-Tolerance Management Tools 314
15.9.3 Cloud Development Tools 314
15.9.4 Support Systems 314
15.10 Summary 315
References 315

PART 4 RESOURCE MANAGEMENT   321

CHAPTER 16 **The HARNESS Platform: A Hardware- and Network-Enhanced Software System for Cloud Computing** **323**
Jose G.F. Coutinho, Mark Stillwell, Katerina Argyraki, George Ioannidis, Anca Iordache, Christoph Kleineweber, Alexandros Koliousis, John McGlone, Guillaume Pierre, Carmelo Ragusa, Peter Sanders, Thorsten Schütt, Teng Yu, Alexander Wolf
16.1 Introduction 323
16.2 Related Work 324
16.3 Overview 325
16.4 Managing Heterogeneity 327
16.4.1 Hierarchical Resource Management 328
16.4.2 Agnostic Resource Management 329
16.4.3 Ranking Allocation Requests 331
16.4.4 HARNESS API 334
16.5 Prototype Description 336
16.5.1 The Platform Layer 336
16.5.2 The Infrastructure Layer 338
16.5.3 The Virtual Execution Layer 339
16.6 Evaluation 340
16.6.1 Executing HPC Applications on the Cloud 340
16.6.2 Resource Scheduling with Network Constraints 345
16.7 Conclusion 349
Project Resources 350
References 350
Acknowledgements 351

CHAPTER 17 **Auditable Version Control Systems in Untrusted Public Clouds 353**
Bo Chen, Reza Curtmola, Jun Dai
17.1 Motivation and Contributions 353
17.2 Background Knowledge 355

17.2.1   Data Organization in Version Control Systems 355
17.2.2   Remote Data Integrity Checking (RDIC) 357
17.3   System and Adversarial Model 357
17.4   Auditable Version Control Systems 358
17.4.1   Definition of AVCS 358
17.4.2   An AVCS Construction 359
17.5   Discussion 362
17.6   Other RDIC Approaches for Version Control Systems 363
17.7   Evaluation 363
17.7.1   Theoretical Evaluation 363
17.7.2   Experimental Evaluation 364
17.8   Conclusion 365
References 365

CHAPTER 18   **Scientific Workflow Management System for Clouds** **367**
Maria A. Rodriguez, Rajkumar Buyya
18.1   Introduction 367
18.2   Background 368
18.3   Workflow Management Systems for Clouds 370
18.4   Cloudbus Workflow Management System 372
18.5   Cloud-Based Extensions to the Workflow Engine 374
18.6   Performance Evaluation 379
18.6.1   WRPS 379
18.6.2   Montage 379
18.6.3   Setup of Experimental Infrastructure 380
18.6.4   Montage Setup 381
18.6.5   Results 382
18.7   Summary and Conclusions 385
References 386

PART 5   LOOKING AHEAD   389

CHAPTER 19   **Outlook and Future Directions** **391**
Maritta Heisel, Rami Bahsoon, Nour Ali, Bruce Maxim,
Ivan Mistrik
19.1   New or Advanced Applications 391
19.2   Advanced Supporting Technologies 394
19.3   Architecturally Significant Requirements 395
19.4   Challenges for the Architecting Process 397
19.5   Further Reading 401
References 402

Glossary 403
Author Index 407
Subject Index 425

CONTRIBUTORS

Nour Ali
University of Brighton, UK

Katerina Argyraki
EPFL, Switzerland

Ioannis N. Athanasiadis
Wageningen University, Information Technology, Wageningen, The Netherlands

Cigdem Avci Salma
Wageningen University, Information Technology, Wageningen, The Netherlands

Rami Bahsoon
School of Computer Science, University of Birmingham, UK

Alistair Barros
Science and Engineering Faculty, Queensland University of Technology (QUT), Brisbane, QLD, Australia

Stephen Bonner
Institute of Advanced Research Computing, Durham University, United Kingdom

John Brennan
Institute of Advanced Research Computing, Durham University, United Kingdom

Rajkumar Buyya
Cloud Computing and Distributed Systems (CLOUDS) Laboratory, School of Computing and Information Systems, The University of Melbourne, Australia

Bo Chen
Department of Computer Science, University of Memphis, Memphis, TN, USA

Tao Chen
School of Computer Science, University of Birmingham, UK

Mandy Chessell
IBM, Winchester, Hampshire, United Kingdom

Jose G.F. Coutinho
Imperial College London, UK

Reza Curtmola
Department of Computer Science, New Jersey Institute of Technology, Newark, NJ, USA

Jun Dai
Southwestern University of Finance and Economics, Chengdu, Sichuan, China
Rutgers University–Newark, Newark, NJ, USA

Anastasija Efremovska
Vrije Universiteit Amsterdam, The Netherlands

Robert Eikermann
Software Engineering, RWTH Aachen University, Aachen, Germany

Colin Fidge
Science and Engineering Faculty, Queensland University of Technology (QUT), Brisbane, QLD, Australia

Andrei Furda
Science and Engineering Faculty, Queensland University of Technology (QUT), Brisbane, QLD, Australia

Saurabh Garg
School of Engineering and ICT, University of Tasmania, Tasmania, Australia

Ian Gorton
Northeastern University, United States

Wilhelm Hasselbring
Kiel University, Germany

Robert Heinrich
Karlsruhe Institute of Technology, Germany

Maritta Heisel
Universität Duisburg-Essen, Germany

George Ioannidis
EPFL, Switzerland

Anca Iordache
Université de Rennes 1, France

Reiner Jung
Kiel University, Germany

Christoph Kleineweber
Zuse Institute Berlin, Germany

Alexandros Koliousis
Imperial College London, UK

Ibad Kureshi
Institute of Advanced Research Computing, Durham University, United Kingdom

Patricia Lago
Vrije Universiteit Amsterdam, The Netherlands

Markus Look
Software Engineering, RWTH Aachen University, Aachen, Germany

Darshan Lopes
Capgemini UK, UK

Bruce Maxim
University of Michigan-Dearborn, USA

John McGlone
SAP Labs, USA

Ivan Mistrik
Independent Researcher, Germany

Alp Oral
Wageningen University, Information Technology, Wageningen, The Netherlands
Microsoft, Vancouver, Canada

Fiona O'Sullivan
Capgemini UK, UK

Kevin Palmer
Capgemini UK, UK

Guillaume Pierre
Université de Rennes 1, France

Deepak Poola
The University of Melbourne, Australia

Carlos Queiroz
The Association of Computing Machinery (ACM), Singapore

Carmelo Ragusa
SAP, UK

Kotagiri Ramamohanarao
The University of Melbourne, Australia

Ralf Reussner
Karlsruhe Institute of Technology, Germany

Maria A. Rodriguez
Cloud Computing and Distributed Systems (CLOUDS) Laboratory, School of Computing and Information Systems, The University of Melbourne, Australia

Alexander Roth
Software Engineering, RWTH Aachen University, Aachen, Germany

Berhard Rumpe
Software Engineering, RWTH Aachen University, Aachen, Germany

Mark Ryan
School of Computer Science, University of Birmingham, UK

Mohsen Amini Salehi
The University of Louisiana Lafayette, USA

Peter Sanders
Maxeler Technologies, UK

Thorsten Schütt
Zuse Institute Berlin, Germany

Mark Stillwell
Imperial College London, UK

Bedir Tekinerdogan
Wageningen University, Information Technology, Wageningen, The Netherlands

Georgios Theodoropoulos
Institute of Advanced Research Computing, Durham University, United Kingdom

Tim Vincent
IBM, Toronto, Ontario, Canada

Alexander Wolf
University of California, Santa Cruz, USA

Dan Wolfson
IBM, Austin, TX, USA

Andreas Wortmann
Software Engineering, RWTH Aachen University, Aachen, Germany

Jiangshan Yu
School of Computer Science, University of Birmingham, UK

Teng Yu
Imperial College London, UK

Xinwei Zhao
School of Engineering and ICT, University of Tasmania, Tasmania, Australia

Olaf Zimmermann
University of Applied Sciences of Eastern Switzerland (HSR FHO), Rapperswil, Switzerland

Christian Zirkelbach
Kiel University, Germany

ABOUT THE EDITORS

Ivan Mistrik is a researcher in software-intensive systems engineering. He is a computer scientist who is interested in system and software engineering and in system and software architecture, in particular: life cycle system/software engineering, requirements engineering, relating software requirements and architectures, knowledge management in software development, rationale-based software development, aligning enterprise/system/software architectures, value-based software engineering, agile software architectures, and collaborative system/software engineering. He has more than 40 years' experience in the field of computer systems engineering as an information systems developer, R&D leader, SE/SA research analyst, educator in computer sciences, and ICT management consultant. During the past 40 years, he has been primarily working at various R&D institutions in USA and Germany and has done consulting on a variety of large international projects sponsored by ESA, EU, NASA, NATO, and UN. He has also taught university-level computer sciences courses in software engineering, software architecture, distributed information systems, and human–computer interaction. He is the author or coauthor of more than 90 articles and papers in international journals, conferences, books, and workshops. Ivan Mistrik has written a number of editorials for special issues and edited books. He has also written over 120 technical reports and presented over 70 scientific/technical talks. He has served in many program committees and panels of reputable international conferences and organized a number of scientific workshops. He was the lead-editor of ten books between 2006 and 2016: *Rationale Management in Software Engineering; Rationale-Based Software Engineering; Collaborative Software Engineering; Relating Software Requirements and Architecture; Aligning Enterprise, System, and Software Architectures; Agile Software Architecture; Economics-driven Software Architecture; Relating System Quality and Software Architecture; Software Quality Assurance; Managing Trade-Offs in Adaptable Software Architectures.*

Nour Ali is a Principal Lecturer at the University of Brighton since December, 2012. She holds a PhD in Software Engineering from the Polytechnic University of Valencia-Spain for her work in Ambients in Aspect-Oriented Software Architecture. She is a Fellow of UK Higher Education Academy (HEA). Her research area encompasses service oriented architecture, software architecture, self-adaptation and mobile systems. In 2014, the University of Brighton granted her a Rising Stars award in Service Oriented Architecture Recovery and Consistency. She is currently the Principal Investigator for the Royal Society Newton grant, "An Autonomic Architectural Approach for Health Care Systems," and is the Knowledge Supervisor for the Knowledge Transfer Partnership project for migrating legacy software systems using architecture centric approach. She has also been the Principal Investigator for an Enterprise Ireland Commercialisation Project in Architecture Recovery and Consistency and coinvestigator in several funded projects. Dr. Ali serves on the Programme Committee for several conferences (e.g., ICWS, ICMS, HPCC, etc.) and journals (e.g., JSS and JIST). She has cochaired and coorganized several workshops such as the IEEE International Workshop on Engineering Mobile Service Oriented Systems (EMSOS) and the IEEE Workshop on Future of Software Engineering for/in the Cloud. She was the coeditor of the JSS Special Issue on the Future of Software Engineering for/in the Cloud published in 2013 and has coedited three books including "Agile and lean service-oriented development: foundations, theory, and practice" published in 2012. She is the Application

Track chair for International Conference on Web Services (ICWS 2016). Her personal website is: http://www.cem.brighton.ac.uk/staff/na179/.

Rami Bahsoon is a Senior Lecturer Software Engineering (Assoc. Prof.) and founding member of the Software Engineering Research group and the Cloud Software Engineering interest group at the University of Birmingham, UK. He holds a PhD in Software Architecture from University College London. During his PhD, he was awarded a fellowship to attend London Business School (LBS) for MBA studies in technology strategy and strategy dynamics. Bahsoon's research interests are in Cloud software Engineering, Software Architectures, Self-adaptive and Managed Software Engineering, Security Software Engineering, Relating software requirements (nonfunctional requirements) to software architectures, testing and regression testing, software maintenance and evolution, software metrics, empirical evaluation, Software Sustainability and Economics-driven Software Engineering research. His Birmingham Group comprises 10 PhD students and was among the first groups worldwide to carry fundamental research on cloud software engineering and software architectures evidenced by publications to top-tier venues such as IEEE Transactions on Cloud Computing, IEEE Transactions on Software Engineering, IEEE Transactions on Services Computing, IEEE Computer, ICWS, IEEE Cloud, WICSA, SEAMS/ICSE, UCC, HPCC, among others. His group has been working on self-adaptive and managed architectures for supporting the development and evolution of dependable ultra-large software systems covering cloud; dynamic resource allocation and federation in cloud; self-aware cloud; cloud elasticity, autoscaling and dynamic management of Quality of Service (QoS); utility models for service composition; volunteer services computing. Bahsoon had founded the IEEE International Software Engineering IN/FOR the Cloud workshop (in its 6th version now) in conjunction with IEEE Services and IEEE Cloud, the leading venue for cloud research. He was the lead editor for a special issue on the Future of Software Engineering for/In the Cloud and another on Architecture and Mobility and with the Journal of Systems and Software, a leading software engineering journal. Bahsoon has coedited a book on Software Architectures for Cloud and Big Data (Elsevier). He coedited another three books on Software Architecture and Software Quality (Elsevier 2014); Economics-Driven Software Architecture (Elsevier 2014); Aligning Enterprise, System, and Software Architectures (IGI Global in 2012). He has acted as the workshop chair for IEEE Services 2014, IEEE Cloud, IEEE Big Data, ICWS; the Doctoral Symposium chair of IEEE/ACM Utility and Cloud Computing Conference (UCC 2014 and UCC2016); track chair for Utility and Cloud Computing of IEEE HPCC 2014; Visionary Track chair for IEEE Services (2015); Emerging Technologies Track Chair for IEEE Services (2016); IEEE Big Data UK Satellite session chair (2015) on Big Data Software Engineering for Cloud and Mobile Services (2015); Big Data Software Engineering for Cloud, Edge Computing and Mobility; workshop chair for ECSA 2016 and programme chair for IEEE Services 2017. He is a member of EPSRC Associate College Board and acted as a panellist for the NSF/EPSRC Software Grand Challenge for expertise in cloud software engineering, had reviewed for major EU/UK funding bodies and software engineering and service science conferences and journals. His website is: https://www.cs.bham.ac.uk/~rzb/.

Maritta Heisel is a Full Professor for software engineering at the University Duisburg–Essen, Germany, since 2004. Her research interests include the development of dependable software, pattern- and component-based software development, requirements engineering (including quality requirements), software architecture, and software evolution. She is particularly interested in incorporating security and privacy considerations into software development processes and in integrating the development of safe and secure software. She has published over 100 scientific papers in various fields of software engineering. She is a member of the board of paluno – The Ruhr Institute for Software Technology.

She is a member of the European Workshop on Industrial Computer Systems Reliability, Safety and Security (EWICS). EWICS runs the annual International Conference on Computer Safety, Reliability and Security (SAFECOMP), for which Maritta Heisel is a regular program committee member. She also served as a member of the steering committee of the working group on secure ICT research and innovation established by the European Union in the context of the NIS (Network and Information Security) Public–Private Platform, and is coeditor of a deliverable "Cybersecurity Education Snapshot for workforce development in the EU". Furthermore, she has been appointed as an independent expert and project proposal evaluator by the European Commission. She was a member of the Network of Excellence on Engineering Future Internet Software Services and Systems (NESSoS), which was funded by the European Union. Furthermore, she was involved in different projects, investigating the derivation of design alternatives based on quality requirements, and developing a support tool for documenting security requirements for cloud computing systems, checking their consistency, and generating documentation for the certification of cloud computing systems. Her personal website is: https://www.uni-due.de/swe/maritta.

Bruce Maxim is Associate Professor of Computer and Information Science at the University of Michigan-Dearborn. He has worked as a software engineer, project manager, educator, author, and consultant for more than 30 years. His professional experience includes managing research information systems at the University of Michigan Medical School, directing instructional computing for the University medical campus, and working as a statistical programmer in the School of Public Health. He served as the chief technology officer for a game development company. His research interests include software engineering, human computer interaction, game design, social media, artificial intelligence, and software engineering education. He is coauthor of nine books, including a best-selling introductory computer science text and a best-selling software engineering text. He has published a number of papers on software quality, project management, computer algorithm animation, game development, and engineering education. He is the chief-architect of the ABET accredited software engineering program at University of Michigan-Dearborn. He established the GAME Lab in the University of Michigan-Dearborn College of Engineering and Computer Science. He has supervised several hundred industry-based software development projects at both the graduate and undergraduate levels. He is the recipient of several distinguished teaching awards and a distinguished community service award. He is a member of Sigma Xi, Upsilon Pi Epsilon, Pi Mu Epsilon, Association of Computing Machinery, IEEE Computer Society, American Society for Engineering Education, Society of Women Engineers, and International Game Developers Association. His personal website is: http://www-personal.umd.umich.edu/~bmaxim/.

FOREWORD BY MANDY CHESSELL

AMNESIA OR PROGRESS?

Over the last few years, big data processing techniques and practices have matured. We no longer hear claims that the sheer volume of "big data" renders old fashioned, complex and time-consuming practices, such as data quality management, obsolete. In fact, many practices that were developed for data warehousing are being introduced into big data projects. There is a rise in the demand for data modelers, and technologies such as SQL and ETL engines are being ported and enhanced to execute on big data platforms.

So what have we gained in this movement to big data? Was it just a case of collective industry amnesia as we cast aside the years of information management experience developed, often painfully, from large-scale data warehouse projects, or has something significant happened in information management?

THE LEGACY OF DATA WAREHOUSING

During the big data frenzy, the use of data warehouses has not diminished in absolute terms. However, they no longer represent the only approach to collating and managing information outside of the operational systems that originate data.

The shift away from data warehouses was driven by cost, flexibility and time to value. A data warehouse aims to construct a coherent view of an organization's operation. This takes time because most organizations do not operate in a coherent manner. It takes thought and cross-organizational agreements to determine how the disparate operations are reconciled. This time and effort was perceived as expensive. To reduce this cost, the information governance program pushed greater conformity back into the operational systems feeding the data warehouse in a way that gave it a reputation for stifling innovation.

Thus people looked for a new approach to deliver a more agile and flexible data capability that would enable a more data-rich operating model for the organization.

The big data teams used new technology, new techniques and seemed to deliver proof of concepts, and their initial projects with lightning speed. However, as the volume and variety of data grew, the big data projects began to stall, amid a wave of concerns about the safety and trustworthiness of the data they hosted. Organizations started to question if big data had really brought them any gains over the data warehouse and began looking for another miracle technology.

LOOKING BACK AT THE IMPACT OF BIG DATA TECHNOLOGY

Despite the problems, the result of the big data movement is significant, but not as revolutionary as enthusiasts originally thought. Big data projects have been dogged with the same types of problems related to data understanding, data quality and project over-runs as data warehouse projects. There is increasing recognition that extracting, transforming, linking and collating data from heterogeneous systems is innately hard and although big data processing makes it faster and cheaper to process data, it does not remove much of the complexity and skill needed.

For the more thoughtful organizations there is a realization that information management techniques should largely be agnostic to the data platform and the type of data. The result is that:

1. Data warehouses are seen as complementary rather than competitive to big data platforms. Their use is focused on highly optimized processing of data for standard reports and dashboards. The big data platforms offer generic capability for all types of data, which is useful for analytics development and experimentation plus production workload that are less time-critical in nature.
2. Data is processed selectively from raw format to finished data service in an agile and modular fashion. There is no longer an attempt to make all data fit into a single data model.
3. Common data models are used to create consistency between data service implementations, not to create a single coherent view of the organization's operation.
4. The data governance program is becoming targeted and selective rather than a set of standards applied to all data. It operates across all platforms.
5. Metadata is being used operationally for online data catalogs, virtualized access and active governance of data.
6. Techniques for data quality, lifecycle management and protection are being homogenized to support all types of structured and unstructured data.
7. Data is seen by the business as an asset and its use is now a discussion at the boardroom level.

Information management is getting harder due the diversity of information producers today. However, the big data movement has forced a significant step forward in information management practices beyond those developed for the data warehouse, and as a result we are better placed to manage this.

THE IMPACT OF CLOUD TECHNOLOGY

The movement to cloud is the next great playground. Business teams can select and purchase new services without involving anyone from the IT. This appears to remove a bottleneck to progress – particularly when a mature organization is trying to transform it operations. However, from a data point of view, these new cloud services are creating new silos of data distributed across different providers' data centers and the relief it offers to organizations will hit a similar wall as big data when they try to integrate their new services with their existing business.

There are also technical challenges still to be addressed. Cloud computing aims to virtualize infrastructure and IT services so that they can be seamlessly shared, to reduce cost and flexibility.

Data presents a challenge to cloud environments because it is a physical resource in an infrastructure that aims to scale by virtualizing resources.

How does an organization position data and workload across a hybrid multi-cloud ecosystem in a way that enables their business to operate coherently and efficiently?

Today this is a labor intensive, manual effort that needs significant research and investment to automate. These different infrastructure environments do not currently capture and exchange enough metadata and operational information to make this possible, even for a static environment. Given that organizations today are continuously evolving, the ecosystem must be able to dynamically evolve with it.

CONCLUSION

This is indeed an exciting time for practitioners in data-related professions. The technology is advancing, enabling the economic processing of many more types of data in many more types of systems.

To take full advantage of these advancements, information management needs to step above the technology landscape and focus on managing the movement, consumption and management of information as a coherent backbone of the organization. Supporting this backbone is a variety of technology that is selected and tuned to the workload requirements of the organization's operations.

This information backbone has to assume it is operating in a hybrid, multicloud ecosystem. Thus information management and governance capabilities need to be consistently embedded in cloud platforms from all vendors and on premises systems. They need open interfaces and well-defined behaviors to enable cloud brokerage services to correctly position both data and workloads on the most effective processing platform whilst keeping track of the organization's assets as a coherent enterprise-wide view.

Mandy Chessell
IBM's Hursley Laboratory, UK

FOREWORD BY IAN GORTON

There are many estimates of the size of the digital data that exists in the world right now, and as many predictions of how it will grow. For example, one source predicts that digital data will grow from a recently estimated 500 exabytes to 40 zettabytes in the next 5 years. That's exponential growth with a bullet. It's impossible to be accurate, of course, but at these volumes a few percentage points error is really neither here nor there. You really only have to be a dweller in the Internet age to experience this exponential growth of data, right there, through your browser windows.

Organizations working at these scales of data, and writing the software to meaningfully process it, live at the leading edge of software engineering. Tens of thousands of talented engineers work at the Internet pioneers (Google, Amazon, Facebook, Netflix, Microsoft, etc.), crafting scalable, high performance software infrastructures and applications that serve billions of requests on the Internet from consumers. These systems execute on globally distributed computing systems, housed in huge data centers scattered across the globe – these are the fabric of the global computing cloud. More and more, commercial and government organizations are migrating their core systems into this computing cloud, benefiting from economies of scale. Organizations buying and owning their own computing infrastructure is starting to sound so last century.

Many of the foundations of research in software architecture were established 15 to 20 years ago, before scalability became the dominant quality attribute for many modern applications. It is therefore timely indeed for the academic community to examine long hold tenets in software architecture principles and practices. Recognizing the core characteristics of these systems – capacity must grow exponentially and costs linearly – throws a whole new twist on architecture practices. For example, why produce architecture documentation when the architecture changes monthly? Do architecture reviews that take 2 days to produce results make sense in a world dominated by microservice-based systems? How can we create and manage useful architecture knowledge in a fast-paced, ever evolving development environment? How can we enable architects to explore the whole range of possible solution approaches given a huge design space created by open source technologies? How can we estimate the likely effects on performance of competing architecture evolution strategies?

It is in this context that I am happy to see this compendium of chapters, the first to turn the spotlight of software architecture research on scalability. It draws together some excellent research, descriptions of the state-of-the-art, and thoughtful reflections about where our discipline can fruitfully contribute to engineering practices in this scalable, big data world. The opportunities are truly huge as the problems are so immense. It just requires the software architecture community to shift gears, work closely with industry, and hypothesize new approaches for testing and validation at scale. With luck, this book will act as a catalyst and inspiration for this gear shift – it's about time.

Ian Gorton
North Eastern University, Seattle, WA, USA

PREFACE

The relation of software architectures to functional and quality requirements is of particular importance in cloud computing. Requirements are the basis for deriving software architectures. Furthermore, the environment in which the software will operate is an important aspect to consider in developing high-quality software. That environment has to be taken into account explicitly. One and the same software may be appropriate (e.g., secure) in one environment, but inadequate (e.g., not sufficiently secure) in a different environment. While these considerations are important for every software development task, there are many challenges specific to cloud and big data. In this book, our goal is to collect chapters on systems and architectures for cloud and big data and, more specifically, how software architectures can manage challenges in advanced big data processing.

INTRODUCTION

Software architecture is the earliest design artifact, which realizes the requirements of a software system. It is the manifestation of the earliest design decisions, which comprise the architectural structure (i.e., components and interfaces), the architectural topology (i.e., the architectural style), the architectural infrastructure (e.g., the middleware), the relationship among them, and their relation to other software artifacts (e.g., detailed design and implementation) and the environment. The architecture of a system can also guide the evolution of qualities such as security, reliability, availability, scalability and real-time performance over time. The properties of a particular architecture, whether structural or behavioral, can have global impacts on the software system. Poor architectural realization can threaten the trustworthiness of a system and slow down its evolution. The architectural properties of a system also determine the extent to which it can meet its business and strategic objectives. Consistent with this view is the trend toward focusing software architecture documentation in meeting stakeholder needs and communicating how the software solution addresses their concerns and the business objectives.

Big data is about extracting valuable information from data in order to use it in decision making in business, science, and society. Big data is an emerging paradigm applied to datasets whose size is beyond the ability of commonly used software tools to capture, manage, and process the data within a tolerable elapsed time. Such datasets are often from various sources (Variety), yet unstructured such as social media, sensors, scientific applications, surveillance, video and image archives, Internet texts and documents, Internet search indexing, medical records, business transactions and web logs; and are of large size (Volume) with fast data in/out (Velocity). More importantly, big data has to be of high value (Value) and establish trust in it for business decision making (Veracity). Various technologies are being discussed to support the handling of big data such as massively parallel processing databases, scalable storage systems, cloud computing platforms, and MapReduce. Innovative software architectures play a key role in advanced big data processing.

As the new-generation distributed computing platform, cloud computing environments offer high efficiency and low cost for data-intensive computation in big data applications. Cloud resources and services are available in pay-as-you-go mode, which brings extraordinary flexibility and cost-effectiveness as well as zero investment in the customer's own computing infrastructure. However, these advantages come at a price – people no longer have direct control over their own data. Based on this view, data security becomes a major concern in the adoption of cloud computing.

WHY A NEW BOOK ON SOFTWARE ARCHITECTURE FOR BIG DATA AND THE CLOUD?

We believe that cloud architecture is an emerging and important topic right now. Coupled with the increased number of applications, migrating to mobile devices that make use of cloud storage and cloud software services will see a marked increase in usage, but we are not sure software designers have thought through the changes needed to their applications to use cloud capabilities wisely. Likewise, big data is on everyone's radar right now. Working with big data is tricky, once you get past the knowledge discovery tasks. The real challenge to including big data in data architecture is structuring the data to allow for efficient searching, sorting, and updating (especially if parallel hardware or parallel algorithms are involved).

The area of cloud and big data is rapidly developing, with conferences/workshops exploring opportunities that cloud and big data technology offers to software engineering, both in practice and in research. However, most of these are focused on the challenges imposed by building big data software systems. There is no single resource that brings together research on how software architectures can solve these challenges. The editors of this book have varied and complementary backgrounds in requirements and architecture, specifically in software architectures for cloud and big data. They also have expertise in software engineering for cloud and big data. This book aims to collect together work across different disciplines in software engineering for cloud and big data.

This new book makes a valuable contribution to this existing body of knowledge in terms of state-of-the-art techniques, methodologies, tools, best practices, and guidelines for software quality assurance and points out directions for future software engineering research and practice. This book discusses systematic and disciplined approaches to building software architectures for cloud and big data. We invited chapters on all aspects of software architecture for cloud and big data, including novel and high-quality research related approaches on innovative software development environments and tools for big data processing.

The book provides opportunities for further dissemination of state-of-the-art methods and techniques for representing and evaluating these systems. We asked authors to ensure that all of their chapters will consider the practical application of the topic through case studies, experiments, empirical validation, or systematic comparisons with other approaches already in practice. Topics of interest included, but were not limited to: innovative software architecture for big data processing; theory, frameworks, methodologies, and architecture for cloud and big data; big data technologies; big data visualization and software architectures; innovative software development environments and tools for big data processing; cloud software as a service; software security, privacy with big data; new programming models for big data processing; software simulation and debugging environments for big data processing; research challenges in software architecture for cloud and big data; architecture refactoring for cloud and big data; modeling the software architecture of big data-oriented software systems; and architectures for organizing big data in clouds.

BOOK OUTLINE

In Chapter 1 we present an overview of software architecture for big data and the cloud. The cloud has revolutionized the way we look at software architectures. The emergence of the cloud and its "as-service" layers (e.g., software, platform, databases, infrastructure as services, etc.) has significantly induced the architecture of software systems. Cloud marketplaces, multitenancies, federation, elastic and on-demand access have enabled new modalities to the way we incept, compose, architect, deploy, maintain and evolve architectures of software systems. Properties related to dynamic access of resources; resource pooling; rapid elasticity and utility service provision; economies of scale; dynamicity and multitenancy are arguably the emergent "cloud-architecture significant properties." These properties have influenced not only the behavior of the software systems benefiting from the cloud, but also its structure, style, and topology. It has also moved architecting practices towards architecting for uncertainty, where architecture design decisions are more complex and require us to anticipate the extent to which they can operate in dynamic environments and cope with operational uncertainties and continuous changes. More interestingly, the cloud business model has also moved architecting towards economics-driven architecting, where utilities, risk avoidance, utilization, technical debt monitoring, and optimizing for Service Level Agreements (SLA) are among the business objectives. In this context, architecting in/for the cloud has become an exercise that requires continuous alignments between enterprise and technical objectives. Several architecture styles and architecture-centric development processes that leverage the benefits of the cloud and big data have emerged. The fundamentals of these styles cannot be understood in isolation in what we term as "cloud-architecturally significant requirements." The chapter will review these requirements and explain their implications on architecting for/in the cloud in the presence of big data. It will also roadmap opportunities for researchers and practitioners in software architecture for cloud and big data.

We have divided the rest of the book into five key parts, grouping chapters by their link to these key themes: concepts and models, evaluation of architecture models, big data technologies, resource management, and future directions. Part I papers examine concepts and models. Here the five chapters provide a broad outline of the area of software architectural concepts as applied to big data and the cloud.

PART I: CONCEPTS AND MODELS

Part I of this book consists of five chapters focusing on concepts and models which are useful for understanding big data and cloud computing architectures. Chapter 2, by Ian Groton, discusses issues related to hyperscalability and the changing face of software architecture. Hyperscale systems are pushing the limits of software engineering knowledge on multiple horizons. To address this explosion of data and processing requirements, we need to build systems that can be scaled rapidly with controllable costs and schedules. Hyperscalable systems can grow their capacity and processing capabilities exponentially to serve a potentially global user base, while scaling linearly the resources and costs needed to deliver and operate the system. Successful solutions are not confined to the software architecture and algorithms that comprise an application. Approaches to data architectures and deployment platforms are indelibly intertwined with the software design, and all these dimensions must be considered together in order to meet system scalability requirements. This chapter describes some of the basic principles that underpin system design at scale.

Chapter 3, by Mandy Chessell, Dan Wolfson, and Tim Vincent, discusses different types of systems involved in big data architecture, how the data flows between them, how these data flows intercept with the analytics lifecycle,[1] providing self-service access to data, backed with information governance that creates trust and confidence both to share and consume data. As an industry we need to improve the time to value and success rate of big data projects. This is going to take: better architecture methods that support different big data arenas; tools that automatically manage the metadata and context data necessary to pass data between processing zones; and standard structures for this data to allow for interoperability between cloud services and on premises systems.

Domain-driven design of big data systems based on reference architectures is discussed by Cigdem Avci Salma, Bedir Tekinerdogan, and Ioannis N. Athanasiadis in Chapter 4. Big data has become a very important driver for innovation and growth for various application domains. These application domains impose different requirements on the big data system. Designing a big system as such needs to be carefully considered to realize a system's business goals. In this chapter, the authors have adopted a domain-driven design approach in which they provide a family feature model and reference architecture based on a domain analysis process. The family feature model covers the common and variant features of a broad set of applications, while the reference architecture provides a reusable architecture for deriving concrete application architectures. The authors illustrate their approach by considering Facebook and Twitter as case studies.

Robert Heinrich, Reiner Jung, Christian Zirkelbach, Wilhelm Hasselbring, and Ralf Reussner consider architectural run-time models for quality-aware DevOps in cloud applications in Chapter 5. Cloud-based software applications are designed to change often and rapidly during operations to provide constant quality of service. As a result the boundary between development and operations is becoming increasingly blurred. DevOps is a set of practices for the integrated consideration of developing and operating software. Software architecture is a central artifact in DevOps practices. Architectural information must be available during operations. Existing architectural models used in the development phase differ from those used in the operation phase in terms of abstraction, purpose and content. This chapter presents the iObserve approach to address these differences and allow for phase-spanning usage of architectural models.

In Chapter 6, Tao Chen and Rami Bahsoon present novel ideas for facilitating cloud autoscaling. They examine the similarities between a cloud ecosystem, represented by a collection of cloud-based services with a natural ecosystem. They investigate how the ecological view can be adopted to explain how cloud-based services evolve, and explore the key factors that drive stable and sustainable cloud-based services. To achieve this goal they discuss how to transpose ecological principles, theories and models into autoscaling cloud analogues that spontaneously improve long-term stability and sustainability of a cloud ecosystem.

---

[1]The data analytics lifecycle is the process that organizes and manages the tasks and activities associated with the analysis of big data.

PART II: ANALYZING AND EVALUATING

The four chapters that make up Part II of this book focus on the analysis and evaluation of several big data and cloud architectural models. The production, processing, and consumption of big data require that all the agents involved in those operations be able to authenticate each other reliably. Authentication of servers and services on the Internet is a surprisingly hard problem. Much research has been done to enhance certificate management in order to create more secure and reliable cloud architectures. However, none of it has been widely adopted, yet. Chapter 7 written by Jiangshan Yu and Mark Ryan provides a survey with critical analysis of the existing proposals for managing public key certificates. Of the three solution categories reviewed, they argue that solutions based on transparent public logs have had the most success in the real world. They present an evaluation framework which should be helpful for future research on designing alternative certificate management systems to secure the Internet.

Performance monitoring in cloud-based big data systems is an important challenge that has not been fully solved, yet. In Chapter 8, Bedir Tekinerdogan, and Alp Oral discuss several potential solutions including caching and scalability. However, none of these approaches solves the problem of disruptive tenants that impede the performance of other tenants. Problems that are difficult to solve using the conventional caching and scalability approaches can be addressed using performance isolation. The authors discuss several performance isolation strategies and describe how the Tork application framework can be used to integrate performance isolation mechanisms found in existing cloud-based big data systems. In this chapter, they propose a framework and a systematic approach for performance isolation in cloud-based big data systems. They present an architectural design for a cloud-based big data system and discuss the integration of feasible performance isolation approaches. They evaluate their approach using PublicFeed, a social media application that is based on a cloud-based big data platform.

Anastasija Efremovska and Patricia Lago discuss the risks and benefits found in software cloud migration in Chapter 9. Multiple factors need to be considered when migrating to the cloud, which include financial, legal, security, organizational, technical risks and benefits, as well as general measures. The body of knowledge on relevant migration factors is mostly neglected in practice and scattered in the scientific literature. Security and legal concerns are no longer considered the greatest issues in cloud migration. Issues like post-migration costs and the potential impact of the migration on organization staff are gaining importance. Migration that was once considered a one-time task has now become a long term project. The authors present a list of factors that can help decision makers in assessing the risks and benefits of moving a software application to the cloud. These can also be used as a base to produce a more complete list of requirements when rearchitecting preexisting software and ease their migration to the cloud.

Big data has only recently been accepted as a recognizable IT discipline. It could be argued that it represents the next major paradigmatic shift in information systems thinking. Big data solutions represent a significant challenge for some organizations. In Chapter 10, Darshan Lopes, Kevin Palmer, and Fiona O'Sullivan present a practitioners perspective on big data. This chapter focuses on four key areas associated with big data that require consideration from a practical and implementation perspective: big data as a new paradigm, product considerations for big data, issues related to using the cloud for hosting big data, and big data implementation frameworks and migration patterns. There is no magic bullet for getting the right big data implementation. But the authors argue that using a combination of business problem focus, open source solutions, power of cloud, and understanding of transition to big data architecture can accelerate the journey and minimize the investment risk.

PART III: TECHNOLOGIES

Technologies used in several big data applications are discussed in the five chapters that make up Part III of this book. In the era of big data, an unprecedented amount of data is generated every second. Real time analytics has become a force for transforming organizations that are looking to increase their consumer base and profit. Real time stream processing systems have gained a lot of attention in social media companies such as Twitter and LinkedIn. In Chapter 11, Xinwei Zhao, Saurabh Garg, Carlos Queiroz, and Rajkumar Buyya propose a taxonomy that can be used to characterize and classify various stream systems. Based on this taxonomy, they compare several open source stream computing platforms. They observe that each platform offers very specific special features that make its architecture unique and that some features make a stream processing platform more applicable than others for different scenarios. The performance of a stream processing system will be always limited by the capacity of the underlying cluster environment where real processing is done. None of the systems surveyed allow the use of cloud computing resources which can scale up and down according to the volume and velocity of data that needs to be processed.

In Chapter 12, Robert Eikermann, Markus Look, Alexander Roth, Bernhard Rumpe, and Andreas Wortmann present a vision of model-driven cloud architecture engineering that relies on reusable service components. This approach enables developers of cloud services and architecture to efficiently build upon existing services. These services exist in the context of ecosystems providing important base services to support reuse, service composition, and user data management. For the latter, the notion of a Digital Me provides benefits for all participating roles: it facilitates data access control and data update for service users and it liberates service developers from providing data management features. Furthermore, it always yields the most up-to-date user data available. Using a generative approach, services for the digitized world can be developed more efficiently on a better suitable, namely higher, level abstraction. This ultimately enables each role, participating in service development, to contribute their domain expertise to dedicated challenges and facilitates service component reuse.

Enterprise applications are data-centric information systems that are being increasingly deployed as Software-as-a-Service (SaaS) Cloud offerings. Such service-oriented enterprise applications allow multiple tenants (i.e., groups of service consumers) to share the computational and storage capabilities of a single cloud application instance. A multitenant SaaS architecture lowers both deployment and maintenance costs. The cost reductions motivate architects to reengineer existing enterprise applications to support multitenancy at the application level. However, in order to preserve data integrity and data confidentiality, the reengineering process must guarantee that different tenants allocated to the same application instance cannot access one another's data. Chapter 13 by Andrei Furda, Colin Fidge, Alistair Barros, and Olaf Zimmermann presents a method and a set of architectural patterns for systematically reengineering data-sensitive enterprise applications into secure multitenant software services that can be deployed to public and private cloud offerings. Architectural refactoring is introduced as a novel reengineering practice and the necessary steps in multitenant refactoring are described from planning to execution to validation (including testing and code reviews). The authors present a realistic case study to illustrate the refactoring process.

Chapter 14 by Stephen Bonner, Ibad Kureshi, John Brennan, and Georgios Theodoropoulos explores the rise of big data and the hardware and software computational strategies that have evolved to deal with this paradigm. Starting with the concept of data-intensive computing, different facets of data processing such as Map/Reduce, machine learning, and streaming data are explored. The evolution of different frameworks such as Hadoop and Spark are outlined, and an assessment of the modular offerings within these frameworks is compared with a detailed analysis of the different functionalities and features. The hardware considerations required to move from compute-intensive to data-intensive are outlined along with the impact of cloud computing on big data. New systems like Apache Spark have been able to push application performance further by utilizing memory locality. The move to in-memory computation has also expanded the number of paradigms these data intensive frameworks are able to perform. The ability to utilize multiple computing paradigms within the same application will result in a new generation of data intensive applications being created.

During recent years, workflows have emerged as an important abstraction for collaborative research and managing complex large-scale distributed data analytics. Workflows are becoming prevalent in distributed environments, such as clusters, grids, and clouds. These environments provide complex infrastructures that aid workflows in scaling and parallel execution of their components. Workflow management systems need to be robust to guard against performance variations and be tolerant against failures. In Chapter 15, Deepak Poola, Mohsen Amini Salehi, Kotagiri Ramamohanarao, and Rajkumar Buyya provide a detailed understanding of faults from a generic viewpoint (e.g., transient, intermittent, and permanent) and a processor viewpoint (such as crash, fail-stop, and byzantine). They also describe several techniques such as replication, provenance, and trust-based approaches used to resolve these faults and provide transparent and seamless experience to workflow users. In addition, they classify various failure models, metrics, tools, and support systems. This chapter provides an insight into failure models and metrics. These can be used by developers to reason about the quality of the schedule and help quantify the fault tolerance of a schedule.

PART IV: RESOURCE MANAGEMENT

Three chapters make up Part IV of this book focusing on managing the architectural resources required for big data and cloud computing. In Chapter 16, Jose Gabriel de Figueiredo Coutinho, Mark Stillwell, Katerina Argyraki, George Ioannidis, Anca Iordache, Christoph Kleineweber, Alexandros Koliousis, John McGlone, Guillaume Pierre, Carmelo Ragusa, Peter Sanders, Thorsten Schütt, Teng Yu, and Alexander Wolf present the HARNESS integrated platform architecture, which is capable of managing resources such as CPUs (Central Processing Units), DFEs (Data Flow Engines), network middle boxes, and SSDs (Solid Straight Drives). The HARNESS architecture is based on a novel hierarchical management approach, designed to make cloud platform systems resilient to new forms of heterogeneity, allowing the introduction of new types of resources without having to redesign the entire system. The HARNESS platform layer automates the process of selecting resources to satisfy application-specific goals (e.g., low completion time and/or low monetary cost) specified by cloud tenants. The HARNESS infrastructure layer is managed by a collection of resource managers, each designed for a specific type of devices incorporated in the HARNESS cloud. The HARNESS enhanced cloud platform stack fully embraces heterogeneity, allowing a more complex and richer context in which to make price/performance tradeoffs and other resource optimizations.

Software development usually relies on a version control system (VCS) to automate the management of source code, documentation, and configuration files. To reduce the cost of storing and managing repositories, data owners often turn to public clouds. Unfortunately, public cloud providers are not necessarily trusted for various reasons. Bo Chen, Reza Curtmola, and Jun Dai introduce the definition of Auditable Version Control Systems (AVCS) in Chapter 17 and instantiate AVCS construction for skip delta-based version control systems which rely on mechanisms to ensure all the versions of a file are retrievable from an untrusted version control server over time. The authors describe an AVCS construction has the following features: (i) the data owner has the ability to check the integrity of all versions in the VCS repository, (ii) the cost of performing integrity checking on all the versions of a file is asymptotically the same as the cost of checking one file version, (iii) it allows the data owner to check the correctness of the version retrieved from the VCS repository, and (iv) it only requires the same amount of storage on the client like a regular (unsecure) VCS system.

Infrastructure-as-a-Service clouds offer access to a scalable virtualized infrastructure on a pay-per-use-basis. This is greatly beneficial for the deployment of scientific workflows. Considerable effort is being made to develop and update existing workflow management systems to support the cloud resource model. The majority of existing systems are designed to work with traditional distributed platforms such as grids and clusters in which the resources are limited and readily-available. In contrast, clouds offer access to elastic and abundant resources that can be provisioned and deprovisioned on-demand. In Chapter 18, Maria A. Rodriguez and Rajkumar Buyya present the use of Workflow Management Systems (WMSs) in cloud computing environments. The authors present a reference architecture for a cloud WMS and explain its key components which include a user interface with workflow modeling tools, submission services, a workflow engine capable of making resource provisioning and scheduling decisions, a set of task and resource monitoring tools, and a set of cloud information services. Efforts to extend an existing workflow system, the Cloudbus WMS, to enable the deployment of scientific applications in cloud computing environments are described. The authors present a case study to demonstrate the added functionality and evaluate the performance and cost of a well-known astronomy application on Microsoft Azure.

PART V: LOOKING AHEAD

In Part V of this book we discuss future directions for software architectural work as applied to big data and cloud computing. The importance of clouds and big data will undoubtedly grow in the future. New technologies will change individual and public life substantially, and enterprises will experience unprecedented new possibilities of operating. As with all new technologies, there are chances and risks, and they have to be applied wisely so that the benefits outweigh the drawbacks. This book reports on the state-of-the-art in software architectures for big data and the cloud. Future developments will build on that state-of-the-art, which constitutes valuable knowledge for all who want to be part of the exciting endeavor of building the digital future.

Ivan Mistrik
Nour Ali
Rami Bahsoon
Maritta Heisel
Bruce R. Maxim

INTRODUCTION. SOFTWARE ARCHITECTURE FOR CLOUD AND BIG DATA: AN OPEN QUEST FOR THE ARCHITECTURALLY SIGNIFICANT REQUIREMENTS

Rami Bahsoon*, Nour Ali†, Maritta Heisel‡, Bruce Maxim§, Ivan Mistrik¶

*University of Birmingham, UK †University of Brighton, UK ‡Universität Duisburg-Essen, Germany §University of Michigan-Dearborn, USA ¶Independent Researcher, Germany

1.1 A PERSPECTIVE INTO SOFTWARE ARCHITECTURE FOR CLOUD AND BIG DATA

Cloud has revolutionized the way we look at software architectures. The emergence of cloud and its "as-a-service" layers (e.g., software, platform, data, infrastructure-as-a-service, etc.) have significantly induced the architecture of software systems. Cloud marketplaces, multitenancies, federation, elastic and on-demand access have enabled new modalities to the way we incept, compose, architect, deploy, maintain, and evolve architectures of software systems. Properties related to dynamic access of resources, resource pooling, rapid elasticity and utility service provision, economies of scale, dynamicity and multitenancy are arguably the emergent "architecturally significant requirements" [1] related to the cloud. These properties have influenced not only the behavior of the software system benefiting from the cloud, but also its structure, style, and topology. It has also moved architecting practices towards architecting for uncertainty, where architecture design decisions are mere complex to anticipate the extent to which they can operate in dynamic environments, and cope with operational uncertainties and continuous changes [2]. More interestingly, the cloud business model has also transformed architecting into economics-driven architecting, where utility monitoring, risk avoidance, utilization, technical debt monitoring, and optimizing for Service Level Agreements (SLA) are among the business objectives. In this context, architecting in/for the cloud has become an exercise that requires continuous alignments between enterprise and technical objectives.

The unbounded scalability of the cloud has "accidentally" led to "data farming", due to the volume and variety of data accumulated and/or assimilated across various service cloud layers and constituent architectural components. The accidental presence of the phenomena had steered a new hype for "big data" and a need for architecting for big data in the presence of the cloud. The hype has consequently provided new opportunities and modalities for data-driven services. In addition, data has introduced new constraints and requirements of architecturally significant nature.

Software Architecture for Big Data and the Cloud. DOI: 10.1016/B978-0-12-805467-3.00001-6
Copyright © 2017 Elsevier Inc. All rights reserved.

Architecting for the cloud and data is difficult to decouple. The coupling has led to new architecture styles and design paradigms that are designed with the evolution of data and its management as first class entities. Several architecture styles and architecture-centric development processes that leverage the benefits of the cloud and big data have emerged. The fundamentals of these styles cannot be understood in isolation in what we term as "cloud architecturally significant requirements."

We quest for cloud architecturally significant requirements and explain their implications on architecting for/in the cloud in the presence of big data. We posit that properties that relate to multitenancy, dynamism and elasticity, service Level Agreements (SLAs) constraints, value-seeking architecting through autonomic decisions, cloud marketplaces, big data management for volume, velocity, veracity, and scale are essentially architecturally significant requirements that are implied by the cloud as a distributed on-demand operating environment. Awareness of these requirements can help architects and practitioners to formulate architecture design decisions and choices, which are cloud-explicit. We hope to provide insights that can help in the systematic architecting for cloud-based systems and lessen generality and ad hoc practices.

1.2 CLOUD ARCHITECTURALLY SIGNIFICANT REQUIREMENTS AND THEIR DESIGN IMPLICATIONS

The software architecture community had come to the conclusion that not all nonfunctional requirements or quality attributes (QA) can have measurable or significant effects on software architectures, their design decisions and choice. Consequently, architecturally significant requirements were advocated as the determinants for this category of requirements that relate to architectures of software systems [1,10]. The observation is valid without any doubt: not all requirements can have direct implications on the architecture, constraint its process, and/or explicitly affect the choice of architecture design decisions, tactics, style, etc. Though it may be difficult to objectively determine the architectural significance nature of these requirements, researchers have suggested some indicators [1], which can relate to the extent to which requirements are important and unique to the operation of the system; its responsibility in affecting functionalities and nonfunctionalities that are visible within the architecture; the significant character of the requirement to the stakeholders involved; observable effects on Service Level Agreements performance; business objectives and constraints and/or technical debts implication of the choice. Nevertheless, difficulties arise from the fact that these indicators cannot be clearly assessed and can be observed across various trade-off points.

In the context of the cloud, many indicators are fundamentally linked to the characteristics of the paradigm itself and its distribution environment. Cloud-architecture significant requirements stem from cloud properties that relate to the fundamentals of elastic computing, scalability, multitenancy of the cloud, etc. This implies that the cloud environment and the environment economies of scale are key determinants to these requirements. They can consequently affect the way we resolve trade-offs and decide on cloud-based architecture design decisions, styles, etc.

Cloud architecturally significant requirements and measurable effects can be observed on Services Level Agreements (SLA) compliance and violations. The choice of architecture design decisions is essentially SLA-centric; where SLA promises mandate design choices. Conversely, architecture design decisions and choices tend to inform, refine, and elaborate SLAs. The process is continuous; it is intertwined, interleaved, and informed by the requirements of various multitenants. The challenge is that the process has to reconcile various multitenant requirements and their constraints. This begs the question: is it possible to classify multitenants and relate their *commonality* requirements to architecture design decisions and choices of cloud-based systems? How do *variability* requirements within multitenancy inform of these choices? These questions are difficult for researchers to answer without understanding the anticipated behavior of the tenant, the dynamism of their behavior and the environment.

1.2.1 DYNAMISM AND ELASTICITY AS CLOUD ARCHITECTURALLY SIGNIFICANT REQUIREMENTS

Cloud is fundamentally dynamic. Dynamism induces the architecture of cloud-based systems in several ways. It can be implied from the fundamental properties of the cloud that have to do with *elastic computing* and multitenancy. Elasticity is defined as "the degree to which a system is able to adapt to workload changes by provisioning and de-provisioning resources in an autonomic manner, such that at each point in time the available resources match the current demand as closely as possible" [9]. Dynamism can be inherited from cloud service providers, where performance and service provision instability are the norms. As the cloud is a shared environment, it is imperative that architecting process for the cloud transits into resource and capacity planning in the realm of dynamism and benefiting from the economies of scale. The objective is to optimize for Quality of Services (QoS) provision and to improve cloud-based services utilization.

Dynamism is essentially a cloud architecturally significant requirement. It calls for new tactics and architecture strategies for predicting behavior in the cloud environment and proactively resolving complex trade-offs at runtime. It can also constrain the design of load balancing tactics and scheduling mechanisms that are essential for scalable, available, and dependable architectures. Dynamism makes uncertainty and unpredictability a pronounced concern in the architecting process; it begs for architecture-centric solutions that tame it. Solutions need to exploit various types of machine learning, planning, and intelligence to predict and consequently plan for realizing behavioral requirements. It also calls for architectural control and actuating mechanisms for managing trade-offs and mitigating their implications on various quality trade-offs. Analytic solutions that are grounded on market-based control, strategy dynamics, economics and finance are among the widely used techniques for managing and coping with dynamism.

One pending issue and open challenge that faces architects is to scale these decisions to cope with various levels of dynamism, ranging from relatively stable to dynamic and/or excessively hyper. Autonomic solutions are advocated in the heart of the architecture design process, where architecture design decisions are judged by their ability to deal with operational and evolution uncertainties. Among the autonomic decisions that architects consider is matching cloud users' requests with the resources capable of meeting users' requirements within the specified SLA constraints. Architectures are designed to dynamically allocate resources, effectively monitor resources' states and rapidly adapt to changes in workload. Architectures should seamlessly and efficiently resolve conflicting user goals and requirements, where scale, heterogeneity, dynamism, and complex trade-offs for nonfunctional requirements are the norm.

1.2.2 MULTITENANCY AS CLOUD ARCHITECTURALLY SIGNIFICANT REQUIREMENT

By multitenants we mean a software architecture which is designed to support instantiation, where multitenants can have a dedicated share of instances, including configuration, user management, individual tenant functionality, data and nonfunctional properties. Designing for multitenancy is a challenging exercise, as architects need to design instantiation taking into account multiple users in a given tenancy and across multiple ones. Architects need to consider the diverse needs, wishes, context, requirements, and quality-of-services constraints within and across tenants. They have to architect, realizing the commonality, variability, veracity, diversity, and scale of both functional and nonfunctional requirements supporting individuals, tenants, and the operating environment. Architects need to predict what may seem unpredictable from variation in workload patterns, likely sudden spikes or a one-off, etc. within and across tenants. Architects need to formulate design decisions and tactics that are flexible enough to cater for continuous changes in users' requirements in a single tenancy and across multitenancy. They also need to consider how changes associated with adapting to new environments relate to the cloud, how mobility, Fog, Edge, Internet of Things (IoT) and federation can affect design decisions and their evolution over time. Architects also need to predict changes in functional and nonfunctional requirements during the lifetime of the cloud-based system while it evolves. It is imperative that dynamic and "hyper" scale is the norm, where a new multitenant can join the environment and others may leave. Architectural design frameworks need to provide mechanisms to deal with similar uncertainties and to provide fairness and prevent "greed" in situations where providers stretch the economies of scales by accommodating more than what the environment can normally handle.

1.2.3 SERVICE LEVEL AGREEMENTS (SLAS) CONSTRAINTS AS CLOUD ARCHITECTURALLY SIGNIFICANT REQUIREMENT

Service Level Agreements (SLAs) constraints and specifications are essentially cloud architecturally significant requirements. Cloud-based system architects are challenged by the need for aligning Service Level Agreements (SLAs) with the architecture and its services provision, whether they are functional or nonfunctional in nature. Any violation of these agreements relating to performance, availability, reliability, security, compliance, etc., could lead to degradation of the provider's reputation or penalties in the form of monetary or service credit repayment [3]. Henceforth, architecting becomes a "strategy" game and challenge, where architects need to take cost-effective and efficient decisions, anticipate the risks and value of these decisions against likely or unpredictable changes in requirements and operating environments. This transits architecting process into service-level agreement-centric and value-driven design for operation and evolution, where alignment of the business objectives and technical drivers are at the heart of the process. Architecture design decisions hope to guarantee that violations for SLAs can be reduced by ensuring that critical requirements are provisioned through dependable resources. Therefore, the problem at hand is what architectural strategies, tactics and styles could help cloud providers meet the dynamic requirements of cloud-based systems, while adhering to service level terms. Aspects of the SLA life cycle, such as service discovery, SLA negotiation and reconciliation, monitoring and reporting can liken themselves with architecture tactics and components that meet these objectives.

1.2.4 CLOUD MARKETPLACES AS ARCHITECTURALLY SIGNIFICANT REQUIREMENT

Several cloud marketplaces have emerged, offering cloud application developers and architects ready means for online access and use of software applications and instances. Cloud-based architectures, an emerging class of architectures, can be composed of web-services, which can be leased or bought off the cloud marketplaces. It is believed that the value of the application and its underlying architecture is a function of the value of the individual web-services composing the application. These architectures can "trade" instances of abstract web services off the cloud, which can serve as a basis for dynamic synthesis and composition of the architecture. That is, for a given abstract service A, there exist multiple concrete services $Ai \ldots An$ in the market offering comparable functionalities, but differing in their price and Quality of Service (QoS) provision. Cloud is also emerging as a marketplace for service provision, where the selection of concrete web service instances from cloud-based market as a dynamic "search problem", which needs to be optimized to reduce probable risks [7,5], QoS and price [4], and technical debt [6].

Cloud-based architectures encompass a set of architecture strategies and tactics, which can take advantage of "goods" (e.g., service instances) traded in this market. Market mechanisms have lent themselves neatly to the notion of valuation of cost and benefits via utilities. "Buyers" are cloud-based application architectures, and sellers are vendors and providers of the services, which realize quality attributes, functional requirements, price and environmental constraints [7]. The formulation has enabled new modalities to the way we develop, maintain and deploy cloud-based architectures, where decentralization, scalability, modularity, substitutability are among the selling features. This has effectively steered new architecting paradigms, such as microservices [12], DevOps, etc.

The emergence of cloud marketplaces and instantiation has enabled dynamic composition of such architectures through substitution, where maximizing value, and minimizing debts and risks can be among objectives. Technical debt in cloud-based architectures can be attributed to suboptimal, poor and/or quick substitution and composition decisions [6]. This can be related to situations, where (i) the selected service features do not fully match the requirements of the application; fixes may be required to reengineer the solution to better fit the requirements, (ii) composing the service may have negative impact on the overall quality of the architecture; the composition may negatively affect the overall utility of the architecture and qualities like scalability, reliability, security, real time performance and the overall stability, (iii) in the absence of publically available benchmarks and historical performance data to verify the service provision and its compliance, uninformed quick selection and substitution decisions may carry likely risks, which can lead to Service Level Agreement (SLA) violations, (iv) the potentials of the architecture following composition are not fully utilized and the operational cost tends to exceed that of the generated benefits, (v) poor and quick decisions may add a value in the short-term, but can introduce long-term debt in situations where scaling up is unavoidable. Technical debt can also occur accidentally: cloud service providers may rush the release of their services introducing technical debt, which can be attributed to pressures to meet deadline and catch up the market. This can be, for example, through falsely accelerating the velocity by reducing testing and verification of the features delivered with the services. In situations where the service(s) are selected based on the sole trust of the service provider, the choice may accidentally introduce a debt, which is often left to the application developer to visualize and manage. As Agile Service Networks (ASN) become a reality, tools and techniques that allow organizations to autonomously evaluate the long-term value of the structure, the technical debt introduced by selection and substitution decisions will be needed. The impact of dynamic composition decisions of the architecture on value creation must be calculable, and actionable by autonomic software, which can self-manage the architecture for value creation, debt reduction, and long-term sustainability.

1.2.5 SEEKING VALUE AS CLOUD ARCHITECTURALLY SIGNIFICANT REQUIREMENT

Cloud-based software architectures can dynamically evolve to seek value [4]. The evolution of such architectures shall add value to the enterprise, end users, cloud provider and environment in which they operate. We viewed evolution of cloud-based application through continuous adaptations as a value-seeking and value-maximizing activity. The added value can be attributed to the Operational flexibility primitives of the cloud. Value can be linked to Service Level Agreements (SLA) compliance, Quality of Service (QoS) improvements, revenue streams for cloud providers and the multitenant cloud consumers, better utilization of the cloud economies of scale, environmental sustainability and CO_2 footprint reduction. At runtime, cloud-based architectures can specify the type of web-services to meet their functional and nonfunctional requirements. They can specify their constraints for price, computing power, energy consumption, and demands to virtualized and physical resources. Indeed, the need for web service substitution could be attributed to a business objective or a technical one, such as changes in load, the need to scale up, improving the current system' QoS, reducing the operational cost, or by upgrading to a new web service, which has been released in the marketplace. If the architecture wishes to create an added value, it can dynamically substitute its services. Scenarios, where federated clouds with different specialized and standardized services collaborate can be envisaged. These collaborations can be leveraged by an enterprise to construct cloud-based architectures, which are dynamic and self-adaptive by changing the web services they utilize. The recognition of Agile Service Networks (ASN) that spring up in modern business practices is a testament to this.

A common way of representing value for architecture tactics (e.g., provision of resource to improve QoS) is to formulate this using utility functions. This could take different forms (e.g., additive utility), where each formulation impacts the market's ability to reach desirable emergent state(s). There are many existing market mechanisms in the microeconomics literature. Each theoretically studied mechanism can be shown to reach some known solution concept (e.g., Nash equilibria). A self-adaptive mechanism, which uses these utility models, can assist analysts, architects and enterprises in providing built-in support for an autonomic architecture management supporting continuous evolution for added value. The inputs to these modes can be continuous data and feeds available through published benchmarks (e.g., cloudharmony.com; spec.org), which can continuously steer the selection and composition of cloud-based architectures. IT analysts, planners, and software architects and engineers can use simulation toolkits, which facilitate the scientific and engineering queries, what-if, sensitivity and cost-benefit analyses for sustainability and value. The use of microeconomic trading mechanisms such as the Continuous Double Auction (CDA), for example, has inspired the design of decentralized, robust, and scalable self-adaptive architecture for the cloud [4]. The work demonstrates how value-based reasoning can dynamically and adaptively steer the evolution of cloud-based architectures for value added by optimizing for utilities expressing QoS concerns. The space of strategies that a buyer (i.e., architecture) may choose during its interaction is yet another dimension. A buyer may be risk averse when trading web services instances, which will sustain or improve the utility of the architecture. These instances shall provide the assurance for SLA compliance and reduce the risk in likely violations [5]. In a market context, value can be estimated through tracking an underlying asset (also referred to as twin asset). The premise is that the twin asset can serve the evaluation through analogy in the absence of historical performance data of the asset under valuation, expert judgment, etc. [8].

1.3 BIG DATA MANAGEMENT AS CLOUD ARCHITECTURALLY SIGNIFICANT REQUIREMENT

The popularity, availability, unbounded scalability and service provision across various cloud layers, software, storage, infrastructure, platform, etc., had "accidentally" led to farming of data. The phenomena have hyped and strengthen what is known as big data, presence and opportunities. However, the hype has introduced new challenges to the architecting process, where data-centric architecting has become unavoidable and among the main drivers. The hype can be attributed to the natural incubation of data, represented by its volume, veracity and variety accumulated and/or assimilated across various cloud service layers and constituent architectural components.

Though big data is concerned with extracting valuable information from data spanning areas of society, business, science, medicine, engineering, entertainment, logistics among the many others, its presence within/from the cloud has constrained the architecting processes and product, and enabled new data-driven services. Such datasets are often from various sources (Variety), yet unstructured, such as social media, sensors, scientific applications, surveillance, video and image archives, Internet texts and documents, Internet search indexing, medical records, business transactions and web logs; and are of large size (Volume) with fast data in/out (Velocity). More importantly, big data has to be of high value (Value) and establish trust in it for business decision making (Veracity). Various technologies are being discussed to support the handling of big data such as massively parallel processing databases, scalable storage systems, cloud computing platforms and MapReduce.

Architecting for the cloud and big data is difficult to decouple. The coupling has led to new architecture styles and design paradigms that are designed with the evolution of data and its management as first class entities. The elasticity, multitenancy and the unbounded scalability of the cloud have steered new opportunities for data-driven architecting. The hype has provided new modalities for data-driven services. In addition, data has introduced new constraints and requirements of architecturally significant nature. The architecting process is challenged by having data assimilation, aggregation, classification and intelligent data analysis at the heart of the architecting process where data security, privacy, scalability, performance, availability and integrity and associated trade-offs are among the architecture significant requirements that influence architecture design decisions.

Database schema unification, portability, adaptation, search and mining efficiency, and their associated nonfunctional requirement trade-offs become pronounced cloud architecturally significant requirements that constraint and inform the architecture design process. The coupling of cloud and data has led to new opportunities for utilizing data through data as services and available via marketplaces, etc. Conversely, publically available service provision data and benchmarks have informed the composition decisions of cloud-based architectures, guided by historical information in relation to likely behavior and its dependability provision, cost, value, and risks. In dynamic and continuously evolving context, the challenge is to understand how value can be captured modeled, analyzed, and how the various trade-offs are involved.

Big data architectures, in the realm of the cloud, can essentially relate to architectures of data-driven services enabled by the cloud. The commonly used data-driven services relate to analytics services; these services are enabled and steered by the cloud as high-performance, scalable and on-demand "high-refresh" computing paradigms. Discussions on big data architectures can also relate to fundamentals of inducing the architecture with specific big data technologies and their architecturally significant requirements implications such as parallelism and concurrency.

1.3.1 BIG DATA ANALYTICS ENABLED BY THE CLOUD AND ITS ARCHITECTURALLY SIGNIFICANT REQUIREMENTS

Buyya et al. [11] investigated the architecture elements of big data analytics enabled by the cloud. Among the architecture significant requirements that big data analytics architecture need to consider is context related. Contextual information compiles information, such as logs of infrastructure operations, product releases, business metrics, and data compiled from social networks analysis among the others. In other words, the contextual architecture elements tend to refer to a broad spectrum of information processed from various media, whether they are structured or unstructured, technical, business, organization, sentiment, etc. The variety of contextual related data calls for the inception of other architectural elements, which are essential for big data analytics. The essential architectural elements have to do with the selection of appropriate sources of data for prediction; data filtering, requiring a search for most relevant data to be included in the selection, prediction and modeling; data extraction and ensuring the timeliness of the extracted data in relation to decisions, architecture reaction which are based on this data.

Other important architecturally significant requirements that relate to analytics have to do with the integrity, persistence, reliability, scalability, and general dependability of the raw data and the processed information. These requirements crosscut the entire lifecycle of dealing with the context ranging from selection, filtering, modeling, prediction, refreshing, and timeliness, etc.

The nature of the data can impose requirements of architecture significance. For example, data and information that deal with identities can raise ethical concerns and can call for solutions that maintain privacy and security of the identities, where data is arguably the individual's asset, and compliance for confidentiality can be a pronounced constraint. Architecture solutions need to consider locality vs. distribution, decentralization vs. centralization of the computation and transmission. Solutions need also to consider the motion of data and devise architecture solutions that cater for constraints for full, limited or no motion. Data exploitation and sharing under the realm of cloud data-as-service needs to consider compliance related requirements among the other requirements. Data of public use and interest can also introduce its own architecture challenge for solutions that cater for trust monitoring, scalability, availability, dependability and decay of the data and processed information to the beneficial services.

1.3.2 ARCHITECTURALLY SIGNIFICANT REQUIREMENTS IN REALM OF COMPETING BIG DATA TECHNOLOGIES

Several big data technologies exist. It is an architecture challenge to select the "right" technology that induces the architecting process and solution. Examples of widely used technologies include but are not limited to Hadoop/YARM, Spark, Pig and Hive, Mahout, and Cassandra, CouchDB, BlinkDB, HDFS. These frameworks are engineered to serve specific functionalities and features for data analytic, data parallel processing, etc.

For example, Hadoop/YARM is a general-purpose, distributed, application management framework that supersedes MapReduce framework for processing data in Hadoop clusters. The Map phase of MapReduce is concerned with the parallel processing of data. In this phase, the data is split into discrete fragments for processing. In the Reduce phase, the output of the map phase is aggregated to generate the outcome. The framework promises efficient and scalable processing of data across various nodes. MapReduce can be affected at the nodes that process that data. The premise is that it significantly reduces the network I/O, keeping I/O on the local disk or rack. The architecture principle that underlies this model is that the computation is localized; processing takes place at the data side as opposed to moving the data itself to the computation node. The principle acknowledges that limiting the motion of data can have implication on scalability, performance, security of both data and computation.

MapReduce has limited capabilities when supporting real-time and/or near real-time processing such as stream processing. This is because MapReduce has been essentially designed for batch-processing. Storm, on the other hand, addresses this limitation and is suitable for processing unbounded streams of data, enabling real-time processing of large volumes of high-velocity data. Storm claims to be capable of processing over a million records per second on a cluster node. Spark provides an environment and interface for programming entire clusters; it can focus on implicit data parallelism and fault-tolerance. Domain-specific applications that benefit from STORM include real-time customer service management, cybersecurity and threat analytics, data monetization, operational dashboards, etc.

Other related environments and tooling such as Pig and Hive (high level query languages/tools that ease the complexity of writing MapReduce queries), Mahout (providing high-level analytics tasks that create scalable machine learning algorithms to deal with Recommendation, Classification, and Clustering), and Cassandra, CouchDB, BlinkDB, HDFS (file systems and NOSQL databases) have also provided new opportunities for inducing and realizing architectures that meet modern needs.

Architecture styles can be induced by these technologies and can benefit from the tooling support. Each technology and tooling support provides pragmatic architecture realizations and ready solutions influenced by their strengths and limitations. It can also enable effective and efficient analytics, with minimum resource consumption. The choice can address recurring problems that relate to batch processing, parallel processing, data motion and related trade-offs.

REFERENCES

[1] C. Lianping, A. Babar, B. Nuseibeh, Characterizing architecturally significant requirements, IEEE Softw. 30 (2) (2013) 38–45, http://dx.doi.org/10.1109/MS.2012.174.
[2] T. Chen, R. Bahsoon, Self-adaptive and online QoS modeling for cloud-based software services, IEEE Trans. Softw. Eng. (2016), http://dx.doi.org/10.1109/TSE.2016.2608826.
[3] F. Faniyi, R. Bahsoon, A systematic review of service level management in the cloud, ACM Comput. Surv. 48 (3) (2016) 43:1–43:27.
[4] V. Nallur, R. Bahsoon, A decentralized self-adaptation mechanism for service-based applications in the cloud, IEEE Trans. Softw. Eng. (2013).
[5] F. Alrebeish, R. Bahsoon, Implementing design diversity using portfolio thinking to dynamically and adaptively manage the allocation of web services in the cloud, IEEE Trans. Cloud Comput. 3 (3) (2015) 318–331, 2015.
[6] E. Alzaghoul, R. Bahsoon, CloudMTD: using real options to manage technical debt in cloud-based service selection, in: The Fourth International Workshop on Managing Technical Debt. The 35th ACM/IEEE International Conference on Software Engineering, San Francisco, CA, ACM Press, 2013.

[7] F. Faniyi, R. Bahsoon, Self-managing SLA compliance in cloud architectures: a market-based approach, in: Proceedings of the International ACM Sigsoft Symposium on Architecting Critical Systems, Bertinoro, Italy, ACM Press, 2012.

[8] R. Bahsoon, W. Emmerich, An economics-driven approach for valuing scalability in distributed architectures, in: Proc. of the 7th Working IEEE/IFIP Conference on Software Architecture (WICSA 2008), Vancouver, Canada, IEEE Computer Society Press, 2008.

[9] N. Herbst, S. Kounev, R. Reussner, Elasticity in cloud computing: what it is, and what it is not, in: Proceedings of the 10th International Conference on Autonomic Computing (ICAC 2013), San Jose, CA, June 24–28, 2012.

[10] P.C. Clements, L. Bass, Relating business goals to architecturally significant requirements for software systems (CMU/SEI-2010-TN-018). Retrieved from Pittsburgh, PA, USA, 2010.

[11] R. Buyya, K. Ramamohanarao, C. Leckie, R. Calheiros, A. Dastjerdi, S. Versteeg, Big data analytics-enhanced cloud computing: challenges, architectural elements, and future directions, in: IEEE 21st International Conference on Parallel and Distributed Systems (ICPADS), 2015.

[12] S. Hassan, R. Bahsoon, Microservices and their design trade-offs: a self-adaptive roadmap, in: The 13th IEEE International Conference on Services Computing (SCC), June 27–July 2, 2016, San Francisco, USA, 2016.

CONCEPTS AND MODELS

HYPERSCALABILITY – THE CHANGING FACE OF SOFTWARE ARCHITECTURE

2

Ian Gorton

Northeastern University, United States

2.1 INTRODUCTION

It seems difficult to believe that websites such as Youtube.com (debuted in November 2005) and Facebook.com (public access in 2006) have been around for barely a decade. In 2015 Youtube had more than a billion users, who watched 4 billion videos per day and uploaded 300 hr of video per minute.[1] In 2009, Facebook stored 15 billion photos, occupying 1.5 petabytes (PBs) and at that time growing at a rate of 30 million photos per day. In 2015, Facebook users uploaded 2 billion photos each day, requiring 40 PB of new disk capacity daily.[2]

Traffic and storage magnitudes such as these will not become smaller or easier to deal with in the future. In terms of this rate of growth, Youtube and Facebook are by no means unique. With the imminent explosion of the Internet-of-Things – up to 50 billion new devices are forecast by 2020[3] – the scale of the systems we build to capture, analyze, and exploit this ballooning data will continue to grow exponentially.

The scale of contemporary Internet-based systems, along with their rate of growth, is daunting. Data repositories are growing at phenomenal rates, and new data centers hosting tens of thousands of machines are being built all over the world to store, process, and analyze this data. Societal change driven by these systems has been immense in the last decade, and the rate of innovation is only set to grow. We have truly entered the era of big data.

To address this explosion of data and processing requirements, we need to build systems that can be scaled rapidly with controllable costs and schedules. In this chapter, we refer to such systems as *hyperscalable* systems. Hyperscalable systems can grow their capacity and processing capabilities exponentially to serve a potentially global user base, while scaling linearly the resources and costs needed to deliver and operate the system. An example of a hyperscalable system is Pinterest.com.[4] Pinterest provides a virtual pin board to which users can attach and share content and ideas. From January 2011 to October 2012, their requests load doubled every six weeks to reach tens of billions of page views

---

[1] http://expandedramblings.com/index.php/youtube-statistics/ viewed October 2015.

[2] http://www.nextplatform.com/2015/05/07/cold-storage-heats-up-at-facebook/.

[3] http://www.cisco.com/c/dam/en_us/about/ac79/docs/innov/IoT_IBSG_0411FINAL.pdf.

[4] http://highscalability.com/blog/2013/4/15/scaling-pinterest-from-0-to-10s-of-billions-of-page-views-a.html.

Software Architecture for Big Data and the Cloud. DOI: 10.1016/B978-0-12-805467-3.00002-8

each month. During this time they grew from two founders and one engineer to 40 engineers in total – if engineering growth had kept pace with request loads then the engineering team would have been more than 50,000! At the same time, their cloud-based data storage grew by more than 10×, and while processing resources grew significantly, they cost only $52 per hour at peak and as little as $15 per hour during the night to operate.[5]

Experience building hyperscalable systems has clearly demonstrated that requirements for extreme scale challenge and break many dearly held tenets of software engineering [1]. For example, hyperscale systems cannot be thoroughly system tested before deployment due to their scale and need to run 24 × 7. Hence new, innovative engineering approaches must be adopted to enable systems to rapidly scale at a pace that keeps up with business and functional requirements, and at acceptable, predictable costs [2].

This chapter is about engineering systems at hyperscale for both cloud and private data center hosted deployments. It describes the characteristics of hyperscale systems, and some of the core principles that are necessary to ensure hyperscalability. These principles are illustrated by state-of-the-art approaches and technologies that are used to engineering hyperscalable systems.

2.2 HYPERSCALABLE SYSTEMS

As a quality attribute description, *scalability* is a widely used term in the software industry. Therefore, before we discuss hyperscalable systems, let's analyze in this section precisely what can be meant by "scalability." We will then build upon this understanding to describe hyper scalable systems.

2.2.1 SCALABILITY

Scalability is widely and intuitively understood in the software engineering and research community as something along the lines of being able to increase a system's capacity as its processing load grows. An example of this from the top of a Google search for "What is scalability?" is from Microsoft's MSDN[6]:

"Scalability is the ability of a system to expand to meet your business needs. You scale a system by adding extra hardware or by upgrading the existing hardware without changing much of the application."

This emphasizes expanding hardware capacity without changing "much" of an application. "Much" seems a rather imprecise term, but the general gist of the meaning of the definition is clear. The software architecture literature, for example, [3], follows along these lines, augmenting the definition by differentiating vertical (bigger machines) and horizontal (more machines) scalability. These are also commonly known as scale up and scale out, respectively.

Other attempts to crystallize a universal definition for scalability exist, focusing on achieving speedups in parallel systems [4], and discussing the different *dimensions* of a problem that are related to a system's requirements that are important when discussing scalability [5–9]. The dimensions discussed in these papers, such as CPUs, memory, network and disk, are interestingly related to com-

---

[5]http://highscalability.com/blog/2012/5/21/pinterest-architecture-update-18-million-visitors-10x-growth.html.
[6]https://msdn.microsoft.com/en-us/library/aa578023.aspx.

putation, not data. Others cogently describe the influence of processes and people as well as technical design on achieving scalability [26]. These efforts collectively leave little doubt that scalability is a multidimensional problem.

Scale up and scale out are indeed the primary mechanisms for expanding a system's computational capacity. However, these definitions obscure some fundamental complexities concerning both computational scaling, and project context. These essentially revolve around inherent limits in parallelism that exist in applications and limit scalability, and the dimensions of cost and effort associated with achieving scalability requirements. Let's examine these two issues in detail.

2.2.2 SCALABILITY LIMITS

In the fast moving age of computing, 1967 is the equivalent of times when Neanderthals roamed the earth. It is however the year that Amdahl's Law was first presented [10]. Simply stated, Amdahl's law places a theoretical limit on the speedup possible, in terms of latency to complete a task, for a given workload based on the proportional of a task that must be executed sequentially. For example, a data analysis task takes 10 min to execute for a 1 TB data set. The data set can be partitioned and processed in parallel without dependencies between tasks, but the results of each of these parallel tasks need to be merged serially to produce results once the parallel tasks are complete. If the results processing takes 1 min (10% of the runtime), then the overall latency for the task cannot be less than 1 min. As Fig. 2.1 shows, this limits the speedup of the task to $10\times$.

Amdahl's Law was derived in the context of multiprocessor computers and parallel processing for scientific problems. This explains a well-known limitation, namely that it only applies for a fixed size input. This enables the theoretical maximum speedup for a given algorithm to be estimated on a given input data size. In the era of big data, Amdahl's Law is therefore only applicable to problems that have relatively stable input sizes, for example, performing real-time (e.g., 5 s) facial recognition from cameras installed in a large building. After installation, the number of cameras is mostly stable, providing a fixed size problem to solve.

Gustavson's Law [11] reformulates Amdahl's Law to take into account that as computational power increases, the resources can be used to process larger problems in the same time frame. In our facial recognition example, a larger compute cluster would make it possible to process higher resolution or more frequent images from the cameras and still meet the real-time performance constraints. Gustafson's Law is more applicable to the cloud computing environment, where it is possible to provision computational resources on demand to process larger data sets with a latency that meets business needs. This means that as an organization's problem size grows, for example, by acquiring more customers or selling more goods, they can provision more compute power to perform processing and analysis in roughly constant time.

These two laws apply to problems that can be parallelized easily and have approximately $O(n)$ runtimes. For algorithms that are sensitive to input size, for example, that execute with polynomial ($O(n^e)$, $e > 1$) run times, speedups by applying more concurrency to larger problem sizes will be less than that predicted by Gustafson's Law [12]. Many common algorithms (e.g., quicksort) have worst case polynomial run times, as well as many powerful data mining and machine learning techniques. Scaling these requires more craft than simply throwing more compute power at the problem.[7]

---

[7] http://www.amazon.com/Data-Algorithms-Recipes-Scaling-Hadoop/dp/1491906189.

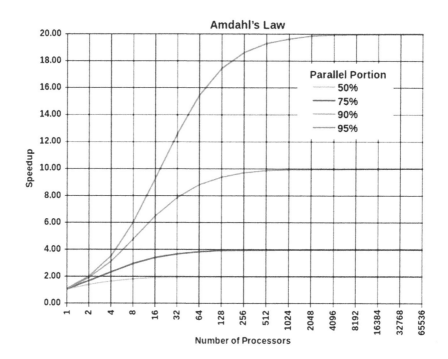

FIGURE 2.1

Amdahl's Law (from https://en.wikipedia.org/wiki/Amdahl%27s_law licensed under CC BY-SA 3.0)

Even if an input data set can be easily partitioned and processed in parallel, the problem of data skew often raises its ugly head. Data skew causes highly variable run times for the tasks that process data partitions in parallel [13]. For example, an application may wish to do a comparison of customer transactions by country. A simple way to process the data in parallel is to allocate the data for all the customers from a single country to a single parallel task, and to provision as many tasks as there are countries. However, if the data set contains 100 million customers in China, and 500 customers in Australia, then the task to process the Chinese customers will take significantly longer than the task to process the Australians. As the customer comparison cannot be completed until the analysis of all countries is complete, the execution time is limited by the time taken to process the data from China.

Data skew is essentially a load imbalance problem, and is commonly observed across different applications, workloads, and business domains. A common approach to dealing with skew is to allocate finer grain partitions to increase parallelism (e.g., process customers in China by province) and reduce task latency. Of course, finer granularity increases overheads and resources, so is not always a panacea. Techniques for both statically and dynamically handling data skew are the subject of ongoing research [14].

In summary, approaches to scaling a problem revolve around scaling up and out computational resources. However, there are fundamental limits to how different types of problems scale, both algorithmically and in terms of their data access patterns. This places an upper bound on how much faster

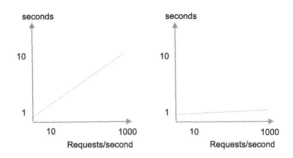

FIGURE 2.2

Scaling an application

a problem can be solved, or what size data sets can be processed in a timely fashion, no matter how many resources can be provisioned to solve a problem.

2.2.3 SCALABILITY COSTS

Unlike engineers from other professions who build and manipulate physical artifacts (e.g., cars, bridges), software engineers primarily manipulate symbolic representations of solutions to problems. These are called programs. While there are physical constraints to consider (e.g., the speed of light for data transmission) when building programs, software is not encumbered by the laws of physics and the complexity of physical construction that other engineering disciplines must deal with.

Perhaps because software is essentially a symbolic artefact with no tangible form for nonengineers to comprehend, we often have expectations of software systems that we would be plainly bizarre for physical artifacts. For example, the Sydney Harbor Bridge was completed in 1932. The traffic volume it carries today far exceeds the capacity it is capable of handling at peak times, causing very significant delays for drivers every single day. However, no one would ever suggest that the capacity of the bridge be doubled or trebled, because the original structure was not built to bear the increased load. Even if it were feasible,[8] the immense costs and work involved, as well as disruption, would be obvious to everyone. With software systems, complexity is hidden to all except those who care to dig into the details.

Let's take a simple hypothetical example to examine this phenomenon in the context of scalability. Assume we have a web-based (web server and database) system that can service a load of 10 concurrent requests with a mean response time of 1 s. We get a business requirement to scale up this system to handle 1000 concurrent requests with the same response time. Without making any changes, a simple test of this system reveals the performance shown in Fig. 2.2 (left). As the request load increases, we see the mean response time steadily grow to 10 s with the projected load. Clearly, this is not scalable and cannot satisfy our requirements in its current deployment configuration.

---

[8]The story of the expansion of the Auckland Harbor Bridge is instructive – https://en.wikipedia.org/wiki/Auckland_Harbour_Bridge#.27Nippon_clip-ons.27.

Clearly, some engineering effort is needed in order to achieve the required performance. Fig. 2.2 (right) shows the system's performance after it has been modified. It now provides the specified response time with 1000 concurrent requests. Hence we have successfully scaled the system.

A major question looms though, namely, how much effort was required to achieve this performance? Perhaps it was simply a case of running the web server on a more powerful (virtual) machine. Administratively performing such a reprovisioning on a cloud might take 30 min at most. Slightly more complex would be reconfiguring the system to run multiple instances of the web server to increase capacity. Again, this should be a simple, low cost configuration change for the application. These would be excellent outcomes.

However, scaling a system isn't always so easy. The reasons for this are many and varied, but here are some possibilities:

1. The database becomes less responsive with 1000 requests, requiring an upgrade to a new machine.
2. The Web server generates a lot of content dynamically and this reduces response time under load. A possible solution is to alter the code to cache content and reuse it from the cache.
3. The request load creates hot spots in the database when many requests try to access and update the same records simultaneously. This requires a schema redesign and subsequent reloading of the database, as well as code changes to the data access layer.
4. The web server framework that was selected emphasized ease of development over scalability. The model it enforces means that the code simply cannot be scaled to meet the request load requirements, and a complete rewrite is required.

There's a myriad of other potential causes, but hopefully these illustrate the increasing effort that might be required as we move from possibility (1) to possibility (4).

Now let's assume option (1), upgrading the database server, requires 15 hr of effort and a few thousand dollars for a new server. This is not prohibitively expensive. And let's assume option (4), a rewrite of the web application layer, requires 10,000 hr of development due to implementing in a new language (e.g., Java instead of Ruby). Options (2) and (3) fall somewhere in between options (1) and (4). The cost of 10,000 hr of development is seriously significant. Even worse, while the development is underway, the application may be losing market share and hence money due to its inability to satisfy client requests loads. These kinds of situations can cause systems and businesses to fail.

This simple scenario illustrates how the dimensions of cost and effort are inextricably tied to scalability as a quality attribute. If a system is not designed intrinsically to scale, then the downstream costs and resources of increasing its capacity in order to meet requirements may be massive. For some applications, such as Healthcare.gov,[9] these costs are borne and the system is modified eventually to meet business needs. For others, such as Oregon's health care exchange,[10] an inability to scale rapidly at low cost can be an expensive ($303 million) death knell.

We would never expect that someone would attempt to scale up the capacity of a suburban home to become a 50 floor office building. The home doesn't have the architecture, materials and foundations for this to be even a remote possibility without being completely demolished and rebuilt. Similarly, we shouldn't expect software systems that do not employ scalable architectures, mechanisms, and

---

[9]http://www.cio.com/article/2380827/developer/developer-6-software-development-lessons-from-healthcare-gov-s-failed-launch.html.

[10]http://www.informationweek.com/healthcare/policy-and-regulation/oregon-dumps-failed-health-insurance-exchange/d/d-id/1234875.

technologies to be quickly changed to meet greater capacity needs. The foundations of scale need to be built in from the beginning, with the recognition that the components will evolve over time. By employing design and development principles that promote scalability, we are able to more rapidly and cheaply scale up systems to meet rapidly growing demands. Systems with these properties are hyper scalable systems.

2.2.4 HYPERSCALABILITY

Let's explore the quality attribute of hyperscalability through another simple example. Assume you become the lead engineer for a system that manages a large data collection that is used for both high performance and historical analysis. This might be an Internet-scale application that collects and mines data from user traffic for marketing and advertising purposes. Or it might be a data collection instrument such as a high resolution radio telescope that is constantly scanning the universe and captures data for astronomical analysis and exploration. The exact application doesn't matter for our purposes here.

In your first meeting with the existing technical team and system stakeholders, the current system status is described and future growth projections discussed. The data collection is currently 1 PB in size, and is projected to double in size every 4 months (because of increased user traffic, higher resolution instrumentation, etc.). This means in three years (9×4 months), the data collection will be 2^9, or 512 PB in size. At the end of the meeting, you are tasked with projecting out anticipated operational, development and maintenance resources needed to facilitate this exponential data growth rate. The current budget is \$2 million. What budget is needed in 3 yr?

Fig. 2.3 plots various budget growth rates over this two year period. The y-axis represents millions of dollars on a logarithmic scale, with each 4 months period represented on the x-axis. If the budget grows at the same exponential rate as the data, you will need \$1024 million in 3 yr. Good luck selling that to your stakeholders! If your budget grows by a constant \$500K for each doubling in data size, you will only need a budget of \$6.5 million in 3 yr. The graph also shows budget growth rates of 25% and 50% every 4 months, and a growth rate of constant \$1 million per 4 months. Clearly, the system sponsors are likely to be more responsive to projections for constant, linear growth. This decouples the costs from the absolute data size that your system manages.

This leads us to a definition of hyperscalable systems:

Hyperscalable systems exhibit exponential growth rates in computational resources while exhibiting linear growth rates in the operational costs of resources required to build, operate, support, and evolve the required software and hardware resources.

In this context:

- **Computational resources** refer to everything required to execute the system. This includes data storage, both on- and offline, processing resources such as CPU nodes and network bandwidth (from dedicated data centers or shared cloud based), and physical resources such as data center construction and power consumption. In big data systems, growth in data size is typically the driving dimension of exponential growth.
- **Operational costs** are all those that are associated with utilizing the computational resources. These include software development costs for evolving existing and building new features, data management platform costs (software and hardware), operations, training and customer support costs, and cost of acquisition of processing nodes (purchase, cloud-based).

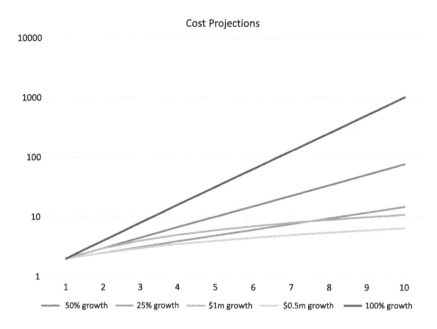

FIGURE 2.3

Cost growth projections in $ millions (y-axis) over a 3 yr period (x-axis in 4 month increments)

The need to scale rapidly therefore is foundational to hyperscalable systems. If they are unable to scale to meet business needs, or achieve scalability but at costs that will become unsustainable, they will fail. Scale is the primary influence on design and engineering, as it is the key quality needed for survival. When design tradeoffs are inevitably needed, the option that promotes scaling wins. Other qualities must of course be achieved too – for example, availability and security – but scale drives decisions forward.

The remainder of this chapter discusses some software engineering principles and approaches that are fundamental to building hyperscalable systems.

2.3 PRINCIPLES OF HYPERSCALABLE SYSTEMS

Hyperscalable systems are immense endeavors, and likely represent some of the most complex achievements that humans have ever built. As with any systems of such complexity, a number of principles underpin their engineering. In this section, we describe some general principles that hold for any hyperscalable system. These principles can help designers continually validate major design decisions across development iterations, and hence provide a guide through the complex collection of design trade-offs that all hyperscale systems require.

2.3.1 AUTOMATE AND OPTIMIZE TO CONTROL COSTS

There are typically two major costs in engineering software systems, namely people and resources (e.g., CPU, disk, network – see above definition of hyperscale systems). As a system's scale increases, inevitably more engineers are needed to design and deploy software, and more compute, network, storage, power, and facility costs are needed to support the system. These consequently are the major source of costs that must be controlled as systems grow.

There are two basic approaches to controlling these costs. First, automation of a whole spectrum engineering and deployment tasks is fundamental, as this reduces human costs and enables organizations to keep team sizes small. Second, optimization of software and data storage makes it possible to reduce the deployment footprint of system while maintaining its capacity to handle requests. As the scale of a system grows, optimizations result in significant absolute costs savings, as we will describe in the following sections.

2.3.1.1 Automation

Modern software engineering is replete with automated processes, for example, automated build and testing. For hyperscale systems, these approaches are equally important. Other characteristics of engineering at scale, however, require further automation. Let's examine a variety of these below.

When you upgrade the features of a site such as netflix.com, it's not possible to bring the whole system down, deploy the new version and start it up again. Internet systems aim for 100% availability. They must be upgraded and tested while live. Automated unit and subsystems test pipelines are still crucial to validate functional correctness, but it is pragmatically impossible to test every component under the load that they will experience in production (imagine the costs and time of setting up a test environment with 100 PB of data and simulating the load of 10 million concurrent users). The only way to test is to deploy the new features in the live system and monitor how they behave.

Testing in a live system is something that goes against established software engineering practices, but this is routinely done in hyperscale systems without bringing down the application. This is achieved through deploying a new component side by side with the replaced component, and directing only a portion (e.g., 1%) of the request load to the new component. By monitoring the behavior of the new functions, errors can be quickly and automatically detected, and the component can be undeployed and fixed if needed. If the component behaves correctly under a light load, the load can be gradually increased so that the performance of the new code under more realistic loads can be tested. If all goes smoothly, the new component will process the full request load and the old version is completely replaced [15].

Automated testing can be extended beyond single component testing to proactive failure injection for the whole system. The primary example of such automation is Netflix's Simian Army.[11] This contains a collection of *monkeys* that can be configured to cause failures in a running system. This makes it possible to discover unanticipated system-wide failure modes in a controlled manner, before these failures are inevitably triggered by the system's production load.

Examples of the Simian Army are:

---

[11] http://techblog.netflix.com/2011/07/netflix-simian-army.html.

- Chaos Monkey: The Chaos Monkey can be configured to randomly kill live virtual machines in a running system. This simulates random failures and enables an engineering team to validate the robustness of their systems.
- Latency Monkey: This introduces delays into the communications between the components in a system, making it possible to test the behavior of the calling components when they experience delays in their dependent components. This is particularly useful when testing the fault-tolerance of a new component by simulating the failure of its dependencies (by introducing long latencies), without making these dependencies unavailable to the rest of the system.
- Security Monkey: This can be configured to test for security vulnerabilities, and check the validity of certificates so that they do not expire unexpectedly.

Testing is not the only engineering task that benefits immensely from automation. Here are some more examples.

Applications that acquire and persist data at rapid rates must continually grow their storage resources while maintaining consistent access times to data. This requires that new database servers be continually added at a rate sufficient to handle data growth and that the data be sharded and balanced across the servers so that contention and hotspots are minimized. Manually rebalancing data across many shards is obviously time consuming and infeasible at scale. Consequently, many scalable database technologies will automatically rebalance data across servers based on a trigger such as adding a new server or detecting imbalance across existing server nodes. Consistent hashing schemes [16] provide the most efficient mechanism to perform this rebalancing as they minimize the amount of data that must be moved between shards as the database key space is repartitioned across available server nodes. An automated, efficient database expansion and rebalancing mechanism is fundamental requirement for hyperscale systems.

Many systems experience cyclic request loads, where peak loads are often an order of magnitude (or more) greater than average loads. Traditionally this has required a system to over-provision processing resources to be able to handle peaks loads. During average or low load periods, this means many of the resources remain idle. For such cyclic loads, the canonical example being Netflix's predictable diurnal load cycle,[12] it is possible to create an elastic solution that handles peaks by temporarily provisioning new cloud-based resources as required, and tearing these down to save costs once the peaks are over. Elastic solutions can be either customized to an application to detect growing and decreases load phases and act accordingly, or can exploit cloud-provider approaches such as AWS' Elastic Load Balancing.[13] By only paying for processing resources when needed, resource costs can be driven down to approximate the cost of the resources needed to process the average load.

2.3.1.2 Optimization

Premature optimization has been seen as an anathema in software engineering for 40 yr or more [17]. However, at hyperscale, even relatively small optimizations can result in significant cost savings. As an example, if by optimizing the web server layer, an application can reduce the number of web servers needed from 1000, to 900, this will both save 10% operational costs and create capacity to handle

---

[12]http://techblog.netflix.com/2012/01/auto-scaling-in-amazon-cloud.html.
[13]https://aws.amazon.com/elasticloadbalancing/.

increased request loads with 1000 servers. Optimization is therefore fundamental to developing hyper scale systems, as it enables a system to "do more with less."

A well-known example of effective optimization is Facebook's work on a translating PHP to C++, known as HPHPc [18]. Facebook extensively used PHP to build their website. Using HPHPc, the PHP is converted to C++, compiled and executed by the VM (rather than interpreting PHP opcodes). This approach provided up to 6× increased throughput for web page generation. HPHPc was recently replaced by a virtual machine-based solution known as HHVM,[14] and this now provides better performance than the original HPHPc. These innovations enable Facebook to handle greater traffic volumes with less resources, and hence drive down operational costs. Of course, for many organizations, undertaking an effort to write a compiler or virtual machine to optimize their applications is not feasible. Importantly though, the major Internet companies commonly open source the technologies they develop, making it possible for the community to benefit from their innovations. Examples are from Netflix[15] and LinkedIn.[16]

Algorithmic optimization is also fundamental at hyperscale. Linear or near linear complexity algorithms will provide faster and more consistent performance and utilize less resources. This becomes important as the size of the problem increases. Many problems can be amenable to approximate algorithms [19], which sample typically a random subset of the data set and produce results that are within a known bound (the confidence level) of the optimal result. For example, processing a random sample of tweets to understand trending topics, or a random sample of sales from supermarkets spread across the country are algorithms that are amenable to approximation. Approximate algorithms are also known as sublinear algorithms.

2.3.2 SIMPLE SOLUTIONS PROMOTE SCALABILITY

Most of us are taught at an early age that if a deal sounds too good to be true, it probably is. Common sense tells us investments that are guaranteed to grow at 100 percent a year are almost certainly bogus or illegal, so we ignore them. Unfortunately, when building scalable software systems, we commonly see common sense tossed out of the window when competing design alternatives and technologies are evaluated as candidates for major components of big data systems.

Let's take a simple example: Strong consistency in databases is the bedrock of transactional systems and relational databases. Implementing strong consistency, however, is expensive. This is especially true in distributed databases due to the necessary overheads such as locking, communication latencies, complex failure and recovery modes associated with distributed commit protocols. To build highly scalable and available systems, the NoSQL [1] database movement has consequently weakened the consistency models we can expect from databases. This trend has occurred for a good reason: weak consistency models are inherently more efficient to implement because the underlying mechanisms required are simpler. Weak consistency models tolerate inconsistency in the face of unavailable replicas, trading off response time and hence scalability against consistency. The inevitable trade-off is that the burden of handling replica inconsistencies is placed on the programmer, with varying degrees of

---

[14]http://hhvm.com/.

[15]https://netflix.github.io/.

[16]https://engineering.linkedin.com/open-source.

support depending on the precise mechanisms used in the database (e.g., vector clocks, versioning, timestamps).

In response, relational databases and the collection of NewSQL[17] technologies are now turning to new implementation models that provide strong consistency. These solutions *"seek to provide the same scalable performance of NoSQL systems for online transaction processing (read-write) workloads while still maintaining the ACID guarantees of a traditional database system."*

This approach sounds attractive, and some of the open source technologies that exploit main memory and single-threading such as VoltDB[18] show immense promise. But fundamentally, achieving strong consistency requires more complexity, and as the scale of the problem grows, it is almost certainly not going to scale as well as weak consistency models. Even advanced technologies such as Google's F1[19] that utilized GPS/atomic clocks, suffer from relatively high write latencies in order to maintain consistency.

As always however, there's no free lunch. Simpler, weak consistency models will give your application greater scalability, but there are trade-offs. You probably have to de-normalize your data model and, hence, manage any duplication this introduces. Application code has to handle the inevitable conflicts that arise with weak consistency models when concurrent writes occur at different replicas for the same database key. But, if your data and workload are amenable to a weak consistency model (and many are, even ones we think of as needing strong consistency[20]), it will be a path to scalability. This principle is depicted below in Fig. 2.4.

Another example of the second principle is the scalability of messaging or publish subscribe frameworks. Most of these offer the option of reliable messaging by persisting message queues so that they can survive node failure. Persistence requires writing messages to disk, and hence is inevitably going to be slower and less scalable than a memory-based queue. Memory-based queues are susceptible to message loss, but will provide significantly better throughput and capacity than their persistent counterparts.

There is one more key point to remember. Even though one design mechanism may be fundamentally more scalable than another, the implementation of the mechanism and how you utilize it in applications, determines the precise scalability you can expect in your system. Poorly implemented scalable mechanisms will not scale well, and from experience these are not uncommon. The same applies to inappropriate usage of a scalable mechanism in an application design, such as trying to use a batch solution like Hadoop for real-time querying.

Adhering to this principle requires thinking about the fundamental distributed systems and database design principals and mechanisms that underpin designs. Even simple rules of thumb[21] can be enormously beneficial when considering how a design may scale. Ignoring this principal can lead to systems that are beautifully engineered to satisfy functional and quality attribute requirements, but are unable to scale to meet ever growing demands.[22]

---

[17] http://en.wikipedia.org/wiki/NewSQL.

[18] https://voltdb.com/.

[19] http://research.google.com/pubs/pub38125.html.

[20] https://cloud.google.com/datastore/docs/articles/balancing-strong-and-eventual-consistency-with-google-cloud-datastore/.

[21] http://perspectives.mvdirona.com/2009/10/17/JeffDeanDesignLessonsAndAdviceFromBuildingLargeScaleDistributed Systems.aspx.

[22] http://www.theregister.co.uk/2014/02/19/some_firstwave_big_data_projects_written_down_says_deloitte/.

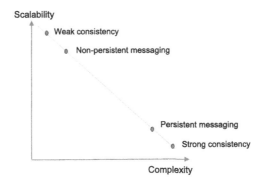

FIGURE 2.4

Scalability versus complexity

2.3.3 UTILIZE STATELESS SERVICES

State management is a much debated and oft misunderstood issue. Many frameworks, for example, the Java Enterprise Edition (JEE), support managing state in the application logic tier by providing explicit abstractions and application programming interfaces (APIs) that load the required state from the database into service instance variables, typically for user session state management. Once in memory, all subsequent requests for that session can hit the same service instance, and efficiently access and manipulate the data that's needed. From a programming perspective, stateful services are convenient and easy.

Unfortunately, from a scalability perspective, stateful solutions are a poor idea for many reasons. First, they consume server resources for the duration of a session, which may span many minutes. Session lengths are often unpredictable, so having many (long-lived) instances on some servers and few on others may create a load imbalance that the system must somehow manage. If a system's load is not balanced, then it has underutilized resources and its capacity cannot be fully utilized. This inhibits scalability and wastes money.

In addition, when sessions do not terminate cleanly (e.g., a user does not log out), an instance remains in memory and consumes resources unnecessarily before some inactive timeout occurs and the resources are reclaimed. Finally, if a server becomes inaccessible due to failure or a network partition, you need some logic, somewhere, to handle the exception and recreate the state on another server.

As we build systems that must manage many millions of concurrent sessions, stateful services become hard to scale. Stateless services, where any service instance can serve any request in a timely fashion, are the scalable solution. There main approach to building stateless systems requires the client to pass a secure session identifier with each request. This identifier becomes the unique key that identifies the session state that is maintained by the server in a cache or database. This state is accessed as needed when new client requests for the session arrive. This allows client request to be served by any stateless server in a replicated server farm. If a server fails while servicing a request, the client can reissue the request to be processed by another server, which leverages the shared session state. Also, new server nodes can be started at any time to add capacity. Finally, if a client becomes inactive on a session, the state associated with that session can simple be discarded (typically based on some timeout value), and the session key invalidated.

As examples, RESTful interfaces are stateless and communicate conversational state using hypermedia links [20]. Netflix's hyperscalable architecture is built upon a foundation of stateless services,[23] and Amazon's AWS cloud platform promotes stateless services to deliver scalability.[24]

2.3.4 OBSERVABILITY IS FUNDAMENTAL TO SUCCESS AT HYPERSCALE

The term *observability* defines the capabilities that make it possible to monitor, analyze, and both proactively and reactively respond to events that occur at runtime in software system. As systems evolve towards hyperscale, it's essential to observe and reason about changes in behavior so that the system can be operated and evolved reliably. The adage of "you can't manage what you don't monitor" is especially true for complex, distributed systems that have an overwhelming number of moving parts, both hardware and software, that interact with each other in many subtle and unanticipated ways.

Here's a simplified example of the problems that can arise in large scale systems. Two separately developed, completely independent business transactions were providing the expected response times when querying a horizontally partitioned database. Suddenly, one transaction slowed down, intermittently, making it occasionally nonresponsive to user needs. Extensive investigations over several days, including detailed logging in production and attempts to recreate the situation in test, eventually led to identifying the root cause. Essentially, periodic and brief request spikes for one of the transactions were overloading a small number of database nodes. During these overload conditions, when the other transaction was invoked, it attempted to read data using a secondary index that was distributed across all nodes. These secondary index reads from the overloaded nodes were taking tens of seconds to respond, leading to unacceptable latencies for those transactions.

How could observability have helped discover the root cause of this problem more quickly? If the developers could have analyzed performance data to visualize transaction volumes for the first transaction against latencies for the second, it would have been immediately obvious that there was a correlation. This would have highlighted the areas of the code that should be investigated, as it was this subtle, unanticipated interaction that was the root cause of the high transaction latencies. Observability in the applications would have recorded transaction latencies and made this data queryable for both real-time and post-mortem analysis.

Detailed performance data at the business transaction level doesn't come for free from databases or web and applications servers. Capturing the necessary performance data to perform this type of analysis requires:

1. Applications to be instrumented with application-relevant measures for observability,
2. A data collection capability to capture and store observability data from the distributed components of the application,
3. Powerful analysis capabilities for developers and operators to gain rapid insights from observability data.

By necessity, Internet companies operating at hyperscale have built their own observability solutions. These solutions are extensive and powerful, and have been built at considerable cost, specifically

---

[23] https://www.nginx.com/blog/microservices-at-netflix-architectural-best-practices/.
[24] http://highscalability.com/blog/2010/8/16/scaling-an-aws-infrastructure-tools-and-patterns.html.

for each's operational environments. Twitter's solution provides an excellent general blueprint for observability,[25] and Netflix gives a comprehensive discussion of the requirements for a hyperscale observability framework.[26] While these efforts help other organizations with the design of an observability capability, they place the burden of detailed design and implementation on each organization building a hyperscalable system. In a massively distributed system, this burden can be enormous both in cost, effort, and risk.

In recent work, we have taken the conceptual architecture described by Twitter and built a reference implementation for a model-driven observability framework. Model-driven approaches facilitate rapid customization of a framework and eliminate custom code for each deployment, hence reducing costs and effort. In our initial experiments, this framework has been able to efficiently collect and aggregate runtime performance metrics in a big data system with 1000s of storage nodes [21]. The project includes:

1. A model-driven architecture, toolset, and runtime framework that allows a designer to describe a heterogeneous big data storage system as a model, and deploy the model automatically to configure an observability framework.
2. A reference implementation of the architecture, using the open source Eclipse package to implement the model-driven design client, the open source *collectd* package to implement the metric collection component, and the open source *Grafana* package to implement the metrics aggregation and visualization component.
3. Performance and availability results from initial experiments, using the reference implementation.

The initial metamodel and implementation focuses on *polyglot persistence* [1], which employs multiple heterogeneous data stores (often NoSQL/NewSQL) within a single big data system. The reference implementation[27] is suitable for further research to address the challenges of observability in big data systems.

The architecture uses model-driven engineering [22] to automate metric collection, aggregation, and visualization. The main run time elements of the observability system architecture are shown in the top-level component and connector diagram in Fig. 2.5. There are two clients, one for each of the main user roles, *modeling* and *observing*, discussed above. The *Server Tier* includes the *Metric Engine*, which implements dynamic metric aggregation and handles concerns related to dependability of connections to *Collection Daemons*. The *Server Tier* also includes the *Grafana Server*, which handles metric visualization. The *Model Handler* in the *Server Tier* propagates changes to the design-time model, and the *Notification Server* augments the interactive metric visualization with automated notification of user-defined exception conditions.

The *Storage Tier* provides persistent storage of metric streams and notifications. All metrics for each database are stored as a time series to facilitate visualization and analysis. Metrics are stored with metadata to enable dynamic discovery of the metrics. This is necessary to accommodate changes in monitoring configurations after an existing model has been upgraded and deployed as a new version.

The *Metric Monitoring Tier* uses *Observability Daemons* on each database node to collect metrics from the local database instance and operating system. The daemons exploit database-specific and operating system APIs to periodically sample metrics and forward these to the *Metric Engine*.

---

[25] https://blog.twitter.com/2013/observability-at-twitter.

[26] http://techblog.netflix.com/2014/01/improving-netflixs-operational.html.

[27] Available at https://github.com/johnrklein/obs-prototype.

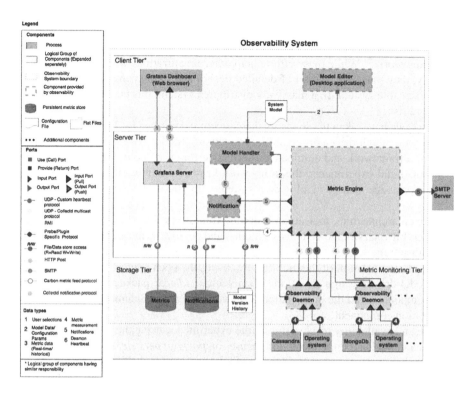

FIGURE 2.5

Observability system architecture (component and connector view)

We performed a series of stress tests on a deployed instance of the observability framework executing on AWS and managing 10,000 simulated database nodes. The metrics collection interval was configured initially at 30 s, and every 5 min was reduced by 5 s. The system operated normally until the sample frequency reached 15 s. At this point, some metrics were not written to disk. This situation continued to deteriorate as we reduced the sampling interval to 5 s. The framework continued to operate but data loss grew.

Examining execution traces from these tests, we saw the CPU, memory, and network utilization levels remained low. Disk writes, however, grew to a peak of 32.7 MB/s. This leads us to believe that the Whisper database[28] in the Grafana server was unable to sustain this relatively heavy write load. This clearly shows that any observability solution for hyperscale systems must be able to sustain heavy write loads. Utilizing a distributed, write-oriented database such as Cassandra or a high throughput file system should provide the write performance required, and we intend to investigate this in future work.

---

[28]http://graphite.wikidot.com/whisper.

2.4 **RELATED WORK**

The software engineering research community mainly focuses on scalable systems in two subareas of the discipline, namely Systems of Systems (SoSs) and Ultra large Systems (ULSs). We'll discuss these briefly below.

The term Systems of Systems was coined by Maier [23] in 1996. The main focus was to examine and define the characteristics of systems that grow in scale and complexity through the integration of several independently developed subsystems. Maier defined a set of characteristics that an SoS should exhibit, namely:

- Subsystems are independently useful and can be acquired and operated stand alone, independent of the SoS they can participate in.
- The SoS evolves over time, gradually incorporating new elements and new features in each element.
- Major functionalities of the SoS are achieved through interactions across many subsystems.
- Subsystems are geographically distributed and interact through exchanging messages and information.

The terminology of SoS emerged from Maier's work in the systems engineering domain, with a specific focus on defense systems (a telltale sign of this is the use of the word *acquired* in the above – defense agencies typically acquire (i.e., buy) systems rather than build them). System engineers build incredible complex artifacts, almost always involving physical elements such as a satellite systems or aircraft or submarines. There is considerable software complexity to consider, but this is not the focus of system engineers, or the original target of the SoS work. While the term has been adopted by a small pocket of the software engineering community involved in large scale (typically defense) systems, it is not a term that had gained any traction in the software industry or research community at large. In many ways, the terms Enterprise Application Integration (EAI) and Service Oriented Architecture (SOA) supplanted the need for SoS to be fruitfully considered in software engineering.

The Ultra Large Scale systems project [24] (ULSs) from the Software Engineering Institute built on Maier's work, but sharpened it to have a more specific software and scale focus. While their original target domain was again defense systems, the work clearly articulated the existence of ULSs in domains such as smart cities, the electrical power grid, and intelligent transport systems. The key features of ULSs can be summarized as:

- Decentralization in multiple dimensions – development, operations, data, evolution and design;
- Complex, ever evolving and inevitably conflicting requirements;
- Continuous evolution of the heterogeneous operational system. It can't be stopped to upgrade;
- System usage drives new insights and evolution;
- Software and hardware failures are the norm.

The original ULS book was published in 2006, just as the revolution in Internet scale systems was starting to gather pace. Undoubtedly, the ULS work was visionary, and the above characteristics apply to the systems built today by Google, Amazon, Facebook, Netflix and the like. In many ways, ULSs have rapidly become commonplace in today's world, and their complexity will only continue to grow.

The ULS authors defined a research agenda and roadmap, and the following quote nicely encapsulates their intent:

"We need a new science to support the design of all levels of the systems that will eventually produce the ULS systems we can envision, but not implement effectively, today."

Ten years later, we all use ULSs every day through our web browser. They can be built, operated and continuously evolved. The Internet scale revolution became the catalyst for the creation of new technologies, tools, and development methodologies alluded to by the "new science" in the above quotation. In addition, business imperatives, not a focus of the ULS work, forced the economic considerations of scale to rapidly come to the forefront and shape the inventions that have become foundational to engineering the hyperscale systems that are the subject of this chapter.

For observability, we know of no solutions that can be adopted and rapidly tailored for deployment at hyperscale. General distributed system monitoring tools have existed for many years. Commercial tools such as AppDynamics[29] are comprehensive products, but like there commercial counterparts in the database arena, license costs rapidly become an issue as systems scale across hundreds and thousands of servers. Open source equivalents such as Nagios[30] and Ganglia[31] are also widely used, and a useful comparison of technologies in this space can be found in [25]. Adopting these technologies and tailoring them to highly heterogeneous execution environments to observe application-relevant measures, as well as making them operate at the scale required by the next generation of big data applications, will however represent a major challenge for any development organization.

2.5 CONCLUSIONS

The ability to rapidly scale at low costs is a defining characteristic of many modern applications. Driven by ever growing data volumes and needs for valuable discoveries from analyzing vast data repositories, the challenges of building these systems will only increase. Systems that are unable to economically scale are destined for limited impact and short life times.

Hyperscale systems are pushing the limits of software engineering knowledge on multiple horizons. Successful solutions are not confined to the software architecture and algorithms that comprise an application. Approaches to data architectures and deployment platforms are indelibly intertwined with the software design, and all these dimensions must be considered together in order to meet system scalability requirements. This chapter has described some of the basic principles that underpin system design at scale, and it is the hope of this work that it will spark new research that builds upon the body of software engineering. Scale really does change everything,[32] and as an engineering profession this is a journey that has only just begun.

REFERENCES

[1] P.J. Sadalage, M. Fowler, NoSQL Distilled, Addison-Wesley Professional, 2012.

---

[29] http://www.appdynamics.com/.
[30] http://en.wikipedia.org/wiki/Nagios.
[31] http://en.wikipedia.org/wiki/Ganglia_%28software%29.
[32] http://resources.sei.cmu.edu/library/asset-view.cfm?assetid=20942.

[2] M. Nygard, Release It!, Pragmatic Bookshelf, 2007.

[3] L. Bass, P. Clements, R. Kazman, Software Architecture in Practice, 3rd edition, Addison-Wesley, 2013.

[4] Mark D. Hill, What is scalability?, Comput. Archit. News 18 (4) (December 1990) 18–21, http://dx.doi.org/10.1145/121973.121975.

[5] Leticia Duboc, David S. Rosenblum, Tony Wicks, A framework for modelling and analysis of software systems scalability, in: Proceedings of the 28th International Conference on Software Engineering (ICSE '06), ACM, New York, NY, USA, 2006, pp. 949–952.

[6] A.B. Bondi, Characteristics of scalability and their impact on performance, in: Proc. Second Int'l Workshop on Software and Performance, ACM Press, 2000, pp. 195–203.

[7] G. Brataas, P. Hughes, Exploring architectural scalability, in: Proc. Fourth Int'l Workshop on Software and Performance, ACM Press, 2004, pp. 125–129.

[8] L. Eeckhout, H. Vandierendonck, K. De Bosschere, Quantifying the impact of input data sets on program behavior and its applications, J. Instr.-Level Parallelism 5 (2003).

[9] D.B. Gustavson, The many dimensions of scalability, in: COMPCON, 1994, pp. 60–63.

[10] Gene M. Amdahl, Validity of the single processor approach to achieving large-scale computing capabilities (pdf), in: AFIPS Conference Proceedings, vol. 30, 1967, pp. 483–485.

[11] John L. Gustafson, Reevaluating Amdahl's law, Commun. ACM 31 (5) (May 1988) 532–533, http://dx.doi.org/10.1145/42411.42415.

[12] Lawrence Snyder, Type architectures, shared memory, and the corollary of modest potential, Annu. Rev. Comput. Sci. 1 (1986) 289–317.

[13] Yanpei Chen, Sara Alspaugh, Randy Katz, Interactive analytical processing in big data systems: a cross-industry study of MapReduce workloads, Proc. VLDB Endow. 5 (12) (August 2012) 1802–1813, http://dx.doi.org/10.14778/2367502.2367519.

[14] Y. Kwon, K. Ren, M. Balazinska, B. Howe, Managing skew in hadoop, IEEE Data Eng. Bull. 36 (1) (2013) 24–33.

[15] Len Bass, Ingo Weber, Liming Zhu, Devops: A Software Architect's Perspective, Addison-Wesley, 2015.

[16] D. Karger, E. Lehman, T. Leighton, R. Panigrahy, M. Levine, D. Lewin, Consistent hashing and random trees: distributed caching protocols for relieving hot spots on the world wide web, in: Proceedings of the Twenty-Ninth Annual ACM Symposium on Theory of Computing, ACM Press, New York, NY, USA, 1997, pp. 654–663.

[17] Donald E. Knuth, Structured programming with go to statements, ACM Comput. Surv. 6 (4) (December 1974) 261–301, http://dx.doi.org/10.1145/356635.356640.

[18] Haiping Zhao, Iain Proctor, Minghui Yang, Xin Qi, Mark Williams, Qi Gao, Guilherme Ottoni, Andrew Paroski, Scott MacVicar, Jason Evans, Stephen Tu, The HipHop compiler for PHP, SIGPLAN Not. 47 (10) (October 2012) 575–586, http://dx.doi.org/10.1145/2398857.2384658.

[19] Dan Wang, Zhu Han, Sublinear Algorithms for Big Data Applications, Springer-Verlag, 2015.

[20] Jim Webber, Savas Parastatidis, Ian Robinson, REST in Practice: Hypermedia and Systems Architecture, O'Reilly Media, 2010.

[21] John Klein, Ian Gorton, Model-driven observability for big data storage, in: Procs WICSA 2016, Venice, Italy, IEEE, April 2016.

[22] M. Brambilla, J. Cabot, M. Wimmer, Model-Driven Software Engineering in Practice, Morgan & Claypool, 2012.

[23] M.W. Maier, Architecting principles for systems-of-systems, Syst. Eng. 1 (1998) 267–284.

[24] Peter H. Feiler, Kevin Sullivan, Kurt C. Wallnau, Richard P. Gabriel, John B. Goodenough, Richard C. Linger, Thomas A. Longstaff, Rick Kazman, Mark H. Klein, Linda M. Northrop, Douglas Schmidt, Ultra-Large-Scale Systems: The Software Challenge of the Future, Software Engineering Institute, ISBN 0-9786956-0-7, 2006.

[25] http://en.wikipedia.org/wiki/Comparison_of_network_monitoring_systems.

[26] Martin L. Abbott, Michael T. Fisher, The Art of Scalability: Scalable Web Architecture, Processes, and Organizations for the Modern Enterprise, Pearson Education, 2009.

ARCHITECTING TO DELIVER VALUE FROM A BIG DATA AND HYBRID CLOUD ARCHITECTURE

3

Mandy Chessell*, Dan Wolfson†, Tim Vincent‡

*IBM, Winchester, Hampshire, United Kingdom †IBM, Austin, TX, USA ‡IBM, Toronto, Ontario, Canada

3.1 INTRODUCTION

This chapter describes the enterprise architecture implications of making extensive use of big data and analytics. It is based on our experiences over the last four years of working with a variety of organizations, both large and small, from multiple industries that have all wanted to derive value from analyzing big data. It summarizes our observations of the different architectures they have employed, extracting what has been successful and why.

Ultimately, these solutions must deliver value to the organization. This could be in the form of better customer service, new products and services, better use of resources, and reduced risk. We have seen examples of ingenious analytics on big data that never moved beyond a proof-of-concept because it was impractical for one reason or another. So we will focus on the practicalities of a solution's operation and evolution in our evaluations. In particular:

- How easy is it to acquire the necessary data and build the analytics?
- How easy is it to deploy the analytics into the appropriate processes that then deliver value to the organization?
- How easy is it to gather data on the effectiveness of the analytics so that it can continuously be improved?

Most big data solutions interface with the real world and therefore need to adapt to their changing environment. They are also still pretty experimental, as their developers explore the different possibilities with the data they have. So a part of any big data architecture includes an aspect of agility in the way analytics and data are used. We call this agile process the "Analytics Lifecycle."

3.2 SUPPORTING THE ANALYTICS LIFECYCLE

The analytics lifecycle is the process that a person or team undertakes to develop new analytics. Fig. 3.1 is a simplified version of the CRISP-DM method [1], which is an industry standard analytics development method that supports the analytics lifecycle. There are three high-level phases.

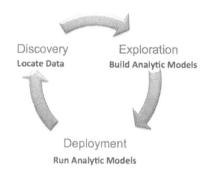

FIGURE 3.1

The analytics lifecycle

Discovery is the process of identifying the data that is potentially useful to feed the new analytics model. Often it involves searching for potentially useful data sets and acquiring them in a form that the analytics tools can operate on in the exploration phase. Typically, this means it can be transformed by the analytics tools without impacting the original source and includes a history of the values as they have changed over time.

Exploration is the iterative process of understanding the patterns in the data and building the analytics implementation to produce the new insight. This may involve further transformation and integration of new data followed by repeated execution of data queries and candidate analytic algorithms until the desired results are achieved.

Deployment is the process of taking the analytics implementation and integrating it with the data in a system that will bring new value to the organization.

All three phases of the analytics lifecycle have their challenges. Discovery often involves battling with the challenge of locating potentially useful information, getting permission to use it, and then getting reliable, on-going access to this data. Exploration is focused on understanding, correlating and identifying where the useful patterns in the data are located and how they can deliver value to the business. However, for many organizations, the major stumbling point in their big data projects is deployment. In simple terms, the analytics has to be deployed where its data is available and there is an opportunity to take action and record the result for future refinement of the analytics. The desire for real-time execution of analytics is expanding the scope of the deployment step beyond the analytics development environment to include the integration of the analytics into operational systems.

- The target operational system may require a different data structure to the one used to develop the analytic model.
- The analytic processing may need to be broken into a number of pieces that are deployed into different places and run at different times in order to access the appropriate data. The results must then be reunited to achieve the overall analytic result.
- Then there is the logic to take action on the resulting insight. This may be an automated action, an alert to a person, or new data displayed on a screen.

- The target operational system needs to collect data around the use of the model to provide the analytics teams with data for on-going validation and training of the model to absorb new data elements and adjust the models as the world evolves.[1]
- Finally, operational systems typically have stringent service level agreements around availability and integrity, which means that extensive quality assurance must take place before new function can go live.

This means the initial deployment of analytics on big data might be a fully-fledged software IT project with all of the checks and steps that implies.

Once the analytics is live, it will need to be constantly verified and improved to maintain its effectiveness as the business environment evolves.

Part of the original deployment of the analytics should have also included the collection of instrumentation data for the analytics. This comprises the data passed to the analytics, the results of the analytics execution, and the outcome of acting on this recommendation. The data scientists will use this instrumentation data to assess the effectiveness of the analytics and improve it as necessary. If the initial deployment is done well, refreshing the analytics implementation should be a routine process once the new analytics have been tested.[2]

Due to the workload generated by the development of new analytics, both the discovery and the exploration phases are typically supported by a specialized analytics system that stores copies of data from many sources. New data is constantly fed into its data stores, as it is generated by the organization, enabling the analytics developers to discover, review, select, and explore data from across the organization as they build their analytics. The specialized analytics system may also support the deployment of analytics.

For big data, where the volume and variety of data needs cheap storage and a flexible processing environment, the specialized analytics system is called a data lake and it is typically implemented using Apache Hadoop technology.

3.3 THE ROLE OF DATA LAKES

A data lake is an analytics system that supports the storing and processing of all types of data [2]. Typically, data from multiple systems, licensed data sets from external partners, and open public data are stored in their original form in the data lake. In the discovery phase, the team building analytic models select data sets from the data lake and potentially supplement this data with new sources.

In the exploration phase, they work with the data in their analytics tools to build new analytic models that can be used to improve operations in the organization. The analytic models may be used once to answer a specific question, deployed into the data lake itself to execute on incoming data as it arrives to derive new data (insight) or deployed in another system. Fig. 3.2 illustrates the data lake in action.

---

[1]While this is sometimes called model drift, it is more accurate to call this world drift, because it is the world that is changing, not the model.

[2]For many organizations – A/B or Champion/Challenger testing is an ongoing, never-ending process. They continually look for new and better approaches.

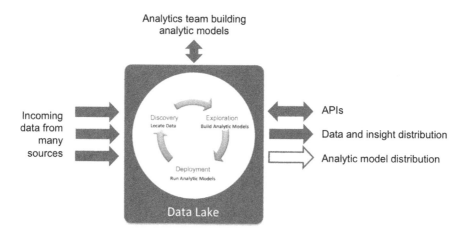

FIGURE 3.2

Interactions with a data lake

In Fig. 3.2, data is flowing in from the left side. Along the top, the analytics teams are working on building new analytic models through discovery and exploration. Some of these models may be deployed into the data lake.

On the right shows the output of the data lake. Systems may access the original data and new insight derived from running the analytic models through APIs. Alternatively, data and insight from the data lake may be distributed to other systems as events or in batch. Finally, the data lake may have distributed analytic models for deployment into other systems.

3.4 KEY DESIGN FEATURES THAT MAKE A DATA LAKE SUCCESSFUL

The data lake approach has received some criticism in recent years, and has even been characterized as a "data swamp" [3]. The root cause of this criticism is that without proper governance and cataloguing of data in the data lake, people are frequently not able to locate the data they need, and even when they do find some potentially useful data, they are not sure where it came from and do not trust it. On the supply side, there is often resistance to add valuable data sources to a data lake because there are no controls on how it will be used.

In our work with clients around data lakes, particularly in regulated industries, we have extending the notion of a simple data lake with metadata management and governance. This architecture is published under the title of a "data reservoir" to highlight that it is a managed data lake [4–6]. The aim is to create an ecosystem where there is trust both to share and consume data.

One of the key differences in the managed data lake is that it potentially includes multiple data platforms, such as Apache Hadoop, streaming technology, relational databases, and No SQL databases. The aim is to site workload and data on the most appropriate platform whilst governing all of the platforms consistently. The managed data lake is surrounded by services that create a consistent interface to the data and analytics irrespective of which platform they are deployed on. The result is an environment where business users and data scientist can innovate with data and analytics whilst the IT team is able to take advantage of the latest innovations in technology.

The following components deliver the managed data lake:

- Data repositories that provide organized data sets from many sources.
- A catalog of the data repositories with details information about their content, lineage and ownership. This enables the discovery phase of the analytics lifecycle by helping the analytics team identify and locate the right data to use in their work.
- Support for self-service population and management of sandboxes, data preparation tools and tools for building new analytics. This supports the exploration phase.
- Production level support for the execution of analytics within the repositories. This supports the deployment phase.
- Ongoing exchange of data in and out of the data lake connecting it to the latest sources of data and distributing new insight.
- Operational information governance and data security services to protect and maintain the data within the care of the data lake.

The success of any data lake is largely due to the investment in the catalog and the governance around it because it must become an environment where there is trust and confidence both to the share data and to consume it. Data lakes that operate without this discipline become an ever-increasing collection of duplicated data where no one is sure what is available and so gets their own copy of data from the source systems for each project. The data left lying around in the data lake becomes a cost, security and privacy liability for the owning organization.

That withstanding, the centralized data lake is an increasing popular approach to creating a big data and analytics environment for an organization's general use. However, it is not always the most appropriate approach.

3.5 ARCHITECTURE EXAMPLE – CONTEXT MANAGEMENT IN THE IOT

Our next architecture relates to big data in an Internet of Things (IoT) solution. The example comes from the field of home monitoring for the elderly [7]. The idea is to monitor the activity in an elderly or vulnerable person's home to detect whether they are performing their usual activities, or there is a problem, such as they have fallen and are hurt, or they did not get out of bed, so may be ill. The aim is to provide simple monitoring without a major invasion of their privacy – such as through using cameras.

The solution involves adding sensors to chairs, kettle, bed, front door, bathroom, and other areas that can detect normal activity. The readings from these sensors can be used to determine if the individual living in the home is ok.

Early architectures for IoT big data solutions had all of the data from the sensors being pumped into a central data lake that was responsible for parsing the raw data, making decisions on actions and then sending the commands back to the devices if needed. However, this has proved impractical for a number of reasons:

- The data transfer times between the monitored environment and the data lake makes the control feedback sluggish.
- The monitored environment has no autonomous action if there are network communications issues.
- The data lake processing is complex since it has to understand all of the complexity of the monitored environments. There is a lot of variation in the types of sensors, how they work and the types of data they generate.
- The central data lake processing is fragile since it is impacted by changes in the monitored environments – such as a broken sensor being replaced by a new sensor from a different manufacturer.

Each of these reasons impacts the ability to scale the solution. The central processing also creates concerns over privacy of the individual given the volume of data about their lives that is being transmitted [8].

A more scalable design pushes processing close to sensors. So a small processing box in each home that manages the data from the sensors and outputs status and alerts as required. Any local changes to the sensors in the home are handled by the local system. The local system does not transmit details of every activity in the home – just that there is activity going on – or that something is potentially wrong.

The value of this approach is that details of the physical deployment of the sensors are replaced by meaningful messages such as "no activity detected since time t" are shared with the central data lake and the individual has an increased level of privacy because only relevant activity is shared beyond the home.

Processing IoT data close to it origin is becoming the best practice approach for IoT solution design. However, there is still a need to transmit a portion of the data back to a central processing point (such as a data lake) in order to enhance the analytic models, or perform historical analysis.

We have seen this pattern used in smart electrical power grids where the physical deployment of components in the power distribution equipment is so complex and volatile, whilst action must be taken very quickly when problems arise. A similar approach is being adopted for automobile automation.

3.6 BIG DATA ORIGINS AND CHARACTERISTICS

The IoT monitoring case study reminds us that big data is not born in the data lake. The areas of growth in data are broadly grouped into:

- Data coming from sensors that are reporting the state of the environment and the activity around them;
- Unstructured data such as text, audio and video media. This information is generated through social media and other collaboration technology and well as the wealth of document publishing channels that we have today.

However, structured data from operational systems (enterprise data) is still significant in big data analytics because it provides the context where the analytics will need to operate if they are to impact the way that the organization operates.

As we examine different big data architectures it is helpful to group related systems into categories that define the types of big data they are processing.

3.7 THE SYSTEMS THAT CAPTURE AND PROCESS BIG DATA

An organization that is focused on becoming a digital enterprise is typically investing in either or both of the following types of systems [9].

- Systems of Engagement (SoE) – these systems interact with people. They include mobile apps and social media services. They are systems that are dedicated to supporting people in many aspects of their daily life. As a result they generate a lot of data about the activities of each individual and have the potential to understand the interests and needs of these individuals. Analytics are often used to make personalized recommendations to individuals.
- Systems of Automation (SoA) – these systems interact with the environment, using sensors and other physical devices to capture data about an asset or a particular location. They are also called Internet of Things (IoT) systems. The big data from these systems is typically streams of events related to the activity around the location or asset. The system of automation uses this input to understand the situation and to make changes to various controls to correct an issue, or make use of an opportunity. Analytics are typically used to predict the likelihood of particular future events based on recent activity.

In addition, the category called System of Record (SoR) is part of this classification scheme. Systems of Record cover the traditional systems that drive an organization's operation. They are considered to represent a reliable, all but localized view of a particular part of the organization's operation. They may also be the target deployment for analytics. So although they do not produce big data from their core operation, they are relevant to this discussion because:

- Their data provides organization context to big data processing. For example, these systems record the transactions of the business. This is the ultimate gauge on the organization's success.
- The transactions also link to the people, products, assets and requests that drive the business. Often the identifiers of these objects are used in correlation in the big data environment.
- They may be a target deployment system for analytics or the insight generated from the big data processing.
- They may be instrumented or monitored by a process that produces log data that requires big data processing to parse, interpret and act on.

An organization's data lake can then be thought of as a System of Insight (SoI) [9] in this classification scheme. They gather data from a wide variety of data sources and aim to blend them together to create a broader picture of the activity across the organization. These systems generate what we refer to as "data gravity." This mean the presence of such a wide variety of data draws people, such as data scientists, and new applications towards it. It therefore also becomes an environment supporting the entire analytics lifecycle plus a distribution point for data and insights to a wide range of applications.

These system categories are illustrated in Fig. 3.3, along with the types of data likely to be generated by these systems.

Each of these types of systems is both collecting and processing key data that is needed by the organization to operate coherently across all of the channels it uses to connect with its customers, business partners and employees. Thus, there is considerable data flow between these systems.

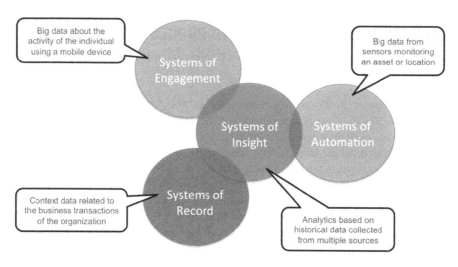

FIGURE 3.3

System categories and the data they produce

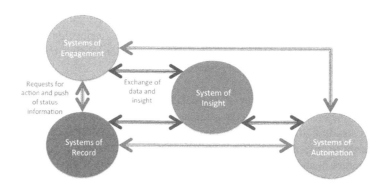

FIGURE 3.4

Interaction between the system categories

In addition, these systems may be hosted either on premise or in the cloud.

In Fig. 3.4, we have added the data integration flows. The blue arrows represent API calls requesting requests to perform an action or service and the green arrows represent bulk movement of the data itself for further processing and analysis. Notice how the data lake (System of Insight) typically acts as a hub for data movement and analysis.

If organizations were flat, egalitarian constructs, then Fig. 3.4 describes an interesting technical challenge to designing data formats and structures that allow each type of system to acquire the data it needs in an efficient form for its processing and run analytic models generated from the data lake. Data would be synchronized between systems as and when it is needed.

The reality is that many organizations are deeply siloed. These silos are designed to divide up the work of the organization into functional units that can be effectively managed. Data is generated by systems owned and operated within these silos. Some big data solutions can be localized within a single silo, combining only its data with potentially data from outside the organization. However, it is more common that a big data solution is aiming to create a coordinated decision making capability for the organization that therefore needs data to flow laterally between silos.

The increasing use of cloud-based services can add to this complexity, creating new technical silos that must be bridged. Cloud-based services extend the technological capabilities of an organization, potentially supporting innovative platforms and functions. Cloud-based services often retain and maintain data that is useful for analytics. The challenge is often in gaining access to that data and combining it with data from other places.

3.8 OPERATING ACROSS ORGANIZATIONAL SILOS

The broader the scope of the big data solution, the more complex it becomes. Not only does it involve crossing the organization's political silos, requiring negotiation and collaboration between people, but also crossing the organization's process silos, requiring the integration of data that has been created with very different assumptions and context.

Blending data from multiple processes as we have already discussed can be complex. Often raw data is full of local, tribal knowledge that makes it unintelligible to external systems. Examples of tribal knowledge include:

- Use of code enumerations to represent valid values for fields. For example, using 0 for "Mr", 1 for "Mrs", 2 for "Miss", 3 for "Dr", 4 for "Sir", 5 for Professor, and so on for courtesy title.
- Inventive use of data fields – for example, using the fifth line of the address for messages to the postman such as "Leave parcel by gate" because the application will then print it on the envelope.
- Local interpretations of common terms.
- Local knowledge on how much to trust the data in the systems and where it came from.
- Local identifiers for people, organizations and shared assets and services.

This tribal knowledge has to be encoded and associated with the data to make it relevant and understandable to an external team using the data. This can be done either by changing the data so it is self-describing, or having metadata that augments the data.

Thus more thought must be given to the way data is acquired and managed to ensure it is processed properly. A similar thought process is required for the insight generated from the data and any resulting action and outcome if it is going to be used outside of the system producing the insight.

Experience also tells us that no organization beyond the control of a single person finds it easy to have a single unifying system for innovation. The nature of innovation is such that it is often opportunistic, slightly maverick, and unplanned. So expecting it to all happen in a single system of insight is unrealistic. As data becomes more important to an organization, multiple silos are likely to develop big data solutions. However, there is clearly value in enabling an organization to act coherently and take advantage of the big data generated from its full range of activities.

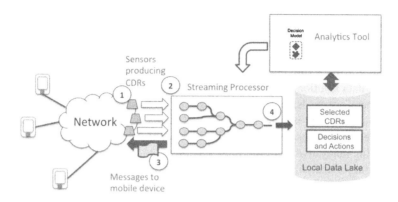

FIGURE 3.5

Mobile device use analysis for a CSP

Combining the need innovate with the need to act coherently – two seeming contradicting require-ments – suggests that enterprise needs to accept that there will be multiple solutions using big data for innovation and the enterprise architecture must to account for this.

We will use two examples of next best action solutions that come from the telecommunications industry. Each aims to offer personalized customer service to people as they interact with a service.

3.9 ARCHITECTURE EXAMPLE – LOCAL PROCESSING OF BIG DATA

The first example of a next best action solution only processes the big data generated from a system of engagement [10].

In this example, a real-time streaming engine in a communication service provider (CSP) [11] is receiving Call Detail Records (CDRs) [12] and related data feeds from mobile phones where the subscriber has a pay-as-you-go service. With a pay-as-you-go service, the CSP has no information of their subscribers. The aim of the big data solution is to analyze the activity on each device to build a profile of the person's behavior that is then used to present offers to the individual. For example, the analytics may notice that the subscriber spends a significant time on Facebook, and so an offer could be made for an enhanced package that gives them unlimited, or faster response time on Facebook. The aim is to create a deeper relationship with the subscriber to reduce the chance of them moving to a different CSP.

Fig. 3.5 shows this architecture.

The interaction of the components shown in Fig. 3.5 is as follows:

1. Call detail records and related data that logs the communication activity from the mobile devices are generated by the network.
2. The streaming processor receives this data and parses, categorizes and analyzes the communication from each mobile device.

3. When appropriate, it sends messages back to an individual mobile device with an offer.

4. The streaming processor also logs the results of its analysis and the outcome of any offer, enabling the data scientists to tune the analytics from the local data lake.

The beauty of this type of big data application is that it is self-contained. All of the analysis is on the data from the mobile device, and the resulting action is executed with messages to the device. The project team can focus on understanding the data they are receiving, gaining proficiency with the streaming technology, and developing the analytics that determines the offers. They are likely to only have one stakeholder and the project can be rolled out incrementally as more advanced analytics are developed.

Make no mistake; this is still a challenging project, since the team is handling both volume and velocity of data. However, the variety of data is missing and this is an important simplification.

Our next architecture expands out from this first architecture, to analyze subscriber interaction from many different types of channels and products and take action on the combined results.

3.10 **ARCHITECTURE EXAMPLE – CREATING A MULTICHANNEL VIEW**

Mature CSPs tend to provide a broad range of services that reflect the development of the telecommunications industry. For example, they may offer landlines for homes and offices, broadband services, as well as mobile phone services. These services typically have one of more contracts associated with them, potentially grouped around a household. The challenge for the CSP is to offer the best package for the contract holder lest they lose all or part of the business to a competitor.

Fig. 3.6 shows a simplified version of the architecture for a multichannel big data solution [13]. The location of the big data solution shown in Fig. 3.5 is highlighted in red and labeled (1) – although some of its plumbing changes, as insight from the CDRs must now be passed to the centralized decision service, and actions that need to be delivered to a particular device are passed back.

The interaction of the components shown in Fig. 3.6 is as follows:

1. Specialized processes receive, parse and extract unstructured data from different sources to understand the behavior of people using each of the different channels of activity. When certain events occur, they trigger an event that is sent to the real-time decisions subsystem (see step 7).

2. The results of the specialized processes are gathered into the Data Lake and where appropriate, onto the Customer Activity system (this maintains a list of recent activity for each customer that is organized for real-time access).

3. The analytics team use data from the system of insight to build analytics.

4. The analytics is deployed to the specialized processes, into the system of insight and/or the real-time decisions subsystem.

5. The activity of the customer generates more data for the specialized processes, and where they interact directly with the CSP's systems, requests for recommendations on offers to make to the customer.

6. The request for a recommendation, either directly from the channel systems, or from an event detected by the specialized processes, results in a call to the real-time decisions subsystem.

7. Inside the real-time decisions subsystem is a Complex Event Processor (CEP) monitoring the events around a customer over different time windows. This may generate additional requests for recom-

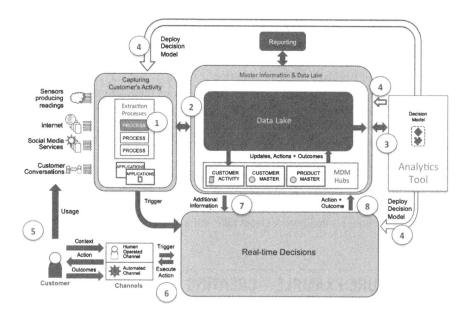

FIGURE 3.6

Multichannel next best action solution

mendations. There are one or more decision engines processing the requests for recommendations. They use the context from the request for a recommendation plus the data from the MDM hubs to make a decision. The resulting recommendation is either returned to the requestor, or sent asynchronously on a different channel.

8. The decision and any outcome are fed back to the data lake.

The striking difference between the architectures shown in Figs. 3.5 and 3.6 is the amount of data movement and data integration logic is required in addition to the analytics. This represents the delta for any big data solution that is processing a variety of data from many different sources. Many of the techniques found in traditional data warehouse solutions become necessary in the big data solution to capture, parse, enrich, correlate, and combine data. In addition, there is infrastructure required to communicate actions back out to the channels and gather results.

Projects of this size often experience delays as teams negotiate access to data and coordinate the rollout of enhancements to systems maintained by different teams. This adds politics to the complexity of the architecture in terms of access to the data, funding of changes required to existing systems and who realizes the benefit of the ultimate value from the actions taken by the big data solution.

In some organizations, the politics are so complex that they make the technical part of the solution seem simple. They are certainly a key factor in whether this type of big data solution is practical for a particular organization.

3.11 **APPLICATION INDEPENDENT DATA**

There is one type of system in Fig. 3.6 architecture that seems to sit a little uncomfortably within the system categories shown in Figs. 3.3 and 3.4. It is the Master Data Management (MDM) hubs.

An MDM hub is one of a number of reference data systems that greatly simplify the integration of all types of data across an ecosystem and as such is used by all of the different system categories. The MDM hub specifically manages the identifiers and core attributes of key objects that are the focus of the ecosystem. These objects could be about people and organizations (customers, employees, business partners), locations, products and offerings, or assets. These objects are often described in many of the systems producing the data for the big data solution and each system assigns a different identifier to their copies of the object. There are often differences in the attributes assigned to the object in each system as they gather and process the values under different conditions. The MDM hub maintains a registry of these objects, listing the identifiers from each system and the authoritative values for the core attributes. Ideally, the MDM hub is used to synchronize the core values in the other systems so the raw data entering the big data solution is reasonably consistent. Either way, the MDM hub is a key source of information for the big data solution when combining data from multiple systems. Organizations that want to operate complex big data solutions find that an investment in MDM pays dividends in facilitating the matching of data from many sources. They should be thought of as the oil that eases the friction of data exchange between the silos.

Other reference systems that aid the integration if data in addition to the MDM hub are the code hub for reconciling code table values [14] from different systems and the metadata catalogue of systems and data for the ecosystem.

3.12 **METADATA AND GOVERNANCE**

Metadata is descriptive data about data. In a data warehouse environment, the metadata is typically limited to the structural schemas used to organize the data in different zones in the warehouse. For the more advanced environments, metadata may also include data lineage and measured quality information of the systems supplying data to the warehouse.

A big data environment is more dynamic than a data warehouse environment and it is continuously pulling in data from a much greater pool of sources. It quickly becomes impossible for the individuals running the big data environment to remember the origin and content of all the data sets it contains. As a result, metadata capture and management becomes a key part of the big data environment. Given the volume, variety and velocity of the data, metadata management must be automated. Similarly fulfilling governance requirements for data must also be automated as much as possible.

Enabling this automation adds to the types of metadata that must be maintained since governance is driven from the business context, not from the technical implementation around the data. For example, the secrecy required for a company's financial reports is very high just before the results are reported. However, once they have been released, they are public information. The technology used to store the data has not changed. However, time has changed the business impact of an unauthorized disclosure of the information, and thus the governance program providing the data protection has to be aware of that context.

Similar examples from data quality management, lifecycle management and data protection illustrate that the requirements that drive information governance come from the business significance of the data and how it is to be used. This means the metadata must capture both the technical implementation of the data and the business context of its creation and use so that governance requirements and actions can be assigned appropriately.

Earlier on in this chapter, we introduced the concept of the managed data lake where metadata and governance were a key part of ensuring a data lake remains a useful resource rather than becoming a data swamp. This is a necessary first step in getting the most value out of big data. However, from the different big data solutions reviewed in this chapter, big data is not born in the data lake. It comes from other systems and contexts. Metadata and governance needs to extend to these systems, and be incorporated into the data flows and processing throughout the solution.

3.13 **CONCLUSIONS**

Deriving value from big data involves processing the right data in the right location and taking action on the results. Innovative data science is only the start of the journey. Big data projects that can process data and act on it close to its origin are more likely to be successful than projects that incorporate systems operated by multiple silos in the organization. This is because they are simpler technically; they meet fewer political hurdles and deliver value while the original stakeholder is still in place. However, it is this second type of project is often addressing the use cases that have the higher value.

As an industry we need to improve the time to value and success rate of big data projects. From a technical point of view, this is going to take:

- Better architecture method around identifying the appropriate systems that support the different types of big data processing needed within a solution.
- Tools and runtimes that automatically manage the metadata and context data necessary to pass data between processing systems.
- Standard structures for this metadata and context data to allow interoperability between cloud services and on premises systems. Hybrid cloud brokers and gateways could then support these standards.

Organizations will also need to rethink their attribute and relationship with data.

Organizations that wish to be data-driven and embark on these broad big data projects need to think deeply about the barriers created by their existing silos, and whether these silos are appropriate for their future digital business. For many, becoming a digital business is going to involve tearing up the current organization chart and organizing around data. This is likely to create new executive roles that bring data oriented skills to the boardroom.

Metadata management and information governance needs a greater focus at the business level. It must be deeply embedded in the systems that are involved in processing data – not just the data platforms associated with a data lake. Metadata must cover both the technical implementation of the data and its processing engines, as well as the business context of where the data was created, its use and the governance requirements associated with it. This metadata then must be an active part of the way data is managed, keeping it up-to-date and relevant to the needs of the organization.

3.14 **OUTLOOK AND FUTURE DIRECTIONS**

The big data space is still evolving. New types of data platforms and processing engines are appearing with a regular cadence and data-oriented roles, such as Chief Data Officer and data scientist, are in high demand. As cloud adoption grows, we see an increasing amount of data that is born on the cloud. This will increase the demand for big data processing systems to also reside in the cloud.

From a data perspective, these trends spell greater chaos, since the origin and consumption of data increasing occurs in systems operated by different organizations. If it was hard to get data management right within an organization then what chance of getting it right in a multiorganizational situation?

This suggests a fundamental change to IT technology in the way it manages data. A system should treat the data it holds as a sharable resource rather than as its own private asset. This means it need to be described both in a human and machine-readable way and accessible through open interfaces. We need a greater level of standardization in the way that data is described, at multiple levels:

- Cataloguing of the data presents and its structure,
- Ownership and custodian responsibility,
- Business meaning and the rules around its use,
- Levels of confidence in its quality and timeliness,
- Classifications, licensing and regulations around its use.

With systems consistently describing their data in this way, exchanging metadata with data as it is copied between systems becomes much easier. The consumer then receives data accompanied by a rich description of its origin, history and related characteristics.

Technically, this is not difficult to do. There are many metadata standards that we could adopt and the processing overload on a system is not that high. Today it does not happen because metadata is treated as an optional capability – used mainly for documentation. However, if metadata is used to give the business a greater visibility and control over the data stored in their many systems then its value rises and so does the investment in it.

There are vendors who sell metadata solutions to help capture and manage metadata. Tools to provide integration capabilities, reports or virtualization interfaces, sit on top of this metadata and use it to interact with the underlying data sources. So using metadata to drive software capability is not new. It is the lifecycle of this metadata that needs to change.

In today's tools, metadata is created retrospectively, an expensive undertaking – the cost coming from the time of subject matter experts to document the origin, meaning and use of metadata. Each vendor uses its own formats so metadata is only exchangeable with additional metadata bridges and brokers.

As data rises in importance to society, it is time to move metadata from an optional extra capability to an embedded capability that systems maintain by default. Open source is potentially offering us a solution in the new Apache Atlas project [15,16]. It aims to provide an open source implementation for an embeddable metadata management and governance capability.

The metadata standards that Apache Atlas adopts would become de facto standards. So where cloud platforms, big data platforms and tools vendors wish to use their proprietary implementation; they can implement these standards in their interchange code.

So what would be the benefit to a ubiquitous metadata and governance capability? Most importantly, data would become visible and consumable to big data and analytics solutions [17]. This would allow an organization to get greater value from their data. The increased value creates a greater interest from all parts of an organization, government and society in general and the human constraints on big data solutions begin to ease.

REFERENCES

[1] Pete Chapman, Julian Clinton, Randy Kerber, Thomas Khabaza, Thomas Reinartz, Colin Shearer, Rüdiger Wirth, CRISP-DM 1.0, Step-by-step data mining guide, ftp://ftp.software.ibm.com/software/analytics/spss/support/Modeler/Documentation/14/UserManual/CRISP-DM.pdf.

[2] Data lake, https://en.wiktionary.org/wiki/data_lake.

[3] Gartner says beware of the data lake fallacy, Gartner Press Release, http://www.gartner.com/newsroom/id/2809117.

[4] Mandy Chessell, Ferd Scheepers, Nhan Nguyen, Ruud van Kessel, Ron van der Starre, REDP5120: governing and managing big data for analytics and decision makers, http://www.redbooks.ibm.com/redpieces/abstracts/redp5120.html?Open.

[5] Mandy Chessell, Nigel L. Jones, Jay Limburn, David Radley, Kevin Shank, SG24-8274-00, designing and operating a data reservoir, http://www.redbooks.ibm.com/Redbooks.nsf/RedpieceAbstracts/sg248274.html.

[6] Mandy Chessell, Building a data reservoir to use big data with confidence, http://www.ibmbigdatahub.com/blog/building-data-reservoir-use-big-data-confidence.

[7] Bolzano case study, http://www-03.ibm.com/press/us/en/pressrelease/28465.wss.

[8] A guide to the best practices in ensuring privacy in big data solutions is covered by the "Privacy by Design resolution", https://www.ipc.on.ca/site_documents/pbd-resolution.pdf.

[9] Brian Hopkins, Systems of insight will power digital business, http://blogs.forrester.com/brian_hopkins/15-04-27-systems_of_insight_will_power_digital_business.

[10] Arvind Sathi, et al., Advanced Analytics Platform (AAP), http://www.ibm.com/developerworks/library/ba-adv-analytics-platform1/index.html.

[11] Communications service provider, https://en.wikipedia.org/wiki/Communications_service_provider.

[12] Call detail record, https://en.wikipedia.org/wiki/Call_detail_record.

[13] Mandy Chessell, REDP4888, smarter analytics: driving customer interactions with the IBM next best action solution, http://www.redbooks.ibm.com/abstracts/redp4888.html?Open.

[14] Dan Wolfson, Going with the flow, http://www.ibmbigdatahub.com/blog/going-flow.

[15] Mandy Chessell, Insight Out: the case for open metadata and governance, http://www.ibmbigdatahub.com/blog/insightout-case-open-metadata-and-governance.

[16] Mandy Chessell, Insight Out: the role of apache atlas in the open metadata ecosystem, http://www.ibmbigdatahub.com/blog/insightout-role-apache-atlas-open-metadata-ecosystem.

[17] Tim Vincent, Bill O'Connell, Insight Ops: the road to a collaborative self-service model, http://www.ibmbigdatahub.com/blog/insight-ops-road-collaborative-self-service-model.

DOMAIN-DRIVEN DESIGN OF BIG DATA SYSTEMS BASED ON A REFERENCE ARCHITECTURE

4

Cigdem Avci Salma, Bedir Tekinerdogan, Ioannis N. Athanasiadis
Wageningen University, Information Technology, Wageningen, The Netherlands

4.1 INTRODUCTION

The idea of creating business value from data has always been an important concern. Many businesses have searched for ways to extract information from data in order to discover new insights and make smarter decisions. Together with the advancements of disruptive technologies such as Cloud Computing and Internet of Things, the ability to capture and store vast amounts of data has grown at an unprecedented rate which soon did not scale with traditional data management techniques. Yet, to cope with the rapidly increasing volume, variety and velocity [14] of the generated data, we can now adopt the available novel technical capacity and the infrastructure to aggregate and analyze big data. This situation has led to new and unforeseen opportunities for many organizations.

Big data has now indeed become a very important driver for innovation and growth for various industries such as health, administration, agriculture, and education [33,34]. These systems usually require considerable financial commitments and huge scale software and system deployments. To meet the business goals by means of the valorization of the big data, proper design is crucial. Unfortunately, developing big data systems is not straightforward and, despite high expectations, big data projects might fail due to the lack of selection of the right features and a proper design of the big data architecture.

In this chapter, we propose a domain-driven approach for designing big data systems based on feature modeling [15]. A feature model is a domain model that defines common and variant features of a domain. We report on our domain analysis of big data systems that has resulted in a feature model. This model includes common and variant features of big data systems and is used as a basis for designing big data architectures.

Besides the common and variant features, other drivers could also be employed throughout the methodology of the derivation of the big data software architectures such as requirements/use cases and nonfunctional requirements [31,32]. In many commercial organizations, there is a maturity curve that they go through, from using Hadoop as a cheap storage area for data they think might be useful, to specialist technology for a small group of data scientists and then to a corporate resource where people can locate useful data and perform ad hoc analysis on it. As the solutions mature, often they broaden the variety of data processed, and this brings in additional components. There is also a difference in the technology components required if the big data architecture is for analytics development, production

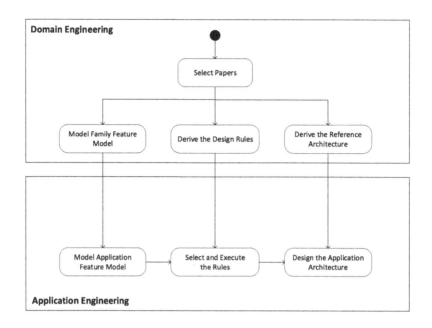

FIGURE 4.1

Adopted approach for domain-driven big data systems

use, or both. These aspects drive the roll-out of big data technology and hence of components needed for each iteration. Especially, many aspects that drive the selection of technology of the environment are driven by nonfunctional requirements. For example, the choice of processing via batch or streaming is based on the rate of data input compared with the urgency to process and consume data values. Therefore, it is important that these aspects be reflected in the model of variability. The model will be extended to drive the architecture from such business requirements as a future work.

The remainder of the chapter is organized as follows. In Section 4.2, we discuss the overall domain-driven approach that we use. Section 4.3 elaborates on the feature model for big data systems. Section 4.4 explains the approach to derive the application architectures via utilizing the feature model for big data. Section 4.5 provides the related work, and finally, Section 4.6 concludes the chapter.

4.2 DOMAIN-DRIVEN DESIGN APPROACH

The domain-driven approach for deriving big data architectures is shown in Fig. 4.1.

In essence the approach consists of two key activities, domain engineering [12] and application engineering. In the domain engineering activity, first the set of relevant papers is selected. The papers are used as input for deriving a domain model (i.e., feature model), reference architecture and the design rules. The list of papers that we have selected is shown in Table 4.1. Besides theoretical papers and white papers, we have also looked at documentation of reference architectures as defined by Big

Table 4.1 List of papers to derive the reference architecture of Big Data systems (in alphabetical order)

1	B. Geerdink, "A Reference Architecture for Big Data Solutions" [11]
2	C. Ballard et al., Information Governance Principles and Practices for a Big Data Landscape. IBM Redbooks, 2014 [3]
3	D. Chapelle, "Big Data & Analytics Reference Architecture." An Oracle White Paper (2013) [6]
4	M. Maier, A. Serebrenik, and I.T.P. Vanderfeesten, "Towards a Big Data Reference Architecture." (2013) [16]
5	NIST Big Data PWG, Draft NIST Big Data Interoperability Framework: Volume 6, Reference Architecture (2014) [17]
6	N. Marz, and J. Warren, "Big Data: Principles and best practices of scalable realtime data systems." Manning Publications Co. (2015) [18]
7	Oracle, Information Management and Big Data A Reference Architecture, An Oracle White Paper, February (2013) [20]
8	P. Pääkkönen, and D. Pakkala, "Reference Architecture and Classification of Technologies, Products and Services for Big Data Systems." Big Data Research (2015) [21]
9	S. Soares, "Big Data Governance." Information Asset, LLC (2012) [23]

Data System Infrastructure vendors. In order to assure sufficient coverage, papers were searched via and selected from three different electronic libraries which are IEEE Xplore, Google Scholar and ScienceDirect. The reference architecture in each paper among the outcome paper set is analyzed in terms of the feature set that it covers, in order to ensure that the maximum known feature coverage is reached without repetition. For feature modeling, we selected each paper of Table 4.1 and extracted the features and constraints which we used to build up the model. The feature model was evaluated after each paper by the authors.

The approach further follows the guidelines as defined by domain analysis process, which is defined as a systematic process for analyzing and modeling a domain. Domain analysis consists of Domain Scoping and Domain Modeling [13,7]. Domain scoping includes the definition of the domain of interest, the stakeholders, and their goals. In our case the domain is the domain of big data system architectures.

Based on the selected papers, the domain modeling is started, which results in a domain model. The domain model is typically derived using a commonality and variability analysis for the concepts of the selected papers. Among the domain modeling approaches, feature modeling is extensively used [13,28]. Features, their relationships, and dependencies are described in a model as a feature diagram or tables. A feature diagram is constructed as a tree, where the root symbolizes a concept (e.g., a software system), and its descendent nodes are the features. The commonalities and variations of the system properties that are aligned with the stakeholders' concerns are identified and classified as the features. The types of parent–child relationship for a feature tree are: mandatory, optional, or (one or more subfeatures have to be chosen), alternative (xor). To limit the configuration space, the feature constraints can be put in the following form (and in other ways): A excludes B.

In parallel or after the domain modeling process, the reference architecture is defined that presents the generic architecture for the various big data systems. According to Angelov et al. [1], "*a software reference architecture is a generic architecture for a class of information systems that is used as a foundation for the design of concrete architectures from this class.*" Software Engineering Institute (SEI) defines the reference architecture as "*a reference model mapped onto software elements that implements the functionality defined in the reference model*" [35]; and the reference model is described

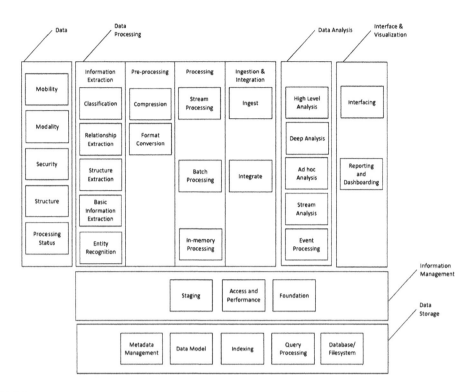

FIGURE 4.2

Big data reference architecture

as "*a division of functionality into elements together with the data flow among those elements*" [35]. A reference architecture presents the architectural best practices by various means such as standards, design patterns, and can be employed by software architects as a base from the beginning to the end of a project. The reference architecture has to be further customized to align with the requirements of the particular organization. Based on the selected papers, by means of using valid reference architectures via induction, we have defined a reference architecture for big data systems, as given in Fig. 4.2. In principle, big data systems have Data Storage, Information Management, Data Processing, Data Analysis, and Interface and Visualization components. A top level view of the reference architecture is provided in Fig. 4.1; however, each component has a more detailed coverage [22]. Especially the information management components which can be listed as catalog, security, lifecycle management, quality management, and logging are included by means of the Staging, Access and Performance and Foundation subcomponents. Often they imply a cultural change around the data use in the big data environment – which is one of the costliest parts of the big data program. We will explain these in more detail in the subsequent sections.

We can identify several other reference architectures in the literature. The reference architecture that we have derived is very similar to the other reference architectures. The reason for this is that we have considered also several other reference architectures when we defined our own reference model. Each reference architecture typically has a different goal (e.g., explaining, describing, deriving designs). The goal of our reference architecture is to support the design of big data systems. When designing the reference architecture, we have tried to define the scope of the applications to be as broad as possible. For this purpose, we have considered the key big data concerns that are required for the majority of the big data systems. In addition, we have also considered both commonality and variability of the reference architecture. As such we aimed to achieve the generic level that is useful, in general. However, the validation of this reference architecture, like all reference architectures, is not straightforward. We have used the reference architecture for the derivation of the two different application architectures (Facebook and Twitter), and the reference architecture can also be used for other applications.

Together with the domain model and the reference architecture, we also derived the design rules from the literature. A design rule defines a design action based on a given condition. In our approach the condition is defined by a selection or deselection of a feature in the family feature diagram. A selection of a feature as such will result in the adaptation of the big data system.

In the application engineering process the family feature model, domain design rules, and reference architecture are used to derive the application architecture for a given big data system project. The family feature model covers the features of the overall big data system domain. To describe the features of a particular big data project, we derive the *application feature model* from the family feature model. The application architecture is derived using the application feature model and the reference architecture. For this the domain design rules are executed based on the selected features. Hence, a selection of different application feature models will trigger different domain design rules which will lead to a different application architecture. We define the family feature model as well as the application engineering process in more detail in the following sections.

4.3 **RELATED WORK**

In the literature we can identify different approaches for defining reference architectures. Galster and Avgeriou [9] propose a methodology to define empirically-grounded reference architectures. The approach consists of the following steps: decision on the type of reference architecture, selection of design strategy, empirical acquisition of data, construction of a reference architecture, enabling the reference architecture variability, and finally evaluation of the reference architecture. Our approach is at an earlier stage than that of [9]. We do not select a reference architecture from the literature but rather first define the reference architecture that is then used to derive the application architectures.

Architecture description languages (ADLs) have been proposed to model architectures. For a long time there has been little consensus on the key characteristics of an ADL. Different types of ADL have also been introduced. Some ADLs have been defined to model a particular application domain, others are more general-purpose. Also the formal precision of the ADLs differs; some have a clear formal foundation while others are less formal. Several researchers have attempted to provide clear guidelines for characterizing and distinguishing ADLs, by providing comparison and evaluation frameworks. Medvidovic and Taylor [19] have proposed a definition and a classification framework for ADL, which states that an ADL must explicitly model components, connectors, and their configurations. Furthermore, they state that tool support for architecture-based development and evolution is needed. These four elements of an ADL include other subelements to characterize and compare ADLs. The focus in the framework is thus on architectural modeling features and tool support. In fact, we could analyze also existing ADLs based on the approach in this paper. That could be complementary to earlier evaluations of ADLs.

Architectural tactics [2] aim at identifying architectural decisions related to a quality attribute requirement and composing these into an architecture design. Defining explicit viewpoints for quality concerns can help us to model and reason about the application of architectural tactics [25]. In our approach we did not explicitly consider the notion of architectural tactics. However, we explicitly identified and described the design decisions. These can be considered similar to and complementary with architectural tactics. The advantage of the method in [2] is picking up concrete scenarios at the initial steps of design, which are also important derivers of architectural design in terms of functional/nonfunctional requirements. We would like to include the step of picking concrete scenarios in our approach as a future enhancement. On the other side in our approach, the variability of the architecture is represented in a more concrete way with the derivation of the feature model.

Architectural Perspectives [8] are a collection of activities, tactics, and guidelines to modify a set of existing views to document and analyze quality properties. Architectural perspectives as such are basically guidelines that work on multiple views together. We have primarily focused on the design of the reference architecture with respect to functional concerns. It might be interesting to look at integrating the guidelines provided by the Architectural Perspectives and the design of big data architectures. Utilizing the both approaches advantages, Domain Driven Design's concrete feature coverage and the Architectural Perspectives' quality assurance, the resulting application could have a more complete design.

Several software architecture analysis approaches have been introduced for addressing quality properties. The goal of these approaches is to assess whether or not a given architecture design satisfies desired concerns including quality requirements. For analyzing and validating the reference architecture, we have applied two real case studies (Facebook and Twitter). We were able to derive the architecture based on the reference architectures. For further more detailed analysis, we could use the existing architecture analysis approaches. We consider this as part of our future work in which we will investigate the impact of quality concerns on big data architectures.

A "description driven" approach is used to design a big data system in [10]. The crucial elements are identified and their high-level descriptions are stored in a model which is clearly separated from its instances. The description driven approach follows the principals of pure object-oriented design. In principle, our approach can be categorized as a description-driven approach since we first describe the feature model and then try to derive the design for the particular applications.

Three principles to design big data systems are listed in [4], and are: "support a variety of analysis methods", "one size does not fit all", "make data accessible".

4.4 FEATURE MODEL OF BIG DATA SYSTEMS

The top level feature diagram of big data systems that we have derived is shown in Fig. 4.3. A more detailed description of the feature diagram has been presented in our earlier work [22]. A big data system consists of the mandatory features Data, Data Storage, Information Management, Data Analysis, Data Processing, Interface and Visualization, and the optional feature, System Orchestrator. In the following subsections we will discuss each of these features in more detail.

FIGURE 4.3

Top-level feature model for big data system

4.4.1 DATA

Data is the feature that defines the data types in terms of their usage, state, and representation. Hence, data in big data systems can be classified with respect to five dimensions: mobility, structure, processing, security [3], and modality. Mobility addresses the status of the data during processing and analysis activities and can be either *batch* or *streaming*. While the design of the batch processing modules should be aligned with the quality goals in terms of scalability, the design of the stream processing activities affects the performance of the system. In [18] and [6] mobility is referred as a feature of the reference architecture.

Another subfeature of the Data feature in big data systems is Structure. Depending on the source of the data, it can be of the following three structural phases: Unstructured, Semistructured, or Structured. The formation of the data processing, analysis and storage modules highly depends on the structure of the data.

The *Processing* feature defines the processing state of the data. Initially, the data in big data systems is *raw*, and can be *processed* and *analyzed*. From the data integrity perspective, different use cases can call for different level of trust [3]. Some other possible modalities of big data are textual, audio and video.

Security is not explicitly discussed in the early big data reference architectures, which glossed over this difficulty. In order to cover the early reference architectures, the security feature of the data is presented as optional. But it should be implied that nowadays it is a major part of the big data landscape, particularly in the industries where data about people and financial/intellectual property is managed by the big data solutions.

4.4.2 INFORMATION MANAGEMENT

The *Information Management* feature represents the governance of the data in terms of security, privacy, integration, and quality. It is composed of three subfeatures, and is typically implemented as layers, namely the staging, access and performance, and foundation layers. The staging layer is an abstraction of the data acquisition process. It calibrates the data receiving rate and prepares data for further processing. The access and performance layer is utilized for data access and navigation. Finally, the foundation layer isolates data in storage from the business processes so that data is ensured to be resilient to changes. (Please see [22] for more details.)

4.4.3 INTERFACE AND VISUALIZATION

The *Interface and Visualization* feature provides interaction of the big data system with the user and other applications. While reporting and dashboarding feature is used only for information presentation, the user and application interface features can provide interactive services for the users and applications. The retrieval of data via the user interfaces will require interactive response, which needs advanced optimization techniques. (Please see [22] for more details.)

4.4.4 DATA PROCESSING

Preprocessing steps, such as compression, aim to prepare data and to facilitate processing activities. Information supply chains within the big data environment that refines data from its source format into a variety of different consumable formats for analysis and use are also covered within preprocessing activities, such as format conversion. Depending on the state of the data, processing can be classified either as stream processing (e.g., filtering, annotation) or batch processing (e.g., cleaning, combining and replication). For further processing, depending on the requirements of the system, information extraction, data integration, in-memory processing, and data ingestion activities can be employed.

Classification, entity recognition, relationship extraction, and structure extraction can be listed among the information extraction features. Data fusion, entity recognition and schema integration are the basic data integration activities. Under the category of in-memory data processing, as opposed to processing in the hard disks, high speed query processing and results caching are among possible features to be utilized. Furthermore, data ingestion which involves data obtaining and processing activities for later use is another optional data processing feature. (Please see [22] for further details.) (See also Fig. 4.4.)

4.4.5 DATA STORAGE

Data storage feature consists of query processing, indexing, distributed file system, data model, metadata management, and database subfeatures. Besides traditional data storage features, such as metadata management, relational model and relational database, a big data system can also employ features for streaming data (i.e., in-stream query processing) and for storing various data structures, with nonrelational models (i.e., NoSQL).

4.4.6 DATA ANALYSIS

Data analysis is one of the major features of a big data system. Stream analysis, high level analysis, ad hoc analysis, event processing, and deep analysis are its subfeatures that take part in the reference architectures in the selected papers (see Fig. 4.5).

4.4.7 FEATURE CONSTRAINTS

Based on the family feature diagram, we can derive many different feature configurations. However, not all feature combinations are feasible and need to be ruled out when defining the application feature model. To this end, feature constraints are used to limit the configuration space so that invalid configurations are prevented. Obviously, features which do not have a parent–child relationship are not allowed to substitute each other. Initially we can consider the constraints that are related to the mobility of the data which is either streaming or batch. For query processing on streaming data such as in sensor networks, response time gains high importance. Therefore real-time query processing is employed in such cases and as a feature constraint and real-time query processing implies streaming data. Similarly, for in-stream processing, the system does not use additional memory and does not employ time intensive storage operations, and in-stream processing implies streaming modality of the data. Besides, data acquisition feature is required to capture and analyze streaming data.

OLAP Cube is a multidimensional dataset, and OLAP data is generally stored in relational data stores or ad-hoc data management systems. While OLAP Cube implies batch processing, streaming OLAP Cubes (StreamCube) are specialized for stream processing. (See Table 4.2.)

FIGURE 4.4

Feature diagram for data processing

Data Fusion is defined as integrating and synthesizing data from multiple sources. For this feature model, we categorized the data sources depending on their modality and restricted Data Fusion to imply at least two different modalities.

Security feature of the big data systems is not discussed in detail for most of the application architectures in the known literature. In case the security feature is included in the application features, data security and privacy feature in the information management component becomes vital.

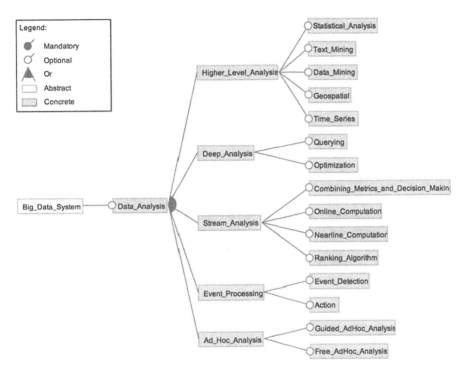

FIGURE 4.5

Feature diagram for data analysis

Table 4.2 Feature constraints

Real Time Query Processing • Streaming
In-Stream Processing • Streaming
Cube Generation • Batch
Database Snapshots • Batch
Relational Database • Relational Modal
NoSQL • Unstructured
Security • Data Security and Privacy
In-Memory File System • In-Memory processing
In-Memory Database • In-Memory Processing
Streaming • Data Acquisition
Parallel Distributed File System • Metadata Management
Object Storage File System • Data Security and Privacy
Document Data Model • NoSQL
Graph Data Model • NoSQL
Key-Value Data Model • NoSQL
Multiple Types of Data • Metadata Management
Ad Hoc Analysis • Information Virtualization
Graph Data Model • Internode Communication
Data Integration • Multiple Sources • Format Conversion

Another processing technique is in-memory processing which benefits from data stored in RAM as it is much quicker to access. In-memory databases and file systems are key features that support in-memory processing.

Schema Integration is a concept related with the distributed, heterogeneous databases which creates a global schema or access to local schemas and, together with the Parallel Distributed File Systems, requires high quality metadata. Therefore metadata management feature has to be employed when multiple data types are covered in the application architecture.

NoSQL is the category of the databases which are nonrelational. The data models other than relational data model that are listed in the feature model, namely document data model, graph data model, and key-value data model, imply the NoSQL databases.

Information virtualization is essential for ad hoc analysis because sandboxing, which is a basic virtualization technique, can support the analyst by means of isolating the data so that the data store will not be affected from a failure caused by the ad hoc analysis.

Finally, the graph data model leads to a very dense data that is distributed among the nodes. The edge information will be distributed across the boundaries as well. Therefore, to gather the edge information among the nodes, inter-node communication is extensively used, and so if the architecture of the system does not support internode communication, the system has low performance for the graph problems.

4.5 DERIVING THE APPLICATION ARCHITECTURES AND EXAMPLE

In the following sections, we define the big data application architecture derivation approach using the feature model that we defined in the previous sections. Afterwards, we apply the methodology to some well-known big data applications to derive application architectures.

4.5.1 FEATURE MODELING

In the previous sections, we defined the family feature model of the big data systems, which supports the reference architecture. We also summarized the feature constraints of this family feature model.

To derive an application architecture, considering the requirements of the application, initially the necessary features and their subfeatures are selected from the family feature model. Then the application feature model is checked against the feature constraints of the family feature model, and the inconsistency is fixed by means of including or excluding the related features from the application feature model. As an example, an application which is based on streaming data requires in-stream processing and real time querying features to be included for the data acquisition. For the same application, without having batch data requirements, selecting the OLAP cube generation feature causes inconsistency.

4.5.2 DESIGN RULE MODELING

Design rules are developed using the features and the feature constraints. The rules have the structure according to a predefined design rule definition language, i.e., "if <feature> is selected then [action] <feature> on node [name]" statement. The design rule set which covers all the features and their constraints should be formed. Among the design rules, there can also be other reference design rules which define the connection between the derived features. Examples of design rules are listed below:

DR1: If AD HOC ANALYSIS is selected then enable INFORMATION VIRTUALISATION on component INFORMATION MANAGEMENT SERVER

DR2: If GRAPH DATABASE MODEL is selected then deploy INTER-NODE COMMUNICATION on component INFORMATION MANAGEMENT

DR3: If MULTIPLE DATA TYPES is selected then load METADATA MANAGEMENT on component DATA STORAGE

DR4: If STREAMING is selected then enable DATA ACQUISITION on component INFORMATION MANAGEMENT SERVER

DR5: If REAL-TIME QUERY PROCESSING is selected then enable DATA ACQUISITION on component INFORMATION MANAGEMENT SERVER

DR6: If IN-MEMORY DATA STORAGE is selected then enable IN-MEMORY DATA PROCESSING on component DATA PROCESSING SERVER

DR7: If OBJECT STORAGE FILE SYSTEM is selected then enable DATA SECURITY AND PRIVACY on component INFORMATION MANAGEMENT SERVER

DR8: If PARALLEL DISTRIBUTED FILE SYSTEM is selected then load METADATA MANAGEMENT on component DATA STORAGE

DR9: If DOCUMENT DATA MODEL is selected then load NoSQL on component DATA STORAGE

DR10: If GRAPH DATA MODEL is selected then load NoSQL on component DATA STORAGE

DR11: If KEY-VALUE DATA MODEL is selected then load NoSQL on component DATA STORAGE

DR12: If RELATIONAL MODEL is selected then load RELATIONAL DATABASE on component DATA STORAGE

DR13: If MULTIPLE DATA TYPES and DATA INTEGRATION is selected then load FORMAT CONVERSION on component PRE-PROCESSING

The focus of the paper is, in fact, on providing a systematic approach for deriving an application architecture using a family feature diagram and a reference architecture. We have provided the reference architecture and family feature diagram in a sufficiently detailed manner to illustrate the process. Both the reference architecture and family feature model, as well as the adopted design rules, could be further elaborated by considering additional knowledge sources. The design rules that we have adopted are used to illustrate the derivation of the application architecture for the given example applications (Facebook, Twitter). For deriving the rules, we considered the selected primary studies and looked for the reference to the features of big data systems. Very often the rules were not explicitly described, and we had to interpret and describe the design rules. As part of our future work, we will extend the design rules when considering additional primary studies.

4.5.3 ASSOCIATING DESIGN DECISIONS WITH FEATURES

So far, the application feature model has been derived and the design rule set has been developed. The next step is determining the design rule set for the application feature model. For this purpose, the selected features in the application feature model are matched with the features included in the definitions of the design rules. The matching subset of the design rules is the input for the next step.

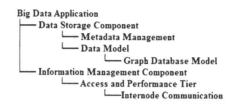

FIGURE 4.6

Big data application tree

For example, having the three rules defined in the previous section, when we select Multiple Data Types and Graph Database features for our application, the corresponding design rule set is associated with these features as follows:

Feature	Associated Design Rule
Multiple Data Types	DR3
Graph Database	DR2

4.5.4 GENERATION OF THE APPLICATION ARCHITECTURE AND THE DEPLOYMENT DIAGRAM

In this step, we have the feature model and the design rule set for the application. The aim of this step is to obtain the corresponding application architecture. In principle, this can be done manually but since the features, reference architecture, and design rules can be specified in a precise manner we could also provide automated support for this. Combining the feature model and the corresponding subset of the design rules via joining both sets on the matching features, we obtain a tree-like hierarchical structure. The structure represents the feature hierarchy and the matching design approach which is defined in the design rule set. Afterwards, these rules have to be transformed to an architecture specification. Therefore, a simple architecture description language can be defined with basic types such as device, execution, and connection. By using an ADL, the application design rules have to be converted to architectural description. Finally, the ADL instance enables the user to draw the deployment diagram.

The graphical representation of the combination of the derived features and the corresponding design rule set from the example in the previous section is shown in Fig. 4.6.

A possible ADL instance, which is obtained via transformation of our derived design rule set, can be as follows:

```
<Device name="MetadataManagement" id="4" component="DataStorage"/>
<Device name="DataModel" id="5" component="DataStorage">
<Execution id="1">GraphDatabaseModel</Execution>
<Device/>
<Device name="AccessAndPerformance" id="6" component="InformationManagement">
<Execution id="2">InternodeCommunication</Execution>
<Connection srcID="0" destID="1"/>
<Connection srcID="2" destID="1"/>
<Device/>
```

FIGURE 4.7

Facebook application tree

4.5.5 DERIVING BIG DATA ARCHITECTURES OF EXISTING SYSTEMS

In the previous section we have defined the family feature model for big data systems. The family feature model defines different possible big data systems. We can use the family feature model to characterize and define a particular big data system by selecting the corresponding features. In this section, we will illustrate this for two big data systems, namely Facebook and Twitter.

4.5.5.1 Facebook

Facebook software architecture is discussed in [29]. This architecture includes Data, Data Storage, Information Management, Data Analysis, Data Processing, and Interface, and Visualization features. Event Processing, Data Integration, Data Fusion, Entity Resolution, and Schema Integration are not defined as part of the architecture. Moreover, the architecture emphasizes the structure and mobility of data, but does not clarify its modality and security perspectives.

We cannot describe the derivation of the whole application architecture in one section; however, we are going to derive the components related to two selected features of the Facebook system. Facebook uses Scribe to collect the log data in real time which means that log data has the streaming feature. Besides, we know that Facebook system carries out ad hoc analysis on the stored data. Therefore, we select these two features from the family feature model as part of the application feature set. As the second step, we associate these two features with the related design rules from the design rule set of the family feature model as follows:

DR1: If **AD HOC ANALYSIS** is selected then enable INFORMATION VIRTUALISATION on component INFORMATION MANAGEMENT SERVER

DR2: If **STREAMING** is selected then enable DATA ACQUISITION on component INFORMATION MANAGEMENT SERVER

To generate the application architecture and the deployment diagram, we should convert the design rules to an ADL instance. (See Fig. 4.7.)

A possible ADL instance, which is obtained via transformation of our derived design rule set, can be as follows:

```
<Device name="AdHocAnalysis" id="4" component="DataAnalysis"/>
<Device name="AccessAndPerformance" id="6" component="InformationManagement">
<Execution id="2">InternodeCommunication</Execution>
<Connection srcID="0" destID="1"/>
<Connection srcID="2" destID="1"/>
<Device/>
```

```
<Device name="Staging" id="7" component="InformationManagement">
<Execution id="3">DataAcquisition</Execution>
<Device/>
```

Finally, the deployment diagram can be generated automatically by mapping the ADL instance to the DSL instance and generating the corresponding layout and connections.

We reviewed the papers related to the Facebook application architecture to check the validity of the derived application architecture [29,36,37]. In [36], the ad hoc analysis component is described as follows: "A badly written ad hoc job can hog the resources in the cluster, thereby starving the production jobs and in the absence of sophisticated sandboxing techniques, the separation of the clusters for ad hoc and production jobs has become the practical choice for us in order to avoid such scenarios." The data acquisition (gathering) component is mentioned in [37]: "The first set of applications requires realtime concurrent, but sequential, read access to a very large stream of realtime data being stored in HDFS. An example system generating and storing such data is Scribe, an open source distributed log aggregation service created by and used extensively at Facebook. Previously, data generated by Scribe was stored in expensive and hard to manage NFS servers. Two main applications that fall into this category are Realtime Analytics and MySQL backups." Anjos et al. [38] discuss the internode communication: "Distributing the data introduces other complications such as latency when communication is needed between nodes within a cluster or even between different clusters. Clever partitioning of the graph can minimize these problems. Instead of randomly distributing vertices of the graph across servers an algorithm could make sure that we minimize the internode communication and thus the latency. A typical query in a social network like Facebook is to fetch information from all your friends (neighboring vertices). The latency of this query may be significantly lowered by localizing these vertices to the same server. Facebook utilizes this by first calculating a good partitioning using Giraph and then distributing the information in their relational databases according to the suggested partitioning."

4.5.5.2 Twitter

The features of the Twitter data are listed as streaming and unstructured [27]. Data security and modality are not included in the architectural design. Especially real-time query processing and metadata management are important features of the system, while its data integration capability is limited. The architecture also employs in-memory processing. Ingestion is covered in the architectural descriptions. We use the real-time query processing [30] and in-memory data storage features of the family feature model for deriving the related part of the application architecture of Twitter. The related design rules from the design rule set of the family feature model are as follows:

DR1: If **REAL-TIME QUERY PROCESSING** is selected then enable DATA ACQUISITION on component INFORMATION MANAGEMENT SERVER
DR2: If **IN-MEMORY DATA STORAGE** is selected then enable IN-MEMORY DATA PROCESSING on component DATA PROCESSING SERVER

Afterwards, we convert the design rules to an ADL instance to generate the application architecture and the deployment diagram. (See Fig. 4.8.)

A possible ADL instance, which is obtained via transformation of our derived design rule set, can be as follows:

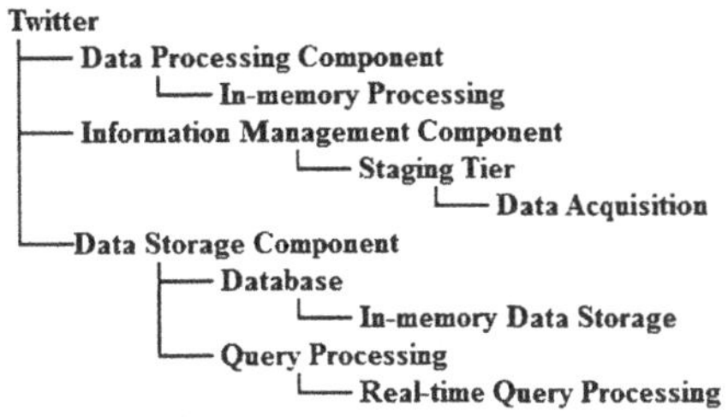

```
Twitter
    ├── Data Processing Component
    │       └── In-memory Processing
    ├── Information Management Component
    │                └── Staging Tier
    │                        └── Data Acquisition
    └──Data Storage Component
            ├── Database
            │        └── In-memory Data Storage
            └── Query Processing
                     └── Real-time Query Processing
```

FIGURE 4.8

Twitter application tree

```
<Device name="InMemoryProcessing" id="4" component="DataProcessing"/>
<Device name="Database" id="6" component="DataStorage">
<Execution id="2">InMemoryDataStorage</Execution>
<Device/>
<Device name="Staging" id="7" component="InformationManagement">
<Execution id="3">DataAcquisition</Execution>
<Device/>
```

In [38], Twitter's in-memory processing component, which is also included in the derived application architecture, is discussed as follows: "An interesting design decision we made early in the Wtf project [5] was to assume in-memory processing on a single server. At first, this may seem like an odd choice, running counter to the prevailing wisdom of "scaling out" on cheap, commodity clusters instead of "scaling up" with more cores and more memory. This decision was driven by two rationales: first, because the alternative (a partitioned, distributed graph processing engine) is significantly more complex and difficult to build, and, second, because we could! We elaborate on these two arguments below. In 2010, our calculations showed that storing the entire Twitter graph in memory on a single machine was feasible." The data acquisition is mentioned in [24]: "The input stream of a Storm cluster is handled by a component called a spout. The spout passes the data to a component called a bolt, which transforms it in some way. A bolt either persists the data in some sort of storage, or passes it to some other bolt. You can imagine a Storm cluster as a chain of bolt components that each make some kind of transformation on the data exposed by the spout." Also in-memory data storage is implied in [38]: "Twitter graph is assumed to be stored in memory on one server." Finally in [26], we can observe that Twitter architecture employs real-time processing components (servers and search engines).

4.5.5.3 Energy management system

Energy Management System (EMS) defined in [38] as a monitoring tool to track the buildings' energy consumption. Real time query processing, data acquisition, in-memory data storage, multiple types of data, and data integration features are emphasized in the architectural description of the system. It uses a traditional relational DBMS to store historical data. We use the real-time query processing, relational modal, data integration, multiple types of data, and in-memory data storage features of the family feature model for deriving the related part of the application architecture of EMS. (See also Fig. 4.9.) The related design rules from the design rule set of the family feature model are as follows:

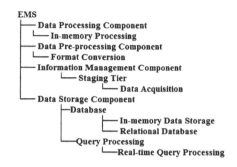

FIGURE 4.9

EMS application tree

DR1: If **REAL-TIME QUERY PROCESSING** is selected then enable DATA ACQUISITION on component INFORMATION MANAGEMENT SERVER

DR2: If **IN-MEMORY DATA STORAGE** is selected then enable IN-MEMORY DATA PROCESSING on component DATA PROCESSING SERVER

DR3: If **RELATIONAL MODEL** is selected then load RELATIONAL DATABASE on component DATA STORAGE

DR4: If **MULTIPLE DATA TYPES** and **DATA INTEGRATION** is selected then load FORMAT CONVERSION on component PRE-PROCESSING

A possible ADL instance, which is obtained via transformation of our derived design rule set, can be as follows:

```
<Device name="InMemoryProcessing" id="4" component="DataProcessing"/>
<Device name="FormatConversion" id="4" component="DataPreProcessing"/>
<Device name="Database" id="6" component="DataStorage">
<Execution id="2">InMemoryDataStorage</Execution>
<Execution id="3">RelationalDatabase</Execution>
<Device/>
<Device name="QueryProcessing" id="6" component="DataStorage">
<Execution id="5">RealTimeQueryProcessing</Execution>
<Device/>
<Device name="Staging" id="7" component="InformationManagement">
<Execution id="4">DataAcquisition</Execution>
<Device/>
```

4.6 CONCLUSION

Big data has become a very important driver for innovation and growth for various application domains. They impose different requirements on the big data system. Designing a big system as such needs to be carefully considered to realize the business goals. In this paper we have adopted a domain-driven design approach in which we provided a family feature model and a reference architecture based on a domain-analysis process. The family feature model covers the common and variant features of a broad set of applications, while the reference architecture provides a reusable architecture for deriving concrete application architectures. We were able to derive a broad set of features that characterize multiple different big data systems. With the further development in big data research, we can enhance the feature model in the future. Similarly, we have derived the reference architecture based on a domain-analysis process. The reference architecture as such appeared to be generic and representative of the various big data systems. We have discussed the design of an application architecture that can be considered as a function of a selection of features from the family feature model that in its turn can be coupled to a design decision on the reference architecture. We have indicated that we can derive the design rules to further support this process. With further research we could derive more design rules and integrate them in the overall process for supporting the architect in deriving a feasible big data architecture. We have been able to illustrate the approach for the case of Facebook, Twitter and EMS and to derive their application architecture. We have shown that besides the specialized application architectures such as Facebook and Twitter, EMS's more generic architecture can also be successfully derived using our approach. As a lesson learned, it should be mentioned that a complete set of design rules and proper derivation of the feature model is vital to applying the approach. In our future work we plan to elaborate on the approach and provide automated support for the design of big data architectures. Besides, the model will be extended to derive the architecture from the business requirements that trigger the evolution of the software architecture of a big data system.

REFERENCES

[1] S. Angelov, P. Grefen, D. Greefhorst, A classification of software reference architectures: analyzing their success and effectiveness, in: Joint Working IEEE/IFIP Conference on Software Architecture, 2009 & European Conference on Software Architecture. WICSA/ECSA 2009, IEEE, 2009, pp. 141–150.

[2] F. Bachmann, L. Bass, M. Klein, Architectural Tactics: A Step Toward Methodical Architectural Design, Technical Report CMU/SEI-2003-TR-004, Pittsburgh, PA 2003.

[3] C. Ballard, C. Compert, T. Jesionowski, I. Milman, B. Plants, B. Rosen, H. Smith, Information Governance Principles and Practices for a Big Data Landscape, IBM Redbooks, 2014.

[4] E. Begoli, J. Horey, Design principles for effective knowledge discovery from big data, in: 2012 Joint Working IEEE/IFIP Conference on Software Architecture (WICSA) and European Conference on Software Architecture (ECSA), IEEE, 2012, pp. 215–218.

[5] P. Gupta, et al., Wtf: the who to follow service at Twitter, in: Proceedings of the 22nd International Conference on World Wide Web, International World Wide Web Conferences Steering Committee, 2013.

[6] D. Chapelle, Big Data & Analytics Reference Architecture, An Oracle White Paper, 2013.

[7] K. Czarnecki, C. Hwan, P. Kim, K.T. Kalleberg, Feature models are views on ontologies, in: 10th International Software Product Line Conference, IEEE, 2006, pp. 41–51.

[8] E. Woods, N. Rozanski, Using architectural perspectives, in: 5th Working IEEE/IFIP Conference on Software Architecture, WICSA'05, IEEE, 2005, pp. 25–35.

[9] M. Galster, P. Avgeriou, Empirically-grounded reference architectures: a proposal, in: Proceedings of the Joint ACM SIGSOFT Conference–QoSA and ACM SIGSOFT Symposium–ISARCS on Quality of Software Architectures–QoSA and Architecting Critical Systems–ISARCS, ACM, 2011, pp. 153–158.

[10] R. McClatchey, A. Branson, J. Shamdasani, Z. Kovacs, Designing traceability into big data systems, arXiv preprint arXiv:1502.01545, 2015.

[11] B. Geerdink, A reference architecture for big data solutions introducing a model to perform predictive analytics using big data technology, in: 8th International Conference for Internet Technology and Secured Transactions (ICITST), IEEE, 2013, pp. 71–76.

[12] M. Harsu, A Survey on Domain Engineering, Tampere University of Technology, 2002.

[13] K.C. Kang, S.G. Cohen, J.A. Hess, W.E. Novak, A.S. Peterson, Feature-Oriented Domain Analysis (FODA) Feasibility Study (No. CMU/SEI-90-TR-21), Carnegie-Mellon Univ./Software Engineering Inst., Pittsburgh, PA, 1990.

[14] D. Laney, 3D Data Management: Controlling Data Volume, Velocity and Variety, Meta-Group Report #949, 2001.

[15] K. Lee, K.C. Kang, J. Lee, Concepts and guidelines of feature modeling for product line software engineering, in: Software Reuse: Methods, Techniques, and Tools, Springer, Berlin, Heidelberg, 2002, pp. 62–77.

[16] M. Maier, A. Serebrenik, I.T.P. Vanderfeesten, Towards a big data reference architecture, 2013.

[17] W. May, Draft NIST Big Data Interoperability Framework: Volume 6 Reference Architecture, 2014.

[18] N. Marz, J. Warren, Big Data: Principles and Best Practices of Scalable Realtime Data Systems, Manning Publications Co., 2015.

[19] N. Medvidovic, R.N. Taylor, A classification and comparison framework for software architecture description languages, IEEE Trans. Softw. Eng. 26 (1) (2000) 70–93.

[20] Oracle, Information Management and Big Data a Reference Architecture, An Oracle White Paper, 2013.

[21] P. Pääkkönen, D. Pakkala, Reference architecture and classification of technologies, products and services for big data systems, Big Data Res. 2 (4) (2015) 166–186.

[22] C. Avci Salma, B. Tekinerdogan, I. Athanasiadis, Feature driven survey of big data systems, in: Proc. of IoTBD, April 2016.

[23] S. Soares, Big Data Governance, Information Asset, LLC, 2012.

[24] J. Leibiusky, G. Eisbruch, D. Simonassi, Getting Started with Storm, O'Reilly Media, Inc., 2012.

[25] N. Rozanski, E. Woods, Software Systems Architecture – Working With Stakeholders Using Viewpoints and Perspectives, Addison-Wesley, 2005.

[26] G. Mishne, et al., Fast data in the era of big data: Twitter's real-time related query suggestion architecture, in: Proceedings of the 2013 ACM SIGMOD International Conference on Management of Data, ACM, 2013.

[27] B. Tekinerdogan, S. Bilir, C. Abatlevi, Integrating platform selection rules in the model driven architecture approach, in: Model Driven Architecture, Springer, Berlin, Heidelberg, 2005, pp. 159–173.

[28] B. Tekinerdogan, K. Öztürk, Feature-driven design of SaaS architectures, in: Software Engineering Frameworks for the Cloud Computing Paradigm, Springer, London, 2013, pp. 189–212.

[29] A. Thusoo, Z. Shao, S. Anthony, D. Borthakur, N. Jain, J. Sen Sarma, R. Murthy, H. Liu, Data warehousing and analytics infrastructure at Facebook, in: Proceedings of the 2010 ACM SIGMOD International Conference on Management of Data, ACM, 2010, pp. 1013–1020.

[30] G. Mishne, J. Dalton, Z. Li, A. Sharma, J. Lin, Fast data in the era of big data: Twitter's real-time related query suggestion architecture, in: Proceedings of the 2013 ACM SIGMOD International Conference on Management of Data, ACM, 2013, pp. 1147–1158.

[31] I. Gorton, J. Klein, Distribution, data, deployment: software architecture convergence in big data systems, IEEE Softw. 32 (3) (2015) 78–85.

[32] R. McClatchey, A. Branson, J. Shamdasani, Z. Kovacs, Designing traceability into big data systems, arXiv preprint arXiv:1502.01545, 2015.

[33] E. Begoli, J. Horey, Design principles for effective knowledge discovery from big data, in: Joint Working IEEE/IFIP Conference on Software Architecture (WICSA) and European Conference on Software Architecture (ECSA), IEEE, 2012, pp. 215–218.

[34] P. Xuan, Y. Zheng, S. Sarupria, A. Apon, SciFlow: a dataflow-driven model architecture for scientific computing using Hadoop, in: IEEE International Conference on Big Data, IEEE, 2013, pp. 36–44.

[35] Glossary, Software Engineering Institute, http://www.sei.cmu.edu/architecture/start/glossary/.

[36] A. Thusoo, et al., Data warehousing and analytics infrastructure at Facebook, in: Proceedings of the 2010 ACM SIGMOD International Conference on Management of Data, ACM, 2010.

[37] D. Borthakur, J.S. Sarma, J. Gray, K. Muthukkaruppan, N. Spiegelberg, H. Kuang, K. Ranganathan, D. Molkov, A. Menon, S. Rash, R. Schmidt, A. Aiyer, Apache Hadoop goes realtime at Facebook, in: Proceedings of the 2011 ACM SIGMOD International Conference on Management of data, ACM, 2011, pp. 1071–1080.

[38] D. Anjos, P. Carreira, A.P. Francisco, Real-time integration of building energy data, in: 2014 IEEE International Congress on Big Data, IEEE, 2014.

AN ARCHITECTURAL MODEL-BASED APPROACH TO QUALITY-AWARE DEVOPS IN CLOUD APPLICATIONS*

5

Robert Heinrich*, Reiner Jung†, Christian Zirkelbach†, Wilhelm Hasselbring†, Ralf Reussner*

*Karlsruhe Institute of Technology, Germany †Kiel University, Germany

5.1 INTRODUCTION

Cloud Computing technologies have been developed for storing and processing data using distributed resources which are often located in third party data centers. Constructing software systems by incorporating and composing cloud services offers many advantages like flexibility and scalability. Still, considerable challenges come along with these technologies such as increased complexity, fragility, and changes during operations that are unforeseeable at development time. As cloud-based systems are designed to change rapidly, they require increased communication and collaboration between software developers and operators, a strong integration of building, evolving and adaptation activities, as well as architectures satisfying deployability in heterogeneous contexts.

DevOps is an umbrella term of practices for enabling software developers and operators to work more closely and thus reducing the time between changing a system and putting the change into normal production, while ensuring high quality [2]. DevOps practices contribute to an integration of the roles of developer and operator. Software architecture is an essential artifact for both, developers and operators. The phase-spanning consideration of software architecture is foundation of DevOps practices. Besides life cycle processes and responsibilities, DevOps practices have strong impact on the software architecture. New architectural styles such as microservices [26] emerged to satisfy needs for scalability, deployability, and continuous delivery.

By merely introducing new architectural styles, however, the actual problems in collaboration and communication among developers and operators are not solved. Existing architectural models used in the development phase differ from those used in the operation phase in terms of purpose (finding appropriate design vs. reflecting current system configurations), abstraction (component-based vs. close to implementation level), and content (static vs. dynamic). Consequences of these differences are lim-

*This work was partially supported by the DFG (German Research Foundation) under the Priority Programme SPP1593: Design For Future – Managed Software Evolution and the MWK (Ministry of Science, Research and the Arts Baden-Württemberg) in the funding line Research Seed Capital (RiSC).

ited reuse of development models during operations and limited phase-spanning consideration of the software architecture.

In this chapter, we propose the iObserve approach for the reuse of architectural development models of cloud-based software applications during the operation phase. We enrich and update the development models with operational observations to construct architectural runtime models. A technology-independent monitoring approach is applied for operational observation. iObserve maintains the semantic relationships between monitoring outcomes and architectural models. We introduce a cloud-based software application as an illustrative example in Section 5.2 before we describe current differences in architectural models among development and operations in Section 5.3. An overview of the iObserve approach is given in Section 5.4. We describe concepts of the iObserve approach to address the differences in architectural models in Section 5.5. A megamodel integrates development models, code generation, monitoring, runtime model updates, as well as adaptation candidate generation and execution. The combination of descriptive and prescriptive architectural models improves the communication and collaboration between operators and developers once a software system is in operation phase. The consideration of static and dynamic content in architectural models supports operation-level adaptations. The application of these concepts is described in Section 5.6. We mention limitations of iObserve in Section 5.7. Related work is discussed in Section 5.8. The chapter concludes with a summary and listing of future work in Section 5.9.

5.2 A CLOUD-BASED SOFTWARE APPLICATION

We use an illustrative example in this chapter built upon an established community case study – the Common Component Modeling Example (CoCoME) [20] – and an associated evolution scenario [18]. CoCoME resembles a trading system as it may be applied in a supermarket chain. It implements processes at a single cash desk for processing sales, like scanning products or paying, as well as enterprise-wide administrative tasks, like ordering products or inventory management. The detailed design and implementation of CoCoME is described in [16] and the source code is available for download.[1] We refer to the Java Enterprise implementation of CoCoME in this chapter.

CoCoME uses a database service hosted on data centers that are distributed around the globe, as shown in Fig. 5.1. The figure illustrates the CoCoME core application and the global reach of prospective cloud providers that offer Database-as-a-Service (DBaaS). During development, architectural models are created and analyzed for quality aspects like performance, e.g., using the Palladio approach for software architecture modeling and simulation [29]. If an appropriate design has been found, the system is implemented into source code and deployed on the cloud. This is the point where developers hand over the system to operators to put it in production.

During system operations, an advertisement campaign of the supermarket chain leads to an increased amount of sales and thus to variations in the application's usage profile and intensity. Increased usage intensity causes an upcoming performance bottleneck due to limited capacities in the given service offering of the cloud provider currently hosting the database. For the sake of simplicity, we assume each cloud provider owns exactly one data center. Migrating or replicating the database from one data

---

[1] https://github.com/cocome-community-case-study.

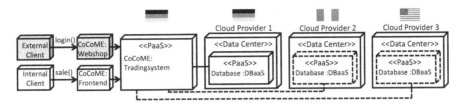

FIGURE 5.1

Actual (solid line) and conceivable (dashed line) component deployment of a cloud-based software application within a global reach of prospective data centers

center to another may solve the scalability issues. Conceivable component deployments are illustrated by dashed lines in Fig. 5.1. However, migrating or replicating the database may cause privacy issues if sensitive data are transferred outside the European Union [18]. Privacy has been analyzed for CoCoME in [32,33]. In cloud-based software applications there is often a trade-off between performance and privacy as further discussed in Section 5.5.2. These privacy issues cannot be foreseen at development time as prospective cloud providers are unknown. In order to analyze upcoming quality flaws during operations and react on them, operators need to observe the system and run analyses based on a model that represents the current application configuration and usage during operations. This model is called an architectural runtime model [15]. However, there are often differences between architectural models used in development and operations which hamper a phase-spanning consideration of the architecture as discussed based on the example in the following.

5.3 DIFFERENCES IN ARCHITECTURAL MODELS AMONG DEVELOPMENT AND OPERATIONS

This section discusses three differences in architectural models among development and operations – the level of abstraction, the use of prescriptive and descriptive models, and the differences in static and dynamic content reflected by the architectural models.

There are **different abstraction levels** of architectural models in development and operations. Architectural models especially in early phases of development commonly adhere to a component-based paradigm (e.g., [38,12]). Architectural models used in operations are closer to an implementation level of abstraction. In the CoCoME example, developers specify software components and their interactions in architectural models. Component-based models allow for keeping track of the architecture and structure the system by encapsulated components interconnected via interfaces. During operations the system is observed and architectural models are created from monitoring data. This monitoring data is related to source code artifacts (e.g., service calls or class signatures). For example, observing the sales service of CoCoME (cf. `sale()` in Fig. 5.1) results in monitoring records for the service itself and all invoked internal services. In addition, the class signature is recorded per service. Yet, no information about the component structure is provided by monitoring. Models derived from the data are close to implementation level, e.g., depict the dependencies between invoked services. Thus, it is hard to reproduce development component models from monitoring data as knowledge about the initial component structure and component boundaries is missing. This knowledge is important for system comprehension and reverse engineering.

For supporting DevOps practices it is useful to **combine prescriptive and descriptive architectural models**. However, a combination of both kinds of model can seldom be found. Prescriptive architectural models are employed during development to document the system to be designed and implemented. During operations, descriptive architectural models are used to reflect the actual state of the running system. Thus, descriptive architectural models are again often created from observation data. Currently there is no phase-spanning notion of software architecture which impedes the combination of prescriptive and descriptive models. In the CoCoME scenario a prescriptive model may be applied during development to make early quality predictions or to make quality predictions for evolutionary changes conducted by developers. An example of an evolutionary change is adding a web shop component (highlighted grey in Fig. 5.1) to the trading system [18]. Such a change will have strong impact on various quality properties like privacy, security, performance, and reliability. Developers may want to analyze such quality properties in advance before implementing the change. Descriptive architectural models are applied in the CoCoME example during operations to describe the current system state, potentially after adaptations to the system, e.g., the number of replicated components or the actual geographical location of a migrated component. Developers can modify the descriptive models according to evolutionary changes to construct prescriptive models for quality analysis.

There is **different content (static vs. dynamic)** in architectural models used in development and operations. Architectural models are applied during development to describe the static software design and structure. During operations, architectural models show dynamic content like object stacks in memory, service utilization, and response times of services. Visualization of dynamic content allows the operators to investigate current bottlenecks, analyze for anomalies, and support the decision process for human intervention. In the CoCoME example, a development view of the architecture may comprise the component types, package structure, and class declarations of the application. The operations view may contain charts of resource consumption for the several parts of the architecture and events occurred during operations visualized in sort of a dashboard.

5.4 THE iObserve APPROACH

The iObserve approach [13,15] specifies operation-level adaptation and development-level evolution as two mutual, interwoven processes that affect each other. Fig. 5.2 gives an overview of iObserve. The figure is inspired by [27]. The evolution activities are performed by human developers, while the adaption activities are executed automatically by predefined procedures where possible without human intervention.

iObserve tackles architectural challenges in DevOps by following the MAPE (Monitor, Analyze, Plan, Execute) control loop model. MAPE is a feedback cycle commonly used for managing system adaptation [5]. The MAPE loop is extended with models and transformations between them to facilitate the transition between operation-level adaptation and development-level evolution. The executed software application is observed and used to update the architectural runtime model. Based on the up-to-date model, the current application configuration is analyzed to reveal anomalies and predict quality flaws. The architectural runtime model is then applied as input either for adaptation or evolution activities depending on the outcome of a planning step. In the adaptation process an adaptation

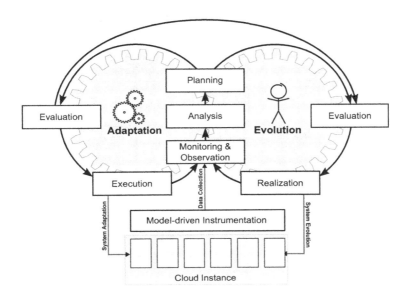

FIGURE 5.2

Overview of the iObserve approach

plan is selected and evaluated to mitigate deviations. Finally, the plan is executed to update the application architecture and configuration. In the evolution process changes are designed, evaluated and implemented by human developers.

iObserve applies an architectural runtime model that is usable for automatized adaptation and is simultaneously comprehensible for humans during evolution [17]. Foundation is a model-driven engineering approach [13] that models the software architecture and deployment in a component-oriented fashion and generates the artifacts to be executed during operations. Therefore, iObserve relies on the Palladio Component Model (PCM) [29] as an architecture metamodel. The PCM consists of several partial metamodels reflecting different architectural views on a software application. The repository model describes components and their interfaces stored in a repository. The components' inner behavior is described in so-called service effect specifications. The system model specifies the software architecture by composing components from the repository. The resource environment model provides a specification of the processing resources (CPU, hard disk, and network) while the allocation model specifies the deployment of the components to the resources. The usage model describes the user behavior and usage intensity. Quality-relevant properties, like resource demands of actions and processing rates of resources, are part of the models. Changes during operations relevant in the iObserve context affect the application usage and deployment. In particular, we focus on changes in user behavior and usage intensity, migration and (de)-replication of components, and (de)-allocation of execution contexts [15]. These changes are reflected in the PCM by modifying the usage model and allocation model.

The PCM in its current form is focused on single quality aspects, like performance and reliability, yet does not reflect, for instance, privacy aspects which are relevant in the scope of iObserve. To

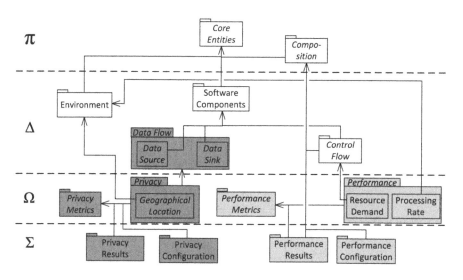

FIGURE 5.3

Exemplary instantiation of the reference architecture for performance and privacy

enable a more comprehensive representation of quality aspects in the PCM, we apply a metamodel modularization and extension approach [36] for component-based architecture description languages. Following a reference architecture, the information to be represented in the architecture metamodel is divided into four dimensions – paradigm, domain, quality and analysis – as depicted in Fig. 5.3. Each rectangle with a register symbol in the figure represents a modular metamodel that extends another metamodel and can itself be extended. Each rectangle without a register symbol represents a class or attribute that extends a metamodel. The paradigm layer (π) defines a foundational structure without any semantics, e.g., object oriented design or componentization. Here components and interfaces are specified as core entities. Further, composition by connectors is specified. The domain layer (Δ) extends π and assigns domain-specific semantics to its abstract first class entities. In the context of the iObserve approach Δ will capture software systems whereas in general any Δ layer is possible, e.g., for embedded or mechatronic systems. For software systems, Δ introduces the modules software components and environment. The control flow module extends software components by abstraction of the component behavior similar to flowcharts. Additionally, the software components module is enriched with information whether a component is source or sink of a dataflow. Dataflows are represented by inter-component communications via service calls. The quality layer (Ω) defines the inherent quality aspects of Δ concepts. It contains primarily second class entities, which enrich the first class entities of Δ. In the iObserve approach, the Ω layer comprises performance (light grey) and privacy (dark grey) aspects visualized in Fig. 5.3. For performance modeling the control flow module is extended with performance-relevant annotations for resource demands of actions and processing rates of resource containers within the execution environment. The performance metrics module contains the metamodeled metrics and corresponding units. For privacy modeling the dataflows, together with information about the geographical location of resource containers, form the basis for privacy analysis. The privacy metrics module comprises metamodeled privacy policies. The analysis layer (Σ) is required if models are used for analyses or simulation. In the iObserve context the performance results module contains a metamodel of service response times. The performance configuration module covers the model-based representation of analysis settings like simulated time span and number of measurements. Analogously, the privacy results module comprises a metamodel of privacy checks including their results. The privacy configuration model covers settings for a privacy check like sensitivity information for data and a blacklist or whitelist of geographical locations. Technical details of privacy analyses conducted in the iObserve context are given in [32,33].

Applying the reference architecture enables us adding all iObserve-specific content in a modular and noninvasive way without bloating the PCM. Further details on the application of the reference architecture to the PCM are given in [36].

The cloud application is instrumented with monitoring probes to keep it causally connected with the architectural runtime model. As technical basis for instrumentation, we choose the fast and reliable Kieker monitoring framework [21].

5.5 ADDRESSING THE DIFFERENCES IN ARCHITECTURAL MODELS

In this section, we describe concepts provided by the iObserve approach to address the three kinds of differences in architectural models among development and operations. The application of the concepts is demonstrated using the CoCoME example in Section 5.6.

5.5.1 THE iObserve MEGAMODEL

The iObserve approach applies a megamodel to bridge the divergent levels of abstraction in architectural models used in development and operations. Megamodels describe the relationships of models, metamodels, and transformations [8]. The iObserve megamodel depicted in Fig. 5.4 serves as an umbrella to integrate development models, code generation, monitoring, runtime model updates, as well as adaptation candidate generation and execution. Fig. 5.4 extends a previously published megamodel [15] by models and transformations for planning and execution. Rectangles depict models and metamodels, respectively. Solid lines represent transformations between models while diamonds indicate multiple input or output models of a transformation. Dashed lines reflect the conformance of a model to a metamodel, and, in case of implementation artifacts, the instance of relationship between operations data and development data types.

The iObserve megamodel exhibits four sections defined by two dimensions: one for development vs. operations, and one for model vs. implementation level. On the development side at model level, the megamodel depicts the combination of an architectural model with our model-driven monitoring approach [23]. The monitoring approach comprises an instrumentation record language (IRL) to define the data structures used for monitoring in a record type model. Further, the monitoring approach comprises an instrumentation aspect language (IAL) to specify the collection of data and the probe placement in an instrumentation model. The architectural model, the record type model, and the instrumentation model are applied for generating source code artifacts of the application and the corresponding monitoring probes. On the operations side at model level, monitoring data that adheres to source code artifacts like Java classes is associated with the elements of the architectural runtime model. Thus, the iObserve megamodel enables the reuse of development models during operation

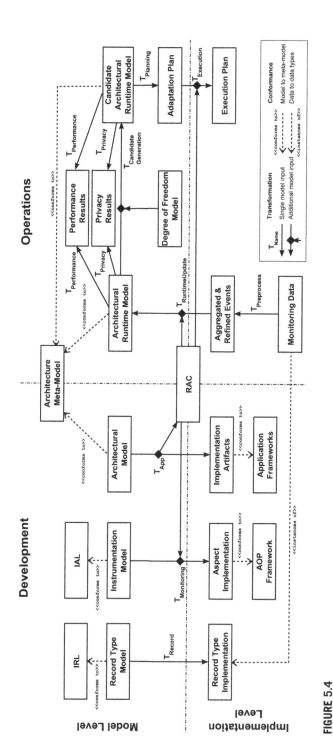

FIGURE 5.4

Overview of the iObserve megamodel

phase by updating them based on operational observations. Moreover, the operation side shows the generation of adaptation candidate models and the adaptation plan construction.

At implementation level, the megamodel depicts development and operations artifacts. The development artifacts comprise the generated implementation of the record types, the instrumentation aspects which implement the probes, and the technology specific artifacts which implement the application, like Servlets and Enterprise Java Beans in the Java Enterprise context. The operations side shows the monitoring data and their aggregation together with an execution plan describing the precise steps for adaptation on implementation level.

The Runtime Architecture Correspondence Model (RAC) is the central element of the megamodel and crucial for the use of an architectural model at development and operations. The RAC relates architectural model elements to implementation artifacts, like classes and services. It is created during code generation by the transformation T_{App}, as depicted in Fig. 5.4, or may be specified by hand in scenarios where the code is implemented by a developer. The RAC is also used for the generation and configuration of probes by our model-driven monitoring approach. Monitoring data is a continuous data stream which may comprise large amounts of events, i.e., millions of events per second in large enterprise applications [9]. iObserve first filters and aggregates the monitoring data ($T_{Preprocess}$). Then, iObserve allocates the monitoring data to architectural model elements, and finally uses the aggregated information to update the architectural runtime model by the transformation $T_{RuntimeUpdate}$.

Therefore, the architectural runtime model relates development and operation phases. It allows for phase-spanning consideration of software architecture. Furthermore, it enables quality analyses based on the architecture specification and thus contributes to quality-aware DevOps. Since we update development models by operational observations, our models contain all design decisions, e.g., about component boundaries and the distribution of the application to several execution containers.

Further, in iObserve, the level of abstraction of the initial architectural model and the updated model is maintained, due to:

(a) both the initial architectural model and the architectural runtime model, which rely on the same metamodel (the PCM),

(b) the decomposition of a development model element in one or more source code artifacts which is recorded in the RAC during code generation, and

(c) restoring while transforming monitoring events related to the source code artifacts to the component-based architectural runtime model.

As a consequence, using the iObserve approach changes in the operation phase can be seamlessly integrated with evolutionary changes in the development phase. Operators get access to higher level abstractions through which to view and manipulate the running application while developers can integrate tightly with adaptations that have been made for operational reasons.

5.5.2 DESCRIPTIVE AND PRESCRIPTIVE ARCHITECTURAL MODELS IN iObserve

The iObserve approach applies descriptive and prescriptive architectural runtime models for realizing the MAPE control loop as depicted in Fig. 5.5. In the Monitor phase, iObserve uses information gathered by probes to maintain the semantic relationship between the descriptive architectural runtime model and the underlying cloud application. Descriptive architectural runtime models are applied in the Analyze phase to reveal quality flaws like performance bottlenecks or violations of privacy policies and thus trigger adaptations. If a performance or privacy issue has been recognized, adaptation candi-

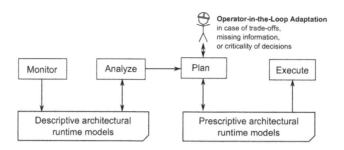

FIGURE 5.5

Descriptive and prescriptive architectural runtime models in the MAPE loop of our operator-in-the-loop adaptation approach [19]

dates are generated by the transformation $T_{CandidateGeneration}$ in form of candidate architectural runtime models in the Plan phase as depicted in Fig. 5.4. These prescriptive candidate models are generated based on a degree of freedom model that specifies variation points in the software architecture. We apply the PCM-based design space exploration approach PerOpteryx [24] to the architectural runtime models to find adaptation candidates and rank them regarding quality aspects like performance and costs. PerOpteryx provides a Pareto frontier of optimal design candidates.

Trade-offs between various quality aspects must be considered while planning for adaptation. In the cloud context there is often a trade-off between performance, costs, and privacy. The application usage effects on the performance of the application. Elasticity rules trigger the migration or replication of software components among geographically distributed data centers. Both migration and replication may increase performance; however, they may lead to violation of privacy policies and increasing costs. We apply PerOpteryx for analyzing trade-offs between performance and costs. Including privacy in design optimization and trade-off analysis is a subject of current work [34].

Once an adaptation candidate has been selected, the model is operationalized by deriving concrete tasks of a plan for adaptation execution. These tasks are derived by the transformation $T_{Planning}$ while comparing a candidate model to the original model and applying the KAMP approach to architecture-based change impact analysis [30]. KAMP provides for each change to the architecture elements a set of tasks to implement the change and has already been applied for deriving work plans for solving performance and scalability problems [14]. The aggregation of the tasks forms the adaptation plan which is transferred in the Execution phase to an execution plan at implementation level by $T_{Execution}$.

In case that no specific model among the candidates can be selected fully automatically, e.g., when there are trade-offs between quality aspects, or if an adaptation plan cannot be derived fully automatically, the human operator (cf. Fig. 5.5) chooses among the presented adaptation alternatives. Also when no candidate model can be generated, e.g., due to lack of information or criticality of decision, the operator will be involved.

5.5.3 STATIC AND DYNAMIC CONTENT IN ARCHITECTURAL MODELS

iObserve applies the PCM as an architecture metamodel for modeling usage profiles, the software architecture and deployment as well as quality properties. The PCM is well suited to reflect static system

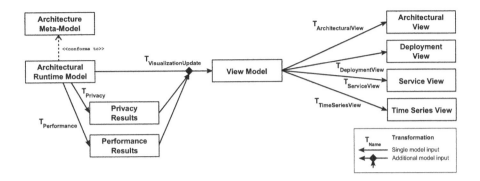

FIGURE 5.6

Extension of the iObserve megamodel for live visualization

design and structure and due to the extensions of iObserve it is also able to reflect adaptations during operation phase gathered by monitoring the software system, e.g., component migration or replication. To further improve the support of human operators and thus facilitate operator-in-the-loop adaptation [19], iObserve is extended by live visualization of software architectures. Key for live visualization and model inspection (e.g., for performance and privacy) are dynamic attributes of the application, which are collected by our monitoring framework.

Existing live visualization approaches, as listed in [10], provide interactive visualizations of the deployed application and its internal structure. They monitor and aggregate events during operations to create and update their architectural models. However, they lack static design information, such as component structure, do not provide analyses for privacy, and cannot relate monitoring data to the application architecture defined during development. Consequently, model visualizations of these approaches relate to the implementation level of abstraction. This hinders communication between operators and developers about issues occurred during operations as they use different models.

In iObserve, we eliminate this drawback by combining static and dynamic content, like in-memory object creation, communication, and execution traces, in an architectural runtime model. This is possible through the mapping capabilities of the RAC which provides model traces relating source code artifacts to architectural model elements. iObserve is inspired by visualization concepts of the live visualization approach ExplorViz [10]. ExplorViz provides two views, called landscape and application level perspective. The first provides an aggregated view on the deployment of software applications solely based on dynamic information. The second allows for viewing the internal structure of a service. The visualizations of iObserve provide similar views. In contrast to ExplorViz, iObserve also allows for utilizing static information which provides further insights into the state of the software application. To provide the information to the operator, iObserve uses a view model depicted in Fig. 5.6. The view model is created or updated by the transformation $T_{VisualizationUpdate}$ and subsequently used to generate the specific views. In detail, $T_{VisualizationUpdate}$ is triggered after the architectural runtime model has been updated and the results of the performance and privacy analysis are available. $T_{VisualizationUpdate}$ collects information from the architectural runtime model regarding execution contexts, services, and communication on type and instance level as simple named entities. It associates results of the privacy and performance analyses as well as time series information to these entities, together with other properties, such as call traces, user interaction, and system utilization. While this might seem like a duplication of information, the view model is designed to be a concise representation to support the presentation of different views for the operator. In contrast to the architectural runtime model, the entities do not exhibit any semantics. Instead, they contain information prepared for visualization.

Based on the view model, three views for architecture, deployment, and service are generated by the transformations $T_{ArchitecturalView}$, $T_{DeploymentView}$, and $T_{ServiceView}$. The views are continuously updated triggered by changes in the view model. Furthermore, the transformations are parametrized by operator selections and are reexecuted based on changes to operator selections. Examples based on the CoCoME scenario are given in Section 5.6.3.

To reduce the visual complexity the architectural view and deployment view display multiple instances of a service in an aggregated form. By operator choice, the aggregated services can be selectively expanded showing every service instance. This allows for investigating the state of the software application in more detail. For example, if the response time of a service does not conform to constraints, the aggregated service shows a warning like the box representing the aggregated service is highlighted. The operator can now expand the aggregated view of the service and see all instances. The layout is updated accordingly and only the instances violating the constraint are now highlighted. To further investigate the response time issue, the operator may select the individual service and continue the investigation in the service view. The service view is the adopted application level perspective of ExplorViz, which can now rely on the iObserve view model and present information on a package and component level.

The communication between services is shown as arrows pointing from the caller to the callee. The thickness of the arrow indicates the intensity of the communication, which can be either throughput or number of requests per second. The view model contains both values, while the architecture and deployment view can only visualize one value at a time. In the service view, communication is depicted as lines representing the call traces. The thickness of the lines increase based on number of requests per second.

The three views are limited to the visualization of the current application state including aggregated information on response times and communication intensities. However, in many cases it is important to inspect these values over time. Therefore, execution contexts, services, communication, call traces, and components can be selected and corresponding time series data is displayed in addition to the three views. The time series view is created or updated by $T_{TimeSeriesView}$, which is executed only in case a time series is displayed. The transformation is therefore parameterized based on the selection in one of the three views.

5.6 APPLYING iObserve TO CoCoME

In this section, we sketch the application of parts of the iObserve approach based on the CoCoME example. We assume code has been generated initially by the transformation T_{App} and the correspondences between architectural model elements and the Java classes have been stored in the RAC. Further, the application is deployed and running.

5.6.1 APPLYING THE iObserve MEGAMODEL

The observation of the running application using the Kieker monitoring framework produces a stream of heterogeneous events. Following the CoCoME scenario, increased usage intensity of the application triggers changes in the workload specification of the architectural model. iObserve filters out single entry and exit events to services of the application (e.g., the sales service) and aggregates them to sequences of events. The sequences are input to the calculation of the new usage intensity which is then transformed to the PCM workload specification.

The $T_{Preprocess}$ transformation pipeline depicted in Fig. 5.4 listens to the stream of monitoring events related to entry level services and creates an entry call event for each invocation of the sales service. The transformation aggregates the sales service together with other entry calls (e.g., for reporting or browsing the product catalogue) by exploiting user session information contained in the monitored events. All observed user sessions are combined in a graph-based entry call sequence model to calculate usage-related properties such as path probabilities, loop iterations or usage intensities. The sequence model is input to the $T_{RuntimeUpdate}$ transformation.

$T_{RuntimeUpdate}$ comprises transformations to modify the architectural runtime model according to changes in usage, deployment, and allocation. In the CoCoME scenario, we monitored increased invocations to the sales service which triggers $T_{RuntimeUpdate}$ to modify the workload specification within the PCM usage model. As there might be various usage profiles for different user roles in the model, the transformation takes a look into the RAC to identify the workload specification to be updated for the observed sales service. Note, only the PCM usage model is modified. The other partial models of the PCM (cf. Section 5.4) are taken as they are. If the architectural runtime model is created initially, the other partial models are taken from the architectural model on development side. Otherwise, the models are taken from the existing architectural runtime model. The result of this transformation pipeline is an updated descriptive architectural runtime model.

Similar procedures are applied for observing and processing other changes during operation like migration and (de-)replication of software components and (de-)allocation of execution contexts [15].

In the CoCoME scenario deployment changes (i.e., migration and (de-)replication) are evoked in the planning phase and therefore already contained in a prescriptive architectural runtime model (cf. Section 5.6.2). Nevertheless, iObserve is capable to observe and processes deployment changes. iObserve first filters out deployment events from the stream of monitoring events. In contrast to aforementioned entry and exit events, a preprocessing of deployment events is not necessary. A deployment event can be directly mapped to the corresponding resource environment in the architectural runtime model as it contains information about deployed classes and the deployment target (i.e., the resource container). For each deployment event $T_{RuntimeUpdate}$ modifies the resource environment. The RAC is required to identify components corresponding to the observed classes. The same procedure is executed for undeployment events. Moreover, new execution contexts become available (allocation) or existing ones disappear (de-allocation) without creating distinct (de-)allocation events. Yet, as a deployment always requires an existing execution context, we can apply the deployment target information contained in the (un-)deployment events to update the resource environment with respect to (de-)allocation. $T_{RuntimeUpdate}$ checks whether (de-)allocation was observed and, if necessary, updates the resource environment before the deployment is updated.

5.6.2 APPLYING DESCRIPTIVE AND PRESCRIPTIVE ARCHITECTURAL MODELS

After the descriptive architectural runtime model is updated by aforementioned transformations it can be applied for quality analysis. In the CoCoME scenario, the model is analyzed for performance using simulators of the Palladio approach [29]. Based on the PCM, including the usage model updated by transformations, the response time distribution for each service of the CoCoME application is simulated. The simulation is depicted as $T_{Performance}$ in Fig. 5.4 pointing to the performance results model. The simulation indicates upcoming performance bottlenecks caused by increased usage intensity due to the advertise campaign. More precisely, the average response time of the sales services increases by increased usage intensity. For mitigating the performance issues iObserve automatically generates various prescriptive adaptation candidate models by the transformation $T_{CandidateGeneration}$. For candidate generation the degree of freedom in the CoCoME scenario is deployment. Therefore, various candidate models are generated using evolutionary algorithms [24] each differing in deployment of the database service to data centers. This includes replication and migration of the database service.

During candidate generation, the candidate models are analyzed for performance ($T_{Performance}$) and additionally for privacy ($T_{Privacy}$). For privacy, dataflows are analyzed by constraint checking techniques to ensure that sensitive data do not exceed the EU borders. As CoCoME contains data of different sensitivity we do not peremptorily exclude data centers outside the EU. Data with low sensitivity can be located outside the EU. If privacy violations are identified, the candidate is discarded. This means it is not further evolved to generate new candidates.

Once an appropriate candidate is found, the system is adapted based on the prescriptive model ($T_{Execution}$). If no candidate model can be generated based on the given degrees of freedom (e.g., if there are no alternative data centers) or if no appropriate candidate model can be identified (e.g., if all candidates that satisfy privacy show performance issues), the human operator is involved for decision making. This is supported by visualization techniques discussed in the next section.

5.6.3 APPLYING LIVE VISUALIZATION

The deployment of the CoCoME cloud application is presented in a 2D live visualization in Fig. 5.7. The visualization has been created from the view model using the transformation $T_{DeploymentView}$. The system border of CoCoME is depicted by the outer box which comprises the execution contexts named WebNode, DataCenter, Adapter, and LogicNode. Inside these execution contexts the single services of CoCoME are shown connected by arrows. Note that the services depicted are composite services each consisting of hierarchically aggregated services. The execution contexts can be virtual machines and dedicated servers, which can be dynamically allocated and deallocated.

The arrow pointing from WebService to CashDesk indicates intensive communication between the two services. Furthermore, the direction indicates that the WebService is calling the CashDesk service. Based on the intensity of the communication, the operator may decide to replicate the CashDesk service. However, before triggering a replication, the operator may want to know more about the service and its communication. Therefore, the operator selects the execution context LogicNode, the CashDesk service, and the TCP connection between WebService and CashDesk to inspect their properties, like the current resource consumption. Consequently, the transformation $T_{DeploymentView}$ is reexecuted parametrized by the operator selections. The properties are presented on the right side of

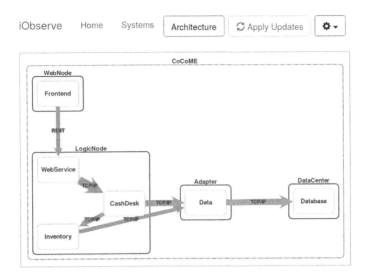

FIGURE 5.7

Deployment view of iObserve depicting a running CoCoME instance

Fig. 5.7 in a small table. In addition, time series data and statistics, such as throughput and response time, can be viewed as time series graphs in the side pane as well by triggering the transformation $T_{TimeSeriesView}$.

To support the operator, the views indicate bottlenecks and violations of constraints by highlighting the specific elements. In Fig. 5.7, the Inventory service is highlighted indicating a warning level issue based on an SLA violation.

The operator can now consult time series on performance and other properties provided on the side pane, or inspect the interior of the service utilizing the 3D service and component view of ExplorViz depicted in Fig. 5.8. In the figure, the LogicNode is shown in a 3D live visualization including the Inventory and CashDesk service. The green blocks represent the static package structure of the services, which are alternating colored for better identification. Packages can be opened to show contained classes, like the application.store package, or closed to provide an aggregated view, like the data.store package. The blue pillars visualize dynamic stacks of object instantiations. The communication, based on call traces, is depicted by the orange lines between the classes and packages. Fig. 5.8 indicates intensive internal communication between classes of the data and application package. This could be the cause of the SLA violation. Based on the visualization, the operator is able to identify potential performance bottlenecks. For further investigation, the operator can inspect the call traces and determine the invoked methods in the classes. If the cause cannot be found on this level, the operator can hand over the information to the developer who then can inspect the related source code, through an integrated source code view or external tools, and the architectural model to identify implementation errors.

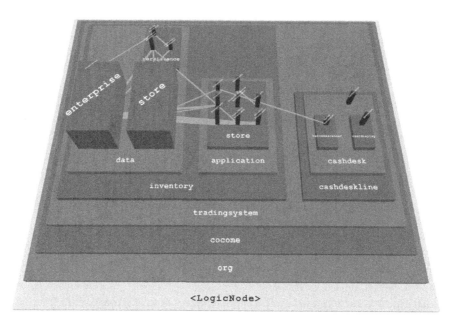

FIGURE 5.8

Service and component view of iObserve visualized in ExplorViz depicting the LogicNode with the Inventory and CashDesk service

5.7 LIMITATIONS

In this section we describe limitations of iObserve identified while applying the approach to the Co-CoME community case study.

Currently iObserve is limited to observation and processing of changes in the application's usage and deployment, i.e., migration and (de-)replication of software components and (de-)allocation of execution contexts. These are the most common changes for cloud-based software applications discussed in literature [15]. iObserve can be extended for additional types of changes easily by adding new monitoring probe specifications and new transformations to the megamodel.

iObserve focuses on the software application architecture and does not consider internal events of the cloud infrastructure. Thus, the impact of infrastructure internals, e.g., changes in the technology stack or internal replications, on the application's quality is not considered. We use a PAAS cloud. Therefore, we assume we can observe all events needed from the perspective of an application developer and operator. Nevertheless, SAAS-based services can be represented in the architectural model and may be supported by additional monitoring technologies in the future development of iObserve.

Increased criticality and limited observability of cloud-based applications require involving humans in the operation and adaptation process [19]. The iObserve approach supports human engagement at several points in the process. Humans are supported by visualization of the current situation and reveling consequences of design decisions. At the end, the human operator still needs knowledge and experience to make a good decision. However, due to the support given by iObserve decision making is expected to be much easier.

A common limitation of runtime modeling approaches is the accuracy of the model depends on the length of the time span of observation. If the time span is too short, services invoked seldom may not be observed or probabilities calculated may be inaccurate.

5.8 RELATED WORK

Work related to the concepts proposed in this chapter can be distinguished into four major categories: (i) approaches for reusing development models during operations, (ii) approaches for model extraction from observation data, (iii) approaches for architecture conformance checking, and (iv) approaches for trace visualization.

Work on *reusing development models* during operations (e.g., [25,22,6]) employs development models as foundation for reflecting software systems during operations. Bencomo et al. [3] give an overview of runtime modeling and analysis approaches. The work in [25] reuses sequence diagrams to verify running applications against their specifications. However, the approach does not include any updating mechanism that changes the model whenever the reflected system is being alternated. Consequently, changes during operation phase are not supported. Other than this, the runtime models in [22] and [6] are modified during operations. These approaches employ workflow specifications created during development phase in order to carry out performance and reliability analyses during operation phase. The approaches update the workflow models with respect to quality properties (e.g., response times) of the services bound to the workflow. However, these approaches do not reflect component-based software architectures. Further, this work updates the model with respect to single parameters and does not change the model's structure.

Work on *model extraction* creates and updates model content during operations. Approaches such as [35,31,1] establish the semantic relationships between executed applications and runtime models based on monitoring events (for a comprehensive list of approaches see [37]). Starting with a "blank" model, these approaches create model content during operation phase from scratch, e.g., by observing and interpreting service traces. Therefore, they disregard information that cannot be gathered from monitoring data, such as development perspectives on component structures and component boundaries. For instance, the work in [1] exploits process mining techniques for extracting state machine models from event logs. Without knowledge about the component structure created during development, the extracted states cannot be mapped to the application architecture specified in development phase. In consequence, the model hierarchy is flat and unstructured, which hinders software developers and operators in understanding the application at hand. Further, the work reflects processes but neither components nor their relationships. Other than this, the work in [31] extracts components and their relationships from observations for architecture comparison. With this approach we share the application of transformation rules to update a runtime model based on monitoring events. The resulting model in [31] is coarse-grained, which is sufficient for their purposes. However, when conducting performance and privacy analyses the observation and reflection of resource consumptions is crucial. Reflecting the consumption by the means of usage profiles requires processing event sets rather than single events, which outruns the capacity of this approach. Further, the observation and analysis of usage and component changes causes complex relationships between the investigated applications, probe types, and runtime models, which is not discussed in [31].

Work on *architecture conformance checking* compares the static source code of a software application to an architectural model or architectural constraints. An early approach of architecture conformance checking is based on Sotograph and allows for comparing different source code versions with an architectural model to detect architecture degradation [4]. A unifying approach [7] integrates different conformance checking tools and provides a common rule based interface to them. As a rule based approach no explicit architecture model is used. Passos et al. [28] investigate three different conformance check approaches based on dependency matrices, source code queries and reflexion models. All these approaches rely only on static information and cannot capture the deployment of a software application. Furthermore, they try to recover the architecture or architectural properties based on the source code without knowledge of the actual relationship of code and architectural model. In iObserve, we use the RAC to ensure that the correct code is related to the architecture and, due to operational observations, we are able to include dynamic properties in our analyses.

Related work on *trace visualization* utilizes concepts similar to those proposed in the paper. The visualizations of iObserve are inspired by ExplorViz [10] and therefore most related to this approach. ExplorViz creates views based on monitoring data, however, neglects development decisions. The TraceCrawler approach [11] visualizes prerecorded program traces relating to a single software service. Therefore, TraceCrawler implements an offline analysis, while iObserve focuses on live visualization of multiple software systems in a large software landscape. The visualization of TraceCrawler is based on a 3D graph metaphor where each instance of a class is represented by a box and the invocation is represented by edges between these boxes [11]. This individual representation of instances and invocations can lead to a complex web of boxes and edges which are hard to comprehend. Therefore, we use an aggregated view, where each class is represented by a single box and edges are drawn between classes instead of instances. The amount of instances is represented through the height of a box, and the number of invocations determines the thickness of edges. The CodeCity approach [40] uses a city metaphor for large-scale software systems, like ExplorViz. However, CodeCity is only able to visualize static properties of source code, like classes and packages, where iObserve, ExplorViz, and TraceCrawler include dynamic content. Furthermore, CodeCity visualizes the whole application in class level detail at once. In contrast, we employ a top-down driven hierarchical approach, which allows for inspecting single packages interactively.

To summarize, development models reused during operation phase provide good comprehensibility to humans, but are not updated with respect to structural changes yet. However, structural updates are required to reflect changes during operations like replication or migration as further described in [15]. Work on model extraction automatically creates runtime models from scratch. As development decisions on the application architectures cannot be fully derived from monitoring events the resulting models lack understandability. Approaches on architecture conformance checking neglect dynamic properties since they are limited to the conformance between static source code and architectural models. The visualization of models is essential to support understandability. Most visualization approaches reflect only static models and source code, which cannot provide insight in operational properties. Approaches like TraceCrawler incorporate monitoring data, however, are not able to provide live visualizations, which are necessary to support operators. ExplorViz offers live visualization but neglects development decisions.

Moreover, there are approaches for model synchronization using triple graph grammars for instance. Trollmann and Albayrak [39] propose a triple graph for synchronizing Enterprise Java Beans and component models. However, data do not result from monitoring a running application.

5.9 CONCLUSION

In this chapter we proposed the iObserve approach to address architectural challenges in DevOps of cloud-based software applications. The iObserve megamodel bridges different abstraction levels among architectural models in development and operations. iObserve employs descriptive and prescriptive architectural runtime models in the context of the MAPE control loop. Extending the iObserve megamodel for live visualizations allows for depicting static as well as dynamic content in architectural models used in operator-in-the-loop adaptation.

In the future, we plan to further investigate the planning and execution phases of iObserve. Besides further analyzing design space exploration and optimization approaches to find optimal architectural runtime model candidates, we will investigate the execution of adaptation plans to allow for a maximum degree of automation where adaptation is possible without human intervention. Our live visualization supports cases where human intervention is required. We will extend the visualization approach by additional 3D views to further improve support of human operators. We will conduct experiments for evaluating our architectural runtime models with respect to fidelity, usefulness for human inspection, and scalability.

Moreover, we will extend and revise the PCM following our reference architecture for metamodel modularization and extension to support additional quality aspects that may become relevant in the iObserve context.

REFERENCES

[1] W. van der Aalst, M. Schonenberg, M. Song, Time prediction based on process mining, Inf. Sci. 36 (2) (2011) 450–475.
[2] L. Bass, I. Weber, L. Zhu, DevOps: A Software Architect's Perspective, Addison–Wesley Professional, 2015.
[3] N. Bencomo, R. France, B.H.C. Cheng, U. Amann, Models@run.time, Springer, 2014.
[4] W. Bischofberger, J. Kühl, S. Löffler, Sotograph – A Pragmatic Approach to Source Code Architecture Conformance Checking, LNCS, vol. 3047, 2004, pp. 1–9.
[5] Y. Brun, et al., Engineering self-adaptive systems through feedback loops, in: Software Engineering for Self-Adaptive Systems, Springer, 2009, pp. 48–70.
[6] G. Canfora, M. Di Penta, R. Esposito, M.L. Villani, A framework for QoS-aware binding and re-binding of composite web services, J. Syst. Softw. 81 (10) (2008) 1754–1769.
[7] A. Caracciola, M. Lungu, O. Nierstrasz, A unified approach to architecture conformance checking, in: 12th Working IEEE/IFIP Conference on Software Architecture, ACM, 2015, pp. 41–50.
[8] J.-M. Favre, Foundations of model (driven) (reverse) engineering – episode I: Story of the fidus papyrus and the solarus, in: Dagstuhl Post-Proceedings, 2004.
[9] F. Fittkau, S. Frey, W. Hasselbring, Cloud user-centric enhancements of the simulator CloudSim to improve cloud deployment option analysis, in: European Conference on Service-Oriented and Cloud Computing, Springer, 2012.
[10] F. Fittkau, A. Krause, W. Hasselbring, Software landscape and application visualization for system comprehension with ExplorViz, Inf. Softw. Technol. (2016), http://dx.doi.org/10.1016/j.infsof.2016.07.004.
[11] O. Greevy, M. Lanza, C. Wysseier, Visualizing live software systems in 3D, in: ACM Symposium on Software Visualization, 2006, pp. 47–56.

[12] W. Hasselbring, Component-based software engineering, in: Handbook of Software Engineering and Knowledge Engineering, World Scientific Publishing, Singapore, 2002, pp. 289–305.

[13] W. Hasselbring, R. Heinrich, R. Jung, A. Metzger, K. Pohl, R. Reussner, E. Schmieders, iObserve: Integrated Observation and Modeling Techniques to Support Adaptation and Evolution of Software Systems, Technical Report 1309, Kiel University, Kiel, Germany, 2013.

[14] C. Heger, R. Heinrich, Deriving work plans for solving performance and scalability problems, in: Computer Performance Engineering, in: Lecture Notes in Computer Science, vol. 8721, Springer, 2014, pp. 104–118.

[15] R. Heinrich, Architectural run-time models for performance and privacy analysis in dynamic cloud applications, ACM SIGMETRICS Perform. Eval. Rev. 43 (4) (2016) 13–22.

[16] R. Heinrich, Kiana Rostami, Ralf Reussner, The CoCoME Platform for Collaborative Empirical Research on Information System Evolution, Technical Report 2016, 2; Karlsruhe Reports in Informatics, KIT, 2016.

[17] R. Heinrich, E. Schmieders, R. Jung, K. Rostami, A. Metzger, W. Hasselbring, R. Reussner, K. Pohl, Integrating run-time observations and design component models for cloud system analysis, in: 9th Int'l Workshop on Models@run.time, 2014, pp. 41–46, CEUR Vol-1270.

[18] R. Heinrich, S. Gärtner, T.-M. Hesse, T. Ruhroth, R. Reussner, K. Schneider, B. Paech, J. Jürjens, A platform for empirical research on information system evolution, in: 27th Int'l Conference on Software Engineering and Knowledge Engineering, KSI Research Inc., 2015, pp. 415–420.

[19] R. Heinrich, R. Jung, E. Schmieders, A. Metzger, W. Hasselbring, R. Reussner, K. Pohl, Architectural run-time models for operator-in-the-loop adaptation of cloud applications, in: IEEE 9th Symposium on the Maintenance and Evolution of Service-Oriented Systems and Cloud-Based Environments, IEEE, 2015.

[20] S. Herold, et al., CoCoME – the common component modeling example, in: The Common Component Modeling Example, Springer, 2008, pp. 16–53.

[21] A. v. Hoorn, J. Waller, W. Hasselbring, Kieker: a framework for application performance monitoring and dynamic software analysis, in: 3rd Int'l Conference on Performance Engineering, ICPE 2012, ACM, 2012, pp. 247–248.

[22] D. Ivanovic, M. Carro, M. Hermenegildo, Constraint-based runtime prediction of SLA violations in service orchestrations, in: Service-Oriented Computing, Springer, 2011, pp. 62–76.

[23] R. Jung, R. Heinrich, E. Schmieders, Model-driven instrumentation with Kieker and Palladio to forecast dynamic applications, in: Symposium on Software Performance, 2013, pp. 99–108, CEUR Vol-1083.

[24] A. Koziolek, H. Koziolek, R. Reussner, PerOpteryx: automated application of tactics in multi-objective software architecture optimization, in: ACM SIGSOFT Conference on Quality of Software Architectures, 2011.

[25] B. Morin, O. Barais, J.-M. Jezequel, F. Fleurey, A. Solberg, Models@run.time to support dynamic adaptation, IEEE Comput. 42 (10) (2009) 44–51.

[26] S. Newman, Building Microservices, O'Reilly, 2015.

[27] P. Oreizy, N. Medvidovic, R.N. Taylor, Runtime software adaptation: framework, approaches, and styles, in: Companion of the 30th Int'l Conference on Software Engineering, ACM, 2008, pp. 899–910.

[28] L. Passos, R. Terra, M.T. Valente, R. Diniz, N. das Chagas Mendonca, Static architecture-conformance checking: an illustrative overview, IEEE Softw. 27 (5) (2010).

[29] Ralf H. Reussner, et al. (Eds.), Modeling and Simulating Software Architectures – The Palladio Approach, MIT Press, ISBN 978-0-262-03476-0, 2016.

[30] K. Rostami, J. Stammel, R. Heinrich, R. Reussner, Architecture-based assessment and planning of change requests, in: 11th International ACM SIGSOFT Conference on Quality of Software Architectures, ACM, 2015, pp. 21–30.

[31] B. Schmerl, J. Aldrich, D. Garlan, R. Kazman, H. Yan, Discovering architectures from running systems, IEEE Trans. Softw. Eng. 32 (7) (2006) 454–466.

[32] E. Schmieders, A. Metzger, K. Pohl, A runtime model approach for data geo-location checks of cloud services, in: International Conference on Service-Oriented Computing, Springer, 2014, pp. 306–320.

[33] E. Schmieders, A. Metzger, K. Pohl, Runtime model-based privacy checks of big data cloud services, in: International Conference on Service-Oriented Computing, Springer, 2015, pp. 71–86.

[34] S. Seifermann, Architectural data flow analysis, in: 13th Working IEEE/IFIP Conference on Software Architecture, IEEE, 2016.

[35] H. Song, G. Huang, F. Chauvel, Y. Xiong, Z. Hu, Y. Sun, H. Mei, Supporting runtime software architecture: a bidirectional-transformation-based approach, J. Syst. Softw. 84 (5) (2011) 711–723.

[36] M. Strittmatter, K. Rostami, R. Heinrich, R. Reussner, A modular reference structure for component-based architecture description languages, in: 2nd International Workshop on Model-Driven Engineering for Component-Based Systems, CEUR, 2015, pp. 36–41.

[37] M. Szvetits, U. Zdun, Systematic literature review of the objectives, techniques, kinds, and architectures of models at runtime, Softw. Syst. Model. 15 (1) (2016) 31–69.

[38] C. Szyperski, Component Software: Beyond Object-Oriented Programming, 2nd edition, Addison–Wesley, 2002.

[39] Frank Trollmann, Sahin Albayrak, Extending model synchronization results from triple graph grammars to multiple models, in: Theory and Practice of Model Transformations, in: LNCS, vol. 9765, Springer, 2016, pp. 91–106.

[40] R. Wettel, M. Lanza, Visualizing software systems as cities, in: 4th International Workshop on Visualizing Software for Understanding and Analysis, VISSOFT 2007, 2007.

BRIDGING ECOLOGY AND CLOUD: TRANSPOSING ECOLOGICAL PERSPECTIVE TO ENABLE BETTER CLOUD AUTOSCALING

6

Tao Chen, Rami Bahsoon

School of Computer Science, University of Birmingham, UK

6.1 INTRODUCTION

In cloud environment, the quality of service (QoS) and cost/energy objectives for cloud-based services can be tuned by accessing software configurations (e.g., the number of service threads, size of connection pool, and session lifetime) and hardware resources (e.g., the CPU, memory, and Virtual Machine) that are shared, leased, and priced as utilities. Such a feature is fundamentally facilitated through autoscaling: an automatic and elastic process, typically running on a Physical Machine (PM), that adapts software configurations and hardware resources provisioning on-demand according to the changing environmental conditions (e.g., the workload).

What make the cloud autoscaling challenging are the dynamic, uncertainty and possible trade-offs on objectives (i.e., QoS and cost/energy objectives) exhibited in the process. In cloud, dynamics and uncertainty arise from the unpredictable environmental conditions and QoS interference – a scenario where the competing demands of some of the services can interfere with the QoS of others, provided that there are many cloud-based services run on a shared infrastructure. Trade-offs are associated with runtime autoscaling decisions as to the appropriate amount of scaling applied to software configurations and hardware resources. These trade-offs can be, for example, whether to choose throughput over cost or which competing cloud-based services to focus on.

To address those challenges, prior efforts in cloud autoscaling have relied on rules-based control [14], control theoretic mechanisms [22], and computational intelligence techniques [5], with particular focus on improving the optimality, elasticity, and scalability of the autoscaling system. However, the runtime stability and sustainability in the cloud, which are mainly concerned with the long-term benefit for both cloud consumers and provider, have not been explicitly tackled. Here, *sustainability* refers to the ability of cloud to endure the stress caused by dynamic and uncertain events, e.g., workload and QoS interference, with an aim to continually optimize QoS attributes of all cloud-based services while minimizing their costs and energy consumptions. The longer the time when no violation of Service Level Agreement (SLA) and budget requirements occur, the better the *stability*. Following the intuition that *computer systems can be better understood, controlled, and developed when viewed from the perspective of living systems* [12], we argue that the perspective of ecology and natural ecosystem[1] is a new, yet neat view for computer science researchers to design a novel autoscaling system in the cloud. In particular, understanding stability and sustainability of natural ecosystems, as well as how we can better manage them spontaneously, has been the core research theme for ecologists. These will therefore provide many useful insights for researches in cloud autoscaling.

In this article, we explore the potential benefit of using ecological view when designing an autoscaling system in the cloud. From the ecological point of view, we intend to render the cloud environment as a natural ecosystem and to design autoscaling system in the cloud derived/inspired from ecological techniques. We then propose a sensible translation of ecological principles, theories, and models into cloud autoscaling analogues. Particularly, we have explored the biotic characterizations of cloud-based services and the underlying cloud primitives w.r.t. the principles of living organisms/species, nonliving components, habitats, biodiversity, disturbances, species competition, trophic web, and natural evolution. We propose an ecology-inspired self-aware architectural pattern extending on the self-aware patterns from our prior work [11]. The new pattern explicitly caters for the key levels of biotic information, which are also systematically linked to the original principles of self-awareness. Finally, we highlight the challenges and opportunities for future investigations of ecology-inspired autoscaling in the cloud.

6.2 MOTIVATION

Elastic autoscaling in the cloud has been an increasingly important research topic since the emergence of cloud computing paradigm. Efforts have been spent to deal with the dynamics, uncertainty and trade-offs exhibited in the autoscaling process [14,22,5,7]. Nevertheless, how autoscaling can improve the stability and sustainability of the cloud as a whole has not been explicitly studied in prior work. Undoubtedly, stability and sustainability are among the most desirable attributes of cloud computing. Table 6.1 illustrates the benefits of explicitly considering stability and sustainability when autoscaling in the cloud.

Natural ecosystems are considered to be robust, efficient, and scalable systems that are capable to cope with dynamics and uncertainty, possessing several properties that may be useful in cloud autoscaling systems. These properties include self-awareness, self-adaptivity, and the ability to provide solutions for complex scenarios [17], e.g., resolving trade-offs. Many of these properties can be understood via well-known ecological models [16], which provide a theoretical basis for the occurrence of self-awareness and self-adaptivity, resulting from the interactions among the individuals and their environment, leading to complex and emergent behaviors [17] (e.g., evolution driven by natural selection).

Among others, stability and sustainability are the most desirable attributes in natural ecosystem and they have been studied by the ecologists for decades. We advocate that the well-established ecological principles, theories, and models can provide rich source of inspiration to spontaneously improve the stability and sustainability of the cloud as a whole. This will allow all the cloud-based services to stay robust and generate minimal overhead when optimizing their objectives and complying their SLA/bud-

---

[1]We will discuss this in details in Section 6.3.

Table 6.1 Comparing autoscaling in the cloud with/without tackling stability and sustainability

With stability and sustainability	Without stability and sustainability
Improve QoS, cost and energy from a long-term perspective	Improve QoS, cost and energy, but might only be effective in short-terms
Resilient to extreme cases, e.g., sudden and spiked workloads	Vulnerable to extreme cases, e.g., sudden and spiked workloads
Aim for less scalings and smaller overhead	Easy to result in unnecessary scalings and larger overhead

get requirements. However, this begs the question: *How can we systematically incorporate the natural ecosystem and cloud autoscaling?*

6.3 NATURAL ECOSYSTEM

From the ecological perspective, the term *ecosystem* refers to a natural community where all the living organisms (e.g., plants and animals) and nonliving components (e.g., air, light, and water) exhibit dynamic, and uncertain interactions with each others and the environment, emerging as a system [20].

The dynamics in an ecosystem is represented by trophic web – an interaction network that models the consumer–resource relationship, for examples, predator–prey or organism–resources. The trophic web often consists of different trophic levels, each of which represents a family of functionally consistent species. The consumer–resource relationship takes place between different trophic levels. The foundation of a trophic web are the autotrophic species (e.g., most plants) who can produce complex organic compounds from nonliving components. In contrast, higher levels in the trophic web are heterotrophic species (e.g., animals) who cannot fix carbon and use organic carbon for growth. There is a special kind of mixotrophic species that use a mix of different sources of energy and carbon, e.g., the venus flytrap and oriental hornet.

An ecosystem might face disturbances caused by either natural or human induced stress, e.g., tornado and deforestation are examples of natural and human-induced stress, respectively. Sustainability often refers to the endurance of an ecosystem in the presence of disturbances. Better sustainability of an ecosystem implies better stability – an ecosystem is said stable if, when disturbances occur, it is not affected or it is able to quickly resume its prior stable state after disturbances.

According to the well-recognized insurance hypothesis [21], ecologists have acknowledged that better stability and sustainability of an ecosystem can be achieved on higher biodiversity. This is because an ecosystem with large diversity of species will be able to respond to the disturbances in different ways, and thus it is more likely to resume the previous stable state as some species can compensate for those that disappear.

Biodiversity is a corollary of evolution, which describes the ability of a species to survive and reproduce. This is attributed to the fact that a species contains different individuals whose concrete characteristics vary, e.g., their genetic code and habits. Driven by the natural selection during evolution, new species might be created and the incapable ones might disappear. Evolution might lead to the change of an ecological niche, which represents how the species responds to the changes of resources and competitors. Changing the niche could also imply conversion of the habitat (e.g., land or sea) that

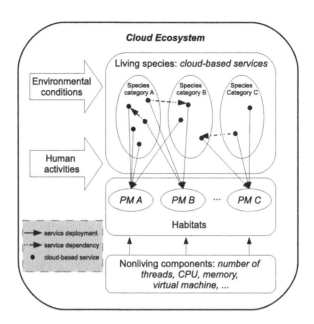

FIGURE 6.1

The architecture of cloud ecosystem

is used by the species, e.g., the ancestors of whales were living on land. According to the competitive exclusion principle [15], evolution is one of the results of competition, in which the benefit of one species can be lowered by the presence of the others – this might be due to the limited supply of certain resources. A special case, namely coevolution, occurs if one species changes in response to the changes in others.

6.4 TRANSPOSING ECOLOGICAL PRINCIPLES, THEORIES AND MODELS TO CLOUD ECOSYSTEM

Existing ecology researches have provided many insights on how we can better preserve the natural ecosystem, particularly with an aim to improve its stability and sustainability. Our hope is to learn and investigate how these insights can be used to derive better elastic autoscaling in the cloud. In fact, as we will show below, the collection of cloud-based services operates in a way that has many similarities to the natural ecosystem, and therefore emerging as a *cloud ecosystem.*

Ecosystem. The 3-layered architecture of cloud ecosystem is illustrated in Fig. 6.1. At the top layer, the cloud-based services are regarded as living organisms, which are categorized as species within the cloud ecosystem. These species can be fundamentally classified based on the nature of the services, e.g., their functional dependency to other services and whether it is a commercial web service or a scientific service, etc. This is similar to the general classification of species in the natural ecosystem, e.g., plants, animals and microorganisms. Such classification might be useful for us to study the characteristics of the species in a cloud ecosystem. At the intermediate layer, one or more species might coexist in a habitat, i.e., a PM that encapsulates the necessary nonliving components. Here, different PMs might be heterogeneous, leading to various forms of habitat. In such a context, the nonliving components can be the fine-grained and reusable software configurations (e.g., thread of service) and hardware resources (e.g., CPU and memory), as shown in the bottom layer. In particular, the software configurations are counterparts of infinite natural resources (e.g., light and air) while the hardware resources are the components that are subject to limited supply, e.g., soil and water in the natural ecosystem. Externally, the cloud ecosystem would be affected by disturbances, including both environmental conditions and human activities: the former refer to the factors that are controlled by neither the cloud provider nor service owners, e.g., the workload and the size of incoming jobs. The later, on the other hand, represent the activities that would influence cloud-based services, as conducted by the service owners or cloud provider.

Similar to the natural ecosystem, the cloud ecosystem reacts to the emergent disturbances and preserves stability in the same pattern: When disturbances occur (e.g., sudden changes in workload), the organisms (cloud-based services) would have to amend their demand for nonliving components (e.g., CPU, memory) or demand for the other species of organisms (when the services have functional dependency), in order to survive in the cloud ecosystem. In certain cases, organisms, or even the entire species, would need to change the habitat (VM migration), creating opportunities for multiple species in the same habitats. All these facts imply evolution that changes the biodiversity, e.g., the demand of services, their underlying VM and neighboring services are changed. In the following, we will explain the mapping between ecological principles and cloud autoscaling system in detail.

Trophic web. The notion of trophic web can also find a matching principle in a cloud ecosystem. As we can see from Fig. 6.2, the functional dependency between cloud-based services can be modeled as a predator–prey relationship, e.g., one or more business services (predator) can depend on a database service (prey). In the natural ecosystem, a larger population of species A (predator) usually means a smaller population of species B (prey), until at some point in time this A declines due to a lack of B. In contrast to the predator–prey relationship, the cloud ecosystem would not change the quantity of services, but could affect their ability in serving requests and jobs. For example, when the number of predator services increases, their prey services can gradually reach their limit in handling requests, which would be equivalent to "dying out". Consequently, the predator services would decline due to the "dying out" of their prey, unless they can evolve themselves to seek alternatives. On the other hand, the correlation between cloud-based services and the software/hardware resources is clearly an organism–resources relationship. It is obvious to see that the species in a cloud ecosystem can only be either autotrophic or mixotrophic because, on the one hand, they directly consume the nonliving components and, on the other hand, they may rely on the organic carbon from the other species.

Disturbances. Similar to natural ecosystems, the cloud ecosystem exhibits various forms of disturbances caused by the environmental conditions. These disturbances can be naturally induced stress, e.g., the changes in colocated services and cohosted Virtual Machines (VMs), changes of software configurations and hardware resources provisioning, and VMs migration/replication. Humans, i.e., service owners and cloud providers, might also create stress by changing the SLA and budgets requirements, deploying/removing cloud-based services or amending the prices for renting software and hardware resources.

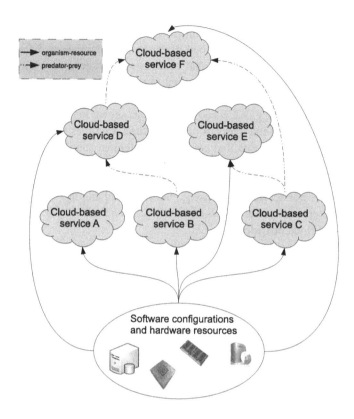

FIGURE 6.2

The trophic web of cloud ecosystem

Biodiversity and evolution. In the cloud ecosystem, the species, or cloud-based services, differ depending on their QoS sensitivity to different software configurations and hardware resources, as well as their SLA and budget requirements. In addition, there can be a large diversity of the cloud-based services running on the same PM, or habitat. These are clear evidences of biodiversity in the cloud ecosystem. Through elastic autoscaling, evolution in the cloud ecosystem refers to changing the ability of cloud-based services in accessing the software configurations and hardware resources, and possibly the deployment of services. This fact allows such evolution to directly influence the biodiversity in the cloud ecosystem. Precisely, evolution can be regarded on two levels: (i) at the microevolution level, where cloud-based services can continually evolve by changing their software configurations and hardware resource provisioning based on their demand; and (ii) at the macroevolution level, where adding/removing cloud-based services and VM migration/replication can cause changes to their habitats.

Species competition. QoS interference is a good example of species competition in the cloud ecosystem, as the cloud-based services running on the same habitat are competing for resources when the supply is limited. Consequently, they need to either evolve themselves (through autoscaling) or die out (crash or be removed by the owners due to severe SLA violations). This phenomena in cloud also play a role of a counterpart to the coevolution principle in a natural ecosystem: to mitigate QoS interference, two or more cloud-based services might need to evolve in response to each other.

6.5 ECOLOGY-INSPIRED SELF-AWARE PATTERN

We now describe our preliminary research outcome that extends the self-aware patterns to incorporate ecological principles and biotic information for cloud autoscaling. As systematically documented in our handbook [11,10], self-aware patterns describe sets of capabilities (i.e., levels of awareness) to acquire knowledge for a *node* which, in the context of self-aware computing systems, can refer to a process, machine, or any conceptual part of a software system being managed. Similar to the original self-aware patterns, the ability to acquire knowledge also plays a crucial role in ecology-inspired patterns, but it particularly focuses on acquiring different levels of biotic information and knowledge. Specifically, when describing ecology-inspired pattern in cloud autoscaling, a *node* refers to an autoscaling process, which maintains biotic information and manages a group of species (i.e., cloud-based services) separated by their categories and/or habitats (i.e., PMs). As mentioned in previous sections, different groups of species and the nonliving components form the cloud ecosystem.

A possible ecology-inspired pattern and the corresponding self-aware capabilities are shown in Fig. 6.3. The key capabilities to acquire biotic information in the pattern can be discussed as follows:

- **Disturbance-Awareness.** This is the basic level of awareness in an ecology-inspired pattern. It may acquire knowledge about either natural or human induced stress. It corresponds to the stimulus-awareness in self-aware patterns.
  - *Example.* The cloud autoscaling process is able to sense different forms of disturbances, e.g., changes in workload, the neighboring services/VMs, changes in pricing/requirements and availability of software/hardware resources. For instance, with disturbance-awareness, the cloud ecosystem is able to identify the source of stimulus and react upon.
- *Trophic-web-Awareness.* Interactions within ecosystem are expressed in a trophic web and therefore awareness of such a web is essential to capture the occurrences of possible interactions. In particular, this type of awareness could acquire knowledge about either internal or external interactions. For example, the relationships between species in the corresponding group are clearly internal interactions; while those between different groups or even different ecosystems can be seen as external interactions. This awareness also permits coevolution, i.e., two or more species might need to evolve in response to each other. For instance, coevolution on two or more services implies that scaling decisions for one could have potential implications on the others. As a result, when making scaling decisions, implications on all services involved in the coevolution need to be catered for. To this end, Trophic-web-Awareness helps us to measure, understand and quantify those implications, thus enabling the evolution of one service with respect to the others, leading to better-informed decision making process. Trophic-web-Awareness corresponds to the Interaction-awareness in self-aware patterns.
  - *Example.* The cloud autoscaling process is able to recognize the relationships between cloud-based services and software/hardware resources, their functional dependency, and the topology. Specifically, when disturbances are detected, cloud-based services would need to evolve in or-

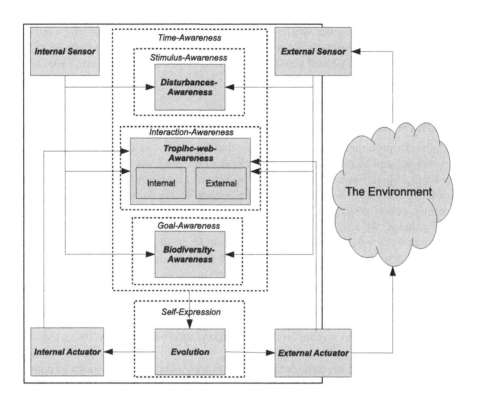

FIGURE 6.3

The ecology-inspired pattern

der to maintain stability. Knowledge of the trophic web can help us to explore the direction of evolution, e.g., assess the effects of a certain way of evolution, and comply with the constraints imposed by dependency and topology.

- ***Biodiversity-Awareness.*** Increasing biodiversity is the key to improving stability and sustainability of an ecosystem. Awareness of biodiversity permits the ability to reason about and acknowledge the effects of evolutions w.r.t. stability and sustainability for the entire ecosystem. Therefore, it corresponds to the Goal-awareness in self-aware patterns.
  - *Example.* The cloud autoscaling process is able to reason about how different forms of evolution can affect the biodiversity which, in turn, influences the long-term stability and sustainability related to QoS, cost and energy consumption in the cloud ecosystem. Such awareness could produce explicit answers on *when* the cloud should scale and *what* is the amount of scaling that leads to higher biodiversity. Concretely, biodiversity serves as the metric to assess the direction of evolution, thus providing guidance for the cloud ecosystem to maintain high biodiversity.
- ***Evolution.*** Evolution of an ecosystem can be regarded on two levels: (i) at the microevolution level, where the species can evolve themselves to adapt to the environment or the other species; and

(ii) at the macroevolution level, where the species can change their habitats. This corresponds to the Self-expression in self-aware patterns.
- *Example.* The cloud autoscaling process is able to know *how* the cloud ecosystem can evolve. This is concerned with whether vertical scaling, horizontal scaling, or both should be triggered. Here vertical scaling implies evolution at the microlevel, in which the cloud-based services can adapt their software configurations and hardware resource provisioning based on their demand. Similarly, horizontal scaling means evolution at the macrolevel, e.g., adding/removing cloud-based services and VM migration/replication, which can cause changes to their habitats.

All the levels of awareness in the cloud ecosystem can be connected to the Time-awareness from the self-aware patterns. This is because the natural ecosystem, which exists for millions of years, can often gain rich benefits from its long history. In the context of a computing system, such historical data can be relevant to disturbances, changes of trophic web, and evolution of the biodiversity. As a result, historical knowledge plays an integral role in our ecology-inspired pattern, for example, evolution of the biodiversity could gain insights from the past biodiversity levels, including their implication on the current cloud ecosystem and the entire path of evolution. This information can help us guide both the micro- and macrolevel evolution.

6.6 OPPORTUNITIES AND CHALLENGES

We have already shown that the cloud ecosystem exhibits many similarities to the natural ecosystem. Presumably, when cloud autoscaling leads to a higher level of biodiversity, global stability and sustainability of the cloud ecosystem would be expected to improve. This direction of research will create several opportunities and challenges:

- Autoscaling in the entire cloud is a complex and large-scale control problem. The notion of evolution from the natural ecosystem can provide inspiration about how to ensure high biodiversity in the cloud ecosystem, and thus improve global stability and sustainability. However, incorporating the control mechanisms of biodiversity and cloud autoscaling is a research challenge. Additionally, selecting the right measurements and form of biodiversity for cloud ecosystem is also a difficult issue. We expect to obtain similar perception as our prior work [7,9,3] when applying ecological principles to this challenge.
- Dynamics and uncertainty in the cloud significantly influence the design of an autoscaling system due to the time-varying workload, QoS interference, and the behaviors of cloud-based services. We hope that the mechanisms and models from the trophic web can better handle the dynamics and uncertainty. These mechanisms and models can provide us with insight about the interactions in different trophic levels and competition between species (i.e., cloud-based services). In addition, ecologists have applied several metrics (e.g., Shannon entropy) to quantify biodiversity in the trophic web. The challenge is how the trophic web can be used to correlate the QoS with cloud configurations and resources; and how it might influence the decision making of autoscaling.
- QoS interference and trade-offs are important issues in autoscaling decision making. Here, trade-offs do not only refer to the naturally conflicted objectives of the same cloud-based service (e.g., throughput vs. cost/energy), but also to the conflicted objectives for different cloud-based services

caused by QoS interference. While QoS interference might be tackled using computational intelligence [4,8,6,5], it is still challenging to study how the insights of species competition and coevolution can be used to resolve the trade-offs and to mitigate the effects of QoS interference in the cloud.

6.7 RELATED WORK

There have been some successful attempts in applying ecological principles, theories, and models to address issues in computer science. Examples can be found in the area of software engineering [19], collaborative adaptive systems [1,18], distributed computing [2], and grid computing [13]. However, there have been very limited efforts on adopting the ecological point of view for cloud autoscaling.

Among others, ECOS [19] is a research project that adopts ecological models to analyze the evolution of open-source software. Particularly, ecology-inspired methods are used to understand and better explain how the projects evolve, and what the factors are that drive the success of these projects. The goal is to optimize the fitness of software projects, leading to better stability of open-source software ecosystem.

Briscoe and Wilde [2] intend to apply ecological thinking to create scalable and self-organizing approaches for distributed evolutionary computing. The aim is to maintain a stable evolution of the processes in distributed environment, i.e., what processes should run independently or incorporated.

Ecology-inspired approach has been used in grid computing [13] with an aim to handle dynamics, uncertainty, diversity, and evolution in grid services. However, the authors focused on subscription, discovery, selection, and composition of grid-based services, as opposed to the cloud autoscaling of software configurations and hardware resources in our work.

The EU funded, multidisciplinary project DEVERISTY [1] is possibly the closest work to our research. DEVERISTY exploits the analogy with natural ecosystems in order to come up with better principles and mechanisms for handling the emergence of diversity in collaborative adaptive systems. The objective is to increase diversity in software systems and thus achieve better stability, as well as ability to react to unpredicted events [18]. Such an objective is consistent with our work, but we have particularly focused on the context of cloud computing and autoscaling, which exhibit some unique characteristics.

6.8 CONCLUSION

In this article, we have presented an intuitive and sensible transposition of ecological perspective to the context of cloud autoscaling. Deriving from existing self-aware software patterns, we have also proposed an architecture pattern for enabling such a transition, with respect to the different principles of natural ecosystem, including disturbance, trophic-web, biodiversity and (co-)evolution. The challenges for this direction of research were also discussed.

Cloud computing will continue to attract more and more participants for its scalable, elastic and on-demand promises. Stability and sustainability can quickly become critical quality indicators of cloud-based services, leading to several new challenges. Until recently, there has been an increasing interest in investigating the assurance of long term benefits in the cloud via autoscaling. To the best of our knowledge, there is no known method that is explicitly developed for the long term benefit of stability and sustainability of cloud-based services. In this premise, the well-established ecological principles appear to be a neat solution for those challenges, as we have discussed in this article. This will further advance the existing view of the cloud and its autoscaling.

As future work, we aim to explicitly tackle the aforementioned research challenges, particularly focusing on the design of ecology driven mechanisms to handle dynamics and uncertainty exhibited in the cloud.

REFERENCES

[1] B. Baudry, M. Monperrus, C. Mony, F. Chauvel, F. Fleurey, S. Clarke, Diversify: ecology-inspired software evolution for diversity emergence, in: IEEE Conference on Software Maintenance, Reengineering and Reverse Engineering (CSMR-WCRE), 2014 Software Evolution Week, Feb. 2014, pp. 395–398.

[2] G. Briscoe, P. De Wilde, Ecosystem-oriented distributed evolutionary computing, in: 2012 12th UK Workshop on Computational Intelligence (UKCI), Sept. 2012, pp. 1–8.

[3] T. Chen, R. Bahsoon, Self-adaptive and sensitivity-aware QoS modeling for the cloud, in: Proceedings of the 8th International Symposium on Software Engineering for Adaptive and Self-Managing Systems, SEAMS'13, IEEE Press, Piscataway, NJ, USA, 2013, pp. 43–52.

[4] T. Chen, R. Bahsoon, Symbiotic and sensitivity-aware architecture for globally-optimal benefit in self-adaptive cloud, in: Proceedings of the 9th International Symposium on Software Engineering for Adaptive and Self-Managing Systems, 2014, pp. 85–94.

[5] T. Chen, R. Bahsoon, Self-adaptive trade-off decision making for autoscaling cloud-based services, IEEE Trans. Serv. Comput. (2015), http://dx.doi.org/10.1109/TSC.2015.2499770.

[6] T. Chen, R. Bahsoon, Towards a smarter cloud: self-aware autoscaling of cloud configurations and resources, Computer 48 (9) (Sept. 2015).

[7] T. Chen, R. Bahsoon, Self-adaptive and online QoS modeling for cloud-based software services, IEEE Trans. Softw. Eng. (2016), http://dx.doi.org/10.1109/TSE.2016.2608826.

[8] T. Chen, R. Bahsoon, G. Theodoropoulos, Dynamic QoS optimization architecture for cloud-based DDDAS, in: 2013 International Conference on Computational Science, Proc. Comput. Sci. 18 (2013) 1881–1890.

[9] T. Chen, R. Bahsoon, X. Yao, Online QoS modeling in the cloud: a hybrid and adaptive multi-learners approach, in: Proceedings of the IEEE/ACM 7th International Conference on Utility and Cloud Computing, 2014, pp. 327–336.

[10] T. Chen, F. Faniyi, R. Bahsoon, Design Patterns and Primitives: Introduction of Components and Patterns for SACS, Springer International Publishing, Cham, 2016, pp. 53–78.

[11] T. Chen, F. Faniyi, R. Bahsoon, P.R. Lewis, X. Yao, L.L. Minku, L. Esterle, The handbook of engineering self-aware and self-expressive systems, preprint arXiv:1409.1793, 2014.

[12] S. Forrest, J. Balthrop, M. Glickman, D. Ackley, Computation in the wild, in: Robust Design: A Repertoire of Biological, Ecological, and Engineering Case Studies, 2005, pp. 207–230.

[13] L. Gao, Y. Ding, L. Ren, A novel ecological network-based computation platform as a grid middleware system, Int. J. Intell. Syst. 19 (10) (2004) 859–884.

[14] R. Han, L. Guo, M. Ghanem, Y. Guo, Lightweight resource scaling for cloud applications, in: 12th IEEE/ACM International Symposium on Cluster, Cloud and Grid Computing, May 2012, pp. 644–651.

[15] G. Hardin, et al., The competitive exclusion principle, Science 131 (3409) (1960) 1292–1297.

[16] S.P. Hubbell, The Unified Neutral Theory of Biodiversity and Biogeography, MPB, vol. 32, Princeton University Press, 2001.

[17] S.A. Levin, Ecosystems and the biosphere as complex adaptive systems, Ecosystems 1 (5) (1998) 431–436.

[18] D. Mendez, B. Baudry, M. Monperrus, Empirical evidence of large-scale diversity in API usage of object-oriented software, in: 2013 IEEE 13th International Working Conference on Source Code Analysis and Manipulation (SCAM), IEEE, 2013, pp. 43–52.

[19] T. Mens, M. Claes, P. Grosjean, Ecos: ecological studies of open source software ecosystems, in: IEEE Conference on Software Maintenance, Reengineering and Reverse Engineering, 2014, pp. 403–406.

[20] S.T. Pickett, W. Carson, Ecology: individuals, populations and communities, Brittonia 39 (3) (1987).

[21] S. Yachi, M. Loreau, Biodiversity and ecosystem productivity in a fluctuating environment: the insurance hypothesis, Proc. Natl. Acad. Sci. 96 (4) (1999) 1463–1468.

[22] Q. Zhu, G. Agrawal, Resource provisioning with budget constraints for adaptive applications in cloud environments, IEEE Trans. Serv. Comput. 5 (4) (2012) 497–511.

ACKNOWLEDGEMENT

This work is supported by the Paul and Yuanbi Ramsay Research Funding Award form the School of Computer Science, University of Birmingham, UK.

ANALYZING AND EVALUATING

EVALUATING WEB PKIS

7

Jiangshan Yu, Mark Ryan

School of Computer Science, University of Birmingham, UK

7.1 INTRODUCTION

The term big data refers to the massive amounts of digital information generated from multiple sources, such as social media sites, climate monitoring sensors, digital pictures and videos, online payment records, smart phones, and IoT devices. Security and privacy issues are magnified by velocity, volume, and variety of big data, such as large-scale cloud infrastructures, diversity of data sources and formats, streaming nature of data acquisition and high volume inter-cloud migration.

Ensuring the security of big data requires encryption, and in particular, requires *public key encryption*. The producers of big data (sensors, websites, etc.) will have public keys, and the consumers may also have public keys. The main practical difficulty in deploying public key cryptography is to ensure that the correct public key is being used. *Public key infrastructure* (PKI) [1] is the name given to the policies and procedures needed to create, manage, and distribute public-key certificates in order to use public key encryption securely.

Putting good PKI in place would provide a range of benefits for big data. As mentioned above, it would allow public key encryption. But it also enables a range of other uses and applications of public keys, such as digital signatures, secure multiparty computation, privacy-preserving data mining, and proofs of possession and proofs of knowledge [2–5].

To give an intuition of potential security and privacy applications of PKI in big data, we present some example scenarios. We then explain on a high level how PKI would help enable these applications.

- **Entity authenticity.** A web user needs to verify that a social network web server it is communicating with is really the correct one. To achieve this, the web server typically sends its public key to the user's web browser. The browser needs PKI to ensure that the public key being used really is the bank's public key [6–8].
- **Data authenticity**. A server needs to ensure that data it receives from a sensor is authentic. To achieve this, the sensor can digitally sign the data. The server requires PKI in order to be sure of using the correct public key to verify the sensor's signature [9,10].
- **Data confidentiality.** Data exchanged between two parties should be secure, namely only the sender and the recipient should be able to read the data. To achieve this, the two parties need to establish a *session key* between them. If each of them has a public key and PKI is in place, then there are several protocols [11–13] they can use to establish the session key.
- **Data integrity.** Any unintended changes to the exchanged data between two parties (for example, two embedded devices in an *ad hoc* network) should be prevented, or at least, detected. There are

several ways to achieve this (for example, one can use digital signatures or message authentication codes [14]), but they all rely on PKI to manage the public keys of the devices.

- **Privacy-preserving data mining.** Suppose a data owner wants to subcontract the processing of customer data (e.g., social security numbers or health records) to a third party. This data is sensitive, and should not be divulged freely. A variety of cryptographic techniques can be used [15,16], such as *fully homomorphic encryption* (which allows the third party to compute with ciphertexts) [17–21] and *multiparty computation* (which allows the third party to contribute to a computation without seeing all the plaintext data) [22,23]. All these techniques require various parties to have public keys, and PKI is needed to ensure their correct management.

- **Verifiability of computational results.** When subcontracting data processing in the example above, another party may wish to verify that the processing has been done correctly. Once again, there are several techniques in cryptography that can achieve this. *Verifiable computing* is the name given to this field [24–27]. It starts from the assumption that the parties have public keys and there is a PKI in place to manage them.

7.2 AN OVERVIEW OF PKI

The purpose of PKI is to ensure that a party has an authentic copy of the genuine public key of another party. For example, when a user logs in to Facebook through his/her web browser, the web session will be secured by the public key of the Facebook server. If the user's web browser accepts an inauthentic public key for Facebook created by an attacker, then the traffic (including log-in credentials) can be intercepted and manipulated by the attacker.

The authenticity of keys is assured at present by *certificate authorities* (CAs). In the given example, the browser is presented with a public key certificate for Facebook, which is intended to be unforgeable evidence that the given public key is the correct one for the web site. A public key certificate is a digital document declaring that the recorded subject owns the public key presented in the certificate. It contains a public key, the identity of the key owner, and a signature of an entity that has verified the certificate's contents are correct. In a typical PKI scheme, the signer is a trusted party called certificate authority (CA), usually a company (e.g., VeriSign and Comodo) which charges customers to issue certificates for them. The user's browser is pre-configured to accept certificates from certain known CAs. A typical installation of Firefox has about 100 root certificates in its database. Each root CA can empower many intermediate CAs. The EFF SSL observatory has observed more than 1500 CAs [28].

Unfortunately, CA model that has been in use on the web for the last 20 years is vulnerable to attacks. The main weakness of CA model is that CAs must be assumed to be trustworthy. If a CA is dishonest or compromised, it may issue certificates asserting the authenticity of fake keys; those keys could be created by an attacker or by the CA itself. In practice, the assumption of honesty does not scale up very well. As already mentioned, a browser typically has hundreds of CAs registered in it, and the user cannot be expected to have evaluated the trustworthiness and security of all of them. This fact has been exploited by attackers [29–34]. In 2011, two CAs were compromised: Comodo [35] and DigiNotar [36]. In both cases, certificates for high-profile sites were illegitimately obtained (e.g., Google, Yahoo, Skype, etc.). In the second case, these certificates were reportedly used in a *man in the middle* (MITM) attack [37]. See [38] for a survey on CA compromises.

Another problem with CA model is the *certificate revocation management*. The CA model itself does not provide any effective way for managing certificate revocation. In common practice, Certificate Revocation Lists (CRL) [39–41], On-line Certificate Status Protocol (OCSP), and certificate revocation trees [42–44] are used to handle certificate revocation. In order to remove the need for on-the-fly revocation checking, they mostly involve periodically pushing revocation lists to browsers. However, such solutions create a window during which the browser's revocation lists are out of date until the next push.

Several protocols are proposed to strengthen the current certificate management system. However, none of them have been widely adopted, yet. On the one side, this is partly because the replacement of a large scale system is challenging. On the other side, this is also because new proposals each have different sets of advantages and disadvantages, and it may not be clear what features are really needed in given applications.

Clark and van Oorschot [45] have presented an analysis on TLS mechanism and issues, by concerning themselves with crypto weakness and implementation issues of HTTPS, and trust issues of certificate management. However, they left the public log based certificate management systems out of the analysis. The use of public logs is now the dominant trend in managing web certificates. The main idea of public log based certificate management systems is to make certificate management transparent by using public auditable logs to record all issued certificates. Clients will only accept a certificate if it is recorded in the log. Site owners can compare their own local record with the log to check whether a mis-issued certificate has been recorded in the log. This gives the site owners the ability to verify issued certificates for their sites, and make the certificate management transparent.

Kim et al. [46] have presented a comparison of web certificate management mainly based on the duration of compromise and duration of unavailability. The former shows, given the compromise of a domain's private key, how long the domain can be impersonated; and the later concerns the unavailability time period of a domain's certificate in a system.

The above two works are broad and they evaluate web certificate management systems from different perspectives. However, some important aspects are not considered in the existing work. For example, *offline verification* is one of the desired properties that have been left out from the above analyses. This property ensures that internet users can verify a received certificate without having to communicate with other parties. This is extremely useful when a user needs to connect from a captive portal in an airport or in a hotel, since the user's device cannot make other connections before he/she paid for the internet connection. In addition, this property also reduces the communication cost for certificate verification, as the verifier is not required to have extra connections for verifying a certificate.

Another important property not considered by the existing works is *trust agility* [47] – it allows users to freely make decisions on which certificate management service provider they wish to trust, for establishing secure communications with domain servers. In particular, we discovered a new aspect of trust agility, namely independence of trust. It requires that one or more service providers cannot influence another service provider's service. It is in particular useful in the scenario where there exists a set of service providers, and users need to put their trust in a subset of these service providers for certificate management. If a system does not offer this feature, then it means that even if the set of service providers chosen by a user is trustworthy, a malicious service provider that is not trusted by the user can still influence the certificate verification result, and put the user at risk of accepting fake certificates. Since the independence of trust is more strict, it is possible that a system offers the generic trust agility, but it does not offer independence of trust. In this case, users are free to make their trust decisions, but servers that are not trusted by the user are still able to affect the certificate management services delivered to the user.

One more example of desired properties that is not considered by the existing evaluation frameworks is called *anti-oligopoly*. It is proposed in [48] as a foundational property. This property observes that the present-day certificate authority model requires a fixed set of global certificate authorities to be known to every browser, which implies an oligopoly. In fact, the current set of CAs trusted by the browser is dominated by US organizations. This means that US government agencies are likely to be able to control these organizations. This cannot be considered satisfactory in the presence of mutual distrust between nations regarding cybersecurity and citizen surveillance, and also trade sanctions which may prevent the USA offering services (such as CA services) to certain other countries.

To help research in securing the web certificate management, we classify 16 prominent proposals into different categories, and provide a qualitative analysis on selected proposals based on 15 criteria.

7.3 DESIRED FEATURES AND SECURITY CONCERNS

To evaluate different systems in a systemic way, we list the desired features and security concerns for web certificate management systems.

1. Trust

- *Trust agility* [47] allows users to freely decide which entities they want to trust for confirming public key information of domain servers, and to revise their decision at any time.

   In particular, we observed one aspect of the trust agility that has not been discovered in the literature, namely independence of trust. It requires that the trust relations between service providers will not influence the trust relations between clients and the service providers they trust. In other words, one or more service providers cannot influence another service provider's service to its clients.
- *Free of trusted parties* is the property saying that no party is required to be trusted for certificate issuance and revocation. For example, a certificate authority in the CA model is required to be trusted by all browsers, so the CA model does not provide *free of trusted parties*. This property is the strongest of all trust-related features.
- *Verifiable trusted parties* is the property saying that the behavior of trusted parties is transparent and can be efficiently verified by users.
- *Anti-oligopoly* [48] is the feature that prevents the monopoly or oligopoly of certificate management services. To achieve this, the trust on any service provider (e.g., CAs) should be minimized, and the system should support self-issued certificates.

2. Availability

- *Offline verification* is a feature such that in a system clients can verify a given key or certificate without having to connect to other parties.

   This feature is desired when a user needs to connect from a captive portal – a login page or payment page – before using the Internet. The use of captive portal is very common in public places, for example, airports or hotels. When a user is presented a captive portal, the user cannot establish a connection with any party to check the obtained public key as no internet is available. In addition, this feature also reduces the communication cost and network latency, as it does not require additional connections.

- *Built-in key revocation* requires the system to have its own mechanism to effectively manage certificate revocation, rather than relaying on existing revocation protocols (e.g., certificate revocation list (CRL) or online certificate status protocol (OCSP)).

The current certificate revocation management protocols (e.g., CRL and OCSP) have different limitations and cannot offer satisfactory services. So it is necessary for systems to have an integrated revocation mechanism to effectively manage certificate revocations.

- *Scalability* is the property enabling a system to handle increasing real world workload. It is important that a system is capable of supporting enrolment from existing and potential future HTTPS servers.
- *Multiple certificate support* says that the certificate verification system allows a domain to have multiple certificates. The fact that many sites have multiple certificates emphasizes the importance of this feature.
- *Timely key verification* says that the period from the time a domain owner establishes a key and the time a user can verify the key is short.

This is a feature that has not been prominent in the literature. It is useful when a domain server updates its certificates. A system that does not offer this feature would cause the problem that the newly issued certificate cannot be verified and will not be accepted by web browsers within a short time period after the certificate issuance. This reduces availability.

3. Security

- *First connection protection* is the feature that protects the first connection between two communication parties.

This is useful to prevent attacks on "trust on first use"-based systems. In addition, it is likely to be the first connection when a user connects to a captive portal. So the system should protect users' first connection to a domain server.

- *Denial of service (DoS) attack protection* is the security guarantee that prevents attacks on the key verification infrastructure in order to deny the verification services.

This feature is useful to prevent attacks that attempt to block the verification servers to stop users verifying the received certificates.

- *Use of mis-issued certificate prevention* measures whether the system can prevent MITM attacks launched by an attacker with mis-issued certificates. In other words, even if an attacker has obtained a mis-issued certificate, web browsers should still not accept this certificate. This gives users extra security guarantee against compromised CAs.
- *Use of mis-issued certificate detection* measures whether the system provides features allowing one to detect MITM attacks launched by using mis-issued certificates.

This is a weaker security guarantee, as it can only detect attacks rather than prevent attacks. However, CAs are businesses, and they are willing to maintain their reputation to keep their customers. So they might not launch attacks if their attacks are detected. So this feature still offers some sensible security guarantee.

- *Provably secure* measures if the security of a given system is formally verified.

  It is well-known that security protocols are notoriously difficult to get right, and the only way to avoid this is with systematic verification.

4. Usability

- *No user involvement* is a feature related to usability, such that the key verification result and the decision of accepting or rejecting a certificate do not need the extra involvement of users.

  This is an important feature to have as users are not qualified to make decisions on the browser warnings, and they will likely click through security warnings [50].

5. Privacy

- *Protecting browsing history* says that the system does not leak users browsing history to other parties. In a PKI, if a user needs to ask another party to verify a received certificate, then the user's browsing activity is leaked to the verification party, as the subject of the to be verified certificate is very likely the website that the user is going to visit.

7.4 EXISTING PROPOSALS

Several protocols are proposed to strengthen the current certificate management system. According to the principles of each design, we classify leading certificate management systems into three categories, namely *difference observation*, *scope restriction*, and *certificate management transparency*, as presented in Table 7.1.

7.4.1 CLASSIC

The CA-based certificate management system is the current deployed PKI. It is highly usable and scalable. Unfortunately, it requires users to fully trust all certificate authorities, and the trust cannot be modified without sacrificing users' ability to securely communicate with some domains. As a result, it does not provide trust agility, implies an oligopoly (on CA), and cannot easily prevent or detect MITM attacks when a CA is compromised.

7.4.2 DIFFERENCE OBSERVATION

Difference observation is a concept aiming to detect untrustworthy CAs, by enabling a browser to verify if the received certificates are different from those that other people are being offered [51–54,47].

7.4.2.1 Perspectives

In 2008, Wendlandt, Andersen and Perrig implemented a Firefox add-on, called *Perspectives* [51]. It is proposed to improve the security of trust-on-first-use authentication by asking different observers

Table 7.1 Existing prominent proposals

Category	Existing proposals
Classic	CA-based certificate management system
Difference observation	Perspectives (2008) [51]; DoubleCheck (2009) [52]
	Convergence (2011) [47]; Certificate Patrol (2011) [53]; CertLock (2011) [54]; TACK (2012) [55]
Scope restriction	Public key pinning (2011) [56]; DANE (2011) [57]; CAge (2013) [58]
Certificate management transparency	Sovereign Keys (2012) [59]; Certificate Transparency (2012) [60]
	AKI (2013) [46]; CIRT (2014) [61]; ARPKI (2014) [62]; DTKI (2014) [48], [49]

(a.k.a. notary servers) to detect inconsistent public keys of the same server. In Perspectives, observers are decentralized and independent. Each observer stores all observed keys or certificates with corresponding timestamps, and periodically checks updates and revocations. When a client wants to make a secure connection with a domain server, the client requests the server's public key from the server and from multiple observers, then compares the received keys. If the obtained public keys are consistent, the client considers the public key is trustworthy and uses this key to establish a secure connection. Otherwise, it might indicate that an attacker has launched man-in-the-middle (MITM) attack by offering a different public key to the client. So the client needs to make a decision on whether to use the obtained key or not.

- **Strength**
  Perspectives makes MITM attacks using mis-issued certificates difficult to launch without being detected, as an attacker would have to additionally intercept all connections between observers and the victim. In addition, it provides trust agility as users can choose which observer they want to use for certificate verification. Moreover, since it supports self-signed certificates, and does not require a fixed set of observers, it provides anti-oligopoly.
- **Weakness**
  With Perspectives, if a server has multiple public keys or certificates, then clients will likely get a warning of receiving inconsistent public keys. This is due to the fact that a client might receive two different genuine certificates of the same domain from the domain server and an observer. In addition, a new public key or a new server will suffer an unavailability period in the system. Since observers periodically check new public keys and revocations, the latest information about new public keys and revocations will not be immediately available from the observers. So, Perspectives does not offer timely key verification. Also, when a browser receives the latest genuine one from the server, and the revoked one from observers, then the browser will show a pop-up window warning the user that two different keys are observed, although what the server provided is a valid certificate. Such faulty warnings reduce usability of the system. Moreover, if two different certificates are detected, then the user needs to make a decision on whether to continue the connection. However, users are not qualified to make such a decision and they are likely to click through the warnings [50]. Furthermore, any observer can learn a user's browsing history when the user requests verification

on a certificate. Last, it does not work when a user needs to connect from a captive portal, as no internet is available for connecting to an observer.

7.4.2.2 DoubleCheck

In 2009, Alicherry and Keromytis [52] proposed *DoubleCheck* to solve the issue of leaking user browsing history, and the issue that new keys might suffer an unavailable period in Perspectives. The main idea is to query the certificate from a target server twice: once through a TLS connection, and once through *Tor* [63].

- **Strength**
  Compared to Perspectives, it additionally protects user browsing history, and new keys does not suffer from an unavailability period. Moreover, it can be deployed without requiring any new infrastructure.
- **Weakness**
  The use of *Tor* adds extra time cost (up to 15 s [54]) for each certificate verification. In addition, a user is likely to get a warning when a server has multiple certificates. Also, when a warning is given, a user will need to make a decision on which certificate to trust, and they are likely to click through the warning. Moreover, it will not work when a user needs to connect from a captive portal.

7.4.2.3 Convergence

Marlinspike proposed *Convergence* [47], a Firefox add-on and an improvement on *Perspectives*, in Black Hat 2011. In Convergence, to protect users' browsing history, instead of directly communicating with notary servers (i.e., observers), users randomly choose one notary server to pass the client request to other notary servers, through an onion routing like mechanism. So the intermediate notary server does not know what a requester is requesting, and the end notary server does not know who is the requester. In addition, to reduce the number of connections a user has to make, users store verified certificates in their browser cache and only query notary servers when they received a different one. Moreover, rather than querying the certificate of a domain server from a notary server, users send the certificate received from the server to notary servers. The notary server will request a certificate from the domain server if the received certificate does not match the notary's cache.

- **Strength**
  As an improvement of Perspectives, it additionally supports timely key verification, does not require users to make decisions on which certificate to trust, and it protects user privacy. Moreover, it offers offline verification if the site has been visited before.
- **Weakness**
  Similar to Perspectives, Convergence does not support multiple certificates, and does not protect users when they are connected to a captive portal.

7.4.2.4 Certificate patrol

Certificate Patrol [53] is another Firefox add-on for managing web certificates. It monitors and stores all SSL certificates a browser has obtained. Since the validity period of a certificate is fairly long, it is unlikely that a certificate was changed in a short time. So, when a different certificate is observed, it is possible that one of them is a mis-issued certificate used by attackers. With Certificate Patrol, if the newly received certificate is different from the previously stored certificate of the same domain, the browser will display to the user the difference between the two certificates, and the user needs to make a decision on whether to trust the newly received one.

- **Strength**
  It is a lightweight tool to protect user browsing history, and to offer an extra layer of security – it can help users detect any change of the previously received certificate.
- **Weakness**
  This add-on will not work if a domain has multiple certificates, and it requires users to make decisions. In addition, it does not protect user's first connection to a website or user connection from a captive portal.

7.4.2.5 CertLock

CertLock [54] is a Firefox add-on for monitoring CAs' location. In particular, it observes the country of the CA which issued the received certificate. On the detection that two CAs from different countries have issued certificates for the same site, the browser will display a warning to the user.

- **Strength**
  CertLock can help users detect attacks in some specific scenario. For example, a site authorized certificate authority CA_1 in country A is to issue certificate for its domain. A malicious government agency in country B wants to intercept the communication between users and the site. The malicious government agency can compel a certificate authority CA_2 located in country B to issue fake certificates for the site, then uses this mis-issued certificate to launch MITM attacks. CertLock can help users detect such attacks.
- **Weakness**
  CertLock won't be able to detect attacks using fake certificates that are issued by CAs in the same country. In addition, a false warning will be displayed if a site has switched from a CA in country A to a CA in country B. In addition, it still relies on the CA trust model, so it does not offer trust agility or anti-oligopoly. Also, it cannot protect user's first connection and a user who is connected to a captive portal.

7.4.2.6 TACK

In 2012, Marlinspike and Perrin proposed *trust assertions for certificate keys* (TACK) [55] to remove the need of trusting CAs. In TACK, a domain server generates a TACK private/public key pair, and uses the TACK private key to certify its TLS public keys. After a client observes a consistent TACK public key of a domain multiple times, it pins the public key to the domain name, and trusts this "pin" for a period, and accepts the public key if it is certified by the private key corresponding to the observed TACK public key. If a certificate becomes compromised and the observed information has not been pinned, then the client must delete the observed TACK information and restart the observation process. To be scalable, TACK will need an online pin store, where users can share their observed pins. However, the problem of how to design a secure pin store for users to share their observations, while prevent attackers to spoof or poison the store, remains unsolved.

- **Strength**

  TACK removes the need of CA, offers trust agility, does not require users to any trusted party, and provides anti-oligopoly. Once local observations are built, TACK allows offline verification and supports multiple certificates.

- **Weakness**

  Since TACK relies on visit patterns by clients to pin the domain's public key, the first several connections to a domain server will not be protected, and every new TACK key pair or new domain suffers an initial unavailability period. In addition, the revoked key will still be accepted by the client if the client still trusts its previous observation.

  To be scalable, TACK requires an online store to share TACK keys observed by different clients. The use of such online stores make TACK difficult to provide the independence of trust required by trust agility. Indeed, a client Alice might choose to trust some stores or clients for the TACK keys they observed. However, the store or clients trusted by Alice might put their trust on other stores and clients. This transitive trust relation could effect Alice's trust option and Alice's observation on the TACK keys. Currently, it is hard to judge whether TACK offers the independence of trust required by trust agility, as the online store is not designed, yet.

7.4.3 SCOPE RESTRICTION

Scope restriction is the concept aiming to reduce the power of CAs by restricting the domain scope that a CA can vouch for.

7.4.3.1 Public key pinning (PKP)

Public key pinning (a.k.a. certificate pinning) is a mechanism for domain servers to specify which CAs are authorized to certify public keys for a given domain. Langley et al. implemented it in Google Chrome [64].

Scalability is a main challenge for key pinning, due to the need of prior knowledge of the mapping between each domain server and CAs. Public key pinning extension for HTTP [65] addresses the scalability challenge by allowing a domain server to declare the authorized CAs for its sites in an HTTP header.

- **Strength**

  As PKP is a way to restrict CAs' power by specifying which CAs are authorized for a given website, it protects user communications against attackers who have mis-issued certificates from CAs that are not authorized for the victim. In addition, PKP allows a website to have multiple certificates, does support offline verification, and is scalable with the PKP extension for HTTP.

- **Weakness**

  The weakness of PKP is that it cannot completely protect all user connections. For example, it cannot protect when a user does not have a pin of a website, which is generally the case for the first connection. Also, it cannot protect the connection when the pin is expired in the user browser. Moreover, it cannot effectively detect attacks when a CA has mis-issued certificates for the domains that the CA is pinned for. Furthermore, it does not offer trust agility or anti-oligopoly.

7.4.3.2 DANE

Domain name system (DNS)-based authentication of named entities (DANE) [66,67] binds the public key information to a domain name by using DNS Security Extensions (DNSSEC). More specifically, DANE enables a domain server to certify its public keys by storing the public keys in its DNS records. This DNS record is valid only if it is correctly signed as specified in DNSSEC [68]. So, the parent domain servers are the authority of their child domains. In other words, only the parent domain can certify public keys of its child domains. In this way, DANE limits the damage of dishonest or compromised authorities.

- **Strength**
  Compared to PKP, DANE is highly scalable since it is based on DNSSEC. In addition, it can protect a user even when the user connects from a captive portal.
- **Weakness**
  The security of DANE strongly relies on the trustworthiness of parent domains according to the DNS hierarchy. As a result, ICANN, top-level domains (TLDs), and second-level domains (SLDs) become very powerful and fully trusted CAs. So, DANE does not provide trust agility and anti-oligopoly. In addition, domain servers cannot choose which CA they want to get service from, as they have to get their keys to be certified by their parent domain.

7.4.3.3 CAge

In 2013, Kasten, Wustrow and Halderman proposed *CAge* [58] to restrict the scope of domains that a CA can certify public keys for. According to the data observed in [69], they show that only a small number of CAs have signed certificates for TLDs. Based on this observation, *CAge* suggests to limit a CA's certification scope by only allowing a CA to issue certificates on a restricted set of TLDs. CAge limits the scale of MITM attacks using mis-issued certificates, but cannot completely solve this problem.

- **Strength**
  As all systems in the category of scope restriction, CAge reduces the damage from a compromised CA by limiting the set of domains that a CA can vouch for.
- **Weakness**
  Since CAge is still based on the CA trust model although with restrictions on a CA's ability, it does not offer trust agility or anti-oligopoly. In addition, domain servers have less flexibility to choose which CA they want to use, because only a subset of CAs will be eligible for certifying keys for given domains.

7.4.4 CERTIFICATE MANAGEMENT TRANSPARENCY

Certificate management transparency is the concept aiming to make CA's behavior transparent. The basic idea is to use a publicly visible log to record issued certificates. So interested parties can check the log to detect any mis-issued certificates.

7.4.4.1 Sovereign keys

Sovereign Keys (SK) [70] aims to get rid of browser certificate warnings, by allowing domain owners to establish a long term ("sovereign") key and by providing a mechanism by which a browser can hard-fail if it doesn't succeed in establishing security via that key. A sovereign key is a long-term key used to cross-sign operational TLS keys, and it is stored in an append-only log on a "timeline server", which is abundantly mirrored.

When a browser connects to a website, it sends a query to a mirror of the "timeline server" to check if the site has a sovereign key. If the site does have a sovereign key, then the browser only accepts a certificate for this site if the certificate is issued by CAs and is cross-signed by the sovereign key. If the certificate is not cross-signed, then rather than emit certificate warnings, the browser will try to find a way to make a sovereign key connection to the site. There are several ways to establish a connection without having a cross-signed certificate. The strongest way is to compute a hash of the sovereign key, and use that as the .onion address of the Tor hidden service which allows the secure connection. Weaker ways include stapling to the sovereign key and trying to connect through other means such as proxy and VPN, until the browser gets a verified connection.

- **Strength**

  SK introduces the first public log based PKI. It eliminates browser certificate warnings, reduces the trust put on CAs, allows a site to have multiple certificates, and prevents attacks from an attacker who compromised CAs.

- **Weakness**

  Sovereign Keys doesn't have an efficient way for the timeline server and mirrors to prove their correct behavior. The only way for verifying it is to download and verify the entire log. So internet users and domain owners have to trust mirrors of time-line servers. Additionally, it doesn't provide any mechanism for key revocation, either of TLS keys or sovereign keys. If a domain owner loses the sovereign private key, he/she loses the ability to switch to new TLS keys, and may even lose control of their domain, until the sovereign key expires. Another security concern is that if a site does not have a sovereign key yet, then a determined attacker could register his own sovereign key for the site and intercept secure connections made to the site.

7.4.4.2 Certificate transparency

Certificate transparency (CT) [60] is proposed by Google aiming to allow domain owners to efficiently detect mis-issued certificates, by making certificate issuance transparent.

The basic idea is to use public auditable logs to record all issued certificates. In this way, interested parties can monitor the log to verify all of CAs' behavior. To enforce CAs to publish all issued certificates into the log, web browsers only accept certificates if a verifiable evidence is provided to prove that the certificate is present in the log.

In more detail, domain owners request from the log maintainer signed confirmations saying that their certificates are included in the log, and then they can provide this confirmation together with the corresponding certificate to web browsers. Browsers only accept a certificate if both the certificate and the signed confirmation are valid. Browsers also need to periodically verify received signed confirmation against the public log to check if the certificate is indeed being inserted in the log.

To reduce the trust put on CAs and log maintainers, CT uses an append-only log which is organized as an append-only Merkle tree. In the tree, data items (i.e., certificates or references to certificates) are stored left-to-right in chronological order at the leaves, and added by extending the tree to the right. This structure enables the log maintainer to provide two types of verifiable cryptographic proofs: (a) a proof that the log contains a given certificate, and (b) a proof that a snapshot of the log is an extension of another snapshot (i.e., only appends have taken place between the two snapshot). The time and size for proof generation and verification are logarithmic in the number of certificates recorded in the log. To ensure the log maintainer is behaving correctly, CT requires monitors to check the consistency of logs.

- **Strength**
  Since CA's behavior is transparent, CT does not require users to blindly trust CAs, i.e., the behavior of CAs is verifiable. This makes CT to offer trust agility. In addition, CT enables domain owners to readily detect any mis-issued certificates.
- **Weakness**
  A main weakness of CT is that users still have to trust "monitors" for verifying the behavior of logs. In addition, CT does not provide an efficient scheme for key revocation. Also, CT does not provide anti-oligopoly, because although the set of log servers are not fixed, it doesn't have any method to allocate different domains to different logs. In CT, when a domain owner wants to check whether mis-issued certificates are recorded in logs, he needs to contact all existing logs, and download all certificates in each of the logs, because there is no way to prove to the domain owner that no certificates for his domain is in the log, or to prove that the log maintainer has showed all certificates in the log for his domain to him. Thus, to be able to detect fake certificates, CT has to keep a very small number of log maintainers. This prevents new log providers being flexibly created, creating an oligopoly. Another limitation is that CT can only detect mis-issued certificates, rather than prevent attacks that use mis-issued certificates.

7.4.4.3 Accountable key infrastructure

Accountable key infrastructure (AKI) [46] also uses public logs to make certificate management more transparent.

Similar to SK, AKI allows domain owners to define their own security policy by specifying several additional attributes of a certificate, such as which CA and log maintainer a domain owner wants to get services from, what is the minimum number of CA signatures to validate a certificate for her domain, etc. To obtain a certificate, a domain owner contacts at least a minimum number of CAs that she wishes to trust based on the policy, and to cross sign her public key with her security policy. Then she requests log maintainers to update her certificate, and expects a signed proof that the certificate is recorded in the log. Clients only accept a certificate if the certificate satisfies defined security policy, and is currently recorded in the log.

To be able to manage key revocations, AKI stores only the current valid certificates of domains in a public log. The log is organized as a hash tree, where the certificates stored in leaves are ordered lexicographically.

To detect mis-behaviors, AKI uses the "checks-and-balances" idea that allows parties to monitor each other's behavior. So AKI limits the requirement to trust any party. Moreover, AKI prevents attacks that use fake certificates rather than merely detecting such attacks (as in CT).

- **Strength**
  AKI extends the previous architectures in several ways. First, it allows multiple CAs to sign a single certificate. Additionally, the domain can specify in its certificate which CAs and logs are allowed to attest to the certificate's authenticity. These features provide resilience against a certificate signed by

a compromised or unauthorized CA. AKI can also handle key loss or compromise through cool-off periods. For example, if a domain loses its private key and registers a new certificate not signed by its old private key, the new certificate will be subject to a cool-off period (e.g., three days) during which the certificate is publicly visible but not usable. This ensures that even if an adversary obtains and registers a fake certificate, the domain has the opportunity to contact the CAs and logs to resolve the issue.

- **Weakness**

  To ensure that any log server can provide a proof for a domain's certificate, AKI logs maintain a globally consistent view of the entries that they have for a given domain name. This applies for every certificate operation (registration, update, and revocation), meaning that even frequent certificate updates (such as in the case of short-lived certificates) are subject to successful log synchronization. In addition, AKI requires that each domain name only has one active and valid certificate associate with it at any given time. Moreover, AKI needs to rely on third parties, called validators, to ensure that the log is maintained without improper modifications, and to assume that CAs, public log maintainers, and validators do not collude together.

7.4.4.4 *Certificate issuance and revocation transparency*

Certificate issuance and revocation transparency (CIRT) [61] improves certificate transparency by providing transparent key revocation, and reducing reliance on trusted parties.

To provide an effective way for certificate revocation, CIRT proposes a new log structure that consists of two tree structures presenting the same set of data. The first tree is called a ChronTree, which is an append-only Merkle tree (as in CT) ordered chronologically. The second tree is called LexTree, which is a Merkle tree ordered lexicographically by the subject of the certificate. The ChronTree stores in the leaves a pair (C, h), where C is a certificate appended in the ChronTree, and h is the hash root value of the LexTree in which the last inserted data is C. The LexTree stores $h(d_i)$ in every node for some i, where d is an ordered list of certificates that has the same subject. The last element in the list is the current valid certificate of the subject.

This log structure enables the log maintainer to provide efficient proofs that (a) some data is present in the log, (b) any data having a given attribute (e.g., an identity) is absent from the log, (c) some data is the latest valid one in the log, and (d) the current log is extended from a previous version.

Loosely speaking, by proving a proof that a certificate C is the last element in an ordered list d, and $h(d)$ is present in the LexTree of the log, a verifier is ensured that C is the currently valid certificate, i.e., not revoked. Due to the use of two different trees presenting the same set of data, it is crucial to ensure that the data presented by the two trees are consistent. To verify the consistency of the two trees, CIRT distributes the monitoring role among user browsers. To do so, each user browser verifies if a randomly selected certificate stored in the ChronTree is also in the LexTree. If the number of such random verification is big enough, then the consistency between the two trees is likely to be verified.

- **Strength**

  CIRT provides a solution for managing both certificate issuance and revocation by using a new log structure, and reduces reliance on trusted parties by using user side random verifications. It also allows a domain to have multiple certificates, and to update keys timely. In addition, similar to all other systems in certificate management transparency category, it does not need users to be involved.

- **Weakness**

  A weakness of CIRT is that it can only detect attacks that use fake certificates; it cannot prevent them. Also, since CIRT was proposed for email applications, it does not support the multiplicity of log maintainers that would be required for web certificates.

7.4.4.5 Attack resilient public-key infrastructure

Attack Resilient Public-Key Infrastructure (ARPKI) [62] is an improvement on AKI. In ARPKI, a client can designate n service providers (e.g., CAs and log maintainers), and only needs to contact one CA to register her certificate. Each of the designated service providers will monitor the behavior of other designated service providers. As a result, ARPKI prevents attacks even when $n - 1$ service providers are colluding together, whereas in AKI, an adversary who successfully compromises two out of three designated service providers can successfully launch attacks [62].

- **Strength**

  ARPKI is the first formally verified log-based PKI system. Its security properties are proved by using a protocol verification tool called Tamarin prover [71]. The verification uses several abstractions during modeling. For example, they represent its underlying log structure (a Merkle tree) as a list.

- **Weakness**

  The weakness of ARPKI is that all n designated service providers have to be involved in all the processes (i.e., certificate registration, confirmation, and update), which would cause considerable extra latencies and the delay of client connections.

7.4.4.6 Distributed transparent key infrastructure

Distributed Transparent Key Infrastructure (DTKI) [48] is an improvement on CIRT [61].

In DTKI, each domain owner has two types of keys – TLS keys and a master key. Browsers only accept a certificate if it is issued by the corresponding master key. Both master keys and TLS keys are recorded in public auditable logs. So dishonest CAs and log maintainers cannot issue fake certificates for a domain unless they have the corresponding master key.

To support multiple logs, DTKI has two different types of log maintainers, namely certificate log maintainers (CLMs) and the mapping log maintainer (MLM). Each CLM maintains a database of all certificates for a particular set of domains for which it is responsible. DTKI does not fix the set of certificate logs, but the MLM is unique. The MLM maintains association between certificate logs and the domains they are responsible for. So an internet user can query the MLM for the association, and query the corresponding CLM for the certificate of the target domain. All log maintainers are not required to be trusted, as they behave transparently, and can provide the same set of efficient proofs as in CIRT. Similar to CIRT, the consistency between logs are verified by user side random verification, and the behavior of all trusted parties is efficiently verifiable.

The complex data structure in systems like CIRT and DTKI prevents them to use the verification method proposed for ARPKI, as the method requires abstractions on the underlying log data structure. To bridge this gap, in DTKI, the underlying log structure of DTKI is formalized, and the properties of log structures are formally proved. Then, the security property of the protocol is proved by using Tamarin prover.

- **Strength**

  It is the first system which allows all parties to collude together, while still being able to prevent MITM attacks using mis-issued certificates rather than merely detect them. It formalizes its underlying log data structure, and formally proved its security properties also by using Tamarin prover. DTKI requires a single global mapping log server, which might imply a monopoly. However, the mapping log is a lightweight governing party, is not required to be trusted, is not involved in every day communications, and it does not directly manage certificates for sites. So, DTKI provides anti-oligopoly at some level.

- **Weakness**

  The weakness of DTKI is that it adds extra latency compared to other systems, its complexity makes it difficult to be deployed, and it suffers from the same problem of SK, namely a domain owner who loses the sovereign key also loses the ability to switch to new operational keys until the SK expires.

7.5 OBSERVATIONS

Based on the above analysis, we observed the advantage and weakness in each category. This section discusses the observations based on different perspectives, i.e., on the property perspective and on the system perspective. In addition, this section summarizes our observations regarding the leading proposals in Table 7.2.

7.5.1 PROPERTY PERSPECTIVE

We summarize our observations on different system categories according to the perspective of identified properties.

Trust agility

The current CA model does not provide this feature, since any compromised CA can issue valid certificates for any domain server. Similarly, systems in the category of *Scope restriction* also do not provide this feature, because they merely restrict the set of domains that CAs can issue certificates for. Most systems in *difference observation* offer this feature, as anyone can be a notary server, and users can select which notary servers they want to trust, and any notary server will not be influenced by other notary servers.

Anti-oligopoly

Systems in the category of *difference observation* normally provide this feature, as the number of observers is not fixed. In addition, the certificate verification result relies on the out-of-band checking through a different path. So, as far as the observed certificates are the same, the client will accept them. Thus, the role of CA is minimized.

Offline verification

In the current CA model, clients only need to verify the validity of the received certificate. So, it satisfies offline verification. Systems in the category of *scope restriction* also provide this feature, as the way they work is similar to the current CA model, but with some restrictions.

Table 7.2 Evaluation of proposals

Desired features	Classic	Difference observation			Scope restriction		Certificate management transparency		
	CA-based	Perspectives	Convergence	TACK	PKP	DANE	CT	ARPKI	DTKI
Trust									
Trust agility	×	√	√	√²	×	×	√	√	√
Free of trusted parties	×	×	×	√²	×	×	×	×	×
Verifiable trusted parties	×	×	×	×	×	×	√	√	√
Anti-oligopoly	×	√	√	√	×	×	×	√	√
Availability									
Offline verification	√	×	⊗¹	√	√	×	√	√	×
Built-in key revocation	×	×	×	×	×	×	×	√	√
Scalability	√	√	√	×²	√	√	√	×	√
Multiple certificate support	√	×	×	√	√	√	√	√	√
Timely key verification	√	×	√	×	√	√	√	√	√
Security									
First connection protection	√	√	⊗³	×	√	√	√	√	√
DOS attack protection	√	×	×	√²	×	×	√	√	√
Use of mis-issued certificate prevention	×	√	√	√	⊗⁴	⊗⁴	×	√	√
Use of mis-issued certificate detection	×	√	√	√	⊗⁴	⊗⁴	√	√	√
Provably secure	×	×	×	×	×	×	×	√	√
Usability									
No user involvement	√	×	√	×	√	√	√	√	√
Privacy									
Protecting browsing history	√	×	√	√²	√	√	√	√	√

√ – The subject offers this feature.

⊗ – The subject offers this feature but with other concerns.

× – The subject does not offer this feature.

1 This feature is satisfied if and only if the received public key/certificate can be found in the local cache.

2 We consider the case without using an online crowd-sourced pin store. If an online pin store is used, then the result might be different depending on how the store is designed. (The pin store has not been proposed, yet.)

3 This feature is satisfied if and only if the received public key certificate can be found in the local cache, and the subject of the certificate has not updated its certificate.

4 This feature is satisfied if the malicious CA is not authorized for the victim domain.

Most systems in the category of *certificate management transparency* offer this feature as well, because in these systems the proofs to be verified about a certificate are provided together with the certificate. In contrast, most systems in the difference observation category don't offer this feature, because with these systems, clients have to make additional connections to verify the certificates they obtained.

Built-in key revocation

Most systems in the category of *difference observation* and *scope restriction* do not provide this feature. Most systems in the category of *certificate management transparency* do offer this feature. For example, CIRT proposed a way to manage certificate revocation by using an advanced log structure; and AKI and ARPKI manage certificate revocation by only recording the latest certificates of domains in their logs.

Multiple certificate support

The current CA model offers this feature. Systems in the category of *difference observation* generally don't provide this feature. Because when clients see different certificates of the same website from different paths or observers, a warning will be displayed to clients even if the received certificates are all genuine. Systems in the category of *scope restriction* and *certificate management transparency* provide this feature.

Timely key verification

Systems in *difference observation* are likely not to provide this feature, as the observers might not be always up to date with all domains.

First connection protection

Systems such as Certificate Patrol, CertLock, and TACK in *difference observation* do not provide this feature, because they verify the certificate based on what has been observed in the previous connections.

Denial of service (DoS) attack protection

The CA model offers this feature. All systems in the category of *scope restriction* and most systems in the category of *certificate management transparency* provide this feature as well. However, some systems in *difference observation* require out-of-band observation, so they will not provide this feature, as the verification server can be blocked.

Use of mis-issued certificate prevention

All systems in *difference observation*, and some systems in the category of *certificate management transparency*, provide this feature. In contrast, systems in the category of *scope restriction* do not provide this feature if the mis-issued certificate is issued by a CA who is authorized for the victim domain. For example, DANE cannot prevent MITM attacks when the fake certificate used by an attacker is issued by the parent domain of the victim domain.

Use of mis-issued certificate detection

All systems in *difference observation* and in *certificate management transparency* provide this feature.

7.5.2 SYSTEM PERSPECTIVE

As shown in the table, systems in the category of *difference observation* provide better trust-related features. However, they can have difficulties in providing better availability, because the observer might not have the latest update, the systems in general do not provide an effective key revocation management, and they require user involvement to make decisions. Moreover, they can suffer from DoS attacks on the observers.

Systems in the category of *scope restriction* provide better usability and availability. However, they have only restricted the power of each trusted parties, but Internet users still need to trust them. This can limit the damage from attacks launched by malicious CAs, but cannot completely solve the problem.

Systems in the category of *certificate management transparency* provide better security and availability. However, anti-monopoly might be a problem for these systems. DTKI shows the possibility of providing anti-monopoly, but it still needs lightweight governing party. It is desired to provide a fully distributed system and still be able to remove the need of trusted parties.

All proposed systems have different advantages compared to the current PKI, and they are trying to solve different problems. However, none of them is satisfactory as a replacement of the current PKI, as the authors were not concerned with all desired features while designing web PKI alternatives.

7.6 CONCLUSION

The production, processing, and consumption of big data requires that all the agents involved in those operations can authenticate each other reliably. Unfortunately, authentication of servers and services on the Internet is a surprisingly hard problem. The classical CA model that we have been relying upon for 20 years is no longer adequate.

We reviewed solutions proposed, and divided them into three categories. Of the three categories, the last one, based on transparent public logs, has had the most success in the real world. Unfortunately, the version of this idea being implemented by Google doesn't handle revocation, and doesn't properly allow a multiplicity of log maintainers. We have reviewed solutions that do allow these additional features, and we think that those solutions are the most comprehensive so far.

We hope our evaluation framework will help the ongoing research on web certificate management alternatives.

REFERENCES

[1] P. Yee, Updates to the Internet X.509 public key infrastructure certificate and certificate revocation list (CRL) profile, RFC 6818 (Proposed Standard), Internet Engineering Task Force, Jan. 2013.
[2] W. Mao, Modern Cryptography: Theory and Practice, HP Professional Series, Prentice Hall PTR, 2004. [Online]. Available: http://books.google.com/books?id=H42WQgAACAAJ.
[3] N. Ferguson, B. Schneier, Practical Cryptography, Wiley, 2003.
[4] B. Schneier, Applied Cryptography – Protocols, Algorithms, and Source Code in C, 2nd ed., Wiley, 1996.
[5] N.P. Smart, Cryptography Made Simple, Information Security and Cryptography, Springer, 2016. [Online]. Available: http://dx.doi.org/10.1007/978-3-319-21936-3.
[6] E. Rescorla, HTTP over TLS, RFC 2818 (Informational), Internet Engineering Task Force, May 2000. [Online]. Available: http://www.ietf.org/rfc/rfc2818.txt.
[7] T. Dierks, E. Rescorla, The transport layer security (TLS) protocol version 1.1, RFC 4346 (Proposed Standard), Internet Engineering Task Force, Apr. 2006. [Online]. Available: http://www.ietf.org/rfc/rfc4346.txt.
[8] S. Turner, T. Polk, Prohibiting secure sockets layer (SSL) version 2.0, RFC 6176 (Proposed Standard), Internet Engineering Task Force, Mar. 2011. [Online]. Available: http://www.ietf.org/rfc/rfc6176.txt.

[9] J.L. Massey, Cryptography—a selective survey, Digit. Commun. 85 (1986) 3–25.

[10] A. Aziz, W. Diffie, Privacy and authentication for wireless local area networks, IEEE Pers. Commun. 1 (1) (1994) 25–31.

[11] W. Diffie, M.E. Hellman, New directions in cryptography, IEEE Trans. Inf. Theory 22 (6) (November 1976) 644–654.

[12] W. Diffie, P.C. van Oorschot, M.J. Wiener, Authentication and authenticated key exchanges, Des. Codes Cryptogr. 2 (2) (1992) 107–125. [Online]. Available: http://dx.doi.org/10.1007/BF00124891.

[13] H.H. Kilinc, T. Yanik, A survey of SIP authentication and key agreement schemes, IEEE Commun. Surv. Tutor. 16 (2) (2014) 1005–1023.

[14] S. Turner, L. Chen, Updated security considerations for the MD5 message-digest and the HMAC-MD5 algorithms, RFC 6151 (Informational), Internet Engineering Task Force, Mar. 2011.

[15] C. Dwork, K. Nissim, Privacy-preserving datamining on vertically partitioned databases, in: Advances in Cryptology – CRYPTO 2004, 24th Annual International Cryptology Conference, Santa Barbara, California, USA, August 15–19, 2004, Proceedings, 2004, pp. 528–544.

[16] B. Pinkas, Cryptographic techniques for privacy-preserving data mining, ACM SIGKDD Explor. Newsl. 4 (2) (2002) 12–19.

[17] M. van Dijk, C. Gentry, S. Halevi, V. Vaikuntanathan, Fully homomorphic encryption over the integers, in: Advances in Cryptology – EUROCRYPT 2010, 29th Annual International Conference on the Theory and Applications of Cryptographic Techniques, French Riviera, May 30–June 3, 2010, Proceedings, 2010, pp. 24–43.

[18] C. Gentry, A Fully Homomorphic Encryption Scheme, PhD dissertation, Stanford University, 2009.

[19] C. Fontaine, F. Galand, A survey of homomorphic encryption for nonspecialists, EURASIP J. Multimed. Inf. Secur. 2007 (1) (2007) 1–10.

[20] V. Vaikuntanathan, Computing blindfolded: new developments in fully homomorphic encryption, in: IEEE 52nd Annual Symposium on Foundations of Computer Science, FOCS 2011, Palm Springs, CA, USA, October 22–25, 2011, 2011, pp. 5–16.

[21] C. Fontaine, F. Galand, A survey of homomorphic encryption for nonspecialists, EURASIP J. Inf. Secur. 2007 (2007).

[22] W. Du, M.J. Atallah, Secure multi-party computation problems and their applications: a review and open problems, in: Proceedings of the New Security Paradigms Workshop 2001, Cloudcroft, New Mexico, USA, September 10–13, 2001, 2001, pp. 13–22.

[23] S. Goldwasser, Multi-party computations: past and present, in: Proceedings of the Sixteenth Annual ACM Symposium on Principles of Distributed Computing, Santa Barbara, California, USA, August 21–24, 1997, 1997, pp. 1–6.

[24] K. Yang, X. Jia, K. Ren, Secure and verifiable policy update outsourcing for big data access control in the cloud, IEEE Trans. Parallel Distrib. Syst. 26 (12) (2015) 3461–3470.

[25] Q. Zheng, S. Xu, Verifiable delegated set intersection operations on outsourced encrypted data, in: 2015 IEEE International Conference on Cloud Engineering, IC2E 2015, Tempe, AZ, USA, March 9–13, 2015, 2015, pp. 175–184.

[26] Q. Zheng, S. Xu, G. Ateniese, VABKS: verifiable attribute-based keyword search over outsourced encrypted data, in: 2014 IEEE Conference on Computer Communications, INFOCOM 2014, Toronto, Canada, April 27–May 2, 2014, 2014, pp. 522–530.

[27] J. Wang, X. Chen, X. Huang, I. You, Y. Xiang, Verifiable auditing for outsourced database in cloud computing, IEEE Trans. Comput. 64 (11) (2015) 3293–3303.

[28] The EFF SSL Observatory. [Online]. Available: https://www.eff.org/observatory.

[29] P. Eckersley, Iranian Hackers Obtain Fraudulent HTTPS Certificates: How Close to a Web Security Meltdown Did We Get?, Electronic Frontier Foundation, 2011. [Online]. Available: https://www.eff.org/deeplinks/2011/03/iranian-hackers-obtain-fraudulent-https.

[30] J. Leyden, Trustwave admits crafting SSL snooping certificate: allowing bosses to spy on staff was wrong, says security biz, The Register (2012). [Online]. Available: www.theregister.co.uk/2012/02/09/tustwave_disavows_mitm_digital_cert.

[31] MS01-017: Erroneous VeriSign-issued digital certificates pose spoofing hazard, Microsoft Support. [Online]. Available: http://support.microsoft.com/kb/293818.

[32] P. Roberts, Phony SSL certificates issued for Google, Yahoo, Skype, others, Threat Post, March 2011. [Online]. Available: http://threatpost.com/phony-ssl-certificates-issued-google-yahoo-skype-others-032311.

[33] T. Sterling, Second firm warns of concern after dutch hack, Yahoo! News, September 2011. [Online]. Available: http://news.yahoo.com/second-firm-warns-concern-dutch-hack-215940770.html.

[34] L.O.M.N. Falliere, E. Chien, W32.stuxnet Dossier, Technical report, Symantec Corporation, 2011.

[35] J. Appelbaum, Detecting certificate authority compromises and web browser collusion, Tor Blog, 2011.

[36] Black Tulip Report of the Investigation Into the DigiNotar Certificate Authority Breach, Tech. Report, Fox-IT, 2012.

[37] C. Arthur, Rogue web certificate could have been used to attack Iran dissidents, The Guardian, 2011.

[38] A. Niemann, J. Brendel, A survey on CA compromises, 2013. [Online]. Available: https://www.cdc.informatik.tu-darmstadt.de/fileadmin/user_upload/Group_CDC/Documents/Lehre/SS13/Seminar/CPS/cps2014_submission_8.pdf.

[39] D. Cooper, S. Santesson, S. Farrell, S. Boeyen, R. Housley, W. Polk, Internet X.509 public key infrastructure certificate and certificate revocation list (CRL) profile, RFC 5280 (Proposed Standard), Internet Engineering Task Force, May 2008, updated by RFC 6818. [Online]. Available: http://www.ietf.org/rfc/rfc5280.txt.

[40] R.L. Rivest, Can we eliminate certificate revocation lists?, in: Financial Cryptography, Springer, 1998, pp. 178–183.

[41] A. Langley, Revocation checking and Chrome's CRL, ImperialViolet (blog), 2012.

[42] P. Kocher, A quick introduction to certificate revocation trees, unpublished work, 1998.

[43] K. Nissim, M. Naor, Certificate revocation and certificate update, in: USENIX Security, Citeseer, 1998.

[44] B. Laurie, E. Kasper, Revocation transparency, Google Research, September 2012.

[45] J. Clark, P.C. van Oorschot, SoK: SSL and HTTPS: revisiting past challenges and evaluating certificate trust model enhancements, in: IEEE Symposium on Security and Privacy, 2013, pp. 511–525.

[46] T.H.-J. Kim, L.-S. Huang, A. Perrig, C. Jackson, V. Gligor, Accountable key infrastructure (AKI): a proposal for a public-key validation infrastructure, in: The 22nd International World Wide Web Conference (WWW 2013), 2013.

[47] M. Marlinspike, SSL and the future of authenticity, in: Black Hat, USA, 2011.

[48] J. Yu, V. Cheval, M. Ryan, DTKI: a new formalized PKI with no trusted parties, CoRR, vol. abs/1408.1023, 2014. [Online]. Available: http://arxiv.org/abs/1408.1023.

[49] J. Yu, V. Cheval, M. Ryan, DTKI: a new formalized PKI with no trusted parties, Comput. J. 59 (11) (2016) 1695–1713.

[50] D. Akhawe, A.P. Felt, Alice in warningland: a large-scale field study of browser security warning effectiveness, in: Usenix Security, 2013, pp. 257–272.

[51] D. Wendlandt, D.G. Andersen, A. Perrig, Perspectives: improving SSH-style host authentication with multi-path probing, in: USENIX Annual Technical Conference, 2008, pp. 321–334.

[52] M. Alicherry, A.D. Keromytis, DoubleCheck: multi-path verification against man-in-the-middle attacks, in: ISCC, 2009, pp. 557–563.

[53] Certificate patrol. [Online]. Available: http://patrol.psyced.org.

[54] C. Soghoian, S. Stamm, Certified lies: detecting and defeating government interception attacks against SSL, in: Financial Cryptography, 2011, pp. 250–259.

[55] M. Marlinspike, T. Perrin, Internet-draft: trust assertions for certificate keys (TACK), 2012. [Online]. Available: http://tack.io/index.html.

[56] Public key pinning, http://www.imperialviolet.org/2011/05/04/pinning.html, May 2011.

[57] R.L. Barnes, Dane: taking TLS authentication to the next level using DNSSEC, IETF J. (October 2011).

[58] J. Kasten, E. Wustrow, J.A. Halderman, CAge: taming certificate authorities by inferring restricted scopes, in: Financial Cryptography, 2013.

[59] P. Eckersley, Internet-draft: sovereign key cryptography for internet domains, 2012. [Online]. Available: https://www.eff.org/sovereign-keys.

[60] B. Laurie, A. Langley, E. Kasper, Certificate transparency, RFC 6962 (Experimental), Internet Engineering Task Force, 2013.

[61] M. Ryan, Enhanced certificate transparency and end-to-end encrypted mail, in: NDSS, 2014.

[62] T.H. Kim, P. Gupta, J. Han, E. Owusu, J.I. Hong, A. Perrig, D. Gao, ARPKI: attack resilient public-key infrastructure, in: ACM CCS, 2014.

[63] R. Dingledine, N. Mathewson, P. Syverson, Tor: the second-generation onion router, in: Proceedings of the 13th USENIX Security Symposium, 2004, pp. 303–320.

[64] A. Langley, Public-key pinning, ImperialViolet (blog), 2011.

[65] C. Evans, C. Palmer, R. Sleevi, Internet-draft: public key pinning extension for http, Oct. 2014, draft 21.

[66] R. Barnes, Use cases and requirements for DNS-based authentication of named entities (DANE), RFC 6394 (Informational), Internet Engineering Task Force, Oct. 2011. [Online]. Available: http://www.ietf.org/rfc/rfc6394.txt.

[67] P. Hoffman, J. Schlyter, The DNS-based authentication of named entities (DANE) transport layer security (TLS) protocol: TLSA, RFC 6698 (Proposed Standard), Internet Engineering Task Force, Aug. 2012. [Online]. Available: http://www.ietf.org/rfc/rfc6698.txt.

[68] S. Weiler, D. Blacka, Clarifications and implementation notes for DNS security (DNSSEC), RFC 6840 (Proposed Standard), Internet Engineering Task Force, Feb. 2013. [Online]. Available: http://www.ietf.org/rfc/rfc6840.txt.

[69] N. Heninger, Z. Durumeric, E. Wustrow, J.A. Halderman, Mining your Ps and Qs: detection of widespread weak keys in network devices, in: Proceedings of the 21st USENIX Conference on Security Symposium, in: Security'12, USENIX Association, Berkeley, CA, USA, 2012, p. 35. [Online]. Available: http://dl.acm.org/citation.cfm?id=2362793.2362828.

[70] P. Eckersley, Sovereign key cryptography for internet domains, Internet Draft, 2012.

[71] S. Meier, B. Schmidt, C. Cremers, D.A. Basin, The TAMARIN prover for the symbolic analysis of security protocols, in: Computer Aided Verification – 25th International Conference, CAV 2013, Saint Petersburg, Russia, July 13–19, 2013, Proceedings, 2013, pp. 696–701.

PERFORMANCE ISOLATION IN CLOUD-BASED BIG DATA ARCHITECTURES

8

Bedir Tekinerdogan*, Alp Oral*,†

*Wageningen University, Information Technology, Wageningen, The Netherlands †Microsoft, Vancouver, Canada

8.1 INTRODUCTION

In the last decade, the ability to capture and store vast amounts of structured and unstructured data has grown at an unprecedented rate. Traditional data management techniques and tools did not scale with the generated mass scale of data and the need to capture, store, analyze, and process this data within acceptable time [10]. To address these problems, the term big data has been introduced which can be explained according to three V's: Volume (amount of data), Velocity (speed of data), and Variety (range of data types and sources). Big data has now become a very important driver for innovation and growth for various industries such as health, administration, agriculture, defense, and education. To cope with the problems of rapidly increasing volume, variety and velocity of the generated data novel technical capacity and the infrastructure has been developed to aggregate and analyze big data. One of the important approaches is the integration of cloud computing with big data. Big data is now often stored on a distributed storage based on cloud computing rather than local storage. Cloud computing is based on services that are hosted on providers over the Internet. Hereby, services are fully managed by the provider, whereas consumers can acquire the required amount of services on demand, use applications without installation and access their personal files through any computer with Internet access. Cloud computing provides a powerful technology for data storage and data analytics to perform massive-scale and complex computing. As such, cloud computing eliminates the need to maintain expensive computing hardware, dedicated storage, and software applications.

A typical cloud-based big data system has many different tenants [7], which require access to the server's functionality. In a *nonisolated* cloud system, the different clients can freely use the resources of the BCS. Hereby, disruptive tenants who exceed their limits can easily cause degradation of performance of the provided services for other tenants. To meet performance demands of the multiple tenants and meet fairness criteria, various performance isolation approaches have been introduced including artificial delay, round robin, blacklist, and thread pool. Each of these performance isolation approaches adopts different strategies to avoid the performance interference in case of multiple concurrent tenant needs.

In this paper, we propose a framework and a systematic approach for performance isolation in cloud-based big data systems. To this end, we present an architecture design [18] of cloud-based big data systems and discuss the integration of feasible performance isolation approaches. We evaluate our approach using *PublicFeed*, a social media application that is based on a cloud-based big data platform.

The remainder of the paper is organized as follows. In Section 8.2, we provide the background on cloud computing, and big data architecture. Section 8.3 presents the case study with the problem statement. Section 8.4 presents the state-of-the-art on performance monitoring in cloud-based big data systems. Section 8.5 describes the application framework that integrates performance monitoring with big data systems. In Section 8.6, provides the evaluation of the proposed framework and the approach. Section 8.7 presents the discussion. Section 8.8 presents the related work and finally Section 8.9 concludes the paper.

8.2 BACKGROUND
8.2.1 CLOUD COMPUTING

In general, three types of cloud computing models are defined [16,17,15]. These are Infrastructure as a Service (IaaS), Platform as a Service (PaaS), and Software as a Service (SaaS). The IaaS model shares hardware resources among the users. Cloud providers typically bill IaaS services according to the utilization of hardware resources by the users. The PaaS model is the basis for the computing platform based upon hardware resources. It is typically an application engine similar to an operating system or a database engine, which binds the hardware resources (IaaS layer) to the software (SaaS layer). The SaaS model is the software layer, which contains the business model. In the SaaS layer, clients are not allowed to modify the lower levels such as hardware resources and application platform. Clients of SaaS systems are typically the end-users that use the SaaS services on-demand basis. We can distinguish between thin clients and rich clients (or thick/fat clients). A thin client is heavily dependent on the computation power and functionality of the server. A rich client is a computer that provides itself rich functionality independent of the central server.

In principle, SaaS has a multitier architecture with multiple thin clients. In Fig. 8.1 the multiplicity of the client nodes is shown through the asterisk symbol (∗). In SaaS systems the thin clients rent and access the software functionality from providers on the Internet. As such the cloud client includes only one-layer User Layer which usually includes a web browser and/or the functionality to access the web services of the providers. This layer includes, for example, data integration and presentation. The SaaS providers usually include the layers of Distribution Layer, Presentation Layer, Business Service Layer, Application Service Layer, Data Access Layer, Data Storage Layer, and Supporting Service Layer.

Distribution Layer defines the functionality for load balancing and routing. *Presentation Layer* represents the formatted data to the users and adapts the user interactions. The *Application and Business Service Layer* represents services such as identity management, application integration services, and communication services. *Data Access Layer* represents the functionality for accessing the database through a database management system. *Data Storage Layer* includes the databases. Finally, the *Supporting Service Layer* includes functionality that supports the horizontal layers and may include functionality such as monitoring, billing, additional security services, and fault management. Each of these layers can be further decomposed into sub-layers.

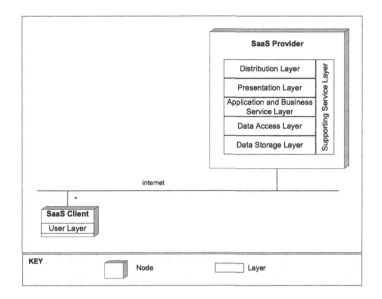

FIGURE 8.1

SaaS reference architecture

8.2.2 BIG DATA ARCHITECTURE

Obviously, an appropriate big data architecture design will play a fundamental role to meet the big data processing needs. Several reference architectures are now being proposed to support the design of big data systems. In this paper, we will adopt the Lambda architecture as defined by Marz [10]. The Lambda architecture is a big data architecture that is designed to satisfy the needs for a robust system that is fault-tolerant, both against hardware failures and human mistakes. Hereby it takes advantage of both batch- and stream-processing methods. In essence, the architecture consists of three layers including batch processing layer, speed (or real-time) processing layer, and serving layer. (See Fig. 8.2.)

The batch processing layer has two functions: (1) managing the master dataset (an immutable, append-only set of raw data), and (2) to precompute the batch views. The master data set is stored using a distributed processing system that can handle very large quantities of data. The batch views are generated by processing all available data. As such, any errors can be fixed by recomputing based on the complete data set, and subsequently updating existing views.

The speed layer processes data streams in real time and deals with recent data only. In essence, there are two basic functions of the speed layer: (1) storing the real time views and (2) processing the incoming data stream so as to update those views. It compensates for the high latency of the batch layer to enable up-to-date results for queries. The speed layer's view is not as accurate and complete as the ones eventually produced by the batch layer, but they are available almost immediately after data is received.

The serving layer indexes the batch views so that they can be queried in low-latency, ad-hoc way. The query merges result from the batch and speed layers to respond to ad-hoc queries by returning precomputed views or building views from the processed data.

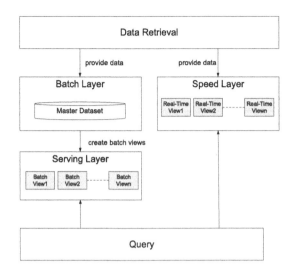

FIGURE 8.2

Lambda architecture for a big data system (adapted from [10])

8.3 CASE STUDY AND PROBLEM STATEMENT

In this section, we describe the case study that is used to illustrate the problem statement.

8.3.1 CASE STUDY

PublicFeed (https://www.publicfeed.com/) is a location and interest based real time social collaborative newsfeed application which has to deal with a variety types of data. The conceptual architecture for PublicFeed is shown in Fig. 8.3.

The architecture represents a cloud-based big data system in which multiple tenants access the big data and the related services via the cloud server. Tenants make requests to fetch results as a data response. In the system, users can register to the system, follow other members in the system, publish feeds, and interact with each other. Registered users are able to publish text feeds, videos, photos and audio files. Feeds have different type of meta-data including uniquely addressing global coordinate, a category, tags, and one of the five different levels of sharing audience selected by Author. Sharing audiences are distinguished based on Country, City, District, Neighbor, and Street levels. System users can real-time follow the feeds for the selected audience level. The selected audience level also covers the subaudience levels such as cities covers districts, neighbors, and street levels. Therefore, the overall data flow in the system is changing for each incoming feed. Given this context, the system can be largely characterized as a big data system from the earlier defined three perspectives of volume, variety, and velocity of the data. The following metric values provide insight in the complexity and size of the current system:

- Total number of users: 212,470

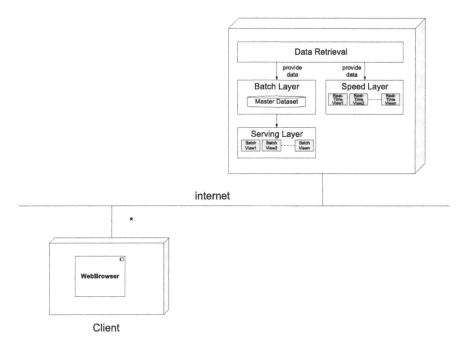

FIGURE 8.3

Conceptual architecture of PublicFeed, a cloud-based big data system

- Total number of registered mobile devices: 61,431
- Total number of different feeds: 147,762
- Total number of different location coordinates assigned to feed: 21,228
- Daily incoming news feeds: 400–1500
- Daily private messages: 5000–20,000
- Daily like/dislike: 3000–9000

The data is generated from end users who wish to share their experiences. The feeds are considered as raw data and further processed. An important information that is extracted is, for example, the *best feeds* that is calculated based on the number of likes. Feed specific interactions are the basic measures for determining the quality of an individual feed. In addition to these interaction data, time of the taken actions also play a key role for this measurement. Individual feed quality affects the overall application, whereas other interactions only affect individual users. An important aspect of the system is the *feed timeline*, which lists 150 feeds, including the user interest, time and sharing audience metrics. Feed timeline is specifically defined for each registered user who has different interests. Besides of the interaction among the users, the system can use a push based notification system that sends information to the clients at specific times and time intervals. Most of the time, this notification is based on other users' actions and is sent to affected users only, but sometimes a broadcast of a specific feed with editorial content might be send to all users. This editorial content is often available due to an unexpected event – for example, in case of an earthquake or any other important event. These notifications need to be instantly sent and cannot be scheduled.

8.3.2 PROBLEM STATEMENT

In the previous case study, the massive number of users together with their interactions can easily result in performance problems. If the actions of users are not perfectly isolated, the system might soon have to cope with disruptive users, who exceed their limits and thereby cause suffering to the regular users who demand the service within their limits. This situation can lead to a loss of trust in the system, which can eventually lead to a business critical situation. Thus, handling the performance problem in a fair way is as important as providing the functional services of the application.

Sometimes it is possible to increase or decrease the performance for some users, as long as this will not violate other customers' minimum service level agreement (SLA) requirements. An extreme solution is the isolation of computational resources for different users. Hereby, the interference of different users is avoided using isolated resource sharing. In practice, this is not a cost-effective solution since several resources can become unnecessary idle. To cope with performance problems two seemingly feasible solutions could be identified caching, and horizontal scalability.

In the case of caching, frequently accessed data is often cached to shorten data access times, reduce latency, and improve input/output. Since the system workload is dependent upon I/O operations, caching as such can be indeed used to improve application performance. Unfortunately, caching is not always feasible and cannot completely solve the problem of fairness. This is in particular the case if the need for cache updates exceeds the required updates of the actual data. For example, in the case study the feed timeline needed to be updated at real time and was based on both individual user interaction and other incoming related feeds. In this situation, the frequency of cache update can occur more than the timeline requests. Hence, caching does not solve the performance and fairness problem, at the optimum level.

Another solution that seems feasible is to ensure performance demands of the multiple tenants by relying on elastic scalability of the cloud system. With elasticity, the system can scale itself up or down according to the minimum necessary computational power to handle all the requests within the minimum requirements of SLA. Unfortunately, relying on elasticity does not solve the problem either. From a general perspective, both performance isolation and elasticity support the realization of SLA, but their objectives are different. The main goal of elasticity is not directly to support performance isolation but rather scalability of the SaaS in general. The system could scale up while there are still disruptive tenants who hamper the performance of other tenants.

Since complete isolation of computational resources, caching, and elasticity do not solve the identified problems at the optimal level, it is important to provide a solid approach, which achieves fairness with respect to performance requirements. We will discuss this in the following section.

8.4 PERFORMANCE MONITORING IN CLOUD-BASED SYSTEMS

In essence, to build a fair system, the following conditions must be satisfied [8,12]:

1. Customers working within their defined limits should not be affected by other customers exceeding their limits. The term *limit* here is referred to as the workload size a tenant is agreed to run on a cloud server. Workload can be considered as the amount of requests within a given time period.
2. Customers exceeding their limits and causing a negative impact of others should be reduced by performance degradation. This eventually makes the system light and responsive to each customer.
3. Customers that have better limits should have better performance compared to customers with lower limits. Performance here can be defined as input/output related parameters such as response time, request rate, etc.

To ensure performance isolation four different architectural solutions are proposed [8,12] (Fig. 8.4):

Artificial delay

This approach generates artificial delay on tenant requests by considering the tenant limitations and its corresponding request rate. The purpose behind this delay is to create backpressure to the disruptive tenant. This strategy expects increased response times for disruptive tenants. The delay time for responses can be calculated dynamically considering the limitations of the tenant, or it may be a constant value for all disruptive tenants. Experiments show that the steady amount of artificial delay cannot keep up performance isolation since it does not prioritize the disruptive requests compared to abiding requests. In this way, the same workload coming from the disruptive requests is handled by the system in a delayed manner.

Round robin

This strategy creates FIFO-queues for each tenant and gives the requests first coming out by the queue in each turn. Since these queues are handled by the request manager layer, the application server does not need to consider prioritizing the requests or tenants. The application layer simply takes the incoming request from the next request provider. The expected outcome of this technique is to distribute utilization of the system among the waiting tenants. When some queues are empty, and there are only few active tenants on the system, the empty queues are skipped and therefore the active tenants are served as much as the workload capacity of the system. Moreover, they use the workload capacity of the offline tenants, which provides a cost-optimized solution while distributing the workload.

Black list

The black list strategy uses two FIFO queues for handling the incoming requests. Typically, the first queue is used to fetch the requests and send to the application server. The second queue is the black list queue and is only served when there are no incoming requests from the first queue. Otherwise every nth request is fetched from the first queue, where n is some large number to process the blacklist queue slowly. When some tenants exceed the request limits, their requests will be redirected to the black list queue to push the distribute tenant back and process them slowly.

Thread pool

This strategy separates the workload resource pool reserved for each tenant by separating each tenants thread pools. Incoming requests first queued in the request manager layer are ordered in an FIFO basis. Subsequently, the thread pools in the application server processes the next incoming requests according to its available workload capacity.

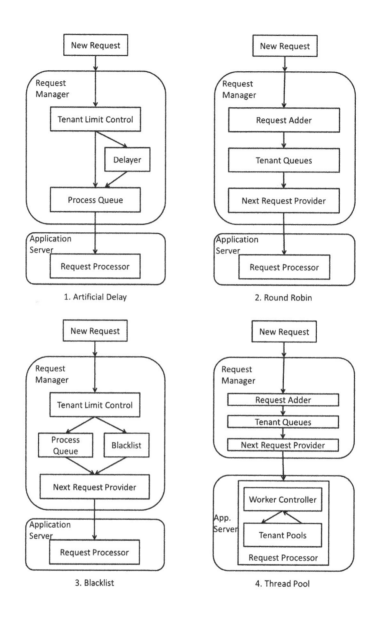

FIGURE 8.4

Proposed performance isolation approaches in Multitenant Applications (adapted from [8])

8.5 APPLICATION FRAMEWORK FOR PERFORMANCE ISOLATION

In this section, we present the so-called Tork application framework that integrates performance isolation with the existing request handling mechanisms. In the conventional case, without performance isolation, incoming requests are first received by load balancers that on their turn redirect these requests to the most feasible application nodes. The selection of the nodes is usually based on the request traffic on the system. This approach provides a balanced request distribution for different end points and utilizes the entire system to reach the best performance. However, during the request handling, existing cloud providers do not use performance isolation strategies at the SaaS. The main reason for this is mainly to prevent unknown impact of disruptive tenants on the SaaS level business logic. In this context, request workloads are usually estimated by counting the amount of incoming requests per second (RPS), and based on this the workload is distributed among the nodes. The RPS calculation by itself, however, does not provide performance isolation and as such need to be enhanced with proper performance isolation approaches, as introduced in Section 8.4.

To meet the performance isolation in the system and calculate the overall system performance, we used the performance isolation metrics in [8,12]. To integrate the performance isolation mechanisms in the practical big data system, we assumed that the following criteria are satisfied:

1. Different entities which are sending requests to the cloud application must be identified, and separated into tenants.
2. To reach the optimal performance balance for a request endpoint, the processing times for different tenant requests should be uniformly distributed.
3. Tenant related requests need to identify themselves from the application (SaaS) layer; they should not depend on a lower layer such as TCP/IP protocol.

The first criterion is necessary to distinguish different tenants and group the same tenants in order to isolate the incoming requests from different tenants. This criterion also determines which entities in the application need isolation. Requests for each tenant may contain various amounts of workloads, which is used to prioritize the tenants.

The second criterion may not be always possible in a real world cloud application. This is because different workloads of different tenants will disrupt the assumption of a uniform distribution. A possible approach for separating the request types with different workloads is choosing the requests according to their I/O formats (such as write only requests and read only requests). Assigning similar workloads to the same endpoint will utilize the system isolation by utilizing the isolation metric predictions for the workloads.

For the third criterion, performance isolation in the SaaS layer requires tenants to identify themselves in the software layer. Therefore, all tenant related, and isolation required requests should send their tenant information in the application logic. Since the tenant information is sent from client to server, this information could be changed and may contain misleading data for the server. Handling wrong tenant data from the cloud server may cause severe performance degradations in this case, and it could create a potential security risk. To accomplish a secure cloud application, this information should be handled correctly and processed to become real tenant identifier. Therefore, during the transportation of real tenant identifier from client to server, it should be encrypted hash keys, or session based temporary keys.

The Tork Framework is designed to satisfy these three key performance isolation requirements. The conceptual architecture of a cloud-based big data system with performance isolation using the Tork framework is shown in Fig. 8.5. The Tork Framework is based on a generic client–server architecture pattern, and supports three node types including, client nodes, application nodes, and database nodes. Tork Framework uses Node.js environment in application nodes and provides JavaScript API library for the client-side development, which is the same language used in Node.js environment. The

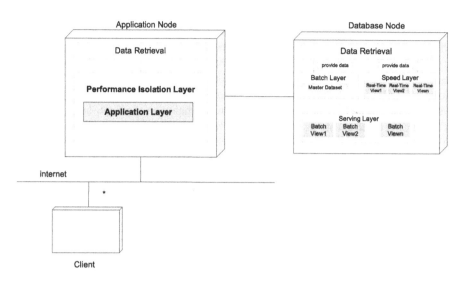

FIGURE 8.5

Performance isolation in a cloud-based big data system

framework can be used to support both the development of thin clients and thick clients. Fig. 8.5 shows an example of a thin client since the application layer is only included in the application node. Alternatively, the client node could also include the application layer. The framework supports both options.

As shown in Fig. 8.5, the Performance Isolation layer includes Application layer that represents the business logic with the performance isolation services of the SaaS application. Hereby, the business logic is based on the model-view-controller (MVC) pattern to process the requests. To realize the performance isolation, the business logic is encapsulated within the performance isolation layer. The available performance isolation algorithms are separately defined as pluggable modules and together define the overall performance isolation layer. Further, each performance isolation algorithm is configurable and can be selected and applied on the incoming business logic requests. The selected performance isolation algorithm basically intercepts the incoming requests and calculates the waiting times based on the request parameters, which is then used to determine the tenant information and the related request end point. As soon as the waiting time condition is satisfied, the intercepted request is applied to the application logic. This sequence of these actions is given in Fig. 8.6.

Besides the overall performance isolation layer, Tork Framework provides built-in common MVC Framework modules for utilizing the productivity of the business logic. Detailed information of these modules is provided in [12]. Encapsulating the usage of existing modules at the SaaS level also provides performance isolation in a more comprehensive way with respect to the business logic. These encapsulated modules may include Data-Grids, Data-Forms, Logging, Login, etc., measuring the performance isolation for unit access modules is a future research topic for the Tork Framework.

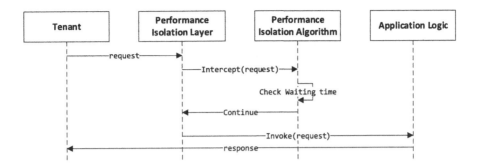

FIGURE 8.6

Sequence of requests using performance isolation

8.6 EVALUATION OF THE FRAMEWORK

To evaluate the results of performance isolation on the Tork Cloud Application Framework, we have adopted the case study of PublicFeed where the elasticity and cache mechanisms of the cloud application could not entirely solve the problem of balanced availability for each active user. To illustrate these critical points, we selected two use cases from a mobile social media application and evaluated the performance isolation algorithms under the selected cases for different scenarios.

PublicFeed provides social media services such as writing location based local news, news-feed timeline, news-feed detail for reading the published news. 10K daily active users currently use this application and their hundreds of concurrent connections operating from the single data store. Most of the functionalities are related with Feed-Timeline requests and Feed-Detail requests for all active users. These requests are served by 2 Node.js application servers for high availability and 1 database server for consistency among application servers. In the current production of the application, these requests are served from Tork Framework without using the performance isolation principles. To measure the effects of performance isolation on the system, we replicated the overall database and application nodes from the production environment, then setup a testing environment to the same cloud network. This environment included 8 vCPU and 15 GB of RAM instance for the database server and 2 vCPU and 8 GB of RAM for the application server. Microsoft SQL Database server is used for storing the overall data of the application and Node.js framework used baseline for the Tork Framework in the application layer.

Since the nature of the application requires consistent real time availability, it does not use caching in the application layers. Instead, it utilizes the database layer by calculating the changing data for each request. Changing data is based on various factors. These factors include user location, their interest of category, published feed time and general popularity of the feeds inside the overall database system. From the perspective of the data velocity that is caused by the disruptive tenants, this system can be considered a transition state of a big data system. Our unique implementation of the proposed approaches in the Tork Framework provides the performance isolation solution for the big data velocity system; therefore, we consider our practical contribution also applicable for the big data systems.

Table 8.1 Scenario parameters to be used in the evaluation framework	
Scenario parameter	**Description**
Number of tenants	Number of active users using the application server
Number of clients	Number of active connections opened by tenants
Number of disruptive tenants	Active users that have more number of concurrent connections
Number of abiding tenants	Active users that have normal or low number of concurrent connections
Concurrent clients per disruptive tenant	Number of active connections takes service for a single active user
Concurrent clients per abiding tenant	Number of active connections takes service for a single abiding user
Service level agreement for requests	Promised request count per tenant per second
Waiting time between client requests	Calculated automatically from SLA parameter. 0 for disruptive tenants, client size/SLA for normal tenants
Adopted performance isolation approach	Selected approach for evaluating the results, it can be Round-Robin, Delay, Black-List or Nonisolated

In our use cases, we measured the isolation metrics based on two scenarios. These scenarios are the cases of low rate of requests and heavy rate of requests. In these scenarios, we used a set of parameters to determine the workload of the system. These parameters are described in Table 8.1.

To measure the isolation metrics, requests counts and response times from the real environment should be collected. To send, collect and measure the results, we have developed a web based simulation client. By using JavaScript and AJAX technologies, this client was able to open multiple concurrent HTTP connections at a time, simulate different tenants, and measure the request rate with corresponding response time for all tenants and all clients.

Since some default security settings for the modern browsers prevent high amount of TCP connections, we used the Mozilla Firefox web browser and changed its socket size limitation to use 10,000 concurrent sockets at a time, which is sufficient for this experiment.

Tenants, client amount of tenants, and their corresponding request rates are configurable from the user interface. Since we assumed that the SLA is based on acceptable request count per second, request rates are indicated as an SLA variable, which determines the usual amount of request rate; therefore, it also determines the disruptive tenants whose request rate is above the usual. These set of parameters needs to be selected before the experiment to determine the test scenario. Set of parameters are grouped into user interface as follows:

Configurations for selecting the use cases and their scenarios

For this case study, there are two use cases and two scenarios for each. These are Feed Detail and Feed Timeline use cases; low load and heavy load scenarios. In the Feed Detail use case, one of the random feed is selected first and all of the information related to this feed is requested by different tenants. Response for Feed Detail use case is a single feed, specialized with the requester tenant's unique interactions. This use case is the most basic read request from database layer. For the Feed Timeline use case, different numbers of tenants request their timeline list. Timeline list is computed at the database layer for each incoming request. Feed Timeline use case utilizes the database via complex calculations more than any other use case in the application. Low load and heavy load scenarios for each use case change the SLA variable of the use case. This affects the simulation software to send more requests per second for abiding tenants.

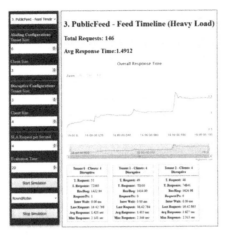 

FIGURE 8.7

Different snapshots of the simulation environment

Configurations for abiding tenant and clients

Since we assumed that requirement for being abiding tenants is using the system within the limits of the SLA, the abiding tenant configuration is used to select the number of abiding active users in this case study. Related clients of these abiding tenants have a request rate within the limits of SLA. Selection of these parameters determines the number of connections that will satisfy SLA conditions. The number of connections will be equal to the tenant size multiplied by the client size.

Configurations for disruptive tenant and clients

Disruptive tenant configuration has the same parameters as the abiding tenant configuration. Disruptive connections do not have any waiting period for making another request to the server. They are constantly making requests and are assumed not to satisfy SLA.

SLA, evaluation time and algorithm configurations

Simulation software uses SLA variable as a number of requests that can be processed per second for a single tenant. When the tenants request more than SLA variable, they violate the SLA, and the related performance isolation algorithm can check this condition and may take appropriate actions. Evaluation time is a period in seconds to measure the performance isolation of the application. During this time, requests are made by clients. Their related request rates and response times are calculated and stored, and the stored data is drawn as a graph. Changing the algorithm configuration notifies the application servers and changes their way of handling requests to the selected algorithm. In addition, changing the algorithm clears the caching mechanisms of the application server that are used for request handling algorithms.

Fig. 8.7 shows two snapshots from the simulation environment during the experiments. After selection of parameters, for each use-case/scenario/algorithm pair, the tenant number of phase experiments should be done to measure the effect of disruption and isolation for the given parameters. Each phase has a duration of evaluation period variable in seconds. In each phase, abiding tenant amounts decrease by one as the disruptive tenant amounts increase by one. In each phase, simulation environment shows

Table 8.2 Evaluation metrics used for performance isolation

Symbol	Meaning
t	A tenant in the system.
D	Set of disruptive tenants exceeding their request rate limits (e.g., defined in the SLA) $\|D\| > 0$.
A	Set of abiding tenants not exceeding their request rate limits (e.g., defined in the SLA) $\|A\| > 0$.
w_t	Workload of the tenant t; $w_t \in W$, $W = \sum_{t \in AUD} w_t$.
W	Total system workload. It can be found by the addition of disruptive and abiding tenants' workloads.
$z_t(W)$	Reflects the QoS provided to tenant t, represented as real number. QoS observation of the individual tenant, which is the function of overall system workload. Lower values correspond to better qualities (low latency response time).
I	Isolation degree of the system. Index is used to separate different isolation values.

the overall response time for the requests and highlights the disruptive tenants' real time. This gives some status clue about the computation resource allocation of the application server, and may even indirectly give status clue about database server during the tests. This way, it is possible to understand whether the test parameters have a meaningful workload effect on the overall application.

8.6.1 EVALUATION RESULTS

Performance isolation is calculated by using the quality of service metrics [8,12]. The metrics that we use have adopted from [8] are shown in Table 8.2. Measuring the isolation depends on at least two other measurements. The initial measurement is the reference value and the second measurement is the disruptive case value. Reference value indicates the quality of service results for all users in the system ($t \in A$) that is indicated as W_{ref}. For the second measurement, a subset of abiding tenants challenges the system isolation by increasing their workload, this point is the disruptive case value and it is measured as W_{disr}. During the measurements of these values, the overall tenant number does not change, therefore the union of A and D remains the same.

The relative differences of these two measured values indicate the QoS of Δz_A, and this is also defined as the reference quality of service compared to the disruptive quality of service. Eq. (8.1) shows the calculation of this comparison [8]:

$$\Delta z_A = \frac{\sum_{t \in A} \left[z_t (W_{disr}) - z_t (W_{ref}) \right]}{\sum_{t \in A} z_t (W_{ref})}. \tag{8.1}$$

Similar to the comparison of the quality of service, relative difference of the workload is measured as it is shown in Eq. (8.2):

$$\Delta W = \frac{\sum_{w_t \in W_{disr}} w_t - \sum_{w_t \in W_{ref}} w_t}{\sum_{w_t \in W_{ref}} W_t}. \tag{8.2}$$

The change in the quality of service and workloads affects the performance isolation in the following way:

$$I_{QoS} = \frac{\Delta z_A}{\Delta W}. \tag{8.3}$$

Table 8.3 Timeline-view scenario performance isolation indices

Approach	Scenario 1: timeline view (low workload)				Scenario 1: timeline view (heavy workload)			
	I_{QoS1}	I_{QoS2}	I_{QoS3}	I_{avg}	I_{QoS1}	I_{QoS2}	I_{QoS3}	I_{avg}
Non-isolated	3.69	4.05	6.14	4.62	2.56	1.58	5.48	3.10
Round robin	1.96	2.43	3.44	2.61	1.74	1.90	3.70	2.45
Delay	2.29	2.75	3.09	2.71	3.93	1.62	4.26	3.28
Black list	0.98	2.43	3.27	2.22	1.22	5.18	4.57	3.66

Table 8.4 Feed-detail scenario performance isolation indices

Approach	Scenario 2: feed detail (low workload)				Scenario 2: feed detail (heavy workload)			
	I_{QoS1}	I_{QoS2}	I_{QoS3}	I_{avg}	I_{QoS1}	I_{QoS2}	I_{QoS3}	I_{avg}
Non-isolated	1.28	1.63	2.13	1.68	1.35	1.86	2.31	1.81
Round robin	1.22	1.62	2.08	1.64	1.26	1.74	2.13	1.71
Delay	5.58	5.27	5.61	5.49	4.31	4.83	4.59	4.58
Black list	1.13	1.50	2.06	1.56	1.42	1.66	1.98	1.68

To disregard the network latency, response time metric is taken as the duration of calculation in the server, until the last byte of the response is flushed. Therefore, average response duration of t variable is calculated by a function of z_t, which results as the workload W. In the experiment, workload size is derived from the request frequencies from the concurrent connections that belong to each tenant.

In this simulation, we considered low and heavy workload scenarios of Timeline-Request and Feed Detail Request use cases. For each case, we have examined 3 active abiding users that have 3 clients, each changing into 3 disruptive users that have 4 clients. Changing from abiding tenants to disruptive tenants in each phase, we found the related quality of service index. These quality-of-service indices are enumerated as I_{QoS1}, I_{QoS2}, and I_{QoS3}. We calculated the averaged isolation metric, I_{avg}, by averaging the quality indices.

Tables 8.3 and 8.4 show the average and steps of the service quality indices for each use case and scenario. For these indices, lower values indicate a more balanced way of workload distribution among tenants which implies better performance isolated system. For the baseline of comparison, nonisolated approach refers to the existing system whereas the others are the results of the proposed isolation algorithms.

For Table 8.3, I_{avg} shows exponential values in the nonisolated as the disruptive tenant size is increased. This means the quality of service is negatively impacted for the abiding tenants due to increase in the workload of the disruptive tenants. Therefore, this use case provides a good example to show the effects of the performance isolation algorithms as we showed the existing system is nonisolated. For the low workload scenario, Round-Robin, Delay and Black List approaches show the increasing I_{avg} as the disruptive tenants are increased. However, this increase looks constant compared to nonisolated system. The Black List approach seems to be the best approach under the low workload scenario. However, Round Robin is the best approach under heavy workload scenario. This is caused by the variation of the workload in the Time Line View scenario. In this scenario, we see that delaying or punishing the tenants due to their disruptive behavior causing worse performance isolation impacts better than the default nonisolated approaches.

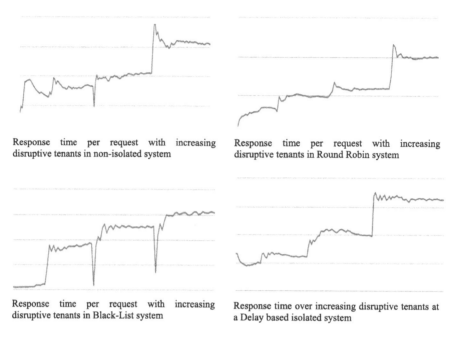

Response time per request with increasing disruptive tenants in non-isolated system

Response time per request with increasing disruptive tenants in Round Robin system

Response time per request with increasing disruptive tenants in Black-List system

Response time over increasing disruptive tenants at a Delay based isolated system

FIGURE 8.8

Response time per request for different performance isolation strategies

In Table 8.4, at the Low Workload scenario we see that the system is not nonisolated at all. Since retrieving a feed detail from the server does not challenge workload, all requests are immediately served from the available computational resource. However, in this case Delay approach shows substantial increase compared to other approaches. This situation shows that delaying requests when the system has available resources causes negative impact on the performance isolation among tenants.

Algorithm – response time characteristics

So far we have analyzed the performance isolation approaches for different workloads. The performance isolation approaches are necessary to guarantee the fairness principle and as such do not violate the expected response times for each tenant. An important question here is how the overall average response time is affected with increasing disruptive tenants.

During the test case we have also investigated this issue by adopting three different phases. At each phase the number of disruptive tenants was increased and the average response time was measured. The results are shown in Fig. 8.8. The horizontal axis of the figures represents the time, while the vertical axis represents the average response time.

From Fig. 8.8 we can conclude that an increased workload from disruptive tenants actually is agnostic to the adopted performance isolation approaches. The average response time appeared to increase proportionally for all the four performance isolation approaches. For the nonisolated approach, the fairness principle will be violated but the average delay time will increase proportionally for each individual tenant. For the other performance isolation approaches, the average response time increases proportionally but fairness is not violated.

8.7 DISCUSSION

We have provided a systematic approach and a corresponding framework to integrate performance isolation within cloud-based big data systems. The study has been carefully planned and evaluated. As such, we believe that the overall approach could be of value for both practitioners and researchers. To define the scope of the work and pave the way for further study, the following issues might need further attention:

One instance is used to simulate all client requests.

For sending all client requests, the evaluation environment is used. This environment is executed on top of a single instance. This means that all of the client requests are sent from the same source. In a real life scenario, client requests may be coming from different nodes and these may belong to different geographical distances to the application server.

Small group of users and clients are used for the tests.

Since all requests can be sent from one computer, there are limiting factors coming from the testing computer. According to these limitations we used three users and four clients for each user, thus totaling 12 concurrent active connections. In a more advanced real life scenario, these numbers may be increased, and the behavior of the application server and database instances may be changed due to different utilization criteria.

DNS lookup times and ingress network traffic for the requests are not considered.

Since all requests are sent from a single computer only, the DNS lookup time is computed once for all requests. This is the first reason why the DNS lookup times are not included in the response times. The second reason is that we assumed real world scenarios for each client, there would thus be only one DNS lookup compute time; this case would not affect the behavior of the overall cloud system. However, in some more advanced real life scenarios, client behavior may vary and active clients may tend to be unique clients that could be from different geographical areas. In this situation, since they connect to the application server at the first time, the DNS lookup time and ingress network traffic may also effect to response time, which may change the results.

Application server is artificially limited for test scenarios.

Since we have limited computational power to simulate all clients, and wanted to examine the performance isolation solutions under heavy utilization, we limited the application server. This limitation is based on CPU throttling of the application layer, and performance isolation layer processes. Therefore, only a limited amount of hardware is used to work for processing the requests. To settle this limitation, first we tried different values of CPU percentages, and selected the best value according to the utilization of the response time. When the response time was increased, and stabilized, responding to all the client requests, we understood that limited hardware amount is utilized for the test cases. However, in general, finding the system limitation given client requests is not a feasible thing to calculate because of the varying workloads and different operating system limitations.

8.8 RELATED WORK

Several cloud application development frameworks have been proposed in the literature. For example, Intercloud [2], Appscale [4], CloudScale [14] and EasySaaS [19] are recent popular frameworks and publications that are focused on scaling multitenant cloud applications. However, none of these explicitly consider performance isolation. Moreover, they primarily provide elasticity solutions for supporting QoS of the cloud application. As stated before, elasticity is important for enhancing performance but it does not directly solve the problem of fairness in case of disruptive tenants.

Performance isolation has been addressed in the literature. Hereby, the focus has been generally on resource efficiency, and performance isolation metrics on multitenant architectures. It is based on resource sharing by optimal placement of customers given a set of resources, and SLA requirements [6,21]. Optimal placement solutions enhance the performance isolation in the application; however, it cannot be considered as an alternative for performance isolation.

Schroeter et al. [13] provide a tenant-aware model that can be reconfigured automatically. This leverages the isolation by placing disruptive tenants into one single node or adding a new node to the system. However, the contribution of the paper is based on elasticity and not directly on performance isolation as we have proposed in this paper.

Lin et al. show an approach to achieve performance isolation on multitenant applications [9]. Hereby, different quality of service is provided to different tenants. The approaches are evaluated based on a test case with changing workloads. However, this approach mainly focuses on differentiating QoS, and does not directly relate to supporting performance isolation.

Wei et al. [20] proposes a technique for isolation of resources by estimating the demands of tenants. Performance isolation is achieved by preventing the disruptive tenants that are responsible for the degradation of the performance on other tenants. The approach is based on static control of resources for the performance isolation and does not use dynamic adaptation of the resources. Further, the approach does not directly consider service level agreement (SLAs), since controlling resources does not directly guarantee fulfilling the SLAs [5].

Performance isolation is actually one way to deal with the problem of performance interference. In [1,3] and [11], instead of admission control and/or isolation, the authors formulate the performance interference problem as an optimization/control problem. Subsequently, they try to mitigate interference by making optimal and the fairest trade-off for all tenants in cloud. In this case for realizing fairness primarily elasticity is adopted. We consider this complementary to the performance isolation approach.

8.9 CONCLUSION

Performance monitoring in cloud-based big data systems is an important challenge that has not been fully solved, yet. We have identified and discussed several potential solutions including caching and scalability. However, none of these approaches completely solves the problem of disruptive tenants that exceed their performance resources and as such impede the performance of other tenants. Considering the fairness criteria, we have discussed that performance isolation is an important concern. Several performance isolation strategies have been identified in the literature. We have provided an approach and discussed the application framework Tork that can be used to integrate performance isolation mechanisms in existing cloud-based big data systems. The framework has been applied to PublicFeed, a social media application that is built on top of a cloud-based big data system. We have reported on the experimental simulations which consider the application of three different performance isolation strategies. Depending on the simulations, we conclude that adopting performance isolation strategies clearly enhances the performance of cloud-based big data systems. Interestingly, the problems that are difficult to solve using the conventional caching and scalability approaches can be supported using performance isolation. In our future work, we will further experiment and simulate with different industrial case studies. Hereby, we will also consider the combination of different performance management approaches of caching, scalability, and performance isolation.

REFERENCES

[1] X. Bu, J. Rao, C. Zhong Xu, Coordinated self-configuration of virtual machines and appliances using a model-free learning approach, IEEE Trans. Parallel Distrib. Syst. 24 (4) (Apr. 2013) 681–690.

[2] R. Buyya, R. Ranjan, R.N. Calheiros, Intercloud: utility-oriented federation of cloud computing environments for scaling of application services, in: Algorithms and Architectures for Parallel Processing, in: LNCS, 2010, pp. 13–31.

[3] T. Chen, R. Bahsoon, Self-adaptive trade-off decision making for autoscaling cloud-based services, IEEE Trans. Serv. Comput. (Nov. 2015).

[4] N. Chohan, et al., Appscale: scalable and open AppEngine application development and deployment, in: Cloud Computing, Springer, Berlin, Heidelberg, 2010, pp. 57–70.

[5] V.C. Emeakaroha, et al., Low level metrics to high level SLAs-LoM2HiS framework: bridging the gap between monitored metrics and SLA parameters in cloud environments, in: 2010 International Conference on High Performance Computing and Simulation (HPCS), IEEE, 2010.

[6] C. Fehling, F. Leymann, R. Mietzner, A framework for optimized distribution of tenants in cloud applications, in: 2010 IEEE 3rd International Conference on Cloud Computing (CLOUD), IEEE, 2010.

[7] D. Jacobs, S. Aulbach, Ruminations on multi-tenant databases, BTW 103 (2007).

[8] R. Krebs, C. Momm, S. Kounev, Metrics and techniques for quantifying performance isolation in cloud environments, Sci. Comput. Program. 90 (2014) 116–134.

[9] H. Lin, K. Sun, S. Zhao, Y. Han, Feedback-control-based performance regulation for multi-tenant applications, in: 2009 15th International Conference on Parallel and Distributed Systems (ICPADS), IEEE, 2009, pp. 134–141.

[10] N. Marz, J. Warren, Big Data: Principles and Best Practices of Scalable Realtime Data Systems, Manning Publications Co., 2015.

[11] R. Nathuji, A. Kansal, A. Ghaffarkhah, Q-clouds: managing performance interference effects for QoS-aware clouds, in: Proceedings of the 5th European Conference on Computer Systems, ACM, 2010.

[12] O.A. Oral, B. Tekinerdogan, Supporting performance isolation in software as a service systems with rich clients, in: 2015 IEEE International Congress on Big Data (BigData Congress), IEEE, 2015.

[13] J. Schroeter, S. Cech, S. Götz, C. Wilke, U. Aßmann, Towards modeling a variable architecture for multi-tenant SaaS-applications, in: Proceedings of the Sixth International Workshop on Variability Modeling of Software-Intensive Systems, ACM, 2012.

[14] Z. Shen, S. Subbiah, X. Gu, J. Wilkes, CloudScale: elastic resource scaling for multi-tenant cloud systems, in: Proceedings of the 2nd ACM Symposium on Cloud Computing, ACM, 2011, p. 5.

[15] K. Öztürk, B. Tekinerdogan, Feature modeling of software as a service domain to support application architecture design, in: Proc. of the Sixth International Conference on Software Engineering Advances (ICSEA 2011), Barcelona, Spain, Oct. 2011.

[16] B. Tekinerdogan, K. Öztürk, Feature-driven design of SaaS architectures, in: Z. Mahmood, S. Saeed (Eds.), Software Engineering Frameworks for Cloud Computing Paradigm, Springer-Verlag, London, 2013, pp. 189–212.

[17] B. Tekinerdogan, K. Öztürk, A. Dogru, Modeling and reasoning about design alternatives of software as a service architectures, in: Proc. Architecting Cloud Computing Applications and Systems Workshop, 9th Working IEEE/IFIP Conference on Software Architecture, 20–24 June 2011, pp. 312–319.

[18] B. Tekinerdogan, Software architecture, in: T. Gonzalez, J.L. Díaz-Herrera (Eds.), Computer Science Handbook, Volume I: Computer Science and Software Engineering, second edition, Taylor and Francis, 2014.

[19] W.T. Tsai, Y. Huang, Q. Shao, EasySaaS: a SaaS development framework, in: 2011 IEEE International Conference on Service-Oriented Computing and Applications (SOCA), IEEE, 2011.

[20] W. Wang, et al., Application-level CPU consumption estimation: towards performance isolation of multi-tenancy web applications, in: 2012 IEEE 5th International Conference on Cloud Computing (Cloud), IEEE, 2012.

[21] Y. Zhang, Z. Wang, B. Gao, C. Guo, W. Sun, X. Li, An effective heuristic for on-line tenant placement problem in SaaS, in: 2010 IEEE International Conference on Web Services (ICWS), IEEE, 2010.

FROM LEGACY TO CLOUD: RISKS AND BENEFITS IN SOFTWARE CLOUD MIGRATION

Anastasija Efremovska, Patricia Lago
Vrije Universiteit Amsterdam, The Netherlands

9.1 INTRODUCTION

The cloud has quickly become a disruptive technology, especially when it comes to the way enterprises run their IT. What began as a pioneering idea of companies such as Amazon and Google, quickly started to gain in popularity among enterprises. The main reason is the tremendous potential in cost savings that can be achieved. As Nati Shalom reports in her article "Moving Enterprise Workloads to the Cloud" [15], on a massive scale the cost savings that can be achieved reach 21% if only three mission-critical applications were moved to the cloud. Another driver towards migration is the maturing of cloud technology in areas that were considered as the biggest deal-breakers for migration such as security or complexity. Different degrees of SLAs and offerings in the form of IaaS, PaaS or SaaS seem to be able to accommodate the plethora of enterprise needs. Yet, all these benefits can be achieved only if the application is suitable for the cloud. This suitability, however, is not limited to the technical characteristics of the application – as many managers still think.

The aim of this chapter is to identify and classify the various factors that influence the success of enterprise application migration to the cloud. If known, addressing these factors can guide enterprises in deciding if a selected cloud environment is right for the considered software applications. The study also helps break the myth that migration is a one-time project.

In the rest of the chapter we first discuss how the literature review was designed and conducted, followed by an overview of the classified extracted data, including general measures and indicators, risks and benefits, and models that guide the migration process. Finally, we present the findings that emerged after examining the data.

9.2 RESEARCH METHOD

This study is based on the systematic literature review method described in [8,13,6]. The review method comprises: defining a research question, identifying keywords and defining a search query for different libraries, data extraction, data analysis and conclusion, containing the findings of the review. The method is tested by first running a pilot study.

Software Architecture for Big Data and the Cloud. DOI: 10.1016/B978-0-12-805467-3.00009-0

9.2.1 PILOT STUDY

The pilot study aims to evaluate and revise the research method on one digital library, in terms of completeness and rigorousness. For this aim we used Google Scholar, which is one of the most voluminous and commonly used digital libraries. The initial research question is formed based on the pilot article "Decision support tools for cloud migration in the enterprise" [12]. The initial search proved to be too general, after which we reduced the context, for example, by explicitly defining *"business application"* or *"enterprise application"* instead of *"business or enterprise"* and *"application"*. In addition, the initial search revealed synonyms that are used in the final search strings. To make sure that the protocol was implemented correctly, we consulted a similar systematic research in the SOA migration field [14].

9.2.2 SEARCH STRATEGY

After the pilot study identified the needed components for a complete review and helped us refine them, the systematic literature review was conducted. The following sections describe the strategy employed by this literature review study.

9.2.2.1 Research question

The purpose of this systematic review is to extract measures, indicators and/or models that can aid companies and individuals evaluate if migrating their enterprise (legacy) software applications to the cloud is feasible, and provide guidelines. Therefore we defined the following research question:

> *"What measures and indicators can be used by enterprises to predict if migrating their applications to the cloud is beneficial?"*

9.2.2.2 Data sources

When conducting the systematic literature review we use the following digital libraries as primary resources: Google Scholar, ACM Digital Library, CiteSeerX, and IEEE Xplore. ACM Digital Library, CiteSeerX, and IEEE Xplore are included in addition to Google Scholar to see if there are any studies that are not retrieved by querying it and these are included in the final set of retrieved studies. CiteSeerX did not return any results so it was not used further.

9.2.2.3 Search query

From the research question defined in Section 9.2.2.1, the following keywords were extracted: *"measure"*, *"indicator"*, *"enterprise"*, *"application"*, *"cloud"*, and *"migration"*. To these search terms we add the keyword *"model"* in order to get all the enterprise application migration models defined, as they may already incorporate measures and indicators relevant for application migration and extract them when possible. We also wanted to see if there are models that can be used as a guideline framework for migration. Furthermore, for all search terms alternative spelling and synonyms were identified. Based on the search terms and their synonyms, we defined the following query string:

> *(Measure OR estimate OR evaluat* OR indicator OR forecasting OR predicting OR prognosis) AND (enterprise OR business) AND (application OR software) AND model AND "cloud (transition OR migration)"*

9.2.2.4 Search process

The first appearance of the term "cloud computing" is commonly connected to 2006 when companies like Google and Amazon started offering the new business model to customers. Antonio Regalado at MIT Technology Review traces it back to 1996 [19]. Other authors trace the initial conception of cloud computing back to the start of ARPANet in the late 1960s [18]. In order not to overlook relevant studies, the search was not limited to a starting year of publication; rather it dates from any article published on the topic until December 15th 2014, when the search was conducted. We applied the search string to the full text of papers, excluding patents, and checked if the pilot study was retrieved. The query in the form specified in Section 9.2.2.3 was suitable for Google Scholar and IEEE Xplore (using the advanced search option for IEEE Xplore) and returned the pilot study. In the case of ACM Digital Library, the query had to be decomposed into 64 separate queries. The resulting set of articles was obtained as an intersection of the sets returned by each separate query.

9.2.2.5 Selection of primary studies

The decision on which papers to include into the set of primary studies was done based on a set of inclusion and exclusion criteria. Studies that satisfied at least one of the exclusion criteria in Table 9.1 were excluded. Studies that met all the inclusion criteria in Table 9.2 were considered as primary studies.

9.2.2.6 Included and excluded studies

From all three libraries, a total of 508 studies were found that matched the query strings (after eliminating multiple copies of the same studies found in more than one library). Table 9.3 provides an overview of the exact number and the percentage of studies found (hits) per digital library. Out of the 508 studies, 367 were eliminated based on reading the title, 99 based on the abstract, and 7 based on the full text. From the 28 studies left, which were taken as primary studies, 12 that contained general measures or models not connected to migrating only one part of an application (such as data, for example) were included in the study. The rest of the articles were not further considered. This decision was made in order to get an overall impression of factors that play a role in migrating any type of application. Studies that were a short version of a more detailed paper published at a later stage were combined in order not to bias the research results with the same model or measures appearing twice. Studies published by the same authors but with complementing findings were included. There was one example of the latter.

9.2.2.7 Search result management

For keeping track of the studies and their reference information we used the Zotero [20] desktop application as well as the browser add-on for Google Chrome. Zotero allows downloading the studies, if they are publicly available, and saving their reference information at the same time. For each digital library, a different Zotero folder was created. Exporting the reference information in a JabRef [21] database format is also possible.

9.2.2.8 Quality assessment of primary studies

The quality of the selected studies was measured according to six general quality criteria that should be satisfied for every well-written study and seven quality criteria that evaluate a study that deals with application cloud migration (see Table 9.4). The quality criteria were taken from the example quality criteria listed in [22] and adapted to fit the purposes of this review. The quality criteria evaluation is

Table 9.1 Exclusion criteria

Exclusion criteria

E1: *The study does not contain (clear) measures or indicators that help estimate the success of enterprise application cloud migration. Rationale:* The measures or indicators proposed are either absent or too general and don't include concrete measures or indicators but are based on poorly supported arguments. *Example:* A paper is concerned with the number of enterprise applications migrated so far, whether they have failed or succeeded, but does not include relevant measures or indicator that relate to the success/failure.

E2: *The study does not relate to software migration to the cloud. Rationale:* 1. The findings are relevant from the business perspective but do not touch upon any technical aspects of software or application migration to the cloud; 2. The study is related to hardware migration; 3. The study has nothing to do with software migration to the cloud. *Example:* 1. Business risk analysis according to specific business models; 2. Live migration of virtual machines; 3. "Review and Update of Standards for Marine Equipment".

E3: *The study is focused on cloud migration of applications for private customers or end-users and cannot be related to enterprise applications. Rationale:* Such studies do not contain any aspects that capture concerns of enterprise applications and may lead to incorrect predictions if used for a large company's decision-making purposes. *Example:* 1. End user satisfaction levels' comparison before and after moving the end-user centered application to the cloud (e.g., moving Spotify application from dedicated servers to the cloud). 2. Video sharing user application popularity measured in percent of views after the application was moved to the cloud. (Measuring the percentage of views is important for this specific application to estimate its popularity between users but this cannot be used in enterprises.)

E4: *The search result is a book, not a paper. Rationale:* Restricted by the duration of this research, reading a whole book that matches the query is too time-consuming. *Example:* [BOOK] "The CIO's Guide to Oracle Products and Solutions".

E5: *The study is developed as part of a commercial research and it includes strong bias towards the commercial company it was developed for. Rationale:* Renowned cloud providers already develop models or give customers guidelines whether their cloud platforms can best suit their company needs. Such commercial research that gives realistic and unbiased results can be used for extracting reliable measures and indicators for cloud migration. If, however, they are biased towards the company and do not give realistic results, they are not useful. *Example:* Analogous example from the pharmaceutical industry: "Drug companies now finance most clinical research on prescription drugs, and there is mounting evidence that they often skew the research they sponsor to make their drugs look better and safer." (http://jama.jamanetwork.com/article.aspx?articleid=182478). A hypothetical example concerning our topic would be: Amazon sponsored research on AWS skews the results for performance, network speed, etc., in order to represent it as the predominant cloud technology on the market.

E6: *The study is not written in English. Rationale:* Because of the multilingual composition of the peer reviewers of the study and the study feasibility, we only focus on papers written in English. *Example:* "TEZĂ DE DOCTORAT".

done in addition to the inclusion/exclusion criteria and serves as an internal metric. For each criterion, the studies were additionally scored on three levels: completely satisfies the criterion (1 point), partially satisfies the criterion (0.5 points), and does not satisfy the criterion (0 points). A study that completely satisfies a criterion has all the elements of that criterion present, and they are clearly described and defined. A study that has only a few elements of the criterion or that is not clearly defined is partially satisfied (e.g., statistical methods used for data aggregation are only listed but not described). Total absence of a criterion' elements (e.g., no data collection method described or defined) means that a particular criterion is not satisfied, resulting in a 0 points score. At the end the total score for the quality of a study was calculated as an average score of the applicable criteria. An average score of 0.7 or above represents high quality papers, a score between 0.3 and 0.7 represents papers of acceptable quality, whereas a score of 0.3 or below excludes the papers.

Table 9.2 Inclusion criteria

Inclusion criteria

I1: *The study proposes either concrete quantitative and/or qualitative measures and indicators or a model that can be used to evaluate the success or failure of enterprise or end-user centered application software migration to the cloud.* *Rationale:* We want to identify quantitative and qualitative measures and indicators that can be easily reused in a general context in an enterprise environment. These measures can be used as a template with which companies can estimate the feasibility of cloud migration of their IT products or as a basis for deriving an estimation model for cloud migration feasibility. If there are models that evaluate the benefits/risks of enterprise application software migration to the cloud, they should be based on qualitative or quantitative measures. We can extract these measures from the models to build our estimation of success template. Nonenterprise (or user) application software migration strategies may include general factors and indicators that are relevant for enterprise applications, too. *Example:* Quantitative measures: I/O and network data-transfer latency rates, CPU clock rate, cost (amount of money); Qualitative measures: security, interoperability issues, noncompliance with regulation, etc.

I2: *The study includes risk and benefit factors recorded based on concrete examples of enterprises that have migrated their applications to the cloud. Rationale:* Enterprise cloud migration is an already tried concept and as such has a few valuable success and failure stories. Based on these examples, quantitative and qualitative measurements can be derived to better estimate future cases. Examples may include: the enterprise size, the application dependencies, the application type, etc. *Example:* Company: R&D Division of a Media Corporation; Company size: 20000 employees worldwide; Division size: 40 employees; Benefits: ease of dealing with volatile number of customers; elastic compute power provisioning (i.e., on-demand extra servers provided and discarded when not needed); Risks: security of data; cloud company being sold to third party, etc.

I3: *The study is developed by researchers and practitioners. Rationale:* Both academic researchers and practitioners are relevant for this study. The academic papers may give the general guidelines, while the practitioners' results could be used to prove/disprove some of the theoretical guidelines proposed by researchers.

I4: *The study is peer-reviewed. Rationale:* Systematic research demands strict quality of content. Papers that are published by reliable sources, such as conference proceedings, journals in the domain, scientific libraries, etc., or peer-reviewed papers can be used for guaranteeing quality and proper information structure. *Example:* 1. "Recent Advances on Soft Computing and Data Mining." Springer, pp. 633–645; 2. ICN 2011, The Tenth International Conference on Networks, pp. 353–358; 3. Example of a not peer-reviewed paper would be a Master's thesis.

Table 9.3 Distribution of studies found in digital libraries

Digital library	Number of studies	Percent (%)
Google scholar	405	80%
IEEE Xplore	59	12%
ACM digital library	44	8%

9.2.3 DATA EXTRACTION

The data extraction from each of the primary studies was facilitated by the data extraction form given in Table 9.5. For each study we recorded the identified measures or indicators, benefits, risks, and models.

Many of the primary studies that were examined did not have the data we needed explicitly shown in the form it was expected in the data extraction form, such as benefits or risks. Therefore extra work was needed to extract or identify these types of measures. Many of the studies included implicit measures that aid migration in the models or frameworks they described, which required even deeper analysis.

Table 9.4 Quality criteria		
Title **Author** **ID**	**General quality criteria (G)**	**Score**
G1	Are the aims and objectives, as well as the motivation, of the study clearly described?	
G2	Is the context in which the study was carried out adequately defined?	
G3	Are the research methodology and its organization clearly stated?	
G4	Is the reporting clear and coherent?	
G5	Does the study provide clearly stated findings with credible results and justified conclusions?	
G6	Do the findings answer the study question(s)?	
	Specific quality criteria (S)	
S1	Have the identified measures and indicators or model for enterprise application cloud migration evaluated on a real world case study?	
S2	If the research paper has a case study company is the size of the company and the choice of it presented and argumentatively supported?	
S3	Are the quantitative measures and indicators identified in the study adequately measured? (Example database size, CPU clock rate, etc.)	
S4	Are the data collection methods described?	
S5	Are the qualitative measures (if any) clearly explained?	
S6	If any statistical models were used in summarizing the results, are they explained and justified?	
S7	Are the identified benefits and risks for enterprise cloud migration diverse (i.e., technical, legal, organizational, financial risks and benefits, etc.)?	

9.2.4 DATA ANALYSIS METHOD

The aim of this review is to identify and categorize different factors that can aid companies evaluate if migrating their legacy application to the cloud is beneficial. In order to achieve this, a method of analyzing the studies was needed. Given that most of the measures we found are qualitative, manual analysis and synthesis was inevitable.

We differentiate benefits and risks as a special kind of factors because they represent an explicit indicator of the possible gains or losses of a migration approach. In this work we use the following definitions of benefits and risks: a *benefit* is an advantage or profit gained from migrating an (enterprise) application to the cloud, whereas a *risk* is an undesirable event that may happen if you migrate your application to the cloud. These measures are typically qualitative in nature. Therefore they do not have any measuring units specified and are characterized only by category.

The risks and benefits categories identified in the pilot study [12] were used as classification categories of all types of measures (including identified benefits and risks), which include the following: *financial, technical, organizational, legal*, and *security*. The studies that categorized their measures either had the same or similar categories or had a more fine-grained technical category. Technical subcategories were translated simply into *technical* as we were interested in the type of the categorization of measures rather than their subcategories. The description of a measure, if identified in multiple studies, was taken from the one that had the most descriptive name or best explanation. If a measure in a study did not specify any category, the most logical category of the set of starting categories identified

Table 9.5 Data extraction form

	Field	Description
1	Study identifier	[A unique ID of the article in the set of all collected articles.]
2	Title	[Title of the study.]
3	Authors	[Authors of the study.]
4	Data source	[The name of the digital library in which the article was found (e.g., IEEE Xplore, Google Scholar, ACM Digital Library, etc.).]
5	Type of the article	[The type of the article (e.g., conference paper, journal article, book chapter, etc.).]
6	Measures or indicator identified	[For each measure or indicator identified, list all the characteristics of it (a, b, c, and d). If there are other characteristics mentioned list them too under e.
	a) Name	a) Name of the measure;
	b) Type	b) Is it a qualitative or quantitative measure;
	c) Measuring unit (if quantitative)	c) Measuring unit (e.g., money unit or speed unit);
	d) Group	d) Hardware type of measure, Economical type of measure, etc.;
	e) Textual description	e) A short description of the measure;
	f) Other	f) Other characteristics not mentioned in a–d.]
7	Model based on the measures (if any)	[Describe the models that are constructed from the measures or identifiers for supporting enterprise application cloud migration success evaluation.]
8	Risks and benefits identified	[List all the risks and benefits identified from the measures and case studies in general, for each list the specifics (a and b). If there are other characteristics list them too in c.
	a) Description	a) Name of the risk or benefit, or a sentence that describes it;
	b) Type	b) Risk or a benefit;
	c) Group	c) Group of the risk or benefit: financial, legal, technical or other type of risk;
	d) Other	d) Other characteristics that may be important but are not mentioned.]
9	Type of company and the application in the case study (if any)	[List the size of the case study company and the enterprise application on which the model or measures were tested, e.g., SME or Large company division and a web application.]
10	Study findings	[Describe the study findings for each of the case studies in which they were applied.]
11	Conclusions	[What is the study conclusion(s).]

was chosen. When we encountered a specific category that was not present in the list of categories, it was replaced with the most logical one.

The found measures and indicators are summarized in a tabular form, augmented with the corresponding narrative description. The description is taken from the source articles, unchanged (if it was present) or reported as a combination of the definitions (if found in multiple articles). A mapping of the measures in one study to the same or similar measures found in other studies was reported in these tables.

The models found in the studies were also evaluated and compared by looking at the proposed steps and the stage of the migration they cover. An evaluation of models for cloud migration is given in [7], which presents a descriptive summary of models/frameworks of migration and an evaluation of their

Table 9.6 Overview of included studies	
Study	**Year**
Khajeh-Hosseini et al. [11]	2010
Varia [16]	2010
Khajeh-Hosseini et al. [12]	2011
Banerjee [4]	2012
Beserra et al. [5]	2012
Khajeh-Hosseini et al. [10]	2012
Vu and Asal [17]	2012
Aggarwal et al. [1]	2013
Alonso et al. [2]	2013
Azarnik et al. [3]	2013
Erfan [9]	2013

missing features. However, our analysis of the models is not based on model completeness – as [7] suggest – but on the perspective they consider for migration and when a certain perspective starts to appear or becomes predominant.

9.3 RESULTS

The analysis of the primary studies identified a set of factors, both general and related to risks and benefits, as well as many models or frameworks designed especially for application migration to the cloud. The analysis also revealed the gaps and quality of the studies. In the next two sections we present an overview of the included studies and their quality, followed by the identified measures and models. While Tables 9.7, 9.8 and 9.9 present only a selection of the identified factors (3 factors for each subcategory), the complete list of factors is also available online at http://tinyurl.com/h6rhhp6.

9.3.1 OVERVIEW OF PRIMARY STUDIES AND QUALITY EVALUATION

An interesting fact found when analyzing the included studies is that 3 out of the 12 studies (also quite detailed and high in quality) share a coauthor, Khajeh-Hosseini (Table 9.6). Most of the primary studies are from 2012 and 2013, whereas the earliest study dates from 2010.

From the 12 initially selected articles, one more was eliminated and further used as a reference. Namely, the article "A Survey of Cloud Computing Migration Issues and Frameworks" [7] is a summary of the quality and completeness of 11 models or frameworks for application migration. The article includes a summary of models that were not evaluated by the authors themselves but were taken from other articles and analyzed as defined or were not available. Therefore we used this article exclusively as an example for evaluating other models found in the rest of the primary studies. Three of the models

Table 9.7 Benefits

ID	Classification category	Source category	Benefit
1	Technical	Technical [12]	Fast access to additional computational resources and specialized skills (e.g., IT specialists who build and maintain clouds). Results in quicker system deployment times.
4	Technical	Technical [12]	Anywhere/anytime/any device (desktop, laptop, mobile, etc.) access to computational resources and applications can be setup without too much effort. This in turn simplifies collaboration amongst users and simplifies application support and maintenance.
5	Technical	Technical [12]; Not specified [9]	Increased system security due to more investment into security by cloud providers (e.g., specialized security teams, greater resilience, protection against network attacks, and quicker disaster recovery procedures).
18	Financial	Financial [12,5]	Reduced costs due to more efficient operations and less infrastructure maintenance costs but also due to economies of scale that can be achieved by cloud providers.
19	Financial	Financial [12]; Unknown [9]; Other [3]	Reduced energy consumption, leads to greener organizations.
26	Financial	Cost [3]	Lower cost of entry as cloud computing does not require heavy investment in physical infrastructure.
28	Organizational	Organizational [12]; Agility [3]	Ability to focus on core business activities and free-up management and IT personnel from mundane tasks (such as hardware support activities) so that they can focus on value-added activities.
30	Organizational	Organizational [12]; Other [3]; Not specified [4]	Opportunity to offer new products or services or trial products to gauge the level of interest from customers.
32	Organizational	Organizational [12]	Reduced risks of technological obsolescence as cloud providers update the infrastructure.

identified in [7] were also found in separate studies and were used to extract measures and indicators from their original articles.

Two articles [2] and [10] do not report on any benefits or risks identified and because of that do not completely satisfy inclusion criterion 2. However, these articles have very detailed models and general measures which have been evaluated on real-world case studies. Therefore, they were included as primary studies.

A shortcoming in most of the articles is that their findings were not evaluated on real-world case studies (or case studies that mimic real applications in general). There were six such articles, and one in particular, even though it states that it is based on the migration of applications in the Iranian telecommunications industry [9], does not specify any details of the company, staff size and composition or characteristics of the migrated applications. Eight of the included studies presented models or frameworks for migration. As can be seen in Fig. 9.1, the average quality of the studies is around 0.8, based on the quality criteria point system (see Section 9.2.2.8).

Table 9.8 Risks

ID	Classification category	Source category	Risk
9	Technical	Application [5]	Application users are located in a region with unreliable Internet connection, which may affect their capacity to communicate reliably with application components deployed on remote cloud servers.
13	Technical	Not specified [17]	Applications processing data streams. Cloud providers rarely support data streams as it can drastically increase costs because of data-intensive remote/intra-cloud communication.
21	Technical	Technical [12]; Outsourcing opportunism risks [3]	Data lock-in for SaaS/PaaS and system lock-in for IaaS.
29	Financial	Financial [5]	Cost to operate the application after migration to the cloud.
31	Financial	Financial [12]	Actual costs may be different from estimates, this can be caused by inaccurate resource estimates, cloud providers changing their prices, or inferior performance (e.g., due to over-utilized servers) resulting in the need for more computation resources than expected.
33	Financial	Financial [12]	Increased costs due to complex system integration problems between existing systems and cloud-based systems. Inability to reduce costs due to unrealizable reductions in the number of system support staff (e.g., due to their knowledge of existing systems).
34	Organizational	Organizational [12]	Private data being exposed due to a change of responsibility for users who have a lack of awareness about where to put different types of data.
35	Organizational	Organizational [12]	Mismatch between existing incident handling procedures and cloud providers' procedures. Lack of information or no access to a cloud's vulnerability information or incident report data. Leads to limited responses from an organization in case of incidents.
37	Organizational	Not specified [11]	Decrease in satisfaction – Support engineers risk decreasing job satisfaction as work may shift from a hands-on technical role to reporting and chasing up issues with third party service providers. Sales and marketing staff risk of decreasing job satisfaction if they are set unrealistic goals regarding the selling of the new cloud based services. Customer care staff also risk decreasing job satisfaction because their ability to perform their job will be dependent upon third parties out of their control resulting in a greater lag between customer queries and resolution.
54	Legal	Legal [12]; Suitability [5]	Unusable software license on the cloud due to the license using traditional per-seat or per-CPU licensing agreements, etc.

9.3.2 BENEFITS AND RISKS

Benefits and risks, as a special type of qualitative measures, are classified according to the five categories defined in Section 9.2.4. Five of the studies that were chosen did not have a category specified for their risks and benefits. Not defining a category for the risks and benefits is more common than in the case of general measures. The reason for this may be the opinion of authors that specifying something as a risk or benefit is self-sufficient and does not need any other classification information.

Table 9.8   (*Continued*)

ID	Classification category	Source category	Risk
56	Legal	Not specified [17]	Applications contain sensitive or important data that cannot be exported to outside the organization or outside the country where the organization is situated.
65	Legal	Legal [12]	Private data stored on the cloud can be accessed by foreign governments due to differences in jurisdictions.
66	Security	Security [12]	Denial of service attacks. Leads to unavailability of resources and increases cloud usage bills.
67	Security	Security [5]	Level of encryption implemented by the provider for communication both within and outside the cloud infrastructure.
70	Security	Security [12]	Insecure or ineffective deletion of data when scaling down resource usage or when changing providers.

Table 9.9   General measures and indicators

ID	Classification category	Source category	Measure/indicator
1	Financial	Economical [1]	Existing investments in IT – For migrating into the cloud, Small and Medium Enterprises (SMEs) are at an advantage over large organizations because they have a limited installed IT base. They may be able to directly move into the cloud. In comparison large organizations huge investments and complexity of hardware, network, application support, administration, customization and integration make it difficult for them to migrate to cloud easily.
6	Financial	Business [2]	Type of elements for billing.
7	Financial	Cloud provider characteristic [5]	Cost and price models for the resources – What are the costs and price models (e.g., per hour on demand, per hour reserved, market bidding) for each type of resource.
8	Security	Technical [1,10]	Data security – Organizations resist sending sensitive applications and confidential information behind the corporate firewall. Data with greater security tolerance however could be ported onto the cloud. Security of data is still the top most inhibiter of cloud adoption.
9	Security	Technical [10,4]; Cloud provider characteristic [5]	Security mechanisms offered by provider – What are the security mechanisms put in place by the provider?
10	Legal	Organizational [1]; Business [2]; Technical [10]	Regulations – Geopolitical issues especially for Governments and financial institutions should be carefully evaluated before making the transition to the cloud. In the Indian context this is especially relevant as most cloud data centers are not located within the country. It is also important to ensure that local regulations relevant to each organization should be adhered to before deciding to move to the cloud.
11	Legal	Business [2]; Organizational [5]	Fulfilment of data privacy laws
12	Organizational	Technical [1]; Organizational [5]	IT skills – Migration to cloud requires IT team with updated skills like virtualization, Web 2.0, etc. These types of challenges need to be addressed prior to deciding the migration to the cloud.

Table 9.9 *(Continued)*

ID	Classification category	Source category	Measure/indicator
13	Organizational	Organizational [1]; Technical [2,10]; Cloud provider characteristic [5]	Service Level Agreements (SLAs) – Another key aspect to consider before migrating to the cloud is whether cloud service providers are able to provide SLAs that the business needs. It should clearly outline service provider responsibilities and penalties for failure to meet agreed service levels.
15	Organizational	Business [2]	More than one business model.
41	Technical	Technical [1]; Application and programming [2]; Application, technical characteristic [5]; Not specified [16]	Architecture and architecture complexity – Simple applications can be easily migrated to the cloud and the amount of effort required moving such applications may not be not too significant. Migration of complex applications however, needs elaborate planning and testing prior to implementation. Legacy applications and existing enterprise applications could require code changes to work on the cloud.
47	Technical	Technical [2,10,4]; Application, technical characteristic [5]	Specific or minimal hardware needs – What is the minimum or specific hardware configuration necessary to run the application?
57	Technical	Application, usage characteristic [5]	Number of users and users' location – How many users access the application and from which locations?

Beserra et al. [5] have much more detailed technical subcategories for the risks and benefits such as *communication, performance, availability*, and *suitability*, which can be useful if the accent is put on the technical aspects of migration.

Especially interesting categorizations were given by Azarnik et al. [3], who use *cost* category in the equivalent sense as the *financial* category. One particularly interesting category of risks they identify is the *outsourcing opportunism risk* (see Table 9.8), which takes into account the risks that may emerge from using cloud providers without (clearly defined) SLAs. If a risk or benefit does not fit any of the four previously mentioned categories, they simply categorize it as *other*.

In general, many of the articles had specific subcategories defined for the categories we use. The list of subcategories for the *technical* benefits and risks category include: *communication, availability, suitability, performance, operational*, and *agility*. In contrast, Azarnik et al. [3] also use super categories for some of the classification categories. Such is the *outsourcing opportunism risk* category, which integrates the *technical, legal*, and *organizational* categories. The distribution of our categories in the studies is given in Fig. 9.2.

Besides the defined super- and subcategories for measures, the following category synonyms were encountered: *cost* or *economic* for the *financial* category, *operational* or *functionality* as technical subcategories, and *political* as a synonym for *organizational*. Selected lists of benefits and risks, along with their original and assigned classification categories, can be found in Tables 9.7 and 9.8, respectively.

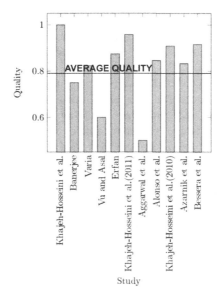

FIGURE 9.1

Quality of primary studies

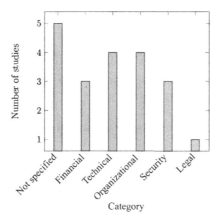

FIGURE 9.2

Benefits and risks categories distribution in primary studies

9.3.3 GENERAL MEASURES

General measures and indicators are those measures that, depending on the values they take and the context in which they are measured, can be seen either as benefits or risks in the process of migration. Without their values, it is difficult to say if they describe an upside or downside of migration. For example, let us consider network bandwidth as a measure. Low bandwidth values are a hindering factor towards the migration decision, if we want to migrate an application that has large bandwidth demands. If the bandwidth values are high enough for the application needs, then bandwidth is a beneficial factor towards migration.

The measures and indicators in the studies were less frequently explicitly listed as measures compared to the risks and benefits. Yet, the classification of measure and indicators was much more easily extracted and more often explicitly specified. There is also a bigger overlap in identified measures and indicators across the studies compared to risks and benefits.

There is an overlap in some of the risks and benefits and the general measures identified. A typical example would be the "bandwidth" general measure which prescribes examining the bandwidth available in the cloud and if it is sufficient for the concrete application. The equivalent risk is "low bandwidth", which describes the unwanted effects of migration if bandwidth was not taken into account.

The classification of general measures is similar to the risks and benefits across the papers (Table 9.9). The *technical* category had the most subcategories: *operational, computational, application-usage characteristics,*[1] *application-technical characteristics,*[2] *application and monitoring, user management and security, IaaS, PaaS, monitoring,* and *multitenancy*. The *financial* category has only one subcategory – *billing*, whereas *organizational* has the *migration strategy characteristics, provisioning, user interaction,* and *SLA* subcategories. Beserra et al. [5] use the *cloud provider characteristics* super category which includes the *security, organizational, financial,* and *technical* categories. Alonso et al. [2], on the other hand, use the *business* supercategory to classify measures in the *financial, organizational,* and *legal* categories. An overview of the general measures and their original categories is shown in Table 9.9, and the categorization across studies is presented in Fig. 9.3.

9.3.4 MODELS AND FRAMEWORKS FOR CLOUD MIGRATION

The analysis of the models and frameworks of migration revealed four distinct types of models, based on the extent to which they cover the migration process:

- **Type 1: Models that focus only on one aspect of migration**

    This is the simplest type of model found, and can be seen more as guidelines. Examples are the *Cost modeling framework* [12] that deals with the financial infrastructure costs and the *Informal migration feasibility assessment framework* [11] that deals with the organizational impact of migration.

- **Type 2: Models that support migration decision making from multiple perspectives**

    These models can be seen as an extension of the type 1 models, which take the diverse nature of factors of migration into account. The factors match the categorization of measures and indicators and comprise of technical, organizational, financial, etc., feasibility assessment. For instance, the

---

[1]This technical subcategory was defined as the usage characteristic of the application and can be seen as a subcategory of the application category Table 9.9.

[2]Technical characteristics is defined as a subcategory of the application category in the corresponding paper; see Table 9.9.

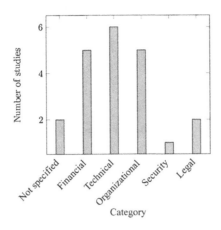

FIGURE 9.3

General measures categories distribution in studies

Cloud Adoption Toolkit [10] includes the *Cost Modeling framework* [12] and augments it with technical feasibility, energy consumption, stakeholder and responsibility analysis. Another example of this type of model is the *ARTIST cloud modernization framework* [2], which in the analyzed study only describes the premigration phase. The full ARTIST framework can be seen as type 4 model, but the paper that describes it only presents the internal tools working rather than the migration and evaluation phases.

- **Type 3: Incremental migration support models**

The incremental migration support model type can be seen as composed of three general stages: *premigration, migration* and *validation/testing*. In the premigration stage the technical characteristics and requirements of the application are determined and profiles of the cloud providers are made. The application characteristics are compared to the profiles and the most suitable one is chosen. The migration phase encompasses the actual moving of the application and data, which is done in two separate steps: either first migrating the application then the data or vice versa. In the validation phase performance tests and optimization of the cloud environment are done. The following frameworks can be classified as type 3 migration models: *AWS cloud migration framework* [16], *The five step methodology to cloud migration* [4], and the *Incremental data-application cloud migration model* [1].

- **Type 4: Multiple perspective integration migration support models**

The type 4 models can be seen as a synthesis of the type 2 and type 3 models. This model explores the multiple perspectives of migration in the pre-migration stage as described in the type 3 model. A representative example is the *Cloudstep* [5] model.

9.4 DISCUSSION

In the following we extract the main findings and lessons learned, followed by the threats to validity that should be kept in mind in the interpretation of the results.

9.4.1 FINDINGS AND LESSONS LEARNED

- **The shortage of migration specialist to perform the migration increases.**

The analysis of measures and indicators revealed a comparable number of organizational and technical risks. One of the risks gaining importance over time is the need of migration specialists in the staff to both perform the migration and be able to monitor the life cycle of the application once it is migrated. This risk was first mentioned in 2010 in the works of [11]. After that it gained popularity from 2013. This risk is important to be pointed out as it defies the belief, common at the time, that outsourcing an application to the cloud is sufficient and does not require further effort.

- **Employees' resistance to migration is a prominent organizational obstacle towards migration to the cloud.**

Another prominent organizational obstacle is the staff's resistance to migration, motivated by fear of losing their job. As a result, possible risks include loss of valuable and experienced engineers and a decrease in the productivity and morale of the rest of the staff. This risk also appears as early as 2010 and has been the most often identified risk.

- **Legal restrictions on data location may prohibit migration.**

From a legal standpoint, migration is most often not possible because of the strict requirements of data location. Namely, many countries' laws require that private and sensitive data of the country and their citizens be kept within the country borders. As cloud providers expand and open more data centers, this risk is slowly, but certainly starting to disappear, at least for the larger Western countries. The appearance of this risk is evident in 2011 and 2012 and slowly disappears in 2013, just to be replaced with the general measure of the type of SLA offered by the cloud providers. The reason lies in the fact that nowadays cloud providers offer the option of keeping certain types of data within country borders and guarantee it through their SLAs. This trend explains the low number of legal risks and measures identified in the studies.

- **Better SLAs offered by cloud providers eliminate many security risks.**

The low amount of security risks can also be explained by the more detailed SLAs offered by cloud providers. Risks such as interception of infrastructure management messages in transit or private data accesses by other customers sharing the same infrastructure are explicitly engineered against by cloud providers and guaranteed in the SLAs they offer. Risks such as Denial of Service attacks cannot be avoided by cloud providers and can happen even if the application does not reside in the cloud.

- **Nowadays software license migration is done along with the migration of software.**

Another advancement, which is visible from the cloud providers' side, is the offering of easy migration of software licenses alongside the application. Cloud providers in cooperation with third party software suppliers offer cloud licenses for a small additional fee for the most commonly used support services, such as Oracle database. So if a company already has a license for a software product, it can easily move to the cloud by extending its existing license.

- **Green computing is an important additional benefit of the migration to the cloud.**

An important benefit emerging from the literature is green computing, which authors relate to energy savings. In [12], the authors enlist, among the additional resources for their study, reduced energy consumption as a benefit that leads to greener organizations. Erfan goes a step further by characterizing cloud computing as a "green IT tool for the 21st century" [9, p. 4], [3, p. 5] identify green computing as a benefit of cloud computing because cloud providers, according to them, are better at managing voltage conversions and cooling as compared to on-premise computing centers, and consequently are more energy-efficient. Furthermore, because cloud providers use virtualization of their servers, they reach better resource utilization that leads to lower energy consumption. Azarnik et al. [3] also believe that businesses today care more about the environment and run companies in a greener way, therefore it is plausible that in the near future they will turn to using cloud computing because of its (promised) green benefits.

- **Migration models vary in the focus and detail of the migration phases.**

As far as the different types of model are concerned, we could not spot any trend across different years. This may be a result of the relatively small number of primary studies. Apparently the depth in which cloud migration is considered in these models is diverse and models of all types are equally appearing in 2010, 2013, and 2014. Our suggestion, based on the primary studies, is to turn the focus to technical, financial, and organizational factors when considering cloud migration. Special care should be taken when calculating the postmigration costs from the financial aspect and the staff impact the migration may have from organizational aspect. A detailed SLA can eliminate the majority of legal and organizational risks and as such is a mandatory ingredient of any migration process. If a migration model or framework is to be used, in the initial phase (considering whether to migrate or not) models of type 1 and 2 are more suitable. When planning the migration itself, however, models of type 4 are preferable as they cover all migration phases.

9.4.2 THREATS TO VALIDITY

Even though this review was performed based on the systematic literature review guidelines provided in scientific literature (Section 9.2), there may still be some threats to its validity. In particular, the following threat to validity was identified: most studies do not have the same classification of measures and indicators or have no explicit classification at all. Therefore most of the classification done in this paper is done based on the context in which the measures are mentioned. The classification is naturally influenced by the specific context reported in the primary study. However, the authors could have defined the measures/indicators for more generic applications.

9.5 CONCLUSION

This study shows that cloud migration factors and models for software applications haven't matured, yet. However, the literature shows clear signs of the increased need for these techniques.

Multiple factors need to be considered when migrating to the cloud, which include financial, legal, security, organizational, and technical risks and benefits, as well as general measures. The field of cloud computing is maturing, and SLA offerings eliminate most security and legal concerns that were noticeable in previous years. However, these risks may still appear depending on the chosen cloud provider or the legal constraints that concern its geographical location. Migration that was once considered a one-time task has now become a long term project. This impacts the organization in multiple aspects in terms of needed technology and knowledge, financial considerations and the effect the potential migration may have on the employees.

There are four types of model for migration that either deal with the initial stage of migration and consider only one or a few aspects, or are designed to guide the whole migration, from the planning phase to postmigration management.

REFERENCES

[1] V. Aggarwal, M. Mathur, N. Saraswat, Comprehensive cloud incremental data-application migration—a proposed model for cloud migration, Int. J. Comput. Appl. Eng. Sci. 3 (1) (2013) 20.
[2] J.M. Alonso, L. Orue-Echevarria, M. Escalante, J. Gorroñogoitia, D. Presenza, Cloud modernization assessment framework: analyzing the impact of a potential migration to cloud, in: 2013 IEEE 7th International Symposium on the Maintenance and Evolution of Service-Oriented and Cloud-Based Systems (MESOCA), IEEE, 2013, pp. 64–73.
[3] A. Azarnik, J. Shayan, M. Alizadeh, S. Karamizadeh, Associated risks of cloud computing for SMEs, Open Int. J. Inform. 1 (1) (2013).
[4] J. Banerjee, Moving to the cloud: workload migration techniques and approaches, in: 2012 19th International Conference on High Performance Computing (HiPC), IEEE, 2012, pp. 1–6.
[5] P.V. Beserra, A. Camara, R. Ximenes, A.B. Albuquerque, N.C. Mendonça, Cloudstep: a step-by-step decision process to support legacy application migration to the cloud, in: 2012 IEEE 6th International Workshop on the Maintenance and Evolution of Service-Oriented and Cloud-Based Systems (MESOCA), IEEE, 2012, September, pp. 7–16.
[6] P. Brereton, B.A. Kitchenham, D. Budgen, M. Turner, M. Khalil, Lessons from applying the systematic literature review process within the software engineering domain, J. Syst. Softw. 80 (4) (2007) 571–583.
[7] A. Cardoso, F. Moreira, P. Simões, A survey of cloud computing migration issues and frameworks, in: New Perspectives in Information Systems and Technologies, Volume 1, Springer International Publishing, 2014, pp. 161–170.
[8] T. Dyba, T. Dingsoyr, G.K. Hanssen, Applying systematic reviews to diverse study types: an experience report, in: Empirical Software Engineering and Measurement – ESEM 2007. First International Symposium, IEEE, 2007, pp. 225–234.
[9] A. Erfan, Determinants of a successful migration to cloud computing in Iranian telecommunication industry, arXiv preprint, arXiv:1310.7353, 2013.
[10] A. Khajeh-Hosseini, D. Greenwood, J.W. Smith, I. Sommerville, The cloud adoption toolkit: supporting cloud adoption decisions in the enterprise, Softw. Pract. Exp. 42 (4) (2012) 447–465.
[11] A. Khajeh-Hosseini, D. Greenwood, I. Sommerville, Cloud migration: a case study of migrating an enterprise it system to IAAS, in: 2010 IEEE 3rd International Conference on Cloud Computing (CLOUD), IEEE, 2010, pp. 450–457.

[12] A. Khajeh-Hosseini, I. Sommerville, J. Bogaerts, P. Teregowda, Decision support tools for cloud migration in the enterprise, in: 2011 IEEE International Conference on Cloud Computing (CLOUD), IEEE, 2011, pp. 541–548.

[13] B. Kitchenham, Procedures for performing systematic reviews, Keele, UK, Keele University 33 (2004) 1–26.

[14] M. Razavian, P. Lago, A survey of SOA migration in industry, in: Service-Oriented Computing, Springer, Berlin, Heidelberg, 2011, pp. 618–626.

[15] N. Shalom, Moving enterprise workloads to the cloud on a massive scale. Available from, http://getcloudify.org/2012/10/30/moving_enterprise_workloads_to_the_cloud_on_a_massive_scale.html, 2012 (accessed 22 March 2017).

[16] J. Varia, Migrating your existing applications to the AWS cloud. A phase-driven approach to cloud migration, 2010.

[17] Q.H. Vu, R. Asal, Legacy application migration to the cloud: practicability and methodology, in: 2012 IEEE Eighth World Congress on Services (SERVICES), IEEE, 2012, pp. 270–277.

[18] A. Mohamed, A history of cloud computing. Available from: http://www.computerweekly.com/feature/A-history-of-cloud-computing, 2009 (accessed 11 January 2016).

[19] N. Regalado, Who coined 'cloud computing'? Available from: http://www.technologyreview.com/news/425970/who-coined-cloud-computing/, 2011 (accessed 11 January 2016).

[20] Zotero.org, computer software. Available from: https://www.zotero.org/ (accessed 15 January 2016).

[21] JabRef.org, computer software. Available from: http://www.jabref.org/ (accessed 15 January 2016).

[22] S. Keele, Guidelines for Performing Systematic Literature Reviews in Software Engineering, Technical report, Ver. 2.3 EBSE, 2007.

BIG DATA: A PRACTITIONERS PERSPECTIVE

10

Darshan Lopes, Kevin Palmer, Fiona O'Sullivan
Capgemini UK, UK

Big data has only recently come into common parlance and been accepted as a recognizable IT discipline over the past few years.

It could be argued that it represents the next major paradigmatic shift in Information Systems thinking. Big data solutions represent a significant challenge for some organizations. There are a huge variety of software products, deployment patterns and solution options that need to be considered to ensure a successful outcome for an organization trying to implement a big data solution.

With that in mind, the chapter will focus on four key areas associated with big data that require consideration from a practical and implementation perspective:

(i) Big Data is a new Paradigm – Differences with Traditional Data Warehouse, Pitfalls and Considerations.

(ii) Product considerations for Big Data – Use of Open Source products for Big Data, Pitfalls and Considerations.

(iii) Use of Cloud for hosting Big Data – Why use Cloud, Pitfalls and Considerations

(iv) Big Data Implementation – Architecture definition, processing framework and migration patterns from Data Warehouse to Big Data

10.1 BIG DATA IS A NEW PARADIGM – DIFFERENCES WITH TRADITIONAL DATA WAREHOUSE, PITFALLS AND CONSIDERATION

Wikipedia defines big data as:

Big data is a broad term for data sets so large or complex that traditional data processing applications are inadequate. [1]

It is generally described by the following characteristics known as the 3 V's – Volume (quantity of data), Velocity (speed at which it is generated), Variety (different types of data).

10.1.1 DIFFERENCES WITH TRADITIONAL DATA WAREHOUSE

Big data is very different from processing within a traditional data warehouse. These differences are highlighted in Table 10.1.

	Traditional data warehouse	Big data
Table 10.1 Differences between traditional data warehouse and big data		
Data format	Structured	Combination of structured and unstructured
Data types	Fixed format	Fixed format, audio, video, PDF, XML, JSON, Binary files + flexible formats
Data size	Typically terabytes	Petabytes and beyond
Storage	Relational data stores	Distributed file system
Operations	Known operations using SQL	Flexible queries using SQL + NoSQL
Repositories	Often fragmented multiple warehouses	Single repository using the concept of a data lake which is constantly gathering and adding data
Schema	Static	Unstructured data, nontransactional, dynamic schemas
		Metadata-driven design
Processing scalability	Scales vertically	Massively Parallel Processing capability

Whilst traditional data warehouses provide insight into the past to answer "What has happened?", whereas big data, using advanced analytics and variety of data, tries to understand the future and to answer not only "What is happening now?" but also "What could happen?".

Big data allows the data consumers to adapt their knowledge of traditional data combined with other data sources using the following capabilities:

- Large scale analytical processing to find previously unknown trends and learnings;
- The capability for flexible queries, allowing unrestricted exploration and experimentation of existing and new data sets;
- Use of SQL (for structured and standardized) or NoSQL; or even a combination if appropriate;
- Use of commodity hardware and open source software.

10.1.2 PITFALLS

10.1.2.1 Insufficient volume of data

It is important not to think of big data just in the context of having a large data volume to manage. An organization may not have the massive volumes of raw data as, say, Twitter or LinkedIn, but it may still have large volumes of business transaction data because of the business problems it is trying to solve. Also, the organization that may not produce large amounts of data itself could benefit from external "ancillary" information to enrich its own understanding of customers, competitors, and industry-wide trends.

10.1.2.2 Not having a business challenge

An organization would benefit from focusing on its specific challenge, be it cost reduction, increasing efficiency, or uncovering new revenue streams. Once the challenge has been established, the question becomes how big data technologies can be utilized. What data sets do I need? What technologies can help? For example, a furniture company wishes to enter Far Eastern markets. By using a combination of social networks, sentiment analysis, and translation capabilities, it can find a much cheaper and quicker alternative to traditional market research enabling its marketing campaign to be quicker online, have increased flexibility and reduced financial outlay. A general principle to keep in mind is to begin with your business needs and then perform a market scan to assess available tools and data appropriate to this need. This is no different to traditional systems' development, where there is no magic shortcut.

10.1.2.3 Ignoring the data quality

The importance of data quality is directly proportionate to the type of analysis required and must be understood by the data owner. For example, data used for statutory reporting must be extremely accurate; however, data used for marketing segmentation provides a more general view and therefore would not require the same level of accuracy.

10.1.2.4 Big data can predict the future

Data alone cannot predict the future. A combination of understood data and well designed, considered analytical models can make reasonable predictions alongside defined assumptions. It is entirely within the data owner's responsibility to understand if and for how long these assumptions will be valid. In some cases very short term predictions might be more than sufficient, and new analytic models can be created continuously as requirements develop.

10.1.3 CONSIDERATIONS

- Focus on the business challenge first and then figure out the technology required to support this challenge.
- Look out for "ancillary" information from sources outside of the boundaries of your organization.
- Quality of data becomes important where the use case requires accurate outcomes from the analytics process.

10.2 PRODUCT CONSIDERATIONS FOR BIG DATA – USE OF OPEN SOURCE PRODUCTS FOR BIG DATA, PITFALLS AND CONSIDERATIONS

The number of products in the area of big data has been growing rapidly to meet the volume, speed, and complexity requirements.

10.2.1 THE USE OF OPEN SOURCE PRODUCT FOR BIG DATA

Whilst many vendor-driven products have evolved to handle analytics, it is important to consider the impact of the open source projects on the big data and analytics solution.

There are three key reasons for looking at the open source projects for the big data:

- Open source projects have been driving the innovation to meet the big data challenges by making the paradigm shift in processing of big data, i.e., taking processing to data, distributed file systems for data storage, and use of commodity or cloud hosting.
- There has been an explosion of new open source projects to meet analytics requirements.

• Cost effective compared to vendor products.

The best-known open source project related to big data processing is Apache Hadoop based on the technical paper written by Google [2]. Apache Hadoop has now spawned a number of related open source initiatives including Spark, HBase, Hive, Pig, and Avro. These Apache open source projects are driving the innovation within the big data world, processing at a faster rate than before, and producing a variety of feature rich platforms. The Apache Hadoop architecture and its ecosystem of related open source projects have become the industry standard for handling the current big data wave and the next wave, the Internet of Things.

10.2.2 PITFALLS

10.2.2.1 Not focusing on business needs and falling to the latest hype

Choosing an open source project based on hype with no business outcome in mind could end up as a costly venture for an organization. The scenario could be that open source project is not ready for enterprise scale production environment or the product does not add any value, only integration complexity. It is therefore important to understand the business problem the open source product is going solve. An organization whilst selecting the open source product needs to ask these questions: How ubiquitous is the software usage? Is it just short-term hype? Is software being used by multiple industries to solve their business problems? What is the maturity of the project? Has it gone beyond its 0.1 version and mature into 1.x or 2.x versions? Does it provide a stable version of bug-free software?

10.2.2.2 Not focusing on operational & nonfunctional requirements

It's not just the functional features that are important, operational and nonfunctional requirement assessment is crucial to successful big data delivery. Does it enable quick installation and deployment? Open source software generally is not written with ease of use in mind in terms of deployment and installation. Does it cover the required security features? Certain security features may not be available in the open source version of the software. For example, MySQL Community Edition does not provide database encryption. What is the upgrade path when new version is released? How are version upgrades managed? Does it provide backward compatibility?

10.2.2.3 Lack of sufficient document and or community base support

An organization should ask these questions: Who can provide support when it fails? What is the SLA for the fix to a bug? Are support contracts available? Is there sufficient documentation available in the open source community for this software product? How large is the community of contributors?

10.2.2.4 Not planning for separate environment to prove version compatibility

Generally, organizations tend to have development, test, and production environments. This is good if the products are relatively stable and unlikely to require frequent product upgrades. But given the rate and space of innovation in the big data products, it is more than likely that new versions with richer features will need to be installed on a frequent basis. To cater for this, organizations need to have a provision for a separate environment to prove any version compatibility proving before deploying the newer version to the development, test, and production environments.

10.2.3 CONSIDERATIONS

- There is no magic here, and good, well-founded technology selection principles still apply.
- Use open source version for quick proving but move to supported versions for product (e.g., Cloudera or Hortonworks System distribution of Hadoop) once selected.
- Conduct a capabilities gap analysis to understand the current state of products involved and gap in capability as a result of the business requirement.
- Maintain a product roadmap of the products involved in the big data solution, including features, current version and future upgrades, and any future compatibility issues.
- Maintain a separate environment to test new versions of the products and compatibility.

10.3 USE OF CLOUD FOR HOSTING BIG DATA – WHY TO USE CLOUD, PITFALLS AND CONSIDERATION

Cloud computing provides a shared multitenancy pool of processing resource to computers and other devices as the demand is required. Cloud computing can be rapidly provisioned and released to with minimal management effort and potentially reduced cost of ownership [3].

10.3.1 WHY TO USE CLOUD?

Adding "Complexity" alongside "Volume", "Velocity", and "Variety" of data, it is easy to follow the principle that to process large volumes of data requires high volume of computer processing power. There are cases where, due to the types of data being queried, the time to execute the query may be significant, and the enterprise has the choice to either accept the time to execute the query, or temporarily increase the processing capacity to reduce the time taken to execute. The cloud model enables such an increase in the processing capacity.

Here are some of the reasons why the cloud is important to big data:

Scalability – The cloud platform is highly scalable and provides the computing power required for the big data. This provides a fast capability to scale up and down as the business demands.

Pay as you go – The cloud model allows for pay-as-you-go model, which means organization only pays for the amount of resources it uses.

Low upfront cost – As a result of the data center and infrastructure already in place and the pay-as-you-go model, there is a low upfront cost, thus reducing operating costs and any high investment failure risk.

Self Service – Organizations are able to acquire the resources as needed via portal interface from the cloud provider.

It makes perfect sense to use the combination of the open source product and cloud model for the big data projects to deliver a solution, which has both cutting edge innovation and can be delivered efficiently with reduced time to market and at lower cost.

10.3.2 PITFALLS

10.3.2.1 Not knowing where the data will be stored

The data centers for the cloud will be spread across different countries and even continents. Organizations need to confirm where their data will end up, as regulatory laws may prevent data from being stored in a different country/continent.

10.3.2.2 Not understanding the SLA with the cloud provider

There should be an explicit service level agreement signed with the cloud provider describing performance, backup and recovery, availability and support.

10.3.2.3 Not understanding how to transfer data to cloud

The organization needs to ensure that the cloud provider has provided data management capability to import/export the data in a secure way.

10.3.2.4 Not knowing the processing profile required as cloud can scale

Whilst the cloud model is pay-as-you-go, it is easy to fall into a trap of paying for computing resources that the enterprise doesn't require all the time, based on lack of knowledge of the required processing resources, processing profile, and especially the design and implementation of poorly performing applications and queries. Designing with performance in mind is far easier (and in the majority of times far cheaper) than trying to add it in or apply it at a later stage. The implementation of a significant number application systems are delayed due to poor performance – it does not meet client expectations – which could have been avoided by taking the approach "design for performance."

10.3.3 CONSIDERATION

- Understand the usage and performance profile of the services being run in the cloud; understand the peaks and troughs of the processing requirements.
- When designing and building applications, performance requirements should be established and considered as early as possible in the development lifecycle.

10.4 BIG DATA IMPLEMENTATION – ARCHITECTURE DEFINITION, PROCESSING FRAMEWORK AND MIGRATION PATTERN FROM DATA WAREHOUSE TO BIG DATA

To understand what is required to implement a big data solution, it is important to understand:

- What is the typical architecture that underpins a big data solution?
- What is the processing framework involved in the big data solution?
- What are the patterns for transitioning from a data warehouse solution to a big data solution?

The diagram (Fig. 10.1) shows a typical big data architecture based on the Apache Hadoop framework.

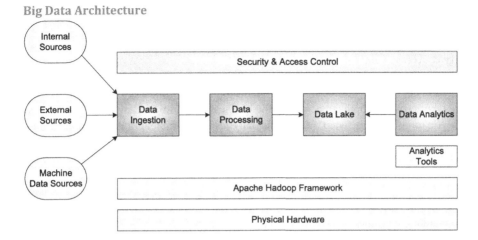

FIGURE 10.1

Big data architecture based on hadoop framework

Data Sources

The data can come from multiple sources:

- Internal – generated internally by the systems
- External – these could be social media generated or commercial packages of data or data from business partners
- Machine Data – data generated by various devices/sensors

Data Ingestion

Data Ingestion is a process of acquiring data from the sources and storing it for further processing.

Data Processing

This transforms the data to the required format or structure to make it effective for big data analytics. This is an optional step.

Data Lake

Data lake is a single repository to store all the data across the organization using a distributed file system.

Data Analytics

This is the part where analytic processing would be applied on the data stored in the data lake.

Apache Hadoop Framework

Apache Hadoop framework is one of the significant frameworks which is fast becoming a de-facto standard that provides the foundation to big data processing. It consists of the following: (a) core modules (HDFS, Hadoop YARN, Hadoop MapReduce) and (b) other Hadoop ecosystem components (Apache Hive, Apache Pig, Apache HBase, Apache Spark).

Physical Hardware

This could be a commodity hardware or cloud infrastructure such as a service platform.

Analytics Tools

These are the analytics products which enable data analytics by providing prepackaged functions or a development framework. Examples include Revolution R, MapR, Pentaho, Tableau, Platfora.

Security & Access Control

What data security should be applied? These could be encryption or tokenization or access control.

Organizations need to think about how to secure the data in-flight or data at rest in multitenancy shared data lake across multiple teams within the business. In addition, they will have to consider what type of analytic tool stack they want. Is a single analytics tool sufficient or is there a need for a stack of analytic tools to meet the multifaceted requirement of big data analytics? Also one has to consider the approach for introducing the new analytics tool in a way that minimizes risks and also reduces time to market.

The diagram in Fig. 10.2 shows the key attributes involved in big data processing. Understanding these attributes will help in the decision making for what big data technologies and design pattern are required to handle the business requirement.

Data Ingestion Type

Is the data being ingested in a batch process or in real time?

Data Ingestion Pattern

How is the data being ingested? Does it involve transferring files, using messages, connecting to RDBMS or via machine events?

Data Ingestion Frequency

How frequently is the data being ingested?

Data Format

What data formats are involved? These could be:

- Structured – predefined or dynamically created schema due to consistent structure, e.g., XML, Delimited files, JSON object.
- Unstructured – when it is not easy to define a schema, e.g., PDF, Audio files, Video files, picture, social media discussions.

Data Analytics Type

What type of analytics is required on the ingested data? Do we require text, visual, sentimental, or predictive analytics?

Data Types

What type of data is involved? These could be:

- Metadata – this is the contextual information of the ingested data.
- Full Record – this is the master data with full details.
- Full Cutover – full copy of the data.
- Delta – only changed attributes or records.
- Event – event generated by devices/sensors.

Data Analytics Type

What type of analytics is required on the ingested data?

Big Data Processing Framework

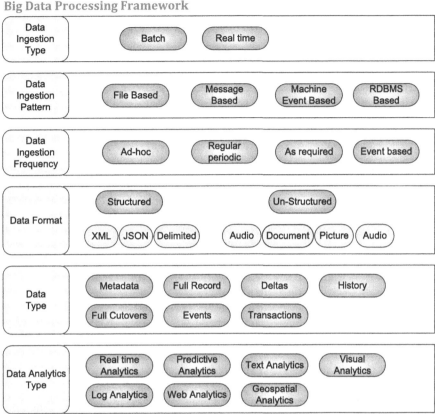

FIGURE 10.2

Big data processing framework

The above framework provides a way to understanding the impact on type of analytics tools required. Is there more focus on visual analytics, for example? It can also be used to understand the impact on the capacity of the infrastructure required by getting a view on the ingestion type and ingestion frequency. If the organization is using a system integrator or hosting on the cloud, this framework will help to think about the SLA required on the infrastructure.

10.4.1 PATTERNS FOR TRANSITIONING FROM DATA WAREHOUSE TO BIG DATA

The traditional data warehouse solution might look as depicted in Fig. 10.3.

The transition to a big data solution could be done via the following patterns:

1. Augmenting the big data solution within the data warehouse solution
2. Using only the big data solution
3. Adopting a hybrid model with coexisting data warehouse and big data solutions

FIGURE 10.3

Traditional data warehouse solution

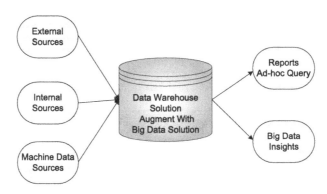

FIGURE 10.4

Big data solution added to a data warehouse solution

1. Augmenting the big data solution within the data warehouse solution

The existing data warehouse solution could be augmented with the big data solution to handle multiple data sources. (See Fig. 10.4.)

Pros:

- Consistent solution
- Minimal impact to existing business service

Cons:

- Licence cost
- Limits on the scalability
- Retained dependency on the legacy solution

Risk Profile

- **Medium Risk** as a result of new technology infusion with old technology

2. Using only the big data solution

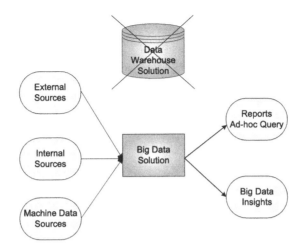

FIGURE 10.5

Single data by decommissioning of data warehouse solution

The existing data warehouse solution could be decommissioned and the new big data solution implemented to handle insights as well as reporting. (See Fig. 10.5.)

Pros:

- Simplifies the IT estate
- Highly scalable
- Commodity hardware

Cons:

- Significant impact to existing business service
- All eggs in one basket

Risk Profile

- **High Risk** as a result of dependency on a single solution for data queries/analytics

3. Adopting a hybrid model with coexisting data warehouse and big data solutions

The existing data warehouse solution could be retained alongside the new big data solution. (See Fig. 10.6.)

Pros:

- Minimal impact to existing business service
- Separation of responsibilities
- Commodity hardware and scalable

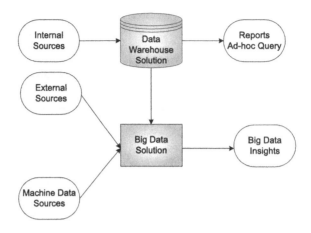

FIGURE 10.6

Hybrid model

Cons:

- Higher cost as a result of maintaining two solutions

Risk Profile

- **Low to Medium Risk** depending on how quickly the big data solution is implemented

Each big data transition pattern has pros and cons associated with it. An organization may want to take a full transformational approach or have high risk appetite and as a result choose the high risk pattern of the single big data solution to cover all use cases. Ultimately, the choice of the pattern selected by the organization depends on (a) risk appetite and (b) funding availability.

10.5 CONCLUSION

This is a significant growth area within the IT industry. As more data is captured and made available to be analyzed, more tools are being developed and released onto the market to exploit the data. Some of these tools are open source, some are open source with vendor-provided support, and others need specific software licence.

The most important "V" of the big data is finding the value in the data. There is no magic bullet for getting the right big data implementation. But using a combination of business problem focus, open source solution, power of the cloud, and understanding the transition to big data architecture can accelerate the journey and minimize the investment risk.

REFERENCES

[1] https://en.wikipedia.org/wiki/Big_data.
[2] http://research.google.com/archive/gfs.html.
[3] https://en.wikipedia.org/wiki/Cloud_computing.

TECHNOLOGIES

A TAXONOMY AND SURVEY OF STREAM PROCESSING SYSTEMS

11

Xinwei Zhao*, **Saurabh Garg***, **Carlos Queiroz**†, **Rajkumar Buyya**‡

**School of Engineering and ICT, University of Tasmania, Tasmania, Australia* †*The Association of Computing Machinery (ACM), Singapore* ‡*Cloud Computing and Distributed Systems (CLOUDS) Laboratory, School of Computing and Information Systems, The University of Melbourne, Australia*

11.1 INTRODUCTION

Every second an incredible amount of data is being generated around the world. According to [13], the world has created 90% of all its data in the last two years. Such staggering number indicates that the data nowadays is not only large in its size but also implies the fast speed in its generation and changes. The amount of data generated is so large that it is not only difficult to manage but also process using traditional data management tools. This data is referred as big data in today's context. There are two fundamental aspects that have changed the way data needs to be processed and thus needs a complete paradigm shift: the size of data has evolved to the amount that it has become intractable by existing data management systems, and the rate of change in data is so rapid that processing also needs to be in real-time. To tackle the challenge of processing big data, MapReduce framework was developed by Google, which needs to process millions of webpages every second. Over the last five years with the availability of several open-source implementations of this framework such as Hadoop [34], it has become a dominant framework for solving big data processing problems. However, recently it was observed that "Volume" is not the only challenge of big data processing and that the speed of data generation is also an important challenge that needs to be tackled for processing sensing data which is continuously being generated [8]. There are a number of applications where data is expected to be ingested not only in high volume but also with high speed, requiring real-time analytics or data processing. These applications include: stock trading, network monitoring, social media based business analytics, and so on. More specifically, there is a high demand of real-time data processing on the Internet or in sensors-related business models as the data generated need to be analyzed dynamically. For example, Google needs to count the clicks of websites in real time to decide which webpages are popular, and then use this information to leverage the advertisement fees to earn benefits. Besides, there is also a value associated with each dataset that varies with time. For example, static pages may have validity/value for some months; blogging may have for days, and Twitter messages may be valuable for less than a day. To process and analyze a data set which is changing in its value/validity quite fast, it is not productive to apply traditional method of "store and then analyze later" approach. The reason for this is obvious: firstly, such a large amount of data itself is not easy to manage, and secondly, by the time one will start the analysis, data may lose its value. Since the data almost needs to be processed in a real-time manner, the latency in processing the data should be quite low when compared to batch data processing systems such as Hadoop.

The limitation of the previous approach in managing and analyzing high volume and velocity data in real-time has led to development of sophisticated new distributed techniques and technologies. The processing of data with such features is defined as *"data stream processing"* or *"stream processing"* or sometimes called stream computing. The research in the area of stream processing can be divided into three areas:

- Data stream management systems where online query languages have been explored;
- Online data processing algorithms where the aim is to process the data in single pass; and finally
- The stream processing platforms/engines, which enable implementation and scaling of stream processing-based applications.

Given the high business demand of stream processing platforms, in this chapter, we are specifically focused on the analysis of different stream processing platforms/engines and developing taxonomy of their different features. Current stream processing platforms/systems borrow some features from dataflow systems developed in the 1960s to low level signaling networks developed during the 1980s [38], and then from data stream management systems developed during the 1990s. Stream processing platforms enable specifically the execution and deployment of real-time data processing applications in a scalable and fault-tolerant manner.

In recent years, due to different challenges and requirements posed by different application domains, several open source platforms have emerged for real-time data stream processing. Although different platforms share the concept of handling data as continuous unbounded streams, and process them immediately as the data is collected, they follow different architectural models and offer different capabilities and features. For both research and business communities who want to adopt the stream processing technology, it is important to understand what capabilities and features different stream platforms offer to its end users.

There are several studies that have been conducted on stream processing platforms and large-scale computing platforms. For example, Jagmohan Chauhan et al. [11] have conducted an assessment on Yahoo! S4's technical performance regarding its scalability, loss of events, and fault tolerance. The Samza team performed its own comparison of Samza with other platforms such as Storm and Spark Streaming. Chen et al. [12] have also proposed a brief survey of stream computing platforms such as S4 and Storm. However, currently there is not a single study that synthesizes the features of different stream processing systems and developed a comprehensive set of standard criteria for evaluating and understanding those platforms particularly from point of view of both technical and business issues such as cost. In this chapter, the basic research question that we are answering is *"how to develop a framework that can help the end users to classify different data stream processing platforms using their different characteristics."*

Therefore, to fill this gap, in this chapter, we propose a taxonomy of different features of stream processing platforms that are important from both research and business perspectives. The taxonomy is then used to compare existing stream processing systems to survey current research developments and enable identification of possible future development. As it is not easy to get access to commercial stream processing platforms, the proposed taxonomy is derived after studying different open-source platforms including Data Stream Management Systems (DSMS), Complex Event Processing (CEP) systems, and stream processing systems such as Storm.

The rest of the chapter is organized as follows. Section 11.2 gives a brief background about Stream processing systems/engines. In Section 11.3, we present the taxonomy and different set of criteria that has been utilized to build the taxonomy. Section 11.4 presents a survey of stream processing platforms and other closely related platform. Section 11.5 presents the comparison between the platforms. Section 11.6 concludes the chapter with future directions and research questions.

11.2 STREAM PROCESSING PLATFORMS: A BRIEF BACKGROUND

The stream processing research area has a long history of development that started at least five decades ago. The topics that underpin it include distributed computing, parallel computing, and message-passing. Stephens [38] shows that the earliest research about stream processing can be tracked back to the 1960s in the form of dataflow systems or data management systems. However, during that period only some theoretical development took place without any implementation of a dataflow management system. In the late 1960s, the primary solutions for dataflow management were Database Management Systems (DBMSs) [4], but there were some starting developments to integrate features required for the data streams with the design models of DBMSs. For example, some DBMS at that time implemented a distributed network model in which the different nodes in the network were used to undertake different computational tasks [4]. In the 1970s, researchers proposed new approaches to describe and process dataflow. In 1974, the first dataflow programming language, Lucid, was introduced to allow for limited use of data streams [6]. One important contribution of that decade is the Kahn's Processing Network (KPN) that proposed a distributed computing network model. In the same year, Kahn [18] introduced a network processing model for modeling distributed systems, particularly using First In, First Out (FIFO) communicating channels. The FIFO communication strategy which represents a queuing behavior of input data has been one of the dominant data scheduling strategies over the years. Other than modeling a distributed system, KPNs model was also proven to be useful for modeling signal processing system, which is generally recognized as another early version of stream processing platform [38].

The 1980s was a decade of the booming development of stream processing theory, during which another significant concept, namely synchronous concurrent computation, was introduced [38]. The term synchronous concurrent computation is another way of saying parallel computing. This technology further led to the new advancements in data management technologies to enhance efficiency of different queries, named as reactive systems [38]. The reactive systems used highly concurrent lightweight message passing to quickly respond to the input data events from sensors. The real time behavior of data ingestion components in the reactive systems is one of the most remarkable characteristics of todays' stream processing platforms. In the early 1990s, another development began in the area of DBMS that was started to serve the requirements of applications such as network traffic analysis where data is generated in real time, and continuous queries were required. This development led to introduction of features such as continuous querying, temporal data models which were integrated in the form of Data Stream Management Systems (DSMS). These systems allow persistent queries on both continuous, real-time stream of data and standard database tables. The key feature of these systems is that data can be queried on the fly before it is stored permanently.

The development of these topics progressed during the last five decades, and not until recently that they grew both theoretically and physically mature enough to construct a modern blueprint of Stream processing systems that we are using today. Stream processing platforms are designed to run on top of distributed and parallel computing technologies such as clusters to process real-time stream of data. Dataflow has always been the core element of stream processing system. *Data Streams* or *Streams* in the stream processing context refers to the infinite dataflow within the system. Logically, a stream processing platform is a message-passing system [11], whose data processing activities are driven by the owing data [9] so that the topic of data passing and dataflow management have been drawing all the attention of stream processing researchers over the years.

11.2.1 REQUIREMENTS OF STREAM PROCESSING PLATFORMS/ENGINES

Stream processing is also a solution for the management of big data using different approach than that of batch processing. Michael et al. [39] proposed a general set of requirements for data stream processing engines, which are listed as follows:

- (R1) Keep the data moving: Keep latency at absolute minimum by processing data as soon as captured.
- (R2) Handle stream imperfections: Provide built-in features for handling missing or out-of-order data.
- (R3) Query using SQL on Streams: Allow SQL queries on data streams to build extensive operators.
- (R4) Generate predictable outcomes: Be able to provide guaranteed repeatable and predictable results.
- (R5) Integrate stored and streaming data: Be able to combine different data streams from external sources ingested with different speed.
- (R6) Guarantee Data safety and Availability: Provide fault tolerance features to ensure continuous processing of data.
- (R7) Partition and scale applications automatically: Distribute data and process among multiple processors/CPUs/nodes.
- (R8) Process and respond instantaneously: Achieve the real-time response with minimal overhead for high-volume data streams.

Most stream processing systems are built more or less based on these requirements and essentially work with moving data (data streams) and do the processing in the memory. For example, Yahoo! S4 is claimed to have features like real-time response, as well as being distributed, fault-tolerant, scalable, and pluggable [11] that address the requirements R1, R3, R4, R6, R7, and R8. However, there requirements are not necessarily perfectly encompassed by a stream processing platform as a whole since some of them are in conflict with each other. Bockermann [9] states that the activity of guaranteed data safety and availability (R2) will raise the cost of computation and storage performance, which eventually compromises the throughput of dataflow, eventually leading to adverse effects on latency and real-time response (R1, R8). These conflicting requirements result in some differences in the way they have been emphasized in different stream processing platforms. But in general these requirements are commonly addressed in the design of today's stream processing engines. In addition to these requirements, there are other requirements that are essential both from developer and business perspective before any stream processing platform/engine is adopted for organizational use. Our proposed taxonomy concerns not only the technical design of a stream processing engine, but also tries to point out the criteria essential for commercial adoption. The additional requirements that can be used for the comparison of different stream processing platforms will be discussed in the later sections.

11.2.2 GENERIC MODEL OF MODERN STREAM PROCESSING PLATFORMS/ENGINES

The modern stream processing platform/engine is built on top of distributed and parallel computing technologies. The typical distributed and parallel computer architecture, arranged as a cluster, can be found in all modern stream processing systems like Yahoo! S4, Twitter Storm, and LinkedIn Samza [11,29,33].

The cluster computing technology allows a collection of connected computers to work together providing adequate computing power for the processing of large datasets. Such a feature is so important for stream processing platforms that clusters have become one of its necessary modules for processing high velocity big data. A typical stream processing platform ingests data from external sources such as Facebook, Twitter and databases, and delivers processed results either back to storage or to be published on an online system (or website). Yahoo! S4 [11] is good example where a computer cluster is utilized for large real-time dataset processing. In the example, the S4 platform uses an additional adapter to preprocess raw input data into data events for the cluster with the purpose of better scheduling of event processing tasks [11]. The figure presents an external view of a stream processing platform which can be regarded as a general structure model.

A stream processing platform, in its nature, is a data-passing system, thus the execution module of a stream process platform/engine can be modeled using the dataflow from the sources where data is ingested to the sink which will output the processed data. However, the dataflow in stream processing is quite different from the one in batch processing. According to Babcock et al. [7], the stream processing platforms differ in the following ways:

- Source: data arrives from online sources rather than physical storage like disk or memory.
- Order: Data order and event processing order cannot be controlled by the system.
- Size: data streams are potentially infinite in size, being continuous dataflow.
- Retrieval: data elements generally will be discarded after processing, making it hard to retrieve.

Because of these different features, stream processing systems cannot be designed using the conventional relation model for data management, which is more suitable for the management of static and stored content [7]. Thus, stream processing requires a dynamic model for data management and processing since a stream processing system is in its nature a message-passing system and its activities like programming are driven by the data [9]. As a result, a typical stream processing engine consists of three fundamental elements with respects to the dynamic nature of stream processing system: a source which allows external data passing into the system, a processing node where computation activities are performed, and a sink that passes the processed data out of the system. Fig. 11.1 [9] shows the mechanism of how each individual element addresses the issue of passing data, while in Fig. 11.2, a model combining all the elements shows dataflow execution within a typical stream processing platform.

These elements can be found in all the surveyed stream processing platforms, but some may use a different set of terminology to describe such elements. For instance, while Spring XD inherits totally

FIGURE 11.1

The concept of a data source and a processing node

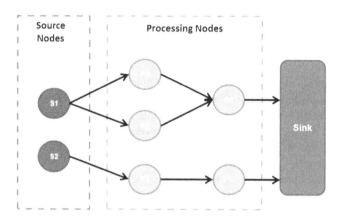

FIGURE 11.2

Dataflow model of a stream processing platform

the same nomenclature, Twitter Storm [29,43] uses spouts for naming the sources, and bolts for the processing nodes.

These different elements are connected following a hierarchical model shown in Fig. 11.2, and each of them implements different stream processing components to perform their specific function. For example, a source node implements an event scheduler to allocate input data tasks to appropriate processing nodes in the cluster, while the processing nodes implements applications to consume and process the data. A real world example is Samza, which uses Apache YARN to perform the tasks like data ingestion and scheduling, while in its cluster, machines will use the "Samza API" to process data events [33].

11.3 TAXONOMY

In the previous section, we gave a general overview of the requirements and design concepts of modern stream processing platforms. However, as mentioned in the previous section, the existing stream processing platforms/engines differ from each other by emphasizing on different processing requirements. Such differences will make the selection of an appropriate stream processing platform difficult. In this section, a taxonomy framework is proposed to characterize and classify various features of stream processing platforms based on two primary aspects as shown in Fig. 11.3: functional and nonfunctional

FIGURE 11.3

High level classification of stream processing platforms

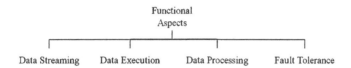

FIGURE 11.4

Functional aspects

aspects. The ultimate goal of our research is to provide a solution for better stream processing platform selection, so that taxonomy has been developed considering both functional and nonfunctional aspects of a stream processing platform. The functional criteria are from a stream application perspective and are about the technical aspects of the stream processing platforms, i.e., what features they have and how they perform. The nonfunctional criteria are related to the qualities of the systems and services other than their functional performances.

11.3.1 FUNCTIONAL ASPECTS

Christian Bockermann [9] identifies two basic functional components of stream processing platforms as:

1. A queueing or message passing component that is responsible for the communication between processing nodes; and
2. An execution component that provides the runtime and environment for the execution of processing nodes.

In this chapter, an extended taxonomy (Fig. 11.4) of stream processing platforms' technical aspects is proposed, in which Issue 1 has been identified as Data Streaming, and Issue 2 has been divided into two parts as Data Execution and Data Processing. In addition, we identified that the issue of fault tolerance is becoming extremely important to today's stream processing platforms, thus it is regarded as one of their fundamental functionalities, which in Bockermann's survey was studied as one of the challenges in stream processing under the discussion of execution environment.

11.3.1.1 Data streaming

As mentioned earlier, a stream processing system is logically a message-passing system, which means that the communication between different stream processing modules is critical to the entire performance of a stream processing platform. There are two fundamental considerations in relation to

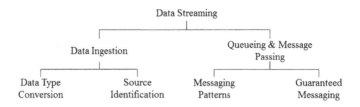

FIGURE 11.5

Data streaming criteria

data streaming. One is the ingestion of data, and another is the queuing & message passing (see Fig. 11.5). Data ingestion is about how to collect data from external sources, while queuing and message passing provides the communication channels which connect different nodes within the system.

Data ingestion. Data ingestion is related to collecting data from identified sources, but it is different from data collection. The difference lies in the additional activity of formatting the data. The ingestion process often involves the addition and alteration of data content and format with the purpose to use it properly later. The reason for this is that at present, the data that are about to be processed presents a high diversity in their types, while a stream processing platform can process only a few particular types of data. This conflicting situation requires the data being processed satisfy the type requirement of stream processing platforms, so that a process of type identification and conversion is needed by a stream processing platform. Currently, some messaging systems, such as Apache Kafka [27], Apache Flume [22], and ZeroMQ [2], provide this type of conversion service as one of their fundamental components to their users whose time is saved from developing special programs to ingest data from conventional sources such as TCP sockets and HTTP POSTs [37]. Data ingestion process involves another functionality, which is acknowledged as the identification of data sources. In general, there are two types of data sources: stored data and streaming data. Although stream process platforms are primarily designed for the processing of large streaming datasets, sometimes stored data is needed to conduct a comprehensive data analysis. Michael Stonebraker et al. [39] use terms "past" and "present" to describe the features of these two categories of data respectively. They imply that in some cases (e.g., in the analysis of "unusual" events) the integration of both "past" and "present" data is so important to the data analysis that they list it as one of the basic requirements of stream processing platforms (R5). Thus, the data ingestion process of a stream processing system should not only be able to ingest real-time data from online sources, but also to ingest data from physical data storage, such as disks and hard drives.

Queueing & message passing. Queueing and message passing is responsible for the communication between different stream processing modules. In Twitter Storm, the streaming modules, spouts and bolts are connected by communication channels provided by ZeroMQ messaging library [26]. In a real-world perspective, different stream processing platforms/engines implement different messaging systems with various patterns of messaging. For distributed architecture, there are four typical message patterns which are widely used [21]:

- *PAIR:* message communication is established strictly within one-to-one peers.

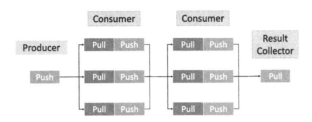

FIGURE 11.6

Push/pull messaging pattern

- *Client/Server:* messages are distributed from server according to the requests sent from clients.
- *Push/Pull (pipeline):* enables the distribution of messages to multiple processors, arranged in pipeline.
- *Publish/Subscribe:* enables the distribution of messages to specific receivers who are interested in the massage content rather than the senders of message.

However, not all of the message patterns are suitable for stream processing which needs to handle high velocity and volume data. For example, the PAIR message pattern's passes messages on one-to-one basis that limits the distribution of large volume of messages. Thus, this pattern is not suitable for a processing node that requests specific data from sources due to unpredictable nature of data content and format. Compared to PAIR and Client/Server, the remaining two patterns do not have the above mentioned problem, making them a common choice of stream processing systems. Push/Pull pattern is a one-way stream processing pattern, in which the downstream nodes will be invoked whenever the upstream nodes finish processing of tasks [28]. As shown in Fig. 11.6, streams go through several processing stages, with no messages' sending upstream.

Pub/Sub is so far the most popular messaging pattern. There is a long list of queueing and messaging systems using pub/sub pattern, such as RabbitMQ [32], Open AMQ [46], Apache ActiveMQ [35], and Apache Kafka. These messaging systems share a common feature that they all have a broker that manages the distribution of messages. In a pub/sub system, streams are called topics. Specifically, a broker is a program that will function like a mediator, which matches the topics subscribed by receivers to the topics published by producers. Fig. 11.7 presents the role of brokers in pub/sub messaging system. Each application could be either the publisher or the subscriber, and the broker will transmit the topics from the publish end to the subscription end.

11.3.1.2 Data execution

A stream processing platform/engine must have an execution component that arranges the data events to appropriate processing nodes. As shown in Fig. 11.8, data execution can be divided into different components such as the scheduling, the scaling, and the distributed computing of data events.

Scheduling. Falt and Yaghob [16] observed that the operation order of processing applications is "closely related to the utilization of the hardware components", indicating that the outcome of the task scheduling will consequently influence the overall performance of the stream processing system. In general, most stream processing platforms, thus, have adopted some scheduling solutions. For exam-

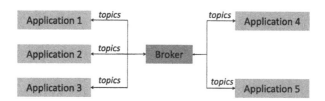

FIGURE 11.7

Pub/sub messaging pattern with a broker

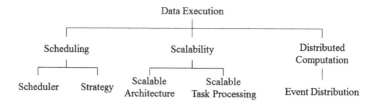

FIGURE 11.8

Data execution criteria

ple, Apache Samza is using the Resource Manager provided by YARN, which contains a pure scheduler application that allocates the computation resources [33], while Yahoo! S4 does not use a scheduler application but use Keys to correlate the processing elements to corresponding processing nodes [11]. Other than the scheduling system, the scheduling strategies will also impact the system's performance in terms of queue size, latency, and data throughput. A stream processing system should allow the users to implement the scheduling strategies, or provide options for users to change the strategy implementations. We survey that there are three commonly applied scheduling strategies:

1. *FIFO:* a scheduling strategy which is the acronym of First-In-First-Out, with which the data events are processed in the sequence of their arrival [25].
2. *Capacity:* a strategy that guarantees the minimum capacity of queue processing, while if there are available resources, it will allocate it to the waiting queues to enlarge its capacity.
3. *Fair:* a strategy that allocates almost the equal capacity to each active task slot, making each job get approximately the same amount of processing time and resources [34].

There is no best strategy or best scheduler. Jiang and Chakravarthy [25] state that, although the FIFO strategy enables high throughput and low latency scheduling pattern, it did not consider the optimal utilization of hardware resources (e.g., CPU, memory, etc.). However, they observed that the capacity-based scheduling strategy may suffer from the overflowing buffer of data events if the volume of tasks is high. Thus, instead of predetermining a scheduling strategy, it is a better solution to allow users to make the decision. For example, Apache Samza has provided a pluggable API to enable the users to integrate their custom scheduler applications [33]. Other streaming engines, like Spark Streaming and Spring XD, enable users to develop scheduling strategies based on their own scheduler patterns (Batch Scheduler, and Cron Scheduler) [37,48], and Twitter Storm which used to use Nimbus to schedule tasks [29] has now the feature of a pluggable scheduler.

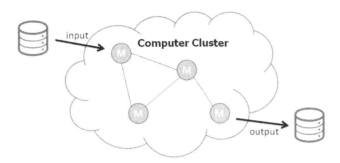

FIGURE 11.9

Simple model of a distributed system

Scalability. Scalability refers to the ability of a multiprocessor system to handle the increasing amount of tasks, or the ability to enlarge the system itself to tackle the growth of tasks [10]. Scalability is one of the most important requirements in the age of big data because systems need to handle the pressure from incoming high volume data sets. A scalable system should scale both in its architecture and its data processing capacity. A scalable architecture connotes that the system can manage the growth of processing nodes without technical and functional errors, such as data loss and node failures. The important challenge faced by a scalable system is the coordination of the nodes within the expanding network to minimize the loss of data, and the monitoring of the status of each node to avoid the risk of significant node failure [47]. Most of the current stream processing platforms such as Storm, S4, Spark Streaming, and Samza provide scalable systems that allow the enlargement of their architectural topology. The scalable capacity, or scalable task processing, is a result of the enlargement of architecture. With added machines, a cluster should be able to perform more tasks with higher throughput.

Distributed computation. Distributed computation is the key component of data execution in stream processing. It is a hard fact that a stream processing system must be a distributed system, which is defined as a collection of independent computers that appears to its users as a single coherent system [42]. Network technologies are applied to realize such coherency by connecting machines within a cluster. In practice, distributed computing in stream processing is responsible for the allocation of jobs and the coordination of the machines in order to perform the event processing in a concurrent manner. It is the core and the foundation of a stream processing platform, the key to realize the processing of lager volume big data. Although different stream processing platforms are different in the design of their cluster topology, the designs are all built up on top of a distributed system pattern shown in Fig. 11.9. Machines in a distributed computer cluster are autonomous and execute the applications whenever events arrive. For example, Yahoo! S4 is using the keyed attributes as the trigger of operations so that a processing node (machine) can autonomously execute the application if an event with corresponding keyed attribute arrives [31].

11.3.1.3 Data processing

The data processing component of a stream processing platform is a group of programs and applications that is implemented on the computing machines to perform tasks like processing and analysis. The most

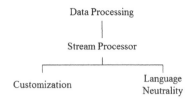

FIGURE 11.10

Data processing criteria

important part of data processing in stream processing platforms is the stream processor, which in its nature is a program that can access the streams and invoke appropriate processing applications based on its algorithmic coding, as shown in Fig. 11.10.

Stream processor. The term "stream processor" has a different meaning from commonly understood meaning of processors as central processing unit (CPU) or graphics processing unit (GPU). The latter processors are physical, while the stream processor refers to a programing code that provides the communication between data streams and stream processing applications to perform processing. Such a program is also known as application programming interface (API), which is defined as a language and message format used by an application program to communicate with the operating system or some other control program such as a database management system (DBMS) or communications protocol. However, a real time stream processing system does not necessarily include a DBMS or APIs to enable ingestion of the data stream directly. For example, Twitter's streaming API provides connection from user's node to the Twitter's stream of tweet data, whose process is like downloading an infinite file. The stream processor can be described further using two aspects: customization and language neutrality. The stream processing platforms should allow users to develop custom processing applications on their nodes so that they can perform analysis in accordance to their expectations. Currently, all of the surveyed platforms in this chapter provide this feature that allows the users to write streaming applications based on provided patterns. For example, Spark Streaming provides Spark's language-integrated API to users which supports common programming language Java and Scala [36].

The application development using APIs should be compatible with different languages to allow users with different ability to harness the power of stream processing platforms. We choose to call this compatibility as "language neutrality" referring to how many different programming languages a stream processing platform accepts. Java is currently being the most popular programming language which is supported by all the surveyed stream processing platforms, primarily because of its features being simple, stable, and sustainable. Other popular languages used for steaming API and application development include Scala, Python, and so on, among which JVM-based languages take up a significant proportion.

11.3.1.4 Fault tolerance

The fault tolerance is identified as one of the most important requirements and a challenge for stream processing systems. Fault tolerance is the concept that is derived from the design of a distributed system, which considers that the failure of a single or multiple processing nodes should not impact the correct operation of the entire system. Conventionally, fault tolerance is described as a system's ability

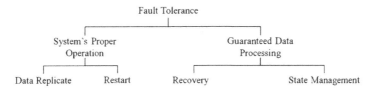

FIGURE 11.11

Fault tolerance

to replicate important data before a failure happens, and to restart the failed node to make it functional again. However, currently fault tolerance also includes a new concept of guaranteed data processing, which ensures the data will be fully processed even though a failure happens. Briefly speaking, fault tolerance concerns two things: the proper operation of the entire system and the guaranteed processing of data messages, as shown in Fig. 11.11. The fault tolerance design of a distributed system has to handle different failure situations to maintain proper operation of the system. In a distributed architecture, there will be two situations of failure: the failure of centralized components within the cluster, which are commonly known as the processing nodes, and the failure of parallel applications that perform data processing, which run on the worker nodes within the cluster [29,44]. While a node within the cluster fails, the primary solution is that the system should be able to replicate the key data and reassign the data processing tasks to another node. However, if an application fails to respond, the system should be able to restart the node that runs the application, in order to recover the application from complete failure.

Besides the correct operation, fault tolerance in a stream processing system also guarantees the completeness of message processing, which means that it tries to prevent the system from losing data. Guaranteed data processing is actually a guarantee of the message delivery in each surveyed platform. For example, Twitter Storm uses the combination of Kestrel queue and time-out function to manage the state of message, in which the message will not enter the processing stage until the previous message has been fully processed, or fail to process completely within given timeout [29]. Other platforms may use a messaging system such as Kafka [27] to guarantee that the message is delivered at least once. The "at least once" messaging approach ensures that there is no data loss, but it is likely to cause duplication in some fault scenario, in which the same message could be sent twice to the consumer [33].

11.3.2 NONFUNCTIONAL ASPECTS

While the functional requirements concern the technical behavior of a stream processing system, nonfunctional requirements concern the results and effects of its behavior. Nonfunctional requirements define the overall qualities or attributes of the resulting system, and they include safety, security, reliability, and some management issues such as costs, time, and schedule. The most important nonfunctional criteria for selection of a stream processing system are cost, technical support, and the user community (see Fig. 11.12).

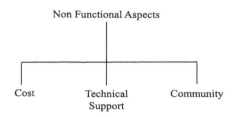

FIGURE 11.12

Nonfunctional aspects

FIGURE 11.13

Stream processing platforms' cost

11.3.2.1 Cost

The cost of a stream processing platform consists of several components; each refers to different usage stage. As shown in Fig. 11.13, installation, development, and maintenance are the three basic stages that a system has to go through, and each of them involves a significant amount of cost. Installation cost includes the licensing cost and installation support cost. However, as the target systems in our survey are all open-source, there is no licensing cost for each of them, but still it is important to include such cost into the study because it will help in development of a decision making framework that can be generalized to suit the selection of all kinds of stream processing platforms. Also it may include the cost of hiring a specialized professional for installation support. For example, the average on-going development and maintenance cost of Apache Storm [26] counts to about US $1,700 million per three years [24], which is so significant figure that a consumer cannot neglect. Among the cost, payments to experts and experienced personnel take up the largest proportion.

There will be development and maintenance costs after the installation of a stream processing platform. Users have to develop applications on top of the platforms to fit their particular purpose for big data analytics. The primary activities involved in the development stage include planning and programming, which requires the involvement of professional personnel whose payments take up the largest proportion of development cost. Besides, the stream processing platform is a complex system consisting of numerous hardware and software, which requires careful and on-going maintenance to ensure its proper operation. The implementation of a stream processing platform is always an important decision from a long-term perspective, so that users have to carefully address the problem before selecting one solution.

11.3.2.2 Technical support

Technical support is the service that the stream processing platform developer can offer to users. Similarly to how we classify the cost, a classification of technical support is based on the stages involved, as shown in Fig. 11.14. From the users' perspective, the essence of technical support is the availability

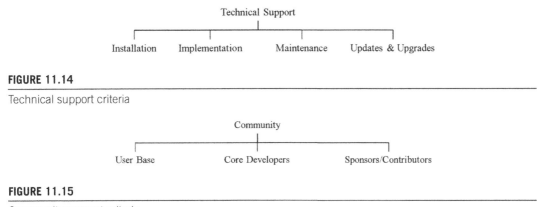

FIGURE 11.14

Technical support criteria

FIGURE 11.15

Community support criteria

of instruction and consultation that can be offered by the platforms' technical team or the community. Besides, how convenient it is for the consumers to reach the support is another consideration. In short, technical support is one of the most important factors that contribute to the overall customer satisfaction, which from a commercial perspective indicates whether a platform is successful or not.

11.3.2.3 User community

One also needs to study the community support available for the stream processing platforms. There are three primary communities included in the community aspect: the user community, the developer community, and the contributor community, as shown in Fig. 11.15. These communities can provide essential support in regards to the issues such as development, operation, and maintenance of the stream processing platforms. The user base of a platform reflects its popularity. The difference of popularity between each platform is very likely to be a result of the comparison of their functionalities. A larger user base always means that there will be more feedback about a particular platform that a user can access and utilize. Feedback is extremely meaningful when users attempt to gain deep insight into the platform's performance from either the advantageous or the disadvantageous side. The core developers and contributors of a stream processing platform will be the source of supporting information. Users can acquire technical information like manual, update, and upgrades from these sources, and sometimes users can ask for a change or update in case of issues such as bugs or their individual use case.

11.4 A SURVEY OF STREAM PROCESSING PLATFORMS

In the previous section, we presented a taxonomy framework that can be used to judge the functional and nonfunctional features of a stream processing platform. As we always stressed, the goal of our research is to enable future development in this research area and also to enable selection of proper stream processing system based on user's need. In this section, we conduct a survey of different stream processing platforms based on our proposed taxonomy. The survey includes three versions of stream processing systems: Data Stream Management System (DSMS), Complex Event Processing (CEP) system, and stream processing platform/engine. All of them can be identified as a stream processing system, but they differ in their goals. DSMS aims to handle the continuous online queries with pre-defined query language like CQL [17], which are more closely related to that of a DBMS. Complex event processing systems have a higher goal to identify the important events through stream data analytics. Both DSMS and CEP systems tackle a limited range of data types [5,30]. The stream processing platforms in general can handle a broader range of different formats.

11.4.1 DATA STREAM MANAGEMENT SYSTEMS

The Data Stream Management Systems (DSMS) are the earliest version of the stream processing systems. They encompass the functions of a conventional database management system (DBMS), but further offer the ability to execute continuously incoming data queries to enable real-time data processing. The evolution of DSMS from DBMS is a result of the world's demand for high velocity data querying, especially in the industries where sensors are heavily used [17]. DSMS is not the key focus of this article; one can find more details about DSMS from the following references. Arasu et al. [5] give a detailed introduction about the models and issues related to Data Stream Management Systems which is a valuable reference of the important concepts related to DSMSs. Geisler further presents the general architecture of DSMS [17]. There are several other data stream management systems that are developed for different purposes. For instance, there is a distributed spatiotemporal DSMS named PLACE which is used for monitoring moving objects, and XStream is used for the tracking and processing of signals [45,19]. Other systems, like Borealis, NILE and Medusa, are designed as general purpose data query processing DSMSs [20,1].

11.4.2 COMPLEX EVENT PROCESSING SYSTEMS

The Data Stream Management System provides a solution for real-time data query processing. However, as DSMS handles only generic data without identifying interesting situations known as events. Thus, the Complex Event Processing (CEP) systems have been developed for this purpose. In [14], the improvements of CEP upon DSMS have been explained in detail; however, the most essential development in CEP systems is that they associate semantics with the data so that the system can detect, filter, and combine the data, or so-called event notifications from external sources to understand the events. Compared to generic queries answered by DSMS, events are higher-level analytics results which enable people to better understand their environments and take appropriate actions.

Though CEP is not capable of processing of unstructured data compared to stream computing platforms, it is efficient in analyzing the structured or semistructured data. Currently there are many CEP systems that are available for either business or research purpose, e.g., Oracle Event Processing, Microsoft StreamInsight [3], SQLStream s-Server [23] and StreamBase [40]. Besides the systems introduced above, there are other CEP platforms that share a similar set of characteristics, such as Esper, Cayuga, and Apama [15,41]. These systems have a bit different architecture than those surveyed, but overall they are all following the same concept of a stream processing system.

11.4.3 STREAM PROCESSING PLATFORMS/ENGINES

11.4.3.1 Apache storm

Storm is a distributed stream processing platform that was originally created by Nathan Marz and then acquired by Twitter who turned Storm into a free and open source streaming engine. Currently the Storm project is undergoing incubation in the Apache Software Foundation, sponsored by the Apache Incubator. Storm's architecture model is commonly known as topology, which mostly follows the general pattern we mentioned in the previous sections. The source node in Storm is named spout, which emits data into the cluster. Processing nodes in Storm are called bolts. The data stream in storm is an unbounded sequence of tuples having a formatted structure. Storm topology is a parallel architecture in which nodes execute concurrently to perform different tasks. Users can specify the degree of parallelism for each node to optimize the resources spent on tasks with different complexity.

11.4.3.2 Yahoo! S4

S4 (Simple Scalable Stream Processing System) is a distributed real-time data processing system developed by Yahoo. Yahoo! S4 architecture is inspired by the MapReduce model. However, unlike MapReduce which has a limitation on scaling, Yahoo! S4 is capable of scaling to a large cluster size to handle frequent real-time data [11]. Similar to other distributed and parallel systems, Yahoo! S4 has a cluster consisting of computing machines, known as processing nodes (PNs). A processing node is the host of processing elements (PEs) which perform data processing tasks on events. The data stream within S4 is a sequence of events. The adapter is responsible for the conversion of raw data into events before delivering the events into the S4 cluster. When a processing node receives input events, it will assign it to associate PE via the communication layer. ZooKeeper plays a role as PN coordinator to assign and distribute events to different PEs in different stages.

11.4.3.3 Apache Samza

Samza is the stream processing framework of LinkedIn, and it is now another incubator project of Apache Software Foundation. The platform is scalable, distributed, pluggable, and fault tolerant, and it has recently released its new version as an open source project. However, the new version has some limitations on its fault tolerance semantics according to the Samza development team. The framework is highly integrated with Hadoop YARN, the next generation cluster manager, so that the architecture of Samza is very similar to that of Hadoop. Samza consists of three layers: a streaming layer, an execution layer, and a processing layer [33]. Samza heavily relies on dynamic message passing and thus includes a message processing system like Kafka, adopted for data streaming.

11.4.3.4 Spring XD

Spring XD is a unified big data processing engine, which means it can be used either for batch data processing or real-time streaming data processing. It is now licensed by Apache as one of the free and open source big data processing systems. The goal of Spring XD is to simplify the development of big data applications. The Spring XD uses cluster technology to build up its core architecture. The entire structure is similar to the general model discussed in the previous section, consisting of a source, a cluster of processing nodes, and a sink. However, the Spring XD is using another term called XD nodes to represent both the source nodes and processing nodes. The XD nodes could be either the entering point (source) or the exiting point (sink) of streams. The XD admin plays a role of a centralized tasks controller who undertakes tasks such as scheduling, deploying, and distributing messages. Since

Spring XD is a unified system, it has some special components to address the different requirements of batch processing and real-time stream processing of incoming data streams, which refer to taps and jobs. Taps provide a noninvasive way to consume stream data to perform real-time analytics. The term noninvasive means that taps will not affect the content of original streams.

11.4.3.5 Spark streaming

Spark Streaming is an extended tool of the core Spark engine to enable this large-scale data processing engine to process live data streams. The role of Spark Streaming is very similar to the client adapter used by Yahoo! S4. Currently, Spark Streaming is developed by Apache Software Foundation, which is responsible for the testing, updates, and release of each Spark version. It is important to know that Spark Streaming is not the data processing engine. The engine is named Apache Spark, but without Spark Streaming the engine cannot perform real-time data analytics. Spark Streaming runs as a filter of streams that divides the input streams into batches of data, and dispatches them into the Spark engine for further processing. The Spark engine consists of many machines to form a computing cluster, which is used in a similar manner as in other surveyed platforms. The most special feature of Spark Streaming is how it treats data streams. The data streams within Spark Streaming are called discretized streams, or DStream, which is, in fact, a continuous sequence of immutable datasets, known as Resilient Distributed Datasets (RDDs). All RDDs in a DStream contain data within certain interval, so that they can be clearly separated and ordered for parallel processing.

11.5 COMPARISON STUDY OF THE STREAM PROCESSING PLATFORMS

In this section, we combined all the information we collected to perform a comparison study of all the surveyed stream processing platforms. The criteria used for the comparison are based on our proposed taxonomy framework. Tables 11.1–11.4 give an overview of the features of all surveyed platforms. Due to unavailability of public data for nonfunctional aspects such as cost, these tables only reveal the differences for all the functional criteria. In the following section, we compare different stream processing systems emphasizing metrics such as Scalability, Messaging and Distribution, and Fault Tolerance.

11.5.1 SCALABILITY

The scalability of a stream processing platform is represented by its ability to integrate and coordinate new processing nodes, as well as the ability to partition the tasks to newly added machines. As shown in Table 11.1, although all the streaming engines claim to be scalable, the ways they scale are slightly different. The first difference is the complexity of scalability. Storm, Samza, Spring XD, and Spark Streaming all allow users to add nodes dynamically, and the engine will automatically define the parallelism for the new nodes. In contrast, Yahoo! S4 requires a redefinition of the nodes' parallelism before they can be added into the cluster, which adds up to the difficulty of scaling.

Table 11.1 Comparison based on data execution

| System | | Scheduling | Scalability | | Distributed computing |
		Scheduler	Scalable architecture	Scalable task processing	Distributed event processing
DSMS	STREAM	Global scheduler with round-robin scheme	X	X	X
	Aurora	A state-based scheduler & a feedback-based scheduler	X	X	X
Complex event processing system	SQLStream	A user-defined scheduler	✓	✓	✓
	Oracle event processing	Oracle enterprise scheduler	✓	✓	✓
	Microsoft StreamInsight	StreamInsight scheduler	✓	✓	✓
	StreamBase CEP	–	✓	✓	✓
Stream processing platform	Apache storm	Nimbus	✓	✓	✓
	Yahoo! S4	–	✓	✓	✓
	Apache Samza	YARN	✓	✓	✓
	Spring XD	Cron scheduler	✓	✓	✓
	Spark Streaming	Batch scheduler	✓	✓	✓

(Table header spanning: Features → Data execution, with Scheduling, Scalability, Distributed computing as sub-groups)

11.5.2 MESSAGING & DISTRIBUTION

As shown in Table 11.2, the surveyed platforms differ in their concept for messaging, though the publish/subscribe approach is the most popular and adopted by three of them (Samza, Spring XD, and Spark Streaming). The advantage of pub/sub pattern messaging is that it can handle the complexity of input messages from different sources. Differently, Storm and S4 use pipeline pattern for message passing, while Storm is a pull model and S4 is a push model. Both models ensure a fast and direct passing of messages, with low latency. However, the pipeline being a form of linear transmission method makes it unsuitable for distribution of a highly complex volume of messages, compared to pub/sub pattern which is using a broker to coordinate the events according to the demands of users.

11.5.3 DATA PROCESSING/STREAM PROCESSORS

As discussed before, most stream processing platforms use JVM which makes Java the main language for programming new applications. However, Storm allows programming in more or less all the languages. SpringXD only allows programming of processing units using Java.

Table 11.2 Comparison based on data streaming features

Systems		Features		
		Data streaming		
		Data ingestion		Messaging & queueing
		Data type conversion	Source	Messaging queueing pattern
DSMS	STREAM	X	Stored data	push model
	Aurora	X	Streaming data, stored data	Push/pull model
Complex event processing system	SQLStream	✓	Streaming data, stored data	Kafka pub/sub model with broker
	Oracle event processing	✓	Streaming data, stored data	Point-to-point, pub/sub model
	Microsoft StreamInsight	✓	Streaming data, stored data	Push/pull model
	StreamBase CEP	✓	Streaming data, stored data	RabbitMQ pub/sub model with broker
Stream processing platform	Apache storm	✓	Streaming data, stored data	Pull model pipeline
	Yahoo! S4	✓	Streaming data, stored data	Push model pipeline
	Apache Samza	✓	Streaming data, stored data	Kafka pub/sub model with brokers
	Spring XD	✓	Streaming data, stored data	Kafka pub/sub model with brokers
	Spark streaming		Streaming data, stored data	Kafka pub/sub model with brokers

11.5.4 FAULT TOLERANCE

Fault tolerance is a necessary function of any stream platform to provide reliable processing of big data. As shown in Table 11.4, each surveyed platform in this article ensures the proper operation of the entire system whenever there is a failure of nodes. However, the platforms differ in the way they tackle the issue of data loss. All of the platforms ensure the data can be recovered from faults, but they are using different approaches to realize this goal. While Storm is using a stateless method to reprocess the duplicated data, the other four engines' approach is stateful – recovering the data from the state where the last checkpoint is tracked. In particular, Spark Streaming uses a set of high frequency checkpoints to track the state of data processing, which consequently allows a faster recovery of data as compared to the other three engines which work with checkpoints.

11.6 CONCLUSIONS AND FUTURE DIRECTIONS

Big data problems have brought many changes in the way data is processed and managed over time. Today, data is not just posing challenge in terms of volume but also in terms of its high speed generation. The data quality and validity varies from source to source, and thus are difficult to process. This issue has led to the development of several stream processing engines/platforms by different companies such as Yahoo, LinkedIn, etc. Besides better performance in terms of latency, stream processing overcomes another shortcoming of batch data processing systems, i.e., scaling with high "velocity"

Table 11.3 Comparison based on data processing			
Systems			**Features** Data processing Stream processors
		Customized operators	**Language neutrality**
DSMS	STREAM	–	CQL
	Aurora	–	–
Complex event processing system	SQLStream	–	SQL
	Oracle event processing	✓	Java. SQL
	Microsoft StreamInsight	✓	C#
	StreamBase CEP	✓	Java
Stream processing platform	Apache storm	✓	Any Programing Languages (JVM or Non-JVM)
	Yahoo! S4	✓	Java, C + +, Python, etc.
	Apache Samza	✓	Only JVM Languages
	Spring XD	✓	Java
	Spark streaming	✓	Java, Scala, Python

data. Availability of several platforms also resulted in another challenge for user organizations in terms of selecting the most appropriate stream processing platform for their needs. In this chapter, we proposed a taxonomy that facilitated the comparison of different features offered by the stream processing platforms. Based on this taxonomy we presented a survey and comparison study of five open source stream processing engines. Our comparison study provides an insight of how to select the best platform for a given use case.

From the comparison of different open source stream processing platforms based on our proposed taxonomy, we observed that each platform offers very specific special feature that makes its architecture unique. However, some features make a stream processing platform more applicable for different scenarios. For example, if the organization's data volume changes dynamically, it is better to choose a platform such as Storm which allows dynamic addition of nodes rather than Yahoo! S4. Similarly, if an organization wants to process all the data that is ingested into the system, the guaranteed data processing feature is what it should look for. In contrast to commercial offerings, organizations can save on licensing fees by using open-source platforms. However, the support given for maintenance of such platforms becomes an important factor in making decisions about adopting a particular platform. The user base and support given for each platform varies quite drastically. Storm has the largest user base and also supports services. Yahoo! S4 comes with almost no support.

Based on the survey, it also becomes clear that the performance of a stream processing system depends on multiple factors. However, the performance will always be limited by the capacity of the underlying cluster environment in which real processing is done. More or less every system that was surveyed does not allow using cloud computing resources which can scale up and down according to the volume and velocity of data that needs to be processed. Moreover, the job scheduling mechanisms used by the systems are not very sophisticated and do not take into the consideration the performance

Table 11.4 Comparison based on fault tolerance features

Systems		Features			
		Fault tolerance			
		Proper operation of the system		Guaranteed data processing	
		Replication	Restart	Data recovery	State management
DSMS	STREAM	–	–	–	–
	Aurora	–	–	–	–
Complex event processing system	SQLStream	✓	✓	✓	Stateful management using checkpoints
	Oracle event processing	✓	✓	✓	Stateful management
	Microsoft StreamInsight	✓	✓	✓	Stateful management using checkpoints
	StreamBase CEP	✓	✓	✓	Stateful management using synchronization
Stream processing platform	Apache storm	✓	✓	✓	Stateless management
	Yahoo! S4	✓	✓	✓	Stateful management using checkpoints

of underlying infrastructure which can be quite heterogeneous in some cases. In the future, we would like to conduct a cost and risk analysis of different streaming platforms and conduct a more extensive comparison study. The current taxonomy is derived after studying different open-source stream processing platforms, which limits the scope of our taxonomy. To overcome this limitation, we would also study some key commercially available stream processing platforms such as IBM Stream.

REFERENCES

[1] D.J. Abadi, Y. Ahmad, M. Balazinska, U. Cetintemel, M. Cherniack, J.-H. Hwang, et al., The design of the Borealis stream processing engine, Cidr 5 (2005) 277–289.
[2] F. Akgul, Zeromq, Packt Publishing Ltd., 2013.
[3] M. Ali, An introduction to Microsoft SQL server StreamInsight, in: Proceedings of the 1st International Conference and Exhibition on Computing for Geospatial Research & Application, 2010, p. 66.
[4] H.C. Andrade, B. Gedik, D.S. Turaga, Fundamentals of Stream Processing: Application Design, Systems, and Analytics, Cambridge University Press, 2014.
[5] A. Arasu, B. Babcock, S. Babu, J. Cieslewicz, M. Datar, K. Ito, R. Motwani, U. Srivastava, J. Widom, STREAM: the stanford data stream management system, in: M. Garofalakis, J. Gehrke, R. Rastogi (Eds.), Data Stream Management: Processing High-Speed Data Streams, Springer, Berlin, Heidelberg, ISBN 978-3-540-28608-0, 2016, pp. 317–336.
[6] E.A. Ashcroft, W.W. Wadge, Lucid, the dataflow programming language, APIC Stud. Data Process. 22 (1985).
[7] B. Babcock, S. Babu, M. Datar, R. Motwani, J. Widom, Models and issues in data stream systems, in: Proceedings of the Twenty-First ACM SIGMOD-SIGACT-SIGART Symposium on Principles of Database Systems, 2002.
[8] M. Beyer, Gartner says solving 'big data' challenge involves more than just managing volumes of data. URL http://www.gartner.com/newsroom/id/1731916, 2011.
[9] C. Bockermann, A Survey of the Stream Processing Landscape, Tech. Rep. No. 6. TU Dortmund, Germany, 2014, 5.
[10] A.B. Bondi, Characteristics of scalability and their impact on performance, in: Proceedings of the 2nd International Workshop on Software and Performance, 2000, pp. 195–203.

[11] J. Chauhan, S.A. Chowdhury, D. Makaroff, Performance evaluation of Yahoo! S4: a first look, in: 2012 Seventh International Conference on P2P, Parallel, Grid, Cloud and Internet Computing (3PGCIC), 2012.

[12] C.P. Chen, C.-Y. Zhang, Data-intensive applications, challenges, techniques and technologies: a survey on big data, Inf. Sci. 275 (2014) 314–347.

[13] M. Chen, S. Mao, Y. Liu, Big data: a survey, Mob. Netw. Appl. 19 (2) (2014) 171–209.

[14] G. Cugola, A. Margara, Processing flows of information: from data stream to complex event processing, ACM Comput. Surv. 44 (3) (2012) 15.

[15] A.J. Demers, J. Gehrke, B. Panda, M. Riedewald, V. Sharma, W.M. White, et al., Cayuga: a general purpose event monitoring system, Cidr 7 (2007) 412–422.

[16] Z. Falt, J. Yaghob, Task scheduling in data stream processing, in: Dateso, 2011, pp. 85–96.

[17] S. Geisler, Data stream management systems, in: Data Exchange, Information, and Streams, 2013, pp. 275–304.

[18] K. Gilles, The semantics of a simple language for parallel programming, in: Proceedings of the IFIP Congress, in: Information Processing, vol. 74, 1974, pp. 471–475.

[19] L. Girod, Y. Mei, R. Newton, S. Rost, A. Thiagarajan, H. Balakrishnan, S. Madden, Xstream: a signal-oriented data stream management system, in: IEEE 24th International Conference on Data Engineering, 2008, ICDE 2008, 2008, pp. 1180–1189.

[20] M.A. Hammad, M.F. Mokbel, M.H. Ali, W.G. Aref, A.C. Catlin, A.K. Elmagarmid, et al., Nile: a query processing engine for data streams, in: Proceedings of 20th International Conference on Data Engineering, 2004, 2004, p. 851.

[21] P. Hintjens, Zeromq: Messaging for Many Applications, O'Reilly Media, Inc., 2013.

[22] S. Hoffman, Apache UME: Distributed Log Collection for Hadoop, Packt Publishing Ltd., 2015.

[23] J. Hyde, Data in flight, Queue 7 (11) (2009) 20.

[24] ITG, Business Care for Enterprise Big Data Deployments: Comparing Costs, Benefits, and Risks for Use of IBM InfoSphere Streams and Open Source Storm, Tech. Rep., International Technology Group (ITG), Santa Cruz, California, 2013.

[25] Q. Jiang, S. Chakravarthy, Scheduling strategies for a data stream management system, in: Computer Science & Engineering, BNCOD, 2004, pp. 16–30.

[26] M.T. Jones, Process Real-Time Big Data with Twitter Storm, IBM Technical Library, 2013.

[27] J. Kreps, N. Narkhede, J. Rao, Kafka: a distributed messaging system for log processing, in: Proceedings of the NetDB, Athen Greece, 2011.

[28] M. Kay, You pull, I'll push: on the polarity of pipelines, in: Proc. Balisage: The Markup Conference, in: Balisage Series on Markup Technologies, vol. 3, 2009.

[29] N. Marz, Storm, Distributed and Fault-Tolerant Real-Time Computation, Tech. Rep. 2014, twitter.com: Twitter.

[30] B. Mozafari, K. Zeng, L. D'antoni, C. Zaniolo, High-performance complex event processing over hierarchical data, ACM Trans. Database Syst. 38 (4) (2013) 21.

[31] L. Neumeyer, B. Robbins, A. Nair, A. Kesari, S4: distributed stream computing platform, in: 2010 IEEE International Conference on Data Mining Workshops (ICDMW), 2010, pp. 170–177.

[32] A. Richardson, et al., Introduction to RabbitMQ. Google UK, Sept. 25, 2008.

[33] A. Samza, Samza documentation, http://samza.incubator.apache.org/.

[34] K. Shvachko, H. Kuang, S. Radia, R. Chansler, The Hadoop distributed file system, in: 2010 IEEE 26th Symposium on Mass Storage Systems and Technologies (MSST), 2010, pp. 1–10.

[35] B. Snyder, D. Bosanac, R. Davies, Introduction to Apache ActiveMQ. ActiveMQ in Action, 6–16.

[36] A. Spark, Spark streaming, https://spark.apache.org/streaming/.

[37] Spring. Spring XD guide, http://docs.spring.io/spring-xd/docs/1.0.0.M4/reference/html/.

[38] R. Stephens, A survey of stream processing, Acta Inform. 34 (7) (1997) 491–541.

[39] M. Stonebraker, U. Cetintemel, S. Zdonik, The 8 requirements of real-time stream processing, SIGMOD Rec. 34 (4) (2005) 42–47.

[40] TIBCO STREAMBASE: A real-time, low latency data processing with a stream processing engine, http://www.tibco.com/resources/demand-webinar/introduction-tibco-streambase-complex-event-processing (last accessed 05/05/2017).

[41] M. Strohbach, H. Ziekow, V. Gazis, N. Akiva, Towards a big data analytics framework for IoT and Smart City applications, in: Modeling and Processing for Next-Generation Big-Data Technologies, Springer, 2015, pp. 257–282.

[42] A.S. Tanenbaum, M. Van Steen, Distributed Systems, Prentice-Hall, 2007.

[43] A. Toshniwal, S. Taneja, A. Shukla, K. Ramasamy, J.M. Patel, S. Kulkarni, et al., Storm@ twitter, in: Proceedings of the 2014 ACM SIGMOD International Conference on Management of Data, 2014, pp. 147–156.

[44] M. Treaster, A survey of fault-tolerance and fault-recovery techniques in parallel systems, arXiv preprint cs/0501002, 2005.

[45] X. Xiong, H.G. Elmongui, X. Chai, W.G. Aref, Place: a distributed spatio-temporal data stream management system for moving objects, in: 2007 International Conference on Mobile Data Management, 2007, pp. 44–51.

[46] X. Xiong, J. Fu, Active status certificate publish and subscribe based on AMQP, in: 2011 International Conference on Computational and Information Sciences (ICCIS), 2011, pp. 725–728.

[47] P. Yalagandula, M. Dahlin, Research Challenges for a Scalable Distributed Information Management System, Computer Science Department, University of Texas at Austin, 2004.

[48] M. Zaharia, T. Das, H. Li, T. Hunter, S. Shenker, I. Stoica, Discretized streams: fault-tolerant streaming computation at scale, in: Proceedings of the Twenty-Fourth ACM Symposium on Operating Systems Principles, 2013, pp. 423–438.

ARCHITECTING CLOUD SERVICES FOR THE DIGITAL ME IN A PRIVACY-AWARE ENVIRONMENT

12

Robert Eikermann, Markus Look, Alexander Roth, Berhard Rumpe, Andreas Wortmann

Software Engineering, RWTH Aachen University, Aachen, Germany

12.1 INTRODUCTION

Interconnectivity and ubiquitous computing are key components in the forthcoming age of digitalization. To support this, and to flexibly keep up with newly arising requirements, software is continuously moving from comprehensive desktop applications to smaller services that interconnect with other services and exploit user data to provide added-value experiences. This shift raises concerns for service users and service developers. For service developers, such a change in design and architecture requires engineering of scalable systems that can be developed and maintained independently. This is reflected in the microservices paradigm currently used within many software projects. In microservice architectures, the individual services contribute small parts of domain functionality. The backbone of such microservice architectures is built up from independently functioning base services providing different platform functionality. Such architectures supply millions of users with services. To scale, cloud computing techniques are used providing the necessary scalability and elasticity. The resulting architectures can compose different services to added-value services based on large sets of user data. For service users, employing added-value services requires provision of personal data to many different, yet partially interconnected services. Each of these may store copies of the data and share this with the services they use. This requires the user to abandon control of their data as well as consistently changing their data throughout various services.

In this chapter we discuss a system-of-systems architecture that centers services around the user as opposed to provider-driven services. For creating such architecture, we support the developer with a model-driven and generative methodology supporting reuse of existing services, automated conversion between different data models, and integration of ecosystems facilitating service composition, user data access control, and user data management. To this end, we motivate the need for flexibly composable cloud services by example (Section 12.2), before we identify challenges for such architectures (Section 12.3). Afterwards, we introduce preliminaries (Section 12.4), present our conceptual building blocks for a system-of-systems architecture (Section 12.5), and explain how code generation can facilitate development of composed added-value services (Section 12.6). The subsequent sections discuss related work (Section 12.7) and our approach (Section 12.8). Finally, we conclude this contribution (Section 12.9).

Software Architecture for Big Data and the Cloud. DOI: 10.1016/B978-0-12-805467-3.00012-0

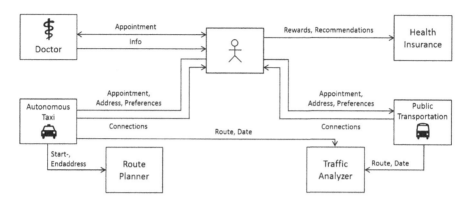

FIGURE 12.1

Overview of available services in our scenario directly or indirectly available through apps on the person's smartphone

12.2 EXAMPLE

This section gives an example scenario to demonstrate the supported forms of use cases. The overall scenario is a person who wants to simplify everyday life processes in order to improve work-life balance. To achieve this, the person already uses several specialized apps on her smartphone. Fig. 12.1 shows systems participating in this scenario. All actions are initiated by the person using her smartphone. In general the person is in good health but likes to participate in several preventive checkups that are recommended by her health insurance. As these preventive checkups often have irregular or long time intervals, her health insurance has a monolithic app where recommendations for checkups are conveniently published. This app uses the Health Insurance Service denoted in Fig. 12.1. She regularly uses this app to inform herself about upcoming preventive checkups. If an examination by her doctor is indicated by the health insurance app, she negotiates an appointment with the doctor. The doctor also has a standalone app to make appointments online. The corresponding service is the Doctor Service in Fig. 12.1. Additionally to the preventive checkup service, the health insurance company also offers a bonus program to reward health supporting behavior of its customers. Our person lives in a larger city and therefore she needs to plan carefully how to get to the doctor's office just in time for her appointment. She can choose from different available mobility offerings performed by the local public transportation company, the new car sharing company that implements a taxi service with autonomous cars or just use her own car. Depending on time and personal preferences she favors one service over the others. As denoted in Fig. 12.1 each, the autonomous taxi and the public transportation company, offer a dedicated service, which is available through a standalone app, to let customers check availability and book trips. Unlike buses, autonomous taxies don't need to stick to a predefined route, and the autonomous taxi internally uses a routing planer for the optimal driveway. The Route Planner has an integrated map annotated with additional information like special streets only available for certain types of vehicles. To overcome high exhaust fumes' concentrations in big cities, bus lanes may also become available for autonomous taxies, or streets may be closed for vehicles exceeding a certain size.

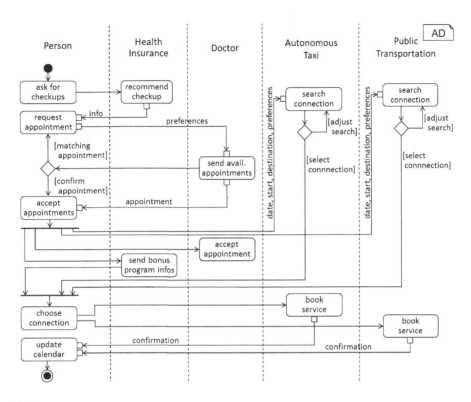

FIGURE 12.2

Activity diagram showing all steps our person has to manually to use different services

Including this, route planning becomes much more dynamic due to high flexibility of available streets. The Traffic Analyzer internally uses several data sources to calculate utilization of all streets.

This data is then extended to a utilization forecast. As a result, the Traffic Analyzer Service is able to provide detailed information about expected time adjustments for routes. In combination with the Route Planner, the Traffic Analyzer Service can be used for a better route selection and estimate the required time for a route. These two services are used in the background by the mobility apps, and our person doesn't come directly in touch with them.

Several apps available on the smartphone, bringing vital services to the users, have to be used separately. Common data must be manually shared between apps, and personal preferences are only collected specifically for each app's use cases. The person from the previously described scenario uses apps where available. In everyday life a combination of different apps and services is often desired. The composition is done manually using the smartphone. Different apps are used in specific order, and data, like personal data or results from previous service calls, is transferred from one app to another. Necessary steps in terms of data transformation and service composition are shown in Fig. 12.2 and described in the following paragraph. Each swimlane in the activity diagram in Fig. 12.2 corresponds to the respective service from Fig. 12.1.

Upcoming preventive checkup recommendations are received through the health insurance app. The person must read the information and decide if this checkup is applicable to her. If this is the case, the app connected to her doctor is used to start an appointment negotiation. In order to be able to use this app, she had to give her personal contact information to the app provider. Even worse she must put a list of her doctors at the app's disposal. This allows her to contact the doctors via the app.

To start an appointment negotiation, she must manually transfer the information from the health insurance app, check general availability in her calendar, and send the appointment request. Attached to that, she has to transfer her personal (timing) preferences into the appointment request because the app only supports appointment preferences in terms of weekdays or availability in the morning, midday or afternoon. The doctor receives this request for an appointment and can check which open slots he can offer. Our person checks if a slot fits well into her time schedule and confirms that slot if applicable. Otherwise she answers with slightly adjusted preferences maybe aiming at appointments a bit more in the future. This is repeated until a suitable slot is found and confirmed. If a suitable slot for an appointment is found, the doctor sends the appointment details to her. The appointment is then displayed in the app and the time information has to be transferred into a calendar item in her calendar app. In doing so, three subsequent steps are initialized. First, the doctor receives a confirmation which appointment was ultimately chosen, which may trigger necessary preparations for the doctor's staff. Second, the health insurance app is used to gather detailed information about available vouchers in the bonus program. Third, our person has to look how to reach the doctor's office. Several providers, like local public transportation or an autonomous taxi service, are present, and each one has a dedicated app available to inform about service details. As our person wants to compare service offerings, she has to use each app but this must be done separately. The apps need information like date and time, home- and doctor's address, and personal preferences. They are very similar for each app but have to be manually entered again. Each app presents a list of mobility offers matching her request. By manually switching between the apps, she can choose the offer most suited for her. As the health insurance app already indicated that the upcoming examination is covered by the bonus program, she does not only need to compare different offers of the mobility services, or consider which offers are eligible for the voucher. As the last option she could also user her own car. Finally, she has to book the chosen offer which includes that she has to enter her personal payment information and submit it to the service provider behind the app. Again, her personal data is spread into another system, and no integrated mechanisms allow her to keep track which data she entered where.

As shown and described in Fig. 12.2, apps on smartphones are already supporting everyday life. However, many apps lack interconnections, so that identical information must be manually transferred from app to app.

12.3 CHALLENGES

Our notion of services follows the W3C, for which "[a] service is an abstract resource that represents a capability of performing tasks that form a coherent functionality from the point of view of providers entities and requesters entities" (https://www.w3.org/TR/ws-gloss/). This entails that a service fulfills a single (coherent) functionality, it is used by requesters, and it may use different providers. Requesters and providers may be persons or other services (i.e., services are meant to be composable). Additionally, services yield a description detailing the interfaces and the semantics of the service. The interfaces define the possible interaction in terms of messages or data types consumed and produced by the service whereas the semantics of the service describes the functionality of the service and the effect of using the service. A single service is a standalone system that relies on other services to fulfill its functionality. This allows for detached development of such a service.

12.3.1 SERVICE COMPOSITION

Research and engineering in services have produced a multitude of different, hardly composable services, which require different representations of the same data types or yield incompatible interfaces [11,24]. Nonetheless, cloud-computing has brought forth a plethora of services that are in use and contribute to large cloud-based architectures. Millions of users use the added-value services of such architectures by providing their personal data to the services. The development of such added-value services, for instance, composing various mobility providers to a comprehensive mobility service is usually done for specific purposes and requires tremendous handcrafting. This is error-prone and ultimately hinders services reuse. Development, integration, and usage of reusable, privacy-aware services yield many challenges to *service developers*, *providers*, and *users*. The challenges for services providers are mainly socio-economical and hence not considered in this article.

12.3.2 TECHNOLOGY ABSTRACTION

Engineering complex services usually reuses existing technologies to avoid reinvention solutions for cross-cutting concerns, such as data distribution, persistency management, or load balancing [22,59, 40,18]. Service developers can choose various technologies to reuse from, but must comprehend and apply these concerns properly. For instance, selection of a proper data store based on the properties of collected data requires expertise in database technologies. Thus, a service developer engineering a service for a specific domain must also become an expert in cross-cutting issues. Similarly, when and how to replicate services to reduce resource consumption when the services are not demanded and to scale-up when demand is high requires proper expertise.

12.3.3 SERVICE AND DATA INTEGRATION

Service developers have the burden of freedom to select from various mechanisms to describe the interfaces of services [21]. Whichever notion is selected may hinder future composition and reuse with other services. Bridging the gap to connect services employing different interface notions requires careful handcrafting. Adapting between, for instance, time-synchronous and asynchronous services requires expertise in both interface kinds. Similarly, the adaptation of data types requested and provided by different services requires further handcrafting. For example, connecting a service requiring a person's place of residence to a service providing the person's address requires correct interpretation of both sets of fields and proper (de-)composition to enable usage of the latter service. This becomes even more complicated if various representations for the same information are available (for instance, different date formats).

12.3.4 TRUSTED USE OF PERSONAL DATA

Added-value services usually exploit (large amounts) user data to provide better user experience [53, 14,32]. However, this usually requires participating users to hand over control of their data (such as medical data or mobility preferences) to the services and subsequently controlling how the data is processed is impossible, revoking it is hardly transparent, and changing it requires to perform updates with each services that was granted a copy of the data (for instance, at user registration). For instance, if our person in the example scenario needs to change her mobility preferences, she currently would require updating this data for all mobility providers she used before. Restoring the users' control over their data and its usage is crucial for trusted added-value services of the future. Providing this data and access management in a centralized, accessible fashion reduces the redundancy of multiple data updates with each service. While the latter may be subject of the services' ecosystem, the individual services must be developed in a fashion to rely on centralized, ecosystem-provided user data only. This also ensures that services can rely on the most up-to-date data easily.

Overall challenges are that service users must be enabled to dynamically compose, specifically tailored to their needs, different monolithic services. To foster this, they have to be able to control data flow, access to data, and consistent change of their data. This includes looking up who accesses which data for which reasons, adding and revoking permissions for specific data and services, and propagate updates to all related services.

Thus, service developers of cloud-based user-centric services operating on big data have to be enabled to:

- Develop services for reuse in different contexts.
- Specify data transformation between services with different interfaces.
- Choose technology depending on the nature and properties of necessary data.
- Retrieve personal data transparently from a Digital Me without collecting superfluous identity information.

12.4 PRELIMINARIES

Large distributed systems, such as the Internet-of-Things, consist of heterogeneous, interacting, software modules that capture various domain expertise. Engineers developing services for such systems must cope with the complexity of integrating solutions formulated by respective domain experts in different general programming languages (GPLs). Integration of these solutions requires comprehension of multiple GPLs, their libraries and communication mechanisms, although these express similar concepts (such as the data types to exchange or the interfaces of services). This lack of conceptual abstraction ultimately increases engineering efforts [18].

Model-driven engineering (MDE) [56,24] is a software development paradigm that lifts abstract models to primary development artifacts. Such models can be domain-specific, focus on important concepts, and avoid the notational noise [58] of GPLs. To this effect, possible models for specific concerns are characterized by domain-specific languages (DSLs), which, for instance, capture concepts of data structures (UML class diagrams [41]), software architectures [35,36], or system behavior [1, 54]. In MDE, models are used for communication, documentation, analysis, and ultimately execution. For the latter, models are either interpreted at run-time [18,2] or translated into GPL artifacts using code generators embodying software engineering expertise [10]. As such models further can be independent of GPL details, they are available for translation into different GPLs and enable us to reuse domain expertise with different programming languages, ecosystems, and services [46]. Multiple domains, including automotive [2,26], avionics [17], robotics [6,45] have employed MDE with various success [34,57].

A prominent kind of DSLs for the description of hierarchical software architectures are architecture description languages (ADLs) [35,34]. One of these languages is the MontiArc [29] component & connector (C&C) ADL, which provides concepts for atomic components and composed components, component interfaces of typed, directed ports, and connectors between these interfaces to architecture developers. Components are black boxes that compute behavior: Atomic components either encapsulate models of other DSLs to describe their behavior or are linked to GPL artifacts [47]. Composed components contain a hierarchy of subcomponents and their behavior emerges from the interaction of their subcomponents. These subcomponents can be atomic or composed again, allowing for architectures of arbitrary complexity with direct access to specific functionality where required. The components exchange messages via their typed ports, which rely on UML/P class diagrams [48] to describe the messages' structures. The encapsulation of components and the flexibility of class diagrams enable for a detached and agile [49] development of components and facilitate a post-deployment integration. With these, service developers can engineer services as components that provide and require services via their stable interfaces of typed ports reuse other services via hierarchical composition. Consequently, cloud-based distributed systems have adopted ADLs for description of services in form of software components as well [23,11,40]. These ADLs feature modeling concepts specific to cloud-based architectures, such as replicating components of message contexts for stateless systems. However, important challenges, such as data migration and privacy-control have yet to be addressed in such systems-of-systems.

Fig. 12.3 depicts a C&C architecture that describes a public transportation service at its top and the related data structures at its bottom. The service enables users to calculate transportation plans based on starting location and destination and considers the user's personal preferences to optimize route calculation. The added-value service Public-TransportationService is composed from three other services. Two of these are specific to the public transportation service, the third (TrafficAnalyzerService) is incorporated from another service provider. This form of tight coupling via integration hides the public transport service's dependency from the traffic prediction service encapsulation ensures it appears as a single, reusable service to potential users. The service also interacts with a banking service and a persistency service (both supplied by different service provides as well) via their public interfaces of typed ports. This loose coupling enables service developers to reuse other services without changing the configuration of their services. The PersistencyService employs the replicating subcomponent Persistence, which replicates itself whenever necessary.

12.5 SYSTEM-OF-SYSTEMS APPROACH

As stated before, modern cloud-computing architectures are made up of several services [33]. These services are composed from other fundamental services to added-value service, relying on personal data. The overall service landscape of such a cloud-computing is huge and quite heterogeneous. The necessary service compositions are manually implemented and specific to the desired service combi-

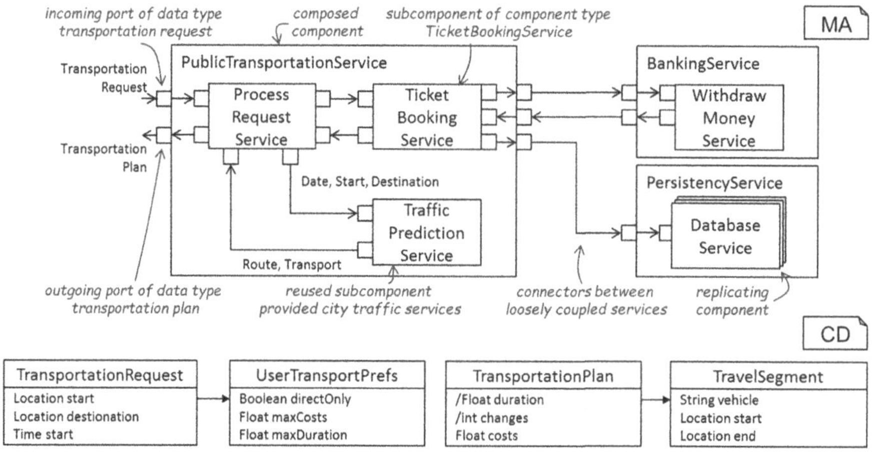

FIGURE 12.3

C&C software architecture for a public transportation service. It consists of composed and atomic components that interact via their interfaces of typed ports. The PublicTransportationService incorporates a services provided by another developer (the TrafficPredictionService) and is loosely coupled to services of other developers. An excerpt of the related UML/P class diagram data types is depicted at its bottom

nation. For alleviating the manual composition of services the different integration and communication challenges, as described have to be tackled.

For this we follow the typical distinction of Infrastructure-as-a-Service (IaaS), Platform-as-a-Service (PaaS), and Service-as-a-Service (SaaS) [59]. Within this contribution we do not consider IaaS and assume that there is always sufficient infrastructure available that can be used on demand in order to be elastic. For the distinction between PaaS and SaaS, we consider PaaS as the layer containing common services used for developing services of the SaaS layer. The SaaS Services are used by persons and typically have some sort of GUI whereas the PaaS services are used by those services in order to ease development [59]. Service provider want to offer high quality functionality, thus the services within our architecture have to be elastic regarding high workloads and responsive to provide such a quality. Furthermore, it should be developed with minimal costs. These requirements pose additional requirements to the service developer. The developer needs to increase reuse of developed services since it is not feasible to reimplement every bit of the desired functionality and the parts that have to be implemented must be easily implementable.

We consider persistency, privacy, service lookup and data transformation services as available platform services. These services can be replicated on demand but are, just like other services, developed in a standalone manner. We start out with the introduction of the Persistence service utilized by our architecture, followed by Data Conversion-, Privacy-, and Personal Data service.

12.5.1 PERSISTENCE SERVICE

The Persistence service, as shown in Fig. 12.4, offers the functionality to store data. Most applications and services need to be able to store data in order to be able to make it available again to other users or

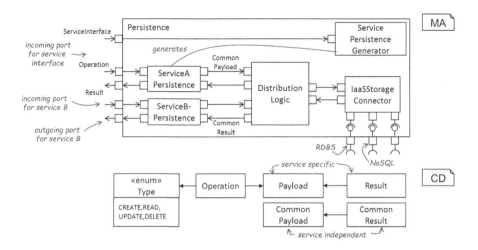

FIGURE 12.4

Persistence component realizes store and retrieve functionality for supported services. The SchedulerPartGenerator component generates a scheduler for each supported service in order to partition data to suitable database back-ends

services. In general object oriented or relational databases [31] and NoSQL databases, such as Apache Cassandra and MongoDB [50] can be distinguished. Each paradigm has its benefits and drawbacks. Relational databases, such as Oracle or PostgreSQL, are especially suited to store structured data. Most of those relational databases are able to fulfill the ACID principles [27] and can therefore ensure consistency. On the downside they may not keep up with processing a huge amount of data. Relational databases organize data in tables with different columns. Each entry of a table is represented as a row. Each data field of a data entry becomes an entry of a column in the corresponding row. Different types of data entries are stored in different tables and merged via join operations. In contrast, NoSQL databases are well suited to process large amounts of data by relaxing the CAP-theorem [8] in terms of not ensuring consistency. Thus, they are the de facto standard supporting digitalization where big data approaches become even more important. They basically provide key value storage functionality and do not support relational structures. On the downside, joins between data are costly.

Nevertheless, both approaches are not mutually exclusive. Moreover, a hybrid approach is necessary that selects the best approach for a certain type of data. This may also lead to splitting up a data model into a structured and a volume part.

The Persistence service consists of the Persistence component that contains several subcomponents, as shown in Fig. 12.4. As stated before we envision a description of a service interface in order to compose them. This description can be sent once to the persistence component where it is used as input for the ServicePersistenceGenerator. This generator generates service specific components and ports within the Persistence component. Thus, each service has an incoming and an outgoing port in order to store or retrieve data. Via the incoming port an Operation is sent. This Operation has a Type that specifies the CRUD type of the operation. Additionally, it has a service specific Payload containing the data. The service specific component ServiceAPersistence receives the Operation and transforms

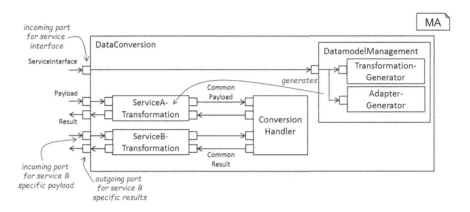

FIGURE 12.5

DataConversion component transform requested data specific to a service. DatamodelManagement component generates and instantiates specific transformation components on demand

the specific payload into a CommonPayload. This CommonPayload is passed on to the DistributionLogic component. The DistributionLogic component decides which database to use based on the incoming payload. The DistributionLogic communicates this decision to the IaaSStorageConnector that directly communicates with a database. In Fig. 12.4 three service ports are given as an example. The RDBS service port is able to store data in a relational database, and the NoSQL service port is able store data in a NoSQL database. For reading data, an Operation with Type read is sent to the Persistence component. The data is loaded into a service independent result from the database and transformed into a service specific result in the ServiceAComponent.

The Persistence service consists of service specific parts and parts necessary for fulfilling the functionality. The latter parts can be implemented once whereas the service specific parts are generated out of an abstract description of a service using the Persistence service. It should be noted that there is not one single Persistence service but several instantiations. For realizing the Digital Me, the Persistence service is necessary since it enables storing the data transparently from the location. Especially since the PersonalData service can instantiate its own Persistence service that stores data in a trusted location.

12.5.2 DATACONVERSION SERVICE

The DataConversion service, as shown in Fig. 12.5, transforms data from one data model to another. This is needed since data models typically do not match. For this the DataConversion service follows the same idea as the Persistence service that was shown in Fig. 12.4. It also uses the common interface description of a using service that can be uploaded to the DataConversion component. The description is delegated to the DatamodelManagement subcomponent that contains two different generator components: the TransformationGenerator and the AdapterGenerator. Both generator components produce parts of the service specific components contained in the DataConversion component. Such service components, i.e., ServiceATransformation and ServiceBTransformation, are located within the DataConversion component. This transformation is able to transform the service specific data model into a generic metamodel. The metamodel itself consists of a Root that contains several Components. The components are designed with a composite pattern. Thus, it has a subclass Directory that can contain multiple components and a subclass Entry that may have a Value. Each Entry has a name, each Value a name and a value. This metamodel is based on the Internet-of-Things data model [30]. The metamodel allows storing heterogeneous kinds of data by using the datatype as the Entry name and each field as a Value. This transformation from and to a metamodel is part of the generated functionality of the service specific components. They make use of the transformation into the metamodel for transforming from and to the different service data models. This is transparent to other services. Other services are able to simply use the service once they have uploaded their interface description. Thus, they can exchange data between different services. This exchange is possible since we use a generative approach, which is presented in the next section. That generative approach connects to services via the DataConversion component by interrupting the data flow with a connection from the incoming port of one service to the outgoing port of the other service. The DataConversion service that is shown in Fig. 12.5 may use the Persistence service in order to store the data of different services in a metamodel data format. The concept of transforming into the metamodel as well as the generation of such transformations has been applied in the COOPERATE research project and has been presented in [21]. It should be noted that the DataConversion service itself is stateless and may therefore have multiple instances and even its own instance of a persistence service.

Within the cloud-architecture we use the DataConversion component to interconnect different services supporting the Digital Me in composing services as needed.

12.5.3 PRIVACY SERVICE

The PrivacyService component depicted in Fig. 12.6 enables connected components to exchange data without the need to expose confidential personal data, like contact addresses. The core functionality is based on the ServiceADataDelivery component. An external component, like ServiceB, connects to the ServiceADataDelivery component port and on the other side the concrete ServiceA is connected. ServiceA has registered at the TokenRegistry and a Token is created. ServiceB uses this Token to establish a connection to ServiceA. Using this indirection in communication between components, components like ServiceA do not have to expose their personal long term contact details to foreign components. This supports the Digital Me by allowing communication by distributing tokens. These tokens could be made publicly available in order to retrieve offers from other services. Unlike the permanent contact address tokens can be easily revoked and such prevent further communication with this token. Additionally, the tokens can have attached limitations, like an expiration date, or the token can only be used by a certain components. Limitations are defined in the TokenRequest and are then connected to the resulting Token. For each component, a DataDelivery component can be generated by the DataDeliveryGenerator component.

12.5.4 LOOKUP SERVICE

The LookUp service supports finding the PersonalData services. It uses the functionality of the Privacy service to make the LookUp service publicly available without direct exploitation of the PersonalData service. Other services have to process the personal data of multiple users. For this, they have to be

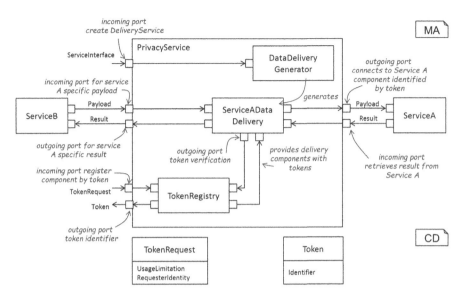

FIGURE 12.6

PrivacyService component ensures decoupled communication between components. Tokens hide away concrete identification and supports temporary access to components

able to find and address the PersonalData service of each single user. Therefore, the LookUp service gets an anonymous token under which a user is known to the service. The LookUp service is able to process this token and to return an instance of the PersonalData service of the respective user. The single services for personal data are all known to a trusted registry within the cloud-architecture described in this paper. The registry is a single endpoint known to all LookUp services. The LookUp service itself can be replicated multiple times within the architecture.

12.5.5 PERSONALDATA SERVICE

Fig. 12.7 shows the PersonalData service. This service uses the previously introduced DataConversion and Persistence services. The PersonalData service is the implementation of the Digital Me as digital representation of a user within the cloud-architecture. The service itself can be instantiated locally, e.g., on the user's phone or remote in a trusted location. Within this paper we assume that the personal data service and especially the Persistence service used by the PersonalData service run on the user's phone. It should be noted that the previously explained services are instantiated multiply. Thus, there is not one single persistence service but several, as stated before. Services querying personal data may use this service. Thus, they post a read Operation to the PersonalData component. This Operation is delegated to the data conversion where it is transformed into the data format of the personal data. The data is loaded from the respective databases transformed back and handed back to the service as a Result.

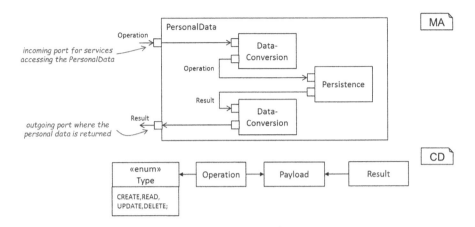

FIGURE 12.7

PersonalData component is composed of DataConversion and Persistence components, to store personal data and provide different data formats through conversions

Overall the fundamental PaaS services of the presented cloud-architecture provide a set of typically used functionality. A service that wants to use other services by composition can connect to those services via the DataConversion service which transforms the data adequately in order to communicate between the different services. If the services want to use personal data of a specific user, they can find the PersonalData service via the LookUp service. Within the PersonalData service the querying service is authenticated and authorized by the Security service. The data is loaded by the Persistence service. On its way back to the querying service the loaded data is transformed into the services data format and anonymized before it is returned. By this the service user can easily reuse the existing services and compose new services.

12.6 GENERATIVE APPROACH

The services, as described in Section 12.5, only provide basic functionality such as persistence and lookup, each of which is developed by a different service provider. In order to develop a new service for the scenario described in Section 12.2, such basic services have to be composed. However, there are two major issues that have to be tackled when developing a new service: *specification of exchanged data* and *service composition*.

Assuming the higher-level service to negotiate an appointment for a person with a doctor, the mobility service is to be developed, as shown in Fig. 12.8. The first step is to define the data that is exchanged by the involved parties. In a privacy-aware environment, users specify what information is exchanged. For example, Fig. 12.1 shows the usage scenario and what information is allowed to be exchanged. First, the doctor is allowed to use a person's address (TAddress) and negotiate appointments (Appointment). Second, a person is allowed to access the doctor's address (DAddress) but not his appointments. Third, the mobility service is allowed to use a person's address, the doctor's

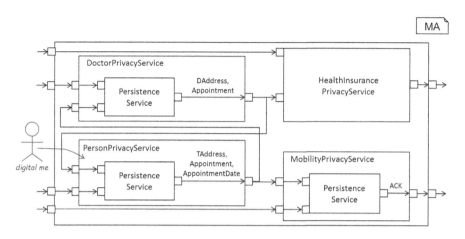

FIGURE 12.8

MontiArc model of the new higher-level service showing only the exchanged data

address, and the date of the appointment. Finally, the health insurance may access the appointment date (AppointmentDate). Such specification of the exchanged data is the foundation for the service developer to develop a new higher-level service.

The next step is the design of the architecture of the overall service by the service developer. One possible description of this new service is shown in Fig. 12.8. It is described using the MontiArc ADL. Such an abstract description can *manually* be realized by implementing the necessary functionality using the basic services. However, when manually implementing such a new service, the service developer has to write glue code for service composition and afterwards adapt services if required. Existing service composition approaches help in realizing such an implementation, such as [53,22], which give an overview of existing composition approaches.

Another way of developing a new higher-level service is a *generative approach*. The main idea is to develop such new services by systematically transforming abstract representations into executable source code. This is done by employing a *code generator*. The example shown in Fig. 12.9 shows a high-level view on the system neglecting privacy, type safety, and even communication concerns. For example, the DoctorPrivacyService requires the address in a different format, which is not considered in the high level. Clearly, such implementation details have to be implemented manually by service providers, when choosing not to use a generative approach.

In order to reduce the required implementation efforts, a generative approach can automatically synthesize a more detailed description of a service, which is based on the aggregation of basic services and respects the particular needs of each basic service. Given the abstract description in Fig. 12.8, a more detailed description as shown in Fig. 12.9 can be generated.

Using the abstract description of each basic service, which specifies how to use the service, type conversion, as well as communication conversion, can be established. For example, in Fig. 12.9 the DoctorPrivacyServiceWrapper can negotiate an appointment with the PersonPrivacyServiceWrapper only by using the LookUp service, which ensures that the digital representation of a Person is used.

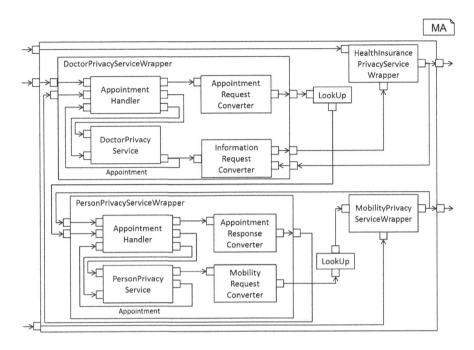

FIGURE 12.9

MontiArc model of the higher-level implementation details including data conversion and additional appointment requests

A generative approach provides essential advantages. First, for each PrivacyService shown in Fig. 12.9 a wrapper is generated, which ensures data conversion and provides additional components to implement business logic, e.g., AppointmentHandler in the DoctorPrivacyServiceWrapper. Hence, the service developer can focus on implementing business logic rather than composition of services. Conversion between different formats can automatically be ensured by adding additional components such as the AddressRequestConverter component, which concerts Appointment into the required format for the PersonPrivacyServiceWrapper component. Second, in a generative approach targeting a privacy-aware environment, additional LookUp components can automatically be added.

12.7 **RELATED WORK**

The related work of our approach domes from different research directions. In Section 12.3 we already described the challenges we faced, such as service composition, technology abstraction, service and data integration, as well as trusted use of personal data. In addition to these challenges, we make use of ADLs as well as generative approaches. For discussing related work, we keep up the identified challenges.

12.7.1 SERVICE COMPOSITION

Most approaches supporting service composition make use of plugin systems, such as OSGi [42], or other plugin architectures [5,43]. These plugin architectures consist of several plugins that are bound to other plugins at runtime. Therefore different services are able to use other services without knowing them beforehand. Typically, service lookup and discovery is done via a service registry. While there are many such architectures, OSGi is the most widespread plugin system.

12.7.2 TECHNOLOGY ABSTRACTION

The technology abstraction is achieved by making use of ADLs and generative approaches. The ADLs have already been discussed in detail in Section 12.4 where we provided preliminaries for the paper and introduced related languages and concepts. Furthermore, we employ generative approaches in order to generate technology specific code from our abstract descriptions, as it has already been proposed in [10,52,4]. However, because abstraction does not always suffice to describe the required functionality, additional approaches to integrate handwritten extensions have to be employed. A detailed overview of currently existing approaches is presented in [19,20]

12.7.3 SERVICE AND DATA INTEGRATION

There are several approaches to service and data integration in the literature. Some focus on finding a common language for modeling data, some focus on finding a common data model, while others focus on semantically integrating different data models in a highly automated fashion. A good overview is given in [28] and in [44]. As an example for approaches that aim at providing a common language for modeling data, the plethora of XML derivatives [3] and their corresponding query languages [7] has to be named. More approaches integrating data via XML are again given in [28]. Apart from that, there are approaches providing a common data model for specific purposes, resulting in different standards. Currently there are data models emerging for nearly all concerns, including Building Information Modeling [16] or sensor streams in the Internet-of-Things approaches [9], to name only a few. Additionally, many ontology approaches emerge, including ontology matching and merging approaches [38,39,13]. Other approaches focus on mapping the different data schemas in an automated fashion in order to automatically integrate the different data [37]. These approaches aim at integrating different data sources [21] or employing machine learning techniques in order to learn the mapping [12,15].

12.7.4 TRUSTED USE OF PERSONAL DATA

A similar approach to our proposed architecture is taken by the di.me project, funded by the European Union. The project focusses on an integrated personal information sphere [51]. Such a personal information sphere contains several digital faces, i.e., data the user selected for sharing with other services. The approach taken by the di.me project allows a fine-grained approach to protecting personal data. Nevertheless, the cloud-architecture in this paper focusses on the composition of services in order to support the user in a digitalized world. This of course includes protecting the information but goes beyond that. Apart from this, the di.me project focusses on a centralized data sharing platform which is a different concept from the approach undertaken within this paper. In [32] an information management assistance system is presented that allows users to find out who has which data and to monitor the data flow. The aim of the cloud-architecture presented within this paper is not only to monitor the flow of data but also to be able to change the data consistently at a single point. In [55], an architecture for privacy-enhanced mobile communities is presented. This architecture contains several services that have to adhere to the architecture specifications. Thus the services are more strongly coupled whereas our architecture aims at the integration of heterogeneous services.

12.8 DISCUSSION

Our approach enables service users to model data access without explicit knowledge about the implementation details facilitating reuse of platform independent models in an agile development environment. However, it does not ensure that the services once granted access to a specific data do neither copy it, nor pass it on. Approaches to data tracing have been presented for homogeneous, enclosed systems, such as the Android Kernel [14]. Whether their practices are feasible for heterogeneous cloud-based services is subject to current research. Having the Digital Me as a single data store for user data introduces a possible bottleneck and honeypot to the ecosystem. However, research big data management and security to fix this is ongoing.

While we presented our approach following a scenario, the approach is not limited to it. The presented basic components are generic regarding the scenario but provide necessary functionality in any software ecosystems. The presented components may not be complete and may have to be extended due to changes in technology or research. Nevertheless, the presented methodology enables providing new components. Additionally, existing components might be extended or updated due to new requirements. This has to be done by the provider of such components. Nevertheless, the design and methodology of the overall approach remain and benefit greatly from the generative approach taken. These benefits are a reduced time-to-market and a significantly improvement in certifying the generated code by certifying the code generator. However, a generative approach can only automatically synthesize wrapper components if the underlying components do exist, such as the basic components presented in Section 12.3. For instance, in cases where no converter is present in the basic services, a service shell is synthesized, allowing service providers to implement the required functionality. A possible approach is to automatically generate OSGi Plugins, which realize the conversion allowing for easy adaptation.

Another disadvantage is that, whenever additional business logic is required such as negotiation of appointments, the business logic has to be implemented manually by the service provider. However, the granularity of the employed modeling languages [25] may not provide a sufficient abstraction such that additional approaches are required to add the wanted granularity. This can, e.g., be achieved by using handwritten extensions such as proposed in [19,20], where an overview of possible handwritten extension approaches is presented.

12.9 CONCLUSION

We have presented a vision of model-driven cloud architecture engineering that relies on reusable service components. It enables developers of cloud services and architecture to efficiently build upon existing services. These services exist in the context of ecosystems providing important base services to support reuse, service composition, and user data management. For the latter, the notion of a Digital Me provides benefits for all participating roles: it facilitates data access control and data update for service users and it liberates service developers from providing data management features. Furthermore, it always yields the most up-to-data user data available. Using a generative approach, services for the digitized world can be developed on a more efficiently on a better suitable, namely higher, level abstraction. This ultimately enables each role, participating in service development, to contribute their domain expertise to dedicated challenges and facilitates service component reuse.

REFERENCES

[1] A. Angerer, R. Smirra, A. Hoffmann, A. Schierl, M. Vistein, W. Reif, A graphical language for real-time critical robot commands, in: Proceedings of the Third International Workshop on Domain-Specific Languages and Models for Robotic Systems, 2012.

[2] M. Broy, F. Huber, B. Schätz, AutoFocus—Ein Werkzeugprototyp zur Entwicklung eingebetteter Systeme, Inform. Forsch. Entwickl. 14 (3) (1999).

[3] S. Boag, D. Chamberlin, M.F. Fernández, D. Florescu, J. Robie, J. Siméon, M. Stefanescu, XQuery 1.0: An XML query language, 2002.

[4] M. Brambilla, J. Cabot, M. Wimmer, Model-Driven Software Engineering in Practice, 1st edition, Morgan & Claypool Publishers, 2012.

[5] D. Birsan, On plug-ins and extensible architectures, Queue 3 (2) (2005) 40–46.

[6] H. Bruyninckx, M. Klotzbücher, N. Hochgeschwender, G. Kraetzschmar, L. Gherardi, D. Brugali, The BRICS component model: a model-based development paradigm for complex robotics software systems, in: Proceedings of the 28th Annual ACM Symposium on Applied Computing, ACM, 2013.

[7] T. Bray, J. Paoli, C.M. Sperberg-McQueen, E. Maler, F. Yergeau, Extensible markup language (XML). World Wide Web Consortium Recommendation REC-xml-19980210, http://www.w3.org/TR/1998/REC-xml-19980210, 1998.

[8] E. Brewer, Pushing the CAP: strategies for consistency and availability, in: Computer, IEEE Computer Society Press, 2012.

[9] P. Barnaghi, W. Wang, L. Dong, C. Wang, A linked-data model for semantic sensor streams, in: Green Computing and Communications (GreenCom), 2013 IEEE and Internet of Things (iThings/CPSCom), IEEE International Conference on and IEEE Cyber, Physical and Social Computing, IEEE, 2013, pp. 468–475.

[10] K. Czarnecki, U.W. Eisenecker, Generative Programming: Methods, Tools, and Applications, Addison-Wesley, ISBN 0201309777, 2000.

[11] E. Cavalcante, A.L. Medeiros, T. Batista, Describing cloud applications architectures, in: Software Architecture, Springer, Berlin, Heidelberg, 2013.

[12] A. Doan, P. Domingos, A.Y. Halevy, Reconciling schemas of disparate data sources: a machine-learning approach, SIGMOD Rec. 30 (2) (2001) 509–520.

[13] L. Ding, P. Kolari, Z. Ding, S. Avancha, Using ontologies in the semantic web: a survey, in: Ontologies, Springer, US, 2007, pp. 79–113.

[14] M. Dam, G. Le Guernic, A. Lundblad, TreeDroid: a tree automaton based approach to enforcing data processing policies, in: Proceedings of the 2012 ACM Conference on Computer and Communications Security, 2012.

[15] A. Doan, J. Madhavan, P. Domingos, A. Halevy, Learning to map between ontologies on the semantic web, in: Proceedings of the 11th International Conference on World Wide Web, ACM, 2002, pp. 662–673.

[16] C. Eastman, C.M. Eastman, P. Teicholz, R. Sacks, K. Liston, BIM Handbook: A Guide to Building Information Modeling for Owners, Managers, Designers, Engineers and Contractors, John Wiley & Sons, 2011.

[17] P.H. Feiler, D.P. Gluch, Model-Based Engineering with AADL: An Introduction to the SAE Architecture Analysis & Design Language, Addison-Wesley, 2012.

[18] R. France, B. Rumpe, Model-driven development of complex software: a research roadmap, in: Future of Software Engineering (FOSE '07), 2007.

[19] T. Greifenberg, K. Hölldobler, C. Kolassa, M. Look, P. Mir Seyed Nazari, K. Müller, A. Navarro Perez, D. Plotnikov, D. Reiß, A. Roth, B. Rumpe, M. Schindler, W. Wortmann, A comparison of mechanisms for integrating handwritten and generated code for object-oriented programming languages, in: Conference on Model-Driven Engineering and Software Development, SciTePress, 2015.

[20] T. Greifenberg, K. Hölldobler, C. Kolassa, M. Look, P. Mir Seyed Nazari, K. Müller, A. Navarro Perez, D. Plotnikov, D. Reiß, A. Roth, B. Rumpe, M. Schindler, W. Wortmann, Integration of handwritten and generated object-oriented code, in: Model-Driven Engineering and Software Development Conference, in: CCIS, vol. 580, Springer, 2015.

[21] T. Greifenberg, M. Look, B. Rumpe, K.A. Ellis, Integrating heterogeneous building and periphery data models at the district level: the NIM approach, in: Proceedings of the 10th European Conference on Product and Process Modelling, ECPPM 2014 – eWork and eBusiness in Architecture, Engineering and Construction, Vienna, Austria, CRC Press/Balkema, Netherlands, 2014.

[22] M. Garrigam, C. Mateos, A. Flores, A. Cechich, A. Zunino, RESTful service composition at a glance: a survey, J. Netw. Comput. Appl. 60 (2016).

[23] M.J. Hadley, Web Application Description Language (WADL), Sun Microsystems, Inc., 2006.

[24] C. Herrmann, H. Krahn, B. Rumpe, M. Schindler, S. Völkel, Scaling-up model-based-development for large heterogeneous systems with compositional modeling, in: Proceedings of the 2009 International Conference on Software Engineering in Research and Practice, vol. 1, 2014.

[25] A. Haber, M. Look, P. Mir Seyed Nazari, A. Navarro Perez, B. Rumpe, S. Völkel, A. Wortmann, Integration of heterogeneous modeling languages via extensible and composable language components, in: Conference on Model-Driven Engineering and Software Development, SciTePress, 2015.

[26] F. Höwing, Effiziente Entwicklung von AUTOSAR-Komponenten mit domänenspezifischen Programmiersprachen, in: INFORMATIK 2007: Informatik trifft Logistik. Band 2. Beiträge der 37. Jahrestagung der Gesellschaft für Informatik e.V. (GI), 24.–27. September 2007 in Bremen, Deutschland, 2007, pp. 551–556, http://subs.emis.de/LNI/Proceedings/Proceedings110/article1774.html.

[27] T. Härder, A. Reuter, Principles of transaction-oriented database recovery, in: ACM Computing Surveys, ACM, 1983.

[28] A. Halevy, A. Rajaraman, J. Ordille, Data integration: the teenage years, in: Proceedings of the 32nd International Conference on Very Large Data Bases, VLDB Endowment, 2006, pp. 9–16.

[29] A. Haber, J.O. Ringert, B. Rumpe, MontiArc – architectural modeling of interactive distributed and cyber-physical systems, 2012.

[30] IoT.est, Internet of things environment for service creation and testing (IoT.est). Available at: http://ict-iotest.eu/iotest/, 2013.

[31] A. Kemper, A. Eickler, Datenbanksysteme: Eine Einführung, Oldenbourg Verlag, 2011.

[32] S. Labitzke, Who got all of my personal data? Enabling users to monitor the proliferation of shared personally identifiable information, in: Privacy and Identity Management for Life, Springer, Berlin, Heidelberg, 2011.

[33] M.W. Maier, Architecting principles for systems-of-systems, in: INCOSE International Symposium, 1996.

[34] I. Malavolta, P. Lago, H. Muccini, P. Pelliccione, A. Tang, What industry needs from architectural languages: a survey, IEEE Trans. Softw. Eng. 39 (6) (2013).

[35] N. Medvidovic, R.N. Taylor, A classification and comparison framework for software architecture description languages, IEEE Trans. Softw. Eng. 26 (1) (2000) 70–93.

[36] N. Medvidovic, E. Dashofy, R.N. Taylor, Moving architectural description from under the technology lamppost, Inf. Soft. Technol. 49 (1) (2007) 12–31, http://dx.doi.org/10.1016/j.infsof.2006.08.006.

[37] T. Milo, S. Zohar, Using schema matching to simplify heterogeneous data translation, VLDB J. 98 (1998) 24–27.

[38] N.F. Noy, M.A. Musen, SMART: automated support for ontology merging and alignment, in: Proc. of the 12th Workshop on Knowledge Acquisition, Modelling, and Management (KAW'99), Banf, Canada, 1999.

[39] N.F. Noy, M.A. Musen, The PROMPT suite: interactive tools for ontology merging and mapping, Int. J. Hum.-Comput. Stud. 59 (6) (2003) 983–1024.

[40] A. Navarro Pérez, B. Rumpe, Modeling cloud architectures as interactive systems, in: MDHPCL@ MoDELS, 2013.

[41] Object Management Group, OMG unified modeling language (OMG UML), Infrastructure Version 2.3 (10-05-03), 2010.

[42] OSGi Alliance, OSGi Service Platform, Release 3, IOS Press, Inc., 2003.

[43] J. Rathlev, Anwendungsentwicklung mit Plug-in-Architekturen: Erfahrungen aus der Praxis, in: Software Engineering, 2011, pp. 183–196.

[44] E. Rahm, P.A. Bernstein, A survey of approaches to automatic schema matching, VLDB J. 10 (4) (2001) 334–350.

[45] A. Ramaswamy, B. Monsuez, A. Tapus, Model-driven software development approaches in robotics research, in: Proceedings of the 6th International Workshop on Modeling in Software Engineering, ACM, 2014.

[46] J.O. Ringert, B. Rumpe, A. Wortmann, Multi-platform generative development of component & connector systems using model and code libraries, in: ModComp Workshop 2014—1st International Workshop on Model-Driven Engineering for Component-Based Systems, Valencia, Spain, in: CEUR Workshop Proceedings, vol. 1281, 2014.

[47] J.O. Ringert, B. Rumpe, A. Wortmann, Language and code generator composition for model-driven engineering of robotics component & connector systems, J. Softw. Eng. Robot. 6 (1) (2015) 33–35.

[48] B. Rumpe, Modellierung mit UML: Sprache, Konzepte und Methodik, 2nd edition, Springer, Berlin, 2011.

[49] B. Rumpe, Agile Modellierung mit UML: Codegenerierung, Testfälle, Refactoring, 2nd edition, Springer, Berlin, 2012.

[50] E. Redmond, J. Wilson, Seven Databases in Seven Weeks: A Guide to Modern Databases and the NoSQL Movement, Pragmatic Bookshelf, 2012.

[51] S. Scerri, R. Gimenez, F. Herman, M. Bourimi, S. Thiel, Digital.me – towards an integrated personal information sphere, in: Proceedings on the Federated Social Web Summit, 2011.

[52] T. Stahl, V. Markus, Model-Driven Software Development, John Wiley & Sons Ltd., 2006.

[53] S.E. Tbahriti, C. Ghedira, B. Medjahed, M. Mrissa, Privacy-enhanced web service composition, IEEE Trans. Serv. Comput. 7 (2) (2014).

[54] U. Thomas, G. Hirzinger, B. Rumpe, C. Schulze, A. Wortmann, A new skill based robot programming language using UML/P statecharts, in: ICRA IEEE International Conference on Robotics and Automation, IEEE, 2013, pp. 461–466.

[55] M. Tschersich, C. Kahl, S. Heim, S. Crane, K. Böttcher, I. Krontiris, K. Rannenberg, Towards privacy-enhanced mobile communities—architecture, concepts and user trials, J. Syst. Softw. 84 (11) (2011) 1947–1960.

[56] M. Völter, T. Stahl, J. Bettin, A. Haase, S. Helsen, K. Czarnecki, B. von Stockfleth, Model-Driven Software Development: Technology, Engineering, Management, Wiley, 2013.

[57] J. Whittle, J. Hutchinson, M. Rouncefield, The state of practice in model-driven engineering, IEEE Softw. 31 (3) (2014).

[58] D.S. Wile, Supporting the DSL spectrum, J. Comput. Inf. Technol. 9 (2001).

[59] Q. Zhang, L. Cheng, R. Boutaba, Cloud computing: state-of-the-art and research challenges, J. Internet Serv. Appl. 1 (1) (2010).

REENGINEERING DATA-CENTRIC INFORMATION SYSTEMS FOR THE CLOUD – A METHOD AND ARCHITECTURAL PATTERNS PROMOTING MULTITENANCY

13

Andrei Furda*, **Colin Fidge***, **Alistair Barros***, **Olaf Zimmermann**[†]

**Science and Engineering Faculty, Queensland University of Technology (QUT), Brisbane, QLD, Australia*
[†]*University of Applied Sciences of Eastern Switzerland (HSR FHO), Rapperswil, Switzerland*

13.1 INTRODUCTION

The Software-as-a-Service (SaaS) deployment model in cloud computing has revolutionized the way enterprises use software applications. SaaS and cloud computing have opened paths to new and unique business opportunities for both large enterprises and start-ups [31,38].

SaaS applications reach their full potentials with respect to cost efficiency and on-demand elasticity when they support *multitenancy* at the application level, i.e., *native multitenancy*. This chapter focuses on this native multitenancy at the application level (as opposed to multiple-instance multitenancy at the virtualized infrastructure level). Multitenant SaaS applications enable multiple groups of consumers (e.g., organizations, departments) to simultaneously access and share application instances [11]. A multitenant SaaS deployment often reduces software maintenance and deployment costs compared to multiple-instance applications that would require a separate application instance for each particular tenant [1,6].

Many traditional enterprise applications were developed before the cloud and SaaS era and were intended to be used by a single organization. Therefore, such applications usually do not support multitenancy. Nevertheless, the combination of a typically large financial investment in legacy enterprise applications, on the one hand, and the high benefits expected from the SaaS business model, on the other hand, motivate architects to reengineer existing enterprise applications to support multitenancy and to deploy them as multitenant SaaS applications in cloud environments [8].

In a multitenant application, confidential data belonging to individual tenants is processed and stored by a shared application instance. Therefore, the reengineering process needs to ensure strict separation of confidential data. It is absolutely crucial that multitenant applications do not allow any tenant's data to be read or modified by other, unauthorized tenants that share the same application instance.

This chapter presents a method and a set of architectural patterns for systematically reengineering data-sensitive enterprise applications into secure multitenant software services that can be deployed to public and private cloud offerings seamlessly. The presented method covers both architectural refactorings and code-level considerations, including appropriate testing and code reviewing techniques that focus on typical defects in multitenant applications.

The chapter is organized as follows. Section 13.2 explains the context of multitenancy in cloud computing. Section 13.3 describes the necessary steps in multitenant refactoring from planning to execution to validation (including testing and code reviews). Section 13.4 introduces the architectural refactoring method and presents architectural solution details. Section 13.5 then describes solution details on testing and code review methods. Section 13.6 presents a fictitious, but realistic and representative, case study implementation distilled from real-world requirements and application architectures, Section 13.7 discusses the research results, and Section 13.8 covers related work. Section 13.9 concludes the chapter with a summary and outlook on future work.

13.2 CONTEXT AND PROBLEM: MULTITENANCY IN CLOUD COMPUTING

Cloud computing has emerged as a logical evolution of Information Technology (IT). It is driven by a worldwide increasing demand for utility priced, on-demand allocated services delivering software applications and IT infrastructure such as data storage. The demand and requirements for such services can, however, only be satisfied by leveraging economies of scale of IT resources, which is enabled by the technical advances in communication (e.g., the Internet), virtualization technologies, and mobile computing. Cloud computing merges the main advantages of its computing precursors, without the costly disadvantages associated with traditional data centers [11,38].

On-demand allocation of resources, utility pricing models, and online accessibility make the adoption of cloud computing ideal for start-up businesses, but even large enterprises are increasingly adopting it [36,38]. Cloud computing technologies and capabilities have enabled new application scenarios, and have also created additional user requirements that were not feasible previously.

New technologies influence both the architectures and the requirements of systems [2]. Thus, the architectures of ideal cloud hosted SaaS applications differ significantly from those of traditional enterprise applications. Consequently, new architectural principles and patterns have emerged, facilitating the IDEAL characteristics of cloud applications: *I*solated state, *D*istribution, *E*lasticity, *A*utomated management, and *L*oose coupling [11].

Many existing enterprise applications were developed decades ago, before the emergence of cloud computing. Due to their high development costs, there is a strong economic incentive to modernize and deploy them as worldwide on-demand accessible SaaS applications in cloud environments. As the architectures of these applications cannot be assumed to adhere to the IDEAL characteristics already, this requires reengineering and *architectural refactoring*, in order to fully take advantage of the new capabilities of cloud computing [44].

SaaS applications achieve a higher level of cost efficiency by sharing component and application instances between multiple organizations, thus eliminating the need to maintain and to deploy individual application instances for each organization. This concept is called *multitenancy*. A tenant is an organizational entity, usually a group of users, who rent access to a SaaS application [8]. Kabbedijk et al. define multitenancy as follows:

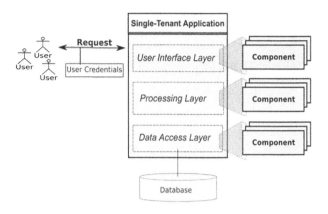

FIGURE 13.1

Single-tenant component based architecture

> *"Multi-tenancy is a property of a system where multiple customers, so-called tenants, transparently share the system's resources, such as services, applications, databases, or hardware, with the aim of lowering costs, while still being able to exclusively configure the system to the needs of the tenant." [19]*

Data security, confidentiality, and integrity are crucial in a multitenant environment [19]. The examples in this chapter show how architectural patterns can be applied to architecturally refactor and to reengineer a single-tenant legacy application (Fig. 13.1) into a modern, multitenant SaaS application (Fig. 13.2). Architectural refactoring refers to changing the internal structure of a system without changing its external behavior [43]. Reengineering, on the other hand, refers to changing the external behavior in order to meet new requirements. The transformation of a single-tenant legacy application into a multitenant SaaS application requires both architectural refactoring and reengineering on the code level. Although the application's external behavior after the transformation appears to remain unchanged from a tenant's (i.e., user's) point of view, it is changed significantly from a designer's and service provider's point of view.

This chapter focuses on how to avoid *data separation defects* that allow unauthorized tenants using the same application instance to access or modify other tenants' confidential data. Tenant data separation defects occur when data belonging to one tenant is made accessible to other, unauthorized tenants. This type of vulnerability could be caused either by software defects or by intentionally placed backdoors.

For a tenant t_i, let e_{ti} denote a data input into a shared component, and a_{ti} denote a data output from the component (i.e., for a tenant). Tenant data separation defects can occur, for example, in the following scenarios (Fig. 13.3):

(i) A service request input e_{t1} from tenant $t1$ (upper left corner) leaks into data storage output a_{t2} that affects a database entry belonging to tenant $t2$ (lower right corner). In this case, tenant $t1$ can modify tenant $t2$ data, resulting in a breach of data integrity for tenant $t2$. For example, this kind of data leak can occur if the data storage procedure writes data into the database using a different tenant ID from the one associated with the requesting tenant. This could happen by accident (e.g., conversion/casting error), or on purpose.

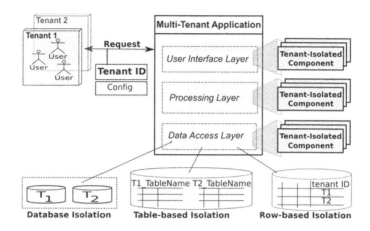

FIGURE 13.2

Multitenant architecture with tenant-isolated components

(ii) A data input from the database e_{t1} (database read operation) meant for tenant $t1$ (lower left corner) reaches a service response output a_{t2} meant for tenant $t2$ (upper right corner). In this case, tenant $t2$ can view tenant $t1$'s data, resulting in a breach of data confidentiality. This kind of data leak can be caused by a procedure that deliberately or accidentally reads data using a tenant ID that differs from the one associated with the requesting tenant.

(iii) Database entries from tenant $t1$'s data store (lower left corner) are copied into tenant $t2$'s data store (lower right corner), and later made accessible as belonging to tenant $t2$ (upper right corner). In this case, tenant $t2$ obtains read access to tenant $t1$'s data, and tenant $t2$'s data integrity is compromised. This is thus a breach of both data confidentiality and data integrity. This kind of data leak can occur, for example, in an application-to-application communication procedure that uses database integration (i.e., through shared database transfer tables). The sending component writes data into a shared transfer table, and triggers the receiving component to read data from the same table [5]. If the tenant ID is modified by either the reading or the writing component, a data leak occurs.

To prevent such data separation effects from happening and to safely architecturally refactor single-tenant applications for multitenancy SaaS Clouds, a *reengineering method* and supporting *architectural patterns* and *architectural refactorings* are required. The next three sections introduce such a method and patterns.

13.3 SOLUTION OVERVIEW: REENGINEERING METHOD AND PROCESS

The purpose of the reengineering method presented here is to assist architects who want to transform a typical single-tenant legacy enterprise application (Fig. 13.1) into a multitenant application that can be deployed in a Cloud environment (Fig. 13.2).

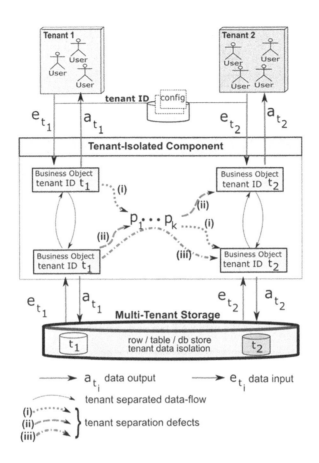

FIGURE 13.3

Illustration of data-flow defects causing data leaks in a multitenant, tenant-isolated component

Enterprise applications are comprehensive information systems that support complex business processes in and across business organizations. Although such applications are built for different purposes and therefore functionally very different, certain commonalities among them exist. For example, the architecture of typical enterprise applications consists of three tiers: a *resource tier* that provides access to a persistent database or other legacy resources, an *application tier* that implements the business logic, and a *presentation tier* that implements the presentation logic for clients and other integrated enterprise applications [10]. Further commonalities are related to how certain recurring software engineering problems are solved through the application of common solutions, so-called patterns. Such patterns are applied in enterprise systems to solve recurring problems related to the logical architecture [12], the integration of enterprise systems [17], or their deployment on cloud computing environments [11].

Aiming to cover a common type of legacy application, the focus here is specifically on Web application architectures that are based on the widely-used Model-View-Controller (MVC) pattern. Fig. 13.4 outlines a reengineering process that comprises three steps (that will be explained in Section 13.4.1),

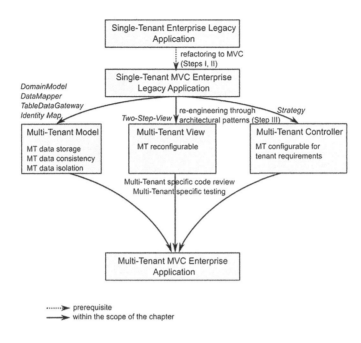

FIGURE 13.4

The reengineering process for enabling multitenancy in a single-tenant legacy application by applying a combination of enterprise application architecture patterns [12]

each of which qualifies as an architectural refactoring according to Zimmermann [43]. Here it is assumed that the architecture of the legacy application is either already based on the MVC pattern, or that it can easily be refactored into a typical Web MVC architecture through standard pattern refactoring techniques [20,34].

Section 13.4 will elaborate on the multitenancy specific requirements for each of the MVC's components, along with architectural solutions using enterprise application architecture patterns. Thus, the resulting architecture is multitenancy capable, and fulfills all architectural requirements that are specific to multitenancy.

At the code level, these requirements, such as tenant data separation, need to be verified through code reviews and regression testing techniques. These techniques will be explained in detail in Section 13.5, using a PHP music library application as an example.

13.4 SOLUTION DETAIL 1: ARCHITECTURAL PATTERNS IN THE METHOD

This section elaborates on the typical architectural requirements that emerge from the new capabilities of cloud environments, and introduces architectural patterns that can be applied to build multitenancy capable systems. First, the typical steps required for modernizing legacy applications for cloud environments are described as architectural refactorings.

At the component level, the new architectural requirements for such applications are identified and architectural patterns are selected that are suitable to exploit the technological benefits and capabilities of cloud environments. Finally, a possible architectural solution is shown by applying a series of suitable architectural patterns that lead to the new envisioned multitenant architecture.

13.4.1 ARCHITECTURAL REENGINEERING STEPS FOR THE CLOUD (ARCHITECTURAL REFACTORING)

A good architecture exploits the technical advantages and capabilities of the target environment, while satisfying the functional and nonfunctional requirements of the system's stakeholders. However, there are additional characteristics, that make an architecture better than "good enough", i.e., "beautiful" [33]. The characteristics that make a "beautiful" architecture stand out from a "good enough" one are support for incremental construction, the ability to easily support changes (persistence), ease of use for both developers and users, and a conceptual integrity that makes it easy to learn [33]. The process described here aims to achieve these objectives.

In this case, a cloud computing environment is the target. The typical properties of cloud environments are (i) on-demand self-service, (ii) broad network access, (iii) measured service, (iv) resource pooling, and (v) rapid elasticity [11,24]. Requirements (i) to (iii) do not directly influence architectural decisions in a multitenancy context. Therefore, the focus is here in particular on architectural decisions that enable *resource pooling* and *rapid elasticity*.

Rapid elasticity refers to the system's ability to quickly allocate additional resources when the workload increases, and to de-allocate them when the workload decreases. Ideally, this capability is supported by the application. To achieve this, the application is scaled horizontally (i.e., scaled-out), by starting up additional service instances that take up the additional workload. These on-demand service instances can be shut down automatically when the workload decreases. An ideal architecture for SaaS applications is therefore service-oriented, and supports dynamic workload balancing across loosely coupled, stateless services. The MVC pattern and modern MVC-based presentation layer frameworks adhere to these characteristics (which, in a reengineering process, can be achieved by Step II in Fig. 13.4).

Resource pooling refers to the system's ability to allow multiple customers (i.e., tenants) to share the allocated resources. At the application level, this means sharing components or application instances, in other words, to enable multitenancy. Ideally, the fact that resources are shared should not be noticed by the tenants. A tenant should not be able to distinguish a multitenant component or application from one that is exclusively dedicated to it. Multitenancy is achieved by specifically designing the architecture to meet the specific multitenancy requirements. The following subsection elaborates these requirements and discusses pattern-based solutions.

From an architectural perspective, as motivated in Section 13.2, cloud applications should expose IDEAL architectural characteristics: isolated state (i.e., stateless components), distribution (i.e., SOA), loose coupling, elasticity (i.e., on-demand allocation and de-allocation), and automated management [11].

To achieve these characteristics, the following architectural reengineering steps are typically required (Fig. 13.4):

(i) Step I: Identify and define the legacy application's functional layers in terms of data access, data processing, and user interface/service interfaces.

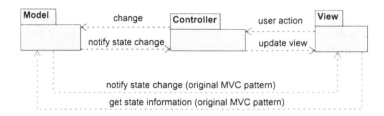

FIGURE 13.5

The Web MVC architectural pattern

(ii) Step II: Decompose each layer into loosely coupled, stateless components that can be deployed as on-demand services elastically.

(iii) Step III: Reengineer the components to support multitenancy. This step is described in detail below, while Steps I and II are beyond the scope of this chapter.

13.4.2 MULTITENANCY REQUIREMENTS AND PATTERNS FOR CLOUD ENVIRONMENTS

The logical architecture of typical enterprise applications is typically structured in three layers (Fig. 13.1): the data access layer, the processing layer, and the presentation layer. This layered structure can also be observed in the Model-View-Controller (MVC) pattern.[1] Therefore, and as already motivated in Section 13.3, it can be assumed that the architecture of the legacy application either resembles MVC already or that it can be first reengineered into a Web MVC application with existing refactoring techniques [20,34].

The MVC pattern is an architectural pattern that leads to a functional decomposition into three groups of components: the Model, the View, and the Controller. The Model components represent application data and data access layer, the View components render data for the user, and the Controller components handle user inputs and manipulate both views and models.

The majority of modern Web applications are based on this pattern; however, most Web application frameworks (e.g., the PHP Zend Framework) implement a slightly modified version of the MVC, the so-called "Web MVC" or "Model 2" pattern (Fig. 13.5) [3,7]. In the original MVC pattern, the View is an Observer of the Model, and thus receives direct notifications when changes in the Model's data occur. On the other hand, in the Web MVC version, these notifications are redirected through the Controller instead, as this is easier to realize with many Web technologies (Fig. 13.5).

The specific requirements which have been identified for multitenancy capable MVC components are explained below [8,39].

---

[1] Two different conceptions exist regarding the MVC pattern: (i) applied at the presentation layer only [12], or (ii) applied across a layered architecture, to separate the presentation layer from the data modeling of the business layer [40]. In this chapter its application across layers is assumed.

13.4.3 THE MULTITENANCY CAPABLE MODEL

Requirement R1: A major requirement for a multitenant MVC Model is its ability to store application domain objects in a multitenant database and to map in-memory domain objects to a multitenant relational database schema. Three database solutions are common for multitenancy (Fig. 13.2) [13]:

(i) A dedicated database instance for each tenant,
(ii) A shared database instance, with a dedicated set of data tables for each tenant, or
(iii) A shared schema in a shared database instance with a tenant ID associating each row to its tenant owner.

An ideal MVC Model should support all three multitenant database options, and also hybrid solutions with a combination of the three options.

Solution for R1: A pattern-based solution is to combine the patterns "Data Mapper" and "Table Data Gateway" [12]. The "Data Mapper" pattern maps in-memory objects to one or multiple relational databases, while the "Table Data Gateway" pattern provides a simple interface for storing and retrieving data from individual database tables (Fig. 13.6). The "Domain Model" pattern [12] combines behavior and data, and is a common pattern in enterprise applications with complex logic [12,41]. In this chapter the domain object is associated with the Tenant class through the tenant ID property. The combination of these patterns decouples the Model from the underlying database technology, allowing the integration of various databases in support of multitenancy.

Requirement R2: The appropriate separation of tenant data is crucial for a multitenant application, and domain objects belonging to different tenants have to be linked to a tenant identifier.

Solution for R2: The "Identity Field" pattern [12] can be used to maintain the identity between the database rows and in-memory domain objects. Each domain object is assigned a tenant ID, which is mapped to the database tenant identifier used to link the data entry with the tenant owner (Fig. 13.6).

Requirement R3: In order to ensure data consistency and separation, a one-to-one relationship between tenant database entries and in-memory domain objects needs to be enforced, and access to tenant domain objects has to be controlled and restricted. Each tenant should be able to access only its own data. At the database level, this can be enforced by ensuring that a tenant ID parameter is mandatory when accessing the database. If a database query ignores the tenant ID parameter, it could access all tenants' data. Such an attempt to access all tenants' data can be discovered at run-time, for example, by introducing a "dummy or sentinel value" that triggers an error when it is accessed [28].

Solution for R3: The "Identity Map" [12] pattern can be applied to avoid reloading identical database rows into different in-memory domain objects. When applying this pattern, all domain objects are loaded and stored in a common data structure, the "Identity Map." Consequently, access to all domain objects can be controlled and restricted by the "Identity Map." Read/write access is only granted to model objects owned by the accessing tenant (Fig. 13.6).

13.4.4 THE MULTITENANCY CAPABLE CONTROLLER

Requirement R4: The Controller handles user input and manipulates data in MVC views and MVC models. Ideally, these functionalities are configurable for each individual tenant. Each tenant should be able to configure the application to handle input, store data, and display the information according to their own business requirements.

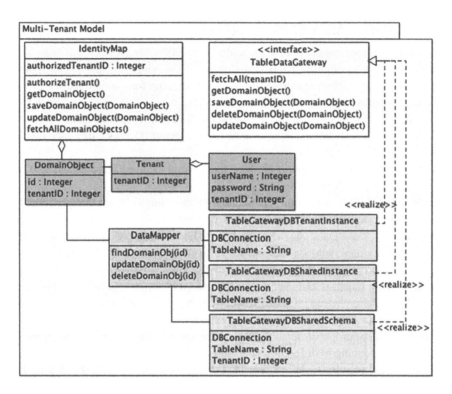

FIGURE 13.6

Multitenant MVC model based on the patterns Identity Map, Domain Model, Identity Field, Data Mapper, and Table Data Gateway

Solution for R4: The "Strategy" pattern [29] allows decoupling the behavior implementation (strategy) from an object, and therefore facilitates the implementation of an individual controller behavior for each tenant (Fig. 13.7).

In single-tenant Web applications, two options are typical for the implementation of controllers: (i) one Controller–multiple Views, and (ii) multiple Controllers–multiple Views (i.e., one Controller per View) [14]. The multitenant equivalents are:

 (i) One Controller per tenant – a group of multiple Views per tenant, and
 (ii) A group of multiple Controllers per tenant – a group of multiple Views per tenant (i.e., each tenant-specific controller handles one tenant-specific view).

13.4.5 THE MULTITENANCY CAPABLE VIEW

Requirement R5: An ideal multitenant application should allow tenants to individually configure the layout of data and the user controls displayed in HTML pages.

Solution for R5: The "Two-Step-View" (Fig. 13.8) pattern allows presentation layer architects to decouple the displayed information from the layout. In the first stage, this pattern forms a logical page,

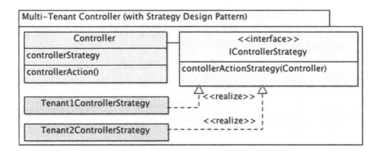

FIGURE 13.7

Multitenant MVC controller based on the strategy pattern

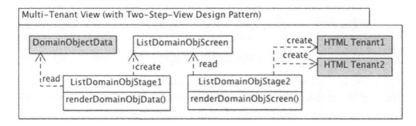

FIGURE 13.8

Multitenant MVC view based on the two-step-view pattern

which is rendered into HTML in a second stage. While the first stage can be application-wide, the second step, which influences the appearance, is individually configurable for tenants (see Section 13.6, for example). The individual tenant-specific creation of HTML pages depends on the tenant ID properties stored in the Domain Object data.

13.5 SOLUTION DETAIL 2: TESTING AND CODE REVIEWS

The pattern-based approach described above enables a developer to create a multitenant architecture. However, the corresponding implementation of this architecture still has to be evaluated for correctness. Most importantly for a multitenant application, it is necessary to ensure that the appropriate separation of tenant data is preserved at the code level. This can be achieved with testing and code review techniques, as explained in this section.

13.5.1 TESTING FOR MULTITENANCY DEFECTS

Enterprise Web applications are difficult to test thoroughly because they often consist of multiple and complex multistage processes and backend system integration flows (that are hard to mock/simulate), and are simultaneously accessed by multiple users [15,25,32]. In such applications that require

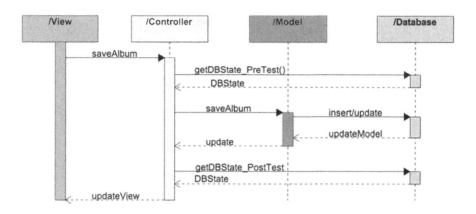

FIGURE 13.9

Sequence diagram of a testing procedure for multitenancy defects

security-testing, tenant data separation defects are especially difficult to find because security leaks may manifest themselves as side-effects on other tenants' data. Such defects can remain undetected by functional black-box testing techniques [35]. The example below illustrates one such tenant data separation defect. Subsequently, a solution using a white-box testing technique is presented.

Example: Confidentiality and Integrity Breach. In this example a multitenant Web application allows users to edit entries of a music album library. Changes made by the user are correctly reflected in the model and in the database (Fig. 13.9). However, in addition to this correct behavior, assume that a software defect allows some edited entries to be duplicated, associated with a different tenant ID, and thus stored in another tenant's data. This software defect results in a breach of data confidentiality for the first (editing) tenant, and a breach of data integrity for the second tenant (as motivated in Fig. 13.3). Such breaches can have a significant negative impact on the business, e.g., harm an application's audit compliance [18].

Since this program completes its intended database update correctly, a typical unit test to ensure that the specific database row has been changed as required will not reveal any problems. Additionally, therefore, a test is needed which checks for the unexpected side-effect that this code has on another tenant's data. In this test the state of the database is retrieved before and after the execution of the program functionality under test (Fig. 13.9). In this example, prior to executing the "saveAlbum" function, the number of rows per tenant is obtained from the database table, and the test ensures that the table is not empty. After executing the "saveAlbum" function, the test obtains again the number of rows, and ensures that it is unchanged (Listing 1).

It is important to highlight that the states of the database are obtained directly from the database, bypassing the Model. These database states consider the data rows and tables of *all* tenants before and after executing a particular program function. The test then asserts, by comparing the states before and after the function, that the tenant data separation property is maintained. In order to assert the tenant data separation property, the database states need to take into account the number of table rows, as well as checksums of all rows (of all tenants) expected to remain unaffected.

```
void testSaveAlbum {
    int rowsBefore = getNoOfRows(AlbumTable);
    assert (numberOfRows > 0);
    editAlbum(..); //function under test
    int rowsAfter = getNumberOfRows(AlbumTable);
    assert(rowsBefore == rowsAfter);
}
```

Listing 1: Pseudocode of the test procedure

The test then asserts that only a single row belonging to the intended tenant is updated, while the checksums (and therefore content) of all other rows remained unaffected. To avoid interference from other updates, this type of test can only run with a single logged-in user. This type of testing should be performed with a small testing database, since a very large multitenant production database would negatively affect the execution performance of the test. This test should be disabled in the production code.

13.5.2 CODE REVIEW FOR MULTITENANCY DEFECTS

Testing often does not reveal all defects or vulnerabilities. For example, a back-door or software defect which allows one particular tenant (with a secret tenant ID) to access all other tenants' data would very likely remain undetected by tests, especially if the privileged tenant had not yet been created at the time of testing. Nevertheless, such tenant data separation defects can be revealed by code reviews.

It is important to note that tenant data separation defects can occur anywhere along data-flow paths between application inputs and outputs (Fig. 13.3 in Section 13.2). Thus, the code reviewing process for finding tenant data separation defects differs from the process for finding security vulnerabilities, which is typically limited to analyzing input and output procedures [9]. To ensure appropriate data separation in a multitenant application, the code reviewer needs to identify and analyze all data-flow paths of input-value/tenant-identifier pairs leading to output-value/tenant-identifier pairs, and ensure that no data output is produced for a different tenant.

For instance, in the code example, the Zend "skeleton" music application, the program was implemented using the "Domain Model" pattern [12]; a common pattern in enterprise applications. Therefore, all objects containing tenant-specific data used as application input or output were encapsulated in classes derived from such a common Domain Object base class. The Domain Object base class and thus all derived subclasses inherit a pair property (data-value, tenant-id) that associates each data value with the tenant owner.

Tenant data separation defects can occur when a multitenant program that receives an input domain object belonging to a tenant, produces at least one output domain object which belongs to a different tenant. In order for this to occur at runtime, at least one internal function needs to violate the tenant data separation property.

The association between tenant data and tenant identifier can be violated in a domain object either by (i) overwriting the tenant identifier with a different one, or (ii) by overwriting the domain object data with other data that belongs to a different tenant. The data-flow of such corrupted domain objects needs to be analyzed, in order to determine whether they can reach an application output.

The code reviewing process needed for finding tenant data separation defects can be summarized as follows:

(i) Identify all procedure invocations which allow data inputs and outputs. Such procedures include, for example, user interfaces (MVC Views), but also database and file system access procedures (MVC Models).

(ii) Find connecting paths of data-flow leading from application inputs to application outputs. Data-flow can occur explicitly, through variable assignments, parameter passing to procedures, and inter-procedural through assignments to and from global and static variables. Data-flow can also occur implicitly through control dependencies, e.g., in code segment "if $(x == \text{false})$ then $y = 0$" the value of variable y is influenced by that of variable x even though there is no assignment between them [27].

(iii) For each identified data-flow path, verify through manual code-reviews that no data-flow exists from input-value/tenant-identifier pairs to a different tenant.

13.5.3 SUMMARY

Table 13.1 summarizes the method and populates the architectural refactoring template from Table A.1 in Appendix 13.A with the multitenancy reengineering knowledge from Sections 13.3, 13.4, and 13.5.

13.6 CASE STUDY (IMPLEMENTATION)

This section demonstrates the applicability of the above reengineering method and pattern-based cloud application architectures with a fictitious, but still representative, sample enterprise application. The method is applied to a typical PHP Web application, which is incrementally transformed from a single-user application into a multitenant SaaS application using two different techniques. The first reengineering technique aims at keeping the number of source code and architecture changes to a minimum, and ignores the use of patterns.

The second reengineering technique that is applied is the one introduced in Section 13.4. The evaluation of the two reengineering techniques confirms that the pattern-based architecture is better suitable to ensure tenant data separation.

The case study application is based on the Zend Framework Skeleton Application [42], and it is a single-user PHP Web application. A PHP case study is used because PHP has evolved into a powerful object-oriented language [23], and is currently one of the most popular server-side programming languages, used, for example, by Facebook, Baidu, Wikipedia, and Twitter [37].

The Zend Skeleton Application is a standard example that demonstrates PHP's capabilities for enterprise applications, and therefore an ideal candidate for our purpose. The Zend Skeleton Application is a music library management system that allows users to enter, edit, delete, and list music albums in a library (Fig. 13.10).

Table 13.1 Architectural refactorings to introduce multitenancy support

Architectural Refactoring (AR)	Introduce multitenancy support to layered application.
Context	An application already applies logical layering and the Model-View-Controller (MVC) pattern on a conceptual level; it is supposed to be deployed into a cloud that has a shared usage model and pools computing and storage resources.
Stakeholder concerns and quality attributes (design forces)	• Security (data privacy, data confidentiality, data integrity) • Accuracy (of calculations and data storage) • Performance • Maintainability • Cost (of deployment and hosting)
Architectural smell	A cloud application has been designed for single-tenant use and therefore does not provide any protection against data separation defects.
Architectural decision(s)	• Cloud deployment model, cloud service model • Approach to tenant isolation • Detailed design of components in MVC pattern
Evolution outline	Upgrade single-user/-tenant component architecture into a multitenant, patterns-based architecture by enhancing the MVC usage with: 1. A Multitenancy Capable Model (with tenant identity-aware domain objects), 2. A Multitenant Two-Step View, and 3. A Multitenancy Capable Controller (strategy-based) as outlined in in Section 13.2 (in Fig. 13.2) and in Section 13.3 (in Fig. 13.4).
Affected architectural elements	All three top-level components in the MVC pattern, as well as the components in Fowler's supporting patterns discussed in Section 13.4 and listed in Table 13.3 in Section 13.6 (e.g., Identity Map, Two-Step View, Strategy).
Execution tasks	1. Implement the enhanced patterns in chosen presentation layer, business logic layer, and data access layer technologies (possibly supported by frameworks). 2. Define tenant identifiers. 3. Update database schemes and system configuration means. 4. Test for multitenancy defects. 5. Review code to validate correct implementation of multitenancy support. 6. Perform security compliance audit (w.r.t. tenant data separation). 7. Monitor application performance at runtime.

13.6.1 MULTITENANCY TRANSFORMATION WITHOUT PATTERNS

The goal of this first transformation is to implement multitenancy with as few code and architecture changes as possible. Starting with the original application (Fig. 13.10), this can be achieved as follows (Fig. 13.11 and Table 13.3).

First, a tenant ID property is added to all domain classes, i.e., in this case the Album class, allowing us to associate each album object with a tenant owner. A new User class includes a tenant ID property through which it associates each user with a tenant. The new authentication controller and the corresponding login view allow users to log-in. The modified Table Gateway class restricts the access

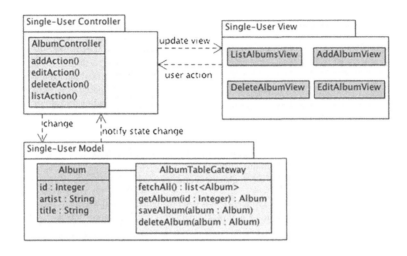

FIGURE 13.10

MVC architecture of the music library management system

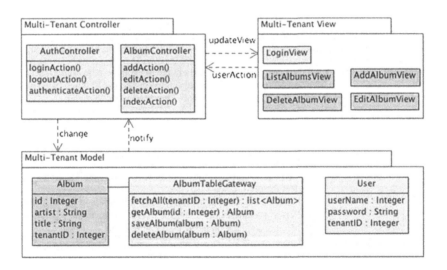

FIGURE 13.11

Reengineering without architectural patterns

to entries associated with the specified tenant. In the database, an additional tenant ID column links each entry to the tenant owner (in a shared multitenant database schema). Authorization checks are implemented as part of the controller actions.

13.6.2 MULTITENANCY TRANSFORMATION WITH PATTERNS

A second version of the Zend Skeleton application can also be produced; however, this time by applying the reengineering method established in Section 13.3 and the architectural patterns introduced in Section 13.4.

The transformation steps in this second version are as follows (Fig. 13.12). In the MVC Model, the "Data Mapper" pattern in implemented in addition to the already existing "Table Data Gateway pattern." This results in a new "Two-Level Data Mapping Gateway" pattern. The first level ("Album Data Mapper") exposes functionalities for retrieving, updating, and deleting an Album object from the Model, while the second level, consisting of the particular realizations of the "Table Data Gateway" interface, implements the data-level read/write access to different types of multitenant databases. Therefore, these patterns facilitate the integration of multitenant databases with database isolation, table-based isolation, or row-based isolation schemas (Fig. 13.2).

The next step is to add the "Identity Map" pattern to the Model, as well as the "Domain Model" with an Identity Field, to form an "Identity-Aware Domain Model" pattern. Through the combination of these patterns, the Model encapsulates the functionality for creating, retrieving, updating, and deleting domain objects in a single class, namely the "Identity Map." In other words, the "Identity Map" is the only access point for data input and output to and from the Controller. Therefore, since the code is not spread out over multiple classes, it is easier to test and review in order to ensure that the Model maintains appropriate tenant data isolation.

In the Controller, the Strategy pattern is implemented with different controller strategies for different tenants. The resulting loose coupling between the strategy implementations and the application's "Album Controller" through the interface "IAlbumControllerStrategy", makes it is easier to add, remove, or modify tenant-specific controller strategy implementations without affecting the rest of the code base. Individual implementations of controller strategies that meet a particular tenant's requirements do not affect other tenants' controller functionalities. The same holds for any software defects in these tenant-specific strategies.

Finally, each MVC View page is transformed into a "Two-Step-View." This decouples the data content from its presentation layout, and allows therefore implementing tenant-specific and individually configurable user interfaces for each tenant. Fig. 13.12 and Table 13.3 summarize the architectural refactoring process.

13.6.3 COMPARISON

The first, patternless transformation version shows that multitenancy functionality can be achieved easily with very few changes of the architecture and source code. However, although the resulting application could be used by multiple tenants, it does not meet the requirements of a multitenant application, including the IDEAL cloud application architecture principles (Table 13.4). This first version is more difficult to integrate with different multitenant database schemas, because the Album Table Gateway is only able to access a single database schema. Additionally, since the MVC Controller and the MVC View are designed for single-tenant use, the implementation is not sufficiently flexible to be easily customized for individual tenant needs. Most importantly, since the source code contains tenant authorization checks at different places (e.g., in each Controller action), it is more difficult to test and code review in order to eliminate tenant data separation defects.

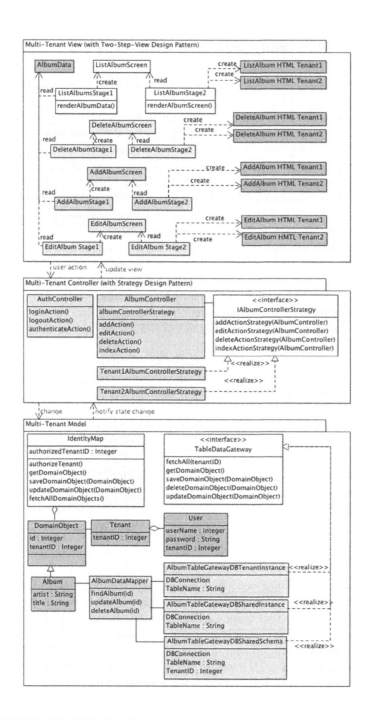

FIGURE 13.12

Pattern-based multitenant capable MVC architecture

Table 13.2 Number of classes and size of the case study application in its transformation stages from a single-user application to the pattern-based version of the multitenant architecture

Application transformation stage	Classes/PHP files	Lines of code
Original Zend Skeleton Application (Modules only, without Zend Framework)	10	561
Multiuser (single-tenant)	18	1021
V1: Multitenant without patterns	18	1052
V2: Multitenant with patterns	28	1344

Table 13.3 Summary of reengineering steps (architectural refactorings). The patterns are introduced by Fowler [12]

	Model	View	Controller
V1: Multitenant without patterns	The tenant ID property is added to class Album	N/A: not tenant-specific configurable	Controller retrieves the tenant ID of the authenticated user. All Controller actions use the tenant ID.
V2: Multitenant with patterns	Added classes: User, Tenant, DomainObject (abstract base class), AlbumDataMapper, IdentityMap, interface ITableDataGateway	Refactored to Two-Step-View (supported by Zend Framework)	Refactored to Strategy pattern. Added interface IAlbumControllerStrategy implemented by tenant-specific AlbumControllers

Table 13.4 Evaluation with respect to "IDEAL" Cloud application characteristics

	Isolated state	Distribution	Elasticity	Automated management	Loose coupling
V1: Multitenant without patterns	Good (stateless components)	Suitable (MVC property)	No (not suitable for horizontal scaling)	No	Weak
V2: Multitenant with patterns	Good (stateless components)	Suitable (MVC property)	Yes (horizontal scaling)	Yes (configurable Controller and View)	Yes

On the other hand, the second, pattern-based version (Fig. 13.12) requires more code and architectural changes (Table 13.2). However, the resulting architecture is superior with respect to its ability for incremental construction, the ability to support changes, and its conceptual integrity. For example, the incremental construction is supported by allowing the addition of new tenant-specific customized controller strategies and Views, without affecting the implementations of other tenant's Controllers and Views. Changes made in such tenant-specific classes do not affect the entire source code base, and are therefore easier to test, debug, and deploy. Furthermore, the use of mature enterprise application architecture patterns improves the conceptual integrity and recognizability of the entire architecture.

Table 13.5 **Evaluation with respect to multitenancy requirements**

Requirement	V1: Multitenant without patterns	V2: Multitenant with patterns
R1 (multitenant storage)	No	Yes
R2 (data separation)	Ad hoc solution	Yes
R3 (limit data access)	No	Yes
R4 (configurable controller)	No	Yes
R5 (configurable view)	No	Yes

The internal coupling properties of the MVC components remain unaffected by the application of the new architectural patterns. The MVC pattern already achieves loose coupling characteristics of its three major components. However, the multitenancy capable MVC Model is more decoupled from the underlying database.

13.7 DISCUSSION

As evidenced in Table 13.5, the pattern-based version of the refactored music library management system fulfills the multitenancy requirements completely, while the nonpattern based version does not do so. Furthermore, the pattern-based version is easier to adapt to different cloud offerings. For example, the loose coupling between the model and the underlying data storage enables the simultaneous integration with multiple cloud storage offerings (Fig. 13.2). Its processing functionalities and user interfaces are easier to configure to individual tenant-specific needs: for instance, the Multitenancy Capable Controller can be configured by allowing each tenant to implement an individual strategy (Fig. 13.7), while the user interface can be configured to display a customizable layout for each individual tenant (Fig. 13.8).

The Multitenancy Capable MVC Model also simplifies the checks of correctness with respect to tenant data separation properties because pattern instances are rather easy to locate in code (assuming that its development adheres to naming conventions and/or uses architecturally evident coding styles). Regression tests, and code reviews can be focused on ensuring that Domain Objects are assigned the correct tenant identifier at the time of construction. Later changes of the tenant identifier can be prevented through code, as well as the cloning of Domain Objects with a different tenant identifier.

The Identity Map is the only interface for passing Domain Objects from and into the model. Therefore, authorization checks implemented in the Identity Map can ensure that each tenant is only granted access to its own Domain Objects. Correctly implemented, these mechanisms guarantee that the tenant data separation property is maintained by the application. Due to the complexity of the required changes and their impact on the entire application, the reengineering process is manual, and would be difficult to automate.

The case study presented in Section 13.6 showed that tenant data separation defects are more likely to happen and are more difficult to detect in the first version (which was developed in an ad hoc manner), in comparison to the second, pattern-based version (whose implementation followed the reengineering method from Section 13.3). This is due to the fact that the data-flow graph of tenant-specific data is significantly simpler in the pattern-based version. On the other hand, the complex data-flow in the ad hoc version leads to difficulties in detecting programming errors.

13.8 **RELATED WORK**

The method described in this chapter concerns the reengineering of legacy applications to support multitenancy, with a specific concern for tenant data separation. Prior work has focused on reengineering legacy applications for cloud migration; however, few publications exist regarding the application of architectural patterns for this purpose. Xuesong et al., for example, proposed guidelines for reengineering legacy Web applications for multitenancy, but they considered only how to deal with the Singleton design pattern in multitenant applications [39]. They did not consider the more commonly-used MVC pattern as done above.

Kabbedijk et al. recently reviewed multitenant understanding in academia and industry, and their definition of multitenant systems was assumed in this chapter [19]. Most interestingly, after studying 761 research papers and 371 industrial blogs, they conclude:

"The results show that most papers propose a solution related to multi-tenancy, but almost no papers report on industrial experiences while implementing multi-tenancy, providing some insight into the maturity of the domain." [19]

Earlier, Bezemer et al. described the challenges of reengineering for multitenancy [8]. However, while they recognized the ability to configure SaaS applications for tenant specific needs, this topic was left open. Similarly, Kousiouris et al. explained the multitenancy challenges of transforming legacy applications, mostly focusing on performance issues [21].

Sengupta et al. discussed the remaining research challenges related to SaaS applications, such as design, testing, maintenance, and optimization [30]. Interestingly, they also highlight refactoring from single-tenant applications as one of the challenges, which is one of the topics addressed in this chapter.

Kun et al. proposed a completely different approach to reengineering source code. They described a middleware layer which intercepts SQL database queries and converts them into multitenant database requests [22]. However, it is not clear from their paper whether their proposal has been implemented or not.

13.9 **SUMMARY AND CONCLUSIONS**

This chapter presented a pattern-based reengineering and architectural refactoring method for transforming legacy enterprise applications designed for single-tenant access into multitenant applications that satisfy the architectural principles required for successful SaaS deployment in cloud environments.

The appropriate separation of tenant data is one of the most critical properties of multi-tenant applications that process sensitive enterprise data because it directly affects the success or failure of SaaS solutions; data separation violations can have disastrous economic and legal consequences for both service consumers and service providers. As a minimum, multitenant SaaS applications should pass a compliance audit to gain evidence and confidence that enterprise data will not be accessible by competitors using the same SaaS solution (in addition to being protected against external attacks). Therefore, the reengineering of legacy applications and the development of new multitenant SaaS solutions should prioritize this critical requirement to preserve tenant data separation on all application and data storage levels. Ideally, the application architecture should make it easier for developers, testers, and compliance auditors to confirm this property, for example, through focussed testing and code reviewing. In this chapter, we presented a method and patterns for doing so.

The multitenancy aware architecture presented in this chapter extends existing enterprise application architecture patterns on the three logical architectural layers (i.e., user interface, business logic processing, and data access) reflected in the Model-View-Controller (MVC) pattern into multitenancy-enabled variants that satisfy five multitenancy-specific requirements. Most importantly, the presented approach preserves the tenant data separation property in order to guarantee data integrity and data confidentiality of sensitive tenant user and application data. Experience with this approach shows that the resulting multitenant software architecture and supporting patterns-based reengineering and architectural refactoring method are better suited for a systematic analysis and testing for the presence of tenant separation defects than ad-hoc evolutions of existing architectures.

A practical case study using a common framework for enterprise PHP applications, the PHP Zend Framework, confirmed the viability and the advantages of the approach. Both an ad-hoc and a pattern-based version of a music library management system were implemented and the two implementations were compared with respect to quality attributes such as developer productivity, maintenance effort, and IDEAL cloud application properties, as well as specific multitenancy SaaS requirements. This evaluation demonstrated that the investment into a pattern-based and method-supported approach to achieving multitenancy can pay off because it reduces the risk of data privacy/integrity breaches (among other security threats) and also simplifies maintenance, compliance auditing, and further evolution of the cloud application (i.e., SaaS offering).

The scope of this chapter was limited to static (architectural) application aspects, and did not include other equally relevant aspects of multitenant systems, such as performance, availability, reliability and fault-tolerance [16], or scalability, load balancing, or RESTful microservices [26]. Future work concerns improving the practical adoption of pattern-oriented architecting and architectural refactoring through Web-enabled architectural knowledge management systems for pattern-based solutions [44], that can be integrated into other tools used by software architects during initial design as well as maintenance and evolution, for instance, modeling and architectural decision management tools [45].

APPENDIX 13.A ARCHITECTURAL REFACTORING (AR) REFERENCE

The introduction of tenant-aware patterns in the three reengineering steps in Fig. 13.4 (i.e., Multitenant Model, Multitenant View, Multitenant Controller) qualifies as an architectural refactoring [44]. Such architectural refactorings can be compiled, curated, and shared in an Architectural Refactoring Tool (ART) [4]. Table A.1 shows the architectural refactoring template underlying Table 13.1 in Section 13.5, which was established in our previous work [43] and is supported by ART.

Table A.1 Decision- and task-centric Architectural Refactoring (AR) template (adapted from [43])	
AR name	**How can the AR be recognized and referenced easily?**
Context	Where (and under which circumstances) is this AR eligible? The context section may include information about the viewpoint and/or abstraction/refinement level in an enterprise architecture management framework.
Stakeholder concerns and quality attributes (design forces)	Which nonfunctional requirements and constraints are affected by this AR?
Architectural smell	When and why should this AR be considered?
Architectural decision(s)	Applying an AR implies revisiting one or more architectural decisions; which ones? Such decisions may deal with pattern, technology, and platform choices.
Evolution outline	Which design elements does the AR comprise of? This is the center piece of the AR, providing a solution sketch. Since the AR describes a design change, two solution sketches may be provided (one illustrating the design before the AR is applied, one the design resulting from the application of the AR). Pitfalls to avoid might also be listed here (e.g., overdoing it).
Affected architectural elements	Which design model elements have to be changed, e.g., subsystems, components and connectors (if modeled explicitly)?
Execution tasks	How can the AR be applied? Execution tasks may include i) tasks to realize structural changes in a design, dealing with components and connectors as well as subsystems and their interfaces, ii) implementation and configuration tasks in development and operations, and iii) documentation and communication tasks such as modeling activities, technical-writing assignments, or design workshop preparation and facilitation.

REFERENCES

[1] W.H. An, H. Cai, L. Fan, B. Gao, C.J. Guo, L.L. Ma, Z.H. Wang, M.J. Zhou, Locating Isolation Points in an Application Under Multi-Tenant Environment, U.P.T. Office. US, International Business Machines Corporation, 2012.

[2] P. Avgeriou, J. Grundy, J.G. Hall, P. Lago, I. Mistrík, Relating Software Requirements and Architectures, Springer-Verlag, 2011.

[3] L. Beighley, M. Morrison, Head First PHP & MySQL, O'Reilly Media, Sebastopol, 2008.

[4] C. Bisig, Ein werkzeugunterstütztes Knowledge Repository für Architectural Refactoring, Masters thesis, HSR Hochschule für Technik Rapperswil, 2016.

[5] J. Boeder, B. Groene, Architecture of SAP ERP: Understand How Successful Software Works, tredition, 2014.

[6] G. Chang Jie, S. Wei, H. Ying, W. Zhi Hu, G. Bo, A framework for native multi-tenancy application development and management, in: The 9th IEEE International Conference on E-Commerce Technology and the 4th IEEE International Conference on Enterprise Computing, E-Commerce, and E-Services, 2007, CEC/EEE 2007, 2007.

[7] J. Coggeshall, Zend Enterprise PHP Patterns, Springer, Dordrecht, 2009.

[8] Cor-Paul Bezemer, A. Zaidman, Challenges of Reengineering into Multi-Tenant SaaS Applications, Delft University of Technology, 2010.

[9] M. Cross, Developer's Guide to Web Application Security, Syngress Press, San Diego, 2007 [Imprint].

[10] D. Duggan, Enterprise Software Architecture and Design: Entities, Services, and Resources, Wiley, Hoboken, 2012.

[11] C. Fehling, F. Leymann, R. Retter, W. Schupeck, P. Arbitter, Cloud Computing Patterns: Fundamentals to Design, Build, and Manage Cloud Applications, Springer, Dordrecht, 2014.

[12] M. Fowler, Patterns of Enterprise Application Architecture, Addison-Wesley, Boston, 2003.

[13] Frederick Chong, Gianpaolo Carraro, R. Wolter, Multi-tenant data architecture. Retrieved from http://msdn.microsoft.com/en-us/library/aa479086.aspx, 2006 (accessed 18 May 2016).

[14] E. Freeman, E. Robson, B. Bates, K. Sierra, Head First Design Patterns, O'Reilly Media, Sebastopol, 2008.

[15] A. Goucher, T. Riley, Beautiful Testing: Leading Professionals Reveal How They Improve Software, O'Reilly Media, Sebastopol, 2009.

[16] R. Hanmer, Patterns for Fault Tolerant Software, Wiley, 2013.

[17] G. Hohpe, B. Woolf, Enterprise Integration Patterns: Designing, Building, and Deploying Messaging Solutions, Addison-Wesley, Boston, London, 2004.

[18] K. Julisch, C. Suter, T. Woitalla, O. Zimmermann, Compliance by design – bridging the chasm between auditors and IT architects, Comput. Secur. 30 (6–7) (2011) 410–426.

[19] J. Kabbedijk, C.-P. Bezemer, S. Jansen, A. Zaidman, Defining multi-tenancy: a systematic mapping study on the academic and the industrial perspective, J. Syst. Softw. 100 (2014) 139–148.

[20] J. Kerievsky, Refactoring to Patterns, Addison-Wesley, Boston, 2005.

[21] G. Kousiouris, D. Kyriazis, A. Menychtas, T. Varvarigou, Legacy applications on the cloud: challenges and enablers focusing on application performance analysis and providers characteristics, in: 2012 IEEE 2nd International Conference on Cloud Computing and Intelligent Systems (CCIS), 2012.

[22] M. Kun, C. Zhenxiang, A. Abraham, Y. Bo, S. Runyuan, A transparent data middleware in support of multi-tenancy, in: 2011 7th International Conference on Next Generation Web Services Practices (NWeSP), 2011.

[23] K. Mcarthur, Pro PHP, Springer, Dordrecht, 2008.

[24] P. Mell, T. Grance, The NIST definition of cloud computing, http://dx.doi.org/10.6028/NIST.SP.800-145, 2011.

[25] G.J. Myers, T. Badgett, T.M. Thomas, C. Sandler, The Art of Software Testing, John Wiley & Sons, Inc., Hoboken, NJ, 2004.

[26] S. Newman, Building Microservices, O'Reilly Media, Inc., 2015.

[27] M. Pistoia, S. Chandra, S.J. Fink, E. Yahav, A survey of static analysis methods for identifying security vulnerabilities in software systems, IBM Syst. J. 46 (2) (2007) 265–288.

[28] C. Ramakrishnan, Data leakage detection in a multi-tenant data architecture, M. Corporation, United States Patent Application US 2014/0130175 A1, 2014.

[29] A. Saray, Professional PHP Design Patterns, Wiley, Hoboken, 2009.

[30] B. Sengupta, A. Roychoudhury, Engineering multi-tenant software-as-a-service systems, in: Proceedings of the 3rd International Workshop on Principles of Engineering Service-Oriented Systems, ACM, Waikiki, Honolulu, HI, USA, 2011, pp. 15–21.

[31] G. Shroff, Enterprise Cloud Computing: Technology, Architecture, Applications, Cambridge University Press, Cambridge, 2010.

[32] Y. Singh, Software Testing, Cambridge University Press, Cambridge, 2011.

[33] D. Spinellis, G. Gousios, Beautiful Architecture: Leading Thinkers Reveal the Hidden Beauty in Software Design, O'Reilly Media, Sebastopol, 2009.

[34] F. Trucchia, J. Romei, Pro PHP Refactoring, Apress, 2010.

[35] M.A. van der Linden, Testing Code Security, Taylor & Francis, Hoboken, 2007.

[36] A. Vance, The cloud: battle of the tech titans, Bloomberg Business. Retrieved from http://www.bloomberg.com/bw/magazine/content/11_11/b4219052599182.htm, 2011, p3 (accessed 18 May 2016).

[37] w3techs, Usage statistics and market share of PHP for websites. Retrieved from https://w3techs.com/technologies/details/pl-php/all/all, 2014 (accessed March 2017).

[38] J. Weinman, Cloudonomics: The Business Value of Cloud Computing, Wiley, Hoboken, 2012.

[39] Z. Xuesong, S. Beijun, T. Xucheng, C. Wei, From isolated tenancy hosted application to multi-tenancy: toward a systematic migration method for web application, in: 2010 IEEE International Conference on Software Engineering and Service Sciences (ICSESS), 2010.

[40] M. Yener, A. Theedom, Professional Java EE Design Patterns, Wiley, Hoboken, 2014.

[41] M. Zandstra, PHP Objects, Patterns, and Practice, Springer, Dordrecht, 2010.

[42] Zend Technologies Ltd., Programmer's reference guide of Zend framework 2. Retrieved from http://framework.zend.com/manual/2.3/en/index.html (accessed 18 May 2016).

[43] O. Zimmermann, Architectural refactoring: a task-centric view on software evolution, IEEE Softw. 32 (2) (2015) 26–29.

[44] O. Zimmermann, Architectural refactoring for the cloud: a decision-centric view on cloud migration, Computing (2016), http://dx.doi.org/10.1007/s00607-016-0520-y. Retrieved from http://link.springer.com/article/10.1007/s00607-016-0520-y (accessed 24 October 2016).

[45] O. Zimmermann, L. Wegmann, H. Koziolek, T. Goldschmidt, Architectural decision guidance across projects-problem space modeling, decision backlog management and cloud computing knowledge, in: 2015 12th Working IEEE/IFIP Conference on Software Architecture (WICSA), IEEE, 2015.

EXPLORING THE EVOLUTION OF BIG DATA TECHNOLOGIES

14

Stephen Bonner, Ibad Kureshi, John Brennan, Georgios Theodoropoulos

Institute of Advanced Research Computing, Durham University, United Kingdom

14.1 INTRODUCTION

Since the adoption of cloud computing, big data has been increasing exponentially in popularity, both computer science and the wider world. This seemingly new paradigm of processing emerges on the heels of e-Commerce and the explosion of Internet-enabled digital devices that allow companies multiple channels and touch points to engage potential customers. The accepted definition of big data is the digital analysis of datasets to extract insights, correlations and causations, and value from data. Different groups have come up with different "Vs" to attempt to formalize the definition of the *big* aspect of this phenomenon. The 3 Vs definition of big data, by Doug Laney for Gartner, states that if it has Volume, Variety and Velocity then the data can be considered *big* [39]. Bernard Marr, in his book Big Data, adds Veracity (or validity) and Value to the original list to create the 5 V's of big data [50]. With Volatility and Variability, Visibility, and Visualization added in some combination to the list by different authors there is now a 7 Vs definition of what constitutes big data [46,3,60,54]. Using sales and advertising as a basis the Vs based definition can be explained as:

- *Volume* – With more data being collected, logged, and generated organizations need larger storage to retain this information and larger compute to process it.
- *Velocity* – Through online transactions and interactions the rate at which the Volume is being created vastly exceeds data generated from person-to-person interactions. Online systems are also expected to react in a timely manner meaning that the data needs to be processed as quickly as it gets ingested.
- *Variety* – A digital transaction gives more than just a sale, even a customer browsing certain sections of an online store is valuable information, whether or not a sale is made. In an online transaction, person A buying Object-X is not the only information that can be extracted. Socio-economic, demographic, and consumer journey information can all be collected to improve future sales and advertising. The problem becomes more complex within the inclusion of data from traditional and social media.
- *Veracity* – Large volumes of disparate data being ingested at high speed are only useful if the information is correct. Incorrectly indexed data or spelling mistakes could make complete datasets useless and thus the veracity is important.
- *Validity* – Inferences derived from the data may also not always be accurate. As the saying goes correlation does not always imply causation and so the validity of the insights derived from the data need to be validated.

- *Value and Volatility* – Value is a multifaceted property of big data. As the volume of data grows the incremental value of each data point begins to decrease. As the variety of data available increases, not all the data may aid in product development, sales, or system management. Data may also lose relevance over time. In this case with the dataset not being a part of the business process how are the costs of retention justified. Big data is not the retention of all data; some data needs to remain volatile.
- *Value and Visibility* – The key motivation behind big data is to extract *value* from the data. Many would argue that this involves extracting hidden meaning from the available data. With valid and valuable data information that is not visible may be extracted to make more informed business decisions.
- *Variability* – An extension of variety, variability exists where a metric of a dataset being collected changes in an unpredictable manner that affects the entire business processes. Unexpected purchasing behavior due to factors external to the supply chain means retailers and vendors would need to dynamically tailor their pricing and advertising strategies accordingly.
- *Visualization* – The adoption of big data within corporate business processes means the data needs to be accessible to all who need it. Large dumps of statistical data may not always be easily interpretable at a glance. Visualizing the data and any inferences is an additional important facet of big data.

14.2 BIG DATA IN OUR DAILY LIVES

Michael Cox and David Ellsworth in their 1997 paper titled "Application-controlled demand paging for out-of-core visualization" used the term big data to refer to the phenomenon of datasets not fitting in memory or on local disk especially in the context of visualization [18]. This is the first use of the term big data in published literature at the time. However, the concept of the data explosion goes back many decades [58]. Within scientific endeavors the Large Hadron Collider program at CERN generated 30 petabytes of data in Phase 1 and is expected to generate approximately 25 gigabytes per second when all 4 experiments are operational in Phase 2 [43]. The Large Synoptic Survey Telescope will generate 15 terabytes of data a night once operational in 2019 [47].

Big data attracted the attention of the wider world through two main seminal developments that came in the form of the Google File System in 2003 [24] and MapReduce in 2004 [20]. The implications of sifting through a multitude of logs, that had hitherto only been methods to debug errors in the system, to profile visitors and target advertising, brought data-centric computing in vogue. Webservers, with their logs and browser cookies, allow organizations to collect detailed information about visitors that includes, but is not restricted to, their device, location, time spent on web pages, journey to the webpage, and the journey beyond. Processing this information through data mining and analytics the visitor's age and gender can be inferred, if not already provided through social media or other account information. Over time the data collected also leads to socio-economic and demographic inferences. All of this helps services, the likes of Google or Facebook, to perfectly target advertising to its visitors, making their platform the perfect channel for other companies to engage their target market.

At its core, the data mining taking place aims to create a profile of the person being observed. The person-centric model being created includes their socio-economic and demographic information, their tastes, and their behavior. Plenty has been written about the use of big data for advertising and so the focus here will be to use the same principles to create a person-centric model that can be applied to new developing paradigms such as Smart Homes. With the advent of the Internet of Things revolution, more metrics can be collected to create holistic models of human behavior. While currently the focus is centered on making devices *Internet enabled*, protocols and encryption techniques are being developed to capture and transport the data deluge to be computed, the *killer apps* will come when this data is processed.

In a futuristic smart home, the agent managing the household will need to make decisions regarding scheduling, brokering, and operation. Here is an example of a hypothetical scenario to understand the decisions the smart home will need to make and the data that is available to it. It is 4 a.m. on a Tuesday in March; the occupants have set their alarms to wake up for 6 a.m. One has a meeting at 9 a.m. with, according to the GPS software, a 1-hour commute beforehand. Several other meeting are scheduled which are geographically dispersed. The other homeowner has nothing scheduled until lunchtime but usually leaves for work at 8:45 a.m. Both have the same entry in their calendars for 6 to 8 p.m. The dishwasher is almost full. The washing machine is full. The weather is going to be clear and sunny, with a 5 mph breeze. Sunrise is at 7:20 a.m. and sunset is at 6:08 p.m. The maximum temperature during the day will be 14°C with a minimum of 9°C during the night. The calendar shows that it will be another early start on Wednesday morning.

The agent can use all this information plus historic information and make the following decisions. The coffee maker with Owner A's coffee preference needs to be triggered at 7:45 and then again at 8:30 with Owner B's preference. After 9 a.m. the dishwasher will have the breakfast crockery and utensils and will be sufficiently filled for a full run. The washing machine too will need to run. When it returns at least one of the two electric cars will need a full recharge if not both. Home lighting and heating will not be required till after 8 p.m. as both owners will be out till then and in case they are present before 6 p.m. it will still be daylight. Due to the early start on Wednesday the homeowners are likely to sleep before 11 p.m. implying, at a maximum, a 3-hour user driven power load. A typical Tuesday night load can be extracted from historical records that include climate control information. Based on previous behavior the home agent can infer that if both homeowners are scheduled to stay out till 8 p.m. then they will eat out and so the home stove will not need to come on. Due to the low wind speeds the wind turbine in the garden is not likely to generate much power; however, the solar panels will be able to generate a predictable amount. The CCTV shows that the homeowners return at 10 p.m. and are not accompanied with any other guests so no changes to the earlier model are needed.

Based on all these metrics and inferences the home can automate most of its processes. Further it can predict how much power load it needs to deliver through the day and what the size of the shortfall will be (if any). The home can negotiate with the power grid and get preferential rates for its deficit requirements. If better rates are given during the day, then the home appliances can be scheduled to run during those times. This saves the solar charged battery power for the time the homeowners are back in or to charge the car.

While this may sound like a utopian Jetsons fantasy, big data, cloud computing, and Internet of things have enabled considerable research and development in this area to make it a reality [35,74,76]. Using the calendar, previous repeated behavioral patterns, data from various Internet enabled devices, and other external sources (e.g., weather services) a smart home can build a complete profile of its occupants, their preferences and their expected behavior. Similar to the model created through people's online behavior that is used in advertising, these highly detailed models are only achievably by processing large quantities of unrelated datasets that need to be sourced from disparate sources. The various devices in the hypothetical scenario continuously generate data that needs to be harvested and used in near real time to account for any changes. This is big data in the home.

14.3 DATA INTENSIVE COMPUTING

The term data intensive computing encapsulates the technology designed to store, manage and process big data [34]. Data intensive computing contains two key areas, applications and frameworks, both of which exploit data parallelism. Data parallelism is the notion that data is distributed among nodes in a parallel computer and therefore can be processed in parallel. It has been argued that data, as opposed to task parallelism, is often the easiest way to create a parallel program [33]. Data intensive frameworks are specialist software, designed to create and run data intensive applications. While data intensive applications are usually data parallel programs, whose main function is the manipulation of massive datasets.

14.3.1 BIG COMPUTE VERSUS BIG DATA

Simply processing large datasets is typically not considered to be big data. Groups like *Conseil Européen pour la Recherche Nucléaire* (CERN) and *Transnational Research In Oncology* (TRIO) have been using High Performance Computing systems and scalable software to analyze very large datasets. However, this is considered *compute-centric processing*. Typically, a mathematical algorithm is used to generate results from the data that forms the input. This is true for computational fluid dynamics, image processing, and traditional genome analysis.

From a components perspective, little differentiates a big data machine from a supercomputer; however, the philosophy of design and interaction of components places these systems in two classes. Table 14.1 outlines the salient differences between big compute and big data systems.

Computers, large and small, are very efficient and quick at processing decimal numbers and mathematical equations. While not always true, typically compute-centric processing takes as input small quantities of data and generates large quantities of data while processing or as output. As the power and thermal limits of silicon were approached, multiple processors were ganged together to parallelize and speed up processing. Compute-centric applications typically parallelize the processing by distributing the data and the instruction to multiple processors that can be as close as being located on the same chip, up to being geographically remote and only accessible over the Internet.

Taking traditional high performance computers (HPC) as an exemplar system, processing elements (PE) are typically located across a tightly coupled local area network operating at network speeds between 1 to 100 Gbps. The biggest bottleneck to a compute-centric parallel program on an HPC system is the network. Complex programs are not able to scale to bigger systems due to large global communication operations. Input data therefore cannot be distributed in the same manner as the instruction set, from one system across the entire parallel machine. A dedicate fast shared storage device is used to make the data available to all processing cores. As all the data is clumped together, even if the data domain is partitioned within the algorithm, each PE still needs to traverse the entire dataset to find the required subset. First and foremost, this is a waste of compute cycles, and secondly it causes unsus-

Table 14.1 Big compute systems vs big data systems

Component	Big compute systems	Big data systems
Data	Centralized shared storage	Local storage managed centrally
Network	High bandwidth and low latency required for scalability	Latency plays minimal role, most bandwidth required during data loading and unloading phases
System Design	Tightly coupled systems	Run on almost anything approach – PEs can be heterogeneous with consumer grade networks
Task Management	Task concurrency required. System can be divided among jobs but each job must run as a single unit	Task and data replication allows for out of order execution of tasks and jobs can also be split
Job Resilience	If a PE involved in a job fails, the job fails and needs to be restarted	Replication of tasks allows for the failure of PE without affecting the job
System Resilience	Systems can cope with loss of PE. Single points of failure: Centralized Storage, Controller Node (redundancy possible), Internal Networking	Built-in redundancy in nearly all components. Default operation includes replication. Single Point of Failure: Internal Networking
Programming Model	Message Passing Interface (MPI), Symmetric multiprocessing (SMP), Parallel Virtual Machine (PVM)	MapReduce, Bulk Synchronous Parallel (BSP)

tainable loads on the storage device (e.g., 50–100 PEs synchronously accessing 1 storage server to find the relevant 1 GB of data to process). For example, if we consider a CFD job with a detailed model (>1 GB) of the object then each PE will request that file and then only load into memory the *chunk* of the model it must process. When designing a typical HPC system (for CFD or FEA workloads) the key metrics in order of importance is processor clock speed, processor density, network interconnect, processing power and network capability of centralized storage, and finally memory per PE.

The main distinction of the big data computing paradigm is that the processing algorithms and systems are usually designed with data centricity in mind. Data centric systems devote the majority of the running time to performing data manipulation and I/O over numerical operations. The optimization of algorithm is secondary to the data management. Within the MapReduce ecosystem (discussed further down) data locality is a major component to the concept of data centricity. Unlike the HPC systems above the data is not stored at a single point. At ingestion time it is in fact divided and replicated across a distributed compute system, and stored local to the processing elements. That way each PE only needs to deal with its local subset of data without needing to search for it. The PEs also do not need to compete with each other for bandwidth over the network. This creative distribution of data ensures that processing instructions only go to the PEs that have direct access to the relevant data. The replication of the data subsets ensures further and much improved parallelization. If two instructions require access to the same subset of data, the replication ensures that two separate PEs can run both instructions simultaneously without any contention for network or disk. When designing a big data system, the metrics to keep in mind are size of PE level storage, speed of PE level storage, memory per PE, processor clock speed, and network interconnect. This is another reason for the penetration of big data within the commercial sector. HPC systems have large power overheads – leading to high processor density, and require highly specialized networking components to deliver performance. Conversely big data systems can be very efficient using high quality workstations loosely coupled with commodity networking equipment. This also makes big data systems easy to deliver over cloud computing infrastructure, lowering the financial barrier to entry.

14.3.2 DATA INTENSIVE APPLICATIONS

There are a variety of computation types that can be considered data intensive. Such applications often use massive quantities of input data to derive some important value from it. Indeed, increasingly a company's success is driven by their ability analyze and draw conclusions from enormous quantities of disperse data sources. The need to derive new information from data has led to the emergence of several sub categories of data intensive applications including:

- *Data Mining* – Data-mining algorithms are a broad class algorithms used to extract certain key features or metrics from a given data. The types of algorithms used and features extracted from data vary upon the domain the data belongs to. The algorithms used to mine astronomy data, for example, would differ from those used to mine financial market data [16].
- *Machine Learning* – Machine learning algorithms are a varied set used broadly to study and learn from datasets with goals including pattern recognition and future prediction. Machine learning is closely related to the data-mining field and recent improvements in algorithms and the power of modern hardware have accelerated progress in the field. The use of larger and more varied training data sets have increased accuracy of any predictions created [42].
- *Real Time Processing* – The introduction of modern software and hardware has increasingly made the real time processing of massive datasets a reality. Such real time analysis is often named stream processing [42]. In stream processing model, data is processed, queried and analyzed immediately as it arrives into the system. Increasingly a data stream from a generation source is sent directly to a compute resource for processing before then being archived for latter access. This is in contrast to the batch processing method, where data is first stored and processed in bulk at a later date.
- *Graph Processing* – Many domains can naturally be represented as graphs as they can capture the inherent interconnecting nature of real world phenomena [8]. Such domains include social networks, semantic web, protein networks and computer networks among others. Due to this, there have emerged a class of algorithms designed specifically to extract metrics and topological features from graph objects, giving valuable and unique insight into the dataset.

14.3.3 DATA INTENSIVE FRAMEWORKS

Data intensive frameworks are a class of software designed to enable the efficient creation and running of data intensive applications. Data intensive applications pose interesting and unique demands on the underlying hardware as data transfer, not processor speeds, limits their performance. As such, data intensive frameworks make important considerations and compromises to optimize for data processing in their architecture design and implementation [68]. The need to process massive quantities of data being generated called for a paradigm shift in the mind-set of system and application designers. This shift called for systems that excel at ingesting, moving, manipulating, and retrieving data on an unprecedented scale. This poses real challenges for both hardware and software. Many of the resulting data intensive frameworks emerged from Internet-focused companies and research institutes, for example MapReduce from Google and Dryad from Microsoft. Data intensive applications prioritize input/output (IO) operations, specifically disk and memory access, over CPU based computation [66]. Both compute and data intensive computing are performed of distributed clusters, usually with a shared-nothing architecture. Although the famous Moore's Law has observed that CPU performance has doubled, due to progress made in the miniaturization of transistors, approximately every two years, IO has experienced a much slower increase in performance. This has led to the notion that compute is considered cheap and data IO is expensive. As data intensive computing is usually performance upon a distributed system, the bandwidth and latency of the network are also an important factor in performance, as large quantities of data needs to be transferred across it. However, the movement of massive datasets across the network has proven to be exceptionally time consuming. For example, a system with a 10 GB network running at 80% utilization, would take approximately 11 days to transfer a dataset 1 petabyte in size [37].

Due to these demands, data intensive frameworks are designed to provide such optimizations as data locality and fault tolerance to optimize the available hardware. There has been a general shift in the management of the complexities introduced by fault tolerance and data locality from hardware to software in the form of data intensive frameworks. In addition, data intensive frameworks mask the complexity of the underlying hardware from the application developer and automatically handle data partitioning, scheduling, and parallelization [33].

14.3.4 MAPREDUCE AND GFS

In 2003 and 2004 Google introduced two key concepts to the research community; both would become some of the cornerstones of the data Intensive computing research landscape. Firstly, Google introduced the concept of MapReduce, which it had developed internally as a conceptually simple, yet extremely powerful new programming paradigm for processing massive datasets in parallel. The second paper introduced was the Google File System (GFS), a distributed and fault resilient file system. The GFS system allows for large files to be split into smaller blocks, which can then be distributed across all nodes in a cluster. These file blocks allow for easy resilience against hardware failure, as each block can be replicated across a range of separate machines. The following sections will give an overview of the design and functionality of both GFS and MapReduce and explain why this model has become so successful for Data Intensive Computing.

14.3.4.1 The Google File System (GFS)

In 2003 Google introduced the distributed and fault tolerant GFS [24]. The GFS was designed to meet many of the same goals as preexisting distributed file systems including scalability, performance, reliability, and robustness. However, Google also designed GFS to meet some specific goals driven by some key observations of their workload. Firstly, Google experienced regular failures of its cluster machines; therefore, a distributed file-system must be extremely fault tolerant and have some form of automatic fault recovery. Secondly, multigigabyte files are common so I/O and file block size must be designed appropriately. Thirdly, the majority of files are appended to, rather than having existing content overwritten or changed, this means optimizations should be focused on appending files. Lastly, the computation engine should be designed and colocated with the distributed file system for best performance [24].

With these goals in mind, Google designed the GFS to partition all input data in 64 MB chunks [24]. This partitioning process helps GFS achieve many of its stated goals. As such, the comparatively large size for the chunks was not chosen by chance. The larger chunk sizes result in several advantages including less metadata, a reduction in the number of open TCP connections and a decrease in lookups. The main disadvantage to this approach is that space on the distributed file system could be wasted if files smaller than the chunk sizes are stored, although Google argues that this is almost never the case [24]. In order to achieve fault tolerance, the chunks of data are replicated to some configurable number of nodes; by default, this value is set at three. If the cluster comprises a sufficient number of nodes, each chunk will be replicated twice in the same rack, with a third being stored in a second rack. If changes are made to a single chunk, the changes are automatically replicated to all the mirrored copies.

From the point of view of the architecture, GFS is conceptually simple, with cluster nodes playing only one of two roles. Firstly, nodes can be data nodes, whose role is to physically store the data chunks on company's local storage and comprise the vast majority of all the cluster nodes. The second class of node is the master node, which stores the metadata for the distributed file system including the equivalent of a partition table, recording upon which nodes chunks are stored and which chunks contain certain files. The GFS has just one master node per cluster. This enables the master node to have a complete view of file system and make sophisticated data placement and partitioning strategies [24]. The master node also ensures that if a data node goes down, the blocks contained on that node are replicated to other nodes, ensuring the block replication is maintained. The one obvious problem with the single master strategy is that it then becomes the single point of failure for the cluster, which seams counterintuitive considering one of the main goals of GFS was resilience against hardware failure. However, the current state of the master node is constantly recorded, so when any failure occurs, another node can take its place instantly [24].

14.3.4.2 MapReduce

MapReduce is both a powerful programming paradigm and a distributed data processing engine, designed to run on large clusters comprised of commodity hardware originally introduced by Google via a 2004 paper [20]. MapReduce was specifically designed as a new way of processing the massive quantities of data required by a company like Google. Its programming model takes inspiration from functional programming and allows users to easily create scalable data parallel applications, whilst the processing engine ensures fault tolerance, data locality and scheduling automatically. MapReduce is not designed as a replacement for traditional parallel processing frameworks such as MPI; instead it is a response to the new class of applications demanded by the big data phenomenon. When Google originally designed the MapReduce system, the following assumptions and principals guided its development [64]:

- MapReduce was designed to be deployed on low-cost and unreliable commodity hardware.
- This hardware was loosely coupled and configured as a Redundant Array of Independent Nodes (RAIN).
- Nodes from the RAIN were assumed to fail and thus could be removed at any time. These failures should have no impact on any running jobs or result in any data loss.
- The MapReduce paradigm was designed to be highly parallel, yet abstract enough to allow for fast and easy algorithm development.

In MapReduce, the compute engine and the distributed file-system are designed together and are tightly coupled. The system utilizes this tightly coupled nature to create the key performance driver of MapReduce – data locality. Data locality ensures that the required computation is moved to the data as the node that holds the data will process it [27]. This is an advantage in a modern compute cluster environment, as data transfer is often the bottleneck in application performance and bringing the compute to the data will remove the need for a costly network transfer.

From a conceptual point of view, MapReduce can be considered as just two distinct phases: Map and Reduce [44]. In order to achieve some of its fault tolerance and scalability goals, the MapReduce system places some limitations on the way end users create their applications. Perhaps the most challenging, from an end user's perspective, is that Map tasks must be written in such a way that they can operate completely independently, and in isolation, on a single chunk of the overall larger dataset. Any operations that require some form of communication must be performed in the Reduce phase, which can aggregate the required result from data passed to it by a series of Mappers. To create a MapReduce application an end user must be able to express the logic required by their algorithms in these two phases, although chaining multiple MapReduce iterations together can accommodate more complicated tasks. It is also possible to create Map only jobs for tasks that do not require any sort of accumulations, such as some data cleaning or validation tasks. From an end user's perspective, one of the key strengths of the MapReduce paradigm is that their applications are completely removed from the often-challenging tasks usually associated with parallel computing. The backend system of MapReduce handles the data distribution, fault tolerance and scheduling for the end user's automatically [64]. This frees users to just focus upon the creation of new algorithms and the parallelization is handled automatically. This lowers the complexity of writing algorithms massively and helps democratize the creation of parallel programs so nonspecialists can harness the power of modern compute clusters [20].

The MapReduce system uses key/value pairs as the input and output for both of the stages. The input data is presented to the Map function as key/value pairs and, after processing, the output is stored as another set of key/value pairs. In between the Map and Reduce phases, common keys in the Map output are grouped together so all the associated values are available for processing in the same Reduce task. The final processing and result from the Reduce task are again output as key/value pairs [20]. One of the key performance drivers of MapReduce is that the Map phase is highly parallel. By default, if the input data resides in m blocks, then m Map tasks will be spawned. As GFS ensures that blocks are distributed across the entire cluster, the Map tasks will be executed on many nodes simultaneously. This is the simplistic model of MapReduce and gives a good representation of how data will flow through an application but it does not discuss some key behind the scenes operations performed by the system.

Greater insight into the operation and intricacies of MapReduce can be gained through the analysis of the word count application, also known as the hello world of MapReduce. For this example application, the input to the program will be a collection of text documents stored on a GFS-like file system and will be completed in a single MapReduce phase. The collection of documents would be split into m 64 MB chunks automatically by the GFS. Once the MapReduce program was launched m Map tasks would be created, wherever possible, upon the nodes containing the relevant file chunks. In the word count application, the role of the Map task is to split the text data contained in the block, using whitespace, into a sequence of individual words. The Map function would then emit its series of intermediate key/value pair with each word located being the key and the value being an integer value of one. Pseudocode representing this process is shown as Code 1.

```
Map:
      void Map(string document) {
            for each word w in document {
                  Emit_Intermediate(w, "1");
            }}
Reduce:
      void Reduce (string word, list<string> values) {
            int count = 0;
            for each v in values {
                  count += StringToInt(v);}
            Emit_Final(word, count);
      }
```

CODE 1

Pseudocode for a MapReduce version of word count

An example output from the Map phase would be $(w1, 1), (w2, 1), ..., (wn, 1)$. The transfer of data between the Map and Reduce phases is handled by a process called shuffle and sort. The role of the shuffle and sort phase is to collect and sort the values associated with a specific key so that they are all presented to a single Reduce task. This phase can be a performance bottleneck, as all the intermediate data from the Mappers is first written back to disk before then being transferred over the network to the nodes that will run the Reduce task. In the word count application an example input to the Reduce function would be $(w1, [11111])$, for a word that had five instances in the original input file. The Reduce function would then simply sum the integer values for all keys and emit the total, along with the original word as the final output of the application – $(w1, 5)$.

Whilst MapReduce has proven to be extremely powerful and popular, it is not without fault and has received some criticism within academic literature [21,56]. The main arguments against MapReduce centers around a few key areas including the comparatively reduced functionality, its lack of suitability for certain computation tasks, a still relatively low-level API and its need for a dedicated cluster resource. When contrasted with other data management and query systems, such as SQL, MapReduce can appear to offer limited functionally. Simple standard relation database operations such as joins are complicated in MapReduce and often require sophisticated solutions. Although several strategies, including Map-side, Reduce-side and Cascade joins, have emerged to enable the functionality, the framework was clearly not designed with workflows involving numerous complicated joins in mind [1]. MapReduce completely removes the data schema used by traditional databases so all data is stored without structure or an index, meaning that it is unable to utilize the possible optimizations offered by structured and semistructured data [21]. The lack of an index means that the entire dataset must be traversed to search for a specific portion of the data, which can be costly, especially with massive datasets. In its original incarnation there is no higher-level language for MapReduce, and users must write their applications using the still low-level API. When compared with writing SQL queries, for example, the MapReduce API has a greater level of complexity and requires more lines of code. In addition, MapReduce code is often less portable and tends to be very data-specific [44]. For certain data processing tasks, particularly those that require many iterations over the same dataset, the MapReduce paradigm is unsuitable. Unfortunately, many state-of-the-art machine learning and graph processing algorithms display exactly these very characteristics [78]. From a system point of view, MapReduce is often deployed on its own dedicated hardware, as the system does not lend itself to resource sharing with competing frameworks such as MPI. This can increase costs for an organization as it potentially must purchase and maintain two clusters if the requirement for both systems is present within the organization.

Despite these limitations, MapReduce has proved to be extremely popular in both industry and academia. Although it should be clear now that MapReduce is best suited for use in a specific class of application, when a massive amount of data needs processing and when the required processing fits well within the data parallel model. The original implementation of MapReduce cannot be, nor was it designed to be, a replacement for parallel processing engines such as MPI or structured database systems such as SQL. Instead it compliments these systems and fills the void when the required workload doesn't fit into either paradigm.

14.4 APACHE HADOOP
14.4.1 HADOOP V1

Apache Hadoop is an open-source project first developed by researchers at Yahoo [4]. It was designed to replicate the functionality of both Google's GFS and MapReduce system. As such, Hadoop originally launched with two components; the Hadoop Distributed File System (HDFS), designed to replicate GFS, and its own implementation of the MapReduce runtime and programming model [67]. Since the code was first made publicly available in 2007, Hadoop has grown to become the de facto standard for big data processing. Since it is a replication of the original Google ideas, Hadoop inherits the same set of strengths and weakness as was previously discussed. The only major differences between them are that Hadoop is written in the Java programming language, compared with the C++ of the original Google system, and that Hadoop is open-source, thus it can be used and modified free of charge.

Hadoop is designed to run on a distributed shared nothing cluster of commodity machines. The original Hadoop implementation runs as a series of daemon processes, with nodes in the cluster taking one of two roles, master or slave. Each of the four separate daemon processes runs within a Java Virtual Machine (JVM). These daemon processes (shown in Fig. 14.1) are:

- *JobTracker* – Master process for the MapReduce component that controls the submission and scheduling of jobs on the cluster. Runs on the master node.
- *NameNode* – Master process for the HDFS that keeps track of how data has been distributed across the available DataNode. Runs on the master node.
- *TaskTracker* – These processes are the worker components of the MapReduce system. The Task-Tracker demons themselves do not perform the computation; instead they control the spawning of separate JVMs for each MapReduce job. These are run upon the slave nodes.
- *DataNode* – These processes control the data stored in the HDFS. These are also run upon the slave nodes.

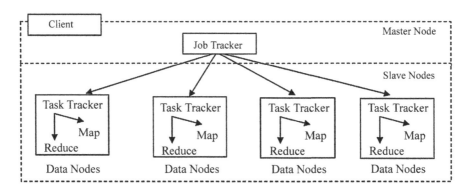

FIGURE 14.1

Interaction between various Hadoop processes [71]

14.4.1.1 The wider ecosystem

Due to the popularity of Hadoop, various research teams have greatly extended its functionality past its original design brief. Many of these projects have been incorporated under the Apache Hadoop banner. These technologies include: HBase, Cassandra, Hive, Pig, Impala, Storm, Giraph, Mahout, and Tez. These systems are designed to introduce additional computing paradigms into the Hadoop ecosystem. Some of the most popular are explored below:

- *HBase* – Apache HBase is an open-source implementation of Google's BigTable system [15]. HBase provides a NoSQL based, fault tolerant, distributed and scalable database layer that resides on top of the HDFS [12]. HBase uses the wide column model from BigTable to store the data, as such it has no schema. Unlike HDFS alone, HBase enables real-time random read and write access to the data contained within a table. HBase provides no traditional query language, so users must access the data via a standard MapReduce job [12].
- *Cassandra* – Apache Cassandra is another database solution for Hadoop that is highly available and scalable, started in 2010 as Facebook's alternative to BigTable [38]. As such Cassandra is similar in functionally to HBase as it is a distributed NoSQL database that can provide high availability, linear scalability and data dissemination across multiple geo-distributed data centers. However, Cassandra supports the Cassandra Query Language (CQL) to provide a way to query data using a limited, SQL-like language [14].
- *Hive* – Apache Hive is a project created by Facebook to provide not only a structured data store, but also a way of querying the data via an SQL-like language called HiveQL [69]. Hive incorporates a query created using HiveQL that is automatically translated into the required number of MapReduce tasks, enabling users who are familiar with SQL to easily start processing data via Hadoop. A key element is that Hive will automatically perform any requested joins [69].
- *Pig* – Apache Pig was created to be a high-level data-flow language, comprising two elements: the Pig data-flow language named Pig-Latin and the Pig execution environment which enables the job to run on a local or Hadoop distributed environment [53]. The Pig-Latin language allows users to express their jobs as a series of operations and transformations to create the desired result. The

included operations include familiar database operations such as filtering, sorts and joins. A key advantage to Pig is that comparatively complex logic can be expressed in a small number of lines as users use a much higher level API. In a similar fashion to Hive, Pig automatically translates these operations into a series of MapReduce iterations [53].

- *Impala* – Apache Impala is a distributed massively parallel processing analytic database engine running on top of Hadoop [36]. The Impala database engine provides a mechanism for producing near real time queries on data stored within a Hive data store, leveraging HiveQL. An Impale service consists of three daemons; the core Impala daemon runs on each DataNode within a system, accepts distributes and coordinates user submitted queries across the cluster. The Impala Statestore monitors the core daemons and maintains state information, which is then redistributed to all core daemons. The Impala Catalog ensures metadata remains up to date across the entire cluster [36].
- *Storm* – Apache Storm is a distributed real-time computation system, based on the original Storm project create at Twitter [70]. Storm makes it easy to reliably process large amounts of streamed data, facilitating real time processing within the Hadoop ecosystem. Storm was designed so it can be used with any programming language through the use of Apache Thrift Topology Definitions. Although the base system is written in the Clojure functional programming language. Storm is comprised of two daemons, Nimbus and the Supervisor. Nimbus is the central orchestration process through which all jobs are delegated to Supervisors. Supervisors spawn and monitor worker threads to complete tasks. These daemons are fast-fail by design, meaning that worker processes are never affected by the failure of Nimbus or Supervisors. Storm has been designed to accept a data stream from a variety of sources including the Twitter streaming API, Apache Kafka, and JMS, although users can create their own stream receivers to accept data from almost any source. Similar to Dryad, Storm's computation model can be considered conceptually as a DAG, where data is streamed along the edges to computational vertices.
- *Giraph* – Apache Giraph is a system for large-scale graph processing, was developed as an open source project able to replicate the functionality of Google's Pregel [17,49]. Giraph processes graph-structured data in iterative *supersteps*. A *superstep* is an embarrassingly parallel problem where a single function is performed on each node within a graph. Changes made to nodes or edges within a *superstep* cascade through the graph on subsequent *supersteps*. Within any step a node can be marked as inactive, and processing continues until this is true for all nodes [32]. Giraph does not require any additional services and simply runs as MapReduce Jobs on standard Hadoop infrastructure.
- *Mahout* – Apache Mahout collection of machine learning libraries that are designed to be scalable and robust, with algorithms focusing in the areas of classification, clustering, filtering, data mining, evolutionary processes and dimensionality reduction [57]. All the original algorithms in Mahout were expressed as MapReduce applications; as such they require no extra daemon services. Recently Apache Mahout has expanded past MapReduce only implementations to include Spark and Flink as well.
- *Flink* – Apache Flink is a distributed data processing system designed with stream processing at its core [13]. Although the system is designed for stream based workloads it can also process batch workloads efficiently by treating them as a special form of a stream application. Users can create Apache Flink applications in either Java or Scala programming languages. Flink jobs can be run upon a Hadoop cluster using YARN, and can even execute Hadoop code from within a job.

14.4.2 HADOOP 2.0

In Hadoop V1, the management and resource negotiation is controlled via the MapReduce runtime. As such, any additional system wishing to access data stored in HDFS must be able to translate itself down to a series of MapReduce tasks. This places a massive restriction of the type of computation that can be performed via Hadoop. To address this, Hadoop 2.0 incorporated a new component called Yet Another Resource Negotiator (YARN) into the software stack [72]. YARN's key advancement is that it separates scheduling decisions from the data processing layer. This means that workflows no longer need to be constructed in terms of MapReduce tasks, potentially manipulated or misused, to achieve completion of work not suited to a MapReduce framework. Examples of this include map-only tasks written for Hadoop 1.0 that would spawn services such as web servers. One of the drawbacks with Hadoop V1 was the single point of failure that the JobTracker daemon represented. If a JobTracker were to fail, the resulting situation would be one where all running jobs within a system would be lost, there was no mechanism for automatic recovery from such a situation and all users would have to manually resubmit jobs for completion once the system was restored. YARN solves this key problem by removing cluster management duties from the JobTracker [72].

The YARN system architecture comprises three separate components, the ResourceManager (RM), the NodeManager (NM), and the ApplicationManager (AM) [72]:

- *ResourceManager* – The RM removes responsibility for scheduling of workflows from the Job-Tracker and serves containers for processing, which are logical bundles of available resources. This process is responsible for global system view collected from communication with the NM and AM, along with overall management of the system through the servicing resource requests made by user job submissions and the AMs. There is also a mechanism whereby the RM can request the return of resources from an AM, if it is deemed to be oversubscribed on the system, or forcibly claw back resources by instructing a NM to terminate containers if it deems too much time has elapsed following a request to an AM. In order to mitigate a single point of failure situation there is a standby RM that can take over responsibility of the system and spawn a new standby RM in the eventuality of a master RM failure. If there is a situation where a node, or NM, fails the RM will detect this, update system global state, report the failure to all running AMs and restart any AMs that were lost due to the failure of the NM.
- *NodeManager* – The NM launches and manages all containers, including AMs, configuring the environment as appropriate from AM, and user, requests received via the RM. Container requirements, including resources and environment, are described through a Container Launch Context (CLC) that are sent with every request for container creation. The NM is also responsible for reporting actual hardware utilization to the RM for maintenance of the global cluster state view. Upon creation all containers are issued a lease to use the requested resources this enables the RM to make better scheduling decisions based on a known lifetime of existing processes. Further, the NM cleans up all processes and files when a container exits, the NM is not aware is a container has exited cleanly or not. Handling of container failure is left to running application framework, i.e., it is up to the AM to know that a container has not exited cleanly and to request a new container via the RM.
- *ApplicationManager* – Bootstrap process, running within a NM spawned container, responsible for the execution of a "job" within the cluster, whether it be set of processes, a logical description of work, or even a long-running service. It requests required resources from the RM and executes code

within other available containers. Also responsible for local job optimization, management for loss of resources (node failure, other than node running AM) and reporting of job based metrics.

14.5 APACHE SPARK

Spark is a general-purpose parallel computing framework designed for computations of increased complexity to be performed upon massive datasets [78]. It's the first general-purpose compute platform to have emerged after the removal of cluster resource management from the MapReduce paradigm. The Spark computing framework grew from work at UC Berkeley and has quickly gained momentum within the data intensive computing community due to its performance and flexibility [9]. The speed increase is due, in part, to the Resilient Distributed Dataset (RDD) abstraction that allows working data be cached in memory, eliminating the need for costly intermediate stage disk writes [78]. At its core, Apache Spark is a cluster-computing platform that provides an API allowing users to create distributed applications, although it has grown to be the key component in the larger Berkley Data Analytics Stack (BDAS). Spark was designed to alleviate some of the constraints of the MapReduce programming model, specifically its poor performance when utilizing the same dataset for iterative compute processes due to its lack of an abstraction for distributed memory access [78]. Spark has been optimized for compute tasks that require the reuse of the same working dataset across multiple parallel operations, especially iterative machine learning and data analytic tasks, whilst also maintaining scalability and fault tolerance [64]. It has been argued that modern data analytic tasks that require the reuse of data are increasingly common in iterative machine learning and graph computation algorithms [77]. Examples of such algorithms include PageRank, used to create a rank of the popularity of web pages and other linked data sources and K-means clustering, used to group common members of a dataset together.

From the application developer's perspective, Spark allows for the creation of standalone programs in Java, Scala, R, and Python. Interestingly Spark also offers users the ability to utilize an interactive shell that runs atop of the cluster, behaving much like an interactive Python interpreter would. Spark has three key advantages for end users over MapReduce. Firstly, user's programs are less complicated to create and often require fewer lines of code. Secondly, users can create more complicated algorithms owing to the increased functionality of the API. Thirdly, due to Spark's speed advantage, user's computation will be completed in less time. Many of Spark's advantages are due to its more expressive and populated API. This higher-level API results in algorithm logic being expressed in fewer lines of code. The creators of Spark illustrate the brevity of Spark code by demonstrating that the word count example, which requires 50+ lines of Java MapReduce code, can be completed in just 3 lines of Scala code. (See Code 2.)

This is achieved via the use of Spark's higher level of API abstraction, allowing users access to a greater range of in-built functionality. Spark also contains concepts that will be familiar to many data scientists, such as data frames and SQL syntax. Compared with writing MapReduce code, Spark can be considered simpler due to the decreased number of nuances and caveats users have to consider during program creation. Another key advantage for end users is the runtime performance when using Spark, which has been shown to be greater than that of MapReduce [77]. In 2014, Spark beat the previous record held by Hadoop MapReduce for the GraySort competition. This competition requires frameworks to sort 100 TB of data in the shortest amount of time. Spark beat Hadoop's record by 49

```
01 val textFile = sc.textFile("hdfs://file.txt")
02 val counts = textFile.flatMap(line => line.split(" "))
              .map(word => (word, 1))
              .reduceByKey(_ + _)
03 counts.foreach(println)
```

CODE 2

Scala code for word count in spark

minutes, taking just a total of 23 minutes to sort the complete dataset [6]. Spark's victory is even more impressive when considering the compute resources consumed by both frameworks for their respective sorts. Spark utilized 1864 less compute nodes than Hadoop, requiring just 206 nodes to Hadoop's 2100 [6]. Other results have shown that Spark has achieved its stated aim of increasing the speed of iterative computing tasks. For example, Spark has been shown to be faster by up-to 20 times for K-means clustering [77] and up-to 8 times for PageRank [75].

From the administrator's perspective, Spark is also an attractive platform. The architecture of its design means that Spark is highly portable and can run on systems ranging from laptops, supercomputers, and the cloud. Spark also integrates well with existing Hadoop deployments, as it can be managed via YARN. In addition, Spark can be controlled via Mesos, an alternative cluster management framework developed by the same team as Spark [30]. Spark can also run in standalone mode, managing its own resources and scheduling. This mode can be configured to run on a single machine for testing and development work. For deployment to the cloud, each release of Spark contains scripts to manage a standalone deployment to Amazon's EC2 cloud. Although Spark's popularity has meant that all the major cloud vendors (Amazon's EC2, Microsoft's Azure and Google's Compute Engine) are offering prebuilt images containing Spark along with additional data intensive frameworks.

14.5.1 RESILIENT DISTRIBUTED DATASETS

The core of Spark is the Resilient Distributed Dataset (RDD) abstraction. An RDD is a read-only collection of data that can be partitioned across a subset of Spark cluster machines and form the main working component [77]. RDDs are so integral to the function of Spark that the entire Spark API can be considered to be a collection of operations to create, transform, and export RDDs. Every algorithm implemented in Spark is effectively a series of transformative operations performed upon data represented as an RDD. The key performance driver of Spark is that an RDD can be cached in memory of the Spark cluster compute nodes and thus can be reused by many iterative tasks. The input data that forms a RDD is partitioned into chunks and distributed across all the nodes in the Spark cluster, with each node then performing computation in parallel upon its own set of chucks. Physically an RDD is a Scala object and can be constructed from a variety of data sources, including files from HDFS or other file system, directly from Scala arrays or from a range of transformations that can be performed upon an existing RDD [77]. A key feature of RDDs is that they can be reconstructed if a RDD partition is lost using a concept called lineage and thus can be considered to be fault tolerant. Spark keeps a record of the lineage of an RDD but tracking the transformation that have been performed to create it. If any part of an RDD is lost then Spark will utilize this linage record to quickly and efficiently re-compute the RDD using the identical operations that created the original version [77]. This method of lineage recomputation removes the need for costly data replication strategies used by other methods for abstracting in-memory storage across a compute cluster. However, if the lineage chain reaches a large enough size, users can manually flag a specific RDD to be check-pointed. Check-pointed RDDs are written to disk or HDFS to avoid the recomputation of long lineage chains. RDDs are not for storing or archiving final result data; this is still handled via HDFS or other file system.

There is a range of parallel operations that can be performed upon a RDD using the Spark Core API. These operations fall into two distinct categories, Transformations and Actions [77]. Transformations contain functions that will create new RDDs from existing data sources, whilst actions trigger computations to calculate a return value from the data or write the data out to external storage. The Transformation operations are lazy, so computation will not occur when these are called. An Action must be called to force the computation to happen. This lazy execution style has several advantages in the optimization of storage and performance for Spark. Spark will inspect a complete sequence of Transformations before a user's application is physically run upon the cluster. This allows for an overall picture of the data lineage to be created so that Spark can evaluate the complete transformation chain. Knowing this complete chain allows Spark to atomically optimize before runtime by only computing with the data required for the final result [9].

The RDD concept has further been expanded via the introduction of Spark DataFrames, [7]. A Spark DataFrame arranges the distributed collection of data into labeled columns similar to a traditional relational database. DataFrames are at a higher level of abstraction then RDDs and include a schema, allowing Spark to perform more automatic optimization at run time by exploiting the structured nature [7]. In addition to the performance improvements, the DataFrames API contains more domain specific functionality not offered by the RDD API, including joins and aggregations familiar to many data scientists.

14.5.2 DATA FLOW AND PROGRAMMING WITH SPARK

To create a program with Spark is very similar to existing data flow languages. End users are only required to write a single class that acts as a high-level program driver. This is in contrast to MapReduce, where 3 classes are required to create a typical program, the driver, mapper and reducer. In Spark, the user created driver program defines how the input data will be transformed to create the desired output. Users can create their applications in Java, Scala, Python or R using the provided APIs. However, Spark is a Scala first platform, meaning that new features in the API are added first in the Scala language. Scala is a functional language, and so can be a bit of a learning curve for users more familiar with OOP. Users of other languages are forced to wait for the latest Spark features to be pushed down steam. The program is submitted on the Spark cluster via the head node, and is then automatically distributed across the cluster so that it can be executed upon the partition of the RDD stored upon each worker node.

The data flow of a Spark program can be considered as follows: Firstly, the driver creates a single or multiple RDDs from a Hadoop or other data source. It then will apply transformations upon the RDD that will create new RDDs. Finally, some number of actions will be invoked upon the transformed RDDs to create the final output from the program. Perhaps the best way to envisage how Spark functions is to consider a typical example application. In this example we will explore how to create a simple log-processing program that will take a log file as input and count the number of times a keyword appears. The overall plan for this application is to take a log file stored on a HDFS, extract only the required lines, load it into memory and count the number of stored lines. To create this application in Spark would require the following steps; firstly, an RDD would be created from the log file stored on the HDFS. The second RDD would be created via the filter transformation; this would filter the original file and only select the lines starting with the string "ERROR." A third RDD would be created using the map transformation to split the string on white space to remove the "ERROR" sub-string from the beginning and load it into memory. Finally, the number of elements would be counted using the inbuilt count function. It may seem inefficient to create three RDDs for such a simple application but as the computation is only triggered when the count Action is called, Spark's execution planning will ensure that only the required data is processed.

Users must still be careful when designing their algorithms to best make use of the Spark system. Spark can still require a fair amount of tuning to achieve optimal performance when running on a cluster.

14.5.3 SPARK PROCESSING ENGINES

In addition to the Spark Core API for creating data flow programs using the RDD abstract, Spark is integrated with a number of additional higher-level APIs that include functionality for specific classes of compute and data problems. As of Spark 2.0.1, the additional APIs are GraphX, MLlib, Spark SQL, and Spark Streaming. These APIs replicate functionality that, if using Hadoop, would require numerous additional domain specific packages to be deployed alongside the base Hadoop. As well as the standard libraries included with Spark, a large number of third-party libraries and APIs are maintained in an online repository and can easily be included by a user when creating their applications.

GraphX is a system that allows users to process graph data using Spark [75]. Its API includes some fundamental operations such as subgraph creation and a variant of Google's Pregel API, the first of the Think Like A Vertex (TLAV) systems [49]. The TLAV paradigm has emerged as the most widely used method for processing massive graphs on distributed systems [51]. GraphX also includes implementations of many of the most commonly used algorithms for graph analysis including PageRank, connected components and triangle counting. As many graph-based algorithms are inherently iterative processes, often values have to be recomputed on the vertices until a particular threshold is reached, they are an ideal class of problems to be performed via Spark. GraphX's performance has been shown to beat other TLAV style frameworks based on Hadoop, as well as other dedicated graph processing systems [8]. A detailed comparison of some of the major graph processing platforms, performed by Batarfi et al. [8], shows that GraphX is often the faster platform at performing the computation, while also consuming fewer resources and generating less network traffic to do so.

MLlib is Spark's distributed machine learning library and provides fast implementations of several key algorithms from the field [52]. Using the DataFrame API, users can create a machine-learning pipeline, mixing several algorithms together to produce the required result. MLlib includes many of the fundamental algorithms of machine learning including linear support vector machines (SVM), logistical regression, random forest and several clustering methods along others [52]. MLlib is shown to be faster and more scalable then its main, Hadoop based, rival Mahout [52].

The Spark SQL library allows for Spark to process and query structured data via standard SQL syntax [7]. Spark SQL can load and query data taken from a variety of sources, and due to sharing some components, is particularly well integrated with Hive. Data can be loaded from mutual sources into a DataFrame, upon which a query can be run. Spark SQL supports all the main SQL data types including bools, integers, floats and strings. Perhaps the most interesting aspect to Spark SQL is that it allows users to combine relational with procedural processing within the same application [7]. Users can, for example, feed the results from an SQL query into functions from the RDD API to create complicated data flows. Spark SQL simultaneously makes Spark more accessible to new users and introduces key optimizations, in the form of DataFrames, for existing ones [7].

The last of the integrated Spark processing engines is Spark Streaming, which allows users to create applications that process data in near real-time [79]. The API has been designed such that writing a stream application is very similar to creating a batch processing application. Users can reuse code from batch processing and even integrate data from historical sources, via the use of join, for example, as the streaming application is running. An application created using Spark Streaming can take input from a variety of sources in including HDFS, Twitter Flume and ZeroMQ. Spark Streaming utilizes the DStreams abstract to represent input stream data as a series of RDDs [79]. Due to the process of creating the RDD's Spark streaming is not real time but can be considered as a micro-batch system.

The DStreams abstraction partitions the input stream into a series of time blocks. Each block contains a few 100 milliseconds of the stream and is stored in an RDD, upon which the standard Spark batch functions can be performed. The performance of Spark Streaming has been shown to scale nearly linearly, and can achieve a throughput rate of 20 MB per second on each node of the Spark cluster [79].

These additional integrated libraries included with Spark are another of its key advantages and set it apart from the Hadoop Ecosystem. Firstly, users need only learn one programming language and set of system APIs. This also benefits system administrators who only have to deploy and configure one software package, versus the many specialized systems that it would require to replicate the same functionality. Secondly, the integration and interoperability enabled between different computing paradigms via the unified Spark stack, allows users to create new classes of applications. This new class of big data applications will be made possible via the integration of previously separate systems. One such example application enabled by this integration is real-time fraud detection for the financial sector. Creating this application in Spark, the user could train the MLlib module on historical data and then use the developed model to detect fraud happening in real-time using the Spark Streaming module. This is just one of the many new applications that could be created using the integrated platform offered via the Spark framework.

14.5.4 HADOOP ECOSYSTEM TAXONOMY

Table 14.2 gives a summary of some of the key differences between, Hadoop V1, Hadoop 2.0, Spark, and Flink. These frameworks are compared on a number of metrics and capabilities.

14.6 THE ROLE OF CLOUD COMPUTING

When comparing the computational requirements for big data systems against traditional high performance computers (HPC), the economic and technological barrier to entry was obviously lower. Both paradigms can make use of commodity systems for proof-of-concept and sometimes as basic implementations for production systems [31,22]. However, to truly scale HPC systems one needs specialist networking with low latency and high bandwidth. As HPCs run on the principle of a single system

Table 14.2 Comparison of various big data ecosystems

	Hadoop	Hadoop 2	Spark	Flink
Execution Model	Batch	Batch, Interactive	Batch, Interactive, Stream	Stream, Batch
Language	Java	Java	Scala, Java, Python, R	Java, Scala
Data Locality	Disk	Disk	Memory, Disk	Memory, Disk
Data Partition	HDFS	HDFS	RDD	HDFS
Data Storage	HDFS	HDFS	HDFS, S3, Tachyon	HDFS, Tachyon, Hbase
Machine Learning	Mahout	Mahout	MLlib	FlinkML
Graph Analytics	Giraph	Giraph	GraphX	Gelly
Streaming	None	Storm	Native	Native
Database	Hive, Hbase	Hive, Hbase	Spark SQL	Table API
Fault Tolerance	Disk Write	Disk Write	Lineage	Checkpoints
Programming Model	Directed Graph	Directed Graph	Directed Acyclic Graph	Directed Acyclic Graph
Security	Access Control List	Kerberos	Kerberos (via YARN)	Access Control List
Bottlenecks	Disk IO, Network IO	Disk IO, Network IO	Memory BW, Network IO	Disk IO, Network IO

image, the performance of a distant processor is expected to be the same or as close to the same as the processor interacting with a user. When a task is initiated, all participatory processing elements (PEs) are required to operate in a timely manner and the occurrence of inter-element dependencies are the norm.

While big data systems are still constrained by Amdahl's Law,[1] systems running Hadoop or Spark type frameworks do not face the type of bottlenecks outlined above. Due to the almost bag-of-tasks approach and greedy scheduling where the same task may be replicated to maximize throughput, performance is very much dependent on the configuration of the PE. At the processing element level, faster CPUs are beneficial but not mandatory. Like any other computing paradigm, the more memory and the faster it is, the better; however, the best commodity memory can deliver great results. As discussed earlier, where big data processing elements differ from their HPC counterparts is the inclusion of high volume and high speed directly attached storage. The penetration of solid-state storage devices has meant that on a performance basis *server grade* hardware and commodity hardware are almost equally matched. With easy and affordable availability of 10 gigabit Ethernet based networking within the commodity market, networking is no longer a bottleneck for organizations implementing local big data systems.

For an organization aiming to incorporate data-centric approaches into their business and product processes, certain other factors play a role in affordability. For a 24 × 7 operational system, with multiple users and operators that is continuously ingesting, processing and delivering data, server grade equipment becomes a necessity. This sort of hardware is designed with resilience and robustness in

---

[1]"The maximum speed up (the maximum number of processors which can be used effectively) is the inverse of the fraction of time the task must proceed on a single thread" [61].

mind for round the clock operation. Server grade hardware, in terms of performance, is matched or slightly better (ECC Memory) than commodity items, but they guarantee reliability. There is a higher price tag attached to this reliability, but it does not just come in the form of capital expenditure on the equipment itself. Server grade hardware requires specialist infrastructure in the form of uninterrupted power supplies with power shaping, industrial cooling units, and server rooms and racks to host the machines. Along with the capital there is a higher operational expense as well. Qualified staff and expensive maintenance contracts are required to manage the infrastructure. As the company expands its data-driven environment, the electrical costs also skyrocket.

To achieve scale, resilience, and robustness, cloud computing provides a cost optimal solution. Within cloud environments (like Amazon's Elastic Compute Cloud) optimized configurations can be found for all the popular data analytics platforms. The developers of the data analytics platforms have configured many of the available images, ensuring the highest quality of the available implementation. Scaling is simpler as the costs do not include capital expenditures for infrastructure such as UPS, rack space, or networking. Operational costs such as electricity and cooling demands also do not change for end user. Table 14.3 shows the different offerings from popular cloud providers.

The pay-per-use model allows for organizations to scale up or down, as the business requires, thus ensuring no waste of money. However, there are some cost considerations that need to be taken into account. For many cloud providers the adage "compute is cheap but bandwidth is expensive" holds true. The phrase refers to the cost in time to move data between peripherals, storage, and the CPU, but it applies to creating compute systems in the cloud and moving data from your local system to the cloud. If an organization needs a large scale big data system for 10 days a month, then for the remaining days it needs to consider the cost of leaving the system running or reprovisioning the whole system when needed and retransferring the data. Cloud services that charge extra for either internode network data traffic make jobs in Hadoop more financially expensive than in Spark, while those that charge more for data at *ingress* or *egress* points may not be as optimal for continuous tear down approaches. Some cloud providers charge extra for HDFS optimized instances, but then exclude internode communications.

The main consideration an organization needs to make, and one of the biggest stumbling blocks, before cloud based deployment of big data solutions is data security and privacy. Depending on the nature of the data, its associated data protection levels, and any service or contractual agreements in place, the public nature of the cloud can be a nonstarter. While the cloud was imagined to be this amorphous collection of resources, in practice they exist across different geo-political boundaries and are thus subjected to a myriad of legal provisions. The United States Patriot Act is a prime example of legislation affecting data privacy [55]. When dealing with customer data organizations can write in clauses in contracts enabling cloud storage of collected information but historic information is still restricted and potentially cannot be included into any data processing framework.

Not every company that needs to develop a model of customer interaction can afford to host its own big bata system. The earlier example of a smart home that aggregates copious amounts of sensor data and then simulates the different possibilities of how the day will proceed would need both a big data system and an HPC cluster. The first is to process the data and create the models, while the second to execute the simulations. Clearly, the homes of the future will not have a data intensive or HPC cluster (or both) in the basement. Cloud computing will be the glue that links the back-office analytics to the real world.

Table 14.3 Offerings of big data on public clouds [29]

	Google	**Microsoft**	**Amazon**	**Cloudera**
Big data storage	Google cloud services	Azure	S3	
MapReduce	AppEngine	Hadoop on Azure	Elastic MapReduce (Hadoop)	MapReduce YARN
Big data analytics	BigQuery	Hadoop on Azure	Elastic MapReduce (Hadoop)	Elastic MapReduce (Hadoop)
Relational database	Cloud SQL	SQL Azure	MySQL or Oracle	MySQL, Oracle, PostgreSQL
NoSQL database	AppEngine Datastore	Table storage	DynamoDB	Apache Accumulo
Streaming processing	Search API	Streaminsight	Nothing prepackaged	Apache Spark
Machine learning	Prediction API	Hadoop + Mahout	Hadoop + Mahout	Hadoop + Oryx
Data import	Network	Network	Network	Network
Data sources	A few sample datasets	Windows Azure marketplace	Public Datasets	Public Datasets
Availability	Some services in private beta	Some services in private beta	Public production	Industries

14.7 THE FUTURE OF BIG DATA PLATFORMS
14.7.1 BIG DATA APPLICATIONS

The use of big data techniques and processing has already been successful in revolutionizing several fields. Areas such as social network analysis, the advertising industry and the management of large computer systems have already benefited. However, big data is poised to be successful in many more including:

- *Healthcare* – There are numerous ways that big data could revolutionize the Healthcare industry. One such area that has been explored is error checking and anomaly detection in medical research datasets [10], although the possibilities for advances across the whole field are endless [59].
- *Governance* – Extending the concept of creating holistic user models, governments are attempting to adopt a person-centric approach to governance. This will lead to customized interactions between the citizenry and local authorities [40]. Through analytics, modeling and simulations, urban authorities hope to be proactive in dealing with potential difficulties rather than reactive [48].
- *Smart Cities* – With the automation of many core operations across urban environments and the deployment of different kinds of sensors where possible, the next step is the integration of these systems. Complex models are being developed that integrate real-time data from the various systems and sensors with simulated environments and humans-in-the-loop to streamline city wide operations and mitigate knock on affects that are caused by problems within one or more systems [19,62].
- *Industry 4.0* – The next revolution in the industrial production processes is the development of agile and flexible systems that are driven by analytics and simulation to respond quickly to problems and variations within the production environment. Intelligent Manufacturing Systems (IMS), using virtual, fractal, bionic, and holonic manufacturing systems, are being developed to provide production

control. The systems not only factor in the factory floor but also the wider supply chain within its decision models [25,41].

- *The Internet of Things (IoT)* – The IoT revolution will be driven by integration of Internet functionality into a range of products and sensors, allowing them to record and transmit data to be sent for analysis [26]. It can be argued that IoT will be the technological backbone used to drive the new class of intelligent Smart Cities and Industry 4.0 applications [26].

To meet the demands of these fields, future big data applications will need ever-greater integration with machine learning to drive intelligent conclusions from the wealth of available data. Many big data applications have traditionally been batch processes, where data was first collected and stored, before being processed at a later date. However, IoT, Healthcare, and Smart Cities applications will need to process data in real-time as they will require instantaneous answers drawn from the stream of data. In addition, all areas will begin to demand subsecond responses to queries on existing data sources.

14.7.2 BIG DATA FRAMEWORKS AND HARDWARE

The evolution of data intensive frameworks has been driven by the roles demanded of them by data intensive applications. The development of the original MapReduce was in response to a new type of workload. Spark was created, in part, as a way to perform many iterative computations over the same working dataset. As such, the role of data intensive frameworks has been evolving since the introduction of MapReduce in 2004, driven by new classes of data intensive problems. Some of the current key roles of a data intensive framework include:

- Provide fault tolerant storage for massive quantities of data from disperse sources.
- Provide a common and expressive set of APIs, written in a variety of languages, enabling users to access and process massive quantities of data.
- Allow users to focus on application development by abstracting away the traditional complexities of parallel computing.
- Automatically schedule jobs to run in parallel across the underlying compute resource, whilst considering aspects such as data locality.

The evolution of data intensive frameworks will continue and will be focused towards increasing the speed of applications, creating more scalable applications and creating easier to use APIs with greater breadth of functionalities. More specifically, data intensive framework evolution will focus on these key areas:

- Continue to increase the possible application performance to meet the demand of sub-second and real-time data analytics by more optimal use of resources and by allowing the applications to scale across larger compute clusters.
- Allow an increasingly diverse range of compute paradigms to interoperate and share access to data and allow the same physical resource to be shared between compute and data centric frameworks.
- Continue to reduce the complexity of creating big data applications with the introduction of more generic and higher-level APIs for developers, along with creating easy deployment methods for data intensive frameworks.

14.7.2.1 Performance and scalability increases

The original performance driver of MapReduce was disk-based data locality and enabling its central philosophy – bring the compute to the data. While this approach was clearly very successful, the need for ever-greater performance, driven by the need for real time analytics, has meant that researchers are looking for new ways to speed-up big data frameworks. There is an argument that network technology has improved to such a degree that it is now able to outpace the speed of local storage. As such, some have claimed that disk-based locality can now be considered irrelevant, as reading from a remote disk is now as fast as local storage due to the modern high-speed networks found in datacenters [2]. While the introduction of technologies like PCIe based NVMe Solid State Disk (SSD) storage will mean that this is not universally true, it can be argued that most data intensive clusters are still using traditional spinning disks due to their lower cost and large capacity [2]. The need for greater performance forced the developers of Spark to abandon disk locality in favor of memory locality. The move to memory-based locality has led to up to an order of magnitude increase in performance over the disk-based Hadoop system [77]. Now that data intensive frameworks are exploiting in-memory processing, future increases in performance will have to come from elsewhere as memory is the currently the fastest storage. It is highly unlikely that CPU caches will increase to a size that can accommodate modern massive datasets. So where is it likely that future increases in performance and scalability will come from? Three possible areas are the use of in-memory storage systems, specialized hardware and continued software improvements.

Whilst there is a move to using memory for dataset processing, current distributed file systems, such as HDFS, still rely on hard drive for the data storage and archiving. Systems such as Spark still have to read input data from disk into main memory before processing can begin, leaving hard drive transfer rates as a bottleneck in application performance. However, there have been efforts to move the storage system for data intensive frameworks into system memory. One example of such system is Alluxio, which aims to offer a fault-tolerant distributed file system, using the speed offered by running elements of itself in-memory to massively increase file write and read times [45]. While Alluxio is not a complete in-memory system, it still utilizes a disk based file system such as HDFS or GlusterFS to provide a persistence copy of the data, it provides a massive performance increase over using those systems alone. Alluxio uses a linage concept, similar to that of Spark's RDD model, to avoid the need for costly data replication strategies, instead the linage of tasks that created a certain dataset is tracked so it can be recomputed on demand [45]. Going forward, there will continue to be developments towards distributed in-memory file systems that are both data locality aware and fault tolerant.

As data intensive frameworks are turning to memory as method for increasing performance, the underlying hardware will need to adapt. One aspect of computer hardware, which has yet to see much adoption for big data workloads, is the Graphics Processing Unit (GPU) [63]. GPUs were first introduced as coprocessors to compute the demanding workload of graphics for video games. However, it was soon noted that they possess characteristics that make them ideal for certain compute intensive workloads. This notion of using a GPU for tasks other than graphics processing is known as General-Purpose computation on Graphics Processing Units (GPGPU). Technologies such as CUDA and OpenCL now allow users direct access to perform their computations upon modern powerful graphics hardware. However, for big data workloads that utilize massive quantities of data, GPUs have some limitations that make them less than ideal [63]. GPUs are unable to directly access data stored on disk or in memory on the host machine, so all required data must be transferred to the memory of the GPU card via the PCIe bus. The PCIe bus has lower bandwidth than memory, so transferring large quantities of data over it can be considered a bottleneck. To compound this problem, GPUs have much smaller amount of memory than is commonly found in big data compute nodes, often over an order of magnitude less, meaning data has to be shuffled in sections. Due to these problems, GPUs have seen little adoption in big data workloads. However, as data intensive workloads diversify and start to include an increasing amount of simulation and machine learning aspects, both of which are classes of computation that GPUs excel at performing, GPUs could become a powerful way to increase performance. GPUs are just one of the forms of coprocessor that could be used to accelerate certain aspects of the modern big data workload, others include FPGAs and the Intel Xeon Phi.

The software used by data intensive frameworks will continue to improve, making better use of the underlying hardware. It has been well established that the bottleneck for many in-memory applications is data transfer over the network [77]. New advances in technology will have to find ways to improve this to further increase performance. Another aspect that future systems could explore is exploiting a greater knowledge of the workload requirements. Having a deeper understanding could enable the system to make intelligent decisions about data preprocessing and hardware scheduling to better optimize resources.

14.7.2.2 Diversification of compute paradigms

MapReduce was originally introduced to perform a specific class of computational problem. Since its introduction the model has been adapted to many diverse computing tasks such as machine learning and graph processing. However, early attempts at porting other paradigms to MapReduce required that they be expressed as a series of MapReduce tasks, limiting functionality. More recently there has been a move away from MapReduce type computation, on data stored in HDFS like file systems. The introduction of YARN addressed this issue by removing the resource negotiation and scheduling from the compute engine, thus MapReduce is now just one of many frameworks that can access data stored in the DFS. As such, systems like Tez and HBase no longer have to abstract down to a series of MapReduce tasks to complete a workflow.

Whilst MapReduce has been very successful at dealing with fault tolerance, data locality, and the obscuring of parallel computing complexities, it is clear that it is not the best approach for every workload. Other frameworks now need to take the successes of the MapReduce framework and apply it to other, more general, data intensive workloads. The move to processing in-memory has increased the number of possible workloads massively, with Spark being able to offer many different compute paradigms. The unification of different compute functionality offered by a system like Spark allows new classes of application to be developed. Such applications could create advanced workflows by, for example, allowing data from relational queries to be fed into graph processing algorithms, with the final results analyzed by machine learning, all within the same framework. To further exploit this potential and enable the creation of the next generation of data intensive applications, future frameworks will need to increase the capability of current implementations and extend the number of available compute paradigms. It has been argued that modern data analytics needs to include simulation and what-if analysis to gain a deeper insight into the data [28]. Future data intensive frameworks will need to include and interoperate with more complex compute focused methods including deep learning and data driven simulation.

14.7.2.3 Simplifying data centric development

Big data processing is typically done on large clusters of shared-nothing commodity machines. One of the key lessons from MapReduce is that it is imperative to develop a programming model that hides the complexity of the underlying system, but provides flexibility by allowing users to extend functionality to meet a variety of computational requirements. Whilst a MapReduce application, when compared with an MPI application, is less complex to create, it can still require a significant amount of coding effort. As data intestine frameworks have evolved, there have been increasing amounts of higher-level APIs which are designed to further decrease the complexities of creating data intensive applications. Current data intensive frameworks, such as Spark, have been very successful at reducing the required amount of code to create a specific application. Future data intensive framework APIs will continue to improve in four key areas; exposing more optimal routines to users, allowing transparent access to disparate data sources, the use of graphical user interfaces (GUI) and allowing interoperability between heterogeneous hardware resources.

- Future higher-level APIs will continue to allow data intensive frameworks to expose optimized routines to application developers, enabling increased performance with minimal effort from the end user. Systems like Spark's Dataframe API have proved that, with careful design, a high-level API can decrease complexity for user while massively increasing performance over lower-level APIs.
- Future big data application will require access to an increasingly diverse range data sources. Future APIs will need to hide this complexity from the end user and allow seamless integration of different data sources (structured and semi- or nonstructured data) being read from a range of locations (HDFS, Stream sources and Databases).
- One, relatively unexplored, way to lower the barrier of entry to data intensive computing is the creation of GUIs to allow users without programming or query writing experience access to data intensive frameworks. The use of a GUI also raises other interesting possibilities such as real time interaction and visualization of datasets.
- APIs will also need to continue to develop in order to hide the complexities of increasingly heterogeneous hardware. If coprocessors are to be used in future big data machines, the data intensive framework APIs will, ideally, hide this from the end user. Users should be able to write their application code, and the framework would select the most appropriate hardware to run it upon. This could also include pushing all or part of the workload into the cloud as needed.

For system administrators, the deployment of data intensive frameworks onto computer hardware can still be a complicated process, especially if an extensive stack is required. Future research is required to investigate methods to atomically deploy a modern big data stack onto computer hardware. These systems should also set and optimize the myriad of configuration parameters that can have a large impact on system performance. One early attempt in this direction is Apache Ambari, although further works still needs under taking, such as integration of the system with cloud infrastructure. Could a system of this type automatically deploy a custom data intensive software stack onto the cloud when a local resource became full and run applications in tandem with the local resource?

14.7.2.4 Physical resource sharing

Computer clusters represent a large investment for any institution that decides they want to perform big data analytics in house rather than in the cloud. Unfortunately, the 3 major paradigms, (HPC, Big Data and Distributed RDBMS) do not share the same physical resource well. The key issue here is that current systems do not share a single scheduler, so are unaware of when a competing framework might be using resources. This is obviously problematic if more than one framework is needed. Institutions have three possible ways of dealing with this issue; run physically separate dedicated resources, separate part of the same physical resource up into dedicated sections or, lastly, by running the various software stacks in a virtualized environment. These methods all have issues, meaning that none are an ideal solution. Purchasing and maintaining separate resources would massively increase expense. Partitioning a single resource could lead utilization and load balancing problems, particularly if one framework is more commonly used. Lastly, virtualizing the software stack could result in less optimal use of the hardware due the overheads inherent in the virtualization process.

To solve this problem, there is currently a great deal of research to develop systems that will allow multiple competing compute frameworks to share the same underlying resource. One such system is Apache Mesos, which allows both Hadoop and MPI to run alongside one another [30]. Mesos works by sitting between the respective frameworks own schedulers and the hardware, deciding which compute resources to offer up to each framework. When a user submits a MapReduce application, for example, the Hadoop scheduler will inform the Mesos master process that it needs some resources. The Mesos master will then decide what of the available resources to offer to Hadoop. If the offer of resources from Mesos does not meet the requirements of the Hadoop job, it can reject the offer and wait for a more suitable offer to be made. If the offer is accepted, Mesos will launch executor tasks to perform the computation. The executor tasks run inside of containers to isolate them from one another [30]. In this way, Mesos acts as the overall controller of compute cluster but still allows the individual frameworks to operate in their own optimal and unique way. Unfortunately, Mesos does not run with standard implementations of the frameworks, as they need additional code to interoperate with the Mesos scheduler. Although the most popular frameworks including Hadoop, Spark and MPICH2 already have Mesos compatible builds available. Mesos is just one such system to tackle the problem; others include Google's Omega [65] and Borg [73] and Microsoft's Apollo [11]. Although the open source nature of Mesos has meant that it has seen good adoption within industry [5]. Whilst Mesos is a good starting position, future work will be needed to expand the system. Such work could include the integration of cloud resources for running containers, more sophisticated resource offers, the integration of more frameworks and support for a more diverse range of hardware.

14.7.3 BIG DATA ON THE ROAD TO EXASCALE

The increase in available data inputs led to the creation of data centric processing frameworks. Traditional large computer systems were geared to scale the processing elements but not increasing input data. This trend does not appear to be changing. In its 2015 Hype Cycle for Emerging Technology, Gartner Inc. put IoT, Advanced Analytics and Machine Learning at the "Peak of Inflated Expectations" with 5–10 years still to go before plateauing out as productive technologies [23]. Over the next 10 years and beyond the size and scope of data will grow considerably and computing paradigms will also have to adapt.

On the technological front, exascale has captured the imagination of experts in the field. Exascale has two facets, the first and the one that gets the most hype is exascale computer systems. Computers capable of calculating 10^{18} floating-point operations a second, or an exaflop, is the next challenge for computing in general and high performance computing in particular. This scale of computing comes with a whole host of challenges: from limitations of the silicon substrate, to the power and thermal limits, and I/O limitations (disk, network, etc.) breaking the exa barrier will be challenging. On the software side as well, compilers and program workflows have not fully addressed the challenges of petascale (10^{15}) computing, and so exascale remains a goal that keeps getting pushed back.

On the data front, reaching exascale is right on the horizon. Datasets that are petabytes and terabytes in size are currently being processed by teraflop and gigaflop capable systems. With the step changes coming, through the phenomenon of Internet of things and person-centric services, workloads that are 1 exabyte (EB) in size will quickly become a reality. Exabyte's of data will be thrust upon businesses and this will be a real challenge to deal with. At that scale the noise ratio becomes much higher and the cost trade-offs also need to be revaluated.

The challenges facing the high performance computing community are the same that will shape the direction of big data. Technologically, scaling big data frameworks to exaflop and petaflop systems will see the same compiler, networking, power, and cost issues as in HPC. Considerable development in both hardware and software is required to deal with the oncoming data deluge.

14.8 CONCLUSION

This chapter has explored the evolution of big data technologies. Since the introduction of MapReduce, the data intensive computing world has been evolving rapidly. The original, inflexible, MapReduce programming model has been expanded to incorporate the full spectrum of data intensive computing paradigms. Now that access to the data stored in a distributed file system has been compartmentalized and separated from the MapReduce programming model, new systems like Apache Spark have been able to push application performance further by utilizing memory locality. MapReduce was only the first step in the democratization of parallel computing, future frameworks will continue this trend and make massive compute power available to nonspecialists. With in-memory processing fully integrated in the big data stack, improving framework performance will require more intelligence from the compilers and middleware to make better use of the available hardware. The move to in-memory computation has also expanded the number of paradigms these data intensive frameworks are able to perform, as the ability to reuse the same working dataset is ideal for both Machine learning and Graph processing. The ability to utilize multiple computing paradigms within the same application, will result in a new generation of data intensive applications being created.

In terms of the possibilities for these applications, returning to the earlier smart home example, in this globally connected world Owner A may be rewarded with an extra strong coffee at his/her 4 p.m. meeting courtesy of a *discussion* between the coffee maker at the meeting place and the home owners home agent that takes place in the cloud and is triggered by the facial recognition system on a CCTV camera.

REFERENCES

[1] F.N. Afrati, J.D. Ullman, Optimizing multiway joins in a map-reduce environment, IEEE Trans. Knowl. Data Eng. 23 (9) (2011) 1282–1298, http://dx.doi.org/10.1109/TKDE.2011.47.

[2] G. Ananthanarayanan, A. Ghodsi, S. Shenker, I. Stoica, Disk-locality in datacenter computing considered irrelevant, in: HotOS'13 Proceedings of the 13th USENIX Conference on Hot Topics in Operating Systems, 2011, pp. 1–5. Retrieved from http://dl.acm.org/citation.cfm?id=1991596.1991613.

[3] M. Ali-ud-din Khan, M.F. Uddin, N. Gupta, Seven V's of big data understanding big data to extract value, in: 2014 Zone 1 Conference of the American Society for Engineering Education (ASEE Zone 1), IEEE, April 2014, pp. 1–5.

[4] Apache, Hadoop, http://hadoop.apache.org, 2009.

[5] Apache, https://mesos.apache.org/documentation/latest/powered-by-mesos/, 2016.

[6] M. Armbrust, T. Das, A. Davidson, A. Ghodsi, A. Or, J. Rosen, R. Xin, et al., Scaling spark in the real world: performance and usability, Proc. VLDB Endow. 8 (12) (2015) 1840–1843, http://dx.doi.org/10.14778/2824032.2824080.

[7] M. Armbrust, R. Xin, M. Zaharia, Spark SQL: relational data processing in spark, in: SIGMOD'15, 2015.

[8] O. Batarfi, R. El Shawi, A.G. Fayoumi, R. Nouri, S.-M.-R. Beheshti, A. Barnawi, S. Sakr, Large scale graph processing systems: survey and an experimental evaluation, Clust. Comput. (2015), http://dx.doi.org/10.1007/s10586-015-0472-6.

[9] B. Bengfort, J. Kim, Data Analytics With Hadoop, Oreilly & Associates Inc, 2015.

[10] S. Bonner, A.S. McGough, I. Kureshi, J. Brennan, G. Theodoropoulos, L. Moss, G. Antoniou, et al., Data quality assessment and anomaly detection via map/reduce and linked data: a case study in the medical domain, in: 2015 IEEE International Conference on Big Data (Big Data), IEEE, 2015, pp. 737–746.

[11] E. Boutin, J. Ekanayake, W. Lin, B. Shi, J. Zhou, Z. Qian, L. Zhou, et al., Apollo: scalable and coordinated scheduling for cloud-scale computing, in: 11th USENIX Symposium on Operating Systems Design and Implementation (OSDI 14), 2014, pp. 285–300.

[12] M. Cafarella, D. Cutting, Apache HBase. Retrieved from https://hbase.apache.org/, 2007.

[13] P. Carbone, A. Katsifodimos, S. Ewen, V. Markl, S. Haridi, K. Tzoumas, Apache flink: stream and batch processing in a single engine, Data Eng. 28 (2015).

[14] Cassandra, from http://cassandra.apache.org/, 2010.

[15] F. Chang, J. Dean, S. Ghemawat, W.C. Hsieh, D.A. Wallach, M. Burrows, R.E. Gruber, et al., BigTable: a distributed storage system for structured data, in: 7th Symposium on Operating Systems Design and Implementation (OSDI'06), November 6–8, Seattle, WA, USA, 2006, pp. 205–218.

[16] P. Chen, C.-Y. Zhang, Data-intensive applications, challenges, techniques and technologies: a survey on big data, Inf. Sci. 275 (2014) 314–347, http://dx.doi.org/10.1016/j.ins.2014.01.015.

[17] A. Ching, C. Kunz, Apache Giraph. Retrieved from https://giraph.apache.org, 2013.

[18] M. Cox, D. Ellsworth, Application-controlled demand paging for out-of-core visualization, in: Proceedings of the 8th Conference on Visualization'97, IEEE Computer Society Press, 1997 (pp. 235-ff).

[19] M. Deakin, The embedded intelligence of smart cities, Intell. Build. Int. 3 (3) (2011) 189–197.

[20] J. Dean, S. Ghemawat, MapReduce: simplified data processing on large clusters, Commun. ACM 51 (2004) 1–13, http://dx.doi.org/10.1145/1327452.1327492.

[21] D. DeWitt, M. Stonebraker, MapReduce: a major step backwards, Database Column 44 (2008) 1–3. Retrieved from http://codepaint.kaist.ac.kr/wp-content/uploads/2014/03/MapReduce.pdf.

[22] D. Eadline, Hadoop 2 Quick-Start Guide: Learn the Essentials of Big Data Computing in the Apache Hadoop 2 Ecosystem, Addison–Wesley Professional, 2015.

[23] Gartner, Newsroom Gartner's 2015 hype cycle for emerging technologies identifies the computing innovations that organizations should monitor. Retrieved from http://www.gartner.com/newsroom/id/31, 2015.

[24] S. Ghemawat, H. Gobioff, S.T. Leung, The Google file system, Oper. Syst. Rev. 37 (5) (2003) 29–43.

[25] W.A. Gruver, D.B. Kotak, E.H. van Leeuwen, D. Norrie, Holonic manufacturing systems: phase II, in: Holonic and Multi-Agent Systems for Manufacturing, Springer, Berlin, Heidelberg, 2003, pp. 1–14.

[26] J. Gubbi, R. Buyya, S. Marusic, M. Palaniswami, Internet of Things (IoT): a vision, architectural elements, and future directions, Future Gener. Comput. Syst. 29 (7) (2013) 1645–1660, http://dx.doi.org/10.1016/j.future.2013.01.010.

[27] Z. Guo, G. Fox, M. Zhou, Investigation of data locality in MapReduce, in: Proceedings – 12th IEEE/ACM International Symposium on Cluster, Cloud and Grid Computing, CCGrid 2012, 2012, pp. 419–426.

[28] P.J. Haas, P.P. Maglio, P.G. Selinger, W. Tan, Data is dead . . . without what-if models, Proc. VLDB Endow. 4 (12) (2011) 1486–1489, http://doi.org/10.1002/num.20576.

[29] I.A.T. Hashem, I. Yaqoob, N.B. Anuar, S. Mokhtar, A. Gani, S.U. Khan, The rise of "big data" on cloud computing: review and open research issues, Inf. Sci. 47 (2015) 98–115.

[30] B. Hindman, A. Konwinski, A. Platform, F.-G. Resource, M. Zaharia, Mesos: a platform for fine-grained resource sharing in the data center, Proc. NSDI 32 (2011). Retrieved from http://static.usenix.org/events/nsdi11/tech/full_papers/Hindman_new.pdf.

[31] V. Holmes, I. Kureshi, Huddersfield university campus grid: QGG of OSCAR clusters, J. Phys. Conf. Ser. 256 (1) (2010).

[32] S. Sherif, Processing large-scale graph data: a guide to current technology, IBM Developerworks, 2013, pp. 1–13.

[33] M. Isard, M. Budiu, Y. Yu, A. Birrell, D. Fetterly, Dryad: distributed data-parallel programs from sequential building blocks, Oper. Syst. Rev. (2007) 59–72, http://dx.doi.org/10.1145/1272996.1273005.

[34] S. Jha, J. Qiu, A. Luckow, P. Mantha, G.C. Fox, A tale of two data-intensive paradigms: applications, abstractions, and architectures, Big Data 2 (1) (2014) 8. Distributed, Parallel, and Cluster Computing. Retrieved from http://arxiv.org/abs/1403.1528.

[35] S.D.T. Kelly, N.K. Suryadevara, S.C. Mukhopadhyay, Towards the implementation of IoT for environmental condition monitoring in homes, IEEE Sens. J. 13 (10) (2013) 3846–3853.

[36] M. Kornacker, A. Behm, V. Bittorf, T. Bobrovytsky, C. Ching, A. Choi, M. Yoder, et al., Impala: a modern, open-source SQL engine for Hadoop, in: 7th Biennial Conference on Innovative Data Systems Research (CIDR'15), 2015.

[37] R.T. Kouzes, G.A. Anderson, S.T. Elbert, I. Gorton, D.K. Gracio, The changing paradigm of data-intensive computing, Computer 42 (2009) 26–34, http://dx.doi.org/10.1109/MC.2009.26.

[38] A. Lakshman, P. Malik, Cassandra, Oper. Syst. Rev. 44 (2) (2010) 35, http://dx.doi.org/10.1145/1773912.1773922.

[39] D. Laney, 3D data management: controlling data volume, velocity and variety, META Group Res. Note 6 (2001) 70.

[40] L. Larroquette, S. Srivastava, Citizen centric governance, J. Dev. Manag. 1 (4) (2013) 439.

[41] J. Lee, B. Bagheri, H.A. Kao, A cyber-physical systems architecture for industry 4.0-based manufacturing systems, Manuf. Lett. 3 (2015) 18–23.

[42] J. Leskovec, A. Rajaraman, J.D. Ullman, Mining of Massive Datasets, Cambridge University Press, 2014.

[43] LHC, CERN Accelerating Science. Processing: What to Record? N.p., 2015. Web. 24 Feb. 2016.

[44] F. Li, B. Ooi, M. Ozsu, S. Wu, Distributed data management using MapReduce, ACM Comput. Surv. 46 (3) (2013) 31:1–31:42, http://dx.doi.org/10.1145/2503009.

[45] H. Li, A. Ghodsi, M. Zaharia, S. Shenker, I. Stoica, Tachyon: reliable, memory speed storage for cluster computing frameworks, in: Proceedings of the ACM Symposium on Cloud Computing – SOCC'14, 2014, pp. 1–15.

[46] R. Livingstone, The 7 Vs of Big Data. Insights. Rob Livingstone Advisory, 21 June 2013. Web. 27 Feb. 2016.

[47] LSST. Data Management. Data Management. N.p., 2015. Web. 24 Feb. 2016.

[48] M. Maciejewski, To do more, better, faster and more cheaply: using big data in public administration, Int. Rev. Adm. Sci. (2016).

[49] G. Malewicz, M. Austern, A. Bik, Pregel: a system for large-scale graph processing, in: Proceedings of the 2010 ACM SIGMOD International Conference on Management of Data, 2010, pp. 135–145.

[50] B. Marr, Big Data: Using SMART Big Data, Analytics and Metrics to Make Better Decisions and Improve Performance, John Wiley & Sons, 2015.

[51] R.R. McCune, T. Weninger, G. Madey, Thinking like a vertex, ACM Comput. Surv. 48 (2) (2015) 1–39, http://dx.doi.org/10.1145/2818185.

[52] X. Meng, J. Bradley, B. Yavuz, E. Sparks, S. Venkataraman, D. Liu, A. Talwalkar, et al., MLlib: machine learning in Apache Spark. CoRR. Retrieved from, http://arxiv.org/abs/1505.06807.

[53] C. Olston, B. Reed, U. Srivastava, R. Kumar, A. Tomkins, Pig Latin: a not-so-foreign language for data processing, in: Proceedings of the 2008 ACM SIGMOD International Conference on Management of Data – SIGMOD'08, 2008, p. 1099.

[54] Optimus Information. Understanding the 7 V's of Big Data. *Blog*. Optimus Information Inc, 18 Aug. 2015. Web. 27 Feb. 2016.

[55] S.A. Osher, Privacy, computers and the patriot act: the fourth amendment isn't dead, but no one will insure it, Fla. L. Rev. 54 (2002) 521.

[56] A. Pavlo, E. Paulson, A. Rasin, D.J. Abadi, D.J. DeWitt, S. Madden, M. Stonebraker, A comparison of approaches to large-scale data analysis, in: Proceedings of the 35th SIGMOD International Conference on Management of Data, 2009, pp. 165–178.

[57] I. Polato, R. Ré, A. Goldman, F. Kon, A comprehensive view of Hadoop research—a systematic literature review, J. Netw. Comput. Appl. 46 (2014) 1–25, http://dx.doi.org/10.1016/j.jnca.2014.07.022.

[58] G. Press, A very short history of big data. FORBES, 2013.

[59] W. Raghupathi, V. Raghupathi, Big data analytics in healthcare: promise and potential, Health Inf. Sci. Syst. 2 (2014) 3, http://dx.doi.org/10.1186/2047-2501-2-3.

[60] M. Van Rijmenam, Connecting Data and People. Datafloq Read RSS. Datafloq, 7 Aug. 2015. Web. 27 Feb. 2016.

[61] D.P. Rodgers, Improvements in multiprocessor system design, Comput. Archit. News 13 (3) (June 1985) 225–231.

[62] C.D.G. Romero, J.K.D. Barriga, J.I.R. Molano, Big data meaning in the architecture of IoT for smart cities, in: International Conference on Data Mining and Big Data, Springer International Publishing, June 2016, pp. 457–465.

[63] M. Saecker, V. Markl, Big data analytics on modern hardware architectures: a technology survey, in: Lecture Notes in Business Information Processing (LNBIP), vol. 138, 2013, pp. 125–149.

[64] S. Sakr, A. Liu, A.G. Fayoumi, The family of MapReduce and large-scale data processing systems, ACM Comput. Surv. 46 (1) (2013) 1–44, http://dx.doi.org/10.1145/2522968.2522979.

[65] M. Schwarzkopf, A. Konwinski, Omega: flexible, scalable schedulers for large compute clusters, in: EuroSys'13 Proceedings of the 8th ACM European Conference on Computer Systems, 2013, pp. 351–364.

[66] J. Shamsi, M.A. Khojaye, M.A. Qasmi, Data-intensive cloud computing: requirements, expectations, challenges, and solutions, J. Grid Comput. 11 (2) (2013) 281–310, http://dx.doi.org/10.1007/s10723-013-9255-6.

[67] K. Shvachko, H. Kuang, S. Radia, R. Chansler, The Hadoop distributed file system, in: 2010 IEEE 26th Symposium on Mass Storage Systems and Technologies, MSST2010, 2010.

[68] D. Singh, C.K. Reddy, A survey on platforms for big data analytics, J. Big Data 2 (1) (2014) 1.

[69] A. Thusoo, J.S. Sarma, N. Jain, Z. Shao, P. Chakka, N. Zhang, R. Murthy, et al., Hive – a petabyte scale data warehouse using Hadoop, in: Proceedings – International Conference on Data Engineering, 2010, pp. 996–1005.

[70] A. Toshniwal, J. Donham, N. Bhagat, S. Mittal, D. Ryaboy, S. Taneja, M. Fu, et al., Storm@twitter, in: Proceedings of the 2014 ACM SIGMOD International Conference on Management of Data – SIGMOD'14, 2014, pp. 147–156.

[71] C. Uzunkaya, T. Ensari, Y. Kavurucu, Hadoop ecosystem and its analysis on tweets, Proc., Soc. Behav. Sci. 195 (2015) 1890–1897.

[72] V.K. Vavilapalli, S. Seth, B. Saha, C. Curino, O. O'Malley, S. Radia, H. Shah, et al., Apache Hadoop YARN, in: Proceedings of the 4th Annual Symposium on Cloud Computing – SOCC'13, ACM Press, New York, New York, USA, 2013, pp. 1–16.

[73] A. Verma, L. Pedrosa, M. Korupolu, D. Oppenheimer, E. Tune, J. Wilkes, Large-scale cluster management at Google with Borg, in: Proceedings of the Tenth European Conference on Computer Systems – EuroSys'15, 2015, pp. 1–17.

[74] M. Wang, G. Zhang, C. Zhang, J. Zhang, C. Li, An IoT-based appliance control system for smart homes, in: 2013 Fourth International Conference on Intelligent Control and Information Processing (ICICIP), IEEE, 2013, pp. 744–747.

[75] R.S. Xin, J.E. Gonzalez, M.J. Franklin, I. Stoica, GraphX: a resilient distributed graph system on spark, in: First International Workshop on Graph Data Management Experiences and Systems, 2013, p. 2.

[76] S.B. Yoginath, K.S. Perumalla, Design of a high-fidelity testing framework for secure electric grid control, in: Proceedings of the 2014 Winter Simulation Conference, IEEE Press, December 2014, pp. 3024–3035.

[77] M. Zaharia, M. Chowdhury, T. Das, A. Dave, Resilient distributed datasets: a fault-tolerant abstraction for in-memory cluster computing, in: NSDI'12 Proceedings of the 9th USENIX Conference on Networked Systems Design and Implementation, 2012, p. 2.

[78] M. Zaharia, M. Chowdhury, M.J. Franklin, S. Shenker, I. Stoica, Spark: cluster computing with working sets, in: HotCloud'10 Proceedings of the 2nd USENIX Conference on Hot Topics in Cloud Computing, 2010, p. 10.

[79] M. Zaharia, T. Das, H. Li, S. Shenker, I. Stoica, Discretized streams: an efficient and fault-tolerant model for stream processing on large clusters, in: Proceedings of the 4th USENIX Conference on Hot Topics in Cloud Computing, 2012, p. 10.

A TAXONOMY AND SURVEY OF FAULT-TOLERANT WORKFLOW MANAGEMENT SYSTEMS IN CLOUD AND DISTRIBUTED COMPUTING ENVIRONMENTS

15

Deepak Poola*, Mohsen Amini Salehi†, Kotagiri Ramamohanarao*, Rajkumar Buyya*

The University of Melbourne, Australia †*The University of Louisiana Lafayette, USA*

15.1 INTRODUCTION

Workflows orchestrate the relationships between dataflow and computational components by managing their inputs and outputs. In the recent years, scientific workflows have emerged as a paradigm for managing complex large scale distributed data analysis and scientific computation. Workflows automate computation, and thereby accelerate the pace of scientific progress easing the process for researchers. In addition to automation, it is also extensively used for scientific reproducibility, result sharing and scientific collaboration among different individuals or organizations. Scientific workflows are deployed in diverse distributed environments, starting from supercomputers and clusters, to grids and currently cloud computing environments [1,2].

Distributed environments usually are large scale infrastructures that accelerate complex workflow computation; they also assist in scaling and parallel execution of the workflow components. The likelihood of failure increases specially for long-running workflows [3]. However, these environments are prone to performance variations and different types of failures. This demands the workflow management systems to be robust against performance variations and fault-tolerant against faults.

Over the years, many different techniques have evolved to make workflow scheduling fault-tolerant in different computing environments. This chapter aims to categorize and classify different fault-tolerant techniques and provide a broad view of fault-tolerance in workflow domain for distributed environments.

Workflow scheduling is a well studied research area. Yu et al. [4] provided a comprehensive view of workflows, different scheduling approaches, and different workflow management systems. However, this work did not throw much light into fault-tolerant techniques in workflows. Plankensteiner et al. [5] have recently studied different fault-tolerant techniques for grid workflows. Nonetheless, they do not provide a detailed view into different fault-tolerant strategies and their variants. More importantly, their work does not encompass other environments like clusters and clouds.

Software Architecture for Big Data and the Cloud. DOI: 10.1016/B978-0-12-805467-3.00015-6

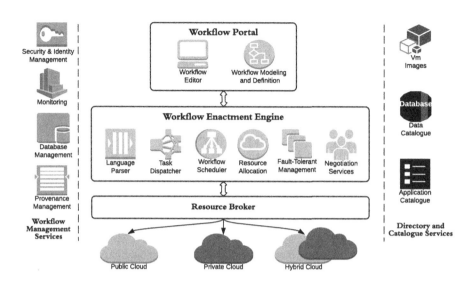

FIGURE 15.1

Architecture of cloud workflow management system. Portal, enactment engine, and resource broker form the core of the WFMS performing vital operations, such as designing, modeling, and resource allocation. To achieve these operations, the workflow management services (left column) provide security, monitoring, database, and provenance management services. In addition, the Directory and Catalogue services (right column) provide catalog and metadata management for the workflow execution

In this chapter, we aim to provide a comprehensive taxonomy of fault-tolerant workflow scheduling techniques in different existing distributed environments. We first start with an introduction to workflows and workflow scheduling. Then, we introduce fault-tolerance and its necessity. We provide an in-depth ontology of faults in Section 15.4. Following which, different fault-tolerant workflow techniques are detailed. In Section 15.6, we describe different approaches used to model failures and also give definition of various metrics used in literature to assess fault-tolerance. Finally, prominent workflow management systems are introduced and a description of relevant tools and support systems that are available for workflow development is provided.

15.2 BACKGROUND
15.2.1 WORKFLOW MANAGEMENT SYSTEMS

Workflow management systems (WFMS) enable automated and seamless execution of workflows. It allows users to define and model workflows, set their deadline and budget limitations, and the environments in which they wish to execute. The WFMS then evaluates these inputs and executes them within the defined constraints.

The prominent components of a typical cloud WFMS is given in Fig. 15.1. The *workflow portal* is used to model and define abstract workflows, i.e., tasks and their dependencies. The *workflow en-*

actment engine takes the abstract workflows and parses them using a language parser. Then, the *task dispatcher* analyzes the dependencies and dispatches the ready tasks to the scheduler. The *scheduler*, based on the defined scheduling algorithms, schedules the workflow task onto a resource. We further discuss about workflow scheduling in the next section. Workflow enactment engine also handles the fault-tolerance of the workflow. It also contains a resource allocation component which allocates resources to the tasks through the resource broker.

The *resource broker* interfaces with the infrastructure layer and provides a unified view to the enactment engine. The resource broker communicates with compute services to provide the desired resource.

The *directory and catalogue services* house information about data objects, the application and the compute resources. This information is used by the enactment engine, and the resource broker to make critical decisions.

Workflow management services, in general, provide important services that are essential for the working of a WFMS. *Security and identify* services ensure authentication and secure access to the WFMS. *Monitoring* tools constantly monitor vital components of the WFMS and raise alarms at appropriate times. *Database management* component provides a reliable storage for intermediate and final data results of the workflows. *Provenance management services* capture important information such as, dynamics of control flows and data, their progressions, execution information, file locations, input and output information, workflow structure, form, workflow evolution, and system information [6]. Provenance is essential for interpreting data, determining its quality and ownership, providing reproducible results, optimizing efficiency, troubleshooting and also to provide fault-tolerance.

15.2.2 WORKFLOW SCHEDULING

As mentioned earlier, a workflow is a collection of tasks connected by control and/or data dependencies. Workflow structure indicates the temporal relationship between tasks. Workflows can be represented either in Directed Acyclic Graph (DAG) (as shown in Fig. 15.3) or non-DAG formats.

Scheduling in workflows maps its tasks on to distributed resources such that the dependencies are not violated. Workflow Scheduling is a well-known NP-Complete problem [7].

The workflow scheduling architecture specifies the placement of the scheduler in a WFMS and it can be broadly categorized into three types as illustrated in Fig. 15.2: *centralized*, *hierarchical*, and *decentralized* [4]. In the *centralized* approach, a centralized scheduler makes all the scheduling decisions for the entire workflow. The drawback of this approach is that it is not scalable; however, it can produce efficient schedules as the centralized scheduler has all the necessary information. In *hierarchical* scheduling, there is a central manager responsible for controlling the workflow execution and assigning the subworkflows to low-level schedulers. The low-level schedulers map tasks of the subworkflows assigned by the central manager. In contrast, *decentralized* scheduling has no central controller. It allows tasks to be scheduled by multiple schedulers, each scheduler communicates with each other and schedules a subworkflow or a task [4].

Workflow schedule planning for workflow applications also known as planning scheme are of two types: *static(offline)* and *dynamic(online)*. *Static* scheme map tasks to resources at the compile time. These algorithms require the knowledge of workflow tasks and resource characteristics beforehand. On the contrary, *dynamic* scheme can make few assumptions before execution and make scheduling

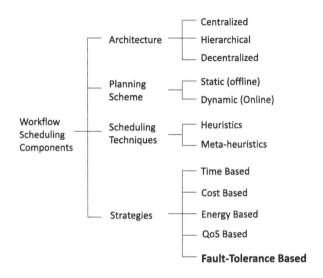

FIGURE 15.2

Components of workflow scheduling

decision just-in-time [8]. Here, both dynamic and static information about environment is used in scheduling decisions.

Further, workflow scheduling techniques are the approaches or methodologies used to map workflow tasks to resources, and it can be classified into two types: *heuristics* and *metaheuristics*. *Heuristic* solutions exploit problem-dependent information to provide an approximate solution trading optimality, completeness, accuracy, and/or processing speed. It is generally used when finding a solution through exhaustive search is impractical. It can be further classified into list based scheduling, cluster based scheduling, and duplication based algorithms [9,10]. On the other hand, *metaheuristics* are more abstract procedures that can be applied to a variety of problems. A metaheuristic approach is problem-independent and treats problems like black boxes. Some of the prominent metaheuristic approaches are genetic algorithms, particle swarm optimization, simulated annealing, and ant colony optimization.

Each scheduling algorithm for any workflow has one or many objectives. The most prominent strategies or objectives used are given in Fig. 15.2. Time, cost, energy, QoS, and fault-tolerance are most commonly used objectives for a workflow scheduling algorithm. Algorithms can be with a single objective or multiple objectives based on the scenario and the problem statement. The rest of the chapter is focused on scheduling algorithms and workflow management systems whose objective is fault-tolerance.

15.3 INTRODUCTION TO FAULT-TOLERANCE

Failure is defined as any deviation of a component of the system from its intended functionality. Resource failures are not the only reason for the system to be unpredictable, factors such as, design faults,

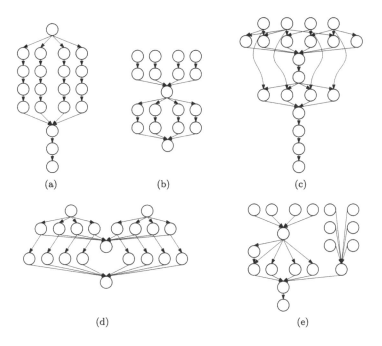

FIGURE 15.3

Examples of the state-of-the-art workflows [11]: (a) Epigenomics: DNA sequence data obtained from the genetic analysis process is split into several chunks and are used to map the epigenetic state of human cells. (b) LIGO: detects gravitational waves of cosmic origin by observing stars and black holes. (c) Montage: creates a mosaic of the sky from several input images. (d) CyberShake: uses the Probabilistic Seismic Hazard Analysis (PSHA) technique to characterize earthquake hazards in a region. (e) SIPHT: searches for small untranslated RNAs encoding genes for all of the bacterial replicas in the NCBI database

performance variations in resources, unavailable files, and data staging issues can be few of the many reasons for unpredictable behaviors.

Developing systems that tolerate these unpredictable behaviors and provide users with seamless experience is the aim of fault-tolerant systems. Fault tolerance is to provide correct and continuous operation albeit faulty components. Fault-tolerance, robustness, reliability, resilience and Quality of Service (QoS) are some of the ambiguous terms used for this. These terminologies are used interchangeably in many works. Significant works are done in this area encompassing numerous fields like job-shop scheduling [12], supply chain [13], and distributed systems [10,14].

Any fault-tolerant WFMS need to address three important questions [14]: (a) What are the factors or uncertainties that the system is fault-tolerant towards? (b) What behavior makes the system fault-tolerant? (c) How to quantify the fault-tolerance, i.e., what is the metric used to measure fault-tolerance?

In this survey we categorize and define the taxonomy of various types of faults that a WFMS in a distributed environment can experience. We further develop an ontology of different fault-tolerant mechanisms that are used until now. Finally we provide numerous metrics that measure fault-tolerance of a particular scheduling algorithm.

15.3.1 NECESSITY FOR FAULT-TOLERANCE IN DISTRIBUTED SYSTEMS

Workflows, generally, are composed of thousands of tasks, with complicated dependencies between the tasks. For example, some prominent workflows (as shown in Fig. 15.3) widely considered are Montage, CyberShake, Broadband, Epigenomics, LIGO Inspiral Analysis, and SIPHT, which are complex scientific workflows from different domains such as astronomy, life sciences, physics, and biology. These workflows are composed of thousands of tasks with various execution times, which are interdependent.

The workflow tasks are executed on distributed resources that are heterogeneous in nature. WFMSs that allocates these workflows uses middleware tools that require to operate congenially in a distributed environment. This very complex and complicated nature of WFMSs and its environment invite numerous uncertainties and chances of failures at various levels.

In particular, in data-intensive workflows that continuously process data, machine failure is inevitable. Thus, failure is a major concern during the execution of data-intensive workflows frameworks, such as MapReduce and Dryad [15]. Both transient (i.e., fail-recovery) and permanent (i.e., fail-stop) failures can occur in data-intensive workflows [16]. For instance, Google reported on average 5 permanent failures in form of machine crashes per MapReduce workflow during March 2006 [17] and at least one disk failure in every run of MapReduce workflow with 4000 tasks.

Necessity for fault-tolerance arises from this very nature of the application and environment. Workflows are applications that are most often used in a collaborative environment spread across the geography involving various people from different domains (e.g., [11]). So many diversities are potential causes for adversities. Hence, to provide a seamless experience over a distributed environment for multiple users of a complex application, fault-tolerance is a paramount requirement of any WFMS.

15.4 TAXONOMY OF FAULTS

Fault is defined as a defect at the lowest level of abstraction. A change in a system state due to a fault is termed as an error. An error can lead to a failure, which is a deviation of the system from its specified behavior [18,19]. Before we discuss about fault-tolerant strategies it is important to understand the fault-detection and identification methodologies and the taxonomy of faults.

Faults can be characterized in an environment through various elements and means. Lackovic et al. [20] provide a detailed list of these element that are illustrated in Fig. 15.4. *Accuracy* of fault detection can be either known or unknown faults. Known faults are those which have been reported before and solutions for such faults are known. *Location* is the part of the environment where the fault occurs. *Originator* is the part of the environment responsible for the fault to occur. *Stage* of the fault refers to the phase of the workflow lifecycle (design, build, testing, and production) when the fault occurred. *Time* is the incidence time in the execution when the fault happened. *Frequency*, as the name suggests identifies the frequency of fault occurrence. *Severity* specifies the difficulty in taking the corrective measures and details the impact of a particular fault. More details of these elements can be found in [20].

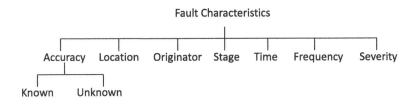

FIGURE 15.4

Elements through which faults can be characterized

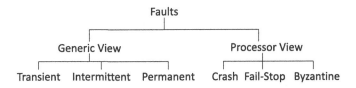

FIGURE 15.5

Faults: views and their classifications

At a high level, faults can be viewed in two different ways, *generic view*, and the *processor view*. The *generic view* of faults can be classified into three major types as shown in Fig. 15.5: *transient*, *intermittent* and *permanent* [20]. *Transient* faults invalidate only the current task execution, on a rerun or restart these fault most likely will not manifest again [21]. *Intermittent* faults appear at infrequent intervals. Finally, *permanent* faults are faults whose defects cannot be reversed.

From a *processor's perspective*, faults can be classified into three classes: *crash*, *fail-stop*, and *byzantine* [19]. This is mostly used for resource or machine failures. In the *crash* failure model, the processor stops executing suddenly at a specific point. In *fail-stop* processor's internal state is assumed to be volatile. The contents are lost when a failure occurs and it cannot be recovered. However, this class of failure does not perform an erroneous state change due to a failure [22]. *Byzantine* faults originate due to random malfunctions like aging or external damage to the infrastructure. These faults can be traced to any processor or messages [23].

Faults in a workflow environment can occur at different levels of abstraction [5]: hardware, operating system, middleware, task, workflow, and user. Some of the prominent faults that occur are network failures, machine crashes, out-of-memory, file not found, authentication issues, file staging errors, uncaught exceptions, data movement issues, and user-defined exceptions. Plankensteiner et al. [5] detail various faults and map them to different level of abstractions.

15.5 TAXONOMY OF FAULT-TOLERANT SCHEDULING ALGORITHMS

This section details the workings of various fault-tolerant techniques used in WFMS. In the rest of this section, each technique is analyzed and their respective taxonomies are provided. Additionally,

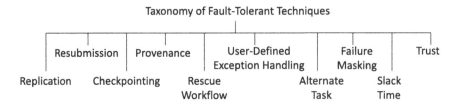

FIGURE 15.6

Taxonomy of workflow scheduling techniques to provide fault-tolerance

prominent works using each of these techniques are explained. Fig. 15.6 provides an overview of various techniques that are used to provide fault-tolerance.

15.5.1 REPLICATION

Redundancy in space is one of the widely used mechanisms for providing fault-tolerance. Redundancy in space means providing additional resources to execute the same task to provide resilience and it is achieved by duplication or replication of resources. There are broadly two variants of redundancy of space, namely, task duplication and data replication.

15.5.1.1 Task duplication

Task duplication creates replica of tasks. Replication of tasks can be done concurrently [24], where all the replicas of a particular task start executing simultaneously. When tasks are replicated concurrently, the child tasks start its execution depending on the schedule type. Fig. 15.7 illustrates the taxonomy of task duplication.

Schedules types, are either *strict* or *lenient*. In *strict* schedule the child task executes only when all the replicas have finished execution [25]. In the *lenient* schedule type, the child tasks start execution as soon as one of the replicas finishes execution [24].

Replication of task can also be performed in a backup mode, where the replicated task is activated when the primary tasks fail [26]. This technique is similar to retry or redundancy in time. However, here, they employ a backup overloading technique, which schedules the backups for multiple tasks in the same time period to effectively utilize the processor time.

Duplication is employed to achieve multiple objectives, the most common being fault-tolerance [25, 27–29]. When one task fails, the redundant task helps in completion of the execution. Additionally, algorithms employ data duplication where data is replicated and prestaged, thereby moving data near computation especially in data intensive workflows to improve performance and reliability [30]. Furthermore, estimating task execution time a priori in a distributed environment is arduous. Replicas are used to circumvent this issue using the result of the earliest completed replica. This minimizes the schedule length to achieve hard deadlines [31–34], as it is effective in handling performance variations [24]. Calheiros et al. [35] replicated tasks in idle time slots to reduce the schedule length. These replicas also increase resource utilization without any extra cost.

Task duplication is achieved by replicating tasks in either *idle cycles* of the resources or *exclusively on new resources*. Some schedules use a *hybrid approach* replicating tasks in both idle cycles and

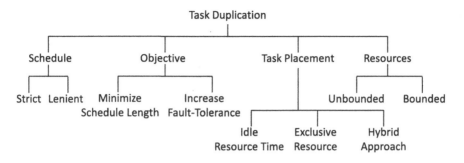

FIGURE 15.7

Different aspects of task duplication technique in providing fault-tolerance

new resources [35]. Idle cycles are those time slots in the resource usage period where the resources are unused by the application. Schedules that replicate in these idle cycles profile resources to find unused time slot, and replicate tasks in those slots. This approach achieves benefits of task duplication and simultaneously considers monetary costs. In most cases, however, these idle slots might not be sufficient to achieve the needed objective. Hence, task duplication algorithms commonly place their task replicas on new resources. These algorithms trade off resource costs to their objectives.

There is a significant body of work in this area encompassing platforms like cluster, grids, and clouds [31,25,27–29,32–34,36]. Resources considered can either be *bounded* or *unbounded* depending on the platform and the technique. Algorithms with bounded resources consider a limited set of resources. Similarly, an unlimited number of resources are assumed in an unbounded system environment. Resource types used can either be *homogeneous* or *heterogeneous* in nature. *Homogeneous* resources have similar characteristics, and *heterogeneous* resources on the contrary vary in their characteristics such as, processing speed, CPU cores, memory, etc. Darbha et al. [31] is one of the early works, which presents an enhanced search and duplication based scheduling algorithm (SDBS) that takes into account the variable task execution time. They consider a distributed system with homogeneous resources and assume an unbounded number of processors in their system.

15.5.1.2 Data replication

Data in workflows are either not replicated (and are stored locally by the processing machines) or is stored on the distributed file system (DFS) where it is automatically replicated (e.g., in Hadoop Distributed File System (HDFS)). Although the former approach is efficient, particularly in data-intensive workflows, it is not fault-tolerant. That is, failure of a server storing data causes the re-execution of the affected tasks. On the other hand, the latter approach offers more fault tolerance but is not efficient due to significant network overhead and increasing the execution time of the workflow.

Hadoop, which is a platform for executing data-intensive workflows, uses a static replication strategy for fault-tolerance. That is, users can manually determine the number of replicas that have to be created from the data. Such static and blind replication approach imposes a significant storage overhead to the underlying system (e.g., cluster or cloud) and slows down the execution of the MapReduce workflow. One approach to cope with this problem is to adjust the replication rate dynamically based on the usage rate of the data. This will reduce the storage and processing cost of the resources [37].

Cost-effective incremental replication (CIR) [38] is a strategy for cloud based workflows that predicts when a workflow is needed to replicate to ensure the reliability requirement of the workflow execution.

There are four major data-replication methods for data-intensive workflows on large-scale distributed systems (e.g., clouds) namely, *synchronous* and *asynchronous* replication, *rack-level* replication, and *selective* replication. These replication methods can be applied on input, intermediate, or output data of a workflow.

In *synchronous* data replication, such as those in HDFS, writers (i.e., producer tasks in a workflow) are blocked until replication finishes. Synchronous replication method leads to a high consistency because if a writer of block A returns, all the replicas of block A are guaranteed to be identical and any reader (i.e., consumer tasks in a workflow) of block A can read any replica. Nonetheless, the drawback of this approach is that the performance of writers might get affected as they have to be blocked. In contrast, *asynchronous* data replication [16] allows writers to proceed without waiting for a replication to complete. The asynchronous data replication consistency is not as accurate as the synchronous method because even if a writer of block A returns, a replica of block A may still be in the replication process. Nonetheless, performance of the writers improves due to the nonblocking nature. For instance, with an asynchronous replication in Hadoop, Map and Reduce tasks can proceed without being blocked.

Rack-level data replication method enforces replication of the data blocks on the same rack in a data center. In cloud data centers machines are organized in racks with a hierarchical network topology. A two-level architecture with a switch for each rack and a core switch is a common network architecture in these data centers. In this network topology the core switch can become bottleneck as it is shared by many racks and machines. That is, there is heterogeneity in network bandwidth where inter-rack bandwidth is scarce compared to intra-rack bandwidth. One example of bandwidth bottleneck is in the Shuffling phase of MapReduce. In this case, as the communication pattern between machines is all-to-all, the core switches become over-utilized whereas rack-level switches are underutilized. Rack-level replication reduces the traffic transferred through the bandwidth-scarce core switch. However, the drawback of the rack-level replication approach is that it cannot tolerate rack-level failures and if a rack fails, all the replicas become unavailable. There are observations that show rack-level failures are infrequent which proves the efficacy of rack-level replication. For instance, one study shows that Google experiences approximately 20 rack failures within a year [39].

Selective data replication is an approach where the data generated by the previous step of the workflow are replicated on the same machine, where they are generated. For instance, in a chained MapReduce workflow, once there is a machine failure at the Map phase, the affected Map tasks can be restarted instantly, if the data generated by the previous Reduce tasks were replicated locally on the same machine. In this manner, the amount of intermediate data that needs to be replicated in the Map phase is reduced remarkably. However, it is not very effective for Reduce phase, because Reduce data are mostly locally consumed.

ISS [16] is a system that extends the APIs of HDFS and implements a combination of three aforementioned replication approaches. It implements a rack-level replication that asynchronously replicates locally-consumed data. The focus of ISS is on the management of intermediate data in Hadoop data-intensive workflows. It takes care of all aspects of managing intermediate data such as writing, reading, Shuffling, and replicating. Therefore, a programming framework that utilizes ISS does not need to consider Shuffling. ISS transparently transfers intermediate data from writers (e.g., Map tasks) to readers (e.g., Reduce tasks).

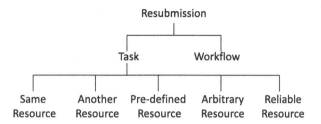

FIGURE 15.8

Taxonomy of resubmission fault-tolerant technique

As mentioned earlier, replicating input data or intermediate data on stable external storage systems (e.g., distributed file systems) is expensive for data-intensive workflows. The overhead is due to data replication, disk I/O, network bandwidth, and serialization which can potentially dominate the workflow execution time [40]. To avoid these overheads, in frameworks such as Pregel [41], which is a system for iterative graph computation, intermediate data are maintained in memory. Resilient Distributed Datasets (RDDs) [40] enables data reuse in a fault-tolerant manner. RDDs are parallel data structures that enable users to persist intermediate data in memory and manipulate them using various operators. It also controls the partitioning of the data to optimize data placement. RDD has been implemented within the Spark [42] framework.

15.5.2 RESUBMISSION

Resubmission tries to reexecute components to mitigate failures. Resubmission or redundancy in time helps recover from transient faults or soft errors. Resubmission is employed as an effective fault-tolerant mechanism by around 80% of the WFMSs [5]. Li et al. [43] claim that 41% of failures are recovered in their work through resubmission. Some of the WFMS that support resubmission for fault-tolerance are Askalon, Chemomentum, GWES, Pegasus, P-Grade, Proactive, Triana, and Unicore [5].

Resubmission can be classified into two levels: *workflow* and *task* resubmission as illustrated in Fig. 15.8. In workflow resubmission, as the name suggests, the entire application or a partial workflow is resubmitted [44].

Task resubmission, retries the same task to mitigate failure. Task retry/resubmission can be either done on the same resource or another resource [5]. Resubmission on the same resource is applicable when a task fails due to a transient failure or due to file staging issues. In other cases this might not be the best approach to mitigate failures. Resubmission of the task can be either done on a fixed predefined resource [45] or on an arbitrary resource or a resource with high reliability. A fixed predefined resource is not necessarily the same resource, but the drawbacks are similar to that. Selecting a resource arbitrarily without a strategy is not the most effective solution to avoid failures. Employing a strategy whilst selecting resources, like choosing resources with high reliability, increases the probability of addressing failures. Zhang et al. [28] rank resources based on a metric called reliability prediction and use this metric to schedule their task retries.

Resources considered can either be homogeneous or heterogeneous in nature. In a heterogeneous resource type environment, different resource selection strategies have different impact on cost and

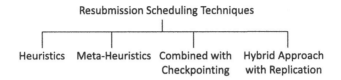

FIGURE 15.9

Different approaches used in resubmission algorithms

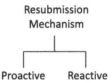

FIGURE 15.10

Classification of resubmission mechanisms

time. A dynamic algorithm must take into consideration deadline and budget restrictions, and select resources that provide fault-tolerance based on these constraints. Clouds providers like Amazon, offer resources in an auction-like mechanism for low cost with low SLAs called spot instances. Poola et al. [46] have proposed a just-in-time dynamic algorithm that uses these low cost instances to provide fault-tolerant schedules considering the deadline constraint. They resubmit tasks upon failures to either spot or on-demand instances based on the criticality of the workflow deadline. This algorithm is shown to provide fault-tolerant schedule whilst reducing costs.

Algorithms usually have a predefined limit for the number of retries that they will attempt [28,47] to resolve a failure. Some algorithms also have a time interval in addition to the number of retries threshold [45]. However, there are algorithms that consider infinite retries as they assume the faults to be transient in nature [48].

Algorithms using resubmission can be broadly classified into four types as shown in Fig. 15.9: *Heuristic* based [43,45,49], *metaheuristic* based [44], *hybrid of resubmission and checkpointing* [28], and *hybrid of resubmission and replication* [50]. Heuristic based approaches are proven to be highly effective, although these solutions are specific to a particular use case and take lot of assumptions. Metaheuristics provide near optimal solutions and are more generic approaches; however, they are usually time and memory consuming. Employing hybrid approaches with checkpointing saves time, does not perform redundant computing, and does not overutilize resources. However, these approaches delay the makespan as resubmission retries a task in case of failures, although, checkpointing reruns from a saved state it still requires additional time delaying the makespan. Replication with redundant approaches wastes resources but does not delay the makespan as the replicas eliminate the necessity of rerunning a task.

Finally, resubmission fault-tolerant mechanism is employed in two major ways (Fig. 15.10): *proactive* and *reactive*. In the *proactive* mechanism [44,51], the algorithm predicts a failure or a performance slowdown of a machine and reschedules it on another resource to avoid delays or failures. In *reactive* mechanism, the algorithms resubmit tasks or a workflow after a failure occurs.

Resubmission in workflow provides resilience for various faults. However, the drawback of this mechanism is the degradation in the total execution time when large number of failures occurs. Resubmission is ideal for an application during the execution phase and replication is well suited at the scheduling phase [50].

15.5.3 CHECKPOINTING

Checkpointing is an effective and widely used fault-tolerant mechanism. In this process, states of the running process are periodically saved to a reliable storage. These saved states are called *checkpoints*. Checkpointing restores the saved state after a failure, i.e., the process will be restarted from its last checkpoint or the saved state. Depending on the host, we can restart the process on the same machine (if it has not failed) or on another machine [52,23]. WFMS actively employ checkpointing as their fault-tolerant mechanism. More than 60% of these systems use checkpointing to provide resilience [5].

A checkpoint data file typically contains data, states and stack segments of the process. It also stores information of open files, pending signals and CPU states [53].

15.5.3.1 Checkpoint selection strategies

How often or when to take checkpoints is an important question while checkpointing. Various systems employ different checkpoint selection strategies. Prominent selection strategies are [53–56]:

- Using event activity as a checkpoint;
- Taking checkpoints at the start and end time of an activity;
- Taking a checkpoint at the beginning and then after each decision activity;
- Letting user define some static stages during build-stage;
- Taking checkpoint when runtime completion duration is greater than maximum activity duration;
- Taking checkpoint when runtime completion duration is greater than mean duration of the activity;
- Reacting when an activity fails;
- Reacting when an important activity finishes completion;
- Reacting after a user defined deadline (e.g., percentage of workflow completion);
- Reacting to system changes like availability of services.
- Using application defined stages;
- Reacting based on linguistic constructs for intervention of programmers.

15.5.3.2 Issues and challenges

Checkpointing provides fault-tolerance against transient faults only. If there is a design fault, checkpointing cannot help recover from it [57]. Another challenge here is to decide on the number of checkpoints to be taken. The more the checkpoints, the higher the overhead, whereas fewer checkpoints leads to excessive loss of computation [58]. The overhead imposed by checkpointing depends on the level that it is applied (e.g., process or virtual machine level). A mathematical model is provided in [59] to calculate the checkpointing overhead of virtual machines.

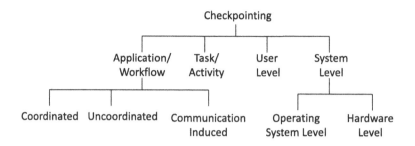

FIGURE 15.11

Taxonomy of checkpointing mechanism

In message-passing systems inter-process dependencies are introduced by messages. When one or more processes fail, these dependencies may lead to a restart even if the processes did not fail. This is called rollback propagation that may lead the system to the initial state. This situation is called a domino effect [54]. The domino effect occurs if checkpoints are taken independently in an uncoordinated fashion in a system. This can be avoided by performing checkpoints in a coordinated manner. Further, if checkpoints are taken to maintain system-wide consistency then the domino effect can be avoided [54].

15.5.3.3 Taxonomy of checkpointing

As shown in Fig. 15.11, there are four major checkpointing approaches: *Application/workflow-level*, *task/activity level*, *user level*, and *system level* implementation.

In *application/workflow-level* checkpointing, implementation is usually performed within the source code, or is automatically injected into the code using external tools. It captures the state of the entire workflow and its intermediate data [58,53]. This can be further classified into *coordinated*, *uncoordinated*, or *communication-induced* [54]. Coordinated approach takes checkpoints in a synchronized fashion to maintain a global state. Recovery in this approach is simple and the domino effect is not experienced in this method. It maintains only one permanent checkpoint on a reliable storage, eliminating the need for garbage collection. The drawback is incurring a large latency in committing the output [54].

Coordinated checkpointing can further be achieved in the following ways: *Nonblocking* Checkpoint Coordination, Checkpointing with *Synchronized Clocks*, *Checkpointing and Communication Reliability*, and *Minimal Checkpoint Coordination*.

Nonblocking Checkpoint Coordination: Here, the initiator takes a checkpoint and broadcasts a checkpoint request to all other activities. Each activity or task takes a checkpoint once it receives this checkpoint request and then further rebroadcasts the request to all tasks/activities.

Checkpointing with Synchronized Clocks: This approach is done with loosely synchronized clocks that trigger local checkpointing for all activities without an initiator.

Checkpointing and Communication Reliability: This protocol saves all the in-transit messages by their destination tasks. These messages are not saved when reliable communication channels are not assumed.

FIGURE 15.12

Workflow-level checkpointing

Minimal Checkpoint Coordination: In this case, only a minimum subset of the tasks/activities is saved as checkpoints. The initiator identifies all activities with which it has communicated since the last checkpoint and sends them a request. Upon receiving the request, each activity further identifies other activities it has communicated since the last checkpoint and sends them a request.

Uncoordinated checkpointing allows each task to decide the frequency and time to saved states. In this method, there is a possibility of domino effect. As this approach is not synchronized, it may take many useless checkpoints that are not part of the global consistent state. This increases overhead and do not enhance the recovery process. Multiple uncoordinated checkpoints force garbage collection to be invoked periodically.

The last type of workflow-level checkpointing is *Communication-Induced Checkpointing*. In this protocol the information about checkpointing is piggybacked in the application messages. The receiver then uses this information to decide whether or not to checkpoint.

Based on the intermediate data, workflow-level checkpointing can also be subcategorized into two types: *lightweight* and *heavyweight* as illustrated in Fig. 15.12. In *lightweight* checkpointing the intermediate data is not stored, only a reference to it is stored assuming that the storage is reliable. Alternatively, *heavyweight* checkpointing stores the intermediate data along with other things in a checkpoint [58,53].

Task-level checkpointing saves the register, stack, memory, and intermediate states for every individual task running on a virtual machine [60] or a processor [58,53]. When a failure occurs, the task can restart from the intermediate saved state and this is especially important when the failures are independent. This helps recover individual units of the application.

User-level checkpointing uses a library to do checkpoints and the application programs are linked to it. This mechanism is not transparent as the applications are modified, recompiled and relinked. The drawback being this approach cannot checkpoint certain shell scripts, system calls, and parallel application as the library may not be able access system files [57].

System-level checkpointing can be done either at the *operating system level* or the *hardware level*. This mechanism is transparent to the user and it does not necessarily modify the application program code. The problem with operating system level checkpointing is that it cannot be portable and modification at the kernel level is not always possible and difficult to achieve [57].

15.5.3.4 Performance optimization

As discussed earlier, optimizing performance in a checkpoint operation is a challenge. The frequency of checkpoints impacts the storage and computation load. Checkpointing schemes can be broadly divided into *online* and *offline* checkpointing schemes as illustrated in Fig. 15.13.

FIGURE 15.13

Checkpointing schemes

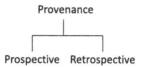

FIGURE 15.14

Forms of provenance

An *offline* checkpointing scheme determines the frequency for a task before its execution. The drawback being it is not an adaptive approach. On the other hand, *online* schemes determine the checkpointing interval dynamically based on the frequency of fault occurrences and the workflow deadline. The dynamic checkpointing is more adaptive and is able to optimize performance of the WFMS.

15.5.3.5 Checkpointing in WFMS

WFMSs employ checkpointing at various levels. At Workflow-level, two types of checkpointing can be employed lightweight and heavyweight as stated earlier. Lightweight checkpointing is used by Chemomentum, GWEE, GWES, Pegasus, P-grade, and Traina WFMS. Similarly, heavyweight checkpointing is employed by GWEE and GWES. Task-level checkpointing is employed by both Pegasus and P-Grade. Proactive WFMS checkpoints at the operating system level [5].

Kepler also checkpoints at the workflow layer [3], whereas, Karajan allows checkpointing the current state of the workflow at a global level. Here, timed or program-directed checkpoints can be taken, or checkpoints can be taken automatically at preconfigured time intervals, or it can be taken manually [61]. SwinDeW-C checkpoints using a minimum time redundancy based selection strategy [62].

15.5.4 PROVENANCE

Provenance is defined as the process of metadata management. It describes the origins of data, the processes involved in its production, and the transformations it has undergone. Provenance can be associated with process(es) that aid data creation [63]. Provenance captures multiple important information like dynamics of control and data flows, their progressions, execution information, file locations, input and output information, workflow structure, form, workflow evolution, and system information [6]. Provenance is essential for interpreting data, determining its quality and ownership, providing reproducible results, optimizing efficiency, troubleshooting, and also to provide fault-tolerance [64,65].

As detailed in Fig. 15.14, provenance can be of two forms: *prospective* and *retrospective* [65]. *Prospective* provenance captures the specifications that need to be followed to generate a data product or class of data products. *Retrospective* provenance captures the executed steps similar to a detailed log of task execution. It also captures information about the execution environment used to derive a specific data product.

Provenance information is used to rerun workflows, these reruns can overcome transient system errors [66]. Provenance allows users to trace state transitions and detect the cause of inconsistencies. It is used to design recovery or undo paths from workflow fault states at the task granularity level. It is used as an effective tool to provide fault-tolerance in several WFMS.

15.5.5 RESCUE WORKFLOW

The rescue workflow technique ignores failed tasks and executes the rest of the workflow until no more forward progress can be made.

A rescue workflow description called rescue DAG containing statistical information of the failed nodes is generated, which is used for later resubmission [4]. Rescue workflow technique is used by Askalon, Kepler and DAGMan [4,62].

15.5.6 USER-DEFINED EXCEPTION HANDLING

In this fault-tolerant technique, users can specify a particular action or a predefined solution for certain task failures in a workflow. Such a technique is called user-defined exception handling [4]. This could also be used to define alternate tasks for predefined type of failures [45].

This mechanism is employed by Karajan, GWES, Proactive, and Kepler among the prominent WFMS [62,5].

15.5.7 ALTERNATE TASK

The alternate task fault-tolerant scheduling technique defines an alternative implementation of a particular task. When the predefined task fails, its alternative implementation is used for execution. This technique is particularly useful when two or more different implementations are available for a task. Each implementation has different execution characteristics but take the same input and produce same outputs. For example, there could be a task with two implementations, where one is less memory or compute intensive but unreliable, while the alternate implementation is memory intensive or compute intensive but more reliable. In such cases, the later implementation can be used as an alternative task.

This technique is also useful to semantically undo the effect of a failed task, that is, alternate tasks can be used to clean up the states and data of a partially executed failed task [4,45].

15.5.8 FAILURE MASKING

Failure masking fault-tolerant technique ensures service availability, despite failures in tasks or resources [57]. This is typically achieved by redundancy, and in the event of failure the services are provided by the active (i.e., surviving) tasks or resources masking failures. Masking can be of two forms: *hierarchical group masking* and *flat group masking*. (See Fig. 15.15.)

FIGURE 15.15

Forms of failure masking

Hierarchical group masking uses a coordinator to monitor the redundant components and decides which copy should replace the failed component. The major drawback of this approach is the single point of failure of the coordinator.

Flat group masking resolves this single point of failure by being symmetric. That is, the redundant components are transparent and a voting process is used to select the replacement in adversity. This approach does not have a single point of failure, but imposes more overhead to the system.

15.5.9 SLACK TIME

Task slack time represents a time window within which the task can be delayed without extending the makespan. It is intuitively related to the robustness of the schedule. Slack time is computed as the minimum spare time on any path from the considered node to the exit node of the workflow. The formal definition of slack is given by Sakellariou and Zhao in [51].

Shi et al. [10] present a robust scheduling for heterogeneous resources using slack time to schedule tasks. They present an ϵ-constraint method where robustness is an objective and deadline is a constraint. This scheduling algorithm tries to find schedules with maximum slack time without exceeding the specified deadline. Similarly, Poola et al. [67] presented a heuristic considering heterogeneous cloud resources, they divided the workflow into partial critical paths and based on the deadline and budget added slack time to these partial critical paths. Slack time added to the schedule enables the schedule time to tolerate performance variations and failures up to a certain extent, without violating the deadline.

15.5.10 TRUST-BASED SCHEDULING ALGORITHMS

Distributed environments have uncertainties and are unreliable, added to this, some service providers may slightly violate SLAs for many reasons including profitability. Therefore, WFMS typically employ trust factor to make the schedule trustworthy. Trust is composed of many attributes including reliability, dependability, honesty, truthfulness, competence, and timeliness [68]. Including trust into workflow management significantly increases fault-tolerance and decreases failure probability of a schedule [68, 69].

Conventionally, trust models are of two types: *identity-based* and *behavior-based*. Identity-based trust model uses trust certificates to verify the reliabilities of components. *Behavior-based* models observe and take the cumulative historical transaction behavior and also feedback of entities to evaluate the reliability [70].

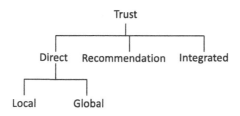

FIGURE 15.16

Methods for evaluating trust in trust-based algorithms used for fault-tolerant WFMS

Trust is evaluated by three major methods as shown in Fig. 15.16: *Direct trust*, *Recommendation Trust*, and *Integrated Trust*. *Direct trust* is derived from the historical transaction between the user and the service. Here, no third party is used to evaluate the trust of the service [70]. Direct trust can be broadly of two types *local trust* and *global trust* [71]. *Local trust* is computed based on a local system's transactions and similarly *global trust* is evaluated considering the entire global system's history. Yang et al. [69] use direct trust in their scheduling algorithm to decrease failure probability of task assignments and to improve the trustworthiness of the execution environment.

Recommendation trust is where the user consults a third party to quantify the trust of a service [70]. *Integration trust* is a combination of both direct and recommendation trust. This is usually done by a weighted approach [71]. Tan et al. [71] have proposed a reliable workflow scheduling algorithm using fuzzy technique. They propose an integrated trust metric combining direct trust and recommendation trust using a weighted approach.

Some of the drawbacks of trust models are: (i) majority of the trust models are designed for a particular environment under multiple assumptions; and (ii) trust is mostly studied in isolation without involving other system components [70].

15.6 MODELING OF FAILURES IN WORKFLOW MANAGEMENT SYSTEMS

Failure models define failure rates, frequencies and other statistically details observed in real systems, these models are used mainly in simulation and prediction systems to recreate failures. Failures can follow Poisson, exponential, Weibull, log-normal, or uniform distributions, as illustrated in Fig. 15.17. Failures can be independent or correlated. Benoit et al. [72] model resource failure through Poisson distribution, they assume failures to be statistically independent and assume a constant failure rate for each processor. Chen and Deelman [48] also assume failure to be independent but use an exponential distribution and also use a non constant failure rate. Dongarra et al's. [73] work is similar to [48], but they assume constant failure rate for each processor.

Weibull distribution is widely used in failure modeling in different ways. Litke et al. [74] use Weibull distribution to estimate the failure probability of the next assigned task for a specific resource based on the estimated execution time of each task on the resource. Plankensteiner et al. [5] use a combination of distribution to model failures. They use Weibull distribution for mean time between failure (MTBF) for clusters and to model the size of failure. Further, they use log-normal distribution to estimate the duration of failure. Rahman et al. [75] use Weibull distribution in their simulation environment

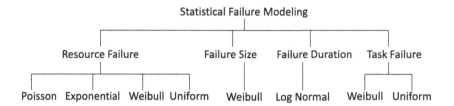

FIGURE 15.17

Distributions used for modeling failures for workflows in distributed environments

to determine whether a task execution will fail or succeed. If a task is likely to fail, they generate a random number from a uniform distribution and if that number is less than the failure probability of a resource at a particular grid, then the task is failed.

Distributions are used to evaluate reliability of tasks and resources. Wang et al. [76] uses exponential distribution to evaluate task reliability based on real-time reputation. The reputation is defined by using their task failure rate.

All the above works consider failures to be independent. However, Javadi et al. [18] consider failures to be spatial and temporally correlated. Spatial correlations of failures imply that multiple failures occur on various nodes with a specified time interval. Temporal correlation denotes skewness in failures over time. They use spherical covariance model to determine temporal failure correlation and Weibull distribution for failure modeling.

15.7 METRICS USED TO QUANTIFY FAULT-TOLERANCE

There are various metrics to measure the robustness or fault-tolerance of a workflow schedule. Each metric measures a different aspect and reports the schedule robustness based on certain constraints and assumptions. We present some prominent metrics used in the literature.

Makespan Standard Deviation reports the standard deviation of the makespan. The narrower the distribution, the better the schedule [77].

Makespan differential Entropy measures the differential entropy of the distribution: if the uncertainty is less, then the schedule is more robust [78].

Mean slack is computed by averaging task slack time, i.e., the amount of time the task can be delayed without delaying the schedule. The slack of a schedule, on the other hand, is the sum of slack times of all the tasks. Hence, the more slack a schedule has, the more failures it can tolerate. Therefore, such a schedule is more robust [78].

Probabilistic metric defines the makespan probability within two bounds. If the probability is high, then the robustness is high. This is because a higher probability indicates that the makespan is close to the average makespan [79].

Lateness likelihood metric gives the probability of the schedule to be late, where a schedule is called late if the makespan exceeds a given deadline. If the lateness likelihood is high, the robustness of the schedule is low [10].

Reliability of a compute service during a given time is defined as follows:

$$Reliability = (1 - (numFailure/n)) * mttf, \qquad (15.1)$$

where *numFailure* is the number of failures experienced by the users, n is the number of users, and *mttf* is the promised mean time to failure [80].

Workflow Failure Ratio is the percentage of failed workflows due to one or more task failures [81].

Request Rejection Ratio is the ratio of number of rejected requests to the total requests [81].

Workflow Success Probability is given as a product of the success probabilities of individual tasks [28].

Standard Length Ratio indicates the performance of the workflow. It is the ratio of turnaround time to the critical path time including the communication time between tasks. Turnaround time is the workflows' running time. A lower value of this metric signifies better performance [28].

Trust metric presents the trustworthiness of a particular resource. It is given by the following equation:

$$Trust(S_i) = w_i * DT(S_i) + (1 - w_i) * RT(S_i), \qquad (15.2)$$

where $DT(S_i)$ is the direct trust based on historical experiences of the ith service, $RT(S_i)$ is the recommendation trust by other users, and w_i is the weight of $DT(S_i)$ and $RT(S_i)$ for the ith service [71].

Failure probability (R_p) is the likelihood of the workflow to fail before the given deadline [10,67], which can be formulated as

$$R_p = (TotalRun - FailedRun)/(TotalRun), \qquad (15.3)$$

where *TotalRun* is number of times the experiment was conducted and *FailedRun* is number of times the constraint, $finish_{t_n} \leqslant D$, was violated. Here, D is the deadline of the workflow and $finish_{t_n}$ is the workflow elapsed time.

Tolerance time (R_t) is the amount of time a workflow can be delayed without violating the deadline constraint. This provides an intuitive measurement of robustness given the same schedule and resource to task mapping, expressing the amount of uncertainties it can further withstand. It is given by

$$R_t = D - finish_{t_n}. \qquad (15.4)$$

15.8 SURVEY OF WORKFLOW MANAGEMENT SYSTEMS AND FRAMEWORKS

This section provides a detailed view of the state-of-the-art WFMSs and also provide information about the different fault-tolerant techniques used, as described in Section 15.5. These WFMSs are summarized in Table 15.1.

15.8.1 ASKALON

Askalon [52] is a WFMS developed at the University of Innsbruck, Austria. It facilitates the development and optimization of applications on grid computing environments [52,4]. The system architecture

Table 15.1 Features, provenance information and fault-tolerant strategies of workflow management systems

WFMS	Features	Provenance	Fault-tolerant strategy
Askalon University of Innsbruck, Austria. http://www.dps.uibk.ac.at/projects/askalon/	• Service Oriented Architecture • Single Access User Portal • UML Workflow Editor • X.509 certificates support • Amazon EC2 API support • Grids and clouds	N/A	Resubmission, replication, checkpointing/restart, migration, user-defined exception, rescue workflow.
Pegasus USC Information Sciences Institute and the University of Wisconsin Madison. http://pegasus.isi.edu/	• Portability/Reuse • Performance and reliability • Scalability • Provenance • Data Management • Desktops, clusters, grids, and clouds	Keeps track of data locations, data results, and software used with its parameters.	Task Resubmission, Workflow Resubmission, workflow-level checkpointing, alternative data sources, rescue workflow.
Triana Cardiff University, United Kingdom.	• Modular java workflow environment • Job queuing • Comprehensive toolbox libraries • Grids and clouds	N/A	Light-weight checkpointing and restart of services are supported at the workflow level. Resubmissions are supported at the task level by the workflow engine, and alternate task technique is also employed.
Unicore 6 Collaboration between German research institutions and industries.	• Support for virtual organizations, X.509 certificates • Improved data management through DataFinder • Supports for each loops and iteration over file-sets • Grids and cluster	N/A	Resubmission and reliability measurement of task and workflows are supported.
Keplar UC Davis, UC Santa Barbara, and UC San Diego. https://kepler-project.org/	• Independently Extensible, Reliable, open and a comprehensive system • Supports multidisciplinary applications • Grids, clusters, and clouds • Easy to use Graphical editor	Data and process provenance information is recorded.	Resubmissions, checkpointing, alternative versions, error-state and user-defined exception handling mechanisms to address issues are employed.
Cloudbus WF Engine The University of Melbourne, Australia. http://cloudbus.org/workflow/	• User-friendly portal for discovery, monitoring and scheduling • Grids, clusters, and clouds	Provenance information of data is recorded.	Failure are handled by resubmitting the tasks to resources.

Table 15.1 (*Continued*)

WFMS	Features	Provenance	Fault-tolerant Strategy
Taverna Created by the myGrid team.	• Capable of performing iterations and looping • Supports data streaming • Grids, clusters, and clouds	Provenance suite records service invocations and workflow results both intermediate and final.	Resubmission and alternate resources.
e-Science Central Newcastle University, United Kingdom. http://www.esciencecentral.co.uk/	• Easy and efficient access through web browser • Provides APIs for external applications • All data are versioned • Private and public clouds	e-SC provenance service collects information regarding all system events.	Provides fine grained security control modeled around groups and user-to-user connections.
SwinDeW-C Swinburne University of Technology, Australia.	• Cloud based peer-to-peer WFMS • Web portal allows users to access entire WFMS • Clouds	data provenance is recorded during workflow execution	Checkpointing is employed. QoS management components includes performance management, data management and security management.

of it consists of the following components: (i) *Scheduler*, which maps single or multiple workflows tasks onto the grid; (ii) *Enactment Engine*, which ensures reliable and fault-tolerant execution of applications; (iii) *Resource Manager*, which is responsible for negotiation, reservation, allocation of resources and automatic deployment of services. It also shields the user from low-level grid middleware technology; (iv) *Performance Analysis*, which supports automatic instrumentation and bottleneck detection (e.g., excessive synchronization, communication, load imbalance, inefficiency, or nonscalability) within the grid; and (v) *Performance Prediction service*, which estimates execution times of workflow activities through a training phase and statistical methods based on a combination of historical data obtained from the training phase and analytical models [82,52].

Askalon uses an XML-based workflow language called AGWL for workflow orchestration. It can be used to specify DAG-constructs, parallel loops and conditional statements such as switch and if/then/else. AGWL can express sequence, parallelism choice and iteration workflow structures. Askalon uses a graphical interface called Teuta to support the graphical specification of grid workflow applications based on the UML activity diagram [82,52].

Askalon can detect faults at the following levels: (i) Hardware level, which includes machine crashes and network failures; (ii) OS level, which comprises exceeded disk quota, out of disk space, and file not found errors; (iii) Middleware-level, accounting for failed authentication, failed job-submission, unreachable services and file staging failures; and (iv) Workflow level, collecting unavailable input data, data movement faults. However, the system cannot detect task-level faults. Further, the system can recover from the following faults at different levels: (i) Hardware level, which includes machine crashes and network failures; (ii) OS level, dealing with exceeded disk quota, out of disk space; (iii) Middleware-level, which includes failed job-submission; and (iv) Workflow level, containing data movement faults. Nonetheless, it does not recover from task level faults and user-defined exceptions. Fault-tolerant techniques like checkpointing, migration, restart, retry, and replication are employed to recover from these faults [5,82,52].

15.8.2 PEGASUS

It is a project of the USC Information Sciences Institute and the Computer Science department at the University of Wisconsin Madison, United States. Pegasus enables scientists to construct workflows in abstract terms by automatically mapping the high-level workflow descriptions onto distributed infrastructures (e.g., Condor, Globus, or Amazon EC2). Multiple workflow applications can be executed in this WFMS [83].

Workflows can be described using DAX a DAG XML description. The abstract workflow describes application components and their dependencies in the form of a DAG [47].

Workflow application can be executed in variety of target platforms including local machine, clusters, grids and clouds. The WFMS executes jobs, manages data, monitors execution and handles failures. Pegasus WFMS has five major components: (i) *Mapper*, which generates an executable workflow from an abstract workflow. It also restructures the workflow to maximize performance. It further adds transformations aiding in data management and provenance generation; (ii) *Local Execution Engine*, which submits jobs to the local scheduling queue by managing dependencies and changing the state; (iii) *Job Scheduler*, which schedules and manages individual jobs on local and remote resources; (iv) *Remote Execution Engine*, which manages execution of one or more tasks on one or more remote nodes; and (v) *Monitoring Component*, which monitors the workflow execution. It records the tasks logs, performance and provenance information in a workflow database. It notifies events such as failures, success, and statuses [84].

Pegasus stores and queries information about the environment, such as storage systems, compute nodes, data location, through various catalogs. Pegasus discovers logical files using the Replica Catalog. It looks up various user executables and binaries in Transformation Catalog. Site Catalog is used to locate computational and storage resources [84,47].

Pegasus has its own lightweight job monitoring service called Kickstart. The mapper embeds all jobs with Kickstart [84]. This helps in getting runtime provenance and performance information of the job. This information is further used for monitoring the application.

Resource selection is done using the knowledge of available resources, their characteristics and the location of the input data. Pegasus supports pluggable components where a customized approach for site selection can be performed. It has few choices of selection algorithms, such as random, round-robin, and min-min.

Pegasus can handle failures dynamically at various levels building on the features of DAGMan and HTCondor. It is equipped to detect and recover from faults. It can detect faults at the following levels: At the Hardware and Operating System levels, it can detect exceeding CPU time limit and file nonexistence. At the level of Middleware, it detects authentication, file staging, and job submission faults. At Task and Workflow levels job crashes and input unavailability are detected. DAGMan helps recover the following failures at different levels: at Hardware level, it can recover from machine crashes and network failures by automatically resubmitting. Middleware faults detected can also be recovered. Data movement faults can also be treated with recovery at task and workflow level. At Workflow level, redundancy is used and lightweight checkpoints are supported [5,84]. If a job fails more than the set number of retries, then the job is marked as a fatal failure. When a workflow fails due to such failures, the DAGMan writes a rescue workflow. The rescue workflow is similar to the original DAG without the fatal failure nodes. This workflow will start from the point of failure. Users can also replan the workflow, in case of workflow failures and move the computation left to an alternate resource. Pegasus uses retries, resubmissions, and checkpointing to achieve fault-tolerance [84].

Monitoring and debugging is also done to equip users to track and monitor their workflows. Three different logs are generated which are used to collect and process data [84]: (i) Pegasus Mapper Log helps relate the information about the abstract workflow from the executable workflow allowing users to correlate user-provided tasks to the jobs created by Pegasus. (ii) Local workflow execution engine logs contain status of each job of the workflow. (iii) Job logs capture provenance information about each job. It contains fine-grained execution statistics for each task. It also includes a web dashboard to facilitate monitoring [84].

15.8.3 TRIANA

Triana [85] is a data-flow system developed at Cardiff University, United Kingdom. It is a combination of an intuitive graphical interface with data analysis tools. It aims to support applications on multiple environments, such as peer-to-peer and grid computing. Triana allows users to integrate their own middleware and services besides providing a vast library of prewritten tools. These tools can be used in a drag-and-drop fashion to orchestrate a workflow.

Triana addresses fault-tolerance in a user-driven and interactive manner. When faults occur, the workflow is halted, displaying a warning, and allowing the user to rectify. At the hardware level, machine crashes and network errors are detected. Missing files and other faults are detected by the workflow engine at the operating system level. Except deadlock and memory leaks that cannot be detected at the middleware and the task level, all other faults can be detected. In the workflow level, data movement and input availability errors are detected. Lightweight checkpointing and restart of services are supported at the workflow level. Retires, alternate task creations, and restarts are supported at the task level by the workflow engine [5].

15.8.4 UNICORE 6

Unicore [86] is a European grid technology developed by collaboration between German research institutions and industries. Its main objective is to access distributed resources in a seamless, secure, and intuitive way. The architecture of UNICORE is divided into three layers, namely, *client layer*, *service layer*, and *systems layer*. In the client layer, various clients, like UNICORE Rich Client (graphical interface), UNICORE command-line (UCC) interface, and High Level API (HiLA), a programming API, are available.

The service layer contains all the vital services and components. This layers has services to maintain a single site or multiple sites. Finally, the system layer has the Target System Interface (TSI) between the UNICORE and the low-level resources. Recently added functionalities to UNICORE 6 contains support for virtual organizations, interactive access based on X.509 certificates using Shibboleth, and improved data management through the integration of DataFinder. GridBeans and JavaGAT help users to support their applications further. UNICORE 6 also introduces for-each-loops and iteration over file-sets in addition to existing workflow constructs. It also supports resubmission and reliability measurement for task and workflows. Added to these new monitoring tools, availability and service functionality are also improved.

15.8.5 KEPLER

The Kepler system [87,88,3] is developed and maintained by the cross-project collaboration consisting of several key institutions: UC Davis, UC Santa Barbara, and UC San Diego. Kepler system allows scientists to exchange, archive, version, and execute their workflows.

Kepler is built on Ptolemy, a dataflow-oriented system. It focuses on an actor-oriented modeling with multiple component interaction semantics. Kepler can perform both static and dynamic checking on workflow and data. Scientists can prototype workflows before the actual implementation. Kepler system provides web service extensions to instantiate any workflow operation. Their grid service enables scientists to use grid resources over the Internet for a distributed workflow. It further supports foreign language interfaces via the Java Native Interface (JNI), giving users the benefits to use existing code and tools. Through Kepler users can link semantically compatible but syntactically incompatible services together (using XSLT, Xquery, etc.). Kepler supports heterogeneous data and file formats through Ecological Metadata Language (EML) ingestion. Fault-tolerance is employed through retries, checkpointing, and alternative versions.

15.8.6 CLOUDBUS WORKFLOW MANAGEMENT SYSTEM

The WFMS [89–91] developed at The University of Melbourne provides an efficient management technique for distributed resources. It aids users by enabling their applications to be represented as a workflow and then execute them on the cloud platform from a higher level of abstraction. The WMS is equipped with an easy-to-use graphical workflow editor for application composition and modification, an XML-based workflow language for structured representation. It further includes a user-friendly portal with discovery, monitoring, and scheduling components.

Workflow monitor of the WFMS enables users to view the status of each task, they can also view the resource and the site where the task is executed. It also provides the failure history of each task. The workflow engine contains workflow language parser, resource discovery, dispatcher, data management, and scheduler. Tuple space model, event-driven approach, and subscription approach make WMS flexible and loosely coupled in design. Failures are handled by resubmitting the tasks to resources without a failure history for such tasks. WMS uses either Aneka [92] and/or Broker [93] to manage applications running on distributed resources.

15.8.7 TRAVERNA

Taverna [94,95] is an open source and domain-independent WFMS created by the myGrid team. It is a suite of tools used to design and execute scientific workflows and aid in silico experimentation. Taverna engine is capable of performing iterations, looping, and data streaming. It can interact with various types of services including web services, data warehouses, grid services, cloud services, and various scripts like R, distributed command-line, or local scripts.

The Traverna server allows workflows to be executed in distributed infrastructures like clusters, grids and clouds. The server has an interface called *Taverna Player* through which users can execute workflows from web browsers or through third-party clients. *Taverna Provenance suite* records service invocations and workflow results both intermediate and final. It also supports pluggable architecture that facilitates extensions and contributions to the core functionalities. Here, retries and alternate resources are used to mitigate failures.

15.8.8 THE E-SCIENCE CENTRAL (E-SC)

The e-Science Central [96] was created in 2008 as a cloud data processing system for e-Science projects. It can be deployed on both private and public clouds. Scientists can upload data, edit, run workflows, and share results using a Web Browser. It also provides an application programming interface through which external application can use the platform's functionality.

The e-SC facilitates data storage management, tools for data analysis, automation tools, and also controlled data sharing. All data are versioned and support reproduction of experiments, aiding investigation into data changes, and their analysis.

The e-SC provenance service collects information regarding all system events and this provenance data model is based on the *Open Provenance Model* (OPM) standard. It also provides fine grained security control modeled around groups and user-to-user connections.

15.8.9 SWINDEW-C

Swinburne Decentralized Workflow for cloud (SwinDeW-C) [62] is a cloud based peer-to-peer WFMS developed at Swinburne University of Technology, Australia. It is developed based on their earlier project for grid called SwinDeW-G. It is built on SwinCloud infrastructure that offers unified computing and storage resources. The architecture of SwinDeW-C can be mapped into four basic layers: *application layer*, *platform layer*, *unified resource layer*, and *fabric layer*.

In SwinDeW-C users should provide workflow specification consisting of task definitions, process structures, and QoS constraints. SwinDeW-C supports two types of peers: An ordinary SwinDeW-C peer is a cloud service node with software service deployed on a virtual machine; and SwinDeW-C coordinator peers, are special nodes with QoS, data, and security management components. The cloud workflow specification is submitted to any coordinated peer, which will evaluate the QoS requirement and determine its acceptance through a negotiation process. A coordinated peer is setup within every service provider. It also has pricing and auditing components. All peers that reside in a service provider communicate with its coordinated peer for resource provisioning. Here, each task is executed by a SwinDeW-C peer during the run-time stage.

SwinDeW-C also allows virtual machines to be created with public clouds providers, such as Amazon, Google, and Microsoft. Checkpointing is employed for providing reliability. Additionally, QoS management components including performance management, data management, and security management are integrated into the coordinated peers.

15.8.10 BIG DATA WORKFLOW FRAMEWORKS: MAPREDUCE, HADOOP, AND SPARK

Recently, big data analytics has gained considerable attention both in academia and industry. Big data analytics is heavily reliant on tools developed for such analytics. In fact, these tools implement a specific form of workflows, known as MapReduce [97].

MapReduce framework is a runtime system for processing big data workflows. The framework usually runs on a dedicated platform (e.g., a cluster). There are currently two major implementations of the MapReduce framework. The original implementation with a proprietary license was developed by Google [97]. After that, Hadoop framework [98] was developed as an open-source product by Yahoo! and widely applied for big data processing.

The MapReduce framework is based on two main input functions, *Map* and *Reduce* that are implemented by the programmer. Each of these functions is executed in parallel on large-scale data across the available computational resources. Map and Reduce collectively form a usually huge workflow to process large datasets. The MapReduce storage functionality for storing input, intermediate, and output data is supported by distributed file systems developed specifically for this framework, such as Hadoop Distributed File System (HDFS) [99] and Google File System (GFS) [100].

More specifically, every MapReduce program is composed of three subsequent phases namely, *Map*, *Shuffle*, and *Reduce*. In the Map phase, the Map function implemented by the user is executed on the input data across the computational resources. The input data is partitioned into chunks and stored in a distributed file system (e.g., HDFS). Each Map task loads some chunks of data from the distributed file system and produces intermediate data that are stored locally on the worker machines. Then, the intermediate data are fed into the Reduce phase. That is, the intermediate data are partitioned to some chunks and processed by the Reduce function, in parallel.

Distributing the intermediate data across computational resources for parallel Reduce processing is called Shuffling. The distribution of intermediate data is accomplished in an all-to-all manner that imposes a communication overhead and often is the bottleneck. Once the intermediate data are distributed, the user-defined Reduce function is executed and the output of the MapReduce is produced. It is also possible to have a chain of MapReduce workflows (a.k.a. multistage MapReduce), such as

Yahoo! WebMap [101]. In these workflows, the output of a MapReduce workflow is the intermediate data for the next MapReduce workflow.

Spark [42] is a framework developed at UC Berkeley and is being utilized for research and production applications. Spark offers a general-purpose programming interface in the Scala programming language [102] for interactive and in-memory data mining across clusters with large datasets. Spark has proven to be faster than Hadoop for iterative applications.

MapReduce has been designed to tolerate faults that commonly occur at large scale infrastructures where there are thousands of computers and hundreds of other devices such as network switches, routers, and power units. Google and Hadoop MapReduce can tolerate crashes of Map and Reduce tasks. If one of these tasks stops, it is detected and a new instance of the same task is launched. In addition, data are stored along with their checksum on disks that enables corruption detection. MapReduce [97] uses a log-based approach for fault tolerance. That is, output of the Map and Reduce phases are logged to the disk [103] (e.g., a local disk or a distributed file system). In this case, if a Map task fails then it is reexecuted with the same partition of data. In case of failure in the Reduce phase, the key/value pairs for that failed Reducer have to be regenerated.

15.8.11 OTHER WORKFLOW MANAGEMENT SYSTEMS

WFMSs are in abundance that can schedule workflows on distributed environments. These WFMS primarily schedule application on clusters and grids. Karajan [61] is one such WFMS, which was implemented to overcome the shortcoming of GridAnt [104]. It was developed at the Argonne National Laboratory. Karajan is based on the definition of hierarchical workflow components.

Imperial College e-Science Network Infrastructure (ICENI) [105] was developed at London e-science center, which provides a component-based grid-middleware. GridFlow [106], Grid Workflow Execution Engine [107], P-Grade [108], Chemomentum [109] are other WFMS that schedule workflow applications on grid platforms. Each of these workflow engine have their own unique properties and have different architectures supported by a wide variety of tools and software.

15.9 TOOLS AND SUPPORT SYSTEMS
15.9.1 DATA MANAGEMENT TOOLS

Workflow enactment engine need to move data from compute nodes to storage resources and also from one node to another. Kepler uses GridFTP [87] to move files, to fetch files from remote locations. Unicore uses a data management system called DataFinder [110]. It provides with management of data objects and hides the specifics of storage systems by abstracting the data management concepts. For archival of data Tivoli Storage Manager[1] could be used. It reduces backup and recovery infrastructure. It can also back up into the cloud with openstack and vCloud integrations. Traditional protocols like HTTP, HTTPS, SFTP are also used for data movement.

---

[1] http://www-03.ibm.com/software/products/en/tivostormana/.

15.9.2 SECURITY AND FAULT-TOLERANCE MANAGEMENT TOOLS

In SwinDeW-C secure communications are ensured through GnuPG,[2] which is a free implementation of OpenPGP. Globus uses the X.509 certificates, an established secure data format. These certificates can be shared among public key based software. Unicore 6 employs an interactive access based on X.509 certificates called Shibboleth[3] that enables Single Sign-On as well as authentication and authorization. The International Grid Trust Federation[4] (IGTF) is a trust service provider that establishes common policies and guidelines. Similarly, The European Grid Trust project[5] provides new security services for applications using GRID middleware layer.

Access control to services can be attained through access control lists (ACLs), which can be attached to data items so that privileges for specific users and groups can be managed. DAGMan offers fault-tolerance to Pegasus through its rescue DAG. Additionally, provenance plays an important role in fault-tolerance. Most WFMS use Open Provenance Model format[6] and the W3C PROV model[7] to achieve and manage provenance information.

15.9.3 CLOUD DEVELOPMENT TOOLS

Infrastructure resources are offered by public and private clouds. Public clouds are offered by many providers like Amazon AWS, Google Compute Engine, Microsoft Azure, IBM cloud, and many others. Private clouds could be built using Openstack, Eucalyptus, and VMware, to name a few. Cloud providers offer many storage solutions that can be used by WFMSs. Some of the storage solutions offered are Amazon S3, Google's BigTable, and the Microsoft Azure Storage. Oracle also offers a cloud based database as a service for business.

Amazon through its Amazon Simple Workflow (SWF)[8] provides a fully-managed task coordinator through which developers can build, run, and scale jobs. Chaos Monkey[9] is a free service that randomly terminates resources in your cloud infrastructures. This helps test the system for failures and help develop fault-tolerant systems in cloud.

15.9.4 SUPPORT SYSTEMS

[my]Experiment [111] is a social network environment for e-Scientist developed by a joint team from the universities of Southampton, Manchester, and Oxford. It provides a platform to discuss issues in development, to share workflows and reuse other workflows. It is a workflow warehouse and a gateway to established environments.

---

[2]https://www.gnupg.org/.

[3]http://www.internet2.edu/products-services/trust-identity-middleware/shibboleth/.

[4]http://www.igtf.net/.

[5]http://www.gridtrust.eu/gridtrust/.

[6]http://openprovenance.org/.

[7]http://www.w3.org/2011/prov.

[8]http://aws.amazon.com/swf/.

[9]https://github.com/Netflix/SimianArmy/wiki/Chaos-Monkey/.

Workflow Generator [112], created by Pegasus provides synthetic workflow examples with their detailed characteristics. They also provide a synthetic workflow generator and traces and execution logs from real workflows.

Failure Trace Archive [113] is a public repository of availability traces of parallel and distributed systems. It also provides tools for their analysis. This will be useful in developing fault-tolerant workflow schedulers.

15.10 SUMMARY

Workflows have emerged as a paradigm for managing complex large scale data analytics and computation. They are largely used in distributed environments such as, grids and clouds to execute their computational tasks. Fault-tolerance is crucial for such large scale complex applications running on failure-prone distributed environments. Given the large body of research in this area, in this chapter, we provided a comprehensive view on fault-tolerance for workflows in various distributed environments.

In particular, this chapter provides a detailed understanding of faults from a generic viewpoint (e.g., transient, intermittent, and permanent) and a processor viewpoint (such as crash, fail-stop, and byzantine). It also describes techniques such as replication, resubmission, checkpointing, provenance, rescue-workflow, exception handling, alternate task, failure masking, slack time, and trust-based approaches used to resolve these faults by which, a transparent and seamless experience to workflow users can be offered.

Apart from the fault-tolerant techniques, this chapter provides an insight into numerous failure models and metrics. Metrics range from makespan oriented, probabilistic, reliability based, and trust-based among others. These metrics inform us about the quality of the schedule and quantify fault-tolerance of a schedule.

Prominent WFMSs are detailed and positioned with respect to their features, characteristics, and uniqueness. Lastly, tools such as those for describing workflow languages, data-management, security, and fault-tolerance, and tools that aid in cloud development and support systems (including social networking environments and workflow generators) are introduced.

In effect, the stance of this chapter is helpful for developers and researchers working in the area of workflow management systems, as it identifies strength and weaknesses in this field and proposes future directions. This chapter provides a holistic view of fault-tolerance in WFMSs and techniques employed by different existing systems. The chapter also identifies the research trends and provides recommendations on future research areas in the area of fault-tolerant workflow management systems.

REFERENCES

[1] G. Juve, E. Deelman, Scientific workflows and clouds, Crossroads 16 (3) (2010) 14–18.
[2] Y. Gil, E. Deelman, M. Ellisman, T. Fahringer, G. Fox, D. Gannon, C. Goble, M. Livny, L. Moreau, J. Myers, Examining the challenges of scientific workflows, Computer 40 (12) (2007) 24–32.
[3] P. Mouallem, D. Crawl, I. Altintas, M. Vouk, U. Yildiz, A fault-tolerance architecture for Kepler-based distributed scientific workflows, in: M. Gertz, B. Ludäscher (Eds.), Scientific and Statistical Database Management, in: Lecture Notes in Computer Science, vol. 6187, 2010, pp. 452–460.

[4] J. Yu, R. Buyya, A taxonomy of scientific workflow systems for grid computing, SIGMOD Rec. 34 (3) (2005) 44–49.

[5] K. Plankensteiner, R. Prodan, T. Fahringer, A. Kertesz, P. Kacsuk, Fault detection, prevention and recovery in current grid workflow systems, in: Grid and Services Evolution, 2009, pp. 1–13.

[6] M.A. Vouk, Cloud computing – issues, research and implementations, CIT, J. Comput. Inf. Technol. 16 (4) (2008) 235–246.

[7] M.R. Garey, D.S. Johnson, Computers and Intractability: A Guide to the Theory of NP-Completeness, W.H. Freeman, New York, 1979, USA.

[8] Y. Kwok, I. Ahmad, Static scheduling algorithms for allocating directed task graphs to multiprocessors, ACM Comput. Surv. 31 (4) (1999) 406–471.

[9] J. Yu, R. Buyya, K. Ramamohanarao, Workflow scheduling algorithms for grid computing, in: F. Xhafa, A. Abraham (Eds.), Metaheuristics for Scheduling in Distributed Computing Environments, Stud. Comput. Intell. 146 (2008) 173–214.

[10] Z. Shi, E. Jeannot, J. Dongarra, Robust task scheduling in non-deterministic heterogeneous computing systems, in: IEEE International Conference on Cluster Computing, 2006, IEEE, 2006, pp. 1–10.

[11] G. Juve, A. Chervenak, E. Deelman, S. Bharathi, G. Mehta, K. Vahi, Characterizing and profiling scientific workflows, Future Gener. Comput. Syst. 29 (2013) 682–692.

[12] V. Leon, S. Wu, H. Robert, Robustness measures and robust scheduling for job shops, IIE Trans. 26 (5) (1994) 32–43.

[13] W. Herroelen, R. Leus, Project scheduling under uncertainty: survey and research potentials, Eur. J. Oper. Res. 165 (2) (2005) 289–306.

[14] J. Smith, H. Siegel, A. Maciejewski, Robust Resource Allocation in Heterogeneous Parallel and Distributed Computing Systems, Wiley Online Library, 2008, USA.

[15] M. Isard, M. Budiu, Y. Yu, A. Birrell, D. Fetterly, Dryad: distributed data-parallel programs from sequential building blocks, in: Proceedings of the 2nd ACM SIGOPS/EuroSys European Conference on Computer Systems, EuroSys'07, 2007, pp. 59–72.

[16] S.Y. Ko, I. Hoque, B. Cho, I. Gupta, Making cloud intermediate data fault-tolerant, in: Proceedings of the 1st ACM Symposium on Cloud Computing, SoCC'10, 2010, pp. 181–192.

[17] J. Dean, Experiences with MapReduce, an abstraction for large-scale computation, in: Proceedings of the 15th International Conference on Parallel Architectures and Compilation Techniques, PACT'06, 2006.

[18] B. Javadi, J. Abawajy, R. Buyya, Failure-aware resource provisioning for hybrid cloud infrastructure, J. Parallel Distrib. Comput. 72 (10) (2012) 1318–1331.

[19] F. Gärtner, Fundamentals of fault-tolerant distributed computing in asynchronous environments, ACM Comput. Surv. 31 (1) (1999) 1–26.

[20] M. Lackovic, D. Talia, R. Tolosana-Calasanz, J. Banares, O. Rana, A taxonomy for the analysis of scientific workflow faults, in: Proceedings of the 13th IEEE International Conference on Computational Science and Engineering, 2010, pp. 398–403.

[21] A. Benoit, L.-C. Canon, E. Jeannot, Y. Robert, Reliability of task graph schedules with transient and fail-stop failures: complexity and algorithms, J. Sched. 15 (5) (2012) 615–627.

[22] R.D. Schlichting, F.B. Schneider, Fail-stop processors: an approach to designing fault-tolerant computing systems, ACM Trans. Comput. Syst. 1 (3) (1983) 222–238.

[23] C. Dabrowski, Reliability in grid computing systems, Concurr. Comput., Pract. Exp. 21 (8) (2009) 927–959.

[24] W. Cirne, F. Brasileiro, D. Paranhos, L. Goes, W. Voorsluys, On the efficacy, efficiency and emergent behavior of task replication in large distributed systems, Parallel Comput. 33 (3) (2007) 213–234.

[25] A. Benoit, M. Hakem, Y. Robert, Fault tolerant scheduling of precedence task graphs on heterogeneous platforms, in: Proceedings of the IEEE International Symposium on Parallel and Distributed Processing, IPDPS 2008, 2008, pp. 1–8.

[26] D. Mosse, R. Melhem, S. Ghosh, Analysis of a fault-tolerant multiprocessor scheduling algorithm, in: Proceedings of the 24th International Symposium on Fault-Tolerant Computing, FTCS-24, 1994, pp. 16–25.

[27] G. Kandaswamy, A. Mandal, D. Reed, Fault tolerance and recovery of scientific workflows on computational grids, in: Proceedings of the 8th IEEE International Symposium on Cluster Computing and the Grid, 2008, pp. 777–782.

[28] Y. Zhang, A. Mandal, C. Koelbel, K. Cooper, Combined fault tolerance and scheduling techniques for workflow applications on computational grids, in: Proceedings of the 9th IEEE/ACM International Symposium on Cluster Computing and the Grid, CCGRID, 2009, pp. 244–251.

[29] K. Hashimoto, T. Tsuchiya, T. Kikuno, Effective scheduling of duplicated tasks for fault tolerance in multiprocessor systems, IEICE Trans. Inf. Syst. 85 (3) (2002) 525–534.

[30] A. Chervenak, E. Deelman, M. Livny, M.H. Su, R. Schuler, S. Bharathi, G. Mehta, K. Vahi, Data placement for scientific applications in distributed environments, in: Proceedings of the 8th IEEE/ACM International Conference on Grid Computing, GRID'07, 2007, pp. 267–274.

[31] S. Darbha, D. Agrawal, A task duplication based optimal scheduling algorithm for variable execution time tasks, in: Proceedings of the International Conference on Parallel Processing, vol. 1, in: ICPP, vol. 2, 1994, pp. 52–56.

[32] S. Ranaweera, D. Agrawal, A task duplication based scheduling algorithm for heterogeneous systems, in: Proceedings of the 14th International Parallel and Distributed Processing Symposium, 2000, pp. 445–450.

[33] A. Dogan, F. Ozguner, LDBS: a duplication based scheduling algorithm for heterogeneous computing systems, in: Proceedings of the International Conference on Parallel Processing, 2002, pp. 352–359.

[34] X. Tang, X. Li, G. Liao, R. Li, List scheduling with duplication for heterogeneous computing systems, J. Parallel Distrib. Comput. 70 (4) (2010) 323–329.

[35] R. Calheiros, R. Buyya, Meeting deadlines of scientific workflows in public clouds with tasks replication, IEEE Trans. Parallel Distrib. Syst. PP (99) (2013) 1.

[36] I. Brandic, D. Music, S. Dustdar, Service mediation and negotiation bootstrapping as first achievements towards self-adaptable grid and cloud services, in: Proceedings of the 6th International Conference Industry Session on Grids Meets Autonomic Computing, GMAC '09, New York, NY, USA, 2009, pp. 1–8.

[37] D. Yuan, L. Cui, X. Liu, Cloud data management for scientific workflows: Research issues, methodologies, and state-of-the-art, in: Proceedings of the 10th International Conference on Semantics, Knowledge and Grids (SKG), 2014, pp. 21–28.

[38] W. Li, Y. Yang, D. Yuan, A novel cost-effective dynamic data replication strategy for reliability in cloud data centres, in: Proceedings of the 9th IEEE International Conference on Dependable, Autonomic and Secure Computing, DASC'11, 2011, pp. 496–502.

[39] J. Dean, Software engineering advice from building large-scale distributed systems, http://research.google.com/people/jeff/stanford-295-talk.pdf, 2007.

[40] M. Zaharia, M. Chowdhury, T. Das, A. Dave, J. Ma, M. McCauley, M.J. Franklin, S. Shenker, I. Stoica, Resilient distributed datasets: a fault-tolerant abstraction for in-memory cluster computing, in: Proceedings of the 9th USENIX Conference on Networked Systems Design and Implementation, NSDI'12, 2012, pp. 2–12.

[41] G. Malewicz, M.H. Austern, A.J.C. Bik, J.C. Dehnert, I. Horn, N. Leiser, G. Czajkowski, Pregel: a system for large-scale graph processing, in: Proceedings of the ACM SIGMOD International Conference on Management of Data, SIGMOD'10, 2010, pp. 135–146.

[42] M. Zaharia, M. Chowdhury, M.J. Franklin, S. Shenker, I. Stoica, Spark: cluster computing with working sets, in: Proceedings of the 2nd USENIX Conference on Hot Topics in Cloud Computing, HotCloud'10, 2010, pp. 10–15.

[43] J. Li, M. Humphrey, Y. Cheah, Y. Ryu, D. Agarwal, K. Jackson, C. van Ingen, Fault tolerance and scaling in e-science cloud applications: observations from the continuing development of MODISAzure, in: Proceedings of the IEEE 6th International Conference on e-Science (e-Science), 2010, pp. 246–253.

[44] F. Berman, H. Casanova, A. Chien, K. Cooper, H. Dail, A. Dasgupta, W. Deng, J. Dongarra, L. Johnsson, K. Kennedy, C. Koelbel, B. Liu, X. Liu, A. Mandal, G. Marin, M. Mazina, J. Mellor-Crummey, C. Mendes, A. Olugbile, M. Patel, D. Reed, Z. Shi, O. Sievert, H. Xia, A. YarKhan, New grid scheduling and rescheduling methods in the grads project, Int. J. Parallel Program. 33 (2–3) (2005) 209–229.

[45] S. Hwang, C. Kesselman, Grid workflow: a flexible failure handling framework for the grid, in: Proceedings of the 12th IEEE International Symposium on High Performance Distributed Computing, 2003, pp. 126–137.

[46] D. Poola, K. Ramamohanarao, R. Buyya, Fault-tolerant workflow scheduling using spot instances on clouds, in: Proceedings of the International Conference on Computational Science in the Procedia Computer Science, in: International Conference on Computational Science, vol. 29, 2014, pp. 523–533.

[47] E. Deelman, G. Singh, M.H. Su, J. Blythe, Y. Gil, C. Kesselman, G. Mehta, K. Vahi, G.B. Berriman, J. Good, A. Laity, J.C. Jacob, D.S. Katz, Pegasus: a framework for mapping complex scientific workflows onto distributed systems, Sci. Program. 13 (3) (2005) 219–237.

[48] W. Chen, E. Deelman, Fault tolerant clustering in scientific workflows, in: Proceedings of the IEEE 8th World Congress on Services, SERVICES, 2012, pp. 9–16.

[49] Z. Yu, W. Shi, An adaptive rescheduling strategy for grid workflow applications, in: Proceedings of the IEEE International Parallel and Distributed Processing Symposium, IPDPS, 2007, pp. 1–8.

[50] K. Plankensteiner, R. Prodan, Meeting soft deadlines in scientific workflows using resubmission impact, IEEE Trans. Parallel Distrib. Syst. 23 (5) (2012) 890–901.

[51] R. Sakellariou, H. Zhao, A low-cost rescheduling policy for efficient mapping of workflows on grid systems, Sci. Program. 12 (4) (2004) 253–262.

[52] T. Fahringer, R. Prodan, R. Duan, J. Hofer, F. Nadeem, F. Nerieri, S. Podlipnig, J. Qin, M. Siddiqui, H. Truong, A. Villazon, M. Wieczorek, Askalon: a development and grid computing environment for scientific workflows, in: I. Taylor, E. Deelman, D. Gannon, M. Shields (Eds.), Workflows for e-Science, 2007, pp. 450–471.

[53] R. Duan, R. Prodan, T. Fahringer, Dee: a distributed fault tolerant workflow enactment engine for grid computing, in: L. Yang, O. Rana, B. Di Martino, J. Dongarra (Eds.), High Performance Computing and Communications, in: Lecture Notes in Computer Science, vol. 3726, 2005, pp. 704–716.

[54] E.N. Elnozahy, L. Alvisi, Y. Wang, D.B. Johnson, A survey of rollback-recovery protocols in message-passing systems, ACM Comput. Surv. 34 (3) (2002) 375–408.

[55] J. Chen, Y. Yang, Adaptive selection of necessary and sufficient checkpoints for dynamic verification of temporal constraints in grid workflow systems, ACM Trans. Auton. Adapt. Syst. 2 (6) (2007).

[56] M.A. Salehi, A.N. Toosi, R. Buyya, Contention management in federated virtualized distributed systems: implementation and evaluation, Softw. Pract. Exp. 44 (3) (2014) 353–368.

[57] I. Egwutuoha, D. Levy, B. Selic, S. Chen, A survey of fault tolerance mechanisms and checkpoint/restart implementations for high performance computing systems, J. Supercomput. 65 (3) (2013) 1302–1326.

[58] R. Tolosana-Calasanz, J. Baòares, P. Álvarez, J. Ezpeleta, O. Rana, An uncoordinated asynchronous checkpointing model for hierarchical scientific workflows, J. Comput. Syst. Sci. 76 (6) (2010) 403–415.

[59] M.A. Salehi, B. Javadi, R. Buyya, Resource provisioning based on preempting virtual machines in distributed systems, Concurr. Comput., Pract. Exp. 26 (2) (2014) 412–433.

[60] M.A. Salehi, J. Abawajy, R. Buyya, Taxonomy of contention management in interconnected distributed systems, in: Computer Science and Software Engineering, Computing Handbook, third edition, 2014, pp. 1–33, Chapter 57.

[61] G. von Laszewski, M. Hategan, D. Kodeboyina, Java COG kit workflow, in: I. Taylor, E. Deelman, D. Gannon, M. Shields (Eds.), Workflows for e-Science, 2007, pp. 340–356.

[62] X. Liu, D. Yuan, G. Zhang, J. Chen, Y. Yang, SwinDeW-C: a peer-to-peer based cloud workflow system, in: B. Furht, A. Escalante (Eds.), Handbook of Cloud Computing, 2010, pp. 309–332.

[63] Y.L. Simmhan, B. Plale, D. Gannon, A survey of data provenance in e-science, SIGMOD Rec. 34 (3) (2005) 31–36.

[64] S.B. Davidson, S.C. Boulakia, A. Eyal, B. Ludäscher, T.M. McPhillips, S. Bowers, M.K. Anand, J. Freire, Provenance in scientific workflow systems, IEEE Data Eng. Bull. 30 (4) (2007) 44–50.

[65] S.B. Davidson, J. Freire, Provenance and scientific workflows: challenges and opportunities, in: Proceedings of the ACM SIGMOD International Conference on Management of Data, SIGMOD'08, New York, NY, USA, 2008, pp. 1345–1350.

[66] Y. Simmhan, R. Barga, C. van Ingen, E. Lazowska, A. Szalay, Building the trident scientific workflow workbench for data management in the cloud, in: Proceedings of the 3rd International Conference on Advanced Engineering Computing and Applications in Sciences, 2009, ADVCOMP'09, 2009, pp. 41–50.

[67] D. Poola, S.K. Garg, R. Buyya, Y. Yang, K. Ramamohanarao, Robust scheduling of scientific workflows with deadline and budget constraints in clouds, in: Proceedings of the 28th IEEE International Conference on Advanced Information Networking and Applications (AINA-2014), 2014, pp. 1–8.

[68] M. Wang, K. Ramamohanarao, J. Chen, Trust-based robust scheduling and runtime adaptation of scientific workflow, Concurr. Comput., Pract. Exp. 21 (16) (2009) 1982–1998.

[69] Y. Yang, X. Peng, Trust-based scheduling strategy for workflow applications in cloud environment, in: Proceedings of the 8th International Conference on P2P, Parallel, Grid, Cloud and Internet Computing (3PGCIC), 2013, pp. 316–320.

[70] W. Li, J. Wu, Q. Zhang, K. Hu, J. Li, Trust-driven and QoS demand clustering analysis based cloud workflow scheduling strategies, Clust. Comput. 17 (3) (2014) 1013–1030.

[71] W. Tan, Y. Sun, L.X. Li, G. Lu, T. Wang, A trust service-oriented scheduling model for workflow applications in cloud computing, IEEE Syst. J. 8 (3) (2014) 868–878.

[72] A. Benoit, M. Hakem, Y. Robert, Multi-criteria scheduling of precedence task graphs on heterogeneous platforms, Comput. J. 53 (6) (2010) 772–785, http://comjnl.oxfordjournals.org/content/53/6/772.full.pdf+html.

[73] J.J. Dongarra, E. Jeannot, E. Saule, Z. Shi, Bi-objective scheduling algorithms for optimizing makespan and reliability on heterogeneous systems, in: Proceedings of the 19th Annual ACM Symposium on Parallel Algorithms and Architectures, SPAA'07, New York, NY, USA, 2007, pp. 280–288.

[74] A. Litke, D. Skoutas, K. Tserpes, T. Varvarigou, Efficient task replication and management for adaptive fault tolerance in mobile grid environments, Future Gener. Comput. Syst. 23 (2) (2007) 163–178.

[75] M. Rahman, R. Ranjan, R. Buyya, Reputation-based dependable scheduling of workflow applications in peer-to-peer grids, Comput. Netw. 54 (18) (2010) 3341–3359.

[76] X. Wang, C.S. Yeo, R. Buyya, J. Su, Optimizing the makespan and reliability for workflow applications with reputation and a look-ahead genetic algorithm, Future Gener. Comput. Syst. 27 (8) (2011) 1124–1134.

[77] L. Canon, E. Jeannot, Evaluation and optimization of the robustness of DAG schedules in heterogeneous environments, IEEE Trans. Parallel Distrib. Syst. 21 (4) (2010) 532–546.

[78] L. Bölöni, D.C. Marinescu, Robust scheduling of metaprograms, J. Sched. 5 (5) (2002) 395–412.

[79] V. Shestak, J. Smith, H. Siegel, A. Maciejewski, A stochastic approach to measuring the robustness of resource allocations in distributed systems, in: Proceedings of the International Conference on Parallel Processing, 2006, ICPP, IEEE, 2006, pp. 459–470.

[80] S.K. Garg, S. Versteeg, R. Buyya, A framework for ranking of cloud computing services, Future Gener. Comput. Syst. 29 (4) (2013) 1012–1023, Special Section: Utility and Cloud Computing.

[81] S. Adabi, A. Movaghar, A.M. Rahmani, Bi-level fuzzy based advanced reservation of cloud workflow applications on distributed grid resources, J. Supercomput. 67 (1) (2014) 175–218.

[82] T. Fahringer, R. Prodan, R. Duan, F. Nerieri, S. Podlipnig, J. Qin, M. Siddiqui, H. Truong, A. Villazon, M. Wieczorek, Askalon: a grid application development and computing environment, in: Proceedings of the 6th IEEE/ACM International Workshop on Grid Computing, GRID'05, Washington, DC, USA, 2005, pp. 122–131.

[83] Pegasus workflow management system, https://pegasus.isi.edu/, 2014 [Online; accessed 01 December 2014].

[84] E. Deelman, K. Vahi, G. Juve, M. Rynge, S. Callaghan, P.J. Maechling, R. Mayani, W. Chen, R.F. da Silva, M. Livny, K. Wenger, Pegasus, a workflow management system for science automation, Future Gener. Comput. Syst. 46 (0) (2015) 17–35.

[85] I. Taylor, M. Shields, I. Wang, A. Harrison, The Triana workflow environment: architecture and applications, in: I. Taylor, E. Deelman, D. Gannon, M. Shields (Eds.), Workflows for e-Science, 2007, pp. 320–339.

[86] A. Streit, P. Bala, A. Beck-Ratzka, K. Benedyczak, S. Bergmann, R. Breu, J. Daivandy, B. Demuth, A. Eifer, A. Giesler, B. Hagemeier, S. Holl, V. Huber, N. Lamla, D. Mallmann, A. Memon, M. Memon, M. Rambadt, M. Riedel, M. Romberg, B. Schuller, T. Schlauch, A. Schreiber, T. Soddemann, W. Ziegler, Unicore 6 – recent and future advancements, Ann. Telecommun. 65 (11–12) (2010) 757–762.

[87] I. Altintas, C. Berkley, E. Jaeger, M. Jones, B. Ludascher, S. Mock, Kepler: an extensible system for design and execution of scientific workflows, in: Proceedings of the 16th International Conference on Scientific and Statistical Database Management, 2004, pp. 423–424.

[88] B. Ludascher, I. Altintas, C. Berkley, D. Higgins, E. Jaeger, M. Jones, E.A. Lee, J. Tao, Y. Zhao, Scientific workflow management and the Kepler system, Concurr. Comput., Pract. Exp. 18 (10) (2006) 1039–1065.

[89] S. Pandey, W. Voorsluys, M. Rahman, R. Buyya, J.E. Dobson, K. Chiu, A grid workflow environment for brain imaging analysis on distributed systems, Concurr. Comput., Pract. Exp. 21 (16) (2009) 2118–2139.

[90] R. Buyya, S. Pandey, C. Vecchiola, Cloudbus toolkit for market-oriented cloud computing, in: M. Jaatun, G. Zhao, C. Rong (Eds.), Cloud Computing, in: Lecture Notes in Computer Science, vol. 5931, 2009, pp. 24–44.

[91] S. Pandey, D. Karunamoorthy, R. Buyya, Workflow engine for clouds, in: Cloud Computing, 2011, pp. 321–344.

[92] C. Vecchiola, X. Chu, R. Buyya, Aneka: a software platform for .net-based cloud computing, in: High Speed and Large Scale Scientific Computing, 2009, pp. 267–295.

[93] S. Venugopal, K. Nadiminti, H. Gibbins, R. Buyya, Designing a resource broker for heterogeneous grids, Softw. Pract. Exp. 38 (8) (2008) 793–825.

[94] T. Oinn, M. Addis, J. Ferris, D. Marvin, M. Senger, M. Greenwood, T. Carver, K. Glover, M.R. Pocock, A. Wipat, P. Li, Taverna: a tool for the composition and enactment of bioinformatics workflows, Bioinformatics 20 (17) (2004) 3045–3054, http://bioinformatics.oxfordjournals.org/content/20/17/3045.full.pdf+html.

[95] K. Wolstencroft, R. Haines, D. Fellows, A. Williams, D. Withers, S. Owen, S. Soiland-Reyes, I. Dunlop, A. Nenadic, P. Fisher, J. Bhagat, K. Belhajjame, F. Bacall, A. Hardisty, A. Nieva de la Hidalga, M.P. Balcazar Vargas, S. Sufi, C. Goble, The taverna workflow suite: designing and executing workflows of web services on the desktop, web or in the cloud, Nucleic Acids Research, http://nar.oxfordjournals.org/content/early/2013/05/02/nar.gkt328.full.pdf+html.

[96] H. Hiden, S. Woodman, P. Watson, J. Cala, Developing cloud applications using the e-science central platform, Philos. Trans. R. Soc. Lond. A, Math. Phys. Eng. Sci. 371 (1983).

[97] J. Dean, S. Ghemawat, MapReduce: simplified data processing on large clusters, Commun. ACM 51 (1) (2008) 107–113.

[98] C. Lam, Hadoop in Action, 1st edition, Greenwich, CT, USA, 2010.

[99] K. Shvachko, H. Kuang, S. Radia, R. Chansler, The Hadoop distributed file system, in: Proceedings of the 26th IEEE Symposium on Mass Storage Systems and Technologies, MSST'10, 2010, pp. 1–10.

[100] S. Ghemawat, H. Gobioff, S. Leung, The Google file system, in: Proceedings of the 19th ACM Symposium on Operating Systems Principles, SOSP'03, 2003, pp. 29–43.

[101] O. Alaçam, M. Dalcı, A usability study of webmaps with eye tracking tool: the effects of iconic representation of information, in: Proceedings of the 13th International Conference on Human–Computer Interaction, 2009, pp. 12–21.

[102] M. Odersky, L. Spoon, B. Venners, Programming in Scala: A Comprehensive Step-by-Step Guide, 1st edition, Artima Press, Walnut Creek, California, 2008, USA.

[103] A. Martin, T. Knauth, S. Creutz, D. Becker, S. Weigert, C. Fetzer, A. Brito, Low-overhead fault tolerance for high-throughput data processing systems, in: Proceedings of the 31st International Conference on Distributed Computing Systems, ICDCS'11, 2011, pp. 689–699.

[104] K. Amin, G. von Laszewski, M. Hategan, N. Zaluzec, S. Hampton, A. Rossi, Gridant: a client-controllable grid workflow system, in: Proceedings of the 37th Annual Hawaii International Conference on System Sciences, 2004, p. 10.

[105] S. McGough, L. Young, A. Afzal, S. Newhouse, J. Darlington, Workflow enactment in ICENI, in: UK e-Science All Hands Meeting, 2004, pp. 894–900.

[106] J. Cao, S.A. Jarvis, S. Saini, G.R. Nudd, Gridflow: workflow management for grid computing, in: Proceedings of the 3rd IEEE/ACM International Symposium on Cluster Computing and the Grid, CCGrid, 2003, pp. 198–205.

[107] E. Elmroth, F. Hernández, J. Tordsson, A light-weight grid workflow execution engine enabling client and middleware independence, in: R. Wyrzykowski, J. Dongarra, K. Karczewski, J. Wasniewski (Eds.), Parallel Processing and Applied Mathematics, in: Lecture Notes in Computer Science, vol. 4967, 2008, pp. 754–761.

[108] P. Kacsuk, G. Sipos, Multi-grid, multi-user workflows in the p-grade grid portal, J. Grid Comput. 3 (3–4) (2005) 221–238.

[109] S.P. Callahan, J. Freire, E. Santos, C.E. Scheidegger, C.T. Silva, H.T. Vo, Vistrails: visualization meets data management, in: Proceedings of the ACM SIGMOD International Conference on Management of Data, SIGMOD'06, New York, NY, USA, 2006, pp. 745–747.

[110] T. Schlauch, A. Schreiber, DataFinder – a scientific data management solution, in: Ensuring the Long-Term Preservation and Value Adding to Scientific and Technical Data, PV, Oberpfaffenhofen, Germany, 2007.

[111] C.A. Goble, D.C. De Roure, myExperiment: social networking for workflow-using e-scientists, in: Proceedings of the 2nd Workshop on Workflows in Support of Large-scale Science, WORKS'07, New York, NY, USA, 2007, pp. 1–2.

[112] Pegasus workflow generator, https://confluence.pegasus.isi.edu/display/pegasus/WorkflowGenerator/2014 [Online; accessed 5 December 2014].

[113] D. Kondo, B. Javadi, A. Iosup, D. Epema, The failure trace archive: Enabling comparative analysis of failures in diverse distributed systems, in: Proceedings of the 10th IEEE/ACM International Conference on Cluster, Cloud and Grid Computing, CCGrid, 2010, IEEE, 2010, pp. 398–407.

PART 4

RESOURCE MANAGEMENT

THE HARNESS PLATFORM: A HARDWARE- AND NETWORK-ENHANCED SOFTWARE SYSTEM FOR CLOUD COMPUTING

16

Jose G.F. Coutinho*, Mark Stillwell*, Katerina Argyraki[†], George Ioannidis[†], Anca Iordache[‡],
Christoph Kleineweber[§], Alexandros Koliousis*, John McGlone[‖], Guillaume Pierre[‡],
Carmelo Ragusa[¶], Peter Sanders**, Thorsten Schütt[§], Teng Yu*, Alexander Wolf[††]

**Imperial College London, UK [†]EPFL, Switzerland [‡]Université de Rennes 1, France [§]Zuse Institute Berlin, Germany
[¶]SAP, UK [‖]SAP Labs, USA **Maxeler Technologies, UK [††]University of California, Santa Cruz, USA*

16.1 INTRODUCTION

Modern cloud computing technologies and interfaces, as demonstrated by the web-service industry, can vastly improve the flexibility and ease-of-use of distributed systems, while simultaneously simplifying administration and reducing downtimes and maintenance costs. However, current data center infrastructures are built primarily to service distributed N-tier web-based applications that run on commodity hardware, leaving out many scientific and engineering applications that have complex task communication interdependencies, and may rely on a variety of heterogeneous accelerator technologies (e.g., GPGPUs, ASICs, FPGAs) to achieve the desired performance. Furthermore, web service applications are engineered to scale horizontally in response to demand, while for many other types of applications there may be a need to select the most appropriate configuration. This involves not only identifying the number and type of resources, but also providing a more complex description of resource requirements, such as the network bandwidth between resources, or the desired FPGA interconnect topology.

To better service workloads stemming from application domains currently not supported by cloud providers, we have designed and implemented an *enhanced cloud platform stack*, HARNESS, that fully embraces heterogeneity. HARNESS handles all types of cloud resources as *first-class entities*, breaking away from the VM-centric model employed by most cloud platforms used today. Moreover, HARNESS is designed to be resilient to different types of heterogeneous resources with its multitier architecture composed of agnostic and cognizant resource managers, and a novel API that provides a common interface to these managers. New types of cloud resources can be integrated into HARNESS, including complex state-of-the-art FPGA accelerator clusters, such as the MPC-X developed and marketed by Maxeler [8]; as well as more abstract resources, such as QoS-guaranteed network links. Our approach provides full control over which resource features and attributes are exposed to cloud tenants. This way, cloud tenants are able to submit fine-grained allocation requests that are tailored to the requirements of their application workloads, instead of relying on a set of predefined configurations (flavors) defined by cloud providers.

This chapter is structured as follows. Section 16.2 describes related work. Section 16.3 provides an overview of the key features of the HARNESS approach. Section 16.4 focuses on how heterogeneous cloud resources are managed within HARNESS. Section 16.5 covers the implementation of a HAR-NESS cloud prototype based on components developed by the project partners. The evaluation of the HARNESS cloud platform and infrastructure is reported in Section 16.6, and Section 16.7 concludes this chapter.

16.2 RELATED WORK

The HARNESS cloud platform provides two autonomous, yet fully integrated, cloud layers:

1. The platform layer, commonly known as Platform-as-a-Service (PaaS), manages the life-cycle of applications deployed in a cloud infrastructure. There are several commercial PaaS systems currently available, including Cloud Foundry [19], Google App Engine [5], Microsoft Azure [9], and OpenShift [32];
2. The infrastructure layer, commonly known as Infrastructure-as-a-Service (IaaS), exposes cloud resources and services that allow applications to run. Notable IaaS systems include Amazon AWS [1], Google Compute Engine [6], and Rackspace Open Cloud [37].

In addition to commercial cloud platforms, there have been a number of EU research projects that focus on solving specific cloud computing problems. For instance, Venus-C [13] is targeting the development, test and deployment of a highly-scalable cloud infrastructure; PaaSage [11] is covering the intelligent and autonomic management of cloud resources that included elastic scalability; CELAR [2] is focusing on the dynamic provisioning of cloud resources; LEADS [7] is working on the automatic management of resources across multiple clouds; BigFoot [12] is designing a scalable system for processing and interacting with large volumes of data; CloudSpaces [4] is focusing on cloud data concerns such as consistency and replication over heterogeneous repositories; and CloudLightning [3] is working on the problem of provisioning heterogeneous cloud resources using a service description language.

An important part of a cloud platform is the **API**, which provides an interface for interacting with its components. Attempts to standardize cloud interfaces have been spearheaded by a number of organizations, most notably Organization for the Advancement of Structured Information Standards (OASIS), Distributed Management Task Force (DMTF) and Open Grid Forum (OGF). The current state of the major available open cloud interface standards is summarized in Table 16.1, and described next:

- The **Topology and Orchestration Specification for Cloud Applications (TOSCA)** [34] standard from OASIS describes how to specify the topology of applications, their components, and the relationships and processes than manage them. This allows the cloud consumer to provide a detailed, but abstract, description of how their application or service functions, while leaving implementation details up to the cloud provider. With TOSCA, cloud users can describe how their distributed application should be deployed (in terms of which services need to communicate with each other), as well as how management actions should be implemented (e.g., start the database before the web service, but after the file server);

Table 16.1 Current open cloud interface standards

Specification	Standards org.	Version	Focus
TOSCA [34]	OASIS	1.0	orchestration
CAMP [33]	OASIS	1.1	deployment
CIMI [18]	DMTF	2.0	infrastructure
OCCI [31]	OGF	1.1	infrastructure

- The **Cloud Application Management for Platforms (CAMP) [33]** standard from OASIS targets PaaS cloud providers. This standard defines how applications can be bundled into a Platform Deployment Package (PDP), and in turn how these PDPs can be deployed and managed through a REST over HTTP interface. It includes descriptions of *platforms*, *platform components* (individual services offered by a platform), *application components* (individual parts an application that run in isolation) and *assemblies* (collections of possibly-communicating application components). Users can specify how application components interact with each other and components of the platform, but infrastructural details are left abstract. For example, a user would not know if their components were executing within shared services, containers or individual virtual machines;
- The **Cloud Management Initiative (CMI) [18]** standard was developed by the Cloud Management Working Group of DMTF. As with most cloud standards it relies on REST over HTTP. While XML is the preferred data transfer format due to the ability to easily verify that data conforms to the appropriate schema, JSON is also allowed. CIMI has predefined resource types defined in the standard, notably networks, volumes, machines, and systems (collections of networks, volumes, and machines), and the actions that may be performed upon a resource are constrained by its type (e.g., machines can be created, destroyed, started, stopped, or rebooted);
- The **Open Cloud Computing Interface (OCCI) [31]** standard comes from OGF, an organization that was previously very active in defining grid computing standards. It is divided into three sections: core, infrastructure, and HTTP rendering. The core specification defines standard data types for describing different types of resources, their capabilities, and how they may be linked together, while the infrastructure specification explicitly defines resource types for compute, network, and storage. The HTTP rendering section defines how to implement OCCI using REST over HTTP. Taken together, these three sections allow OCCI to present similar functionality as found in other IaaS-layer interfaces, such as Amazon EC2 [1], OpenStack Nova [10], and CIMI. However, OCCI is designed to be flexible, and the core specification can be used with extension standards to define new resource types.

16.3 OVERVIEW

A key distinguishing feature of HARNESS, when compared to current state-of-the-art and state-of-the-practice cloud computing platforms, is that it *fully embraces heterogeneity*. More specifically, HARNESS handles resources that are not only different in terms of size and nominal capacity, but also that are intrinsically different from each other, including FPGAs, GPGPUs, middleboxes, hybrid switches, and SSDs, in cloud data center infrastructures. Such support exacerbates the complexity of the management process for both the platform and the infrastructure layers.

While the availability of heterogeneous resources in cloud data centers is not a new concept, the current approach to supporting heterogeneity involves the use of the VM-centric model, where specialized resources are viewed as mere attributes of VMs, e.g., a VM coupled with a GPU or an FPGA. One can also envision a cloud computing platform that handles a closed set of heterogeneous resources; however, it is less obvious how to create a platform that is truly open to new and arbitrary types of cloud resources without having to redesign its underlying architecture and management algorithms. In this context, we have introduced novel aspects to the cloud computing platform design:

- HARNESS supports the allocation of different types of cloud resources, from conceptual (e.g., bandwidth) to complex physical devices (e.g., cluster of FPGAs). In contrast, existing IaaS systems, such as OpenStack [10], expose only one type of compute resource to tenants: virtual machines (VMs) or physical machines (baremetal). On the other hand, database and communication facilities are exposed as high-level services. HARNESS goes beyond the VM-centric model by treating all types of resources as first-class entities, thus cloud tenants can request virtual FPGAs and virtual network links between pairs of resources in the same way VMs are allocated in today's cloud platforms;

- HARNESS allows the side-by-side deployment of commodity and specialized resources, thus dramatically increasing the number of possible resource configurations in which an application can be deployed. In other words, an application may be deployed in many ways by varying the types, the number, and the attributes of resources, each option having its own cost, performance, and utilization footprint. In this context, applications express their wants and needs to the HARNESS platform, as well as the price they are prepared to pay for various levels of service. This expression of wants and needs builds upon what can be expressed through today's simple counts of virtual machines or amounts of storage, to encompass the specific characteristics of specialized technologies;

- HARNESS supports the automatic generation of performance models that guide the selection of well-chosen sets of resources to meet application requirements and service-level objectives. We developed several techniques to reduce the profiling effort of generic applications, including the use of monitoring resource utilization to generate higher-quality performance models at a fraction of time [25], as well as extrapolating production-size inputs using smaller sized datasets;

- HARNESS is designed to be resilient to heterogeneity. We developed a multitier infrastructure system, such that the top level management can perform operations with different levels of agnosticism, so that introducing new types of resources and tailoring a cloud platform to target specialized hardware devices does not lead to a complete redesign of the software architecture and/or its top-level management algorithms;

- The various resource managers that make up the HARNESS infrastructure are governed by a single API specification that handles all types of resources uniformly. Thus, a new type of resource can be incorporated into HARNESS by integrating a resource manager that implements the HARNESS API. Furthermore, cross-cutting functionality such as monitoring, debugging, pricing and security features can be introduced by extending the HARNESS API specification, thus covering all cloud resources types managed by HARNESS.

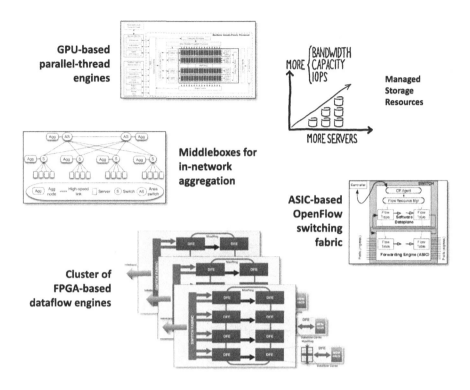

FIGURE 16.1

The HARNESS resource set consists of a group of compute, communication and storage resources. Some of these resources include (clockwise from top): (a) GPU accelerators, (b) managed storage volumes with performance guarantees, (c) hybrid switches that can handle millions of access control rules, (d) a cluster of FPGA-based devices that can be accessed via network, and (e) general-purpose middleboxes that allow application-specific network functions to be performed along network paths

16.4 MANAGING HETEROGENEITY

One of the key problems addressed by the HARNESS project is how to seamlessly incorporate and manage different types of heterogeneous resources in the context of a cloud computing platform. This includes not only supporting resources targeted by the HARNESS consortium (Fig. 16.1), but also generalizing this approach beyond the HARNESS resource set.

There are many challenges in handling heterogeneity in the context of a cloud computing platform. First, in contrast with commodity CPU-based servers, specialized resources are largely invisible to operating systems. Moreover, established cloud infrastructure management software packages, including OpenStack, provide very limited support for these types of resources. Instead, specialized resources must be directly managed by the application programmer, including not just execution of code but also in many cases tasks that are traditionally supported by both hardware and software such as allocation, de-allocation, load balancing, context switching and virtualization. A second challenge in handling heterogeneity is developing a system that does not require redesigning the architecture or

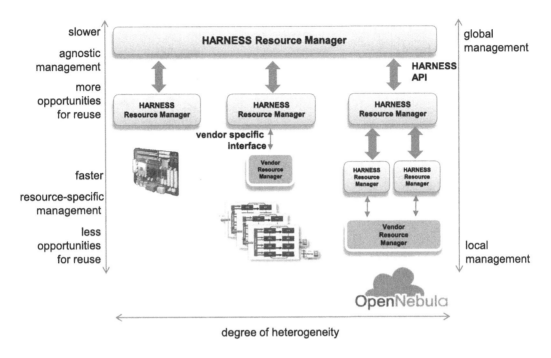

slower
agnostic
management

more
opportunities
for reuse

faster

resource-specific
management

less
opportunities
for reuse

global
management

local
management

degree of heterogeneity

FIGURE 16.2

A heterogeneous cloud computing platform, supporting various types of resources, can be built by composing resource managers that implement the HARNESS API in a hierarchical system

rewriting the allocation algorithms when new types of resources are introduced, considering that each type of resource exposes different control mechanisms, as well as interfaces for acquiring feedback about availability and monitoring. Furthermore, each type of resource exhibits different semantics for expressing capacity and allocation requests.

16.4.1 HIERARCHICAL RESOURCE MANAGEMENT

We have addressed these challenges by designing a cloud computing architecture where runtime resource managers can be combined hierarchically, as illustrated in Fig. 16.2. In this organization, the top levels of the hierarchy are HARNESS resource managers which service requests using the HARNESS API. At the lower levels of the hierarchy we find resource managers, provided by third-party vendors, that handle specific devices using proprietary interfaces. One of the responsibilities of the HARNESS resource managers is to translate agnostic requests defined by the HARNESS API into vendor-specific requests. Supporting multiple hierarchical levels allows a system integrator to design an architecture using separation of concerns, such that each manager can deal with specific types of resources. A typical HARNESS platform deployment has a top-level manager with complete knowledge about all the resources that are available in the system, but very little understanding of how to deal with any of these resources specifically. Any management request (such as reservation or monitoring feedback) are delegated to child managers that have a more direct understanding of the resource(s) in question. A child manager can handle a resource type directly or can delegate the request further down to a more specific resource manager.

Hence, the top levels of the hierarchy have a more agnostic and globalized view of available resources. This view can be acquired dynamically by querying the lower-level resource managers at regular time intervals. As we go down the hierarchy, we find a more localized and cognizant management. The question remains, how does one build an agnostic resource manager that can make allocation decisions without understanding the specific semantics of each type of resource? This is the topic of the next section.

16.4.2 AGNOSTIC RESOURCE MANAGEMENT

The scheduling research community has been aware of and interested in the problem of allocating resources and scheduling tasks on large-scale parallel distributed systems with some degree of heterogeneity for some time. While work in this area generally acknowledges the underlying variations in capabilities between classes of resources, and much has been made of the differences in how time- and space- shared resources (e.g., CPUs vs memory) are partitioned between users and tasks, these works usually assume *uniformity in semantics* presented by the interfaces used to allocate these resources. For example, the authors of [39] assume that a multiresource allocation can be mapped to a normalized Euclidean vector, and that any combination of resource allocation requests can be reasonably serviced by a compute node so long as the vector sum of the allocations assigned to a node does not exceed the vector representing that node's capacity in any dimension.

What we observe, however, is that heterogeneous resources frequently expose complicated semantics that cannot be captured by a simple single- or multidimensional availability metric. This is generally due to internal constraints that disallow certain allocations that would otherwise fall within the total "amount" of resource presented by the device. For an illustrative example of why this is so, consider the MPC-X cluster presented in Fig. 16.3. This type of cluster contains one or more MPC-X nodes, where each node harbors a number of dataflow engine (DFE) devices [35] that are physically interconnected via a ring topology. A DFE is a specialized computation resource employing an FPGA to support reconfigurable designs and 48 GB (or more) RAM for bulk storage. With this setup, applications running on CPU-based machines dispatch computationally intensive tasks to single or multiple DFEs across an Infiniband network. In the context of a cloud platform, we wish to support allocation requests that specify not only the number of DFEs, but also whether these DFEs must be interconnected (RING) or not (GROUP). The choice of topology for allocated DFEs depends on the application. For instance, stencil-based applications can make use of interconnected DFEs (RING) to increase throughput [28]. On the other hand, a GROUP allocation allows the creation of a worker pool, to which tasks are sent to, and are serviced by available DFE workers. In this case, once a DFE allocation is satisfied, the residual capacity must be computed, and that requires understanding how GROUP and RING allocations affect the capacity of the MPC-X cluster.

Also in Fig. 16.3, we consider another type of resource, the XtreemFS storage, which allows users to request storage volumes with specific capacity and performance. As with the MPC-X cluster, to compute the residual capacity of an XtreemFS storage resource requires understanding the inner works of the XtreemFS management algorithms, the physical storage devices used and the corresponding performance models. These performance models indicate, for instance, how performance degrades with

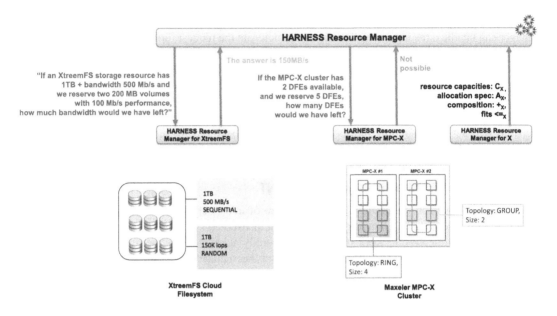

FIGURE 16.3

The top-level manager can allocate abstract resources with the support of child resource managers. To support higher-level management, each child resource manager handling a resource x exposes abstract operators $(+_x, \leq_x)$, the allocation specification (A_x) which defines the space of all valid allocation requests, and the capacities of all available resources of type x (C_x). XtreemFS is a cloud filesystem which manages heterogeneous storage devices. The MPC-X cluster provides a pool of Maxeler dataflow engines (DFEs). A dataflow engine is a physical compute resource which contains an FPGA as the computation fabric and RAM for bulk storage, and can be accessed by one or more CPU-based machines

the number of concurrent users. Additional examples of resources with complex semantics include: a (not necessarily homogeneous) collection of machines capable of running some mix of programs or virtual machines (e.g., a cluster), and a virtual network with embedded processing elements.

To support a central allocation process that has no specific understanding about the type of resources it handles, we use child resource managers, as shown in Fig. 16.3, which oversee the process of translating agnostic management requests from the top-level manager to requests that are specific to a particular type of resource. Each child resource manager is responsible for reporting available resources, servicing allocation and deallocation requests, as well as reporting monitoring information (e.g., resource utilization).

More importantly, child managers report the capacity of all resources to the top-level managers. As previously discussed, an agnostic top-level manager cannot simply look at the descriptions of available resources and reason about their nominal and residual capacities, including understanding whether a sequence of allocation requests can "fit" on or in a resource, as such a capability would require an intimate knowledge about how to interpret the capacity of each type of resource. Moreover, while every resource considered by a resource allocation algorithm has some finite *capacity*, for some resources it may not be possible to fully represent this capacity as a singleton or vector of numerical values, requiring instead a more complex representation.

Rather than ignoring this limitation and modeling finite resource capacities as integers or vectors, as in most works, we assume a more abstract representation, wherein the top-level manager is supplied the following information from the child manager overseeing resources of type x:

(i) The allocation space specification (A_x), e.g., the set of all valid allocation requests for resource of type x;

(ii) An operation of composition $(+_x)$ that groups allocation requests;

(iii) A partial-ordering relation $(\leq_x)$ on the set of basic requests that fulfills the following property: to say that an allocation request $a \in A_x$ is "smaller" than $b \in A_x$ means that servicing a requires less of a resource's capacity than servicing b. More formally, $a \leq_x b$ means that if the residual capacity of resource x is sufficient to service b then it must be sufficient to service a if a was substituted for b.

In Fig. 16.3 we illustrate the interactions between the top-level and child resource managers during the allocation process. The implementation of each abstract operator, including the ordering of both capacities and allocation requests, is specific to each type of resource. Fig. 16.5 presents an example of the ordering of MPC-X allocation requests.

This level of abstraction is necessary to allow the platform to incorporate resources with arbitrary resource allocation semantics, but it can be difficult to adapt standard resource allocation algorithms. In particular, traditional resource allocation approaches have some notion of a numerical quantity that can represent the size of either an item to be placed or the residual capacity of a resource. For example, consider the best-fit strategy commonly used for bin-packing and memory allocation, which simply follows the heuristic that the largest items remaining to be packed will be the ones with the least flexibility as to where they can be placed, and so these should be handled first, and they should be assigned to the resources where there is a minimum of left-over space, so as to minimize underutilized resources. In the next section we will discuss a strategy for ranking resource allocation requests that can be used to adapt conventional allocation algorithms to work with arbitrary heterogeneous resources in an agnostic manner.

16.4.3 RANKING ALLOCATION REQUESTS

The aim of this section is to describe a general procedure for computing a ranking function that can serve as a proxy for the size or the residual capacity of arbitrary resource types [40]. This ranking function can be used as an input to an allocation heuristic. While in this section we focus primarily on the MPC-X device, our technique can be applied deterministically to generate ranking functions for resources with arbitrary resource capacity and allocation representations, extending beyond a simple scalar or vector representation. We demonstrate this process through an illustrative example and argue that the same approach can be applied more broadly to any device for which a HARNESS resource manager can supply the functional interface described in the previous section.

To apply a standard and well established resource allocation algorithm, such as *first-fit* or *best-fit*, to an extended domain of heterogeneous resources, we need some way to compare the relative "size" of requests that may not be related under the inequality defined for the resource type. The standard approach is to base the size of the request on the amount of resource consumed (e.g., number of CPU cores or megabytes of memory). However, we note that for resource allocation among competing

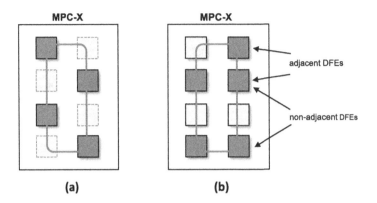

(a)   **(b)**

FIGURE 16.4

To understand the relationship $R_2 \leq G_5$, consider a G_5 allocation corresponding to the selection of five arbitrary DFEs inside an MPC-X box. As can be seen in **(a)**, selecting the fifth DFE implies that at least two of the selected DFEs in a G_5 allocation must be adjacent, i.e., R_2. While this example may lead us to conclude that $R_3 \leq G_5$, note that **(b)** depicts the case of a G_5 allocation that does not hold three adjacent DFEs (R_3)

users what matters is the degree to which satisfying a request limits the possible future uses of the corresponding resource.

Recall that the MPC-X device supports two kinds of resource allocation requests: GROUP and RING requests. A GROUP request contains the number of desired DFE devices inside an MPC-X box, while a RING request requires that all of the allocated devices be interconnected (see Fig. 16.3). We use G_n ($n = 1, \ldots, 8$) to represent GROUP requests and R_n ($n = 1, \ldots, 8$) to represent RING requests. The index of a request represents the number of DFE devices required.

Given our previous definition of inequality, we can see that the following must hold:

$$\forall n \in [1, 7], G_n \leq G_{n+1}, \tag{16.1}$$
$$\forall n \in [1, 7], R_n \leq R_{n+1}, \tag{16.2}$$
$$\forall n \in [1, 8], G_n \leq R_n. \tag{16.3}$$

Furthermore, when considering how DFE devices must be selected in an actual resource allocation for the MPC-X, we can derive the following relationships:

$$G_1 = R_1, \tag{16.4}$$
$$G_7 = R_7, \tag{16.5}$$
$$G_8 = R_8, \tag{16.6}$$
$$R_2 \leq G_5 \tag{16.7}$$
$$R_3 \leq G_6. \tag{16.8}$$

Fig. 16.4 explains relationship (16.7), and the same argument can be extended to relationship (16.8).

In addition, we can include a more constrained relation defined as: $a \preceq b$ iff a is less than b and there is no third allocation request c, distinct from a and b, such that $a \leq c \leq b$. In this case we say that

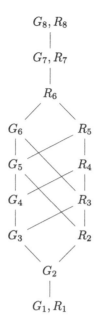

FIGURE 16.5

A lattice-topology for MPC-X resource allocation requests

b covers a, and thus:

$$\forall n \in \{1, 2, 3, 4, 5, 7\}, G_n \preceq G_{n+1}, \tag{16.9}$$

$$\forall n \in [2, 7], R_n \preceq R_{n+1}, \tag{16.10}$$

$$\forall n \in [1, 7], G_n \preceq R_n. \tag{16.11}$$

It should be noted that it is *not* the case that $R_1 \preceq R_2$, as we have $G_1 = R_1$ and therefore $R_1 < G_2 < R_2$. Similarly, G_7 does not cover G_6, as $G_7 = R_7$, and therefore we have $G_6 < R_6 < G_7$.

These covering relationships can be used to form an initial lattice of basic resource allocation requests for the MPC-X device as depicted in Fig. 16.5. As this structure places "larger" requests (e.g., those that either take up more space or put greater constraint on future use of the resource) higher in the hierarchy, this suggests that height might be a reasonable proxy for size. Unfortunately, the relationships between the basic allocation requests for the MPC-X device prevent the easy definition of a consistent height function. For example, we cannot define the height value of G_5 because two nodes immediately under it, G_4 and R_2, are at different levels in the hierarchy.

While the initial lattice structure does not admit a well-defined height function, that is, it is not *modular*, we can use the reverse of *Birkhoff's representation theorem* [17] to extend the nonmodular partially-ordered topology to a modular *downset* lattice (Fig. 16.6). The downset of a basic resource allocation request is a set containing that request and all smaller requests (e.g., the downset of G_3, denoted $G_3 \downarrow$, is the set $\{G_2, G_3\}$). The downset lattice preserves the inequality relationship, but also

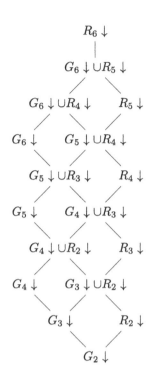

FIGURE 16.6

A *modular* lattice-topology for MPC-X resource allocation requests, which has been derived from the non-modular lattice presented in Fig. 16.5

includes additional nodes labeled with unions of the downsets of basic requests. By constructing a modular lattice, we can define a ranking function for the lattice that obeys the *valuation law*: for any two nodes in the lattice, the sum of their ranks will equal the sum of the ranks of the smallest element larger than both and the largest element smaller than both. For a finite lattice, this is equivalent to stating that for any node the length of every path from that node to the bottom will be the same, and so it is possible to define a consistent ranking function based on the *height*. Note that if requests have the same *height*, then it is up to the allocation algorithm to break ties, for instance, giving priority to the requests that arrived first.

In practice, with the above approach, we can develop an agnostic top-level manager which generates a modular lattice that captures the total ordering of allocation requests and resource capacities, as long as the lower-level manager implements the API described in Section 16.4.4. In this context, this lower-level manager needs only to define the partial ordering between any two resources (i.e., $\leq_x$).

16.4.4 HARNESS API

The HARNESS API provides a uniform interface for resources managers to support hierarchical resource management and agnostic resource allocation as described in Sections 16.4.1 and 16.4.2. Re-

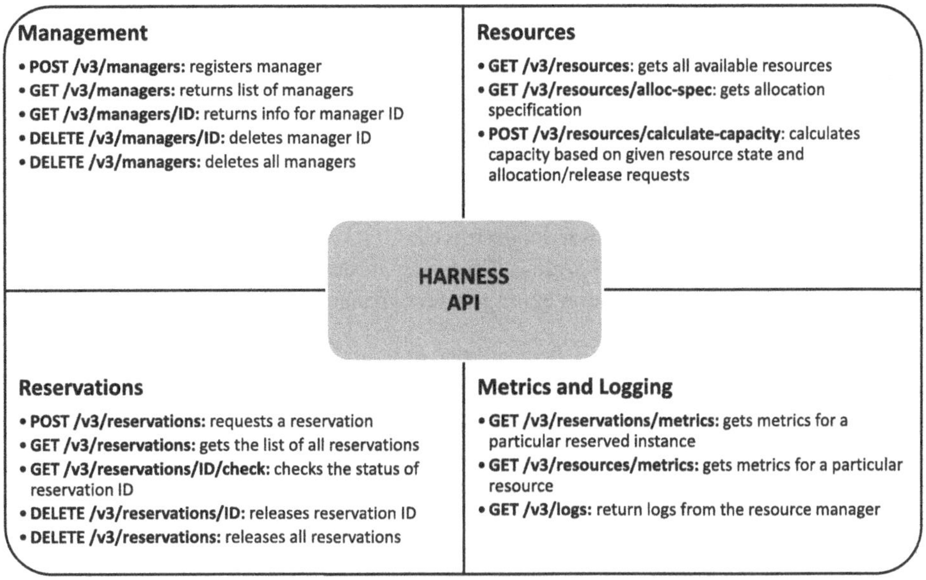

Management

- **POST /v3/managers:** registers manager
- **GET /v3/managers:** returns list of managers
- **GET /v3/managers/ID:** returns info for manager ID
- **DELETE /v3/managers/ID:** deletes manager ID
- **DELETE /v3/managers:** deletes all managers

Resources

- **GET /v3/resources:** gets all available resources
- **GET /v3/resources/alloc-spec:** gets allocation specification
- **POST /v3/resources/calculate-capacity:** calculates capacity based on given resource state and allocation/release requests

HARNESS API

Reservations

- **POST /v3/reservations:** requests a reservation
- **GET /v3/reservations:** gets the list of all reservations
- **GET /v3/reservations/ID/check:** checks the status of reservation ID
- **DELETE /v3/reservations/ID:** releases reservation ID
- **DELETE /v3/reservations:** releases all reservations

Metrics and Logging

- **GET /v3/reservations/metrics:** gets metrics for a particular reserved instance
- **GET /v3/resources/metrics:** gets metrics for a particular resource
- **GET /v3/logs:** return logs from the resource manager

FIGURE 16.7

The HARNESS API provides a REST-based interface for top-level resource managers to handle heterogeneous resources

source managers implementing the HARNESS API (referred to as HARNESS resource managers) can be combined hierarchically taking into account separation of concerns, such that each resource manager handles specific classes of resources at different levels of abstraction. The HARNESS API follows the RESTful style, where interactions are handled through HTTP requests to provide an Infrastructure-as-a-Service (IaaS) platform.

We have successfully employed the HARNESS API to support and manage a wide range of resources that span from physical clusters of FPGAs to conceptual resources such as virtual links. Each HARNESS resource manager exposes a set of resources of a specific type, including their corresponding residual capacities, allowing virtualized instances of these resources to be allocated by defining the required capacity.

While the implementation of the API is specific to a type of resource, the API makes a small number of assumptions about its nature:

(i) A resource has a specific capacity which can be finite or infinite;

(ii) A resource operates on a specific allocation space;

(iii) The availability of a function which computes (or estimates) changes in capacity based on an allocation request;

(iv) Instances of any resource type (e.g., virtual machine) can be created and destroyed;

(v) Resources can be monitored with feedback provided on specific metrics.

We group the HARNESS API functions in four categories (Fig. 16.7):

- **Management** category allows resource managers to register to other HARNESS resource managers in a hierarchical organization;
- **Resources** category provides information about the state of available resources (nominal or residual capacities – C_x), the allocation space specification (A_x), and a method that returns whether the aggregation ($+_x$) of a given set of allocation requests can be serviced ($\leq_x$) by a given resource capacity;
- **Reservations** category allows allocation requests to be submitted, the status of resource instances to be queried, and resource instances to be destroyed;
- **Metrics and Logging** category provides monitoring information about resources and their instances, as well as logging information about resource management.

The HARNESS API sits slightly above the pure infrastructure layer (IaaS). It does not attempt to describe application orchestration like TOSCA or deployment like CAMP (leaving these problems to a PaaS layer), but rather, like OCCI and CIMI is more concerned with allocating and linking infrastructure resources. However, unlike these standards (see Section 16.2 for more details), which come with built-in models of different resource "types", such as machines, VMs, networks, and storage devices, the HARNESS API considers all abstract resources to be of the same type. As can be seen in Fig. 16.3, while resources such as XtreemFS cloud storage and Maxeler MPC-X cluster are inherently different from each other, they are handled transparently as a single type resource, having each a corresponding resource manager that provides an implementation of the HARNESS API.

This allows for a more flexible model that can accommodate a wider array of cloud-enabled devices, as well as supporting cross-cutting services such as pricing and monitoring, which do not have to support multiple resource models. Once resources have been allocated in HARNESS, the deployment phase allows each provisioned resource to be handled using resource-specific mechanisms, including APIs, tools and services, to make full use of their capabilities.

16.5 PROTOTYPE DESCRIPTION

In this section, we describe the HARNESS prototype, presented in Fig. 16.8, which has been implemented to validate our approach. The HARNESS prototype has been deployed in two testbeds: Grid'5000, which allows us to explore a large-scale research infrastructure to support parallel and distributed computing experiments [16]; and the Imperial Cluster testbed, which supports clusters of hardware accelerators and heterogeneous storage.

The HARNESS architecture is split into three layers: (1) a *platform* layer that manages applications, (2) an *infrastructure* layer that is responsible for managing cloud resources, and (3) a *virtual execution* layer where applications are deployed and executed. Next, we explain each HARNESS layer in more detail.

16.5.1 THE PLATFORM LAYER

The platform layer automates the choice of resources to run an application: cloud tenants indicate requirements for job completion time and/or monetary cost. The platform then decides which set of resources best satisfy these objectives and constraints. To execute an application in HARNESS, a cloud

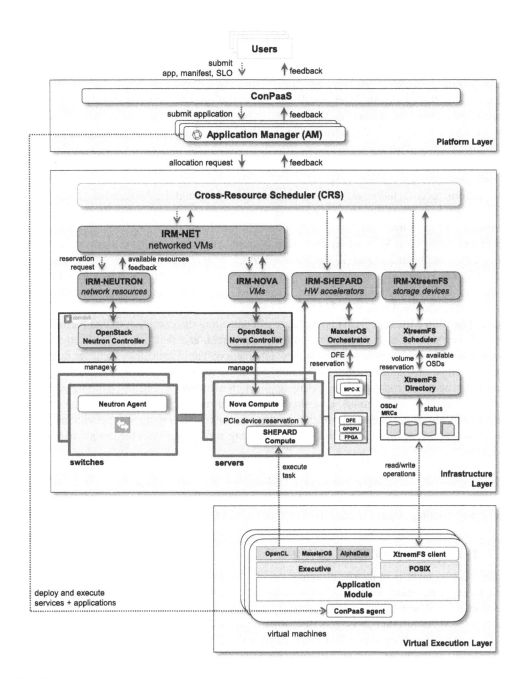

FIGURE 16.8

The HARNESS architecture is composed of three layers: a platform layer that is responsible for managing applications, an infrastructure layer where cloud resources are managed, and a virtual execution layer where applications are deployed and executed user must supply: (i) an application manifest describing the structure of the application and the types of resources it can potentially execute on; (ii) a service-level objective (SLO) defining nonfunctional requirements for this execution, such as the maximum execution latency or the maximum monetary cost; and (iii) the application binaries and scripts. Once this information is supplied, the HARNESS platform deploys the application over a well-chosen sets of resources such that the manifest and the SLO are respected. As mentioned in Section 16.3, an important part of this process is developing performance models that guide this selection. In HARNESS, we developed several techniques to reduce the profiling effort of arbitrary applications, including taking into account monitoring information to generate high-quality performance models at a fraction of time, as well as extrapolating production-size inputs using reduced-size datasets [25].

The platform layer includes two main components: ConPaaS and the Application Manager:

- **ConPaaS** [36] is an integrated runtime environment for elastic cloud platforms. It consists of two key components: (i) a Web server providing a graphical interface where users can submit and manage their applications; and (ii) the *Director* which is in charge of authenticating users and instantiating one Application Manager for each application instance submitted by a user. Once it has created an Application Manager instance, it forwards all subsequent management requests about this application to the Application Manager in charge of the application.
- **The Application Manager (AM)** is in charge of controlling the execution of one particular application. It is a generic and application-agnostic component, and thus a new Application Manager does not need to be developed for every new application. The Application Manager operates in a virtual machine provisioned using the HARNESS cloud resources. This virtual machine contains a specific program in charge of interpreting application manifests and SLOs, building performance models for arbitrary applications, choosing the type and number of resources that an application needs to execute within its SLO, provisioning these resources, deploying the application's code and data in the provisioned resources, and finally collecting application-level feedback during and after execution.

Whenever the *Director* and the Application Manager needs to provision resources in the HARNESS platform (either to create a new Application Manager instance or to run an actual application), it sends a resource provisioning request to the infrastructure layer, which we explain next.

16.5.2 THE INFRASTRUCTURE LAYER

The infrastructure layer is in charge of managing all cloud resources and making them available on demand. Its key components are the CRS (Cross-Resource Scheduler) and the IRMs (Infrastructure Resource Managers). These correspond respectively to the top-level HARNESS resource manager, and the child HARNESS resource managers described in Section 16.4.1. In particular, the CRS handles high-level requests involving multiple resources, while the IRMs are responsible for translating agnostic management requests into resource-specific requests. The currently implemented IRMs are: *IRM-NET* (network resources), *IRM-NOVA* (OpenStack compute resources), *IRM-NEUTRON* (OpenStack network resources), *IRM-SHEPARD* (hardware accelerator resources), and *IRM-XtreemFS* (XtreemFS storage resources). Beneath the IRMs, we have components that manage specific resources, which include OpenStack [10], SHEPARD [30], MaxelerOS Orchestrator [8], and XtreemFS [38].

Below we provide details about some of these components:

- **The Cross-Resource Scheduler (CRS)** is in charge of handling resource provisioning requests [22]. It processes single resource requests, and requests for a *group* of heterogeneous resources with optional placement constraints between resources. For example, an application may request one virtual machine and one FPGA such that the two devices are located close to each other. It uses the network proximity maps provided by *IRM-NET*, and decides which set of physical resources should be chosen to accommodate each request. Once this selection has been made, it delegates the actual provisioning of the resources to corresponding IRMs. Each IRM is in charge of managing some specific type of heterogeneous resources, including VMs, GPGPUs, FPGAs, storage, and network devices.
- **The Network Resource Manager (IRM-NET)** provides the CRS with up-to-date maps of the physical resources which are part of the cloud. These maps contain network proximity measurements realized pairwise between the physical resources, such as latency, and available bandwidth. This information allows the CRS to service allocation requests with placement constraints, such as allocating two VMs with a specific latency requirement between them. This component also handles bandwidth reservations, allowing virtual links to be allocated. Finally, IRM-NET supports subnet and public IP allocations by delegating these requests through IRM-NOVA and IRM-NEUTRON. In particular, users can request one or more subnets and assign VMs to them, and also assign public IPs to individual VMs.
- **The MaxelerOS Orchestrator** supports the allocation of networked DFEs located in MPC-X devices. The MaxelerOS Orchestrator provides a way to reserve DFEs for IRM-SHEPARD. These accelerators are then available to applications over the local network.
- **XtreemFS** is a fault-tolerant distributed file system that provides three kinds of services: (1) the directory service (DIR), (2) the metadata and replica catalog (MRC) server, and (3) the object storage device (OSD) [38]. The DIR tracks status information of the OSDs, MRCs, and volumes. The volume metadata is managed by one MRC. File contents are spread over an arbitrary subset of OSDs. In addition, the XtreemFS Scheduler handles the reservation and release of data volumes to be used by the HARNESS application. Data volumes are characterized by their size, the type of accesses it is optimized for (random vs. sequential), and the number of provisioned IOPS.

16.5.3 THE VIRTUAL EXECUTION LAYER

The virtual execution layer is composed of reserved VMs where the application is deployed and executed (Fig. 16.8). In addition to the application itself, the VMs contain components (APIs and services) that support the deployment and execution processes, including allowing the application to interact with (reserved) resource instances. These components include:

- **The ConPaaS agent,** which performs management actions on behalf of the Application Manager: it configures the VM where the Application Manager resides, installs code/data resources such as GPGPUs, FPGAs and XtreemFS volumes, configures access to heterogeneous resources, starts the application, and finally collects application-level feedback during execution [36];
- **The Executive** is a scheduling process that given a fixed set of provisioned heterogeneous compute resources, selects the most appropriate hardware accelerator for a given application task [20,29];

- **The XtreemFS client** is in charge of mounting XtreemFS volumes in the VMs and making them available as regular local directories [38].

16.6 EVALUATION

In this section, we report two cloud deployment scenarios using HARNESS, which are currently not supported by traditional cloud computing platforms:

- **Executing HPC Applications on the Cloud:** This case study (Section 16.6.1) demonstrates how HPC applications such as RTM (Reverse Time Migration) can exploit hardware accelerators and managed storage volumes as cloud resources using HARNESS. These experiments were performed in the Imperial Cluster testbed;
- **Resource Scheduling with Network Constraints:** This case study (Section 16.6.2) demonstrates the benefits of managed networking when deploying distributed applications such as Hadoop MapReduce in a cloud platform. In this scenario, cloud tenants can reserve bandwidth, which directly affects where jobs are deployed. This work was conducted in Grid'5000 with physical nodes located in Rennes and Nantes.

16.6.1 EXECUTING HPC APPLICATIONS ON THE CLOUD

Reverse Time Migration (RTM) represents a class of computationally intensive applications used to process large amounts of data, thus a subclass of HPC applications. Some of the most computationally intensive geoscience algorithms involve simulating wave propagation through the earth. The objective is typically to create an image of the subsurface from acoustic measurements performed at the surface. To create this image, a low-frequency acoustic source is activated and the reflected sound waves are recorded, typically by tens of thousands of receivers. We term this process a *shot*, and it is repeated many thousands of times while the source and/or receivers are moved to illuminate different areas of the subsurface. The resulting dataset is dozens or hundreds of terabytes in size.

Our experiments were conducted on the Imperial Cluster testbed, which includes 3 physical compute machines, a DFE cluster harboring 24 DFEs, and standard HDD and SSD storage drives. The dataset used in our experiments are based on the Sandia/SEG Salt Model 45 shot subset.[1]

Deploying RTM on a heterogeneous cloud platform. In this experiment, we demonstrate how an HPC application, such as RTM, is deployed and executed in the HARNESS cloud platform. The RTM binary, along with its deployment and initialization scripts, are compressed into a tarball. This tarball is submitted to the HARNESS cloud platform along with the *application manifest*. The application manifest describes the resource configuration space, which allows the Application Manager to derive a valid resource configuration to run the submitted version of RTM.

When the application is submitted, the HARNESS platform creates an instance of the Application Manager which oversees the life-cycle of the application. The Application Manager operates in two modes. In the *profiling* mode, the Application Manager creates a performance model by running the

---

[1]The Sandia/SEG Salt Model 45 shot dataset can be downloaded here: http://wiki.seg.org/wiki/SEG_C3_45_shot.

application on multiple resource configurations and capturing the execution time of each configuration. Associated with the performance model, we have a pricing model which indicates the monetary cost of using a specific resource configuration. With the performance and pricing models, the application manager can translate cost and performance objectives specified in the SLO (e.g., to execute the fastest configuration) into a resource configuration that can best achieve these objectives.

For this experiment, the Application Manager deployed RTM on different resource configurations, varying the number of CPU cores (from 1 to 8), RAM sizes (1024 and 2048 MB), number of dataflow engines (from 1 to 4) and storage performances (10 and 250 MB/s). The pricing model used is as follows:

$$cost(c) = c.num\_dfes \times 9 \times 10^{-1} + c.cpu\_cores \times 5 \times 10^{-4} +$$
$$c.mem\_size \times 3 \times 10^{-5} + c.storage\_perf \times 10^{-5}$$

where for a given configuration c, $c.num\_dfes$ represents the number of DFEs, $c.cpu\_cores$ corresponds to the number of CPU cores, $c.mem\_size$ corresponds to the size of RAM (MB), and $c.storage\_perf$ the storage performance (MB/s). The resulting cost is in €/s. The pricing models presented in this section are loosely based on the current offerings from Amazon EC2 [15]; however, they can be arbitrary and can be updated dynamically to reflect various factors, such as resource availability. The subject of cloud resource pricing is complex, specially when considering heterogeneous resources, and is outside the scope of this chapter.

Fig. 16.9 presents the performance model generated by the Application Manager using the pricing model specified above. The Application Manager automatically selected and profiled 28 configurations, with 5 of these configurations identified as part of the Pareto frontier. The number of profiled configurations is dependent on the profiling algorithm used by the Application Manager [22]. For each configuration, the Application Manager reserves the corresponding resources, and deploys the application. The initialization script supplied with the application automatically detects the configuration attributes, and configures the application to use these resources. For instance, if the configuration specifies 8 CPU cores, then the initialization script configures the OMP_NUM_THREADS environment variable to that number, and allow the application to fully utilize all provisioned CPU resources.

Fig. 16.9 highlights four configurations in the top-right quadrant, which correspond to the slowest and most expensive configurations, and thus the least desirable of all the configurations identified. This is due to the use of slow storage (9 MB/s) which dominates the performance of the job despite the use of DFEs. At the bottom-right quadrant, there are five configurations highlighted that are relatively inexpensive, however they run relatively slow since they do not employ DFEs. Finally, in the center of the figure, we find three highlighted configurations which use a limited number of CPU cores and DFEs, but they do not provide the best trade-off between price and execution time. Instead, the five configurations that provide the best trade-offs are those in the Pareto frontier (see Table 16.2).

With the above configurations and the corresponding pricing, the Application Manager can service SLO-based requests. For instance, if the user requests the fastest configuration under €0.25, the Application Manager would select configuration C, while A would be identified as the cheapest configuration.

Exploiting different DFE topology reservations. The RTM job deployed in HARNESS is both *moldable* and *malleable* [21]. A *moldable* job can adapt to different resource configurations at the start of the program. A *malleable* job, on the other hand, can be reconfigured at run-time during program

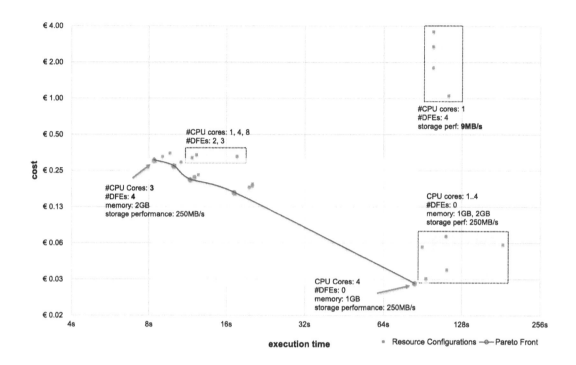

FIGURE 16.9

Performance model for the RTM application automatically generated by the Application Manager

Table 16.2 Five pareto configurations for the RTM application (see Fig. 16.9)

#ID	#DFEs	#CPU cores	RAM (MB)	Storage speed (MB/s)	Execution time (s)	Price (€)
A	0	4	1024	250	84	0.03
B	1	8	2048	250	17	0.17
C	2	1	1024	250	12	0.21
D	3	3	2048	250	10	0.27
E	4	3	2048	250	8	0.31

execution. Both types of jobs provide more flexibility than a *rigid* job which is designed to run on single resource configuration. In the following experiment, we further explore RTM's moldable and malleable properties.

Our implementation of the HARNESS platform supports the *DFE cluster* resource, as presented in Fig. 16.3, with two types of DFE allocation requests: *GROUP* and *RING*. As previously explained, a request for a *GROUP* of N DFEs would provision N DFEs within the same MPC-X box, while requesting N DFEs of a *RING* topology would provision N interconnected DFEs.

Fig. 16.10 shows the performance of a single RTM shot using different problem dimensions and number of DFEs. Multiple DFEs are connected via RING. The characterization of these jobs is sum-

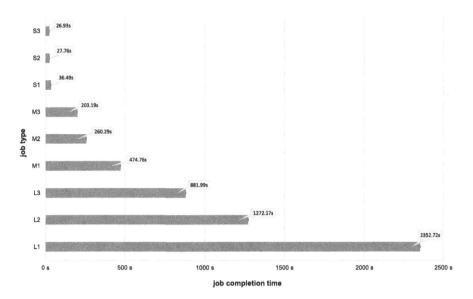

FIGURE 16.10

Performance of a single RTM shot using different problem dimensions (S, M, L) and number of DFEs (1, 2 and 3)

Table 16.3 Three classes of RTM jobs using different number of DFEs

Design	Configuration	Dimension	#iterations
S1	1×DFE	200 × 200 × 200	2000
S2	2×DFEs (ring)	200 × 200 × 200	2000
S3	3×DFEs (ring)	200 × 200 × 200	2000
M1	1×DFEs	400 × 400 × 400	4000
M2	2×DFEs (ring)	400 × 400 × 400	4000
M3	3×DFEs (ring)	400 × 400 × 400	4000
L1	1×DFEs	600 × 600 × 600	6000
L2	2×DFEs (ring)	600 × 600 × 600	6000
L3	3×DFEs (ring)	600 × 600 × 600	6000

marized in Table 16.3. We can see that the number of DFEs makes little impact on smaller jobs, such as $S1$, $S2$, and $S3$. This is due to the fact that smaller workloads will not be able to fully utilize multiple DFEs. Larger jobs, on the other hand, scale better and are able to exploit larger number of DFEs. For instance, $S3$ is only 0.7 times faster than $S1$, while $L3$ is 2.6× faster than $L1$.

Let us now focus on the impact of the DFE topology on completing a multishot RTM job. Fig. 16.11 shows the results of completing an RTM job with varying number of shots. Each shot has a dimension of $600 \times 600 \times 600$, running in 6000 iterations. For each number of shots, we compare the performance of using 3 independent DFEs (GROUP) against 3 interconnected DFEs (RING). The former can pro-

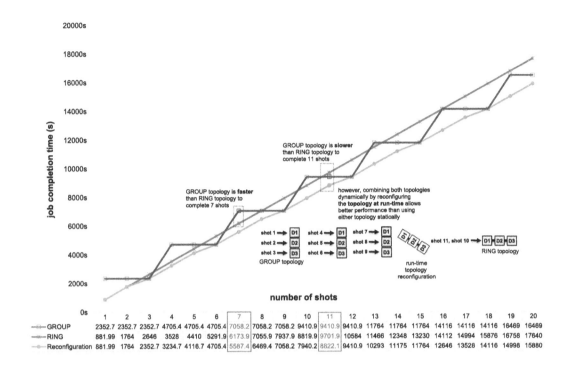

FIGURE 16.11

The effect of different DFE topologies on RTM performance

cess three shots in parallel, while the latter, working as a single compute resource, can only process each shot sequentially. Each independent DFE computes a shot in 2353 s, while the interconnected version computes a shot in 882 s. It can be seen from the figure that depending on the total number of shots, one of the topologies is more efficient than the other. For 7 shots, the independent DFEs run faster, while for 11 shots the interconnected DFEs run faster. Since RTM jobs are moldable, we can optimize their performance by selecting the topology that can provide the best performance according to the number of shots.

We can further speed-up the computation by configuring the RTM job to be *malleable*, so that it adapts during runtime. As can be seen in Fig. 16.11, depending on the number of shots, we can combine both types of topologies to reduce the completion time. For instance, for 11 shots, we can execute 9 shots in three sequences in parallel followed by 2 shots computed with the three DFEs interconnected. This combination yields the best performance (8821 s) when compared to a static configuration using the parallel configuration (9411 s) or the interconnected configuration (9702 s). Malleable jobs can be automatically managed by a runtime scheduler, which decides on the most optimal topology given a set of allocated resources. In our HARNESS prototype, the *Executive* component is responsible for this decision process (see Section 16.5.3).

16.6.2 RESOURCE SCHEDULING WITH NETWORK CONSTRAINTS

The purpose of this case study is to investigate the benefits of managed networking when deploying a distributed application such as the Hadoop-based AdPredictor [23] on a large-scale testbed such as Grid'5000. AdPredictor represents a class of modern industrial-scale applications, commonly known as *recommender systems*, that target either open-source or proprietary on-line services. For example, one such service is Mendeley [26], a free reference organizer and academic social network that recommends related research articles based on user interests. Another such service is Bing [27], a commercial online search engine that recommends commercial products based on user queries. In general, items are matched with users and, due to the modern "data deluge", these computations are usually run in large-scale data centers. The ACM 2012 KDD Cup *track2* dataset [14] has been used to evaluate Ad-Predictor.

Grid'5000 is a large-scale multi-site French public research testbed designed to support parallel and distributed computing experiments. The backbone network infrastructure is provided by the French National Telecommunication Network for Technology, Education and Research RENATER, which offers 11,900 km of optic fiber links and 72 points of presence.

Fig. 16.12 reports the throughput of one MapReduce worker over time where the steady throughput consumption peaks at approximately 200 Mbit/s, excluding any bursts during shuffling. Fig. 16.13 presents the results of an AdPredictor job using the same configuration by varying the available bandwidth between the worker compute hosts. The application exhibits degradation below 200 Mbit/s, which is consistent with our measurements in Fig. 16.12.

Consequently, when a network-bound application, such as AdPredictor, is deployed on a cloud platform that provides *no network performance guarantees*, it will have its performance severely affected if resources have been reserved in a low-bandwidth environment. Note that services like Microsoft Azure [9] enforce a maximum bound on outgoing traffic bandwidth depending on the VM type chosen, not allowing compute and network resources to be tailored independently according to the application needs. HARNESS addresses these issues by exposing network bandwidth and latency as independent resources and constraints, respectively. In this context, applications may define and submit their desired network performance guarantees and the underlying infrastructure will provision them, if available. This highlights a key principle of HARNESS, which allows specialized and commodity resources to be treated as first-class cloud entities.

We report three scenarios conducted in Grid'5000: (a) allocating resources without network constraints; (b) allocating resources using bandwidth reservation requests; and (c) allocating resources with service-level objectives. The testbed used for these experiments consists of 8 physical compute nodes across two different sites: *Rennes* (4 nodes) and *Nantes* (4 nodes). While both sites offer high-speed gigabit connectivity of 1500 Mbit/s, we have emulated heavy network congestion in Nantes, so that the throughput of any network flow in Nantes is limited to 500 Mbit/s.

Allocating without network constraints. In the first experiment we request 1 *master* and three *worker* instances without specifying network constraints. Fig. 16.14 presents all the possible configurations that may result from this allocation request, as each worker may be placed either in Rennes or Nantes. If the tenant specifies no network constraints, any one of these placements may be possible, therefore the end-user will experience a considerable variability in her application's performance over multiple deployments on the same cloud platform. It is evident that the application's execution time is dependent on whether the workers are deployed in the high-bandwidth Rennes cluster, in the con-

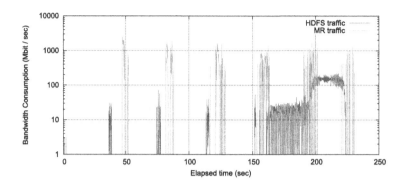

FIGURE 16.12

AdPredictor throughput over time

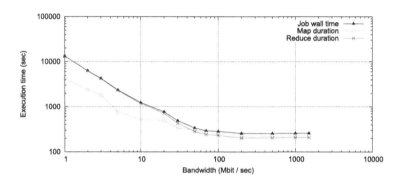

FIGURE 16.13

AdPredictor performance vs bandwidth

gested Nantes cluster, or across both sites. Nevertheless, in this scenario the tenant has no control over the final placement.

Allocating using bandwidth reservation requests. In order to eliminate the suboptimal placements presented in Fig. 16.14, labeled as "2-1", "1-2" and "0-3", which involve at least one of the workers being placed in the congested cluster of Nantes, the tenant can specify a request demanding a reservation of 300 Mbit/s between workers Worker1 and Worker2, Worker1 and Worker3, and Worker2 and Worker3. Consequently, the CRS takes into account this bandwidth reservation request when allocating VMs (containers) for the workers, therefore eliminating the suboptimal placements and deploying all workers in Rennes under the conditions presented in this experiment. Listing 1 presents the reservation request for this scenario, in which four VMs (labeled Master and Worker1–4, respectively) are requested with specific computation requirements, and three resources of type "Link" specify minimum bandwidth requirements between Worker-labeled VMs. Recall that resources of different types can be requested independently from each other and tailored to the specific requirements of an application.

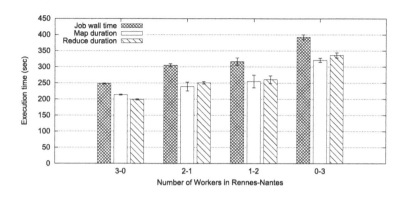

FIGURE 16.14

AdPredictor performance vs resource placement

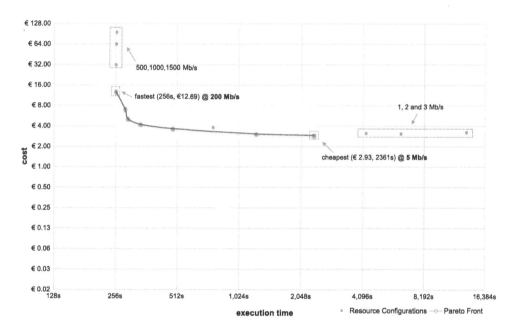

FIGURE 16.15

Performance model generated for AdPredictor running on Grid'5000

Allocating with service-level objectives. In the previous experiment, we requested bandwidth reservation in the application manifest to deploy a Hadoop-based AdPredictor job. In a real scenario, the cloud tenant is more concerned about job completion time and the price of reserving resources. In order for the HARNESS platform to derive a resource configuration that can meet performance

```
{
    "Master": {
        "Type": "Machine",
        "Cores": 4,
        "Memory": 4096
    },
    "Worker1": {
        "Type": "Machine",
        "Cores": 12,
        "Memory": 16384
    },
    "Worker2": {
        "Type": "Machine",
        "Cores": 12,
        "Memory": 16384
    },
    "Worker3": {
        "Type": "Machine",
        "Cores": 12,
        "Memory": 16384
    },
    "Link1": {
        "Type": "Link",
        "Source": "Worker1",
        "Target": "Worker2",
        "Bandwidth": 300
    },
    "Link2": {
        "Type": "Link",
        "Source": "Worker2",
        "Target": "Worker3",
        "Bandwidth": 300
    },
    "Link3": {
        "Type": "Link",
        "Source": "Worker1",
        "Target": "Worker3",
        "Bandwidth": 300
    }
}
```

Listing 1: Reservation request for compute and network resources

or cost objectives, it needs to have a performance model. For this experiment, we have generated a performance model based on profiling AdPredictor with different bandwidth reservation requests.

The pricing model used in our experiments is as follows:

$$cost(c) = c.cpu\_cores \times 5 \times 10^{-4} + c.mem\_size \times 3 \times 10^{-5} +$$
$$c.bandwidth \times 2 \times 10^{-1}$$

The bandwidth unit is Mb/s. With this pricing model, the price of 1 Gb/s bandwidth is roughly equal to one VM with 4 cores and 8 GB RAM.

Fig. 16.15 presents the performance model of AdPredictor running on Grid'5000. It contains 14 points where we vary the bandwidth requirements from 1 Mb/s to 1.5 Gb/s, while maintaining the same compute and storage configuration. It can be seen that different bandwidth reservations have an impact in both pricing and performance. Not all configurations provide a good trade-off between price and execution time, and they are discarded. The remaining configurations, 7 in total, are part of the Pareto frontier. These configurations are then selected to satisfy objectives in terms of pricing (the cheapest configuration costs €2.93 but requires 2361 s to complete) or in terms of completion time (the fastest configuration completes the job in 256 s but costs €12.69).

16.7 CONCLUSION

In this chapter, we presented the HARNESS cloud computing architecture, which supports two distinct layers:

- The *platform layer* manages applications on behalf of cloud tenants. More specifically, it automates the process of selecting a resource configuration that can best satisfy application-specific goals (e.g., low completion time), with each configuration having its own cost, performance, and utilization footprint. To achieve this, the platform layer resorts to application profiling to automatically build performance models. The platform also exploits the fact that application performance characteristics may be observed using smaller inputs, so it employs extrapolated application profiling techniques to reduce the time and cost of profiling;
- The *infrastructure layer* manages heterogeneous resources on behalf of cloud providers. This layer uses a resource management model in which all types of resources are handled as first-class entities, as opposed to the VM-centric model employed by current cloud providers. The infrastructure layer is based on a *multitier management* approach, designed to make cloud computing systems open and resilient to new forms of heterogeneity. This way, introducing new types of resources does not result in having to redesign the entire system. The various resource managers that make up the HARNESS infrastructure are governed by a single API specification that handles all types of resources uniformly. Thus, a new type of cloud resource can be incorporated into the HARNESS infrastructure by providing an implementation of the HARNESS API.

We developed a fully working prototype of the HARNESS cloud computing platform. Our infrastructure layer implementation relies on the following technologies: (a) MaxelerOS Orchestrator for networked DFE reservations; (b) SHEPARD for hardware accelerator reservations; (c) XtreemFS for heterogeneous storage reservations; (d) IRM-NET for network link reservations; and (d) a cross-resource scheduler (CRS) which enfolds all these resource-specific managers to optimize multiple reservation requests alongside (optional) network placement constraints.

Our prototype was evaluated using two testbeds: (1) a heterogeneous compute and storage cluster that includes FPGAs and SSDs where we deployed an HPC application (Reverse-Time Migration), and (2) Grid'5000, a large-scale distributed testbed that spans France to which we deployed a machine learning application (AdPredictor). In our evaluation, we demonstrated how HARNESS fully embraces heterogeneity, allowing the side-by-side deployment of commodity and specialized resources. This support increases the number of possible resource configurations in which an application can be deployed to, bringing wholly new degrees of freedom to the cloud resource allocation and optimization problem.

PROJECT RESOURCES

The source-code of most of the HARNESS prototype components and deployment projects has been released to the public. In particular, the software projects that create the unified HARNESS platform can be downloaded from our GitHub page (https://github.com/harnesscloud). Free-standing software projects created or extended by HARNESS, such as ConPaaS (http://www.conpaas.eu) and XtreemFS (http://www.xtreemfs.org), have their own independent software download sites. A more detailed description of each component available for downloading is found in http://www.harness-project.eu/?page_id=721. Video demonstrations of our final prototype can be accessed in http://www.harness-project.eu/?page_id=862. Technical outcomes of the project not covered in this chapter can be found in the HARNESS whitepaper [24]. Finally, a list of all our project publications and technical reports can be found in our public website: http://www.harness-project.eu/.

REFERENCES
[1] Amazon Web Services. Available at http://aws.amazon.com/.
[2] CELAR project: automatic, multi-grained elasticity provisioning for the cloud. Available at http://www.celarcloud.eu/.
[3] CloudLightning project: self-organising, self-managing heterogeneous cloud. Available at http://cloudlightning.eu/.
[4] CloudSpaces project: an open service platform for the next generation of personal clouds. Available at http://cloudspaces.eu/.
[5] Google App Engine. Available at https://developers.google.com/appengine/.
[6] Google Compute Engine. Available at https://cloud.google.com/products/compute-engine/.
[7] LEADS project: large-scale elastic architecture for data as a service. Available at http://www.leads-project.eu/.
[8] Maxeler Technologies: maximum performance computing. Available at http://maxeler.com/.
[9] Microsoft Azure Services Platform. Available at http://www.azure.net/.
[10] OpenStack: open source software for creating private and public clouds, http://openstack.org.
[11] PaaSage project: a model-based cross cloud development and deployment platform. Available at http://www.paasage.eu/.
[12] The BigFoot project: an OpenStack based analytics-as-a-service solution. Available at http://bigfootproject.eu/.
[13] Venus-C project: virtual multi-disciplinary environments using cloud infrastructures. Available at http://www.venus-c.eu/.
[14] ACM SIGKDD, Predict the click-through rate of ads given the query and user information. Available at http://www.kddcup2012.org/c/kddcup2012-track2/.
[15] Amazon EC2 pricing. Available at http://aws.amazon.com/ec2/pricing/.
[16] D. Balouek, et al., Adding virtualization capabilities to the Grid'5000 testbed, in: Cloud Computing and Services Science, vol. 367, 2013, pp. 3–20.
[17] G. Birkhoff, Lattice Theory, vol. 25, American Mathematical Soc., 1940.
[18] Cloud Management Working Group (CMWG), Cloud Infrastructure Management Interface (CIMI) specification. Available at http://www.dmtf.org/standards/cmwg.
[19] CloudFoundry. Available at http://www.cloudfoundry.com/.
[20] J.G.F. Coutinho, O. Pell, E. O'Neill, P. Sanders, J. McGlone, P. Grigoras, W. Luk, C. Ragusa, HARNESS project: managing heterogeneous computing resources for a cloud platform, in: Reconfigurable Computing: Architectures, Tools, and Applications, Springer, 2014, pp. 324–329.
[21] D.G. Feitelson, L. Rudolph, Towards convergence in job schedulers for parallel supercomputers, in: Proceedings of the Workshop on Job Scheduling Strategies for Parallel Processing, IPPS'96, Springer-Verlag, 1996, pp. 1–26.
[22] FP7 HARNESS Consortium, Heterogeneous Platform Implementation (updated). Technical Report D6.3.3, 2015.
[23] T. Graepel, J.Q. Candela, T. Borchert, R. Herbrich, Web-scale Bayesian click-through rate prediction for sponsored search advertising in Microsoft's Bing search engine, in: Proceedings of the 27th International Conference on Machine Learning (ICML-10), 2010, pp. 13–20.
[24] HARNESS white paper. Available at http://www.harness-project.eu/wp-content/uploads/2015/12/harness-white-paper.pdf.

[25] A. Iordache, E. Buyukkaya, G. Pierre, Heterogeneous resource selection for arbitrary HPC applications in the cloud, in: Proceedings of the 10th International Federated Conference on Distributed Computing Techniques (DAIS 2015), June 2015.

[26] Mendeley. Available at http://www.mendeley.com/.

[27] Microsoft Bing. Available at http://www.bing.com/.

[28] X. Niu, J.G.F. Coutinho, W. Luk, A scalable design approach for stencil computation on reconfigurable clusters, in: Proceedings of the IEEE on Field Programmable Logic and Applications (FPL), 2013.

[29] E. O'Neill, J. McGlone, J.G.F. Coutinho, A. Doole, C. Ragusa, O. Pell, P. Sanders, Cross resource optimisation of database functionality across heterogeneous processors, in: Proc. of the 12th IEEE International Symposium on Parallel and Distributed Processing with Applications, 2014.

[30] E. O'Neill, J. McGlone, P. Milligan, P. Kilpatrick, SHEPARD: scheduling on heterogeneous platforms using application resource demands, in: 2014 22nd Euromicro International Conference on Parallel, Distributed and Network-Based Processing (PDP), Feb. 2014, pp. 213–217.

[31] Open Grid Forum (OGF), Open Cloud Computing Interface (OCCI) specification. Available at http://occi-wg.org.

[32] OpenShift. Available at https://www.openshift.com/.

[33] Organization for the Advancement of Structured Information Standards (OASIS), Cloud application management for platforms (CAMP) v1.1. Available at http://docs.oasis-open.org/camp/camp-spec/v1.1/camp-spec-v1.1.html.

[34] Organization for the Advancement of Structured Information Standards (OASIS), Topology and orchestration specification for cloud applications (TOSCA) v1.0. Available at http://docs.oasis-open.org/tosca/TOSCA/v1.0/TOSCA-v1.0.html.

[35] O. Pell, O. Mencer, H.T. Kuen, W. Luk, Maximum performance computing with dataflow engines, in: High-Performance Computing Using FPGAs, 2013, pp. 747–774.

[36] G. Pierre, C. Stratan, ConPaaS: a platform for hosting elastic cloud applications, IEEE Internet Comput. 16 (5) (Sept. 2012) 88–92.

[37] Rackspace open cloud. Available at https://www.rackspace.com/cloud.

[38] J. Stender, M. Berlin, A. Reinefeld, XtreemFS – a file system for the cloud, in: Data Intensive Storage Services for Cloud Environments, IGI Global, 2013.

[39] M. Stillwell, F. Vivien, H. Casanova, Virtual machine resource allocation for service hosting on heterogeneous distributed platforms, in: Proceedings of the 26th International Parallel and Distributed Processing Symposium, May 2012.

[40] T. Yu, B. Feng, M. Stillwell, J.G.F. Coutinho, et al., Relation-oriented resource allocation for multi-accelerator systems, in: International Conference on Application-Specific Systems, Architectures and Processors (ASAP), 2016.

ACKNOWLEDGEMENTS

Simulations presented in this paper were carried out using the Grid'5000 experimental testbed, being developed under the INRIA ALADDIN development action with support from CNRS, RENATER and several universities as well as other funding bodies (see https://www.grid5000.fr). The HARNESS Project was supported by the European Commission Seventh Framework Programme, grant agreement no 318521.

AUDITABLE VERSION CONTROL SYSTEMS IN UNTRUSTED PUBLIC CLOUDS

17

Bo Chen*, **Reza Curtmola**[†], **Jun Dai**[‡,§]

*Department of Computer Science, University of Memphis, Memphis, TN, USA [†]Department of Computer Science, New Jersey Institute of Technology, Newark, NJ, USA [‡]Southwestern University of Finance and Economics, Chengdu, Sichuan, China [§]Rutgers University–Newark, Newark, NJ, USA

17.1 MOTIVATION AND CONTRIBUTIONS

Software development process usually relies on version control systems (VCS) to automate the management of source code, documentation, and configuration files. A version control system can provide several useful features to software developers. This includes retrieving an arbitrary previous version of the source code in order to locate and fix bugs, rolling back to an early version when the working version is corrupted, or allowing team development in which multiple software developers can work simultaneously on updates. In fact, a version control system is indispensable for managing large software projects. Known version control systems which are extensively used nowadays include CVS [3], Subversion [14], Git [8], and Mercurial [11], etc.

A version control system usually records all changes of the data in a data store, called repository, by which an arbitrary version of the data can be retrieved at any time in the future. Oftentimes, repositories are massive in size and difficult to be stored and managed in local machines. For example, GitHub [9] hosted over 6 million repositories, SourceForge over 324,000 projects [13], and Google Code over 250,000 projects [10]. To reduce the cost of both storing and managing repositories, data owners could turn to public clouds providers. As real-world examples, file hosting service providers like Bitcasa [2] and Dropbox [4] that offer version control functionality to their stored data, rely on a popular public cloud provider Amazon S3 [12] for storage services.

The public cloud providers can offer proficient and cheap storage services. However, they are not necessarily trusted due to various reasons. First, they are vulnerable to various attacks from outside or even inside. Second, they usually rely on complex distributed systems, which are likely vulnerable to various failures caused by hardware, software, or even administrative faults [31]. Additionally, unexpected accidental events may lead to failures of cloud services, e.g., power outage [16,17].

Remote Data Integrity Checking (RDIC) [18,19,30] can be used to address the concerns about the untrusted nature of the public cloud providers that host the VCS repositories. RDIC is a mechanism that has been recently developed to check the integrity of data stored at untrusted, third-party storage service providers. Briefly, RDIC allows a client who initially stores a file at a third-party provider (e.g., a cloud provider) to check later if the provider continues to store the original file in its entirety. This check can be done periodically, depending on the client's needs.

By leveraging RDIC, we are able to ensure all the versions of a file are retrievable from the untrusted VCS server over time, so that the version control system can function properly even in the untrusted public clouds. We introduce AVCS, a novel Auditable Version Control System framework that allows the client to periodically verify the VCS repositories and thus obtain the retrievability guarantee. To reduce storage overhead, modern version control systems adopt "delta encoding" to store versions in a repository, in which only the first is stored in its entirety, and each subsequent file version is stored as the difference from its immediate previous version. These differences are recorded in discrete files called "deltas." Particularly, when each version is stored as the difference from another previous version (i.e., not necessarily the immediate previous version), it will turn to a special "skip delta." Such a skip delta-based encoding can further optimize the combine cost of storage and retrieval of an arbitrary file version. This chapter therefore instantiates the AVCS framework for skip delta-based version control systems. Although portions of this chapter are based on previously published work [24], the chapter contains significantly revised material.

Contributions. The contributions of this chapter are summarized in the following:

- We offer a technical overview of both delta-based and skip delta-based version control systems, which have been designed to work under a benign setting. We make the important observation that the only meaningful operation in real-world modern version control systems is append. Unlike previous approaches that rely on dynamic RDIC and are interesting from a theoretical point of view, ours is the first to take a pragmatic approach for auditing the real-world version control systems.
- We introduce the definition of Auditable Version Control Systems (AVCS), and instantiate the AVCS construction for skip delta-based version control systems. Our AVCS construction relies on RDIC mechanisms to ensure all the versions of a file can be retrieved from the untrusted version control server over time, and is able to provide the following features: (i) In addition to the regular functionality of an unsecure version control system, it offers the data owner the ability to check the integrity of all file versions in the VCS repository. (ii) The cost of performing integrity checking on all the file versions is asymptotically the same with the cost of checking one file version. (iii) It can allow the data owner to check the correctness of a file version retrieved from the VCS repository. (iv) It only requires the same amount of storage on the client side like a regular (unsecure) version control system.
- We summarize all the RDIC approaches for version control systems, and theoretically compare them in term of performance.

Organization. In the remainder of this chapter, we introduce our background knowledge in Section 17.2 as well as our system and adversarial model in Section 17.3. In Section 17.4, we introduce the definition of the AVCS, and present our construction of the AVCS for skip delta-based version control systems. We discuss a few issues faced by our AVCS construction in Section 17.5 and summarize the existing RDIC approaches for version control systems in Section 17.6. In Section 17.7, we provide a theoretic comparison among all the RDIC approaches for version control systems; we also perform experimental evaluations on our approach.

17.2 BACKGROUND KNOWLEDGE
17.2.1 DATA ORGANIZATION IN VERSION CONTROL SYSTEMS

In software development, version control systems have been used broadly in managing source code, documentation, and configuration files. Typically, the VCS clients interact with a VCS server and the VCS server stores all the changes to the data in a main repository, such that an arbitrary version of the data can be retrieved at any time in the future. Each VCS client has a local repository, which stores the working copy (i.e., the version of the data that was last checked out by the client from the main VCS repository), the changes made by the client to the working copy, and some metadata.

A version control system provides several useful features that can allow the users to track and control changes made to the data over time. Such features include operations like commit, update, branch, revert, merge, and log. In practice, the most commonly used operations are *commit* and *retrieve*. Commit refers to the process of submitting the latest changes of data to the main repository, so that the changes to the working copy become permanent. Retrieve refers to the process of replacing the working copy with an older or a newer version stored on the server.

Version control systems using delta encoding. A version control system keeps track of all the changes made to the data over time. In this way, any version of the data can be retrieved if necessary. A key issue here is how to store and organize all those changes in the VCS repository. A straightforward approach could be simply storing each individual data version upon a commit. This simple approach was adopted by CVS [3] when storing binary files. A significant disadvantage of this approach is the large bandwidth and storage space it requires for committing a file version, especially when the file size is large.

By observing that there is always a large amount of duplicate content between each file version and its subsequent file version, modern version control systems adopt "delta encoding" to reduce the storage space being needed. Using delta decoding, a version control system only stores the first version of a file in its entirety, and for each subsequent version of the file, the VCS only stores the difference between this file version and its immediate previous version. All the differences are recorded in discrete files called "deltas."

Therefore, if there are t file versions in total, the VCS server will store them as the initial file and $t - 1$ deltas (see Fig. 17.1). Popular version control systems that use variants of delta encoding include CVS [3], SVN [14], and Git [8]. The delta encoding can significantly reduce the storage space required to store all the file versions. However, it suffers from an expensive retrieval: To retrieve the file version t, the VCS server needs to start from the initial file version and apply all the subsequent deltas up to version t, incurring a cost linear in t (see Fig. 17.1). Considering that source code repositories may have a large number of file versions (e.g., GCC has more than 200,000 versions in its repository [7]), retrieving an arbitrary file version may bring a significant burden to the VCS server.

Version control systems using skip delta encoding. As a special type of delta encoding, the skip delta encoding is designed to further optimize the retrieval cost. Apache Subversion (SVN [14]) is a popular version control system that adopts this type of delta encoding. In skip delta encoding, each new file version is still stored as the difference between it and a previous file version. The main difference between the skip delta encoding and the delta encoding is that this previous file version is not necessarily the immediate previous version. Instead, it can be an arbitrary file version from the initial file version up to the immediate previous file version. This ensures that retrieval of an arbitrary file version t requires significantly less than t applications of deltas by the version control server. In this case, the

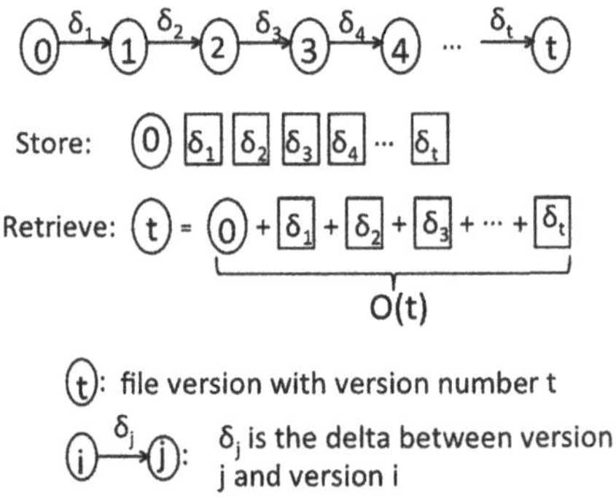

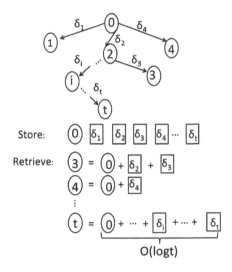

FIGURE 17.1

A delta-based version control system

FIGURE 17.2

A skip delta-based version control system

difference is called a "skip delta" and the old version against which a new version is encoded is called a "skip version."

In particular, if we select the skip version based on the following rule, the complexity for retrieving an arbitrary file version t will be $O(\log(t))$, i.e., we only need to apply at most $\log(t)$ skip deltas in order to recompute the desired file version t starting from the initial file version. Let version j be the skip version of version i. The rule for selecting the skip version j is: Based on the binary representation of i, we change the rightmost bit that has value "1" into a bit with value "0". For example, in Fig. 17.2, version 3's skip version is version 2. This is because the binary representation of 3 is 011, and by changing the rightmost "1" bit into a "0" bit, we can obtain 2.

By using the skip delta encoding, the cost for recovering an arbitrary file version will be logarithmic in the total number of versions. For example, in Fig. 17.2, to reconstruct version 3, we can start from version 0 and apply δ_2 and δ_3; to reconstruct version 4, we can start from version 0 and apply δ_4. The skip version for version 25 is 24, whose skip version is 16, whose skip version is 0. Thus, to reconstruct version 25, we can start from version 0 and apply δ_{16}, δ_{24}, and δ_{25}. We prove that the cost for retrieving an arbitrary file version t is bounded by $O(\log(t))$ [24].

17.2.2 REMOTE DATA INTEGRITY CHECKING (RDIC)

Remote Data Integrity Checking (RDIC) is framework that allows a data owner to verify the integrity of the data outsourced to an untrusted third party. RDIC usually relies on two key steps: (i) Data pre-processing. The data to be outsourced are pre-processed by the data owner, generating metadata (e.g., integrity tags) which can be used to verify whether the data have been tampered with over time; (ii) Periodical checking. After the data have been outsourced, a verifier (e.g., the data owner or a third-party verifier) will periodically issue a challenge request to ask the storage server to prove possession of the outsourced data. The existing PDP [18,19] and PoR [30,20] are two popular RDIC designs, in which the checking step is highly optimized by utilizing a novel "spot-checking" technique. Rather than simply verify the entire outsourced data, which may be prohibitively expensive, the spot-checking technique checks a random subset of the entire outsourced data. Prior work [18,19] shows that if an adversary corrupts a certain amount of the data, the spot-checking technique can detect such a corruption with high probability by checking a few randomly selected blocks.

RDIC has been recently extended to a dynamic setting [22,25,27,33] and a distributed setting [21, 23,26,29].

17.3 SYSTEM AND ADVERSARIAL MODEL

System model. We consider a version control system in which one or more VCS clients store data at a VCS server. The server maintains the main repository, in which all the versions of the data are stored. Each VCS client runs client software. We use the term *client* to refer to the VCS client software and *server* to refer to the server software. Each VCS client maintains a local repository, which stores the working copy, the changes made by the client to the working copy, and the metadata.

From a client's point of view, the interface exposed by the VCS server includes two main operations: *commit* and *retrieve*. Although a VCS system usually provides additional operations including branch, merge, log, etc., we only focus on the most common operations commit and retrieve. We also introduce an additional operation, *check*. This operation allows the client to check if the server possesses all the file versions.

Adversarial model. We consider an adversarial model in which all the VCS clients are trusted and the VCS server may misbehave. This captures real-world scenarios in which the software engineers from a company are collaborating to develop software, and each of them will honestly use the VCS client. However, the VCS server may be hosted in a public cloud provider to reduce operational cost. Due to the untrusted nature of public cloud providers, the VCS server may not function properly.

We consider a rational and economically motivated adversary who may delete the data that were rarely used. The attacks are meaningful only when the adversary can obtain a significant profit. We do not consider attacks in which the server simply corrupts a small portion of the repository (e.g., 1 byte), since such attacks will not bring a significant benefit.

Assumptions. Our design relies on two main assumptions: (i) All the communications are protected (e.g., by SSL/TLS), and the adversary is not able to learn anything from eavesdropping the communications; (ii) The server should respond to any valid requests from the clients. Otherwise, the clients can simply terminate the contract with the service provider.

17.4 AUDITABLE VERSION CONTROL SYSTEMS

A version control system designed for a benign setting cannot work correctly when the VCS server is untrusted. This is usually the case when the server is hosted in the public clouds. We thus introduce a new framework, Auditable Version Control System (AVCS), which can ensure that a version control system is able to function properly even when the VCS server is untrusted and misbehaves.

In this section, we first introduce our definition of the AVCS. By leveraging remote data integrity checking mechanisms, we then instantiate the construction of AVCS for skip delta-based version control systems.

17.4.1 DEFINITION OF AVCS

The AVCS relies on seven polynomial-time algorithms: *KeyGen*, *ComputeDelta*, *GenMetadata*, *GenProof*, *CheckProof*, *GenRetrieveVersionAndProof*, and *CheckRetrieveProof*.

KeyGen is a key generation algorithm run by the client to initiate the entire version control system.

ComputeDelta is a delta generation algorithm run by the client to compute the corresponding delta when committing a new file version.

GenMetadata is a metadata generation algorithm run by the client to generate the verification metadata for a new file version before committing it.

GenProof is an algorithm run by the server to generate a proof of data possession.

CheckProof is an algorithm run by the client to verify the proof of data possession.

GenRetrieveVersionAndProof is an algorithm run by the server to generate the correctness proof of a retrieved file version.

CheckRetrieveProof is an algorithm run by the client to verify the correctness of the retrieved file version.

Utilizing the aforementioned algorithms, we build an AVCS divided into four phases: Setup, Commit, Challenge, and Retrieve.

Setup. The client runs *KeyGen* to generate the private key material and performs other initialization operations.

Commit. To commit a new file version, the client runs *ComputeDelta* and *GenMetadata* to compute the delta and the metadata for the new file version, respectively. The delta and the metadata are both sent to store at the server.

Challenge. Periodically, the verifier (the client or a third-party verifier) challenges the server to obtain a proof that the server continues to store all the file versions stored by the client. The server uses *GenProof* to compute a proof of data possession and sends back the proof. The client then uses *CheckProof* to validate the received proof.

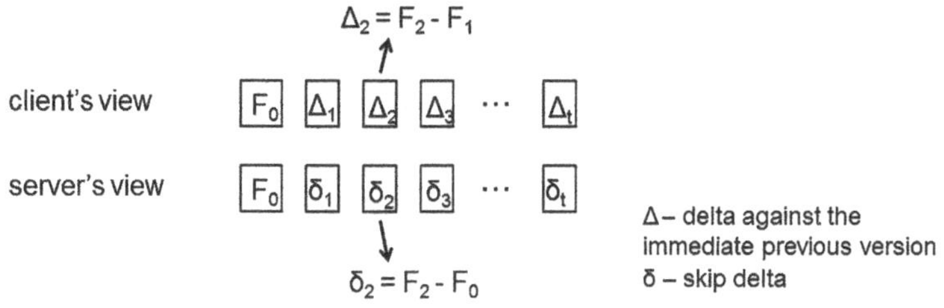

FIGURE 17.3

Inconsistency of the client's and the server's view

Retrieve. The client requests an arbitrary file version. The server runs *GenRetrieveVersionAnd-Proof* to obtain the requested file version, together with a proof of correctness. The client verifies the correctness of the retrieved file by running *CheckRetrieveProof*.

Note that this definition encompasses version control systems that use delta encoding, which also include skip delta-based version control systems.

17.4.2 AN AVCS CONSTRUCTION

Whereas our AVCS definition targets version control systems that use delta encoding in general, in the construction we focus on version control systems that use skip delta encoding, because: First, they are optimized for both storage and retrieval; Second, they are arguably more challenging to secure than version control systems that use delta encoding, due to the additional complexity of computing the skip deltas.

Challenges. To instantiate the AVCS construction for skip delta-based version control systems, we need to address several challenges. These challenges stem from the adversarial nature of the VCS server that is hosted in the untrusted clouds and from the format of a skip delta-based VCS repository being optimized to minimize the server's storage and workload during the Retrieve phase.

The first challenge comes from the gap between the server's and the client's view of the repository. In a general-purpose RDIC protocol (Section 17.2.2), the client and the server have the same view of the outsourced data: the client computes the verification metadata based on the data, and then sends both data and metadata to the server. The server stores these unmodified. Additionally, the server stores and uses the data and metadata to answer the verifier's challenges by computing a proof that convinces the verifier that the server continues to store the exact data outsourced by the data owner.

However, in a skip delta-based VCS, there is a gap between the two views (Fig. 17.3), which makes skip delta-based VCS systems more difficult to audit: Although both the client and server view the main VCS repository as the initial version of the data plus a series of delta files corresponding to subsequent data versions, they have a different understanding of the delta files. To commit a new version t, the client computes and sends to the server a delta that is the difference between the new version and its immediate previous version, i.e., the difference between version t and $t - 1$. However, this delta is different from the skip deltas that are stored by the server: a δ_t file stored by the server is the difference between version t and its "skip version", which is not necessarily the version immediately previous to

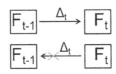

FIGURE 17.4

Delta-encoding is not reversible

version t. Since the client does not have access to the skip deltas stored by the server, it cannot compute the verification metadata over them, as needed in the RDIC protocol.

The second challenge is due to the fact that delta encoding is not reversible. The client may try to retrieve the skip delta computed by the server and then compute the verification metadata based on the retrieved skip delta. However, in an adversarial setting, the client cannot trust the server to provide a correct skip delta value. This is exacerbated by the fact that the delta encoding is not a reversible operation (Fig. 17.4). Specifically, if $\delta_{t-1 \rightarrow t}$ is the difference between versions $t-1$ and t (i.e., $F_t = F_{t-1} + \delta_{t-1 \rightarrow t}$), this does not imply that version $t-1$ can be obtained based on version t and $\delta_{t-1 \rightarrow t}$. The reason comes from the method used by delta encoding to encode update operations between versions, such as insert, update, and delete. If a delete operation was executed on version $t-1$ to obtain version t, then $\delta_{t-1 \rightarrow t}$ encodes only the position of the deleted portion from version $t-1$, so that given version $t-1$ and $\delta_{t-1 \rightarrow t}$, one can obtain version t. However, $\delta_{t-1 \rightarrow t}$ does not encode the actual data that has been deleted. Thus, version $t-1$ cannot be obtained based on version t and $\delta_{t-1 \rightarrow t}$.

High-level idea. We present an AVCS construction that can resolve the aforementioned challenges. The idea behind our construction is that we allow the client and the untrusted server to collaborate to compute the skip deltas. By sacrificing an acceptable amount of communication, we successfully eliminate the need of storing a large number of previous versions in the client (for the purpose of computing skip deltas), and thus are able to conform to the notion of storage outsourcing.

17.4.2.1 Construction details

The version control repository stores t file versions, $F_0, F_1, \ldots, F_{t-1}$. They are stored in the repository using skip delta encoding as: $F_0, \delta_1, \delta_2, \ldots, \delta_{t-1}$ (i.e., the initial file version and $t-1$ skip delta files). We view the entire information pertaining to the t versions of the file F as a virtual file $\tilde{F}$, which is obtained by concatenating the original file version and all the $t-1$ subsequent delta files: $\tilde{F} = F_0||\delta_1||\delta_2||\ldots||\delta_{t-1}$. We view $\tilde{F}$ as a collection of fixed-size blocks, and each block containing s symbols (a symbol is an element from $GF(p)$, where p is a large prime (at least 80 bits)). This view matches the view of a file in an RDIC scheme: To check the integrity of all the versions of F, it is enough to check the integrity of $\tilde{F}$. Let n denote the number of blocks in $\tilde{F}$. As the client keeps committing new file versions, n will grow accordingly (note that n is maintained by the client).

We use two types of verification tags. To check data possession (in the Challenge phase), we use *challenge tags*, which are computed over the blocks in $\tilde{F}$ to facilitate spot checking technique in RDIC (Section 17.2.2). The challenge tag is computed for each block following the manner of private verification tag construction in [32], which is homomorphically verifiable. To check the integrity of individual file versions (in both the Commit and the Retrieve phases), we use *retrieve tags*, each of which is com-

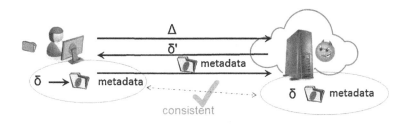

FIGURE 17.5

Overview of the AVCS construction

puted over an entire version of F. The retrieve tag is computed using HMAC [29] over the whole file version and its version number.

In a benign setting, whenever the client commits a new file version, the server computes and stores a skip delta file in the main VCS repository. Under an adversarial setting, to leverage RDIC techniques over the VCS repository, the skip delta files must be accompanied by challenge tags. Since the challenge tags can only be computed by the client, in our construction, we require the client to compute the skip delta, generate the challenge tags over it, and send both the skip delta and the tags to the server. An overview of our AVCS construction is shown in Fig. 17.5.

In the following, we elaborate the design of our AVCS construction for each phase: setup, commit, challenge, and retrieve.

Setup. The client selects two private keys K_1 and K_2 uniformly at random from a large domain (this is determined by the security parameters). It also initializes n as 0.

Commit. As shown in Fig. 17.6, when committing a new version F_i, where $i > 0$, the client must compute the skip delta (δ_{skip}) for F_i. The δ_{skip} must be computed against a certain previous version of the file, called the "skip version" (refer to Section 17.2.1). Let $skip(i)$ be the skip version of version i. Note that the client also has in its local store a copy of F_{i-1}, which is the working copy.

The client will check if $skip(i)$ is version $i - 1$. If it is true, the client can directly compute δ_{skip} such that $F_i = F_{i-1} + \delta_{skip}$. Otherwise, the client computes δ_{skip} by interacting with the VCS server using the following steps (see Fig. 17.6):

1. The client computes the difference between the new version and its immediate previous version, i.e., computes δ such that $F_i = F_{i-1} + \delta$. The client then sends δ to the server.
2. The server recomputes F_{i-1} based on the data in the repository and then computes $F_i = F_{i-1} + \delta$. The server then recomputes $F_{skip(i)}$ (the skip version for F_i) based on the data in the repository and computes the difference between F_i and $F_{skip(i)}$, i.e., it computes $\delta_{reverse}$ such that $F_{skip(i)} = F_i + \delta_{reverse}$. The server sends $\delta_{reverse}$ to the client, together with the retrieve tag for $F_{skip(i)}$.
3. The client computes the skip version, $F_{skip(i)} = F_i + \delta_{reverse}$, and checks the validity of $F_{skip(i)}$ using the retrieve tag received from the server. The client then computes the skip delta for the new file version, i.e., δ_{skip}, such that $F_i = F_{skip(i)} + \delta_{skip}$.

To give an example, when the client commits F_{15}, the client also has the working copy F_{14}, which is the skip version for F_{15}, and the client can compute directly δ_{skip} such that $F_{15} = F_{14} + \delta_{skip}$. However, when the client commits F_{20}, it only has F_{19} in his/her local store and must first retrieve from the server

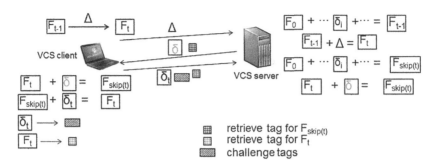

FIGURE 17.6

Commit phase of our AVCS construction

$\delta_{reverse}$ and then compute F_{16}, which is the skip version for F_{20}, as $F_{16} = F_{20} + \delta_{reverse}$. Only then can the client compute δ_{skip} such that $F_{20} = F_{16} + \delta_{skip}$.

After having computed δ_{skip}, the client views δ_{skip} as a collection of blocks, and computes a set of challenge tags using key K_1. The client also computes a retrieve tag R_i for F_i, using key K_2. The set of challenge tags and the retrieve tag R_i will be sent to the VCS server. The client then increases n by x, where x is the number of blocks in δ_{skip}. Note that if the file version being committed is the initial file version F_0, the client directly computes a set of challenge tags and a retrieve tag over F_0.

Challenge. We leverage spot checking technique (see Section 17.2.2) to check the remotely stored CVS repository. Periodically, the client challenges the server to prove data possession of a random subset of the blocks in $\tilde{F}$. The server computes a proof of data possession by using the challenge blocks and their corresponding challenge tags. As the challenge tags are homomorphically verifiable, the server can further reduce the size of the proof by aggregating the challenge blocks and the corresponding challenge tags. The client further checks the proof using key K_1. This spot checking mechanism is quite efficient. For example, when the server corrupts 1% of the repository (i.e., 1% of $\tilde{F}$), then the client can detect this corruption with high probability by randomly checking only a small constant number of blocks (e.g., checking 460 blocks results in a 99% detection probability) [18].

Retrieve. The Retrieve phase is activated when the client wants to replace the working copy with an older or a newer version F_j. The client sends a retrieval request to the server. The server generates the delta (i.e., δ) of F_j against the client's working copy, together with F_j's retrieve tag R_j. Both δ and R_j are returned to the client. The client then computes F_j by applying δ over its working copy, and checks the validity of F_j by using R_j and the key K_2.

17.5 DISCUSSION

Broad applications of the AVCS. One significant advantage of skip delta encoding is that it can be used to handle any formats of data, including source code, audio, image, video, etc. As the AVCS is based on skip delta encoding, it can securely handle any types of data that need to be maintained in a version control manner and need to be stored in an untrusted third party like a public cloud provider.

SVN vs Git. Although Git has been recently gaining popularity compared to SVN, providing guarantees to SVN repositories is still very valuable because there are still plenty of projects and organization that still use SVN. The techniques described in this chapter could be adapted to be applied to Git repositories; we anticipate that devising similar techniques for Git will present fewer challenges, since Git clients clone the entire repository (i.e., all revisions), unlike in SVN where the client usually has only one revision (out of many revisions).

17.6 OTHER RDIC APPROACHES FOR VERSION CONTROL SYSTEMS

DPDP. Erway et al. [27] used a two-level authenticated data structure to provide integrity guarantee for version control systems. Specifically, for each file version, a first-level authenticated data structure is used to organize all the blocks, generating a root for each version. A second-level authenticated data structure is then used to organize all these roots. As the total number of leaves in this two-level authenticated data structure is $t \cdot n$, and verifying a block in the tree-like authenticated data structure usually has a logarithmic complexity, the checking complexity of DPDP will be $O(\log(t \cdot n))$, in which t is the total number of versions and n is the total number of blocks in a version.

DR-DPDP. Etemad et al. [28] proposed DR-DPDP to improve the performance of DPDP. In this approach, they use a first level authenticated data structure to organize all the data blocks of a file version, generating the corresponding root. They then adopt a PDP-like structure [18], rather than an authenticated data structure, to provide integrity guarantee for the roots of the first-level authenticated data structure. Since checking the roots in PDP-like structure can be achieved in constant time, the checking complexity of DR-DPDP can be significantly reduced to $O(1 + \log(n))$.

Other work. Zhang et al. [34] proposed an update tree-based approach. Their scheme adopts a tree structure to organize all the update operations, and thus the checking complexity is logarithmic in the total number of updates, i.e., approximately $O(\log(t))$.

17.7 EVALUATION
17.7.1 THEORETICAL EVALUATION

Theoretical analysis on our AVCS construction. During the Commit phase, the client interacts with the version control server to compute skip deltas. To retrieve any file version from the repository, the server only needs to go through at most $\log(t)$ skip deltas. Therefore, the computation complexity in the server is $O(\log(t))$. The client has to compute the skip version as well as the skip delta, and generate the metadata, which results in a complexity linear to the size of the file version. The communication during the commit phase includes two deltas and a set of challenge tags for a skip delta.

During the Challenge phase, our AVCS uses an efficient spot checking technique: periodically, the client challenges the server, requiring the server to prove data possession of a random subset of data blocks in the entire repository; the server computes a proof by aggregating the selected blocks as well as the corresponding challenge tags. Therefore, both the computation (client and server) and the communication complexities are $O(1)$. This is a major advantage of the AVCS compared to all the

Table 17.1 Comparison of different RDIC approaches for version control systems (t is the number of versions in the repository and n is the number of blocks in a version)

	DPDP [27]	DR-DPDP [28]	AVCS
Communication (Commit phase)	$O(n + \log t)$	$O(n + 1)$	$O(n + 1)$
Server computation (Commit phase)	$O(n + \log t)$	$O(n)$	$O(n \log t)$
Client computation (Commit phase)	$O(n + \log t)$	$O(n + 1)$	$O(n + 1)$
Communication (Challenge phase)	$O(\log n + \log t)$	$O(1 + \log n)$	$O(1)$
Computation (server + client) (Challenge phase)	$O(\log n + \log t)$	$O(1 + \log n)$	$O(1)$
Communication (Retrieve phase)	$O(n + \log t)$	$O(n + 1)$	$O(n + 1)$
Server computation (Retrieve phase)	$O(tn + \log t)$	$O(tn + 1)$	$O(n \log t + 1)$
Client computation (Retrieve phase)	$O(n + \log t)$	$O(n)$	$O(n)$
Client storage	$O(n)$	$O(n)$	$O(n)$
Server storage	$O(nt)$	$O(nt)$	$O(nt)$

previous approaches, in which the checking complexity is proportional to either the repository size or the version size.

During Retrieve phase, the server needs to go through at most $\log(t)$ skip deltas to compute a target file version. Therefore, the server computation complexity is $O(\log(t))$. The client stores locally the working copy which requires $O(n)$ space.

Comparison among different secure version control approaches. We show a performance comparison among our AVCS construction, DPDP [27], and DR-DPDP [28] in Table 17.1. Compared to both DPDP and DR-DPDP, our AVCS has constant complexity in the Challenge phase in terms of both computation and communication. In the Retrieve phase, the AVCS is significantly more efficient than the other approaches in terms of server computation. However, the server computation in the Commit phase of the AVCS is slightly larger than the other approaches due to the overhead for computing the skip deltas. We believe this is not a significant drawback, because: (i) Compared to the other approaches, the AVCS only has an additional logarithmic factor, which is usually small, i.e., for $t = 1,000,000$, $\log(t)$ is 20; (ii) The server is hosted in the public clouds, which are usually capable of handling computation intensive tasks.

17.7.2 EXPERIMENTAL EVALUATION

To understand the impact of AVCS on the real-world VCS systems, we implemented AVCS using a popular open-source version control system, Apache Subversion (SVN) [14] version 1.7.8. As we know, many projects are using SVN for source control management. This includes FreeBSD [6], GCC [7], Wireshark [15], as well as all the open-source projects in Apache Software Foundation [1], etc.

Implementation. We modified the source code of both the client and the server of SVN. For the client, we mainly modified five SVN commands: *svn add*, *svn rm*, *svn commit*, *svn co*, and *svn update*. For the server, we modified the stand-alone server "*svnserve*." The implementation details as well as implementation issues can be found in our conference paper [24].

Experimental results: We evaluated both the computation and the communication overhead during the Commit phase and the computation overhead during the Retrieve phase, for both SSVN and SVN. We selected three representative public SVN repositories for our experimental evaluation: FileZilla [5],

Wireshark [15], and GCC [7]. The Challenge phase has been shown to be very efficient when using spot-checking technique [19], so we do not include it in this evaluation. The detailed experimental results can be found in our conference paper [24], which shows that AVCS only incurs a modest decrease in performance to the original SVN system.

17.8 **CONCLUSION**

In this chapter, we introduce Auditable Version Control System (AVCS), a delta-based version control system designed to function properly in untrusted public clouds. By leveraging remote data integrity checking mechanisms, we instantiate our AVCS for skip delta-based version control systems. Unlike previous approaches that rely on dynamic RDIC and are interesting from a theoretical point of view, ours is the first pragmatic approach for auditing real-world VCS systems. We also summarize all the other RDIC approaches for version control systems, and compare them theoretically.

REFERENCES

[1] APACHE – The Apache Software Foundation. Available at apache.org.
[2] Bitcasa. Available at bitcasa.com.
[3] CVS – Concurrent Versions System. Available at cvs.nongnu.org.
[4] Dropbox. Available at dropbox.com.
[5] Filezilla. Available at filezilla-project.org.
[6] FreeBSD. Available at freebsd.org.
[7] GCC. Available at gcc.gnu.org/.
[8] Git. Available at git-scm.com.
[9] GitHub. Available at github.com.
[10] Google code. Available at code.google.com.
[11] Mercurial. Available at mercurial.selenic.com.
[12] S3. Available at aws.amazon.com/en/s3.
[13] Sourceforge. Available at sourceforge.net.
[14] SVN – Apache subversion. Available at subversion.apache.org.
[15] Wireshark. Available at wireshark.org.
[16] AWS MESSAGE 1 – Summary of the Amazon EC2, Amazon EBS, and Amazon RDS service event in the EU West region. Available at aws.amazon.com/cn/message/2329B7.
[17] AWS MESSAGE 2 – Summary of the AWS service event in the US East region. Available at aws.amazon.com/cn/message/67457.
[18] G. Ateniese, R. Burns, R. Curtmola, J. Herring, O. Khan, L. Kissner, Z. Peterson, D. Song, Remote data checking using provable data possession, ACM Trans. Inf. Syst. Secur. 14 (June 2011).
[19] G. Ateniese, R. Burns, R. Curtmola, J. Herring, L. Kissner, Z. Peterson, D. Song, Provable data possession at untrusted stores, in: Proc. of ACM Conference on Computer and Communications Security (CCS'07), 2007.
[20] K.D. Bowers, A. Juels, A. Oprea, Proofs of retrievability: theory and implementation, in: Proc. of ACM Cloud Computing Security Workshop (CCSW'09), 2009.
[21] K. Bowers, A. Oprea, A. Juels, HAIL: a high-availability and integrity layer for cloud storage, in: Proc. of ACM Conference on Computer and Communications Security (CCS'09), 2009.
[22] D. Cash, A. Kupcu, D. Wichs, Dynamic proofs of retrievability via oblivious RAM, in: Proc. of EUROCRYPT'13, 2013.
[23] Bo Chen, Anil Kumar Ammula, Reza Curtmola, Towards server-side repair for erasure coding-based distributed storage systems, in: The Fifth ACM Conference on Data and Application Security and Privacy (CODASPY'15), 2015.

[24] B. Chen, R. Curtmola, Auditable version control systems, in: Proc. of the 21st Annual Network and Distributed System Security Symposium (NDSS'14), 2014.

[25] B. Chen, R. Curtmola, Robust dynamic provable data possession, in: Proc. of International Workshop on Security and Privacy in Cloud Computing (ICDCS-SPCC'12), 2012.

[26] Bo Chen, Reza Curtmola, Towards self-repairing replication-based storage systems using untrusted clouds, in: The Third ACM Conference on Data and Application Security and Privacy (CODASPY'13), 2013.

[27] C. Erway, A. Kupcu, C. Papamanthou, R. Tamassia, Dynamic provable data possession, in: Proc. of ACM Conference on Computer and Communications Security (CCS'09), 2009.

[28] M. Etemad, A. Kupcu, Transparent, distributed, and replicated dynamic provable data possession, in: Proc. of 11th International Conference on Applied Cryptography and Network Security (ACNS'13), 2013.

[29] H. Krawczyk, M. Bellare, R. Canetti, HMAC: keyed-hashing for message authentication, Internet RFC 2104, February 1997.

[30] A. Juels, B.S. Kaliski, PORs: proofs of retrievability for large files, in: Proc. of ACM Conference on Computer and Communications Security (CCS'07), 2007.

[31] P. Mahajan, S. Setty, S. Lee, A. Clement, L. Alvisi, M. Dahlin, M. Walfish, Depot: cloud storage with minimal trust, ACM Trans. Comput. Syst. 29 (4) (2011) 12.

[32] H. Shacham, B. Waters, Compact proofs of retrievability, in: Proc. of Annual International Conference on the Theory and Application of Cryptology and Information Security (ASIACRYPT'08), 2008.

[33] E. Stefanov, M. van Dijk, A. Oprea, A. Juels, Iris: a scalable cloud file system with efficient integrity checks, in: Proc. of Annual Computer Security Applications Conference (ACSAC'12), 2012.

[34] Y. Zhang, M. Blanton, Efficient dynamic provable possession of remote data via balanced update trees, in: Proc. of 8th ACM Symposium on Information, Computer and Communications Security (ASIACCS'13), 2013.

SCIENTIFIC WORKFLOW MANAGEMENT SYSTEM FOR CLOUDS

18

Maria A. Rodriguez, Rajkumar Buyya

Cloud Computing and Distributed Systems (CLOUDS) Laboratory, School of Computing and Information Systems, The University of Melbourne, Australia

18.1 INTRODUCTION

Workflows are a commonly used application model in computational science. They describe a series of computations that enable the analysis of data in a structured and distributed manner and are commonly expressed as a set of tasks and a set of dependencies between them. These applications offer an efficient way of processing and extracting knowledge from the ever-growing data produced by increasingly powerful tools such as telescopes, particle accelerators, and gravitational wave detectors and have been successfully used to make significant scientific advances in various fields such as biology, physics, medicine, and astronomy [1].

Scientific workflows are often data- and resource-intensive applications and require a distributed platform in order for meaningful results to be obtained in a reasonable amount of time. Their deployment is managed by Workflow Management Systems (WMS) which are responsible for transparently orchestrating the execution of the workflow tasks in a set of distributed compute resources while ensuring the dependencies are preserved. A high-level overview of this process is shown in Fig. 18.1. In general, WMSs provide essential functionality to enable the execution of workflows such as data management and provenance, task scheduling, resource provisioning, and fault tolerance among others.

The latest distributed computing paradigm, cloud computing, offers several advantages for the deployment of these applications. In particular, Infrastructure-as-a-Service (IaaS) clouds offer WMSs an easily accessible, flexible, and scalable infrastructure by leasing virtualized compute resources, or Virtual Machines (VMs). This allows workflows to be easily packaged and deployed and more importantly, enables WMSs to access a virtually infinite pool of heterogeneous VMs that can be elastically acquired and released and are charged on a pay-per-use basis.

In this way, WMSs can use cloud resources opportunistically based on the number and type of tasks that need to be processed at a given point in time. This is a convenient feature as it is common for the task parallelism of scientific workflows to significantly change throughout their execution. The resource pool can be scaled out and in to adjust the number of resources as the execution of the workflow progresses. This facilitates the fulfilment of the quality-of-service (QoS) requirements by allowing the WMS to fine-tune performance while ensuring the available resources are efficiently used.

In this chapter we present an existing WMS and detail its extension to support the cloud computing paradigm. Firstly, we review the concept of scientific workflow and the infrastructure services offered

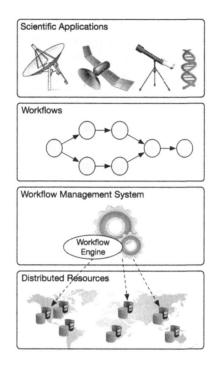

FIGURE 18.1

High-level overview of a scientific workflow deployment in a distributed environment

by clouds as well as existing management solutions for workflow applications. Next, we introduce common functionalities of WMSs designed for cloud environments as well as a general architecture and its components. We then introduce the Cloudbus WMS [2] and detail our implementation of cloud-enabling components to support the dynamic provisioning and deprovisioning of VMs. Finally, with the aim of demonstrating the added functionality, we present a case study on the use of cloud services for a well-known scientific workflow from the astronomy domain.

18.2 BACKGROUND

The concept of workflow has its roots in commercial enterprises as a business process modeling tool. These business workflows aim to automate and optimize the processes of an organization, seen as an ordered sequence of activities, and are a mature research area [3] lead by the Workflow Management Coalition[1] (WfMC), founded in 1993. This notion of workflow has extended to the scientific community where *scientific workflows* are used to support large-scale, complex scientific processes. They are

---

[1]http://www.wfmc.org/.

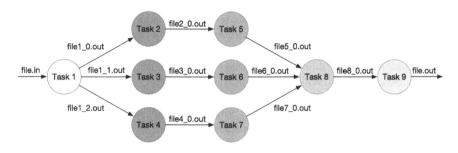

FIGURE 18.2

Sample workflow with nine tasks

designed to conduct experiments and prove scientific hypotheses by managing, analyzing, simulating, and visualizing scientific data [4]. In science, it is common for these applications to be composed of a set of computational tasks and a set of data or control dependencies between the tasks. A sample workflow application can be seen in Fig. 18.2.

Extensive research has been done on the use of scientific workflow systems, particularly in shared infrastructure environments such as grids and dedicated clusters. An example is the Askalon [5] system developed at the University of Innsbruck, Austria. It facilitates the development and optimization of workflows on distributed infrastructures and supports the execution of workflows expressed in an XML-based language called AGWL that enables the specification of looping structures, conditional statements, and Directed Acyclic Graph (DAG) constructs. Another system is Kepler [6], it offers services to design, execute, and share scientific workflows and supports various models of computations such as superscalar and streaming workflows. Taverna [7] is a suite of tools used to design and execute scientific workflows and aid in silico experimentation. The system is capable of interacting with various types of services including web services, data warehouses, and grid services. Finally, Pegasus [8] WMS supports the deployment of workflows in different environments and has the ability to execute workflows expressed as DAGs, manage their data, monitor their execution, and handle failures. A comprehensive taxonomy and survey of these systems is presented by Yu and Buyya [9]; it provides an understanding of existing works from different perspectives such as scheduling, fault management, and data movement.

With the advent of cloud computing, researchers are now focusing on extending existing workflow systems to support the deployment of scientific applications in cloud environments, particularly in IaaS clouds. For instance, the above mentioned products, although initially developed for grids and clusters, have now been enhanced to work with IaaS resources. That is, they are capable of interacting with IaaS vendors that offer VMs for lease with a predefined CPU, memory, storage, and bandwidth capacity. Different resource bundles (i.e., VM types) are available at varying prices and are generally charged per time frame, or billing period. While VMs deliver the compute power, IaaS clouds also offer storage and networking services, providing all the necessary infrastructure for the execution of workflow applications.

WMSs and their users can benefit in different ways from using IaaS resources. As already mentioned, clouds eliminate the need to own any physical resources and users can easily access a flexible and scalable infrastructure on-demand. This not only leads to WMSs being able to customize the type and number of resources used at any point in time but is also beneficial in economical terms. For instance, Deelman et al. [10] studied the cost of running scientific workflows in the cloud. Specifically, they studied the trade-off between cost and performance under different execution and resource provisioning plans as well as storage and networking fees on Amazon AWS. Their findings support the fact that clouds are a cost-effective solution for scientific applications.

Another benefit derives from the fact that scientific workflows are generally legacy applications that contain heterogeneous software components. Virtualization allows for the execution environment of these components to be easily customized. The operating system, software packages, directory structures, and input data files, among others, can all be tailored for a specific component and stored as a VM image. This image can then be easily used to deploy VMs capable of executing the software component they were designed for. Another advantage of using VM images for the deployment of workflow tasks is the fact that they enable scientific validation by supporting experiment reproducibility. Images can be stored and redeployed whenever an experiment needs to be reproduced as they enable the creation of the same exact environment used in previous experiments. The Cloudbus WMS, presented in the sections to follow, is our initiative towards leveraging the aforementioned benefits.

18.3 WORKFLOW MANAGEMENT SYSTEMS FOR CLOUDS

We will begin by introducing a general architectural model for cloud WMSs. In general, a WMS enables the creation, monitoring and execution of scientific workflows and has the capability of transparently managing tasks and data by hiding the orchestration and integration details among the distributed resources [2]. A reference architecture is shown in Fig. 18.3. The depicted components are common to most cloud WMS implementations, however, not all of them are required to have a fully functional system.

User interface. The user interface allows for users to create, edit, submit, and monitor their applications.

Workflow engine. The workflow engine is the core of the system and is responsible for managing the actual execution of the workflow. The parser module within the engine interprets a workflow depicted in a high level language such as XML and creates the corresponding internal workflow representation such as task and data objects. The scheduler and resource provisioning modules work together in planning the execution of the workflow. The resource provisioning module is responsible for selecting and provisioning the cloud resources and the scheduling component applies specific policies that map tasks to available resources, both processes are based on the QoS requirements and scheduling objectives. The performance prediction and runtime estimation module use historical data, data provenance, or time series prediction models, among other methods, to estimate the performance of cloud resources and the amount of time tasks will take to execute on different VMs. This data is used by the resource provisioning and scheduling modules to make accurate and efficient decisions regarding the allocation of tasks. The data management component of the workflow engine manages the movement, placement, and storage of data as required for the workflow execution. Finally, the task dispatcher has the responsibility of interacting with the cloud APIs to dispatch tasks ready for execution onto the available VMs.

Administration and monitoring tools. The administration and monitoring tools of the WMS architecture include modules that enable the dynamic and continuous monitoring of workflow tasks and resource

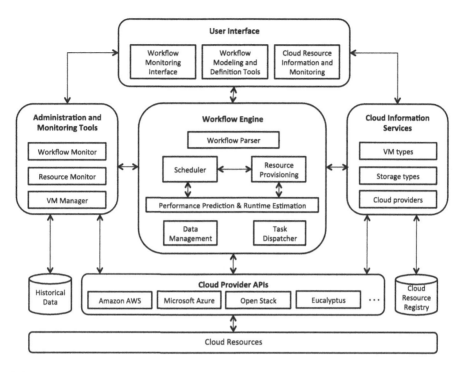

FIGURE 18.3

Reference architecture of a Workflow Management System

performance as well as the management of leased resources, such as VMs. The data collected by these tools can be used by fault tolerance mechanisms or can be stored in a historical database and used by performance prediction methods, for example.

Cloud information services. Another component of the architecture is the cloud information services. This component provides the workflow engine with information about different cloud providers, the resources they offer including their characteristics and prices, location, and any other information required by the engine to make the resource selection and mapping decisions.

Cloud provider APIs. These APIs enable the integration of applications with cloud services. For the scheduling problem described in this chapter, they enable the on-demand provisioning and deprovisioning of VMs, the monitoring of resource usage within a specific VM, access to storage services to save and retrieve data, transferring data in or out of their facilities, and configuring security and network settings, among others. The majority of IaaS APIs are exposed as REST (Representational State Transfer) and SOAP (Simple Object Access Protocol) services, but protocols such as XML-RPC and Javascript are also used. For instance, CloudSigma, Rackspace, Windows Azure, and Amazon EC2 all offer REST-based APIs. As opposed to providing services for a specific platform, other solutions such

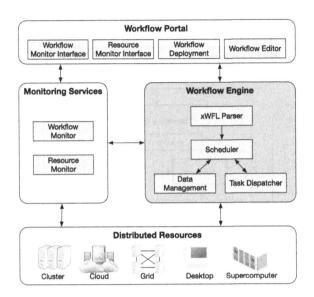

FIGURE 18.4

Key architectural components of the Cloudbus WMS

as Apache JClouds[2] aim to create a cross-platform cloud environment by providing and API to access services from different cloud providers in a transparent manner. Cross-platform interfaces have the advantage of allowing applications to access services from multiple providers without having to rewrite any code, but may have less functionality or other limitations when compared to vendor-specific solutions.

18.4 CLOUDBUS WORKFLOW MANAGEMENT SYSTEM

The Cloudbus WMS was developed at the CLOUDS Laboratory in the University of Melbourne, Australia. It allows scientist to express their applications as workflows and execute them on distributed resources by transparently managing the computational processes and data. Its architecture consists of a subset of the components depicted in Fig. 18.3 and is presented in Fig. 18.4.

The *Workflow Portal* is the entry point to the system. It provides a web-based user interface for scientists to create, edit, submit, and monitor their applications. It provides access to a *Workflow Deployment* page that allows users to upload any necessary data and configuration input files needed to run a workflow. A *Workflow Editor* is also embedded in this component and it provides a GUI that enables users to create or modify a workflow using drag and drop facilities. The workflow is modeled as a DAG with nodes and links that represent tasks and dependencies between tasks. The editor converts

---

[2]Apache JClouds: http://jclouds.apache.org.

the graphical model designed by the users into an XML based workflow language called xWFL which is the format understood by the underlying workflow engine.

The *Workflow Monitor Interface* is also accessed through the portal and it provides a GUI to the *Workflow Monitor* module which is part of the Monitoring Services component. It allows users to observe the execution progress of multiple workflows and to view the final output of an application. Users can monitor the status of every task in a specific workflow, for instance, tasks can be on a ready, executing, stage in, or completed status. Additionally, users have access to information such as the host in which a task is running, the number of jobs being executed, and the failure history of each task. The Workflow Monitor relies on the information produced by the Workflow Engine and the interaction between these two components takes place via an event mechanism using tuple spaces. In broad terms, whenever the state of a task changes, the monitor is notified and as a response to the event, it retrieves the new state and any relevant task metadata from a central database. Finally, the portal offers users access to a *Resource Monitor Interface* which displays the information of all the current available computing resources. The *Resource Monitor* module in the Monitoring Services component is responsible for the collection of this information.

The *Workflow Engine* is the core of the Cloudbus workflow management system; its main responsibilities include scheduling, dispatching, monitoring, and managing the execution of tasks on remote resources. As shown in Fig. 18.4, the workflow engine has four main subsystems: workflow language parser, scheduler, task dispatcher, and data manager.

The workflow portal or any other client application submits a workflow for execution to the engine. The submitted workflow must be specified in the XML-based language, xWFL. This language enables users to define all the characteristics of a workflow such as tasks and their dependencies among others. Aside from the xWFL file, the engine also requires a service and a credential XML-based description files. The service file describes the resources available for processing tasks while the credentials one defines the security credentials needed to access these resources. The existence of these two files demonstrates the type of distributed platforms the engine was originally designed to work with, platforms where the resources are readily available and their type and number remains static throughout the execution of the workflow. Once the system is upgraded to support clouds, the use of these files will be obsolete as resources will be created and destroyed dynamically.

The xWFL file is then processed and interpreted by a subsystem called the workflow language parser. This subsystem creates objects representing tasks, parameters, data constraints and conditions based on the information contained on the XML file. From this point, these objects will constitute the base of the workflow engine as they are the ones containing all the information regarding the workflow that needs to be executed. Once this information is available, the workflow is scheduled and its tasks are mapped onto resources based on a specific scheduling policy. Next, the engine uses the Cloudbus Broker as a task dispatcher.

The Cloudbus Broker [11] provides a set of services that enable the interaction of the workflow engine with remote resources. It mediates access to the distributed resources by discovering them, deploying and monitoring tasks on specific resources, accessing the required data during task execution and consolidating results. An additional component that aids in the execution of the workflow is the data movement service which enables the transfer of data between the engine and remote resources based on protocols such as FTP and GridFTP.

The workflow engine has a decentralized scheduling system that supports just-in-time planning and allows resource allocation to be determined at runtime. Each task has its own scheduler called Task

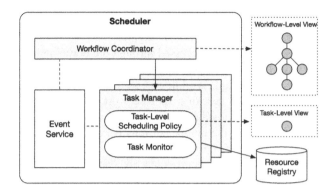

FIGURE 18.5

Key architectural components of the Cloudbus WMS Scheduler

Manager (TM). The TM may implement any scheduling heuristic and is responsible for managing the task processing, resource selection and negotiation, task dispatching and failure handling. At the same time, a Workflow Coordinator (WCO) is responsible for managing the lifetime of every TM as well as the overall workflow execution.

Fig. 18.5 shows the interaction between the different components involved in the scheduling process. The WCO creates and starts a TM based on the task's dependencies and any other specific scheduling heuristic being used. Each TM has a task monitor that continuously checks the status of the remote task and a pool of available resources to which the task can be assigned. The communication between the WCO and the TMs takes place via events registered in a central event service.

Each TM is independent and may have its own scheduling policy, this means that several task managers may run in parallel. Additionally, the behavior of a TM can be influenced by the status of other task managers. For instance, a task manager may need to put its task execution on hold until its parent task finishes running in order for the required input data to be available. For this reason, TMs need to interact with each other just as the WCO needs to interact with every TM; once again this is achieved through events using a tuple space environment.

18.5 CLOUD-BASED EXTENSIONS TO THE WORKFLOW ENGINE

Several extensions and changes were made to the workflow engine component of the Cloudbus WMS in order to support the execution of workflows in IaaS clouds. These extensions allow for scheduling algorithms and resource provisioning strategies to leverage the elastic and on-demand nature of cloud resources, in particular of VMs. The overall architecture of the system and the interaction between the main components remains the same, the extended architecture is shown in Fig. 18.6, where the shaded components are the newly included ones. Each of these components is explained next and a class diagram depicting their implementation is presented in Fig. 18.7.

VM lifecycle manager. A module providing an interface to access VM lifecycle management services offered by IaaS providers. These include leasing, shutting down, restarting, and terminating VMs.

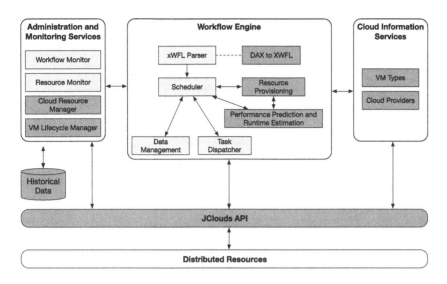

FIGURE 18.6

Key architectural components of the extended Cloudbus WMS

Access to a provider's VM management API is done using Apache JClouds,[3] a Java-based multi-cloud toolkit. It is an open source library that provides portable abstractions for cloud-specific features. It currently supports 30 providers and cloud software stacks such as OpenStack, Amazon, Google, Rackspace, and Azure. The class diagram in Fig. 18.7 shows the methods and IaaS providers currently supported by this module.

The realization of this module also included eliminating the need of having a set of compute services defined in an XML file previous to the execution to the workflow.

Cloud resource manager. An entity responsible of managing the cloud resources used by the engine. It maintains information on the VMs leased from an IaaS provider. Its responsibilities include keeping track of leased, busy, and idle VMs, as well as recording data regarding the lease of VMs such as their lease start and end times.

The following are examples of data that can be accessed through the Cloud Resource Manager:

- Leased VMs: a list of all the VMs that have been leased throughout the lifecycle of the workflow execution.
- Terminated VMs: a list of all the VMs that have been terminated throughout the lifecycle of the workflow execution.
- Active VMs: a list of VMs that are currently leased and active.
- Busy VMs: a list of all VMs that are active and busy with the execution of one or more tasks.
- Idle VMs: a list of all VMs that are active and idle.

---

[3] Apache JClouds http://jclouds.apache.org.

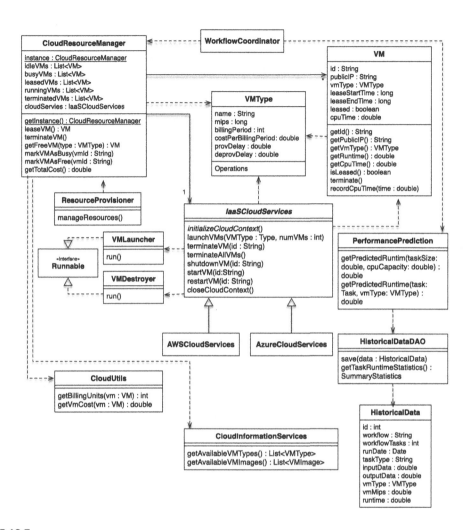

FIGURE 18.7

Class diagram architectural components of the Cloudbus WMS Scheduler

Resource provisioning. An entity responsible of making resource provisioning decisions based on the scheduling objectives and QoS requirements. A basic provisioning strategy was implemented. It monitors the leased VMs every *PROV_POLLING_TIME*. The value for this polling interval is a configurable parameter that can be defined via a properties file. The provisioner then makes the decision to shut VMs down whenever they are idle and approaching their next billing cycle. It does so by considering the time it takes for VMs to be deprovisioned, the time remaining until the VM reaches the next billing cycle, and the time when the next provisioning cycle will occur. If the deprovisioning delay is larger then the time remaining until the next billing cycle then there is no benefit on shutting down the VM as incurring in a new billing cycle is inevitable. Otherwise, the algorithm decides whether the VM can be

---

Algorithm 1 Resource provisioning

1: **procedure** MANAGERESOURCES
2:     VM^{idle} = all leased VMs that are currently idle
3:     **for** each vm_{idle} in VM^{idle} **do**
4:         t_r = time remaining until next billing period
5:         $t_d = Deprovisioning\ delay\ estimate$
6:         **if** $(t_r - t_d \geq 0)$ AND $(t_r - t_d \leq PROV\_POLLING\_TIME)$ **then**
7:             terminate vm_{idle}
8:         **end if**
9:     **end for**
10: **end procedure**

---

left idle and be shutdown on later provisioning cycles without incurring in an additional billing period or if the VM should be deprovisioned in the current cycle to avoid incurring in additional costs. An overview of this strategy is depicted in Algorithm 1. The design provides the flexibility to plug-in different resource provisioning strategies without the need of modifying any other module. For instance, a provisioning strategy that not only decides when to shut-down VMs but also when to lease them based on a utilization metric could also be easily implemented.

Performance prediction and runtime estimation. Two different performance prediction strategies where implemented into a newly created Performance Prediction and Runtime Estimation Module. The first one is a straightforward strategy that allows for the runtime of tasks to be estimated using a measure of the size of a task and the CPU performance of the VM. For this purpose, the xWFL language as well as the existing parser were extended so that the definition of a task includes an optional element indicating its size. In practice, this size can be either the number of instructions (MI), the number of floating point operations (FLOP), or the time complexity of the tasks among others. Additionally, the definition of *compute service* within the engine was extended to include an optional property indicating a measure of the resource's CPU capacity. For this purpose the schema and parsers of the XML-based service file were modified to include the new property as was the *ComputeService* class.

The second strategy is based on the analysis of historical task runtime data. For this purpose, task runtimes are recorded on a historical database which can be later used to estimate the runtime of tasks on particular VM types using statistical tools. The data recorded for each task executed by the engine are depicted in Table 18.1. The current strategy calculates the 95% confidence interval of a task runtime given the task name or type, the workflow it belongs to, the number of tasks in the workflow, the amount of input and output data generated by the task, and the name of the VM type for which the prediction is being made for.

In the future, different prediction algorithms can be seamlessly implemented into this module and used by scheduling algorithms to guide their decisions.

Cloud information services. Through the cloud providers APIs, this module enables the workflow engine to query information regarding the types of services offered by a given provider. Specifically, the implementation leveraged the JClouds API to query the types of VMs available from a given provider as well as the VM images available for use for a given user.

Table 18.1 Contents of the database table recording historical runtime data of tasks

Property	Description
Workflow	Name of the workflow application
Number of Tasks	Total number of tasks in the workflow
Run Date	Date the workflow was deployed
Algorithm	Name of the scheduling algorithm managing the workflow execution
Task Type	Name or type of the workflow task for which the runtime is being recorded
Transferred Input Data	Amount of input data transferred to the task's VM
Transferred Output Data	Amount of output data transferred out of the task's VM
VM Type	Name of the VM type used to run the task
VM CPU Capacity	CPU capacity of the VM type
VM Memory	Memory available for the VM type
VM Bandwidth	Bandwidth of the VM type
Task Runtime	Time taken to complete the task's execution (including input transfer, computations, and output transfer)

DAX to XWFL. The DAX[4] format is a description of an abstract DAG workflow in XML that is used as the primary input into the Pegasus WMS [8], a tool developed at the Information Sciences Institute (ISI), University of Southern California. The extensive research done by this organization in workflows as well as their collaboration with the scientific community makes of the DAX format a popular and commonly used one. For instance, the Pegasus Project[5] has developed a tool in conjunction with the NASA/IPAC project that generates the specification of different Montage workflows in a DAX format. Hence, to take advantage of the existence of these tools as well as workflows described in the DAX format, a DAX-to-xWFL tool was developed as part of this thesis. In this way, the Cloudbus WMS now has the ability to interpret workflows expressed in the DAX format.

Scheduler extension. The existing Scheduler component has been modified to allow the workflow coordinator to have the ability to make scheduling decisions in terms of task to resource mappings. The previous version of the scheduler limited the responsibilities of the coordinator to enforcing the dependency requirements of the workflow. That is, it was responsible for monitoring the status of tasks and releasing those ready for execution by launching their task manager, entity which was then responsible for deciding the resource where the task would be executed. The extended version allows for the workflow coordinator to make all of the scheduling and resource provisioning decisions if required based on its global view of the workflow. Additionally, the WRPS [12] algorithm, which will be introduced in the following section, was implemented and integrated into the workflow coordinator.

---

[4]DAX https://pegasus.isi.edu/documentation/creating_workflows.php.
[5]Pegasus https://pegasus.isi.edu/.

18.6 PERFORMANCE EVALUATION

This section details the deployment of the Montage application on the Cloudbus WMS. The work-flow was scheduled using the WRPS algorithm and Microsoft Azure resources that were dynamically provisioned using the cloud-enabled version of the Cloudbus WMS.

18.6.1 WRPS

WRPS is a resource provisioning and scheduling algorithm for scientific workflows in clouds capable of generating high quality schedules. It has as objectives minimizing the overall cost of using the infrastructure while meeting a user-defined deadline. The algorithm is dynamic to a certain extent to respond to unexpected delays and environmental dynamics common in cloud computing. It also has a static component that allows it to find the optimal schedule for a group of workflow tasks, consequently improving the quality of the schedules it generates. This is done by reducing the workflow into bags of homogeneous tasks and pipelines that share a deadline. The scheduling of these bags is then modeled as a variation of the unbounded knapsack problem which is solved in pseudo-polynomial time using dynamic programming. WRPS considers abundant, heterogeneous, and elastic resources and its provisioning policy results in the VM pool being dynamically scaled in and out throughout the execution of the workflow. For more details, we refer readers to the paper written by Rodriguez and Buyya [12].

18.6.2 MONTAGE

The Montage application is designed to compute mosaics of the sky based on a set of input images. These input images are taken from image archives such as the Two Micron All Sky Survey (2MASS),[6] the Sloan Digital Sky Survey (SDSS),[7] and the Digitised Sky Surveys at the Space Telescope Science Institute.[8] They are first reprojected to the coordinate space of the output mosaic, the background of these reprojected images is then rectified, and finally they are merged together to create the final output mosaic [10].

Fig. 18.8 depicts the structure of the Montage workflow as well as the different computational tasks it performs. The size of the workflow depends on the number of input images used and its structure changes to reflect an increase in the number of inputs, which results in an increase in the number of tasks. For this particular workflow, same-level tasks are of the same type, that is, they perform the same computations but on different sets of data.

The mProjectPP tasks are at the top level of the workflow and hence are the first ones to be executed. They process Flexible Image Transport System (FITS) input images by reprojecting them. There is one mProjectPP task for every FITS input image. In the next level are the mDiffFit tasks. They are responsible for computing the difference between each pair of overlapping images and as a result, their number is determined by the number of overlapping input images. Next is the mConcatFit task, it takes all of the different images as input and fits them using a least squares algorithm. This is a compute-intensive task as a result of its data aggregation nature. The next task is mBgModel which

---

[6]Two Micron All Sky Survey: http://www.ipac.caltech.edu/2mass.
[7]Sloan Digital Sky Survey: http://www.sdss.org.
[8]Digitised Sky Surveys: http://www.stsci.edu/resources/.

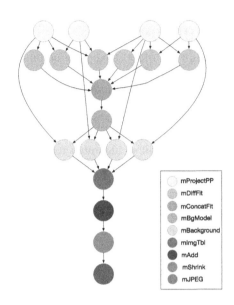

FIGURE 18.8

Sample Montage workflow

determines a background correction to be made to all the images. This correction is the applied to each individual image by the mBackground tasks in the next level of the workflow. Then, the mImgTbl task aggregates metadata from all the images and is followed by the mAdd job. This task is the most computationally intensive and is responsible for the actual aggregation of the images and the creation of the final mosaic. Finally, the size of the final mosaic is reduced by the mShrink task and the output converted to JPEG format by the last workflow task, mJPEG [13].

For this case study, a Montage workflow constructing a 0.5 degree mosaic of the sky was used. This particular instance of the workflow consists of 143 tasks, their type, number, and level are depicted in Table 18.2.

The following are the specific characteristics of the Montage workflow used in this case study:

- Survey, 2mass
- Band, j
- Center, M17
- Width, 0.5
- Height, 0.5

18.6.3 SETUP OF EXPERIMENTAL INFRASTRUCTURE

There are three types of components involved in the execution of a workflow using the Cloudbus WMS. Each of these is deployed on its own compute resource or node. The first component is the actual workflow engine, or *master node*, which is responsible for orchestrating the execution of tasks

Table 18.2 Tasks in a 0.5 degree Montage workflow

Task	Level	Count	Mean runtime (s)	Mean input (MB)	Mean output (MB)
mProjectPP	1	32	35.94	1.66	8.30
mDiffFit	2	73	31.72	16.6	1.02
mConcatFit	3	1	82.99	0.02	0.01
mBgModel	4	1	43.57	0.02	0.001
mBackground	5	32	30.43	8.31	8.30
mImgTbl	6	1	93.92	129.28	0.009
mAdd	7	1	241.50	265.79	51.73
mShrink	8	1	46.43	25.86	6.47
mJPEG	9	1	88.54	6.47	0.20

on *worker nodes*. The lifecycle of these worker nodes is managed by the engine and they contain the actual routines invoked by the workflow tasks. Finally, the *storage node* acts as a central file repository where worker nodes retrieve their input data from and store their output data to. Fig. 18.9 depicts this deployment.

For the experiments performed in this chapter, the VM configuration and location used for each of these components is as follows:

- Master node: Ubuntu 14.4 LTS virtual machine running locally on a MacBook Pro with a 2.9 GHz Intel Core i7 processor and 8 GB RAM. The virtual machine was launched using Virtual Box and had a memory of 2.2 GB and 125.6 GB disk.
- Storage node: Basic A2 Microsoft Azure virtual machine (2 cores, 3.5 GB RAM) with Ubuntu 14.4 LTS installed deployed on the US East region.
- Worker nodes: Dynamically provisioned on Microsoft Azure's US East region using a custom VM image with Montage installed (see Section 18.6.4). The types of VMs where worker nodes could be deployed are depicted in Table 18.3. The A-series are general purpose compute instances while the D-series VMs feature solid state drives (SSDs) and have 60% faster processors than the A-series.

18.6.4 MONTAGE SETUP

This section describes how the Montage routines were setup in the worker nodes VM image. It also explains how the input image files were obtained and how the workflow description XML file was generated.

The Pegasus Project has developed various tools that aid in the deployment of Montage workflows in distributed environments. The installation of Montage on the worker VM image as well as the generation of an XML file describing the workflow were done using these tools.

The first step was to download and install the Montage application, which includes the routines (mProjectPP, mDiffFit, mConcatFit, mBgModel, mBackground, mImgTbl, mAdd, mShrink, and mJPEG) corresponding to each workflow task. For this case study, version 3.3 was installed on a VM running Ubuntu 14.4 LTS. In addition to the task routines, the installation of Montage also includes

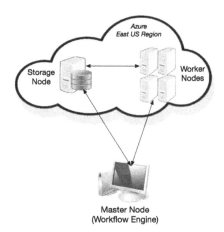

FIGURE 18.9

Cloudbus WMS component deployment

Table 18.3 Types of VMs used to deploy a 0.5 degree Montage workflow

VM name	Cores	RAM (GB)	Disk Size (GB)	Price per minute ($)
A0 (extrasmall)	1	0.75	20	0.000425
A1 (small)	2	1.75	70	0.001275
A2 (medium)	2	3.5	135	0.002548
D1	1	3.5	50	0.001635
D2	2	7	100	0.003270
D11	2	14	100	0.004140

tools used to generate the DAG XML file and download the input image files. Namely, the mDAG and mArchiveExec tools.

The mDAG command generates a DAX XML file containing the description of the workflow in terms of the input files it uses, the tasks, the data dependencies, and the output files produced. This DAX file was then transformed to a xWFL-based one by using the DAX to XWFL tool.

The mArchiveExec command was used to download the input images which were placed in the storage node so that they could be accessed by worker nodes when required.

18.6.5 RESULTS

This section presents the results obtained after executing the 0.5 degree Montage workflow on the Cloudbus WMS under seven different deadlines.

Fig. 18.10A presents the results in terms of the makespan to deadline ratio obtained. The makespan of a workflow is defined as the time it takes for the workflow execution to complete. Ratio values greater than one indicate a makespan larger than the deadline, values equal to one a makespan equal to the deadline, and values smaller than one a makespan smaller than the deadline. Fig. 18.10B depicts

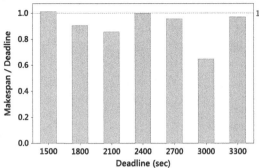

(A) Makespan to deadline ratios obtained for the 0.5 degree Montage execution.

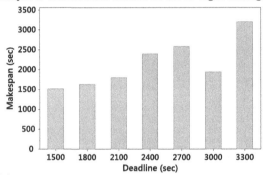

(B) Makespan results obtained for the 0.5 degree Montage execution.

FIGURE 18.10

Makespan and deadline evaluation results for the 0.5 degree Montage execution

the actual makespan values obtained for each deadline. The results presented are the average obtained after running the experiments for each deadline 10 times.

The first deadline of 1500 s is too strict for the workflow execution to be completed on time. On average, it takes approximately 1520 s for the workflow to complete, leading to a ratio of 1.01. This difference between makespan and deadline however is marginal and a 20 s difference is unlikely to have a significant impact on either cost or the usability of the obtained workflow results. The choice of VMs for each deadline interval are presented in Table 18.4. The fact that all of the VMs leased for this deadline interval are of the most powerful VM type (D11), reflects the urgency of the algorithm to complete the workflow execution as fast as possible. The decision to limit the number of VMs to 9 is a direct result of the length of VM provisioning delays. The algorithm recognizes that in some cases it is faster and more efficient to reuse existing VMs rather than leasing new ones.

All of the remaining ratios for the deadlines ranging from 1800 to 3300 s are under one. Clearly, 1800 s is sufficient for the execution of the workflow to complete. This is achieved by leasing 7 D2 VMs and 2 D11 ones. Once again, the deadline is too strict to lease a larger number of VMs but relaxed enough to not have to lease them all of the most powerful type.

Table 18.4 Number of VMs per type leased for the deployment of a 0.5 degree Montage workflow with different deadlines

Deadline (s)	A0	A1	A2	D1	D2	D11
1500	–	–	–	–	–	9
1800	–	–	–	–	7	2
2100	–	13	–	5	–	–
2400	17	2	–	1	–	–
2700	17	2	–	–	–	–
3000	17	–	–	2	–	–
3300	18	–	–	–	–	–

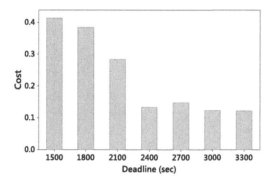

FIGURE 18.11

Cost results obtained for the 0.5 degree Montage execution

As the deadlines becomes more relaxed, WRPS decides it is more efficient to lease a larger number of VMs of less powerful and cheaper types. For a deadline of 2100 s, 13 A1 (small) and 5 D1 VMs are sufficient for the workflow execution to finish well under the deadline with an average ratio of 0.85. From this deadline onwards, the algorithm can finish the workflow execution on time with minimum cost by taking advantage of the cheapest and least powerful VM, the A0 or extra-small. By combining this VM type with more powerful ones when necessary, all of the remaining deadlines are met.

Fig. 18.11 shows the costs of the execution of the workflow for each of the deadlines. As expected, the most expensive scenario occurs when the deadline is the tightest, that is 1500 s. This is a direct result of the provisioning decision to lease the most expensive, and powerful, VM types to finish the execution on time. Overall, except for the deadline of 2400 s, the infrastructure cost consistently decreases as the deadlines become more relaxed. The fact that the cost of running the workflow with a deadline of 2400 s is cheaper than doing it with a deadline of 2700 can be explained by performance and VM provisioning delay variations.

To demonstrate the auto-scaling features introduced into the Cloudbus WMS, Table 18.5 shows the number of VMs used to run the tasks on each level of the Montage workflow for the 2100 s deadline. For the first level mProjectPP tasks, only one A1 VM is used. WRPS estimates that this configuration will allow the mProjectPP tasks to finish by their assigned deadline. The second level

Table 18.5 Number and type of VMs used on the execution of each level of the 0.5 degree Montage workflow with a deadline of 2100 s

Level	Task	Count	A0	A1	A2	D1	D2	D11
1	mProjectPP	32	–	1	–	–	–	–
2	mDiffFit	73	–	13	–	5	–	–
3	mConcatFit	1	–	1	–	–	–	–
4	mBgModel	1	–	1	–	–	–	–
5	mBackground	32	–	1	–	–	–	–
6	mImgTbl	1	–	1	–	–	–	–
7	mAdd	1	–	1	–	–	–	–
8	mShrink	1	–	1	–	–	–	–
9	mJPEG	1	–	1	–	–	–	–

of the workflow contains 73 mDiffFit tasks. Unlike the mProjectPP tasks, these tasks have different starting times, depending on when their mProjectPP parent tasks finished their execution. Based on this, WRPS makes the decision to scale the number of VMs out as mDiffFit tasks become ready for execution. At this point, 13 A1 VMs and 5 D1 Vms, 18 in total, are used to process all the 73 tasks in the level. Next, the parallelism of the workflow is reduced by a data aggregation task, mConcatFit, and as a result the resource pool is scaled in and only one VM of type A1 is left in the resource pool. The next level contains a single mBgModel task and the VM used in the previous level is reused. For the 32 mBackground tasks, WRPS decides they can finish on time by reusing the existing A1 VM. The remaining levels in the workflow contain a single task and hence there is no need to lease more VMs and the workflow finishes its execution with a single A1 VM.

The experiments presented in this section demonstrate how the elasticity and heterogeneity of cloud resources can be leveraged to meet the QoS requirements of workflow applications. In particular, they demonstrate how the performance of the workflow execution in terms of time as well as the cost of using the cloud infrastructure can be controlled by dynamically scaling the number of resources. This enables scientists to benefit from the flexibility, scalability, and pricing model offered by cloud computing. However, evaluating the performance of the Cloudbus WMS with different scheduling algorithms and with larger scientific workflows that have different data and computational requirements and topological structures is an essential future task. In addition to this, as a future work, it is important to evaluate the performance of workflow executions deployed on different cloud providers with different billing periods, VM types, provisioning and deprovisioning delays, and resource performance variations.

18.7 SUMMARY AND CONCLUSIONS

This chapter presented the use of WMSs in cloud computing environments. These distributed platforms offer several advantages for the deployment of scientific applications that stem mainly from their use of virtualized resources and their economic model. For scientific workflows in particular, these benefits include the illusion of unlimited resources, the flexibility of leasing and releasing VMs of different configurations on-demand, paying only for what is used, and the support for legacy applications and experiment reproducibility through virtualization, among others.

We presented a reference architecture for cloud WMSs and explained its key components which include a user interface with workflow modeling tools and submission services, a workflow engine capable of making resource provisioning and scheduling decisions, a set of task and resource monitoring tools, and a set of cloud information services that can be queried to retrieve the supported cloud providers and the type of resources they offer. We then introduced a concrete example of an existing system, the Cloudbus WMS, along with our efforts to extend its functionality to support the elastic cloud resource model. Finally, we demonstrated with a practical scenario the use of the enhanced Cloudbus WMS by deploying a Montage workflow on Microsoft Azure.

The development of cloud-based tools for the deployment of scientific workflows is an emerging field. Systems developed for grids and clusters are being extended to support the cloud resource model and new ones are being developed to support the specific features of the cloud computing paradigm. An example of the latter one is the Workflow as a Service (WaaS) service model. This type of platforms offer to manage the execution of scientific workflows submitted by multiple users on cloud resources at the Platform or Software as a Service level. A recent step towards this is presented by Esteves and Veiga [14]. They define a prototypical middleware framework that embodies the vision of a WaaS system and address issues such as workflow description and WMS integration, cost model, and resource allocation. Hence, as the popularity and use of cloud computing becomes more widespread, so will services such as WaaS.

REFERENCES

[1] Y. Gil, E. Deelman, M. Ellisman, T. Fahringer, G. Fox, D. Gannon, C. Goble, M. Livny, L. Moreau, J. Myers, Examining the challenges of scientific workflows, IEEE Comput. 40 (12) (2007) 26–34.

[2] J. Yu, R. Buyya, A novel architecture for realizing grid workflow using tuple spaces, in: Proceedings of the Fifth IEEE/ACM International Workshop on Grid Computing, IEEE, 2004, pp. 119–128.

[3] U. Yildiz, A. Guabtni, A.H. Ngu, Business versus scientific workflows: a comparative study, in: Proceedings of the Fourth World Conference on Services (SERVICES), IEEE, 2009, pp. 340–343.

[4] A. Barker, J. Van Hemert, Scientific workflow: a survey and research directions, in: Parallel Processing and Applied Mathematics, Springer, 2008, pp. 746–753.

[5] T. Fahringer, R. Prodan, R. Duan, J. Hofer, F. Nadeem, F. Nerieri, S. Podlipnig, J. Qin, M. Siddiqui, H.-L. Truong, et al., Askalon: a development and grid computing environment for scientific workflows, in: Workflows for e-Science, Springer, 2007, pp. 450–471.

[6] B. Ludäscher, I. Altintas, C. Berkley, D. Higgins, E. Jaeger, M. Jones, E.A. Lee, J. Tao, Y. Zhao, Scientific workflow management and the Kepler system, Concurr. Comput., Pract. Exp. 18 (10) (2006) 1039–1065.

[7] K. Wolstencroft, R. Haines, D. Fellows, A. Williams, D. Withers, S. Owen, S. Soiland-Reyes, I. Dunlop, A. Nenadic, P. Fisher, et al., The Taverna workflow suite: designing and executing workflows of web services on the desktop, web or in the cloud, Nucleic Acids Res. 41 (W1) (2013) W557–W561.

[8] E. Deelman, K. Vahi, G. Juve, M. Rynge, S. Callaghan, P.J. Maechling, R. Mayani, W. Chen, R.F. da Silva, M. Livny, et al., Pegasus, a workflow management system for science automation, Future Gener. Comput. Syst. 46 (2015) 17–35.

[9] J. Yu, R. Buyya, A taxonomy of workflow management systems for grid computing, J. Grid Comput. 3 (3–4) (2005) 171–200.

[10] E. Deelman, G. Singh, M. Livny, B. Berriman, J. Good, The cost of doing science on the cloud: the montage example, in: Proceedings of the 2008 ACM/IEEE Conference on Supercomputing, IEEE Press, 2008, p. 50.

[11] S. Venugopal, K. Nadiminti, H. Gibbins, R. Buyya, Designing a resource broker for heterogeneous grids, Softw. Pract. Exp. 38 (8) (2008) 793–825.

[12] M.A. Rodriguez, R. Buyya, A responsive knapsack-based algorithm for resource provisioning and scheduling of scientific workflows in clouds, in: Proceedings of the Forty-Fourth International Conference on Parallel Processing (ICPP), vol. 1, IEEE, 2015, pp. 839–848.

[13] G. Juve, A. Chervenak, E. Deelman, S. Bharathi, G. Mehta, K. Vahi, Characterizing and profiling scientific workflows, Future Gener. Comput. Syst. 29 (3) (2013) 682–692.

[14] S. Esteves, L. Veiga, WaaS: workflow-as-a-service for the cloud with scheduling of continuous and data-intensive workflows, Comput. J. 59 (3) (2016) 371–383.

LOOKING AHEAD

OUTLOOK AND FUTURE DIRECTIONS

19

Maritta Heisel*, Rami Bahsoon[†], Nour Ali[‡], Bruce Maxim[§], Ivan Mistrik[¶]

*Universität Duisburg-Essen, Germany [†]University of Birmingham, UK [‡]University of Brighton, UK [§]University of Michigan-Dearborn, USA [¶]Independent Researcher, Germany

The last decade has seen a paradigm shift in software engineering due to the need of software to process huge amounts of data. This book has extensively discussed several approaches that make use of cloud systems and the processing of big data. However, the current situation will not be the end of the story. The development towards ever larger quantities of data has just begun. Big data is not only about the volume of data but also about the efficiency, velocity, value, and other aspects. The resources of the cloud promise to achieve big data characteristics. This situation will lead to even more and new challenges for software architecture in the context of big data and cloud computing.

In the following, we discuss new trends, challenges and opportunities concerning the future use of big data and clouds, and their impact on software architecture. Being able to handle huge amounts of data and to share computing resources in a cloud make it possible to offer entirely new applications to society. Existing applications will advance and will have the potential to become much more powerful than they are today. In Section 19.1, we highlight some of these new or advanced applications. In Section 19.2 we discuss advances of technologies that support advances in big data applications. In addition, a number of architecturally significant requirements (see Chapter 1 of this book) will be crucial to handle big data and cloud applications in the future. These requirements and their relevance for software architecture are discussed in more detail in Section 19.3. To achieve such requirements, in turn, the architecting processes that are followed in the development of new and advanced applications have to be adjusted accordingly. Section 19.4 presents some of the challenges that architectural processes will face in the future. Of course, this chapter cannot completely cover all of the trends, challenges and opportunities that will shape the future of big data and clouds. In line with its high importance, this topic continuously gains attention. Section 19.5 points readers to other works for further reading.

19.1 NEW OR ADVANCED APPLICATIONS

In the future, gigabytes will not be a relevant quantity of data anymore. Instead, larger chunks of data will be processed on a regular basis, such as terabytes and petabytes. Billions (not only millions) of devices will be connected to the Internet and constantly emit data that will have to be collected and processed. This makes it possible to offer entirely new applications for individuals as well as enterprises, for example, sophisticated ambient-assisted living and remote healthcare systems. Other applications such as social networks and recommender systems will become much more widespread or much more powerful, because the amount of data that can be handled will increase by orders of magnitude. Even today, we can see that our daily lives have changed considerably, because portable devices are continuously connected to the Internet. We constantly upload data, we stay in contact with friends and relatives, and we use more and more sophisticated web services. This is only possible because enormous amounts of data are produced and processed. In the future, new and advanced applications will change our lives even more profoundly. In the following, we briefly describe several advanced or new applications. Further applications (as sources of big data) are enumerated by Yang et al. [8].

Lifelogging. Today, only a relatively limited number of people use activity trackers to measure their body functions (called lifelogging) and obtain statistics about their health and fitness. In the future, this number will grow dramatically. Many existing apps provide advice for a healthy style of living based on data they gather. Such data are not only of value to their producers, but also to third parties. For example, health insurance companies could offer special rates to those users who are willing to share their health data on a regular basis. On the one hand, such applications can contribute much to the well-being of individuals and significantly reduce the costs needed for health systems. On the other hand, however, such applications come with severe risks for privacy.

Ambient-assisted living. In societies where the percentage of elderly people is growing, there is a huge demand to enable elderly people to live at home as long as possible. In ambient-assisted living, the homes of elderly people are equipped with sensors that can detect health problems of a person, for example, when a person falls to the ground and cannot get up again. In such a case, a healthcare provider could be notified automatically. Furthermore, appliances could react to verbal commands, supporting elderly people in their daily activities. Such systems will be of great benefit to individuals and the society; however, they have to be trustworthy.

Internet of Things. The Internet of Things (IoT) is characterized by the fact that sensor networks connect incredible numbers of small devices to the Internet. These devices send their data in regular intervals. All of that sensor data have to be transmitted, (partially) stored, filtered, cleaned, and processed, i.e., big data management techniques have to be used. These techniques will have to be further developed. In particular, to make sense of orders of magnitude more data than is available today will be an extraordinary technological challenge. Based on the sensor data, appropriate actions have to be launched. Such actions depend on the context. For example, the owner of a house could be notified that the stove is turned on even if nobody is at home, or the traffic lights in a city can be controlled according to the overall volume of traffic in the city.

Smart Xs. The Internet of Things is a prerequisite for the advent of smart grids, smart homes, smart cities, smart engineering, and other "smart" applications. For example, smart grids allow consumers of electricity to control their electric appliances so that they are turned on when the price for electricity is low. Furthermore, contracts with electricity providers can be changed frequently, optimizing the cost for power consumption. Smart grids are beneficial because they reduce the overall power consumption and cost of power consumers, but also come with a privacy risk. Smart cities and engineering plants optimize traffic and production flows, but can also be subject to attacks. Apart from compromising security, cyber-attacks can also produce safety risks. When critical infrastructures break down or hospitals are made inoperable, human lives are at stake. Therefore, resilience is an important requirement for smart Xs.

Social Networks. Billions of people use social networks today, and their number will rise in the future. Already today, a study indicates that only the spouse knows a person better than Facebook does. With more data being collected about individuals and better possibilities for analyzing that data, severe privacy issues may arise that have to be addressed. Unfortunately, users of social network sites do not have as much influence on what happens to their data as this would be desirable. A challenge for the future is to empower users, providing them with means to better protect their privacy and to exercise more control over their data.

Recommender Systems. Such systems, even though common already today, will grow in importance and also in power in the future. The amount of data on which a recommendation can be based will grow drastically. However, this does not necessarily mean that the recommendations become more reliable. Recommender systems have to be developed further in such a way that users can better assess the credibility of the given recommendations. Furthermore, recommender systems should be able to adapt to their users, taking characteristics of their personality into account. For such systems (as for social networks), psychology can and should inform software development.

Personalized services. Future cloud and big data technologies will allow personalized services for many people, and the automation of large parts of public services and infrastructures. Such services come with service-level agreements (SLA) that must be met. These may concern performance, but also security and privacy. Measures must be taken at runtime if a service violates the SLA. This involves to develop and apply mechanisms to constantly monitor the fulfillment of the SLA and also mechanisms to replace a service with another one when the SLA is violated. Replacing services is a highly nontrivial task that needs powerful component infrastructures.

Rapid market development. Enterprises will be able to react to changing market conditions much faster than today, because there are more data on which decisions can be based on, and these data can be analyzed in almost real time despite of their size. For example, insurance companies will be able to offer personalized contracts to different groups of people, and to adjust such contracts on a daily basis. The contracts are based on proprietary information such as insurance cases of the company, e.g., how many damage adjustments the insurance company had to make for cases of burglary. In the future, such information will be combined with other sources, for example, police data about committed burglaries in a certain area. In this way, insurance companies can assess the risk for damage adjustments in a much more fine-grained and reliable way than this is possible today.

Homeland security. Our society feels more and more threatened by terrorists and criminals. Public video surveillance will become more widespread than is the case today. Video surveillance produces huge amounts of data, and such data will have to be analyzed automatically. For example, if a video shows a person committing a crime, then that person should be recognized automatically as soon as he or she enters the range of another video camera. US Customs are experimenting with IT-based systems to identify people "who wish to do harm or violate U.S. laws" (see https://www.dhs.gov/obim-biometric-identification-services) when they enter the country. In the future, such systems will become more reliable, because of a broader database and the usage of more sophisticated learning algorithms. There are also attempts to predict the occurrence of crimes. For example, to predict where burglaries will be committed in the next few days, or even using demographic data to predict if an individual will commit a crime in the near future. However, such applications bear a risk of false accusations. Society has to find ways to deal with this problem.

19.2 ADVANCED SUPPORTING TECHNOLOGIES

The innovative applications discussed in Section 19.1 can only be developed successfully when there is also innovation in the underlying supporting technologies.

Machine learning. Machine learning will play a major role in aggregating data to information that humans can interpret. The vast amount of available data also supports machine learning algorithms to work successfully. Sophisticated data analytics algorithms need machine learning techniques. The challenge here is that the learning process must take place in a distributed environment [8].

Data visualization. The importance of data visualization will increase, as organizations relying on big data technology require faster access to useable and comprehensible presentations of the results of data analytics. According to Assunção et al. [2], visualization is needed to support descriptive, predictive, and prescriptive data analysis. These different tasks call for different kinds of visualization approaches. Visualization should not be hampered because of transferring the data to be visualized over a network, which leads to performance issues.

System Interfaces. Big data analytics is challenging and time consuming, requiring expensive software, enormous computational infrastructure and effort. Standards will need to be developed along with new APIs (application programming interfaces) to allow practitioners to switch among analytic products and data sources. New languages will have to be developed to describe data in such a way that big data analytics is supported best. Steps in this direction are the Predictive Model Markup Language (PMML) and the Google Prediction API, as discussed by Assunção et al. [2].

Computing platforms. The most important big data computing paradigm is MapReduce and its implementation Hadoop. With this paradigm, big data processing has become possible at all. MapReduce is an instance of the "data at rest" principle, where data are stored and different queries can be processed on that data. Complex event processing, on the other hand, is an instance of the "data in flight" principle, where the query on the data is fixed, and the query is evaluated on the incoming data, without the need to store the data. Further development of novel computing platforms can be expected, combining the "data at rest" and "data in flight" principles.

Cloud platforms and deployments. Due to their enormous storage requirements, big data applications often make use of cloud platforms. Such platforms may be different in nature (e.g., public or private), but usually offer a set of services, concerning, for example, the configuration of applications, data management, and security. We can expect that those services will be enhanced and augmented in the future. However, the diversity of the services makes it difficult to migrate between different cloud platforms. The question how a migration can be achieved smoothly will deserve more attention in the future.

NoSQL data bases. In the past, relational databases were the most common ones. With a unified data model and the common structured query language SQL, they offered a functionality that met the demands of many applications involving data management. However, relational data bases are not suitable for treating data that stem from various sources and do not adhere to a unique data model. Therefore, NoSQL databases have been developed. They can cope with diverse data and distribution, and they support hyperscalability (see Section 19.3), but come with proprietary APIs (application programming interfaces), which makes porting applications more difficult. Among the new kinds of NoSQL databases that have already been developed are document databases, key-value databases, column-oriented data bases, and graph databases [3,4]. It can be expected that more such novel kinds of data bases will emerge in the future, revolutionizing the way in which big data can be stored and retrieved.

New Cloud Paradigms. Apart from Infrastructure as a Service (IaaS), Platform as a Service (PaaS), and Software as a Service (SaaS), new cloud paradigms have already emerged. They include Data as a Service, Analytics as a Service, Model as a Service, and Storage as a Service [2]. We can imagine that more kinds of useful cloud services will be developed in the future. They will free cloud customers from many tasks that they have to carry out themselves currently, which will lead to an increase in developer productivity and foster a much larger adoption of cloud computing in the future than is currently the case.

Risk management. Big data and cloud computing come with significant risks. Some of them are mentioned in Section 19.1. First and foremost, privacy and security risks have to be mentioned here. However, there also is a considerable risk to draw false conclusions from big data analytics, which puts the entire goal of the analytics in question. Thus, entire business models may turn out to be invalid. Therefore, risk management must accompany big data and cloud applications during their entire lifetime. Risk is composed of the likelihood of an unwanted incident and the negative consequences of that unwanted incident on an asset. Risk management consists of risk identification, risk evaluation, and risk assessment. If an identified risk is assessed to be unacceptable, appropriate risk reduction measures have to be taken. While risk management is common in the context of safety and security-critical systems, it is not yet common to apply it to big data analytics.

Privacy and Security Mechanisms. To reduce privacy and security risks, appropriate mechanisms have to be applied. Currently, such mechanisms consist mainly of encryption or access control. For the novel applications coming with big data and clouds, these simple mechanisms will not suffice any more. For example, homomorphic encryption is a relatively new mechanism that makes it possible to process encrypted data, without the need to decrypt the data before processing. However, the computations that are possible on the encrypted data today are very simple. To support big data analytics on encrypted data, more research is necessary. There also is a need to develop better mechanisms for user empowerment. An example are sticky policies. Here, a security policy is attached to critical data. Such a policy may demand that the data are deleted after some time. However, to date there are no infrastructures available to enforce such policies.

19.3 ARCHITECTURALLY SIGNIFICANT REQUIREMENTS

The novel applications and the further development of their supporting technologies as discussed in the previous sections have far-reaching consequences for advancing the state for the art in software architecture. They result in a number of architecturally significant requirements, as introduced in Chapter 1 of this book. Such requirements are quality requirements (also called nonfunctional requirements), whose fulfillment have an influence on the software architecture of an IT-based system. The architecturally significant requirements are not new; most of them have been discussed extensively in this book. Here, we highlight the importance of these requirements for future developments.

The five Vs. These characteristics of big data, namely Volume, Velocity, Variety, Veracity, and Value, have been drivers for new technologies in recent years. For example, the Variety property spawned the development of NoSQL data bases. Focusing on such characteristics leads to fruitful new research and also new architectural solutions. In the future, it is to be expected that further crucial characteristics of big data and clouds will be discovered (Assunção et al. [2], for example, name "Viability" as a new V) that will lead to further progress in big data and cloud technologies.

Hyper-scalability. As discussed in Chapter 2 of this book, a crucial property of big data systems is their ability to scale in much more extreme ways than this was necessary (and possible) before big data processing came up. Hyperscalable systems are able to support an exponential growth in computing requests even though the available resources only grow linearly. This is an amazing property, which became possible due to a number of principles, such as automation, optimization, simplification, and observability (see Chapter 2). In the future, more mechanisms will have to be found and applied in order to preserve hyperscalability in the presence of the ever-increasing growth rates of big data.

Distribution. Most of the novel applications mentioned above are distributed and rely on the Internet. The distribution of data – though necessary – entails a number of problems that have to be dealt with and need innovation in the future. In Section 19.2, we already mentioned that learning algorithms need to function on distributed data, and that the visualization of distributed data can cause performance problems. Even though distributed data do not suffer from a single point of failure or attack, media report on successful cyber-attacks, involving data theft, or distributed denial-of-service (DDoS) attacks almost every week. However, the existence of enterprises relies on the availability of their services. Client–server systems as they are common today are not robust enough against failure of parts of the Internet, due to, for example, DDoS attacks or censorship by governments. More resilient ways of distribution are necessary, for example, by using peer-to-peer architectures where appropriate. Such architectures are used only sparsely today, because of the large communication overhead involved. A clever combination of client–server and peer-to-peer architectures could lead to more robust services.

Adaptivity. Almost all of the new or advanced applications will need to be adapted to different users and changing circumstances. MAPE-K [5] is an architectural blueprint for self-adaptive systems. It stands for Monitor-Analyze-Plan-Execute plus Knowledge. A monitor component observes events that happen in the environment of the system. The analysis component interprets these events. This is the basis for planning appropriate actions, which are determined by the planning component. The execute component is responsible for enacting the generated plan. All components make use of a common knowledge base. To instantiate such an architectural blueprint in the context of big data and clouds is challenging because of the amount of data to be taken into account for adaptation and the distributed nature of the data sources.

Resilience. In the future, our society will be entirely dependent on functioning computing power and software. Critical infrastructures will be connected to the Internet, and hence can be subject to attacks or failures. Therefore, future systems need to be much more resilient than this is the case today. This involves the need to identify attacks or other adverse circumstances, and to adapt or otherwise react to those circumstances. Developing resilient software architectures will be one of the major challenges for the future.

Trustworthiness. This property is (among others) related to reliability, resilience, security, and performance. It means that users of a system can justifiably place trust in it. For different systems, different properties may be necessary to achieve trustworthiness. For example, in an ambient-assisted living system, it is important that the system correctly identifies health problems of the elderly person and notifies the health care provider in a timely manner, always preserving the privacy of the person. However, trustworthiness cannot be just reduced to these other properties. We also need components in the software architecture that demonstrate to the users that the trustworthiness properties are indeed fulfilled. This is especially difficult for machine learning systems whose specific behavior cannot be predicted from their design only but relies data fed into the learning process as well.

Privacy and Security. While the development of new technologies allowing better services and more automation is certainly welcome, there are also some risks coming with these new technologies that should be taken into account and treated accordingly by research, industry, and politics right from the beginning. With more data being collected about individuals and better possibilities for analyzing that data, severe privacy issues may arise that have to be addressed. But not only privacy, but also security and safety may be at stake. When important public and industrial facilities are connected to the Internet, they will be subject to attacks. The same is true for data stored in clouds. The results of big data processing are only reliable when the underlying data are correct and reliable, and in particular have not been tampered with by attackers. Apart from compromising security, cyber-attacks can also produce safety risks. Therefore, privacy, security, safety, and trust should receive more attention from software architects and data scientists than has been the case in the past. As far as software architecture is concerned, not only software components implementing cryptographic mechanisms or firewalls are needed. Users will need to be empowered to a much larger extent than today. This will involve specific user interface components allowing users to grant or withdraw consent to collect and process their data, informing users about processing, use, and visibility of their data. Since different users have different needs, such components must be personalized and also should be able to adapt to the user (see Adaptivity). Enterprises, in turn, are threatened in their existence by cyber-attacks. Especially when they use clouds, they are no longer in full control of their assets. Security mechanisms must be incorporated in cloud architectures that give reliable security guarantees for cloud customers.

Standards and Certification. Cloud providers must be able to provide credible assurance that they protect their customers' data according to best practices. Today, the ISO 27000 series of standards requires enterprises to develop and maintain a so-called information security management system (ISMS). Such an ISMS not only covers software, but the entire organization of the enterprise. However, establishing an ISMS also needs to implement security controls, thus influencing the software architecture of the software systems used by the enterprise. Currently, only few enterprises are certified according to the ISO 27000 series or other security standards, such as the Common Criteria (ISO/IEC 15408). In the future, this will change drastically, not only because of compliance requirements arising from legislation (see next point), but also because a growing number of attacks will raise the demand for security guarantees.

Compliance. Today, we see a trend toward new regulations and laws concerning data security and privacy. For example, the European Union has passed a new data protection regulation to better protect the privacy of individuals. Furthermore, it is discussed if enterprises will be obliged to report attacks on their IT. Hence, being compliant to the legislation will oblige enterprises and governmental organizations not only to implement protection mechanisms, but also to demonstrate that they have acted according to best practices. Compliance issues have an influence on software architecture, for example, because logging components will have to be integrated in the architecture.

19.4 CHALLENGES FOR THE ARCHITECTING PROCESS

Having identified the architecturally significant requirements that play a role in big data and cloud applications in the future, we now consider the challenges architecting processes will need to cope with.

Systems of Systems and their emergent properties. The use of clouds and big data will go hand in hand with the development of Systems of Systems (SoS) that combine independently developed smaller systems to bigger and more powerful ones with increased complexity and emergent behavior. Such SoS have a high demand of flexibility and adaptability, depending on large amounts of data which are stored in a distributed way. Future applications will be much more complex than they are today. This will result in the need of more advanced engineering methods. For example, the architecting process must take into account how the different subsystems can interoperate to achieve a common goal ("glue architecture"). Furthermore, the emergent properties of the composition must be determined, and it must be decided if they are desirable or not.

Balancing and integrating different architecturally significant requirements. Even though most of the above-mentioned requirements will be relevant for the majority of the novel applications coming with big data and clouds, not all of them will be of equal importance, and some of them might be negligible. Hence, the architecting process must balance the architecturally significant requirements to arrive at an optimal architecture. Performance, for example, conflicts with most other architecturally significant requirements. Therefore, it will not be possible just to add components to the architecture, addressing the different architecturally significant requirements. Instead, clever strategies for reconciling conflicting requirements and approaches for optimizing architectures will be needed.

Evolutionary development. In the future, more applications will make use of big data and clouds. This will involve problems of migration to a different database technology or between different computing and cloud platforms. Hence, software architects have to address the challenge of supporting the migration process. Evolutionary development could be an approach to do so. Here, iterative and incremental development processes are applied. It is to be investigated which aspects of an application are likely to change and which ones are not. The software architecture then should reflect this assessment, because evolutionary development is only successful when changes are cheap and easy to accomplish.

Architecting for hyper and unbounded scale for cloud and big data architecture. Cloud infrastructure, which is essentially as a high-performance service-oriented computing paradigm, is continuously evolving. New computing paradigms which leverage the cloud's capabilities such as Edge, Fog, distributed and federation models, microservices, and the Internet of Things (IoT) have been emerging. As described in Chapter 1 of this book, new architecture significant requirements that are cloud related result from the shared environment, its hyperconnectivity, and continuous evolution. Cloud architecture significant requirements call researchers and practitioners to rethink their practices, which should be aware of cloud fundamentals that relate to elastic computing, dynamism and autoscaling, multitenancies of the cloud, value-driven design for utilizing economies of scale, SLA-centric design in support for multitenancies, to name but a few. The awareness of these requirements challenges the way we systematically architect software systems that operate on the cloud – partially or in whole; interface with other cloud-based services and/or part of the evolving cloud ecosystem. These requirements essentially affect the way we define processes which are cloud-specific; where design and architecture processes should be steered by environment uncertainties, risks mitigation strategies, trade-offs, likely evolution of the services and application ecosystem itself, and the inviting unbounded scale. This transforms the architecting design process into a globally distributed and decentralized exercise, where architecture knowledge and unified design decisions are difficult to incept, elaborate, evaluate, trace and negotiate for conflicts, risks and trade-offs. The challenge calls for cloud-centric architecting processes and tooling support that facilitate architecting in the "wild" and leverage on diversity and wealth of inputs to reach sound and efficient architecture solutions for cloud-based applications and services. In particular, we need to

- define processes which are cloud-aware and embrace decentralization and distribution of the architecting process;
- evaluate architecture design decisions, where cloud-specific properties are core determinants for solutions;
- define cloud-specific architecture knowledge and tooling support which leverage the benefits of diversity, multiperspectives of inputs, etc.;
- provide tooling support for managing and tracing design decisions in the "wild";
- define styles and family of patterns which are suited for given distribution and decentralization contexts.

Multitenancy and service-level agreement-centric architecture solutions. As discussed in Chapter 1, cloud architecturally significant requirements do have measurable effects and can be observed on Services Level Agreements (SLA) compliance and violations. The choice of architecture design decisions should be essentially SLA-aware; where SLA promises should mandate design decisions and choices. Conversely, architecture design decisions and choices need to inform, refine and elaborate SLAs. The process is continuous and is not restricted to the development and predeployment phases. It should be "live" during the operation and evolution of the cloud-software system. The process is intertwined and interleaved and needs to be informed by requirements of various multitenants. The challenge is that the process has to reconcile various multitenant requirements and their constraints, while not compromising the overall "welfare" of the shared environment. This makes architecting rather complex exercise and calls for new approaches for architecting for multitenancy taking into account multiple users in a given tenancy and across multiple ones. Architects need to consider the diverse needs, wishes, context, requirements, and quality-of-services constraints within and across tenants. Architects need to predict what may seem unpredictable from likely changes in requirements, within and across tenants. They also need to consider how changes that relate to adapting to new environments that relate to the cloud, such as mobility, Fog, Edge, Internet of Things (IoT), and federation, can affect design decisions and their evolution over time. Architects need to formulate design decisions and tactics that are flexible enough to cater for continuous changes in users' requirements in a single tenancy and across multitenancy. This calls for novel architecture-centric frameworks that elicit, define, model, evaluate, and realize the commonality, variability, veracity, diversity, and scale of both functional and nonfunctional requirements supporting the individuals, tenants, and the operating environment. These solutions should also provide mechanisms for ensuring fairness and preventing "greed" in situations where providers stretch the economies of scale, by accommodating more than what the environment can normally handle.

Architecting for the unbounded data scale. As explained in Chapter 1, the unbounded scalability of the cloud and its various service layers have "accidentally" lead to "data farming", due to the volume, veracity, and variety of data accumulated and/or assimilated across various service cloud layers and constituent architectural components. There are two fundamental aspects that have changed the way data needs to be processed and thus needs a complete paradigm shift: the size of data has evolved to the amount that it has become intractable by existing data management systems, and the rate of change in data is so rapid that processing also needs to happen in real-time. With analysts estimating data storage growth at 30% to 60% per year, organizations must develop a long-term strategy to address the challenges of managing projects that analyze exponentially growing data sets with predictable linear costs [Ian Gorton, March 7, 2016 – SEI, Pittsburgh]. Henceforth, architecture processes and design decisions shall have managing data, its growth evolution and decay in the heart of the inception, elaboration, evaluation, and operations processes. The process shall provide systematic treatment for architecturally significant requirements that are data related. The treatment shall align the organization's strategies, their long-term business objectives and priorities with the technical decisions for the way data management is designed as a first-class architecture entity. In particular, the architecting process shall explicitly look at effective, efficient and scalable solutions for the way data are assimilated, aggregated, classified and at their intelligent data analysis. Concerns which relate to data security, privacy, scalability, performance, availability, and integrity and associated trade-offs are among the architecture significant requirements that influence architecture design decisions. The choice of data models, their portability, and expressiveness become another first-class concern in the architecting process. The choice is particularly important not only for managing data but for unlocking its potentials in enabling new applications.

Architecting for ubiquitous cloud-based and big data driven systems. The volume of data, especially machine-generated data, is exploding; it is remarkable how fast that data is growing every year, with new sources of data that are emerging. For example, in the year 2000, 800,000 petabytes of data were stored in the world, and it is expected to reach 35 zettabytes by 2020 (according to IBM). Social media plays a key role. Twitter generates 7+ terabytes of data every day. Facebook, 10 terabytes. Mobile devices play a key role as well, as there were estimated 6 billion mobile phones in 2011. Driven by the needs to handle ever growing data collection and integrate diverse applications into systems of systems, scalability is the dominant quality attribute factor for many contemporary software architectures [4]. Architecting for scalability, while ensuring ubiquity and privacy, continues to be one of the challenges that confront architects. This calls for defining and/or extrapolating architecture styles and patterns which have been successful in embracing ubiquity while promising to deliver on other nonfunctional trade-offs.

Ethical-centric architecting for privacy and security. With more data being collected about individuals and better possibilities for analyzing that data, severe privacy issues may arise that have to be addressed as of the architecting phase. The widespread (and often unauthorized) collection of data poses several ethical concerns. Software architects need to become more concerned about how data will be used within the solution and/or within the cloud ecosystem. The architecting inception, elaboration and construction processes should give explicit attention to the benefits and risks of exploiting data and its modalities in the connected world. Architects need to weigh the risks and benefits of exploiting the data; their practices and architecture design choices should seriously look at the potentials of big data practices to further increase the divide between technology haves and have nots. As already mentioned, cyber-attacks can also produce safety risks. Therefore, privacy, security, safety, and trust should require greater attention from software architects and data scientists than it has in the past. Academic computing programs will be pressured to raise the awareness for issues that relate to ethical-centric architecting, architecting for privacy and security and related trade-offs. This cannot be underestimated as a strategy in educating future architects and software engineers for modern distribution paradigms.

19.5 **FURTHER READING**

Recently, a number of publications discussing future trends and challenges for big data and clouds have appeared. Not all of them focus on software architectures. We summarize some of these papers to give the interested reader hints for further information on this topic.

Assunção et al. [2] discuss trends and future directions for big data computing and clouds. They give a thorough overview of data management techniques, including the different "Vs", data storage, integration, processing, and resource management. In the context of model building and scoring, they mention "Data as a Service" as a new cloud computing paradigm, and new languages and APIs to support data analytics. Furthermore, they discuss the role of visualization and user interaction, as well as potential new business models from "Analytics as a Service."

Anagnostopoulos et al. [1] focus on big data, taking a more technical point of view. They describe and compare several Hadoop-based platforms according to the possibility to perform real-time analytics, support for data integration, and supported application domains. Then they systematically analyze the challenges that are relevant for the different tasks in big data management, namely data cleansing, acquisition and capture; storage, sharing and transfer; analysis and collection of results. Ethical considerations are also taken into account.

Nasser and Tariq [6] discuss data challenges (with respect to the different "Vs" and other properties, namely quality, discovery and dogmatism), process challenges, (with respect to the different big data management activities) and management challenges (privacy, security and governance). Furthermore, they discuss possible solutions based on a layered reference architecture called big data technology stack, consisting of seven layers. They contrast different ways to introduce big data technologies in an enterprise, namely the revolutionary, evolutionary, and hybrid approaches.

Gorton and Klein [4] address big data from a software architectural point of view. After discussing NoSQL data bases and the importance of scalability, they enumerate common requirements for big data systems, namely write-heavy workloads, variable request loads, computation-intensive analytics, and high availability. Finally, they show how existing architectural tactics can be adjusted for big data systems. This is achieved by considering three different architectural levels, namely data, distribution, and deployment.

Yang et al. [8] give a comprehensive description of big data and cloud systems, and the corresponding innovation opportunities and challenges. They show how the five "Vs" can be addressed with cloud computing techniques. They identify different sources of big data. They discuss big data technology challenges including data storage, transmission, management, processing, analysis, visualization, integration, architecture, security, privacy challenges, and quality. They sketch the relevant technology landscape, and relate the different technologies to the challenges described before. An elaborate research agenda covers many aspects, from technical ones such as distributed data storage to more cross-disciplinary ones, such as interdisciplinary collaboration. Spatiotemporal aspects play an important role throughout.

Sasi Kiran et al. [7] discuss issues and challenges on big data in cloud computing, based on a multitenant system model with different levels of resource sharing. As future challenges, they identify the problems to find an optimal architecture for an analytics system, guaranteeing the statistical relevance of the analytics results, and distributed data mining.

REFERENCES

[1] I. Anagnostopoulos, S. Zeadally, E. Exposito, Handling big data: research challenges and future directions, J. Supercomput. 72 (2016) 1494, http://dx.doi.org/10.1007/s11227-016-1677-z.

[2] M.D. Assunção, R.N. Calheiros, S. Bianchi, M.A.S. Netto, R. Buyya, Big data computing and clouds: trends and future directions, J. Parallel Distrib. Comput. 79–80 (2015) 3–15.

[3] I. Gorton, J. Klein, Designing scalable software and data architectures, Tutorial at ICSE 2014, 2014.

[4] I. Gorton, J. Klein, Distribution, Data, Deployment: Software Architecture Convergence in Big Data Systems, Technical Report, SEI, May 2014.

[5] J.O. Kephart, D.M. Chess, The vision of autonomic computing, Computer (January 2003).

[6] T. Nasser, R.S. Tariq, Big data challenges, Comput. Eng. Inform. Technol. 4 (3) (2015).

[7] J. Sasi Kiran, M. Sravanthi, K. Preethi, M. Anusha, Recent issues and challenges on big data in cloud computing, IJCST 6 (2) (April–June 2015).

[8] C. Yang, Q. Huang, Z. Li, K. Liu, F. Hu, Big data and cloud computing: innovation opportunities and challenges, Int. J. Digital Earth 10 (1) (2017) 13–53, http://dx.doi.org/10.1080/17538947.2016.1239771.

GLOSSARY

Adaptation is a modification of an executed software application by a human operator or an automated routine. Adaptation is typically conducted to react to changes during operations, like increased usage intensity, and is often focused on modifications in component deployment and allocation of computation resources.

Application Manifest is a file that specifies application's name, version, modules, services, and cloud resource requirements.

Application Programming Interface (API), in the context of cloud services, is a collection of code features (e.g., methods, properties, events, and URLs) that a developer can use in their applications to interact with components of a cloud infrastructure.

Architectural Decision (AD) describes a concrete, architecturally significant design issue (a.k.a. design problem, decision required), for which several potential solutions (a.k.a. options, alternatives) exist.

Architectural pattern expresses a fundamental structural organization schema for software systems. It provides a set of predefined subsystems, specifies their responsibilities, and includes rules and guidelines for organizing the relationships between them.

Architectural Refactoring (AR) is a coordinated set of deliberate architectural activities that removes a particular *architectural smell* and improves at least one quality attribute without changing the scope and functionality of the system. An AR can possibly have a negative influence on other quality attributes, due to conflicting requirements and trade-offs.

Architectural Runtime Model is a runtime model that reflects the component-based architecture of an executed software application. It describes the single software components of the application, their composition and deployment. In the context of iObserve, it also describes the resource environment and usage of the application. The architectural runtime model comprises quality-relevant annotations that are required for analyzing the model using simulation or analysis techniques.

Architectural Smell is a suspicion (or indicator) that something in the architecture is no longer adequate under the current requirements and constraints, which may differ from the originally specified ones.

Architecture Description Language (ADL) describes the architecture of a software system with hierarchical components and their communication points.

Artificial Delay is an enforced delay on disruptive tenants usually with the goal to support performance isolation.

Auditable Version Control System (AVCS) is a *version control system* designed to function properly under an adversarial setting, in which the storage server is untrusted and may misbehave.

Auto-scaling means automatically adjusting the amount of resources used by an application in order to fulfill the application's quality of service requirements.

Biodiversity is the variety of species and their individuals whose concrete characteristics vary (e.g., their genetic code and habits); a high level of biodiversity often implies a strong ability of a species in survive and reproduce.

Black List is a list of disruptive tenants in cloud-based systems which will be handled separately to ensure performance isolation.

Certificate Authority (CA) is a trusted entity that issues digital certificates. A certificate is cryptographically signed data asserting the ownership of a public key by a subject. CAs play an important role in the public key infrastructure.

Cloud Auto-scaling is an automatic and elastic process, typically running on a Physical Machine (PM) that adapts software configurations and hardware resources provisioning on-demand according to changing environmental conditions (e.g., the workload).

Cloud Computing is a subscription-based service that delivers computation as a utility.

Cloud Ecosystem is a multitenant cloud environment where the cloud-based services, their software configuration, and hardware provisioning exhibit dynamic and uncertain interactions with each other and the environment, emerging as a system.

Cloud Migration is the process of moving a software application, or part thereof, to the cloud.

Cloud Stability is the extent, to which the cloud is able to prevent violations of Service Level Agreements (SLA) and budget requirements.

Cloud Sustainability is the ability of a cloud to endure the disturbance/stress caused by dynamic and uncertain events, e.g., workload and QoS interference, with the aim to continually optimize QoS attributes of all cloud-based services while minimizing their costs and energy consumptions.

Code Generation is an essential part of a Code Generator that addresses the systematic synthesis of a concrete implementation from an abstract input model.

Complex Event Processing is processing of multiple data streams from different sources to infer meaningful events.

Data Intensive Frameworks is a class of computing applications which focus on distributing the data across different processing elements for a parallel approach to processing large volumes of data.

Data Lake is an analytics system that supports the storing and processing of all types of data.

Data Locality (a.k.a. Disk Locality, Memory Locality) is the strategy of colocating data with relevant processing elements to avoid global network transfers during processing phases. Two substrategies exist, namely Disk Locality (nonvolatile storage medium, e.g., SSD or spinning disks) and Memory Locality (volatile memory, e.g., RAM).

Data Stream Management Systems are systems similar to database management systems that manage data streams and allow continuous queries.

Data/Information Governance ensures that people roles, processes and technology which provides information is protected and managed appropriately to guarantee that an organization gets the maximum value from it.

Deadline is the time limit for the execution of an application.

Delta Encoding is a coding technique that is utilized by modern version control systems to store the data of a version control repository. In delta encoding, only the first version of a file is stored in its entirety, and each subsequent version of the file is stored as the difference from the immediate previous version. These differences are recorded in discrete files called "deltas".

Design Rules define the reusable design heuristics for designing an application architecture based on selection of features of the family feature model and the reference architecture.

Dataflow Engine (DFE) is a compute device that contains a *Field Programmable Gate Array* (*FPGA*) as the computation fabric and RAM for bulk storage, and is integrated with a host system or shared by multiple host systems.

Disruptive Tenants are customers which have higher request rate to cloud resources than the permitted request rate.

Domain Specific Language (DSL) is a language designed to be useful for a limited set of tasks, in contrast to general-purpose languages that are supposed to be useful for much more generic tasks, crossing multiple application domains.

Domain-driven design is a process for software development based on understanding the problem domain. Typically, it involves the creation of an abstract model about the problem domain which can then be implemented with a particular set of technologies.

Elasticity is the degree to which a cloud-based system is able to adapt to workload changes by provisioning and deprovisioning resources in an autonomic manner such that the available resources match the current demand as closely as possible.

Enterprise Applications are software applications that are designed to fulfill the business needs of organizations. Examples of such applications are Enterprise Resources Planning (ERP), Customer Relationship Management (CRM), and Supply Chain Management (SCM) applications.

Evolution is the modification of a software application by a developer, typically in order to implement new features, migrate the application to a new platform or correct errors.

Failure is defined as any deviation of a component of the system from its intended functionality.

Fault-Tolerance is used to provide correct and continuous operation of fault-prone components.

Feature Constraints prescribe constraints of feature configurations in a feature diagram, with the aim to limit the configuration space, so that invalid configurations are prevented throughout the derivation process.

Feature Model is a domain model that defines the common and variant features of a domain.

Field Programmable Gate Array (FPGA) is an integrated circuit that can be (re)programmed to the required functionality, allowing specific types of workload to be executed orders of magnitude faster than CPUs.

High Performance Computing (HPC) refers to the practice of aggregating computing power from desktops, workstations or servers in a way that delivers much higher performance than one could get out of a single machine.

HTTPS is a protocol for secure communication over a computer network which is widely used on the Internet. It uses *TLS/SSL* to establish an encrypted communication channel, and uses Hypertext Transfer Protocol (HTTP) for communication.

Legacy Software comprises enterprise software applications that are planned to be migrated (in part or in full) to a cloud-based environment.

Machine Learning is a subfield of computer science that evolved from the study of pattern recognition and computational learning theory in artificial intelligence.

Megamodel is a model that describes the relationships of models, meta-models and transformations.

Meta-Data is data that provides information about other data.

Migration factor is a quantity or indicator that influences the process of migrating *legacy software* to the cloud. Several example migration factors are: the general measure, benefits, and risks.

Model-Driven Engineering (MDE) is a software development process where models serve as the primary development artifacts. Those models are not only used for documentation purposes but also for creating a system (semi)automatically.

Montage is a scientific workflow application from the astronomy domain designed to compute mosaics of the sky based on a set of input images.

Multitenancy refers to a software system's ability to transparently fulfill the individual requirements of multiple groups of users (i.e., tenants), while sharing the system's resources such as the database or instances of application components.

Nonisolated Cloud System is a system which does not take into account the possibility of disruptive tenants.

Performance Isolation is a condition in which workload or performance of a single tenant cannot affect the performance of the other tenants.

Processing Elements (PEs) refer to processing end points in large/distributed computational systems. Depending on a system configuration, PEs can be a core, a processor, GPU, or FPGA, etc.

Public Key Infrastructure (PKI) is a system for storing, distributing, and authenticating public keys, so that an entity can ascertain that a given public key belongs to a given entity.

Real time processing systems are systems which can guarantee the processing to be done within a tight deadline.

Reengineering is the process of restructuring and adapting the structure and functionality of a software application in order to improve its qualities or to fulfill new requirements.

Reference Architecture is a software architecture that presents a blueprint for the software system which incorporates best practices by various means such as vocabularies, standards, design patterns, and can be employed by software architects throughout the software lifecycle.

Remote Data Integrity Checking (RDC) is a technique that allows a data owner to check the integrity of data outsourced to an untrusted server, and thus to audit whether the server fulfills its contractual obligations.

Request Rate is the amount of a request sent from a tenant in a particular unit of time.

Resilient Distributed Dataset (RDD) is the primary data abstraction in Apache Spark. RDDs are immutable distributed memory abstractions, each being a partitioned collection of elements that can be operated on in memory through parallel processing on large clusters in a fault-tolerant manner.

Runtime model is a model that reflects the current state of an executed software application. It is constructed or updated based on monitoring data gathered while observing the application.

Scientific Workflow Management System is a system responsible for transparently orchestrating the execution of the workflow tasks in a set of distributed compute resources while ensuring the dependencies are preserved.

Scientific Workflow is an application model used to describe scientific applications by defining a series of computations or tasks and the dependencies between them.

Service Composition is a paradigm where basic services are combined to form a higher level service with increased value for the customer.

Service Level Agreement is Contract between a service provider and the customer that defines the level of service expected from the service provider.

Skip-delta Encoding is a type of delta encoding that is further optimized towards reducing the cost of retrieval. In skip-delta encoding, a new file version is still stored as the difference from a previous file version; however, this difference is not necessarily relative to the immediate previous version, but rather relative to a certain previous version.

Service-Level Objective (SLO) is a file that specifies the objectives (e.g., job completion time or throughput) that must be achieved when running an application.

Software-as-a-Service (SaaS) is a software delivery and licensing model which allows users to access cloud hosted software applications on-demand and pay for the usage on a subscription basis.

Stream Computing is a data-centric high-performance computer system that ingests, manages, analyzes, and passes on (e.g., storage or display) multiple data streams from many sources in real or near real time.

Stream processing is a programming paradigm where a sequence of small operations are applied on each element of a stream.

Stream is a sequence of data tuples that are being generated continuously from a source in real time.

Tenants are the customers that are sharing the same resources of the cloud application.

Thick/Fat/Rich client is a client computer in client–server architecture that provides rich functionality independent of the central server.

Thin client is a lightweight client computer that is purpose-built for remote access to a server to fulfill its computational roles.

Transport Layer Security (TLS) as well as its predecessor Secure Sockets Layer (SSL), is a cryptographic protocol providing communications security over a computer network. It is widely used in web browsing, email, instant messaging, and voice-over-IP (VoIP).

Trophic Web is an interaction network in ecology to model the consumer–resource relationship, for example, predator–prey or organism–resources.

Version Control System (VCS) is a system that provides the ability to track and control the changes made to the data over time, automating the process of version control. It records all changes to the data into a data store called repository so that any version of the data can be retrieved at any time in the future.

Workflow Makespan is the time to complete the execution of a workflow application. It is equal to the completion time, including computation and output data transfer times, of the last workflow task.

Workflow is a collection of tasks connected by control and/or data dependencies. Scientific Workflows automate computation for managing complex large scale distributed data analysis and scientific computation.

AUTHOR INDEX

Note: Page numbers followed by "*f*" indicate figures, and "*t*" indicate tables.

A

Abadi, D.J., 198, 262
Abatlevi, C., 64
Abawajy, J., 290, 299, 304
Abbott, Martin L., 15
Abraham, A., 247, 288
Ackley, D., 92
Adabi, S., 305
Addis, M., 311
Afrati, F.N., 262
Afzal, A., 313
Agarwal, D., 295, 296
Aggarwal, V., 154*t*, 157*t*, 158*t*, 161
Agrawal, D., 292, 293
Agrawal, G., 91, 92
Ahmad, I., 288
Ahmad, Y., 198
Aiyer, A., 64
Akgul, F., 190
Akhawe, D., 110, 111
Akiva, N., 198
Alaçam, O., 313
Albayrak, Sahin, 87
Albuquerque, A.B., 154*t*–157*t*, 158, 158*t*, 160, 161
Aldrich, J., 85, 86
Ali, M., 198
Ali, M.H., 198
Ali, Nour, 1–9, 391–401
Ali-ud-din Khan, M., 253
Alicherry, M., 110, 111*t*, 112
Alizadeh, M., 154*t*–156*t*, 158, 163
Alonso, J.M., 154*t*, 155, 157*t*, 158*t*, 160, 161
Alrebeish, F., 5, 6
Alspaugh, Sara, 16
Altintas, I., 285, 300, 310, 313, 369
Álvarez, P., 297–299
Alvisi, L., 297, 298, 353
Alzaghoul, E., 5
Amann, U., 85

Amdahl, Gene M., 15
Amin, K., 313
An, W.H., 227
Anagnostopoulos, I., 401
Anand, M.K., 300
Ananthanarayanan, G., 276
Andersen, D.G., 110, 111*t*
Anderson, G.A., 259
Andrade, H.C., 185
Angelov, S., 51
Angerer, A., 212
Anjos, D., 64, 65
Anthony, S., 63, 64
Antoniou, G., 274
Anuar, N.B., 274*t*
Anusha, M., 401
Apon, A., 49
Appelbaum, J., 106
Arasu, A., 198
Arbitter, P., 227, 228, 231, 233
Aref, W.G., 198
Argyraki, Katerina, 323–350
Armbrust, M., 268–271
Arthur, C., 106
Asal, R., 154*t*, 156*t*, 157*t*
Ashcroft, E.A., 185
Aßmann, U., 144
Assunção, M.D., 394, 395, 401
Atallah, M.J., 106
Ateniese, G., 106, 353, 357, 362, 363, 365
Athanasiadis, I., 52, 54, 56, 57
Athanasiadis, Ioannis N., 49–67
Aulbach, S., 127
Austern, M.H., 265, 270, 295
Avancha, S., 222
Avci Salma, Cigdem, 49–67
Avgeriou, P., 53, 228
Azarnik, A., 154*t*–156*t*, 158, 163
Aziz, A., 105

B

Babar, A., 1, 2
Babcock, B., 187, 198
Babu, S., 187, 198
Bacall, F., 311
Bachmann, F., 54
Badgett, T., 237
Bagheri, B., 275
Bahsoon, R., 1, 4–7, 91, 92, 97, 99, 100, 144
Bahsoon, Rami, 1–9, 91–101, 391–401
Bala, P., 310
Balakrishnan, H., 198
Balazinska, M., 16, 198
Balcazar Vargas, M.P., 311
Ballard, C., 51*t*, 56
Balouek, D., 336
Balthrop, J., 92
Banares, J., 290, 291
Banerjee, J., 154*t*, 155*t*, 157*t*, 158*t*, 161
Baòares, J., 297–299
Barais, O., 85
Barga, R., 301
Barker, A., 369
Barnaghi, P., 222
Barnawi, A., 258, 270
Barnes, R., 115
Barnes, R.L., 111*t*
Barriga, J.K.D., 274
Barros, Alistair, 227–248
Basin, D.A., 119
Bass, L., 2, 14, 54, 69
Bass, Len, 21
Batarfi, O., 258, 270
Bates, B., 236
Batista, T., 211, 213
Baudry, B., 100
Beck-Ratzka, A., 310
Becker, D., 313
Begoli, E., 49, 54
Beheshti, S.-M.-R., 258, 270
Behm, A., 265
Beighley, L., 234
Beijun, S., 234, 247
Belhajjame, K., 311
Bellare, M., 357, 361
Bencomo, N., 85
Benedyczak, K., 310
Bengfort, B., 267, 269

Benoit, A., 291–293, 303
Bergmann, S., 310
Berkley, C., 310, 313, 369
Berlin, M., 338–340
Berman, F., 295, 296
Bernstein, P.A., 222
Berriman, B., 370, 379
Berriman, G.B., 296, 308, 309
Beserra, P.V., 154*t*–157*t*, 158, 158*t*, 160, 161
Bettin, J., 212
Beyer, M., 183
Bezemer, C.-P., 229, 247
Bezemer, Cor-Paul, 227, 228, 234, 247
Bhagat, J., 311
Bhagat, N., 265
Bharathi, S., 289*f*, 290, 292, 380
Bianchi, S., 394, 395, 401
Bik, A., 265, 270
Bik, A.J.C., 295
Bilir, S., 64
Birkhoff, G., 333
Birrell, A., 256, 259, 290
Birsan, D., 222
Bischofberger, W., 86
Bisig, C., 248
Bittorf, V., 265
Blacka, D., 115
Blanton, M., 363
Blythe, J., 296, 308, 309
Bo, G., 227
Bo, Y., 247
Boag, S., 222
Bobrovytsky, T., 265
Bockermann, C., 186, 187, 189
Boeder, J., 230
Boeyen, S., 107
Bogaerts, J., 148, 152, 154*t*–157*t*, 160, 161, 163
Bölöni, L., 304
Bondi, A.B., 14, 193
Bonner, S., 274
Bonner, Stephen, 253–280
Borchert, T., 345
Borthakur, D., 63, 64
Bosanac, D., 191
Böttcher, K., 223
Boulakia, S.C., 300
Bourimi, M., 222
Boutaba, R., 211, 214

Boutin, E., 279
Bowers, K., 357
Bowers, K.D., 357
Bowers, S., 300
Bradley, J., 270
Brambilla, M., 27, 222
Brandic, I., 293
Branson, A., 49, 54
Brasileiro, F., 292
Brataas, G., 14
Bray, T., 222
Brendel, J., 106
Brennan, J., 274
Brennan, John, 253–280
Brereton, P., 147
Breu, R., 310
Brewer, E., 215
Briscoe, G., 100
Brito, A., 313
Broy, M., 212, 213
Brugali, D., 213
Brun, Y., 72
Bruyninckx, H., 213
Bu, X., 144
Budgen, D., 147
Budiu, M., 256, 259, 290
Burns, R., 353, 357, 362, 363, 365
Burrows, M., 264
Buyukkaya, E., 326, 338
Buyya, R., 8, 143, 275, 285, 287, 288, 290, 292, 293,
    296, 297, 299, 301–305, 310, 311, 368–370, 373,
    378, 379, 394, 395, 401
Buyya, Rajkumar, 183–204, 285–315, 367–386

C
Cabot, J., 27, 222
Cafarella, M., 264
Cai, H., 227
Cala, J., 311
Calheiros, R., 8, 292, 293
Calheiros, R.N., 143, 394, 395, 401
Callaghan, S., 309, 369, 378
Callahan, S.P., 313
Camara, A., 154t–157t, 158, 158t, 160, 161
Candela, J.Q., 345
Canetti, R., 357, 361
Canfora, G., 85
Canon, L., 304

Canon, L.-C., 291
Cao, J., 313
Caracciola, A., 86
Carbone, P., 265
Cardoso, A., 153–155
Carraro, Gianpaolo, 235
Carreira, P., 64, 65
Carro, M., 85
Carson, W., 93
Carver, T., 311
Casanova, H., 295, 296, 329
Cash, D., 357
Catlin, A.C., 198
Cavalcante, E., 211, 213
Cech, S., 144
Cechich, A., 211, 220
Cetintemel, U., 186, 190, 198
Chai, X., 198
Chakka, P., 264
Chakravarthy, S., 192
Chamberlin, D., 222
Chandra, S., 240
Chang, F., 264
Chang Jie, G., 227
Chansler, R., 183, 192, 263, 312
Chapelle, D., 51t, 56
Chapman, Pete, 33
Chauhan, J., 184, 186, 187, 192, 199
Chauvel, F., 85, 100
Cheah, Y., 295, 296
Chen, B., 354, 357, 364, 365
Chen, Bo, 353–365
Chen, C.P., 184
Chen, J., 297, 300–302, 311
Chen, L., 106
Chen, M., 183
Chen, P., 258
Chen, S., 297, 299, 301
Chen, T., 1, 91, 92, 97, 99, 100, 144
Chen, Tao, 91–101
Chen, W., 296, 303, 309, 369, 378
Chen, X., 106
Chen, Yanpei, 16
Cheng, B.H.C., 85
Cheng, L., 211, 214
Cherniack, M., 198
Chervenak, A., 289f, 290, 292, 380
Chess, D.M., 396

Chessell, Mandy, 33–48
Cheval, V., 108, 111*t*, 119
Chien, A., 295, 296
Chien, E., 106
Ching, A., 265
Ching, C., 265
Chiu, K., 310
Cho, B., 290, 294
Chohan, N., 143
Choi, A., 265
Chong, Frederick, 235
Chowdhury, M., 263, 267–269, 276, 277, 295, 313
Chowdhury, S.A., 184, 186, 187, 192, 199
Chu, X., 311
Cieslewicz, J., 198
Cirne, W., 292
Claes, M., 100
Clark, J., 107
Clarke, S., 100
Clement, A., 353
Clements, P., 14
Clements, P.C., 2
Clinton, Julian, 33
Coggeshall, J., 234
Cohen, S.G., 51
Compert, C., 51*t*, 56
Cooper, D., 107
Cooper, K., 292, 293, 295, 296, 305
Coutinho, J.G.F., 329, 331, 339
Coutinho, Jose G.F., 323–350
Cox, M., 254
Crane, S., 223
Crawl, D., 285, 300, 310
Cremers, C., 119
Creutz, S., 313
Cross, M., 239
Cugola, G., 198
Cui, L., 293
Curino, C., 266
Curtmola, R., 353, 354, 357, 362–365
Curtmola, Reza, 353–365
Cutting, D., 264
Czajkowski, G., 295
Czarnecki, K., 51, 212, 213, 222

D

da Silva, R.F., 309, 369, 378
Dabrowski, C., 291, 297

Dahlin, M., 193, 353
Dai, Jun, 353–365
Dail, H., 295, 296
Daivandy, J., 310
Dalcı, M., 313
Dalton, J., 64
Dam, M., 212, 223
D'antoni, L., 198
Darbha, S., 292, 293
Darlington, J., 313
Das, T., 192, 267–269, 271, 276, 277, 295
das Chagas Mendonca, N., 86
Dasgupta, A., 295, 296
Dashofy, E., 212
Dastjerdi, A., 8
Datar, M., 187, 198
Dave, A., 267–269, 276, 277, 295
Davidson, A., 268
Davidson, S.B., 300, 301
Davies, R., 191
De Bosschere, K., 14
De Roure, D.C., 314
De Wilde, P., 100
Deakin, M., 274
Dean, J., 254, 260, 261, 264, 290, 294, 312, 313
Deelman, E., 285, 289*f*, 290, 292, 296, 297, 300, 303, 305, 308, 309, 313, 367, 369, 370, 378–380
Dehnert, J.C., 295
Demers, A.J., 198
Demuth, B., 310
Deng, W., 295, 296
DeWitt, D., 262
DeWitt, D.J., 262
Di Martino, B., 297–299
Di Penta, M., 85
Díaz-Herrera, J.L., 127
Dierks, T., 105
Diffie, W., 105
Ding, L., 222
Ding, Y., 100
Ding, Z., 222
Dingledine, R., 112
Dingsoyr, T., 147
Diniz, R., 86
Doan, A., 222
Dobson, J.E., 310
Dogan, A., 292, 293
Dogru, A., 128

Domingos, P., 222
Dong, L., 222
Dongarra, J., 288, 289, 295–299, 302, 304, 305, 313
Dongarra, J.J., 303
Donham, J., 265
Doole, A., 339
Du, W., 106
Duan, R., 297–299, 305, 308, 369
Duboc, Leticia, 14
Duggan, D., 231
Dunlop, I., 311, 369
Durumeric, Z., 115
Dustdar, S., 293
Dwork, C., 106
Dyba, T., 147

E

Eadline, D., 271
Eastman, C., 222
Eastman, C.M., 222
Eckersley, P., 106, 111*t*, 115
Eeckhout, L., 14
Efremovska, Anastasija, 147–164
Egwutuoha, I., 297, 299, 301
Eickler, A., 215
Eifer, A., 310
Eikermann, Robert, 207–224
Eisbruch, G., 65
Eisenecker, U.W., 213, 222
Ekanayake, J., 279
Elbert, S.T., 259
Ellis, K.A., 211, 217, 222
Ellisman, M., 285, 367
Ellsworth, D., 254
Elmagarmid, A.K., 198
Elmongui, H.G., 198
Elmroth, E., 313
Elnozahy, E.N., 297, 298
Emeakaroha, V.C., 144
Emmerich, W., 7
Ensari, T., 264*f*
Epema, D., 315
Erfan, A., 154*t*, 155, 155*t*, 163
Erway, C., 357, 363, 364, 364*t*
Escalante, A., 300, 301, 311
Escalante, M., 154*t*, 155, 157*t*, 158*t*, 160, 161
Esposito, R., 85
Esterle, L., 92, 97

Esteves, S., 386
Etemad, M., 363, 364, 364*t*
Evans, C., 114
Evans, Jason, 23
Ewen, S., 265
Exposito, E., 401
Eyal, A., 300
Ezpeleta, J., 297–299

F

Fahringer, T., 285, 291, 295, 297–301, 303, 305, 308–310, 367, 369
Falliere, L.O.M.N., 106
Falt, Z., 191
Fan, L., 227
Faniyi, F., 4, 5, 92, 97
Farrell, S., 107
Favre, J.-M., 75
Fayoumi, A.G., 258, 260, 261, 267, 270
Fehling, C., 144, 227, 228, 231, 233
Feiler, P.H., 213
Feiler, Peter H., 29
Feitelson, D.G., 341
Fellows, D., 311, 369
Felt, A.P., 110, 111
Feng, B., 331
Ferguson, N., 105
Fernández, M.F., 222
Ferris, J., 311
Fetterly, D., 256, 259, 290
Fetzer, C., 313
Fidge, Colin, 227–248
Fink, S.J., 240
Fisher, Michael T., 15
Fisher, P., 311, 369
Fittkau, F., 77, 79, 86
Fleurey, F., 85, 100
Flores, A., 211, 220
Florescu, D., 222
Fontaine, C., 106
Forrest, S., 92
Fowler, M., 14, 23, 27, 231, 232*f*, 234, 235, 239, 245*t*
Fox, G., 261, 285, 367
Fox, G.C., 256
France, R., 85, 211, 212
Francisco, A.P., 64, 65
Franklin, M.J., 263, 267, 268, 270, 295, 313
Freeman, E., 236
Freire, J., 300, 301, 313

Frey, S., 77
Fu, J., 191
Fu, M., 265
Furda, Andrei, 227–248
Furht, B., 300, 301, 311

G
Gabriel, Richard P., 29
Galand, F., 106
Galster, M., 53
Gani, A., 274*t*
Gannon, D., 285, 297, 300, 305, 308, 309, 313, 367
Gao, B., 144, 227
Gao, D., 111*t*, 119
Gao, L., 100
Gao, Qi, 23
Garey, M.R., 287
Garg, S.K., 302, 305
Garg, Saurabh, 183–204
Garlan, D., 85, 86
Garofalakis, M., 198
Garrigam, M., 211, 220
Gartner, 279
Gärtner, F., 290, 291
Gärtner, S., 70–72
Gazis, V., 198
Gedik, B., 185
Geerdink, B., 51*t*
Gehrke, J., 198
Geisler, S., 198
Gentry, C., 106
Gertz, M., 285, 300, 310
Ghaffarkhah, A., 144
Ghanem, M., 91, 92
Ghedira, C., 212, 220
Ghemawat, S., 254, 259–261, 264, 312, 313
Gherardi, L., 213
Ghodsi, A., 268, 276
Ghosh, S., 292
Gibbins, H., 311, 373
Giesler, A., 310
Gil, Y., 285, 296, 308, 309, 367
Gilles, K., 185
Gimenez, R., 222
Girod, L., 198
Glickman, M., 92
Gligor, V., 107, 111*t*, 117

Glover, K., 311
Gluch, D.P., 213
Gobioff, H., 254, 259, 260, 312
Goble, C., 285, 311, 367
Goble, C.A., 314
Goes, L., 292
Goldman, A., 265
Goldschmidt, T., 248
Goldwasser, S., 106
Gonzalez, J.E., 268, 270
Gonzalez, T., 127
Good, J., 296, 308, 309, 370, 379
Goodenough, John B., 29
Gorroñogoitia, J., 154*t*, 155, 157*t*, 158*t*, 160, 161
Gorton, I., 49, 259, 394, 400, 401
Gorton, Ian, 13–30
Götz, S., 144
Goucher, A., 237
Gousios, G., 233
Gracio, D.K., 259
Graepel, T., 345
Grance, T., 233
Gray, J., 64
Greefhorst, D., 51
Greenwood, D., 154*t*, 155, 156*t*–158*t*, 160–162
Greenwood, M., 311
Greevy, O., 86
Grefen, P., 51
Greifenberg, T., 211, 217, 222, 223
Grigoras, P., 339
Groene, B., 230
Grosjean, P., 100
Gruber, R.E., 264
Grundy, J., 228
Gruver, W.A., 275
Gu, X., 143
Guabtni, A., 368
Gubbi, J., 275
Guo, C., 144
Guo, C.J., 227
Guo, L., 91, 92
Guo, Y., 91, 92
Guo, Z., 261
Gupta, I., 290, 294
Gupta, N., 253
Gupta, P., 65, 111*t*, 119
Gustafson, John L., 15
Gustavson, D.B., 14

H

Haas, P.J., 277
Haase, A., 212
Haber, A., 213, 223
Hadley, M.J., 213
Hagemeier, B., 310
Haines, R., 311, 369
Hakem, M., 292, 293, 303
Halderman, J.A., 111*t*, 115
Halevi, S., 106
Halevy, A., 222
Halevy, A.Y., 222
Hall, J.G., 228
Hammad, M.A., 198
Hampton, S., 313
Han, J., 111*t*, 119
Han, R., 91, 92
Han, Y., 144
Han, Zhu, 23
Hanmer, R., 248
Hanssen, G.K., 147
Härder, T., 215
Hardin, G., 94
Hardisty, A., 311
Haridi, S., 265
Harrison, A., 309
Harsu, M., 50
Hashem, I.A.T., 274*t*
Hashimoto, K., 292, 293
Hassan, S., 5
Hasselbring, W., 71–73, 75, 77, 78*f*, 79, 84, 86
Hasselbring, Wilhelm, 69–87
Hategan, M., 300, 313
Heger, C., 78
Heim, S., 223
Heinrich, R., 70–75, 78, 78*f*, 79, 81, 84, 86
Heinrich, Robert, 69–87
Heisel, Maritta, 1–9, 391–401
Hellman, M.E., 105
Helsen, S., 212
Heninger, N., 115
Herbrich, R., 345
Herbst, N., 3
Herman, F., 222
Hermenegildo, M., 85
Hernández, F., 313
Herold, S., 70

Herring, J., 353, 357, 362, 363, 365
Herrmann, C., 211, 212
Herroelen, W., 289
Hess, J.A., 51
Hesse, T.-M., 70–72
Hiden, H., 311
Higgins, D., 310, 369
Hill, Mark D., 14
Hindman, B., 268, 279
Hintjens, P., 190
Hirzinger, G., 212
Hochgeschwender, N., 213
Hofer, J., 297, 305, 308, 369
Hoffman, P., 115
Hoffman, S., 190
Hoffmann, A., 212
Hohpe, G., 231
Holl, S., 310
Hölldobler, K., 222, 223
Holmes, V., 271
Hong, J.I., 111*t*, 119
Hopkins, Brian, 39
Hoque, I., 290, 294
Horey, J., 49, 54
Horn, I., 295
Housley, R., 107
Howe, B., 16
Höwing, F., 213
Hsieh, W.C., 264
Hu, F., 392, 394, 401
Hu, K., 302, 303
Hu, Z., 85
Huang, G., 85
Huang, L.-S., 107, 111*t*, 117
Huang, Q., 392, 394, 401
Huang, X., 106
Huang, Y., 143
Hubbell, S.P., 92
Huber, F., 212, 213
Huber, V., 310
Hughes, P., 14
Humphrey, M., 295, 296
Hunter, T., 192
Hutchinson, J., 213
Hwan, C., 51
Hwang, J.-H., 198
Hwang, S., 295, 296, 301
Hyde, J., 198

I

Ioannidis, George, 323–350
Iordache, A., 326, 338
Iordache, Anca, 323–350
Iosup, A., 315
Isard, M., 256, 259, 290
Ito, K., 198
Ivanovic, D., 85

J

Jaatun, M., 310
Jackson, C., 107, 111*t*, 117
Jackson, K., 295, 296
Jacob, J.C., 296, 308, 309
Jacobs, D., 127
Jaeger, E., 310, 313, 369
Jain, N., 63, 64, 264
Jansen, S., 229, 247
Jarvis, S.A., 313
Javadi, B., 290, 297, 304, 315
Jeannot, E., 288, 289, 291, 302–305
Jesionowski, T., 51*t*, 56
Jezequel, J.-M., 85
Jha, S., 256
Jia, X., 106
Jiang, Q., 192
Johnson, D.B., 297, 298
Johnson, D.S., 287
Johnsson, L., 295, 296
Jones, M., 310, 313, 369
Jones, M.T., 190, 196
Jones, Nigel L., 36
Juels, A., 353, 357
Julisch, K., 238
Jung, R., 72, 73, 75, 78*f*, 79, 84
Jung, Reiner, 69–87
Jürjens, J., 70–72
Juve, G., 285, 289*f*, 290, 309, 369, 378, 380

K

Kabbedijk, J., 229, 247
Kacsuk, P., 285, 291, 295, 297, 300, 301, 303, 308–310, 313
Kahl, C., 223
Kaliski, B.S., 353, 357
Kalleberg, K.T., 51
Kandaswamy, G., 292, 293
Kang, K.C., 49, 51

Kansal, A., 144
Kao, H.A., 275
Karamizadeh, S., 154*t*–156*t*, 158, 163
Karczewski, K., 313
Karger, D., 22
Karunamoorthy, D., 310
Kasper, E., 107, 111*t*, 116
Kasten, J., 111*t*, 115
Katsifodimos, A., 265
Katz, D.S., 296, 308, 309
Katz, Randy, 16
Kavurucu, Y., 264*f*
Kay, M., 191
Kazman, R., 14, 85, 86
Kazman, Rick, 29
Keele, S., 149
Kelly, S.D.T., 255
Kemper, A., 215
Kennedy, K., 295, 296
Kephart, J.O., 396
Kerber, Randy, 33
Kerievsky, J., 232, 234
Keromytis, A.D., 110, 111*t*, 112
Kertesz, A., 285, 291, 295, 297, 300, 301, 303, 308–310
Kesari, A., 193
Kesselman, C., 295, 296, 301, 308, 309
Khabaza, Thomas, 33
Khajeh-Hosseini, A., 148, 152, 154*t*, 155, 155*t*–158*t*, 160–163
Khalil, M., 147
Khan, O., 353, 357, 362, 363
Khan, S.U., 274*t*
Khojaye, M.A., 259
Kikuno, T., 292, 293
Kilinc, H.H., 105
Kilpatrick, P., 338
Kim, J., 267, 269
Kim, P., 51
Kim, T.H., 111*t*, 119
Kim, T.H.-J., 107, 111*t*, 117
Kissner, L., 353, 357, 362, 363, 365
Kitchenham, B., 147
Kitchenham, B.A., 147
Klein, J., 49, 394, 400, 401
Klein, John, 27
Klein, M., 54
Klein, Mark H., 29

Kleineweber, Christoph, 323–350
Klotzbücher, M., 213
Knauth, T., 313
Knuth, Donald E., 22
Ko, S.Y., 290, 294
Kocher, P., 107
Kodeboyina, D., 300, 313
Koelbel, C., 292, 293, 295, 296, 305
Kolari, P., 222
Kolassa, C., 222, 223
Koliousis, Alexandros, 323–350
Kon, F., 265
Kondo, D., 315
Konwinski, A., 268, 279
Kornacker, M., 265
Korupolu, M., 279
Kotak, D.B., 275
Kounev, S., 3, 132, 133, 134*f*, 135, 140
Kousiouris, G., 247
Kouzes, R.T., 259
Kovacs, Z., 49, 54
Koziolek, A., 78, 82
Koziolek, H., 78, 82, 248
Kraetzschmar, G., 213
Krahn, H., 211, 212
Krause, A., 79, 86
Krawczyk, H., 357, 361
Krebs, R., 132, 133, 134*f*, 135, 140
Kreps, J., 190, 195
Krontiris, I., 223
Kuang, H., 64, 183, 192, 263, 312
Kuen, H.T., 329
Kühl, J., 86
Kulkarni, S., 188
Kumar, R., 264, 265
Kumar Ammula, Anil, 357
Kun, M., 247
Kunz, C., 265
Kupcu, A., 357, 363, 364, 364*t*
Kureshi, I., 271, 274
Kureshi, Ibad, 253–280
Kwok, Y., 288
Kwon, Y., 16
Kyriazis, D., 247

L

Labitzke, S., 212, 222
Lackovic, M., 290, 291

Lago, P., 148, 213, 228
Lago, Patricia, 147–164
Laity, A., 296, 308, 309
Lakshman, A., 264
Lam, C., 312
Lamla, N., 310
Laney, D., 49, 253
Langley, A., 107, 111*t*, 114, 116
Lanza, M., 86
Larroquette, L., 274
Laurie, B., 107, 111*t*, 116
Lazowska, E., 301
Le Guernic, G., 212, 223
Leckie, C., 8
Lee, E.A., 310, 369
Lee, J., 49, 275
Lee, K., 49
Lee, S., 353
Lehman, E., 22
Leibiusky, J., 65
Leighton, T., 22
Leiser, N., 295
Leon, V., 289
Leskovec, J., 258
Leung, S., 312
Leung, S.T., 254, 259, 260
Leus, R., 289
Levin, S.A., 92
Levine, M., 22
Levy, D., 297, 299, 301
Lewin, D., 22
Lewis, P.R., 92, 97
Leyden, J., 106
Leymann, F., 144, 227, 228, 231, 233
Li, C., 255
Li, F., 261, 262
Li, H., 192, 271, 276
Li, J., 295, 296, 302, 303
Li, L.X., 303, 305
Li, P., 311
Li, R., 292, 293
Li, W., 294, 302, 303
Li, X., 144, 292, 293
Li, Z., 64, 392, 394, 401
Lianping, C., 1, 2
Liao, G., 292, 293
Limburn, Jay, 36
Lin, H., 144

Lin, J., 64
Lin, W., 279
Linger, Richard C., 29
Liston, K., 222
Litke, A., 303
Liu, A., 260, 261, 267
Liu, B., 295, 296
Liu, D., 270
Liu, H., 63, 64
Liu, K., 392, 394, 401
Liu, X., 293, 295, 296, 300, 301, 311
Liu, Y., 183
Livingstone, R., 253
Livny, M., 285, 292, 309, 367, 369, 370, 378, 379
Löffler, S., 86
Longstaff, Thomas A., 29
Look, M., 211, 217, 222, 223
Look, Markus, 207–224
Lopes, Darshan, 167–178
Loreau, M., 93
Lu, G., 303, 305
Luckow, A., 256
Ludäscher, B., 285, 300, 310, 369
Ludascher, B., 310, 313
Luk, W., 329, 339
Lundblad, A., 212, 223
Lungu, M., 86

M
Ma, J., 295
Ma, L.L., 227
Maciejewski, A., 289, 304
Maciejewski, M., 274
MacVicar, Scott, 23
Madden, S., 198, 262
Madey, G., 270
Madhavan, J., 222
Maechling, P.J., 309, 369, 378
Maglio, P.P., 277
Mahajan, P., 353
Mahmood, Z., 128
Maier, M., 51t
Maier, M.W., 29, 213
Makaroff, D., 184, 186, 187, 192, 199
Malavolta, I., 213
Maler, E., 222
Malewicz, G., 265, 270, 295

Malik, P., 264
Mallmann, D., 310
Mandal, A., 292, 293, 295, 296, 305
Mantha, P., 256
Mao, S., 183
Mao, W., 105
Margara, A., 198
Marin, G., 295, 296
Marinescu, D.C., 304
Markl, V., 265, 276
Markus, V., 222
Marlinspike, M., 107, 108, 110, 111t, 112, 113
Marr, B., 253
Martin, A., 313
Marusic, S., 275
Marvin, D., 311
Marz, N., 51t, 56, 127, 129, 130f, 187, 188, 192, 195
Massey, J.L., 105
Mateos, C., 211, 220
Mathewson, N., 112
Mathur, M., 154t, 157t, 158t, 161
Maxim, Bruce, 1–9, 391–401
May, W., 51t
Mayani, R., 309, 369, 378
Mazina, M., 295, 296
Mcarthur, K., 240
McCauley, M., 295
McClatchey, R., 49, 54
McCune, R.R., 270
McGlone, J., 338, 339
McGlone, John, 323–350
McGough, A.S., 274
McGough, S., 313
McPhillips, T.M., 300
Medeiros, A.L., 211, 213
Medjahed, B., 212, 220
Medvidovic, N., 53, 72, 212, 213
Mehta, G., 289f, 290, 292, 296, 308, 309, 380
Mei, H., 85
Mei, Y., 198
Meier, S., 119
Melhem, R., 292
Mell, P., 233
Mellor-Crummey, J., 295, 296
Memon, A., 310
Memon, M., 310
Mencer, O., 329
Mendes, C., 295, 296

Mendez, D., 100
Mendonça, N.C., 154*t*–157*t*, 158, 158*t*, 160, 161
Meng, X., 270
Menon, A., 64
Mens, T., 100
Menychtas, A., 247
Metzger, A., 71–73, 75, 78*f*, 79, 84
Mietzner, R., 144
Milligan, P., 338
Milman, I., 51*t*, 56
Milo, T., 222
Minku, L.L., 92, 97
Mir Seyed Nazari, P., 222, 223
Mishne, G., 64, 65
Mistrík, I., 228
Mistrik, Ivan, 1–9, 391–401
Mittal, S., 265
Mock, S., 310, 313
Mohamed, A., 149
Mokbel, M.F., 198
Mokhtar, S., 274*t*
Molano, J.I.R., 274
Molkov, D., 64
Momm, C., 132, 133, 134*f*, 135, 140
Monperrus, M., 100
Monsuez, B., 213
Mony, C., 100
Moreau, L., 285, 367
Moreira, F., 153–155
Morin, B., 85
Morrison, M., 234
Moss, L., 274
Mosse, D., 292
Motwani, R., 187, 198
Mouallem, P., 285, 300, 310
Movaghar, A., 305
Mozafari, B., 198
Mrissa, M., 212, 220
Muccini, H., 213
Mukhopadhyay, S.C., 255
Müller, K., 222, 223
Murthy, R., 63, 64, 264
Musen, M.A., 222
Music, D., 293
Muthukkaruppan, K., 64
Myers, G.J., 237
Myers, J., 285, 367

N
Nadeem, F., 297, 305, 308, 369
Nadiminti, K., 311, 373
Nair, A., 193
Nallur, V., 5, 6
Naor, M., 107
Narkhede, N., 190, 195
Nasser, T., 401
Nathuji, R., 144
Navarro Pérez, A., 211, 213
Navarro Perez, A., 222, 223
Nenadic, A., 311, 369
Nerieri, F., 297, 305, 308, 369
Netto, M.A.S., 394, 395, 401
Neumeyer, L., 193
Newhouse, S., 313
Newman, S., 69, 248
Newton, R., 198
Ngu, A.H., 368
Nguyen, Nhan, 36
Niemann, A., 106
Nierstrasz, O., 86
Nieva de la Hidalga, A., 311
Nissim, K., 106, 107
Niu, X., 329
Norrie, D., 275
Northrop, Linda M., 29
Nouri, R., 258, 270
Novak, W.E., 51
Noy, N.F., 222
Nudd, G.R., 313
Nuseibeh, B., 1, 2
Nygard, M., 14

O
O'Connell, Bill, 48
Odersky, M., 313
Oinn, T., 311
Olston, C., 264, 265
Olugbile, A., 295, 296
O'Malley, O., 266
O'Neill, E., 338, 339
Ooi, B., 261, 262
Oppenheimer, D., 279
Oprea, A., 357
Or, A., 268
Oral, Alp, 127–145
Oral, O.A., 132, 133, 135, 136, 140
Ordille, J., 222

Oreizy, P., 72
Orue-Echevarria, L., 154*t*, 155, 157*t*, 158*t*, 160, 161
Osher, S.A., 273
O'Sullivan, Fiona, 167–178
Ottoni, Guilherme, 23
Owen, S., 311, 369
Owusu, E., 111*t*, 119
Ozguner, F., 292, 293
Ozsu, M., 261, 262
Öztürk, K., 51, 128

P

Pääkkönen, P., 51*t*
Paech, B., 70–72
Pakkala, D., 51*t*
Palaniswami, M., 275
Palmer, C., 114
Palmer, Kevin, 167–178
Panda, B., 198
Pandey, S., 310
Panigrahy, R., 22
Paoli, J., 222
Papamanthou, C., 357, 363, 364, 364*t*
Paranhos, D., 292
Parastatidis, Savas, 26
Paroski, Andrew, 23
Passos, L., 86
Patel, J.M., 188
Patel, M., 295, 296
Paulson, E., 262
Pavlo, A., 262
Pedrosa, L., 279
Pell, O., 329, 339
Pelliccione, P., 213
Peng, X., 302, 303
Perrig, A., 107, 110, 111*t*, 117, 119
Perrin, T., 111*t*, 113
Perumalla, K.S., 255
Peterson, A.S., 51
Peterson, Z., 353, 357, 362, 363, 365
Pickett, S.T., 93
Pierre, G., 326, 338, 339
Pierre, Guillaume, 323–350
Pinkas, B., 106
Pistoia, M., 240
Plale, B., 300
Plankensteiner, K., 285, 291, 295–297, 300, 301, 303, 308–310

Plants, B., 51*t*, 56
Platform, A., 268, 279
Plotnikov, D., 222, 223
Pocock, M.R., 311
Podlipnig, S., 297, 305, 308, 369
Pohl, K., 71–73, 75, 78*f*, 79, 84
Polato, I., 265
Polk, T., 105
Polk, W., 107
Poola, D., 296, 302, 305
Poola, Deepak, 285–315
Preethi, K., 401
Presenza, D., 154*t*, 155, 157*t*, 158*t*, 160, 161
Press, G., 254
Proctor, Iain, 23
Prodan, R., 285, 291, 295–301, 303, 305, 308–310, 369

Q

Qasmi, M.A., 259
Qi, Xin, 23
Qian, Z., 279
Qin, J., 297, 305, 308, 369
Qiu, J., 256
Queiroz, Carlos, 183–204

R

Radia, S., 183, 192, 263, 266, 312
Radley, David, 36
Raghupathi, V., 274
Raghupathi, W., 274
Ragusa, C., 339
Ragusa, Carmelo, 323–350
Rahm, E., 222
Rahman, M., 303, 310
Rahmani, A.M., 305
Rajaraman, A., 222, 258
Ramakrishnan, C., 235
Ramamohanarao, K., 8, 288, 296, 302, 305
Ramamohanarao, Kotagiri, 285–315
Ramasamy, K., 188
Ramaswamy, A., 213
Rambadt, M., 310
Rana, O., 290, 291, 297–299
Ranaweera, S., 292, 293
Ranganathan, K., 64
Ranjan, R., 143, 303
Rannenberg, K., 223
Rao, J., 144, 190, 195

Rash, S., 64
Rasin, A., 262
Rastogi, R., 198
Rathlev, J., 222
Razavian, M., 148
Ré, R., 265
Reddy, C.K., 258
Redmond, E., 215
Reed, B., 264, 265
Reed, D., 292, 293, 295, 296
Regalado, N., 149
Reif, W., 212
Reinartz, Thomas, 33
Reinefeld, A., 338–340
Reiß, D., 222, 223
Ren, K., 16, 106
Ren, L., 100
Rescorla, E., 105
Resource, F.-G., 268, 279
Retter, R., 227, 228, 231, 233
Reussner, R., 3, 70–75, 78, 78*f*, 79, 82, 84
Reussner, Ralf, 69–87
Reussner, Ralf H., 70, 73, 82
Reuter, A., 215
Richardson, A., 191
Riedel, M., 310
Riedewald, M., 198
Riley, T., 237
Ringert, J.O., 213
Rivest, R.L., 107
Robbins, B., 193
Robert, H., 289
Robert, Y., 291–293, 303
Roberts, P., 106
Robie, J., 222
Robinson, Ian, 26
Robson, E., 236
Rodgers, D.P., 272
Rodriguez, M.A., 378, 379
Rodriguez, Maria A., 367–386
Romberg, M., 310
Romei, J., 232, 234
Romero, C.D.G., 274
Rong, C., 310
Rosen, B., 51*t*, 56
Rosen, J., 268
Rosenblum, David S., 14
Rossi, A., 313

Rost, S., 198
Rostami, K., 73–75, 78
Rostami, Kiana, 70
Roth, A., 222, 223
Roth, Alexander, 207–224
Rouncefield, M., 213
Roychoudhury, A., 247
Rozanski, N., 54
Rudolph, L., 341
Ruhroth, T., 70–72
Rumpe, B., 211–213, 217, 222, 223
Rumpe, Berhard, 207–224
Runyuan, S., 247
Ryaboy, D., 265
Ryan, M., 108, 111*t*, 118, 119
Ryan, Mark, 105–123
Rynge, M., 309, 369, 378
Ryu, Y., 295, 296

S
Sacks, R., 222
Sadalage, P.J., 14, 23, 27
Saecker, M., 276
Saeed, S., 128
Saha, B., 266
Saini, S., 313
Sakellariou, R., 296, 302
Sakr, S., 258, 260, 261, 267, 270
Salehi, M.A., 297, 299
Salehi, Mohsen Amini, 285–315
Samza, A., 187, 188, 192, 195, 199
Sanders, P., 339
Sanders, Peter, 323–350
Sandler, C., 237
Santesson, S., 107
Santos, E., 313
Saraswat, N., 154*t*, 157*t*, 158*t*, 161
Saray, A., 236
Sarma, J.S., 64, 264
Sarupria, S., 49
Sasi Kiran, J., 401
Sathi, Arvind, 42
Saule, E., 303
Scerri, S., 222
Schätz, B., 212, 213
Scheepers, Ferd, 36
Scheidegger, C.E., 313
Schierl, A., 212
Schindler, M., 211, 212, 222, 223

Schlauch, T., 310, 313
Schlichting, R.D., 291
Schlyter, J., 115
Schmerl, B., 85, 86
Schmidt, B., 119
Schmidt, Douglas, 29
Schmidt, R., 64
Schmieders, E., 71–73, 75, 78*f*, 79, 84
Schneider, F.B., 291
Schneider, K., 70–72
Schneier, B., 105
Schonenberg, M., 85
Schreiber, A., 310, 313
Schroeter, J., 144
Schuler, R., 292
Schuller, B., 310
Schulze, C., 212
Schupeck, W., 227, 228, 231, 233
Schütt, Thorsten, 323–350
Schwarzkopf, M., 279
Seifermann, S., 78
Selic, B., 297, 299, 301
Selinger, P.G., 277
Sen Sarma, J., 63, 64
Senger, M., 311
Sengupta, B., 247
Serebrenik, A., 51*t*
Seth, S., 266
Setty, S., 353
Shacham, H., 360
Shah, H., 266
Shalom, N., 147
Shamdasani, J., 49, 54
Shamsi, J., 259
Shank, Kevin, 36
Shao, Q., 143
Shao, Z., 63, 64, 264
Sharma, A., 64
Sharma, V., 198
Shawi, R. El, 258, 270
Shayan, J., 154*t*–156*t*, 158, 163
Shearer, Colin, 33
Shen, Z., 143
Shenker, S., 192, 263, 267, 271, 276, 295, 313
Sherif, S., 265
Shestak, V., 304
Shi, B., 279
Shi, W., 296

Shi, Z., 288, 289, 295, 296, 302–305
Shields, M., 297, 300, 305, 308, 309, 313
Shroff, G., 227
Shukla, A., 188
Shvachko, K., 183, 192, 263, 312
Siddiqui, M., 297, 305, 308, 369
Siegel, H., 289, 304
Sierra, K., 236
Sievert, O., 295, 296
Silva, C.T., 313
Siméon, J., 222
Simmhan, Y., 301
Simmhan, Y.L., 300
Simões, P., 153–155
Simonassi, D., 65
Singh, D., 258
Singh, G., 296, 308, 309, 370, 379
Singh, Y., 237
Sipos, G., 313
Skoutas, D., 303
Sleevi, R., 114
Smart, N.P., 105
Smirra, R., 212
Smith, H., 51*t*, 56
Smith, J., 289, 304
Smith, J.W., 154*t*, 155, 157*t*, 158*t*, 161
Snyder, B., 191
Snyder, Lawrence, 15
Soares, S., 51*t*
Soddemann, T., 310
Soghoian, C., 110, 111*t*, 112, 113
Soiland-Reyes, S., 311, 369
Solberg, A., 85
Sommerville, I., 148, 152, 154*t*, 155, 155*t*–158*t*,
    160–163
Song, D., 353, 357, 362, 363, 365
Song, H., 85
Song, M., 85
Spark, A., 194
Sparks, E., 270
Sperberg-McQueen, C.M., 222
Spiegelberg, N., 64
Spinellis, D., 233
Spoon, L., 313
Sravanthi, M., 401
Srivastava, S., 274
Srivastava, U., 198, 264, 265
Stahl, T., 212, 222

Stamm, S., 110, 111*t*, 112, 113
Stammel, J., 78
Stefanescu, M., 222
Stefanov, E., 357
Stender, J., 338–340
Stephens, R., 184, 185
Sterling, T., 106
Stillwell, M., 329, 331
Stillwell, Mark, 323–350
Stoica, I., 192, 263, 267, 268, 270, 271, 276, 295, 313
Stonebraker, M., 186, 190, 262
Stratan, C., 338, 339
Streit, A., 310
Strittmatter, M., 74, 75
Strohbach, M., 198
Su, J., 304
Su, M.H., 292, 296, 308, 309
Subbiah, S., 143
Sufi, S., 311
Sullivan, Kevin, 29
Sun, K., 144
Sun, W., 144
Sun, Y., 85, 303, 305
Suryadevara, N.K., 255
Suter, C., 238
Syverson, P., 112
Szalay, A., 301
Szvetits, M., 85
Szyperski, C., 71

T

Talia, D., 290, 291
Talwalkar, A., 270
Tamassia, R., 357, 363, 364, 364*t*
Tan, W., 277, 303, 305
Taneja, S., 188, 265
Tanenbaum, A.S., 193
Tang, A., 213
Tang, X., 292, 293
Tao, J., 310, 369
Tapus, A., 213
Tariq, R.S., 401
Taylor, I., 297, 300, 305, 308, 309, 313
Taylor, R.N., 53, 72, 212, 213
Tbahriti, S.E., 212, 220
Teicholz, P., 222
Tekinerdogan, B., 51, 52, 54, 56, 57, 64, 127, 128, 132, 133, 135, 136, 140

Tekinerdogan, Bedir, 49–67, 127–145
Teregowda, P., 148, 152, 154*t*–157*t*, 160, 161, 163
Terra, R., 86
Theedom, A., 234
Theodoropoulos, G., 100, 274
Theodoropoulos, Georgios, 253–280
Thiagarajan, A., 198
Thiel, S., 222
Thomas, T.M., 237
Thomas, U., 212
Thusoo, A., 63, 64, 264
Tolosana-Calasanz, R., 290, 291, 297–299
Tomkins, A., 264, 265
Toosi, A.N., 297
Tordsson, J., 313
Toshniwal, A., 188, 265
Treaster, M., 195
Trollmann, Frank, 87
Trucchia, F., 232, 234
Truong, H., 297, 305, 308
Truong, H.-L., 369
Tsai, W.T., 143
Tschersich, M., 223
Tserpes, K., 303
Tsuchiya, T., 292, 293
Tu, Stephen, 23
Tune, E., 279
Turaga, D.S., 185
Turner, M., 147
Turner, S., 105, 106
Tzoumas, K., 265

U

Uddin, M.F., 253
Ullman, J.D., 258, 262
Uzunkaya, C., 264*f*

V

v. Hoorn, A., 75
Vahi, K., 289*f*, 290, 292, 296, 308, 309, 369, 378, 380
Vaikuntanathan, V., 106
Valente, M.T., 86
van der Aalst, W., 85
van der Linden, M.A., 238
van der Starre, Ron, 36
van Dijk, M., 106, 357
Van Hemert, J., 369
van Ingen, C., 295, 296, 301
van Kessel, Ruud, 36

van Leeuwen, E.H., 275
van Oorschot, P.C., 105, 107
Van Rijmenam, M., 253
Van Steen, M., 193
Vance, A., 228
Vanderfeesten, I.T.P., 51*t*
Vandierendonck, H., 14
Varia, J., 154*t*, 158*t*, 161
Varvarigou, T., 247, 303
Vavilapalli, V.K., 266
Vecchiola, C., 310, 311
Veiga, L., 386
Venkataraman, S., 270
Venners, B., 313
Venugopal, S., 311, 373
Verma, A., 279
Versteeg, S., 8, 305
Villani, M.L., 85
Villazon, A., 297, 305, 308
Vincent, Tim, 33–48
Vistein, M., 212
Vivien, F., 329
Vo, H.T., 313
Völkel, S., 211, 212, 223
Völter, M., 212
von Laszewski, G., 300, 313
von Stockfleth, B., 212
Voorsluys, W., 292, 310
Vouk, M., 285, 300, 310
Vouk, M.A., 287, 300
Vu, Q.H., 154*t*, 156*t*, 157*t*

W

Wadge, W.W., 185
Walfish, M., 353
Wallach, D.A., 264
Waller, J., 75
Wallnau, Kurt C., 29
Wang, C., 222
Wang, Dan, 23
Wang, I., 309
Wang, J., 106
Wang, M., 255, 302
Wang, T., 303, 305
Wang, W., 144, 222
Wang, X., 304
Wang, Y., 297, 298
Wang, Z., 144

Wang, Z.H., 227
Warren, J., 51*t*, 56, 127, 129, 130*f*
Wasniewski, J., 313
Waters, B., 360
Watson, P., 311
Webber, Jim, 26
Weber, I., 69
Weber, Ingo, 21
Wegmann, L., 248
Wei, C., 234, 247
Wei, S., 227
Weigert, S., 313
Weiler, S., 115
Weinman, J., 227, 228
Wendlandt, D., 110, 111*t*
Wenger, K., 309
Weninger, T., 270
Wettel, R., 86
White, W.M., 198
Whittle, J., 213
Wichs, D., 357
Wicks, Tony, 14
Widom, J., 187, 198
Wieczorek, M., 297, 305, 308
Wiener, M.J., 105
Wile, D.S., 212
Wilke, C., 144
Wilkes, J., 143, 279
Williams, A., 311, 369
Williams, Mark, 23
Wilson, J., 215
Wimmer, M., 27, 222
Wipat, A., 311
Wirth, Rüdiger, 33
Withers, D., 311, 369
Woitalla, T., 238
Wolf, Alexander, 323–350
Wolfson, Dan, 33–48
Wolstencroft, K., 311, 369
Wolter, R., 235
Woodman, S., 311
Woods, E., 54
Woolf, B., 231
Wortmann, A., 212, 213, 223
Wortmann, Andreas, 207–224
Wortmann, W., 222, 223
Wu, J., 302, 303
Wu, S., 261, 262, 289

Wustrow, E., 111t, 115
Wyrzykowski, R., 313
Wysseier, C., 86

X
Xhafa, F., 288
Xia, H., 295, 296
Xiang, Y., 106
Ximenes, R., 154t–157t, 158, 158t, 160, 161
Xin, R., 268–271
Xin, R.S., 268, 270
Xiong, X., 191, 198
Xiong, Y., 85
Xu, S., 106
Xuan, P., 49
Xucheng, T., 234, 247
Xuesong, Z., 234, 247

Y
Yachi, S., 93
Yaghob, J., 191
Yahav, E., 240
Yalagandula, P., 193
Yan, H., 85, 86
Yang, C., 392, 394, 401
Yang, K., 106
Yang, L., 297–299
Yang, Minghui, 23
Yang, Y., 294, 297, 300–303, 305, 311
Yanik, T., 105
Yao, X., 92, 97, 99
Yaqoob, I., 274t
YarKhan, A., 295, 296
Yavuz, B., 270
Yee, P., 105
Yener, M., 234
Yeo, C.S., 304
Yergeau, F., 222
Yildiz, U., 285, 300, 310, 368
Ying, H., 227
Yoder, M., 265
Yoginath, S.B., 255
You, I., 106
Young, L., 313
Yu, J., 108, 111t, 119, 285, 287, 288, 301, 305, 368–370
Yu, Jiangshan, 105–123
Yu, T., 331

Yu, Teng, 323–350
Yu, Y., 256, 259, 290
Yu, Z., 296
Yuan, D., 293, 294, 300, 301, 311

Z
Zaharia, M., 192, 263, 267–271, 276, 277, 279, 295, 313
Zaidman, A., 227–229, 234, 247
Zaluzec, N., 313
Zandstra, M., 235
Zaniolo, C., 198
Zdonik, S., 186, 190
Zdun, U., 85
Zeadally, S., 401
Zeng, K., 198
Zhang, C., 255
Zhang, C.-Y., 184, 258
Zhang, G., 255, 300, 301, 311
Zhang, J., 255
Zhang, N., 264
Zhang, Q., 211, 214, 302, 303
Zhang, Y., 144, 292, 293, 295, 296, 305, 363
Zhao, G., 310
Zhao, H., 296, 302
Zhao, Haiping, 23
Zhao, S., 144
Zhao, Xinwei, 183–204
Zhao, Y., 310, 369
Zheng, Q., 106
Zheng, Y., 49
Zhenxiang, C., 247
Zhi Hu, W., 227
Zhong Xu, C., 144
Zhou, J., 279
Zhou, L., 279
Zhou, M., 261
Zhou, M.J., 227
Zhu, L., 69
Zhu, Liming, 21
Zhu, Q., 91, 92
Ziegler, W., 310
Ziekow, H., 198
Zimmermann, O., 228, 229, 232, 238, 248, 249t
Zimmermann, Olaf, 227–248
Zirkelbach, Christian, 69–87
Zohar, S., 222
Zunino, A., 211, 220

SUBJECT INDEX

Note: Page numbers followed by *"f"* indicate figures, *"t"* indicate tables, *"b"* indicate boxes, and *"ge"* indicate glossary terms.

A

Accountable key infrastructure, *see* AKI
ACM (Association of computing machinery), 151*t*, 345
Active users, 137, 138*t*, 139
AD, *see* Architectural decision
Added-value services, 207, 211–213
ADLs (Architecture description languages), 53, 54, 62, 74, 213, 221, 222, 403*ge*
Advanced applications, 391, 392, 396
Agile service networks (ASN), 5, 6
AKI (Accountable key infrastructure), 111*t*, 117–119, 122
Algorithms, 15, 23, 30, 64, 142, 256–258, 261, 267, 268, 270, 287, 288, 292, 293, 296, 358, 378, 378*t*, 379, 383, 384
Allocation requests, 328, 330–332, 334–336, 345
Analytic models, 34*f*, 35, 36, 38, 40
Analytics, 7, 8, 33–35, 37–39, 41–44, 169, 174, 177, 254, 274, 312, 395
Analytics lifecycle, 33, 34, 37
Analytics tools, 34, 35, 174, 175
Apache software foundation, 199, 200, 364
APIs (Application programming interfaces), 25, 36, 40, 194, 267, 269–271, 275, 278, 324, 334, 335, 339, 371, 372, 394, 401*ge*, 403*ge*
Application architectures, 50, 53, 58, 60, 61, 63–65, 67, 73, 79, 85, 86, 228, 248, 404*ge*
Application components, 156, 308, 325, 405*ge*
Application development, 194, 275
Application feature model, 53, 57, 60, 61
Application framework, 128
Application inputs, 239, 240
Application instances, 227–229, 233, 338
Application layer, 133, 136, 137, 143, 312
Application level, 227, 233
Application manager, 338–341, 342*f*
Application manifest, 338, 340, 347, 403*ge*
Application migration, 148, 150, 154, 155

Application nodes, 135–137
Application performance, 132, 261, 276
Application programming interfaces, *see* APIs
Application server, 133, 137, 138*t*, 139, 140, 143
Applications
  cloud-based, 6, 84, 399
  intensive, 256, 258, 275, 277, 278, 340
  new, 39, 201, 271, 338, 391, 392, 400*ge*
  novel, 395, 396, 398
AR (Architectural refactoring), 228–230, 232, 240, 241*t*, 243, 247, 248, 249*t*, 403*ge*
Architects, 1–6, 67, 227, 230, 399, 400*ge*
Architectural decision (AD), 54, 233, 241, 248, 249*t*, 403*ge*
Architectural model elements, 77, 79, 80
Architectural models, 69–72, 75, 77, 79, 81, 83, 84, 86, 87, 184
Architectural patterns, 228, 229, 232–234, 242*f*, 243, 247, 403*ge*
Architectural perspectives, 54, 233
Architectural refactoring, *see* AR
Architectural refactorings, 228–230, 232, 241*t*, 248, 403*ge*
Architectural runtime model, 70–73, 75, 76*f*, 78, 79*f*, 80, 81, 87, 403*ge*
Architectural tactics, 54
Architecture conformance, 85, 86
Architecture description languages, *see* ADLs
Architecture design decisions, 1–4, 399
Architecture metamodel, 73, 74, 78
ARPKI (Attack resilient public-key infrastructure), 111*t*, 119, 122
ASN (Agile service networks), 5, 6
Association of computing machinery, *see* ACM
Attack resilient public-key infrastructure, *see* ARPKI
Attackers, 106, 109, 111, 113, 114, 116, 122, 397
Attacks, 106, 109–111, 113, 114, 116, 117, 119, 123, 357, 358, 392, 396, 397
Auditable version control systems, *see* AVCS

425

AVCS (Auditable version control systems), 354, 358, 362–365, 403*ge*

B
Big data, era of, 13, 15
Big data analytics, 8, 38, 173, 174, 196, 279, 312, 394, 395
Big data applications, 30, 43, 60, 199, 271, 275, 278, 391, 394
Big data architectures, 7, 8, 33, 38, 49, 54, 67, 128, 129, 173*f*, 178, 398
Big data environment, 39, 45, 52, 56
Big data implementation, 167
Big data processing, 39, 46, 129, 169, 170, 173, 174, 183, 263, 278, 312, 391, 394, 396, 397
Big data projects, 34, 46, 49, 171
Big data reference architecture, 52*f*
Big data solutions, 37, 41–46, 48, 56, 167, 171, 172, 175, 176*f*, 177, 178, 273
Big data systems, 19, 23, 27, 49, 50*f*, 52–54, 55*f*, 57, 58, 60, 61, 63, 66, 67, 128, 129, 130*f*, 135, 137, 256, 257*t*, 258, 271–273, 396, 401*ge*
Big data technologies, 8, 50, 168, 174, 280, 393, 394, 401*ge*
Big data workloads, 276, 277
Biodiversity, 92, 93, 95, 96, 98–100, 403*ge*
Browser, 105–108, 110–113, 115, 116, 119, 138, 307*t*

C
CA (Certificate authority), 106, 108–110, 113–120, 122, 403*ge*
CA model, 106–108, 122
  current, 120, 122
Candidate model, 78, 82
CEP (Complex event processor), 43, 185, 197, 198
Certificate authority, *see* CA
Certificate issuance, 108, 109, 118
Certificate management, 107, 117
Certificate management transparency, 110, 115, 122
  category of, 119, 122, 123
Certificate revocation lists, *see* CRL
Certificate transparency, *see* CT
Certificates, 22, 106–113, 116–120, 122, 306*t*, 310, 314, 403*ge*
  multiple, 109, 112–114, 116, 118
  received, 107, 109, 110, 112, 113, 120, 122
Checkpointing, 296–300, 306*t*, 308–310, 312, 315
  workflow-level, 293*f*, 298, 299

CIMI (Cloud infrastructure management interface), 325*t*, 336
Class diagrams, 213, 374, 375, 376*f*
Classification categories, 152, 155–158
Client requests, 25, 111, 112, 138, 143, 359
Clients, 25, 107, 108, 111, 113, 114, 119, 120, 122, 127, 128, 135, 138*t*, 139, 141, 143, 191, 353–355, 357, 358, 359*f*, 360–364, 396, 405*ge*
Cloud, 1–8, 91, 92, 97–101, 147, 148, 150–152, 154, 155*t*–158*t*, 162–164, 273, 278–280, 293, 294, 306*t*, 307*t*, 308, 313–315, 367–370, 395–399, 403*ge*, 404*ge*
Cloud applications, 75, 135, 137, 144, 228, 233, 241*t*, 248, 391, 395, 397, 405*ge*
Cloud architectures, 223, 397, 398
Cloud autoscaling, 91–93, 97, 99, 100
Cloud autoscaling process, 97–99
Cloud-based services, 403*ge*, 404*ge*
Cloud computing, 69, 92, 100, 127, 128, 149, 155*t*, 163, 164, 171, 227, 228, 253, 255, 273, 367, 385, 386, 395, 403*ge*
Cloud computing environments, 15, 231, 233, 285, 385
Cloud computing platform, 7, 326, 327
Cloud ecosystem, 94*f*, 94, 95, 96*f*96–99, 398, 400*ge*, 403*ge*
Cloud environments, 2, 3, 91, 92, 161, 227, 228, 230, 232, 233, 247, 273, 368, 369
Cloud infrastructure management interface, *see* CIMI
Cloud marketplaces, 1, 2, 5
Cloud migration, 148, 150, 151, 153, 161, 163, 247, 403*ge*
Cloud model, 171, 172
Cloud platforms, 47, 150, 171, 311, 324, 326, 329, 340, 345, 394, 398
Cloud provider characteristic, 157*t*, 158*t*, 160
Cloud providers, 4, 6, 70, 71*f*, 71, 95, 128, 155*t*, 156*t*, 157*t*, 161–164, 171, 172, 273, 314, 323, 324, 349, 353, 371, 372, 385
  public, 353, 357, 362
Cloud resources, 279, 323, 324, 326, 337, 338, 340, 349, 367, 370, 374, 375, 385, 386, 404*ge*
Cloud service providers, 3, 5, 158*t*
Cloud services, 46, 69, 223, 273, 311, 353, 368, 371, 403*ge*
Cloud storage, 273
Cloud tenants, 323, 324, 326, 336, 340, 347, 349
Cloud-architecture, 2, 217–219, 222, 223
Cloud-based architectures, 5–7, 213

Cloud-based services, 41, 91, 92, 94–97, 99–101, 223, 398, 403*ge*
  removing, 95, 96, 99
Cloud-based software applications, 70, 71, 84, 87
Cloud-based systems, 2–4, 69, 156, 403*ge*, 404*ge*
Cloudbus WMS, 368, 370, 372*f*, 372, 374, 378–380, 382, 384–386
Cloudbus workflow management system, 373
Clusters, spark, 268, 269, 271
CoCoME (Common component modeling example), 70, 71*f*, 71, 72, 75, 80, 82
CoCoME scenario, 72, 80–82
Coevolution, 94, 97, 100
Common component modeling example, *see* CoCoME
Communication service provider, *see* CSP
Complex event processing system, 198, 201*t*–204*t*
Complex event processor, *see* CEP
Component data processing server, 61, 64, 66
Component data storage, 61, 66
Component information management server, 61, 63, 64, 66
Component structure, 71, 72, 79, 85
Components
  architectural, 1, 7, 372*f*, 374*f*–376*f*, 399
  stateless, 233, 234, 245*t*
Computational resources, 19, 132, 155, 312
Computations, 8, 9, 106, 186, 263, 266, 267, 269, 270, 276, 277, 279, 292, 297, 309, 344, 345, 363, 364, 378, 379, 403*ge*–406*ge*
Connections, 27, 61, 62, 64, 107, 109, 111, 112, 114, 116, 138, 139, 194, 217, 307*t*
Consistency models, weak, 23, 24
Costs, operational, 5, 6, 19, 22, 23, 273, 357
CRL (Certificate revocation lists), 107, 109
Cross-resource scheduler, *see* CRS
CRS (Cross-resource scheduler), 338, 339, 346, 349
CSP (Communication service provider), 42, 42*f*, 43
CT (Certificate transparency), 111*t*, 116–118

D
Data events, 187, 191, 192
Data execution, 191, 193, 201*t*
Data intensive computing, 259
Data lake, 35, 36*f*, 36–38, 40, 43, 44, 46, 168*t*, 173, 404*ge*
Data models, 24, 57, 59*t*, 60, 207, 215–217, 222, 400*ge*
  key-value, 59*t*, 60, 61

Data stream management systems, 184, 185, 197, 198, 404*ge*
Data stream management systems, *see* DSMS
Data systems, cloud-based big, 127, 128, 130, 131*f*, 135, 136*f*, 143, 144
Data warehouse solution, 172, 175, 176*f*, 176, 177
Data-intensive workflows, 290, 293–295
Database management systems, *see* DBMS
Database service, 70, 82, 95
Database-as-a-Service (DBaaS), 70, 71*f*
DataConversion component, 216, 217
DataConversion service, 216, 217, 219
Dataflow engine, *see* DFEs
DBaaS (Database-as-a-Service), 70, 71
DBMS (Database management systems), 185, 194, 198, 404*ge*
Deadline, 5, 286, 296, 302, 305, 379, 382–384, 384*t*, 404*ge*, 405*ge*
Degree montage workflow, 382
Denial of service (DoS), 109, 122
Deployment diagram, 62–64
Descriptive architectural runtime models, 77, 78*f*, 82
Design decisions, 2, 4, 54, 65, 67, 77, 84, 399, 400*ge*
  choice of architecture, 2, 399
Design rule set, 60–65
Design rules, 50, 53, 60–65, 67, 404*ge*
Development models, 70, 75, 85, 86
DFEs (Dataflow engine), 329, 330, 332, 340–342, 342*t*, 343, 343*f*, 343*t*, 344, 404*ge*
Disruptive tenants, 127, 132, 133, 135, 137–142, 144, 403*ge*–405*ge*
Distributed resources, 287, 290, 310, 311, 370, 372, 373
DNS security extensions (DNSSEC), 115
DNSSEC (DNS security extensions), 115
Domain objects, 235, 239, 246
Domain owners, 109, 116, 117, 119, 120
Domain servers, 107–109, 111–115, 120
Domains, 29, 49–51, 54, 74, 107, 109–111, 113–120, 122, 151, 211, 247, 258, 269, 290, 404*ge*
DoS (Denial of service), 109, 122
DSMS (Data stream management systems), 184, 185, 197, 198, 203*t*, 404*ge*
Dynamic content, 70–72, 79, 86, 87

E
EAI (Enterprise application integration), 29
Ecology-inspired pattern, 97, 98*f*, 99

Ecosystem, 36, 45, 93–95, 97, 98, 170, 207, 212, 213, 223, 224
EMS (Energy management system), 65, 67
End-users, 128, 150, 151, 345
Energy management system, *see* EMS
Engines, 184, 185, 187, 188, 190, 191, 197, 200, 202, 261, 277, 370, 371, 373, 375, 377, 381
Enterprise application integration (EAI), 29
Enterprise applications, 148, 150, 151, 153, 231, 235, 239, 240, 404*ge*
  existing, 158, 227, 228
Enterprises, 1, 6, 42, 147, 148, 150–152, 171, 172, 391, 393, 396, 397, 401*ge*
European conference on software architecture, *see* ECSA
Evolution, 4, 6, 29, 33, 53, 67, 73, 92–100, 198, 248, 280, 399, 404*ge*
Exascale, 280
Execution contexts, 73, 79, 80, 82

F

Facebook, 13, 23, 29, 42, 53, 54, 61, 63, 64, 67, 106, 187, 240, 254, 264, 393, 400*ge*
Failure modeling, 303, 304*f*, 304
Failure probability, 302–305
Failures, 21, 22, 25, 150, 151, 194, 195, 257*t*, 260, 265, 266, 285, 290, 291, 295–297, 299, 301–305, 308, 309, 313, 314, 396
Family feature model, 53, 60, 61, 63–67, 404*ge*
Fault-tolerance, 9, 22, 248, 285–290, 292*f*, 292, 293, 295–297, 300–302, 304, 309, 310, 314, 315
Faults, 202, 262, 285, 286, 289–291, 291*f*, 296, 308–310, 313, 315
Feature model, 49–51, 54, 58, 60, 62, 67, 404*ge*
Feature modeling, 49, 51
File versions, 354–358, 360, 361, 363
  arbitrary, 354–357, 359
  new, 355, 358, 360, 361, 405*ge*

G

General-purpose computation on graphics processing units, *see* GPGPUs
Generative approach, 217, 220–224
GFS (Google file system), 254, 259–261, 312
Google file system, *see* GFS
GPGPUs (General-purpose computation on graphics processing units), 276, 323, 325, 339

GPUs (Graphics processing unit), 194, 276, 277, 326, 405*ge*
Graph data model, 59*t*, 60, 61
Graphics processing unit, *see* GPUs
Grid computing, 100, 309
Grids, 285, 293, 306*t*, 307*t*, 308, 311, 313, 315, 369, 386

H

Hadoop, 8, 9, 24, 183, 184, 199, 263–266, 268–270, 272*t*, 272, 2723, 274*t*, 279, 293, 294, 313
Hadoop distributed file system, *see* HDFS
Hardware resources, 19, 91, 95–97, 100, 128, 192
Harness, 194, 261, 323–326, 336, 338, 341, 345, 349, 350
Harness cloud platform, 324, 340
Harness platform, 326, 338, 340, 342, 347
Harness resource managers, 328, 331, 335, 336
HDFS (Hadoop distributed file system), 8, 9, 64, 173, 263, 264, 266, 268–270, 272*t*, 273, 276–278, 293, 294, 312
Heterogeneous resources, 293, 302, 323, 326, 327, 329, 331, 335*f*, 339, 341
High performance computers, *see* HPC
Hosting big data, 167
HPC applications, 340, 349
HPC (High performance computers), 256, 271, 272, 279, 280, 404*ge*
Hyperscalability, 14, 19, 396
Hyperscalable systems, 13, 14, 19, 20, 27, 396
Hyperscale, 14, 22, 23, 26, 30
Hyperscale systems, 14, 20–22, 28, 30

I

IaaS clouds, 369, 374
IEEE Xplore, 51, 148, 149, 151*t*, 153*t*
Implementation level, 69, 71, 75, 77, 78
In-memory processing, 57, 59*t*, 60, 64, 65, 277, 280
In-stream processing, 57, 59*t*, 60
Indicators, 2, 147, 148, 150*t*, 151*t*, 151, 152*t*, 153*t*, 153, 155, 157*t*, 158*t*, 159, 160, 162–164, 403*ge*, 404*ge*
Information, biotic, 92, 97
Input data, 185, 256, 258, 260, 261, 268, 269, 276, 308, 309, 312, 378, 381
Intensive frameworks, 256, 258, 259, 268, 275–278, 280
Internet of things, *see* IoT

IObserve, 70, 72, 73, 77–82, 83*f*, 84*f*, 84, 86, 87, 403*ge*
IObserve approach, 70, 72, 74, 75, 77, 80, 84, 87
IObserve context, 73, 75, 87, 403*ge*
IObserve megamodel, 75, 79*f*, 87
IoT (Internet of things), 4, 37, 39, 49, 170, 255, 275, 279, 280, 392, 398, 399

J
Java virtual machine (JVM), 201, 203*t*, 263

K
Key, private, 107, 113, 116, 118

L
Legacy applications, 152, 158*t*, 231–234, 370, 386
  single-tenant, 229, 232*f*
LookUp service, 217–220

M
Machine crashes, 290, 291, 308–310
Maintenance, 155*t*, 196, 197, 203, 247, 248, 266
Maintenance costs, 196, 323
Managers, top-level, 328, 330*t*, 330 331
Map tasks, 261, 294, 313, 370
MapReduce, 7, 9, 199, 254, 257*t*, 257, 259–263, 267, 269, 275–278, 280, 290, 294, 312, 313, 394
MapReduce application, 261, 265, 278, 279
MapReduce programming model, 267, 280
MapReduce tasks, 264, 266, 277
MapReduce workflow, 290, 293, 312, 313
Mass storage systems and technologies, *see* MSST
MDE, *see* Model-driven engineering
Megamodel, 70, 75, 77, 84, 404*ge*
Metadata, 27, 41, 45–48, 174, 260, 265, 339, 355, 357–359, 363
Metamodel, 74, 75, 77, 217
Migrating, 70, 71, 148, 149, 152, 157*t*, 158*t*, 164
Migration, 73, 78, 81, 82, 84, 86, 147, 148, 153–155, 156*t*–158*t*, 158–164, 306*t*, 308, 394, 398
Migration models, 161, 163
Mis-issued certificates, 107, 109, 113–117, 122
Mobility services, 210, 219
Model level, 75, 76*f*
Model-driven engineering (MDE), 73, 212, 405*ge*
Model-view-controller, *see* MVC
Models
  adversarial, 354, 357
  domain, 49–51, 53, 236*f*, 243, 404*ge*

hybrid, 175, 177, 178*f*
  pull, 201, 202*t*
Modern stream processing platforms, 187, 188
Monitoring approach, 75, 77
Monitoring data, 71, 75, 76*f*, 77, 79, 85, 86, 405*ge*
Montage application, 379, 381
Montage workflows, 378, 379, 380, 380*f*, 381, 381*t*, 384, 384*t*
Multitenancy, 1–4, 7, 160, 174, 228, 232*f*, 232–235, 241, 246–248, 398, 399, 405*ge*
Multitenancy defects, 238*f*, 241*t*
Multitenancy requirements, 233, 246*t*, 246
Multitenant, 3, 4, 231, 235, 241, 245*t*, 246*t*
Multitenant applications, 134*f*, 144, 227, 228, 230, 235, 237, 239, 243, 247
Multitenant databases, 235, 243
Multitenant requirements, various, 2, 3, 399
Multitenant SaaS applications, 227, 229, 240, 247
MVC (Model-view-controller), 136, 231, 234, 235, 240, 241, 248

N
Nodes, master, 260, 263, 380, 381
Nonliving components, 92, 93, 95
Notary servers, 111, 112, 120
Number, total, 131, 344, 363

O
OASIS (Organization for the advancement of structured information standards), 324, 325
Observers, 110–112, 120, 122, 123, 234
OCCI (Open cloud computing interface), 325*t*, 336
OCSP (On-line certificate status protocol), 107, 109
On-line certificate status protocol, *see* OCSP
Open cloud computing interface, *see* OCCI
Open source projects, 169, 170, 199, 265
Operation phase, 69, 70, 77, 79, 85, 86
Operational observations, 70, 77, 86
Operations, proper, 195, 196, 202, 204*t*
Operators, 26, 69–72, 77–80, 82–85, 186, 272
Organization for the advancement of structured information standards, *see* OASIS
Organizational, 155*t*–158*t*, 158

P
Palladio component model, *see* PCM
Parties, 105–110, 115–118, 120, 123, 151, 156*t*, 303, 357, 362, 392
  trusted, 106, 108, 114, 118, 119, 123

PCM (Palladio component model), 73–75, 77, 78, 81, 82, 87
PDPs (Platform deployment package), 325
PE (processing elements), 192, 199, 256, 257, 257*t*, 272, 279, 404*ge*, 405*ge*
Performance isolation, 127, 132–135, 136, 136*f*, 137, 139, 140*t*, 140, 142–145, 405*ge*
Performance isolation approaches, 127, 128, 134*f*, 142, 144
Performance models, 326, 329, 340–341, 342*f*, 347*f*, 348, 349
Performance monitoring, 128, 144
Performance problems, 132, 396
Persistence component, 215, 216
Persistence service, 214–219
Person, 33, 34, 208, 209, 209*f*, 210, 212, 214, 219, 220, 253, 392, 393, 396
Personal data, 207, 209–214, 217–219, 221
Personal data service, 216–219
PKI (Public key infrastructure), 105, 106, 110, 123, 403*ge*, 405*ge*
PKP (Public key pinning), 111, 114, 115
Platform deployment package (PDPs), 325
Platforms, surveyed, 194, 195, 200–202
PNs, *see* Processing nodes
Previous version, immediate, 354, 355, 359, 361, 404*ge*, 405*ge*
Pricing model, 341, 348, 385
Primary studies, 149, 151, 154, 155, 159*f*, 163, 164
Privacy, 7, 8, 37, 38, 56, 59*t*, 61, 71–73, 74, 74*f*, 75, 76*f*, 78, 79, 82, 214, 273, 392, 393, 395–397, 400*ge*, 401*ge*
Processing elements, *see* PE
Processing nodes (PNs), 19, 187, 188, 188*f*, 189, 191, 193, 195, 199
Properties
    tenant data separation, 238, 239, 245*t* 246, 248
    tenant ID, 235, 237, 241, 245*t*
Public clouds, untrusted, 354, 365
Public key infrastructure, *see* PKI
Public key pinning, *see* PKP

Q
QA, *see* Quality attributes
QoS (Quality of services), 3, 5, 6, 91, 93*t*, 98, 99, 140*t*, 144, 288, 289, 312, 367
Quality attributes (QA), 2, 5, 18, 19, 241*t*, 248, 249*t*, 403*ge*

Quality criteria, 149, 152*t*
Quality of services, *see* QoS
Query processing, real-time, 57, 61, 64–66

R
RDIC approaches, 354, 364*t*, 365
Reduce tasks, 261, 262, 294, 313
Reengineering method, 230, 240, 243, 246
Reference architecture, 50, 51*t*, 52–54, 56, 57, 60–62, 66, 67, 74*f*, 75, 87, 129, 370, 371*f*, 386, 404*ge*, 405*ge*
Relational databases, 23, 24, 36, 57, 59*t*, 61, 64, 66, 215, 216, 394
Repository, 37, 73, 353–355, 358–363, 364*t*, 404*ge*, 406*ge*
Request load, 14, 17, 18, 21
Request rate, 133, 138, 139, 404*ge*, 405*ge*
Requesters, 112, 210
Requests, 18, 25, 39, 40, 43, 44, 80, 132, 133, 135, 136, 137*f*, 137, 138*t*, 138, 139, 140, 142*f*, 142, 143, 191, 210, 266, 298, 299, 328–335, 338, 339, 345, 346
Requests per second (RPS), 80, 135, 138
Requirements, significant, 1–4, 7, 8, 391, 395, 397–400
Resource allocation requests, 329, 332, 333*f*, 133, 334*f*
Resource broker, 287
Resource configurations, 341, 347, 349
Resource containers, 74, 81
Resource environment, 81, 403*ge*
Resource instances, 336, 339
Resource managers, 192, 308, 326, 328*f*, 328, 329, 335, 336
    child, 330*f*, 330, 331
Resource pool, 367, 385
Resource pooling, 1, 233
Resource provisioning, 312, 367, 370, 376, 379
Resource relationship, 93, 406*ge*
Resource types, 293, 325, 329, 331, 335
Resources
    allocating, 329, 345
    available, 142, 192, 266, 279, 309, 329, 330, 336, 367, 370, 374, 396
    new, 292, 293
    physical, 6, 19, 275, 279, 339, 369
    remote, 308, 373
    specialized, 326, 327, 349
Retrieve phase, 359, 360, 362, 364

Reverse time migration, *see* RTM

Risks, 4–7, 27, 107, 147, 151, 152*t*, 152, 153*t*, 154, 155. 156*t*, 156, 157*t*, 158–160, 162, 164, 174, 193, 248, 392, 393, 395, 397, 398, 400*ge*, 404*ge*

RPS (Requests per second), 80, 135, 138

RTM jobs, 341, 343, 344

RTM (Reverse time migration), 340, 342

Runtime models, 76*f*, 85, 86, 403*ge*, 405*ge* prescriptive architectural, 77, 78*f*, 81, 87

S

SaaS applications, 136, 227, 228, 233, 247

Sales service, 71, 81, 82

Scheduler, cross-resource, 338, 339, 349

Schedules, 13, 195, 287, 292, 293, 295, 302, 304, 305, 308, 315, 379

Scheduling algorithms, 278*t*, 288, 302, 303, 374, 377–379, 385

Scientific applications, 7, 369, 370, 385, 405*ge*

Scientific workflow management system, 405*ge*

Scientific workflows, 285, 311, 367–370, 379, 385, 386, 405*ge*, 406*ge*

Security risks, 162, 395

Self-aware patterns, 92, 97–99

Server, 22, 23, 25, 30, 64, 65, 105, 108, 111, 112, 123, 128, 135, 139, 141, 142, 191, 357–364, 404*ge*, 405*ge*

Service composition, 207, 209, 219–222, 224, 405*ge*

Service developers, 207, 211–214, 220, 221

Service instance, 5, 25, 80

Service interfaces, 211, 212, 215, 233

Service level agreements, *see* SLAs

Service providers, 5, 107, 108, 119, 210, 213, 214, 219, 220, 223, 247, 302, 312, 358, 405*ge*

Service provision, 5, 7

Service users, 207, 212, 219, 223, 224

Service-level objective, *see* SLO

Services
    aggregated, 80, 82
    basic, 219, 220, 223, 405*ge*
    cloud information, 371, 377, 386
    existing business, 176, 177
    grid, 100, 310, 311, 369
    new, 219, 220
    public transportation, 213, 214*f*
    quality of, 91, 140, 141, 144
    querying, 218, 219
    stateless, 25, 26, 233

Skip version, 356, 357, 359, 361–363

SLAs (Service level agreements), 1, 2, 4–6, 91, 92, 95, 96, 132, 138, 138, 140*t*, 144, 147, 158, 162, 170, 172, 393, 399, 403*ge*

SLO (Service-level objective), 326, 338, 341, 345, 347, 405*ge*

Software applications, 5, 73, 79, 80, 86, 127, 147, 148, 164, 227, 228, 403*ge*–405*ge* executed, 72, 403*ge*, 405*ge*

Software architecture, 1, 2, 4, 30, 67, 69, 70, 72, 73, 77–79, 88, 212, 326, 391, 395–398, 401*ge*, 405*ge*

Software configurations, 91, 95, 96, 99, 100, 403*ge*

Software development, 355, 404*ge*

Solution details, 228

Source category, 155*t*–158*t*

Source code, 70, 83, 86, 240, 243, 298, 353, 364

Spark SQL, 270, 271

Spark streaming, 184, 193, 194, 200–202, 270, 271*t*, 201, 202*t*, 202

Spring, 187, 199–201, 201*t*–203*t*

Stream processing, 9, 57, 184–187, 189, 191, 193, 197, 202, 258, 265, 405*ge*

Stream processing platforms, 184–187, 188*f*, 188, 189*f*, 190, 191, 193, 194, 196*f*, 196–198, 200, 201*t*, 201, 202*t*, 203*t*, 203, 204*t*, 204

Stream processing systems, 184–187, 189–195, 197, 198, 200, 203

Studies, 95, 100, 128, 130, 132, 137, 139, 143, 147–149, 150*t*, 150, 151*t*, 151, 152*t*, 152, 153*t*, 153, 154*t*, 154–156, 158, 160, 161*f*, 161–164, 184, 196, 197, 204, 246
    included, 154*t*, 154, 155
    pilot, 147–149, 152

Subcategories, 152, 154, 158, 160

Subcomponents, 213, 215

System categories, 39, 40*f*, 45, 120

T

Tasks, 15, 16, 78, 191–193, 199, 200, 257*t*, 261, 262, 272, 286, 287, 290–296, 298–305, 308–313, 369, 370, 372–375, 377, 378*t*, 378–380, 381, 381*t*, 382, 384–386
    mProjectPP, 379, 384, 385

Taxonomy, 184, 185, 187, 189, 197, 203, 204, 289, 290, 292

Tenant data separation, 232, 240, 241, 247, 248

Tenant data separation defects, 229, 238–240, 243, 246

Tenant ID, 229, 230, 235, 238, 245*t*

Tenant identifier, 235, 239, 241, 246

Tenant information, 135, 136
Tenant owner, 235, 239, 241, 242
Tenants, 3, 4, 127, 130, 132, 133, 135, 138*t*, 138, 140*t*, 140–142, 144, 228–230, 233, 235–243, 245*t*, 245–247, 345, 346, 399, 405*ge*
   abiding, 138*t*, 138–141
Thin clients, 128, 136, 405*ge*
TLS (Transport layer security), 113, 358, 404*ge*, 405*ge*
Topology and orchestration specification for cloud applications, *see* TOSCA
Tork framework, 135–137
TOSCA (Topology and orchestration specification for cloud applications), 324, 325*t*, 336
Transformations, 34, 62–66, 72, 75, 76*f*, 79*f*, 80–82, 217, 229, 264, 268, 269, 300, 404*ge*
Transport layer security, *see* TLS
Trust, 5, 7, 36, 37, 41, 56, 107, 108, 110, 112–114, 116, 117, 120, 121*t*, 123, 132, 302, 303, 360, 396, 397
   direct, 303, 305
   independence of, 107, 108, 114
   recommendation, 303, 305
Trust agility, 107, 108, 110, 111, 113–115, 117, 120
Trust models, 302, 303

U

ULSs (Ultra large systems), 29, 30
Ultra large systems, *see* ULSs
Uncertainty, 1, 3, 91, 92, 99–101, 289, 290, 302, 304, 305

V

Value, 4–7, 33, 34, 38, 41, 45–47, 80, 140, 143, 159, 183, 184, 217, 253, 254, 356, 382, 391, 392
Value pairs, 261, 262, 313
VCS, *see* Version control systems
VCS clients, 355, 357
VCS server, 355, 357–359, 361, 362
Version, 21, 123, 170, 197, 310, 325*t*, 354–357, 359–361, 363, 364*t*, 364, 381, 403*ge*, 404*ge*, 406*ge*
   new, 21, 27, 170, 171, 199, 356, 359, 361
   pattern-based, 245, 245*t*, 246–248, 364*t*

Version control systems (VCS), 353–355, 357–359, 363–365, 403*ge*, 406*ge*
   delta-based, 354, 356*f*, 358, 359, 365
Virtual machines, *see* VMs
Visualization, 27, 54, 80, 82–84, 86, 253, 254, 278, 394, 396, 401*ge*
VM types, 345, 369, 377, 378, 384, 385
VMs (Virtual machines), 22, 82, 95, 97, 150, 297, 312, 325, 326, 330, 336, 339, 340, 367, 369–371, 374–377, 381, 382*t*, 383, 384*t*, 384, 385*t*, 385

W

WCO (Workflow coordinator), 374, 378
Weakness, 111–120, 263, 315
WMSs (Workflow management systems, WFMS), 285, 286*f*, 286–291, 295, 297, 300–302, 305, 306*t*, 307*t*, 308, 310, 311, 313–315, 367–370, 371*f*, 385
Word count application, 261, 262
Workflow applications, 287, 308, 368, 369, 385, 406*ge*
Workflow coordinator, *see* WCO
Workflow engine, 310, 311, 313, 370, 371, 373, 377, 380, 386
Workflow execution, 286, 287, 294, 308, 367, 369, 370, 374, 375, 378*t*, 382–385
Workflow level, 308–310
Workflow management systems, *see* WMSs
Workflow scheduling, 266, 285–287, 288*f*
Workflow tasks, 287, 290, 367, 370, 378–381, 406*ge*
Workflows, 85, 262, 266, 277, 285–288, 290, 291, 293–295, 297, 300–302, 304*f*, 305, 306, 308–315, 367–370, 372–375, 377, 378*t*, 378–386, 406*ge*
   abstract, 286, 287, 308, 309

Y

YARN (Yet another resource negotiator), 192, 201*t*, 266, 268, 272*t*, 274*t*, 277
Yet another resource negotiator, *see* YARN

Z

Zend skeleton application, 240, 243

Printed in the United States
By Bookmasters